VIENNA AND VERSA

This book brings vividly to life the courtiers and servants of the imperial court in Vienna and the royal court at Paris-Versailles from the sixteenth to the eighteenth century, drawing together a wealth of unpublished material in a comparative context.

Staff, numbers, costs, and hierarchies; daily routines and ceremonies; court favourites and the nature of rulership; the integrative and centripetal forces of the central courtly establishment: all are seen in a long-term, comparative perspective that highlights both the similarities of the two courts and the distinctiveness of the developments in France and the Habsburg lands. In the process, most conventional views of each court – and of court life in general – are challenged, and a new interpretation emerges. Finally, by relocating the household in the heart of the early modern state, *Vienna and Versailles* forces us to rethink the process of state building and the notion of 'absolutism'.

JEROEN DUINDAM is Lecturer in History, Universiteit Utrecht, the Netherlands.

NEW STUDIES IN EUROPEAN HISTORY

Edited by
PETER BALDWIN, University of California, Los Angeles
CHRISTOPHER CLARK, University of Cambridge
JAMES B. COLLINS, Georgetown University
MÍA RODRÍGUEZ-SALGADO, London School of Economics and Political Science
LYNDAL ROPER, Royal Holloway, University of London

This is a new series in early modern and modern European history. Its aim is to publish outstanding works of research, addressed to important themes across a wide geographical range, from southern and central Europe, to Scandinavia and Russia, and from the time of the Renaissance to the Second World War. As it develops the series will comprise focused works of wide contextual range and intellectual ambition.

Books in the series

Royalty and Diplomacy in Europe, 1890–1914
RODERICK R. MCLEAN

Catholic Revival in the Age of the Baroque
Religious Identity in Southwest Germany, 1550–1750
MARC R. FORSTER

Helmuth von Moltke and the Origins of the First World War
ANNIKA MOMBAUER

Peter the Great
The Struggle for Power, 1671–1725
PAUL BUSHKOVITCH

Fatherlands
State Building and Nationhood in Nineteenth-Century Germany
ABIGAIL GREEN

The French Second Empire
An Anatomy of Political Power
ROGER PRICE

Origins of the French Welfare State
The Struggle for Social Reform in France, 1914–1947
PAUL V. DUTTON

Ordinary Prussians
Brandenburg Junkers and Villagers, 1500–1840
WILLIAM W. HAGEN

VIENNA AND VERSAILLES

JEROEN DUINDAM

CAMBRIDGE
UNIVERSITY PRESS

CAMBRIDGE UNIVERSITY PRESS
Cambridge, New York, Melbourne, Madrid, Cape Town, Singapore, São Paulo

Cambridge University Press
The Edinburgh Building, Cambridge CB2 8RU, UK

Published in the United States of America by Cambridge University Press, New York

www.cambridge.org
Information on this title: www.cambridge.org/9780521822626

First published 2003
Reprinted 2006
This digitally printed version 2007

A catalogue record for this publication is available from the British Library

ISBN 978-0-521-82262-6 hardback
ISBN 978-0-521-71476-1 paperback

Contents

Illustrations

Tables

Acknowledgements

The Dutch Organization for Scientific Research (NWO) made possible this book by granting me a sabbatical year, and by contributing, together with the Utrecht University History Department and the Research Institute for History and Culture (OGC), to the costs of travel and accommodation in Vienna and Paris. The Utrecht University Library gave me a variety of privileges assisting my research. In Vienna and Paris, the staffs of all libraries and archives I visited proved willing to fulfil my unreasonable hunger for materials. Among them, Olivier Poncet of the Archives Nationales and Leopold Auer of the Haus- Hof- und Staatsarchiv were particularly helpful.

The number of colleagues involved in the genesis of this book is such that I can only list a small selection of them here. Among my Utrecht colleagues, Hermann von der Dunk, Johan Aalbers, and Wijnand Mijnhardt supported my initiative throughout; Hans Medick, Barbara Stollberg-Rilinger, Ronald Asch, and Heinz Duchhardt provided advice and help. Robert Evans was a source of inspiration as well as help from the very first start of this project; David Parrott and Robert Oresko provided guidance when I had to formulate my plans in a cogent book proposal. Vienna proved to be a city rich not only in materials, but also in human capital. Thomas Fröschl introduced me to Vienna; Stefan Sienell coached me through my first struggles with the German script, and the HHStA inventories. Beatrix Bastl and Susanne Pils were invariably willing to answer my queries. So was Thomas Winkelbauer who later meticulously read my text notwithstanding his own pressing academic work. I enjoyed many fruitful conversations with Andreas Pecar, whom I met working shoulder to shoulder in the Nationalbibliothek: he read the first rough version of this book, and let me read his dissertation in unpublished form. Likewise, Petr Mat'a and Géza Pálffy substantially nuanced my ideas about the two royal crowns in Habsburg possession, and the latter provided a variety of important materials. Jaroslava Hausenblasová kindly sent her publications on Rudolf's court, and Zdenek Hojda offered advice. In a lucky coincidence, Joe Bergin proved to be among the first I would meet in Paris; his company, advice, and finally his reading of several chapters of this book, were very welcome. As the book approached completion others stepped in. Michael Kaiser read the last chapters; Katia Béguin and Nicolas Le Roux read the entire book, and sent me comments as well as relevant articles. Guy Rowlands provided information on the court's guards. My first tentative steps in the field of budgets and currencies were assisted by Oscar Gelderblom, who not only coached me but also led me to the equally helpful Jean-Laurent Rosenthal and Phil Hoffman. Richard Bonney directed me to Joël Félix, who provided more information and L'Averdy's 1768 budget.

Katrin Keller thoroughly read the entire text, providing many corrections and hints; furthermore, she was kind enough to work in the Bildarchiv for several days, selecting my illustrations for the Habsburg court. Leonhard Horowski's comments on the first version of my book formed an invaluable and lengthy essay on the French court, that helped me to improve my text, and reassess several vital points in my argument. Without the coaching of Kate Delaney, finally, this work could never confidently have been written in English: thanks to her invariably rapid and sound corrections, I could write freely, finding a style that seemed to suit me. This work is partly her accomplishment.

Guus and Nol accepted my absences in Vienna and Paris – a feat rendered somewhat easier by the chocolates I brought back for them. Mariella willingly coped with our boisterous little household during my absences. The three of them offered a suitably uncourtly and comfortable counterpoint, reminding me of the daily characteristics of communal living.

Abbreviations

AC	Cimber, Danjou, ed., *Archives curieuses de l'histoire de France*, série I, vol. X (Paris 1836)
AESC	*Annales ESC*
AN	Archives Nationales, Paris
AÖG	*Archiv für Österreichische Geschichte*
AVA	Österreichisches Staatsarchiv: Allgemeines Verwaltungarchiv, Vienna
BI	Bibliothèque de l'Institut, Paris
BM	Bibliothèque Mazarine, Paris
BN	Bibliothèque Nationale de France; MS f: manuscrits français; naf: nouvelles acquisitions françaises; clair: Clairambault
DAR	*Dictionnaire de l'Ancien Régime*, ed. Lucien Bély (Paris 1996)
DGS	*Dictionnaire du Grand Siècle*, ed. François Bluche (Paris 1990)
FHS	*French Historical Studies*
FH	*French History*
JMH	*Journal of Modern History*
HHStA	Österreichisches Staatsarchiv: Haus- Hof- und Staatsarchiv, Vienna. ÄZA: Ältere Zeremonialakten; OMaA: Oberstmarschallamt; OMeA: Obersthofmeisteramt; OMeA Prot: Protokoll in Hofparteiensachen; ZA Prot: Zeremonialprotokolle.
HKA	Hofkammerarchiv, Vienna; HZAB: Hofzahlamtsbücher.
LMA	*Lexikon des Mittelalters*
MIÖG	*Mitteilungen des Instituts für Österreichische Geschichtsforschung*
MRK	*Mitteilungen der Residenzenkommission der Akademie der Wissenschaften zu Göttingen*
MÖStA	*Mitteilungen des Österreichischen Staatsarchivs*
ÖNB	Österreichische Nationalbibliothek, Vienna
ÖZV	Fellner, Thomas and Kretschmayr, Heinrich, eds., *Die österreichische Zentralverwaltung*, I, 3 vols. (Vienna 1907)
WRGB	*Wiener Geschichtsblätter*

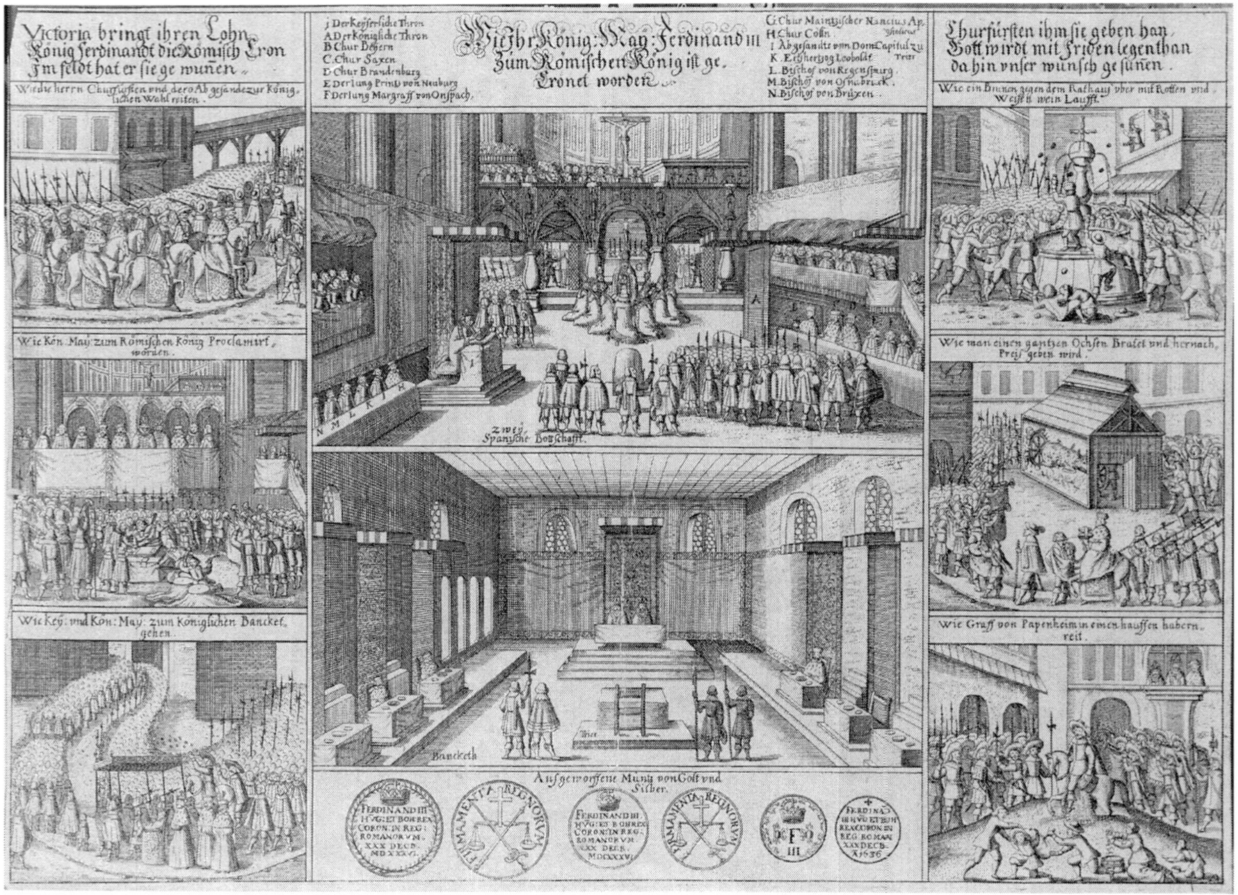

Scenes from Ferdinand III's coronation as King of the Romans, 1636. Note the '*ausgeworffne Müntz*'

PART I

Prelude

CHAPTER 1

Introduction

HOUSEHOLD AND GOVERNMENT

A court, Furetière noted in his 1690 dictionary, is 'the residence of a king or sovereign prince', but also 'the king and his council, or ministers', and 'the officers and the suite of a prince'. To the trinity of palace, council, and retinue, he added a range of meanings connected with either courts of law or refined manners. The 1694 *Dictionnaire de l'Académie*, listing the same associated meanings, primarily described the court as: 'la Maison, les Officiers, les Principaux Seigneurs, & la Justice Ordinaire d'un Roy, d'un Prince' – 'maison' covering dynasty, household, and house. Johann Heinrich Zedler preceded the lengthy discussion of 'Hof' in his *Universal-Lexicon* with the succinct but comprehensive traditional formula: 'Hof wird genennet, wo sich der Fürst aufhält'.[1] All contemporary definitions include both household and government. Indeed, more often than not the officers and attendants following the sovereign and catering for his table, bed, chapel, and stable, had a significant share in the administration of the realm. Moreover, the greater nobles in the vicinity of the court had the right and duty to help and advise the ruler, and the latter was expected to listen to them. From the later Middle Ages until the seventeenth or eighteenth centuries the staffs of most courts expanded – this growth was as relevant for the household as for the administrative services operating within its compass. During and after this phase of expansion, however, household and government slowly but perceptibly drifted apart, a process accompanied by changes in the nature and status of rulership.

[1] Antoine Furetière, *Dictionnaire Universel contenant generalement tous les mots françois* . . . (Paris 1690); *Dictionnaire de l'Académie* (Paris 1694); *Encyclopédie ou dictionnaire raisonné des sciences, des arts et des métiers*, ed. Diderot and D'Alembert (Paris 1756), VI, p. 355, opens with the same description, but soon turns into a critique of courtly vanities; Johann Heinrich Zedler, *Grosses vollständiges Universal-Lexikon aller Wissenschaften und Kunsten* . . . (Leipzig and Halle 1732; repr. Graz 1961), XIII, pp. 405–406; a parallel Spanish description is cited in Glyn Redworth and Fernando Checa, 'The Courts of the Spanish Habsburgs', in J. Adamson, ed., *The Princely Courts of Europe: Ritual, Politics, and Culture under the Ancien Régime 1500–1750* (London 1999), pp. 42–65, here at p. 43: the court is 'the place where the king is to be found with his vassals and his own officials, who constantly advise and wait on him, as well as the great men of the kingdom, who are present'.

Thus, when Louis XVI (1774–92) in 1791 deplored the National Assembly's eagerness to isolate financially and administratively the services rendered to him personally, 'comme si . . . les services rendus à la personne du roi, ne l'étaient pas aussi à l'état', his contention reflected a partisan perspective.[2] In the preceding five centuries rulers themselves had frequently attempted to disengage government and household. The administrative agents and institutions expanding from the later Middle Ages remained linked to the services catering for the ruler's personal needs, but in the course of the early modern age they increasingly operated as an autonomous segment connected only with the apex of the household: the ruler and his circle of advisers. In the sixteenth and early seventeenth centuries, the steady growth of government by paper secured a more conspicuous place at court for administrative specialists of various kinds – a challenge to those among the sword nobles who saw executive power, high court office, and military command as their birthright. Whether subservient to the court's dignitaries, or responsible only to the ruler himself; whether competing with the great nobles, or assimilating with them: high-placed robe administrators had come to stay. Everywhere specialised administrative services grew larger and developed 'bureaucratic' routines. Robe and sword had to come to terms with each other, establishing a new division both of responsibilities and of status.

From the later seventeenth century onwards several practices emerged that further qualified the pre-eminence of the noble household officers and their clans. Through the 'ordre du tableau' Louis XIV's (1643–1715) war minister François-Michel Le Tellier, marquis de Louvois (1641–1691) reorganised promotion in the army, stressing seniority and restricting the privileges of noble status. More importantly, the Sun King did not readily include princes and great nobles in his councils: only the most trusted among his noble companions were allowed to participate in the formal machinery of decision-making. The officers of the royal household were no longer responsible for the government of the realm, and they shared the responsibility for the household staffs with the *sécrétaire d'Etat* for the *maison du roi*. In 1662–1665 and in 1685, the restored English court was much reduced, and it must have lost some of its allure. In the century following the institution of the 'civil list' in 1698, this parliamentary grant sustaining the royal household helped to secure a clearer separation of the budgets of household, warfare, and government.[3] Moreover, it underlined the fact that the court could no longer unequivocally claim to be the centre of the realm.

[2] Louis' declaration is printed in the *Archives Parlementaires de 1787 à 1860*, ed. M. J. Mavidal and M. E. Laurent, première série, vol. XXVII (Paris 1887), pp. 378–383, at p. 379.

[3] See John A. Lynch and E. A. Reitan, 'From Revenue to Civil List, 1689–1702: The Revolution Settlement and the "Mixed and Balanced" Constitution', *Historical Journal* 13 (1970), pp. 571–588; J. Adamson, 'The Tudor and Stuart Courts 1509–1714', in *The Princely Courts of Europe*, pp. 116–117.

Elsewhere, different developments pointed in the same direction. In the years of Frederick III/I (1688–1701–1713), the Prussian court had attempted to emulate the greater European courts. The Soldier-King Frederick William I (1713–1740), however, almost totally abolished his father's household. Frederick the Great (1740–1786) restored a bare minimum, but concentrated on government and military exploits, leaving representative courtly responsibilities to the separate establishments of his spouse and siblings.[4] After the debacle of the Silesian Wars, Maria Theresa (1740–1780) fundamentally reorganised the administration and the army, following enlightened precepts but carefully maintaining the compact of dynasty and magnates. She did put the household, and even noble rank in general, on a more equal footing with the administrative and military hierarchies – a development echoing a similar 1680 Danish ordinance, and Peter the Great's 1722 Table of Ranks.[5] The share of the senior court officers in Maria Theresa's administrative machinery was hardly as comprehensive as had been that of their predecessors, though we can only guess the extent of their influence. Joseph II (1765–1790) further transformed and reduced the Austrian court; his recurring attempts at sweeping reform temporarily upset the balance between elites and dynasty.[6] In France, where the initial bureaucratic impulse had been quite strong, and the administration undoubtedly became more professional in the course of the eighteenth century, the challenge of the robe administrators diminished. The most prominent among the ministerial dynasties were integrated into noble dynasties, several of whom had again secured a key position in the machinery of decision-making around court. In the last decades preceding the Revolution, military and financial debacles did cause fundamental reforms in two quintessentially noble domains: the army was reorganised by the comte de Saint-Germain in 1776, and the royal household was reformed and curtailed from 1780 onwards.

By the end of the eighteenth century, service and merit, traditionally connected with noble status, were no longer necessarily based on genealogy: noble birth and merit could indeed be perceived as opposing principles. Nobilities may or may not have served their rulers, but service itself, on the battlefield, in the bureaucracy, or in finance, became the ennobling principle *par excellence*. European court fashion reflected this evolution: military uniform replaced traditional court dress at the Swedish, Prussian, and Josephine courts – most other

4 Thomas Biskup, 'Queen Elisabeth Christine of Prussia as Consort', paper presented to the conference of the Society for Court Studies, September 1999; the author kindly gave me a copy of his text, to be published in Clarissa Campbell Orr, ed., *Queenship in Europe 1660–1815: The Role of the Consort* (Cambridge 2004). See also Markus Völkel, 'The Hohenzollern Court', in *Princely Courts of Europe*, pp. 211–229.

5 Robert Molesworth, *Etat du Royaume de Danemark, tel qu'il etoit en 1692* (Amsterdam 1695), pp. 205–211, the 'Ordonnance' of 31 December 1680.

6 P. G. M. Dickson, *Finance and Government under Maria Theresia 1740–1780*, 2 vols. (Oxford 1987); Dickson, 'Monarchy and Bureaucracy in Late Eighteenth-Century Austria', *English Historical Review* 110 (1995), pp. 323–367.

courts followed, or sported the simple *frac* instead of the rich French-inspired *habit habillé* and the traditional Habsburg *Mantelkleid*.[7] The forms of social advancement the early modern state had provided for its servants had closely mirrored the traditions and social patterns of the noble elite, creating a multi-layered stratum of service elites that sought to legitimise their position by genealogy; the service elites emerging in the nineteenth century, however, were subject to more rigorous forms of training and selection, and genealogy became less important. This 'modernisation' of the state and its service elites was a long and confused process. We can point to late medieval 'new' monarchies, to the great phases of state building from the sixteenth into the eighteenth centuries; we may want to stress the watershed of 1770–1830, choose to focus on the remarkable mixture of innovation and inflated traditionalism characteristic of nineteenth-century monarchy, or emphasise structural affinities of 'modernising' states in all ages. In no country, however, did the professionalisation of bureaucracies and the insulation of the ruler's household reach a conclusive phase in the early modern age. At some courts the formal connections between household and government remained strong, while the separation achieved on paper in other realms inevitably proved highly permeable because of the accumulation of offices from both spheres in one person or dynasty, and the courtiers' easy access to the ruler's ear.

Emmanuel Siéyès forcefully made this point in his famous 1789 *Qu'est ce que le Tiers Etat* where he deplored the pervasive influence of court nobles.[8] For Siéyès' contemporaries the argument may have been evident, but a further century of bureaucratic development and constitutional debate obscured it. Indeed, with the erosion of monarchy itself in the nineteenth century, the political relevance of court office dwindled as well. Access to the ruler through noble familiarity or domestic service lost its prime importance as other centres of power and patronage came to the fore. Without a doubt, the personal environment of heads of state, whether crowned or chosen, will always retain a certain influence, but the primacy of institutionalised processes of decision-making, and the public functions of representative agencies strictly limit such influences – or force them to domains less visible to public scrutiny, as informal contacts bypassing regular procedures threaten to bring scandal or crisis upon discovery. In the early modern age, household and government were equally 'public', and the household was by no means subservient. Thus, in a process of many centuries, the priorities were inverted: the subservient administrative compartment within

[7] Philip Mansel, 'Monarchy, Uniform, and the Rise of the Frac', *Past & Present* 96 (1982), pp. 103–132, cites the fact that in eighteenth-century France, the fortunes of the silk industry determined the court's decision to maintain the *habit habillé*.

[8] Emmanuel Siéyès, *Qu'est ce que le Tiers Etat*, ed. R. Zappéri (Geneva 1970), pp. 132–133. Siéyès presents robe, sword, and church as functional categories within the 'toute-puissante' aristocracy ruling the court. Compare Malesherbes' complaint to Louis XVI during his short incumbency as secretary of state for the household, AN O 1 749, no. 51, stating that the minister could not reform the court, or give orders to court dignitaries.

the ruler's household now reigns supreme, whereas the modern equivalents of the household are either relegated to a constitutionally defined compartment within the state, or have no formal significance.

Not without reason, nineteenth-century historians looked for the origins of this development in medieval and early modern Europe – one of the contentions of this book is that in doing so, they seriously antedated the isolation and marginalisation of the household. They judged dynastic Europe with the standards of the late nineteenth century, and saw ministers, councils, and bureaucracies in isolation from their courtly environment, treating the early modern household as the largely irrelevant environment of these modern-day institutions. An obsession with the antecedents of the modern state prevented them from granting the household its proper place, and from understanding the crucial unrecorded and informal component of collegial decision-making. In France, the court could be viewed with some indulgence, because it was thought to have consolidated 'national' state building by allowing the 'absolute' rulers to overcome 'feudal' opposition – and establish favourable boundaries. Nineteenth-century German historiography had more difficulties in reconciling the heritage of the Holy Roman Empire and its multi-dynastic mosaic with the ideal of the national state: the multiple courts came to symbolise German impotence, equally ineffectual Habsburg suzerainty, and French triumph. Versailles was equated with the blatant proclamation of victory, demonstrated again in 1871 and 1919. Everywhere, the ideals of national state building dictated the interpretation of dynastic Europe: this prolific generation of historians laid the foundations for our knowledge of the early modern court, and their copious source editions still mould it. Nor was their heritage soon to be corrected by twentieth-century historians. Royalty became ever more marginal, and from the early 1930s until the early 1970s, the court was seen as a quixotic topic, suited only for reactionaries or eccentrics.

REDRESSING THE BALANCE

After fifty years, the court was roused from its historiographical somnolence. Probably, Norbert Elias was the main actor: his epoch-making studies restored the relevance and legitimacy of the court as a theme for research among a generation of historians that had been inclined to ignore it. Indeed, he made it acceptable for those frowning upon the traditional forms of political history, for whom the court and its mannerisms had represented a historical non-entity carrying politically offensive associations. Elias combined the nineteenth century thesis of state building with the equally classic notion of a *civilisation des mœurs* from the later Middle Ages into the eighteenth century; a connection that would hardly have surprised Voltaire or other *philosophes*. They would probably have been slightly more sceptical about the nature of this connection as proposed by

Elias: a change from *Fremdzwang* to *Selbstzwang*. 'External' force dictated more subdued forms of behaviour, but such forms were soon to be embraced as an 'internal' standard, an ideal. Elias chose the court as the focus of this process of 'internalisation', ruler and nobles acting as his main protagonists.[9] Only by losing its power could the nobility set the standards for 'civilisation' in Europe. Elias' conceptual framework thus neatly fitted the perspective of the 'national' historians: again we learn that the court was important because it contributed to the rise of the modern state by annulling the power of that other atavism: nobility. The court was not a centre of noble power; it was a gilded cage for the 'domesticated' grandees. The ruler incited his courtiers to ruin themselves by conspicuous consumption, to engage in ceremonial squabbles with their rivals at court, and thus to gradually dissolve into insignificance under his wary eye. Elias sought and found support for his model mainly in the *mémoires* of the duke of Saint-Simon – a great writer but a *courtisan manqué* and a seriously misleading source for the history of the Sun King's court when used in isolation.

Elias elucidated many patterns of elite behaviour, and some of his conceptions undoubtedly still have great relevance for those studying court life. Rulers may frequently have been shrewd manipulators, nobles hapless victims: it will not do, however, to use such circumstances as logical necessities within a larger argument. Striving to substantiate his grand thesis, Elias excluded the multiple variants of court life that did not fit or that explicitly contradicted his model, in France and elsewhere. The overstatement of the ruler's personal impact, moreover, surprises in an account that incessantly underlines the risks of concentrating on individual actors. By compressing various phases in the interaction of monarch and nobles into one model, Elias strengthened and extended the dominance of the 'myth of Versailles' that arose in the wake of Saint-Simon's memoirs and had already swayed several generations of historians, novelists, as well as, more recently, film-makers. Yet the triumphant restoration of royal power in Louis XIV's early personal reign, starkly contrasting with the defiance of princes and parlements during the *Fronde*; the brilliant first decade of Versailles; the somnolent train of later years marked by financial duress, and the eighteenth-century *raffinements* of a court dominated by an assertive noble elite do not easily fit Elias' monistic view. While Elias mainly discussed France, the scope of his study remained unclear,

[9] Norbert Elias, *Die höfische Gesellschaft. Untersuchungen zur Soziologie des Königtums und der höfischen Aristokratie. Mit einer Einleitung: Soziologie und Geschichtswissenschaft* (Darmstadt and Neuwied 1969); *Über den Prozeß der Zivilisation. Soziogenetische und Psychogenetische Untersuchungen. I: Wandlungen des Verhaltens in den Weltlichen Oberschichten des Abendlandes. II: Wandlungen der Gesellschaft. Entwurf zu einer Theorie der Zivilisation* (Bern 1969). For the earlier historiography of the court and the reception of Elias' works, see Jeroen Duindam, *Myths of Power: Norbert Elias and the Early Modern European Court* (Amsterdam 1995); Duindam, 'Norbert Elias und der frühneuzeitliche Hof. Versuch einer Kritik und Weiterführung', *Historische Anthropologie* 6, 4 (1998), pp. 370–387; Wolfgang Jäger, '"Menschwissenschaft" und historische Sozialwissenschaft. Zur Rezeption von Norbert Elias', *Archiv für Kulturgeschichte* 77 (1995), pp. 85–116; Gerd Schwerhoff, 'Zivilisationsprozeß und Geschichtswissenschaft. Norbert Elias' Forschungsparadigma in historischer Sicht', *Historische Zeitschrift* 266 (1998), pp. 61–105.

and the allure of his statements encouraged others to explicitly generalise them. Thus, in a 'structuralised' form, the Little Duke's rhetoric, barely credible for Versailles itself, was once more accepted as shorthand for court life all over Europe.[10]

Elias' perplexing mélange of grand theory, lucidly formulated analysis, and rather limited research gave rise to a tradition of aulic history with a strong partiality for conceptual ornament and eclectic discourse. The 'role' of the court in 'absolutism' and the 'meaning' of ceremony were deemed more worthy of scholarly attention than the concrete forms of ceremony or the daily routines of the court. Anthropological perspectives, of great relevance for the reassessment of courts in the European past, added emphasis to the notion of 'ritual' and, in an unfortunate conjunction with the post-modern stress on 'de-construction' and rhetoric, strengthened the inclination to wrestle with concepts rather than with concrete data. Moreover, aulic history emerged as a specialised domain with a strong cultural bias, demonstrated by the presence of authors from related

[10] Surprisingly, among French historians of the French court, Elias' views long held sway; notwithstanding the fundamental article by Jacqueline Boucher, 'L'évolution de la maison du Roi: des derniers Valois aux premiers Bourbons', *XVIIe Siècle* 137 (1982), pp. 359–379, putting the Sun King's *maison* into its proper perspective; the brilliant revision of the balance among state, high finance, and nobilities by Daniel Dessert, *Argent, pouvoir et société au grand siècle* (Paris 1984) and his earlier article with J.-L. Journet, 'Le lobby Colbert: un royaume ou une affaire de famille', *AESC* 30, 6 (1975), pp. 1303–1336; the generally well-balanced overview by Jean François Solnon, *La Cour de France* (Paris 1987) corrected many clichés, as did Hélène Himelfarb, 'Versailles: fonctions et légendes', in *Les lieux de mémoire*, ed. Pierre Nora, vol. II: *La Nation* (Paris 1986), pp. 235–292, and to a lesser extent Edouard Pommier, 'Versailles, l'image du souverain', in the same volume on pp. 193–234. See many instructive contributions to the *Dictionnaire de l'Ancien Régime*, ed. Lucien Bély (Paris 1996) and the *Dictionnaire du Grand Siècle*, ed. François Bluche (Paris 1990). The traditional interpretation, reinforced by Elias, was explicitly challenged by Emmanuel Le Roy Ladurie's *Saint-Simon ou le système de la cour* (Paris 1997) paradoxically on the basis mostly of Saint-Simon himself. Gérard Sabatier, *Versailles ou la Figure du Roi* (Paris 1999) a careful, but descriptive study of the great palace, and the dossier on the *logements* compiled by William Ritchey Newton, *L'Espace du roi. La cour de France au château de Versailles 1682–1789* (Paris 2000) do not go beyond the traditional view. On aspects of the court see, for example, the lavishly illustrated Daniel Roche and Daniel Reytier, eds., *Les écuries royales du xvie au xviiie siècle* (Paris 1998), particularly Reytier's 'Un service de la Maison du roi: les écuries de Versailles (1682–1789)', on pp. 61–95, a fine and well-researched overview, that nevertheless dutifully pays lip service to Elias' analysis; the collection 'Les Métiers de Versailles', edited by Béatrix Saule, recently opened with Patricia Bouchenot-Déchin, *Henry Dupuis, jardinier de Louis XIV* (Versailles 2001). Philippe Salvadori's *La Chasse sous l'Ancien Régime* (Paris 1996) adds depth and detail, but does not explicitly attack older conventions; nor does the notably less scholarly work by Roland Jousselin, *Au couvert de roi XVIIe–XVIIIe siècles* (Paris n.d.) mixing original research with unverified assumptions. Two recent works go much further: Nicolas Le Roux, *La faveur du roi. Mignons et courtisans au temps des derniers Valois (vers 1547–vers 1589)* (Paris 2000) provides a detailed analysis of the world of faction and favouritism in the later sixteenth century; Katia Béguin, *Les princes de Condé. Rebelles, courtisans et mécènes dans la France du grand siècle* (Paris 1999) outlines the careers of the Condé princes in the seventeenth century, Henry II, Louis II, and Henry-Jules, carefully demonstrating the compromise of Henry II and Richelieu, the exceptional phase of the *Fronde*, and the lasting importance of the Condé 'nébuleuse' in the later seventeenth century, based on an ever-increasing family fortune. Béguin recently published an innovative analysis of the consequences of Louis XIV's decision to rule without first minister: 'Louis XIV et l'aristocratie: coup de majesté ou retour à la tradition', *Histoire, économie et société* 19, 4 (2000), pp. 497–512. For the Anglo-Saxon revision of absolutism, see below; among other works on the French court: David Potter, *A History of France 1460–1560: The Emergence of a Nation State* (Houndmills and Basingstoke 1995), pp. 57–89, offers a thorough discussion of the French court; Ruth Kleinman, 'Social Dynamics at the French Court: The Household of Anne of Austria', *FHS* 16, 3 (1990), pp. 517–535, is an analysis of the social composition of the household. Leonhard Horowski, 'Pouvez-vous trop donner pour une chose si essentielle? Eine prosopographische Studie der Obersten Chargen am Hof von Versailles', *MRK* 11, 1 (2001), pp. 32–53, offers a wide-ranging discussion of the careers and connections of the highest courtiers, confirming the 'revisionist' thesis.

disciplines such as the history of art, music, theatre, architecture, and language. While the impetus from these disciplines was and remains indispensable, the dominant cultural bias complicated the communication with the field of political history. Thus, the discussion of the 'rhetoric' or 'presentation' of power was not sufficiently connected to the processes of decision-making at court, nor were the rationale or the audiences of courtly splendour systematically analysed. The post-1970 aulic history in its first decades did not suffice to expose the biases of the nineteenth-century heritage; neither could it put into perspective the unwarranted hegemony of Versailles, nor did it effectively integrate the revision of absolutism that gained force in the same years.[11]

Indeed, a fundamental reinterpretation of the early modern state emerged in these decades that should have had many repercussions for the history of the court. Among others, R. J. Knecht, R. Hatton, J. H. Elliott, and R. J. W. Evans, gave a more differentiated and nuanced image of state building, underlining the composite nature of monarchies, the lasting impact of various elites, the nature of political and cultural patronage, faction and favourites at court. Their works made quite clear the relevance of the ruler's personal entourage, and it is hardly a coincidence that the authors mentioned contributed the most distinguished chapters to A. G. Dickens' *The Courts of Europe*.[12] In the 1980s, a range of detailed studies explicitly attacked the notion of 'absolutism', stressing the financial limits of monarchical rule and the resilience of regional powers. The impressive written output of central administrative institutions, the principal source of earlier histories of state building, cannot in itself be seen as 'evidence' of the ruler's power. A proliferation of decrees and state servants does not necessarily coincide with the growing power of the administrative centre of a realm. Moreover, when we can indeed establish such a development, it is far from evident that this necessarily entailed a decline of noble power: elites could gain in the centre what they had lost in the periphery. Absolutism was a conscious

[11] See discussions and bibliography in Duindam, *Myths of Power*, and more recently 'Ceremony at Court: Reflections on an Elusive Subject', *Francia. Forschungen zur westeuropäischen Geschichte* 26, 2 (1999), pp. 131–140; Barbara Stollberg-Rilinger, 'Zeremoniell, Ritual, Symbol. Neue Forschungen zur symbolischen Kommunikation in Spätmittelalter und früher Neuzeit', *Zeitschrift für historische Forschung* 27, 3 (2000), pp. 389–405. In his review of Adamson's *The Princely Courts of Europe*, J. H. Elliott, 'Tediums and Te Deums', *Times Literary Supplement*, 28 April 2000, p. 27, rightly points to the dangers inherent in 'mere antiquarianism'; it is difficult, however, to find a middle way between an 'archeology' of the court concentrating on staffs, numbers, details of ceremonies, etc. and the highly conceptualised and uninformative first phase of 'new aulic history' – a certain level of precision is imperative.

[12] In addition to the contributions to *The Courts of Europe: Politics, Patronage and Royalty 1400–1800*, ed. A. G. Dickens (London 1977), see R. J. Knecht's, 'The Court of Francis I', *European Studies Review* 8 (1982), pp. 1–22; Knecht, *Renaissance Warrior and Patron: The Reign of Francis I* (Cambridge 1994); with Jonathan Brown, J. H. Elliott published *A Palace for a King: The Buen Retiro and the Court of Philip IV* (New Haven and London 1980); his *Spain and Its World 1500–1700: Selected Essays* (New Haven and London 1989) includes a section on the world of the court, as does the volume of essays in honour of Elliott, *Spain, Europe and the Atlantic World*, ed. Richard L. Kagan and Geoffrey Parker (Cambridge 1995), pp. 27–99. R. J. W. Evans' *The Making of the Habsburg Monarchy 1550–1700: An Interpretation* (Oxford 1979), the basis of a new consensus on the Habsburg Lands, does not concentrate on the court; the same holds true for the various volumes edited by Ragnhild Hatton on Louis XIV's reign.

presentation of rulership – an ambition demonstrated on a grand scale, but only partly underpinned by concrete achievement. Nor can we simply take at face value the grandiose presentation of the Sun King's power.[13] Indeed, French 'absolutism', always the prime example, was also the first casualty: William Beik, Daniel Dessert, Joseph Bergin, Roger Mettam, David Parrott, and many others carefully exposed the frailty of earlier historiography.[14] In Germany, conversely, the revision of 'national' historiographies fostered a greater interest in and respect for the Holy Roman Empire, as is evident in the works of authors such as Karl Otmar von Aretin, Volker Press, and Helmut Neuhaus.[15]

Did the revision of absolutism and the new focus on the history of elites give rise to a more mature aulic history? The conference volume edited by Ronald Asch and Adolf Birke, *Princes, Patronage, and the Nobility*, offered a new starting point, combining a detailed down-to-earth discussion of the courts with questions arising from the more conceptualised forms of aulic history. Only towards the end of the 1990s, however, was it followed by various other equally important volumes.[16] Even the most recent works suggest that we are far from a broadly based and well-founded reassessment of the European court. David Starkey, Robert Bucholz, and a range of other historians have established an exceptionally favourable position for the English court. Several studies have contributed to our knowledge of the Spanish court, always relatively strong because of John Elliott's leading example. Elsewhere, results have been less promising: there is no fully convincing study of either the French or the Austrian Habsburg court, and

[13] See the discussion of Louis' presentation in Peter Burke, *The Fabrication of Louis XIV* (New Haven and London 1992), contrasted with eighteenth-century developments in T. C. W. Blanning, *The Culture of Power and the Power of Culture* (Oxford 2002); compare Roger Mettam's more sceptical 'Power, Status and Precedence: Rivalries among the Provincial Elites of Louis XIV's France', *Transactions of the Royal Historical Society* 38 (1988), pp. 43–62, and the judicious analysis of the king's image in popular media by Jens Ivo Engels, *Königsbilder. Sprechen, Singen und Schreiben über den französischen König in der ersten Hälfte des achtzehnten Jahrhunderts*, Pariser Historische Studien 52 (Bonn 2000).

[14] William Beik, *Absolutism and Society in Seventeenth-Century France: State Power and Provincial Aristocracy in Languedoc* (Cambridge 1985); Roger C. Mettam, *Power and Faction in Louis XIV's France* (Oxford and New York 1988); Joseph Bergin, *The Rise of Richelieu* (New Haven 1991) and his *The Making of the French Episcopate (1589–1661)* (New Haven and London 1996); David Parrott, *Richelieu's Army: War, Government and Society in France, 1624–1642* (Cambridge 2001); Dessert, *Argent, pouvoir et société*; also see Sharon Kettering, *Patrons, Brokers and Clients in Seventeenth-Century France* (Oxford 1986); Peter R. Campbell, *Power and Politics in Old Regime France, 1720–1745* (London 1996).

[15] See the judicious reassessments by Peter H. Wilson, *The Holy Roman Empire, 1495–1806* (Basingstoke 1999); Helmut Neuhaus, *Das Reich in der frühen Neuzeit* (Munich 1997), and further literature cited there. Georg Schmidt's challenging *Geschichte des alten Reiches. Staat und Nation in der Frühen Neuzeit 1495–1806* (Munich 1999) opened a new debate; see, for example, Heinz Schilling, 'Reichs-Staat im frühneuzeitliche Nation der deutschen oder teilmodernisiertes Reichssystem. Überlegungen zu Charakter und Aktualität des Alten Reiches', *Historische Zeitschrift* 272, 2 (2001), pp. 377–395.

[16] R. G. Asch and A. Birke, eds., *Princes, Patronage and the Nobility: The Court at the Beginning of the Modern Age c. 1450–1650* (Oxford and London 1991); Adamson, *Princely Courts of Europe*; J. H. Elliott and L. W. B. Brockliss, eds., *The World of the Favourite* (New Haven and London 1999); Maurice Aymard and Marzio A. Romani, eds., *La cour comme institution économique* (Paris 1998); Holger Kruse and Werner Paravicini, eds., *Höfe und Hofordnungen 1200–1600. 5. Symposium der Residenzen-Kommission der Akademie der Wissenschaften in Göttingen* (Sigmaringen 1999), and other volumes in this valuable series, most recently Jan Hirschbiegel and Werner Paravacini, eds., *Das Frauenzimmer. Die Frau bei Hofe in Spätmittelalter und früher Neuzeit 6. Symposium der Residenzen-Kommission der Akademie der Wissenschaften in Göttingen* (Stuttgart 2000).

only few of the Scandinavian, German, and Italian courts have received solid treatment.[17] The fact that the prestigious multi-volume European Science Foundation project on 'the origins of the modern state in Europe' did not choose to include the ruler's household and its relationship to the emerging administrative machinery of government among its major themes, may serve as a reminder that aulic history has been far from effective: the nineteenth-century heritage still has great impact.[18] Only in a small number of works do we find both a solid grasp of this major problem, and the crucial attempt to bring together the predominantly cultural field of court studies with recent work on decision-making in the early modern state.

The sharp divide between household and government is not the only delusive opposition hindering the history of the court. Ceremony more often than not is pictured either as a shrewd manipulation, or as an impregnable fortress of ingrained symbols and signs. Rulers and nobles, or alternatively rulers and estates assemblies, seem to fall into the categories of either friends or foes; court nobles tend be perceived either as a ruling caste or as a captive elite. Neither of these instances of *Trennungsdenken* is helpful: it is the continuing movement between the poles that defines the court, and makes it so interesting. Thus, while one cannot deny the conscious use of ceremony to bolster reputation, it is equally futile to present it as a Machiavellian ruse, monopolised by the sovereign and unconstrained by the hierarchical worldview. Likewise, the 'integration' of noble elites in structures such as army, court, and bureaucracy is clearly supported by historical evidence, but it is not so clear whether this means that a determined ruler 'domesticated' his unruly elites, or that the latter lost their power in the process. Rulers and ministers may have been subject to the same forces. At court, innovation and tradition permanently intertwined, and frequent *ad hoc* attempts to restore an imaginary old order may have had more 'innovative' results than premeditated attempts at change. Nor were sword

[17] On the English court see, for example, David Starkey, ed., *The English Court from the Wars of the Roses to the Civil War* (London 1987); Robert Bucholz, *The Augustan Court: Queen Anne and the Decline of Court Culture* (Stanford 1993); Bucholz and J. C. Sainty, eds., *Officials of the Royal Household, 1660–1837. Part I, Department of the Lord Chamberlain and Associated Offices* (London 1997); Simon Thurley, *The Royal Palaces of Tudor England* (New Haven and London 1993); Ronald G. Asch, *Der Hof Karls I. Vom England. Politik, Provinz und Patronage* (Cologne, Weimar, and Vienna 1993); Simon Adams, 'Favourites and Factions at the Elizabethan Court', in *Princes, Patronage, and the Nobility*, ed. Asch and Birke, pp. 265–287, as well as his short 'The Court as an Economic Institution: The Court of Elizabeth I of England, 1558–1603', in *La cour comme institution économique*, ed. Aymard and Romani, pp. 127–136; Mia Rodriguez-Salgado, 'Honour and Profit in the Court of Philip II of Spain', in *La cour comme institution économique*, pp. 67–86, and Guido Guerzoni, 'The Courts of Este in the First Half of XVIth Century: Socio-economic Aspects', in *La cour comme institution économique*, pp. 89–113; Fabian Persson, *Servants of Fortune: The Swedish Court between 1598 and 1721* (Lund 1999); Olaf Mörke, *'Stadtholder' oder 'Staetholder'?: die Funktion des Hauses Oranien und seines Hofes in der politischen Kultur der Republik der Vereinigten Niederlande im 17. Jahrhundert* (Münster 1997) – this sound study was much influenced by Elias' perspective.

[18] In the important ESF series 'The Origins of the Modern State in Europe', the household falls between the volumes on power elites, Wolfgang Reinhardt, ed., *Power Elites and State Building* (Oxford 1996), and representation, Allan Ellenius, ed., *Iconography, Propaganda, and Legitimation* (Oxford 1998); it is not thoroughly discussed in either of these, and is absent from other volumes in the series.

nobles and estates always agents of tradition, robe administrators and rulers rational innovators.

It is high time to re-establish the concrete outlines of the early modern household, leaving aside the burdensome heritages of contemporary propaganda and national historiography, while evading the biases and dead ends of the first generation of aulic history. Yet it is premature to combine the available knowledge into a general synthesis or 'model'; at the present time this would necessarily lead to a catalogue of ill-assorted instances, or a typology constructed on the basis of insufficient data.[19] A detailed study of one court, on the other hand, does not provide sufficient basis to reconsider the tenacious imagery of Saint-Simon's Versailles. While the range of learned studies of the English court, Aloys Winterling's penetrating 1986 study of the court of the electors of Cologne, or Fabian Persson's well-documented analysis of the Swedish court, conclusively demonstrate that the 'model of Versailles' was not universally valid, this information does not allow us to judge the situation in France. Concentration on France itself is equally inauspicious: without the questions and hints suggested by the study of the sources of another court, it is far more difficult to reassess the French example, and impossible to judge whether it truly was an exception.

Only a comparison of the French court with another major European court fits my purposes. For the sixteenth century, Spain and possibly England are suitable candidates; for the early seventeenth century, Vienna in addition to Spain is an acceptable alternative, yet for the paradigmatic Versailles decades from 1682 to 1715, the Viennese court is the obvious choice.[20] The contacts between the French and Austrian Habsburg courts emerged almost as a consequence of the ties both

[19] The overviews by Volker Bauer, *Die höfische Gesellschaft in Deutschland von der mitte des 17. bis zum Ausgang des 18. Jahrhunderts. Versuch einer Typologie* (Tübingen 1993) and Rainer Müller, *Der Fürstenhof in der frühen Neuzeit* (Munich 1995), useful as they are, indicate that the court needs more detailed study before we can comfortably reach a higher level of synthesis. Peter Claus Hartmann's recent *Kulturgeschichte des Heiligen Römischen Reiches 1648 bis 1806. Verfassung, Religion und Kultur* (Vienna, Cologne, and Graz 2001) includes a rather unsurprising section on 'höfische Kultur', pp. 283–326, based largely on the models of Elias and Krüdener, and the preceding overviews.

[20] On the Austrian Habsburg court see the bibliography in Jeroen Duindam, 'The Court of the Austrian Habsburgs: Locus of a Composite Heritage', *MRK* 8, 2 (1998), pp. 24–58; Ivan Zolger, *Der Hofstaat des Hauses Österreich*, Wiener staatswissenschaftliche Studien 14 (Vienna and Leipzig 1917); R. J. W. Evans, 'The Austrian Habsburgs: The Dynasty as a Political Institution', in *The Courts of Europe*, ed. Dickens, pp. 121–145; Hubert Ch. Ehalt, *Ausdrucksformen absolutistischer Herrschaft. Der Wiener Hof im 17. und 18. Jahrhundert*, Sozial- und Wirtschaftshistorische Studien 14 (Vienna 1980). Major recent contributions include: John P. Spielman, *The City & the Crown: Vienna and the Imperial Court 1600–1740* (West Lafayette, Indiana, 1993); Andreas Pecar, 'Die Ökonomie der Ehre. Ressourcen, Zeremoniell und Selbstdarstellungspraxis des höfischen Adels am Kaiserhof Karls VI. (1711–1740)', unpublished dissertation Cologne (2001); on the practices of governing under Leopold, see: Stefan Sienell, *Die geheime Konferenz unter Kaiser Leopold I. Personelle Strukturen und Methoden zur Entscheidungsfindung am Wiener Hof* (Frankfurt and Bern 2001). Various articles provide information and analysis of court life, for example, Stefan Sienell, 'Die Wiener Hofstaate zur Zeit Leopolds I.', in *Hofgesellschaft und Höflinge an europäischen Fürstenhöfe in der Frühen Neuzeit (15.–18. Jh.)*, ed. Klaus Malettke and Chantal Grell (Münster 2001), pp. 89–111; Mark Hengerer, 'Hofzeremoniell, Organisation und Grundmuster sozialer Differenzierung am Wiener Hof im 17. Jahrhundert', in *Hofgesellschaft und Höflinge*, ed. Malettke and Grell, pp. 337–368; Beatrix Bastl and Gernot Heiss, 'Tafeln bei Hof: die Hochzeitsbankette Kaiser Leopolds I.', *WRGB* 50 (1995), pp. 181–206; Beatrix Bastl, 'Feuerwerk und Schlittenfahrt. Ordnungen zwischen Ritual und Zeremoniell', *WRGB* 51 (1996), pp. 197–229; Bastl and Heiss, 'Hofdamen und Höflinge zur Zeit Leopolds I. Zur Geschichte eines vergessenenen Berufsstandes', *Opera Historica 5* (Ceske Budejovice 1996), pp. 187–234. Currently two research

courts maintained with the Spanish Habsburgs, the greatest European power of the late sixteenth and early seventeenth centuries. Whether in close dynastic union or in permanent rivalry – both for the Valois-Bourbon, and Austrian Habsburg rulers – Spain was the inevitable other. How did this triangle of the two branches of the Habsburgs and their French rival evolve?

TWO RIVALLING DYNASTIES

When Charles VIII of France (1483–1498) crossed the Alps in 1494, he set off a chain of events that would soon give rise to the major dynastic rivalry of early modern Europe, pitting the French Valois dynasty against the Habsburgs. The early successes of the French army, rapidly conquering Italy with its artillery train, proved short-lived, yet subsequent French kings were loath to forget their Italian ambitions. For better or for worse they repeated their efforts, only to be countered by Habsburg Spain and its allies. In 1519, the young king of Spain was elected Emperor Charles V (1519–1556), henceforth confronting the French rulers with an imposing conglomerate of possessions. The Italian wars, dragging on until 1559, gave the Habsburgs Naples and Milan in addition to Spain and its overseas territories, the Habsburg hereditary lands, the Burgundian heritage, and the imperial crown. Such an accumulation made lasting enmity with France, the greatest power of medieval Europe, more than likely, as the French saw themselves encircled by Habsburg domains.

Neither the government nor the succession of the Charles V's unwieldy realms was to remain in one hand. In 1521–1522 a Habsburg family compact laid the foundation for the division between the 'Spanish' and 'Austrian' branches of the dynasty. Emperor Maximilian I's (1493–1519) inheritance, with the exception of the Burgundian lands, would be ruled by Charles' younger brother Ferdinand. When in 1526 the Ottoman armies conquered large parts of Hungary, killing King Louis II Jagiellon of Bohemia and Hungary in the process, Ferdinand in addition obtained these crowns. In 1531, finally, he was elected King of the Romans, or emperor-elect. In 1550–1551 Charles wanted to amend these earlier arrangements, attempting to secure the imperial title for his son Philip. The ageing emperor had to content himself with an impracticable scheme that provided for alternation between the two branches of the dynasty. Ferdinand would succeed him as emperor (1556–1564), but Philip was to be elected as King of the Romans *vivente imperatore*, in Ferdinand's lifetime. When Philip had succeeded Ferdinand, the latter's son Maximilian would be elected following the same procedure, and so on. It all came to nought: the imperial electors did not accept this infringement upon their right to freely designate the new emperor,

projects, and a 'workshop' are devoted to the study of the Habsburg court, see the internet page of the clientage project at: http://www.univie.ac.at/Geschichte/wienerhof/wienerhof2/index.htm.

nor did Ferdinand try hard to overcome their reserves. Maximilian (1564–1576) succeeded his father, and the Austrian Habsburgs would retain the imperial title until 1740. The division between the two branches remained in force until the Spanish branch became extinct with the death of Charles II in 1700.

The senior Spanish and junior Austrian Habsburgs lineages frequently exchanged spouses,[21] and tried hard to maintain a unified front towards the other European dynasties, but their task was not easy. The military priorities of the two branches did not readily coincide: Spain concentrated on its overseas territories, the Mediterranean, France, and Western Europe, whereas the Austrian Habsburgs had to take into account the Ottoman threat on their Eastern borders and the Polish–Swedish constellation on the empire's north-eastern fringes. In the later sixteenth century, moreover, the Austrian Habsburgs were of necessity more lenient vis-à-vis religious heterodoxy than the *Rey Catolico*. Ferdinand I's son Maximilian, married to Charles V's daughter Maria and serving him in Spain as stadholder, chose a religious stance that threatened to alienate both his father and the senior Spanish line. He abandoned his openly heterodox attitudes only in 1560 to secure his election as King of the Romans, confirming his acquiescence by sending his sons Rudolf and Ernst to be educated at Philip II's court. A counter-reformatory stance matching that of the Spanish rulers emerged only in the early seventeenth century. Yet even Ferdinand II (1619–1637), enforcing unambiguously counter-reformatory policies in the Habsburg hereditary lands, still had to reckon with the attitudes of electors and the princes of the empire. The emperors were constantly reminded that they ruled a commonwealth including many Protestant potentates.

Nor did the French threat always bring the branches of the dynasty together. During the Thirty Years' War, the electors and princes of the empire, Catholic and Protestant alike, had looked with a wary eye at the Spanish influences; they suspected that the emperor was at the same time restoring Catholicism and strengthening his dynastic power in the empire with Spanish help. In the Peace of Regensburg (1630) the electors stipulated that war could only be waged after their consent, obstructing Ferdinand II's intervention in the Mantuan crisis.[22] The French played the same card during the Westphalian congress, and the treaty indeed forbade the emperor to support the Spanish cause as long as Spain and France were at war. Further *Wahlkapitulationen*, the conditions the new emperor had to accept upon his election, reiterated that he could wage war only with the explicit consent of the *Reichstag*.[23] This made it even more difficult for the emperors to combine their imperial interests with Habsburg filial piety:

21 See the overview in Brigitte Hamann, ed., *Die Habsburger. Ein biographisches Lexikon* (Vienna 1988), p. 364.

22 See a recent analysis in Michael Kaiser, *Politik und Kriegsführung. Maximilian von Bayern, Tilly und die Katholische Liga im Dreißigjährigen Krieg* (Münster 1999).

23 See, for example, *Die Kaiser der Neuzeit 1519–1918. Heiliges Römisches Reich, Österreich, Deutschland*, ed. A. Schindling and W. Ziegler (Munich 1990), pp. 135–136, 155, 159–161.

Ferdinand III (1637–1657) and Leopold I (1657/8–1705) could not effectively support Philip IV (1621–1665) in his continuing war with France.

After the Peace of the Pyrenees in 1659 the nature and focus of Habsburg–Bourbon rivalry changed. The confirmation of the peace by the marriage of Louis XIV and Maria Teresa resembled the Spanish–French dynastic marriages of 1615, but the context had changed markedly. Typically when in 1661 a squabble arose between the servants of the Spanish and French ambassadors in London, it threatened to become a serious crisis; it hardly was a coincidence that Spain had to send a mission to Louis' court to apologise.[24] Spain, clearly the centre of Habsburg power and in many respects the focal point of European diplomacy in the preceding century, was soon to be eclipsed by France. The 1659 peace, and the subsequent row in London conspicuously demonstrated French ascendancy, but the Spanish example nevertheless retained a great impact on the French court in the first decades of Louis XIV's reign. Only during the critical phase of the Habsburgs in the decades around Philip IV's death in 1665 would the balance shift towards Vienna. The unexpected death of King of the Romans Ferdinand IV in 1654; the 15-month *interregnum* before the election of Leopold I in July 1658; the marriage of Louis XIV with Philip IV's eldest daughter Maria Teresa; the advent of the sickly four-year old Charles II in Spain; no male heirs in either of the two Habsburg realms: the very existence of the dynasty seemed threatened. Neither Leopold's marriage with Philip's daughter from the second bed, Margarita Teresa (1651–1673) nor his second marriage with Claudia Felicitas of Tyrol (1653–1676) changed this: only a third marriage with Eleonora of Pfalz-Neuburg (1655–1720) produced male heirs, Joseph in 1678 and Charles in 1685. By that time, Ludovician France evidently was the major European power, whereas Madrid no longer was the undisputed centre even of the Habsburg dynasty.

Halfway through Louis XIV's reign, the Spanish crown indeed ceased to be the preponderant courtly example and counterpoint for the French. Even at court in Vienna, the Spanish ambassador had trouble securing his precedence among diplomats and princes.[25] Within the limits set by the constitutional intricacies of the empire and the power of estates in the lands more closely tied to Habsburg rule, and thanks to the support of the *kaisertreue* nobles, Leopold's rule was remarkably successful. After the Ottoman siege of Vienna in 1683, hardly the timid emperor's finest hour, Habsburg armies rolled back the Ottomans and their advance was to be halted only in the late 1730s. From the late 1680s onwards, Vienna and Versailles indubitably were the two prime

[24] See Ragnhild Hatton's description in 'Louis XIV and his Fellow Monarchs', in *Louis XIV and Europe*, ed. Ragnhild Hatton (London 1976), p. 18 and n. 10.

[25] See the changing status of the Spanish ambassador, discussed on the basis of *Zeremonialprotokoll* and *Zeremonialakten* by Andrea Sommer-Mathis, 'Theatrum und Ceremoniale. Rang- und Sitzordnungen bei theatralischen Veranstaltungen am Wiener Kaiserhof im 17. und 18. Jahrhundert', in Rahn *Zeremoniell als höfische Ästhetik in Spätmittelalter und Früher Neuzeit*, ed. J. J. Berns and Th. (Tübingen 1995), pp. 511–533.

foci of European court life. The tense relations between the two courts typically emerged in the form of ceremonial conflict during the intermission of hostilities between the peace of Rijswijk (1697) and the War of Spanish Succession. In 1699, the French envoy Louis Hector de Villars visited a *Kammerfest* for archduke Charles; diplomats could attend such festivities from a certain distance. When Villars transgressed the habitual boundaries, he was forcefully expelled by Anton Florian von Liechtenstein, then Archduke Charles' *Ajo* and *Obersthofmeister*. Villars exploited the incident to create a major row, including barely veiled military threats; finally Liechtenstein had to apologise to Villars. The case did not closely resemble the more famous London dispute, nor was the Viennese apology as clear-cut or well-publicised as the earlier Spanish reparation. Nevertheless, it supports the impression that Leopold's court now bore the brunt of French ceremonial and diplomatic challenges.[26]

Once Bourbon rule in Spain had been accepted by the combatants of the War of Spanish Succession (1702–1713/15), a fundamental cause of the Habsburg–Bourbon antagonism disappeared: the 'encirclement' of France by Habsburg territories. The now Austrian Low Countries and the Bourbon and Habsburg possessions in Italy could cause problems, but the more dramatic phase of competition was over. Under the 'last Habsburg', Charles VI (1711–1740), the Viennese court reached its Baroque zenith, while still keeping the influence of French court life at a distance. Finally, both the dynastic rivalry and the decidedly un-French fashions of the Habsburg court fell victim to the great wars of the mid-eighteenth century. For the contemporaries of Versailles' brilliant first decades, Habsburg Vienna was the obvious counterpoint. It had eclipsed Madrid, and was the other major Catholic court. French ambitions in the empire, covered by the status of France as guarantor of the peace of 1648, had prodded Leopold into active defence of the imperial dimension of his dominion. Indeed, the Westphalian settlement was a starting point for the strengthening of the Habsburg position in the empire, and the court was a vital factor in that process. Leopold I increasingly served as the counter-image to Louis XIV, and the emperor benefited from the perception that he successfully defended the empire against French imperialism and the Ottoman threat. Even for many Protestants, the emperor seemed the least of evils.[27]

The very fact that Leopold's rule had a strong imperial dimension can disturb the comparison of his court with that of Louis XIV. There was a permanent confusion of the government of the hereditary Habsburg lands, the

26 See the lengthy discussions of the 1699 dispute in HHStA Staatenabteilung Frankreich, K 8 Varia 1688–1700: 'Aktenstücke welche die Beleidigung betreffen, die dem Französischen Gesandten Herzog Louis Hector de Villars bei einem Hoffeste durch den Obersthofmeister des Erzherzogs Karl, Fürsten Anton von Liechtenstein widerfahren sein soll', fols. 1–75, the threat, for example, on fol. 2: 'wan demselben mit einem Krieg gedienet ist, er alles darzu in Frankreich fertig finden werde . . .'.

27 Burke, *Fabrication of Louis XIV*; Maria Goloubeva, *The Glorification of Emperor Leopold I in Image, Spectacle and Text*, Veröffentlichungen des Instituts für Europäische Geschichte 184 (Mainz 2000).

crowns of Bohemia and Hungary, and the emperor's less concrete rights over the Holy Roman Empire. The clash between the interests of *Hof* and *Reich* – or hereditary lands versus the empire with the kingdoms of Bohemia and Hungary in an intermediate position – more than once complicated the effort to create a more or less unified state. The powerful intermediate stratum of the electors has no close parallel in late seventeenth-century France, where several princely dynasties cherished an increasingly fictional sovereign status not wholly unlike that of minor *Reichsfürsten*. The intricate assemblage of Austrian Habsburg rights and territories helps to put into perspective the overstated concept of French unified monarchy. Most conspicuously, however, it puts into proper perspective the configuration of nobles and ruler at court. The great nobles in the Austrian Habsburg lands formed the backbone of regional government, and had strengthened their position as *Grundherren* – yet the most eminent among them readily served the Habsburg ruler at his court. The very strength of the alliance of dynasty and Catholic *kaisertreue* nobles forces us to cast aside the familiar categories of Versailles: clearly, court office was not inevitably connected to impotence and decline. Turning to Versailles with the experiences of the Hofburg, one is struck not by the obsequiousness of the senior noble officers, but by the marked sense of noble grandeur and liberty they added to the imposing construction of royal power at court – nor can we confidently present this attitude as a compensation for loss of power. This process of reshuffling facts and images exactly serves my purposes, as it forces us to find more balanced explanations for well-known phenomena.

The selection of the Viennese court has one major drawback. Comparing two Catholic courts, I leave aside the complicating problem of confessions and courtly styles. Religious creeds were highly relevant: ceremony has explicit roots in Catholic liturgy, the papal court served as one of the major examples for forms of reverence at court, and Protestants looked with suspicion at the discourse of reputation and decorum.[28] Was courtly splendour typically Catholic, and did Lutheran or Calvinist rulers adopt different forms? Did the abolition of Catholic rituals in the churches lead to a parallel de-sacralisation in the traditions of the household? These questions, frequently surfacing in the literature, but not yet sufficiently analysed, cannot systematically be addressed in this study.

ABOUT THIS BOOK

The court establishments Louis XIV and Leopold I inherited and shaped took form in the later Middle Ages, and were restructured in the period of intense

[28] See the analysis by Milos Vec, *Zeremonialwissenschaft im Fürstenstaat. Studien zur juristischen und politischen Theorie absolutistischer Herrschaftsrepräsentation* (Frankfurt am Main 1998).

struggles in the later sixteenth and early seventeenth centuries. After a short discussion of the diffuse models of court life, and the late medieval background of these courts, I will chart the development of the Bourbon and Habsburg courts in the period from *c.* 1550 to the 1780s. My focus is on the 'apotheosis' of court life emerging after the conflicts of the early seventeenth century. I strive to disentangle the Ludovician court from propaganda, literary embellishment, and eighteenth-century myth-making by comparing it to its Habsburg counterpart, and by looking at earlier as well as later practices at both courts. The eighteenth century itself is relevant also because the style of court life changed in the course of the century, and contemporaries readily projected the images of their polished court onto the more convivial and cruder atmosphere of its seventeenth-century predecessor. Halfway through the century, an ongoing sequence of reforms changed the structures of Habsburg monarchy, in a process that would continue until the end of Joseph II's reign. In the decade preceding the Revolution the Bourbon court too, was once more cast into new forms: staffs were reduced and reformed, and the sway of court office declined. These measures, inspired by a sentiment that undoubtedly was new, in many respects recall earlier ordinances striving to save money and improve efficiency. Only by taking the early modern age in its entirety, can we hope to establish an image that does justice both to the recurring *topoi* of court life, and to the crucial moments of change.

Three ranges of questions define the structure of this book: for all three I aim to provide concrete answers before turning to more speculative discussions and interpretations. Who attended court, and how was this group organised and paid? What were the daily activities of such staffs and officers, and to what extent were these dictated by ceremony? How can we situate the household in the body politic – the position of court officers in the process of decision-making; the mechanisms of patronage, faction, and favouritism; how should we assess the socio-political relevance of the household for the realm as a whole? The court's artistic production, its cultural patronage, and the impact of its example on society at large, however, will be discussed only in the social and political context suggested above.

The sources offer a sufficient basis for my comparison, but they are not equally divided between the Austrian-Habsburg and Valois-Bourbon courts. The central archives of the Habsburg court and their reflections in family archives present a more continuous and systematic heritage than do the series we have for the French court, where negligence, fire, and revolutionary zeal took their toll. In France, however, several rich collections of manuscripts assembled by erudites, genealogists, and ministers help to fill the gaps. These materials present a different, yet roughly equal basis. We cannot say the same for printed sources. From the seventeenth century to this day the French court has attracted much more attention: we have no Dangeau or Sourches for Vienna, let alone a Saint-Simon. Only for the eighteenth century, do we find incidental parallels in Vienna, such as the diary of Khevenhüller-Metsch.[29] The abundant semi-literary sources for the French court, many of them circulating in various forms in the eighteenth century before they were edited and published in one of the monumental French series of such texts, are not invariably helpful: they gave rise to the very images of Ludovician court life that still haunt historiography.[30]

Though I have devoted roughly a decade to study of the court, my direct acquaintance with its archival legacies is of more recent date. Yet archival research was the only reasonable direction of study in a field where tangential discussions have too long obscured our lack of concrete knowledge, and where archival expertise alone did not guarantee immunity from fashionable over-conceptualisation. After having accepted this challenge, I did feel somewhat like a camel trying to get through the needle's eye. The ongoing confrontation between the materials and the accepted ideas of historiography of the court, however, soon turned my novitiate into a highly stimulating exercise. This book strives to bring together these worlds, answering questions and filling gaps in the literature by selective study of relevant archival materials and published sources. The long period and the comparison of two courts allow me, I hope, to analyse developments not otherwise evident; yet these choices prevented me from approaching the depth and precision of an exhaustive archival study of more limited scope. This study should establish an outline of the development of these two courts, and aims to contribute to a general framework of questions allowing us to reappraise the essential features of the early modern court.

[29] Johann Josef Khevenhüller-Metsch, *Aus der Zeit Maria Theresias. Tagebuch des Fürsten Johann Josef Khevenhüller-Metsch, kaiserlichen Obersthofmeisters 1742–1776*, ed. R. Khevenhüller-Metsch and H. Schlitter, 7 vols. (Vienna 1907–1925); *Aus der Zeit Maria Theresias. Tagebuch des Fürsten Johann Josef Khevenhüller-Metsch, kaiserlichen Obersthofmeisters 1742–1776, 1774–1776 und Nachträge*, ed. M. Breunlich-Pawlik and H. Wagner (Vienna 1972) numbered below (p. 329 n. 78) as volume VIII.

[30] The multi-volume collections edited by C. Petitot and L. de Monmerqué, *Collection des mémoires relatifs à l'histoire de France* (Paris 1824–1829); J. Michaud and J. Poujoulat, eds. *Mémoires pour servir à l'histoire de la France depuis le XIIIe siècle jusqu'à la fin du XVIII* (Paris 1836–1844), first series, 32 vols.; *Nouvelle collection des mémoires pour servir à l'histoire de France* (Paris 1850); more recently *Le temps retrouvé*.

CHAPTER 2

The household on the eve of the early modern age

TRADITIONS AND EMULATIONS

A comparison of two major courts inevitably entails a discussion of the Pan-European nature of the court. Europe formed a dense network of dynasties, and rulers were keen on copying the most successful assets of the courts of their rivals and allies.[1] The dynasties of Europe were always exchanging spouses; indeed the success of a dynasty and its court will be reflected in its marital policies, as the Burgundian example conspicuously shows. In the later sixteenth and seventeenth centuries, Spanish brides undoubtedly were the highest prize, but Medici queens were as important in France as Gonzaga empresses in Vienna. Queens and empresses, bringing their establishments and their traditions of ceremony and governance, could cling to their customs and companions, even when these did not easily fit into the structures of their new environment. When dynastic deaths led to the introduction of scions brought up in a foreign environment, these could adopt forms that best suited their tastes, though they always had to take into account the traditions of their new subjects. Less clearly articulated adaptations must have occurred perennially, and without great fuss. Thus, the similarities among the staffs, officers, and traditions of the dynastic courts of Europe need not surprise us: lists of court officers and attendants often offer a multi-language hotch-potch of various traditions.

The expansion of the household and the strengthening of its administrative staffs occurred in a protracted phase of increasing competition and contact among Europe's sovereigns. The vagaries of warfare and succession helped to consolidate larger agglomerates in the patchwork of dynastic territories, giving more weight to the dynasties ruling such composite states. Contacts among these emerging states and the variety of geographically less important territories gradually evolved from the incidental sending of groups of representatives to a more lasting form of representation by resident ambassadors, envoys, or lower

[1] See Malcolm Vale's splendid comparative description of courts and 'court culture', *The Princely Court: Medieval Courts and Culture in North-West Europe, 1270–1380* (Oxford 2001), stressing the parallels and communication among courts. For the early modern age see the wide-ranging but somewhat unfocused introduction to the European dynastic universe by Lucien Bély, *La Société des Princes xvie–xviiie siècle* (Paris 1999).

agents. These diplomats were expected to report the ways of the courts they attended, and thus were instrumental in creating images of court life – and to this day, their reports are among our most important sources for the history of the court. Reputation was a vital concern for many rulers, and splendid households could help to establish or burnish a reputation.

Contemporaries readily discussed the reputations of courts, but few among them were in a position to compare the details of staffs, officers, and ceremonial habits. Reputations generally remained vague. The French court was thought to be exuberant and convivial. Christine de Pisan stressed the open and unconstrained atmosphere at the court of the French King Charles V (1364–1380), where 'toutes manières de gens' approached the ruler when he left the chapel, and his companions attended *lever* and *coucher* without much ado.[2] In the *Cortegiano*, Castiglione still contrasted the 'calm gravity' of the Spaniards with the 'vivacity' of the French.[3] Indeed, the open and accessible nature of French kingship and the unconstrained behaviour of the courtiers long remained proverbial. Nevertheless, it gave birth to a court that came to enjoy a wholly different reputation. An appanage of the French court, the Burgundian court soon surpassed its example in magnificence and refinement. Duke Philip the Good (1419–1467) set new standards most notably for banqueting, for orders of chivalry, and for the management of the court.[4] A rota system was perfected at the Burgundian court, allowing ever more officers to attend court with a certain frequency, without overburdening either the ruler's or the courtiers' finances. Indeed the Burgundian ordinances forbade such officers from attending court at the ruler's expense outside of the allotted periods, or stipulated that they should first obtain permission.[5]

Fifteenth-century Milanese ambassadors contrasted the exquisite politeness and rich apparel of the Burgundian dukes with the simpler habits of the French kings. They thought King Louis XI (1461–1483) was charming, friendly, and familiar – but his court was but a *casa de citadino*, notwithstanding the impressive throne.[6] In Burgundy, on the other hand, the ambassadors, used to the far from

[2] Christine de Pisan, *Le livre des fais et des bonnes mœurs de sage roy Charles V*, ed. S. Solente (Paris 1936; repr. Paris 1977), pp. 43–48.

[3] Baldesar Castiglione, *The Book of the Courtier*, trans. Charles S. Singleton (New York 1959), pp. 115, 134–135.

[4] During the rule of King Charles VI (1380–1429), twelve years old at his accession, Philip the Bold (1363–1404) asked Christine de Pisan to write her 'biography' of Charles V; did the duke order the description of his brother's praiseworthy rule to support the ambitions of his house, or to use it as an example for his own court? See Solente, introduction to *Le livre des fais et des bonnes mœurs*, pp. i–ciii, here pp. xxvi–xxx; and Mary Whiteley, 'Royal and Ducal Palaces in France in the Fourteenth and Fifteenth Centuries: Interior, Ceremony and Function', in *Architecture et vie sociale. L'Organisation intérieure des grandes demeures à la fin du moyen age et à la renaissance. Actes du colloque tenu é Tours du 6 au 10 juin 1988*, ed. Jean Guillaume (Paris 1994), pp. 47–63, here at p. 54.

[5] See Holger Kruse, 'Die Hofordnungen Herzogs Philipps des Guten von Burgund', in *Höfe und Hofordnungen*, ed. Kruse and Paravicini, pp. 141–165.

[6] Gigliola Soldi Rondini, 'Aspects de la vie des cours de France et de Bourgogne par les dépêches des ambassadeurs milanais (seconde moitié du xve siècle)', in *Adelige Sachkultur des Spätmittelalters. Internationaler Kongress krems an der Donau 22. bis 25. September 1980* (Vienna 1982), pp. 195–214, here pp. 202, 213.

negligible splendour of the Milanese court, were impressed by the great banquets and by the solemn ceremonies of the Golden Fleece; even in the Burgundian military camp they found order and splendour. Conversely, when in 1469 Charles the Bold's (1467–1477) representatives were invited by the Habsburg Duke Sigismund of Tyrol (1446–1496) to a banquet in Thann, they were appalled by the bad table manners of their hosts. Sigismund himself outdid the French kings in familiarity, freely mixing in popular dances and jousts.[7] The Burgundian court served as an example for the English King Edward IV's (1461–1483) *Black Book of the Household*, and gave a powerful impetus to chivalrous princely display elsewhere in Europe.[8]

With the Burgundian heritage, the Habsburgs obtained a highly successful model of court life. Consequently, for contemporaries and historians alike, 'Spanish' or 'Spanish-Burgundian' court ceremony came to indicate an ill-defined mixture of solemn forms. Yet the aloofness and ceremonial gravity that were to become a byword for the Spanish court reflected only one aspect of Burgundian court culture – a much more exuberant style of representation can be found in the civic pageantry of the dukes, and it is also evident in the public audiences instituted by Charles the Bold.[9] Charles V adapted to Castilian practices in his early years, yet in 1548 gave his son Philip a Burgundian household that overshadowed, though did not displace, the Castilian *Casa*.[10] Charles V and his successors chose the elements that suited their tastes and needs, and mixed these with the indigenous Castilian forms. The Castilian model of court life thus was inextricably mixed with its reinvention of Burgundian practices, and complicated by the Aragonese and other Spanish traditions.[11] Burgundian

7 Johan Huizinga, *Herfsttij der Middeleeuwen. Studie over levens- en gedachtenvormen der veertiende en vijftiende eeuw in Frankrijk en de Nederlanden* (Haarlem 1963; Eng. trans., *The Waning of the Middle Ages*, 1999), p. 42; Werner Maleczek, 'Sachkultur am Hofe Herzog Sigismund von Tirol', in *Adelige Sachkultur des Spätmittelalters*, pp. 142–143

8 See Werner Paravicini, 'The Court of the Dukes of Burgundy: A Model for Europe?' in *Princes, Patronage, and the Nobility*, ed. Asch and Birke, pp. 69–102, here at pp. 90–96; Christina Hofmann, *Das Spanische Hofzeremoniell von 1500–1700*, Erlanger Historische Studien 8 (Frankfurt, Bern, and New York 1985), particularly pp. 294–296; Hofmann, 'Die Herkunft und Tradierung des Burgundischen Hofzeremoniells', in *Zeremoniell als höfische Ästhetik*, ed. Berns and Rahn, pp. 150–156. Simon Thurley, *The Royal Palaces of Tudor England: Architecture and Court Life 1460–1547* (London 1993), pp. 11–24, discusses the English situation – Edward IV was brother-in-law of Charles the Bold.

9 Peter Arnade, *Burgundian Ceremony and Civic Life in Late Medieval Ghent* (Ithaca 1996).

10 See Mia J. Rodriguez-Salgado, 'Honour and Profit in the Court of Philip II of Spain', in *La cour comme institution économique*, ed. Aymard and Romani, pp. 67–86.

11 For example, the *Leges Palatinae* promulgated in 1337 by James II of Mallorca, adopted by Peter IV for the Aragonese court in 1344, and in all probability known in Castile; in addition to many rules for the ruler's table, the *Leges* decree a more secluded section of the royal apartment, hidden behind antechambers and guarded by officers controlling access. See Gottfried Kerscher, 'Die Strukturierung des Mallorquinischen Hofes um 1330 und der Habitus der Hofgesellschaft', in *Höfe und Hofordnungen*, ed. Kruse and Paravicini, pp. 77–89, here at pp. 83–84; Miguel Angel Ladero Quesada, 'Casa y Corte. L'Hôtel du roi et la Cour comme institutions économiques au temps des Rois Catholiques (1480–1504)', in *La cour comme institution économique*, ed. Aymard and Romani, pp. 43–54, here at p. 44. Hofmann, *Spanische Hofzeremoniell*, pp. 30, 48–50; Paravicini, 'Court of the Dukes of Burgundy', in *Princes, Patronage, and the Nobility*, ed. Asch and Birke, p. 99.

court organisation and counter-reformatory religious zeal became prominent items of the 'Spanish' heritage. A hidden style of rulership as exemplified by portraiture, residences, and ceremony may be Spain's most typical contribution to the traditions of the European court – but it would be unwise to amalgamate this reputation with that of the Burgundians.[12]

The Spanish and the Austrian Habsburgs cultivated the Burgundian parentage of their courts – though in the Austrian case concrete influences remained limited. Yet King Louis XI of France incorporated the larger part of Burgundy in 1477, and his successors tried to introduce Burgundian standards of splendour at their court.[13] In the Low Countries the Burgundian tradition continued and the heritage was soon taken over by the Habsburgs. Thus, Burgundy forms a peculiar *trait d'union* between the Valois-Bourbon and Habsburg courts, and it exemplifies the problems of reputation and emulation – the Spanish-Burgundian household was in many respects a continuation of the establishment of the fourteenth-century French King Charles V enriched by Burgundian practices, and adapted to other circumstances.

Rome long remained the pivot of Christian dynastic Europe, and the pope or his agents arbitrated many a conflict. At most courts, the papal nuncio, the Venetian ambassador, and their Spanish compeer enjoyed privileged positions as the senior diplomats. The Italian constellation of city-states of the fifteenth and sixteenth centuries was as potent a model for court life as for diplomacy. The Italian Wars (1494–1559) helped to broadcast its reputation, and stimulated the Italian presence at other courts. The suave and brilliant reputation of Italian court life as established by Castiglione was not primarily based on court organisation or dignified ceremonial, but on patronage of the arts, magnificence, and the catalogue of virtues presented in the *Cortegiano*.[14] Italian soldiers, courtiers, artisans, musicians, and various instructors were ubiquitous in courtly Europe; they shared their supremacy in some fields with other artists, notably Flemish musicians and painters, but on the whole reigned supreme until their French compeers towards the end of the seventeenth century successfully challenged their semi-monopoly.[15] In the Austrian Habsburg lands and the German principalities, the 'Welsch' assemblage of Italians, Spaniards, and French was at times looked upon with suspicion, a tendency exacerbated by the advent of Protestantism. In France the influence of the Italian language and the prominence of Italian favourites at court were a thorn in the eye of native contestants; though

[12] See the contributions of Fernando Checa Cremades, 'Monarchic Liturgies and the "Hidden King": The Function and Meaning of Spanish Royal Portraiture in the Sixteenth and Seventeenth Centuries', and José Manuel Nieto Soria, 'Propaganda and Legitimation in Castile: Religion and Church, 1250–1500', to *Iconography, Propaganda, and Legitimation*, pp. 89–104 and 105–119, respectively; Arnade, *Burgundian Ceremony and Civic Life.*

[13] See Knecht, 'The Court of Francis I'; and Potter, *A History of France*, pp. 65–70, for numbers.

[14] Yet Angevin Naples seems to have been an example of the aloof and secluded court style, usually connected with Spain.

[15] Jean-François Dubost, *La France Italienne XVIe–XVIIe siècle* (Paris 1997), pp. 270–278.

much the same can be said about the other 'foreign' groups at court, most of all the Spanish.[16]

Did these diverging models for court life stem from a collective forebear or example? Europe's major dynasties cherished artefacts and traditions reaching back into the past. Can we trace these lines to establish a 'genealogy' of court life? If so, we should be more specific – do we look for an ideal of behaviour, for models of ceremonial order, splendour and superb material culture, or court organisation? We can follow the development of *curialitas* or courtliness as an ideal of deportment loosely based on the example of chivalrous medieval court life. The intertwining ideals and anti-ideals of the courtier recur in many forms until the end of monarchy. Similarly, splendour and pageantry or rulers' processions show great resemblance from the range of great ceremonies in imperial Rome to those in any of the major early modern European monarchies.[17] These solemn public appearances tend to be connected to events such as coronations, burials, and entries, or the visit of other rulers. The Roman emperors Diocletian (284–305) and Constantine (306–337) remodelled ceremony after Hellenic rulers, who had themselves been inspired by the Persian example.[18] After the end of the West-Roman empire, the Roman heritage continued in Byzantium, and was taken up in the West by the papacy. The popes, the Carolingian emperors and their royal and imperial successors, must have assembled bits and pieces to re-create a form of *representatio maiestatis* that suited their tastes. Roman Catholic liturgy was to remain one of the main repositories of ceremony: the papal courts in Rome and Avignon pioneered many forms of ceremony that later formed part of the general European courtly heritage.[19] Finally, the fall of Constantinople may have made Western Europe more acutely aware of the Byzantine example; it certainly brought the Ottomans to its threshold. When Sultan Mehmed II (1451–1481) conquered Constantinople, and brought his court there, he used the occasion to establish the first codification of Ottoman ceremonial, the *Kanunnane*

16 In German lands, 'Welsch' was used to indicate the assemblage of Catholic, romanic, southern peoples: Italians, Spanish and French; French writers frequently targeted the combined Spanish and Italian influence. See Eberhard Straub, *Repraesentatio Maiestatis oder Churbayerische Freudensfeste. Die höfischen Feste in der Münchner Residenz vom 16. bis zum Ende des 18. Jahrhunderts*, Miscellanea Bavarica Monacensia 14 (Munich 1969), pp. 117–146: a discussion of Spanish–Italian influences and the exemplary role of Vienna for the German courts.

17 Andreas Alföldi, *Die monarchische Repräsentation im römischen Kaiserreich* (Darmstadt 1980); Helga Scholten, *Der Eunuch in Kaisernähe. Zur politischen und sozialen Bedeutung des praepositus sacri cubiculi im 4. und 5. Jahrhundert n. Chr.* (Frankfurt 1995), Prismata V: Scholten, on p. 171, mentions several categories that are equally prominent in early modern ceremonial sources: public appearances, reception of diplomats, processions, coronations – missing are the dynastic ceremonies of baptism, marriage, burial, and the sequence of feudal ceremonies. See Aloys Winterling, ed, *Zwischen 'Haus' und 'Staat'. Antike Höfe im Vergleich*, Historische Zeitschrift 23 (Munich 1997), particularly Winterling's illuminating typology on pp. 11–25 and his comparison of courts in Antiquity, pp. 151–169; compare Winterling's, *Comitatus: Beiträge zur Erforschung des spätantiken Kaiserhofes* (Berlin 1998).

18 Scholten, *Eunuch in Kaisernähe*, pp. 20, 170–177, 199; compare Gülru Necipoglu, *Architecture, Ceremonial, and Power: The Topkapi Palace in the Fifteenth and Sixteenth Centuries* (Cambridge, MA, and London 1991).

19 See, for example, Sergio Bertelli, 'Rex et Sacerdos: The Holiness of the King in European Civilization', in *Iconography, Propaganda, and Legitimation*, ed. Ellenius, pp. 123–145, and the pertinent remarks on the influence of the papacy made by John Adamson in his introduction to *The Princely Courts of Europe*.

(1477–1481). He was probably inspired by Persian and Arab courts, but Byzantine codices and the image of Alexander the Great were relevant as well.[20]

The suggestion of continuity in ceremony is strong, but it is difficult to establish concrete links.[21] For the insignia of power or the images and artefacts employed in visual arts, we can more confidently establish a chain of emulations. Throne, crown, sceptre, orb, and ring show great continuity, as does the structure of palaces and apartments, with their protective arrangements controlling access. Court staffs and offices, finally, are usually modelled on recurring domestic routines: eating, sleeping, riding, hunting, devotion. All princely households share certain domestic tasks and routines. When we extend our horizon to include Asian and African courts, it becomes evident that we should not exclusively see such similarities as the consequence of mutual influence and emulation.[22] Non-European arrangements for the rulers' palaces and shrines can be as familiar as their household routines, and their attire. Rulers and elites in many ages and regions found similar forms to maintain power and enhance their majesty. A problem familiar to anthropologists arises here: should we strive to chart the diffusion of traditions when we can equally plausibly argue that such patterns originate not in imitation, but independently yet in roughly comparable circumstances? The structural challenges encountered by rulers could be answered in various ways, and examples were always available. Without a doubt, court life had as many ancient examples, and knew as many rebirths, as any other human venture. Such influences, inextricably intertwined, served as a starting point for the expansion of the European court in the later Middle Ages. For my purposes, it is more relevant to understand the structural affinities, and to outline and explain the alternatives different rulers chose, than to establish a tentative sequence of emulation.[23] Intercultural comparison can uncover some universal traits of dynastic establishments, helps to avoid the biases of a perspective narrowly based on Europe,[24] and allows us to go beyond the antiquarianism so

[20] Necipoglu, *Architecture, Ceremonial, and Power*, pp. 15–22.

[21] See the careful discussion in M. McCormick, 'Zeremoniell', in *Lexikon des Mittelalters* (Munich 1977–1999), IX, pp. 546–553, and the regional discussions by several authors, pp. 553–580. On p. 553, 'caerimonia' is cited as 'sorgfältige Verehrung'.

[22] In addition to classics by James Frazer, Sigmund Freud, Marc Bloch, Arthur M. Hocart, Ernst H. Kantorowicz, and Percy Ernst Schramm, see Edwin M. Loeb, 'Die Institution des Sakralen Königtums', *Paideuma* 10 (Wiesbaden 1964), pp. 102–114; Clifford Geertz, *Negara: The Theatre-State in Nineteenth-Century Bali* (Princeton 1980); Claude Tardits, 'L'Etiquette à la cour royale Bamoum (Cameroun)', in *Culture et idéologie dans la genèse de l'état moderne. Actes de la table ronde organisée par le centre national de la recherche scientifique et l'école française de Rome* (Rome and Paris 1984), pp. 179–198, and Tardits, 'L'Espace, indicateur historique, révélateur structural: l'exemple Bamoum' (Cameroun)', *AESC* 40, 6 (1985), pp. 1261–1287; Heinz Duchhardt, Richard Jackson and David Sturdy, eds., *European Monarchy: Its Evolution and Practice from Roman Antiquity to Modern Times* (Stuttgart 1992); John Beattie, *Bunyoro: An African Kingdom* (New York 1969); H. J. M. Claessen and P. Skalnik, eds., *The Early State* (The Hague 1978); David Price, 'The Palace and its Institutions in the Chiefdom of Ngambe', *Paideuma* 31 (1985), pp. 85–103; S. J. Tambiah, *Culture, Thought and Social Action: An Anthropological Perspective* (Cambridge MA 1985).

[23] Huizinga's remark that from the later Middle Ages, the spectacle of rulership and chivalry at many European courts reached new heights, may serve as a starting point for this book, *Herfsttij*, pp. 40–41.

[24] Winterling, 'Hof. Versuch einer idealtypischen Bestimmung anhand der mittelalterlichen und frühneuzeitlichen Geschichte', in *Zwischen 'Haus' und 'Staat'*, pp. 11–25, offers a useful starting point for intercultural comparison.

prominent among contemporary historians of the court and its offices – yet it cannot replace the developmental perspective, roughly outlined below for the staffs and officers of the Valois and Habsburg courts.

EXPANSION AND ORDINANCES

A small group of companions, councillors, guards, and servants following the itinerant rulers formed the core of what was to become a full-fledged court during the later Middle Ages and the early modern age. From the thirteenth to the seventeenth or eighteenth centuries, rising numbers, a proliferation of honorary and administrative tasks, and an increasing sense of majesty changed the face of the court. We can observe the early stages of this metamorphosis in a range of documents that were intended to record and regulate these developments. Supply and transport had to be organised on a larger scale; yet the financial straitjacket dictated frequent attempts to reduce the court, by defining more sharply the rank and number of those entitled to be fed and lodged at court. The closer definition of access to the ruler's hospitality and largesse thus coincided with the establishment of hierarchies of rank and office, a process neatly fitting the growing sense of decorum. Together, these challenges put a premium on written procedures, as relevant for the logistics of the household and for the attempts to make it more orderly, as for the work of the various chanceries, councils, and secretaries.

The ordinances strove to establish an orderly household and government, within the limits of the ruler's financial potential. They were estimates of future costs and attempts to balance the budget by restricting access to food, shelter, and largesse. New rulers, however, could choose to promulgate ordinances to underline their accession to the throne. Finally, whether in combination with the preceding impulses or not, ordinances were a vehicle for general reform of the court. Was the prince the main initiator of such attempts? The sources suggest that he was often loath to be bound by his clerks' written procedures and rules, and ignored them as he saw fit.[25] Princely liberality was too important to be subordinated to the dictates of a balanced budget. When rulers depended on the subsidies of estates in addition to the revenues of their domains, as would often be the case, ordinances could be forced upon the ruler not by his servants in household and government, but by such estates assemblies seeking to bridle his costly appetites through reforms and reductions.

The term ordinance does not indicate a single well-defined source. Roughly, we can distinguish three overlapping categories: *états* or *Hofstaatsverzeichnisse* listing the persons expected to attend court or entitled to remuneration; general ordinances structuring the daily routines at court; and specific instructions for

[25] Kruse, 'Hofordnungen', pp. 155–156; Heinig, 'Theorie und Praxis', p. 242; Bojcov, 'Sitten und Verhaltensformen', pp. 248 (estates), 269–270 (*Räte*) all in *Höfe und Hofordnungen*, ed. Kruse and Paravicini.

the individual staffs or officers of household and government.[26] We incidentally find more comprehensive ordinances including lists and instructions. Such sources, suggesting the numbers of the court and providing a framework of rules, always define the court's senior officers and their staffs.

FRANCE

The Carolingian court harboured a great variety of court officers; we find a smaller selection of these offices at most medieval courts.[27] The court of the early Capetians seems to have known four major officers: the *sénéchal* (*dapifer*, seneschal), *connétable* (*comes stabuli*, master of the stables) *chambrier (camerarius*, chamberlain), and *bouteiller* (*pincerna*, butler; later *échanson*, cupbearer). These four *grands offices*, countersigning royal writ and combining honorary service with major political and military responsibilities, were held by the great feudatories.[28] Later rulers regarded these near-sovereign and *de facto* hereditary offices, and the power accumulated in the dynasties holding them, with some suspicion. When the occasion arose, they granted such offices to less eminent and more trusted nobles, or they even suppressed the titles, leaving only their regional variants. Thus, the *sénéchal* was suppressed in 1190, the *bouteiller* in the reign of Charles VII (1403–1461), the *chambrier* in 1544, and finally the *connétable* in 1626. The archbishop of Rheims held the title of *archichancelier* until the late twelfth century; the *chancelier* (chancellor), a pivotal figure in the royal administration, would usually be a man of the church.

The first ordinances of the French Capetian *hôtel*, the king's inn, were promulgated halfway through the thirteenth century; they included six *métiers*, Parisian corporations catering for the *hôtel*: *paneterie*, *échansonnerie*, *cuisine*, *fruiterie*, directly connected to service at the ruler's table and provisioning; the *écurie* or stable, and the *chambre*.[29] The chamber staff, headed by the *chambrier* assisted by several *chambellans* (chamberlains), was responsible for the king's *coucher* and more generally for the inner rooms of the palace; towards the end of the

[26] Bojcov, 'Sitten und Verhaltensformen', in *Höfe und Hofordnungen*, ed. Kruse and Paravicini, pp. 244–247.

[27] Werner Rösener, 'Hofämter an mittelalterlichen Fürstenhöfen', *Deutsches Archiv für Erforschung des Mittelalters* 45 (1989), pp. 485–550: *Mansionarius–marechal des logis*; *Cubicularius–Chambrier*, versus *Camerarius–Chambellan* in AN O 1 820, no. 1, pp. 94–95, referring to Ducange. See the short descriptions and lengthy genealogies of major servants of the French crown in Père Anselme, *Histoire de la Maison Royale de France et des grands officiers de la couronne* (Paris 1733; repr. New York and London 1967), VIII, pp. 309–824, for the relevant offices.

[28] Rösener, 'Hofämter'; Jean du Tillet, *Recueil des Roys de France leurs couronne et maison, ensemble le rang des grands de France* (Paris 1611; first published in 1577): on pp. 268–318, Du Tillet outlines the major offices, noting their rank, responsibilities, and privileges; a more systematical comparable discussion was later given by Charles Loyseau, see *Les Œuvres du Maistre Charles Loyseau, Avocat en Parlement. Contenant les cinq livres du droit, des offices, les traitez des Seigneuries, des ordres & simples dignitez, du déguerpissement & delaissement par Hypotheque, de la garantie des rentes, & des abus des justices de village* (Paris 1678), Livre IV, chapters I–III, pp. 214–235.

[29] E. Lalou, 'Höfe und Hofordnungen', *LMA*, VI, p. 147, 'Maître de l'Hôtel', 'Métiers'; cf. the later 'Sept Offices' under the *grand maître*: *gobelet*, *cuisine-bouche*, *paneterie*, *échansonnerie*, *cuisine-commun*, *fruiterie*, *fourrière*. Jean François Solnon, 'Maison du Roi', in *DAR*, pp. 777–782, here at p. 778.

thirteenth century, it emancipated itself from the *métiers*. A concise history of the chamber's officers to be found in the archives of the chamberlain's staff, argued that the *chambrier* was responsible for the ruler's private quarters, a role held previously by the Carolingian *cubicularius*. The responsibilities of the Carolingian *camerarius*, the treasury and movable property, on the other hand, had been taken over by the *chambellan*. This division of labour between the *chambrier* and *chambellan* seems not implausible for this period.[30] The *chambrier*, however, came to be replaced in practice by the *premier* or *principal chambellan*; the earlier charge became an honorary asset. When it was abolished in 1544–1545 the *premiers gentilshommes de la chambre* took the prestigious place of the *chambrier*, serving as the *chambellan*'s major deputies.[31] In 1307 the *fourrière*, responsible for travel, quartering, and couriers – or the contacts with the outside world – took the vacant place of the *chambre* among the six *métiers*. In 1315 the *argenterie*, or wardrobe, was instituted within the *chambre*. Along with the chamber and the services for the table, but not dependent on them, the chapel was a constant feature of the court. It included not only the *aumôniers*, *confesseur*, and chaplains, but also a musical establishment.[32] Stables, guards, *vénerie*, and *fauconnerie* as well had developed their own establishments, functioning increasingly independently in the fifteenth century. A department for the *menus plaisirs du roi* emerged in 1483, controlling expenses for the *chambre*, the *argenterie*, and festivities.[33]

In the early thirteenth century the *hôtel* had been reorganised: a new service was added for the table of the household at large, the *commun*. The *métiers* forming the *bouche du roi* still catered for the king's needs. We can conclude that the expansion of the household made this adaptation necessary. Indeed, the responsibility to feed the court during the perennial travels and in the residences, while preventing theft and waste, represented a formidable task. It was made even more daunting by the dictates of princely hospitality and liberality. In this process, the *maître d'hôtel* (steward), first mentioned in the reign of Philip IV (1268–1314), acquired responsibility for the six staffs, and more generally for the 'economy' of the court. Beginning in 1291, one or two *maîtres d'hôtel* oversaw the *hôtel* and its provisioning, soon surpassing the *panetier*, *échanson*, and *tranchant* – these

30 See AN O 1 820, no. 1, pp. 94–95, on p. 95 citing Ducange.

31 E. Lalou, 'Chambrier', *LMA*, II, p. 1677; Lalou, 'Chambellan', *LMA*, II, p. 1671; on the *chambellan*, AN O 1 820, nos. 1, 8; BN MS f 7859, 'Grands Officiers', fols. 153–172, 190–193; on the *premiers gentilshommes* instructions and more history see AN O 1 822, pp. 1–6. The *gentilshommes de la chambre*, created in 1515 in addition to the *valets*, reached impressive numbers in the sixteenth century; see the tables in Potter, *History of France*, p. 66, and Le Roux, *Faveur du roi*, pp. 722–723. The number of the prestigious *premiers gentilshommes de la chambre*, two since their creation in 1544–1545 stabilised at four in Louis XIII's reign, whereas the other *gentilshommes de la chambre* nearly disappeared.

32 See the overview in Georges Minois, *Le confesseur du roi. Les directeurs de conscience sous la monarchie française* (Paris 1988); for musicians at the French court, see Marcelle Benoit, *Versailles et les musiciens du roi, 1661–1733: étude institutionnelle et sociale* (Paris 1971); Marcelle Benoit, *Musiques de cour: chapelle, chambre, écurie, 1661–1733*, La vie musicale en France sous les rois Bourbons 20 (Paris 1971).

33 Potter, *History of France*, p. 63; *DGS*, p. 1015.

offices would retain a largely honorary character.[34] Providing, accounting, and financing the household were increasingly onerous tasks. The *chambre aux deniers* was instituted in the late thirteenth century, controlling the spending of the court, and paying the *officiers domestiques*.[35] From the fourteenth century onwards, the costs of warfare and the royal establishment had risen too high to be paid from the royal domain; extraordinary impositions soon turned into a regular feature of French government, and institutions were created to take care of these 'extraordinary' money sources.[36] In the early sixteenth century, the expanding personnel in the financial sector of the *maison* was still closely connected to the families responsible for state finances.[37] The treasurers and controllers were to be among the best paid servants of the French state.[38] A proliferation of *menus*, *trésoriers*, and *controleurs* checked the expenses for a variety of independently functioning sectors of the court.

Several institutions, most notably the *parlement* (with the assembly of the great spiritual and worldly lords, the *cour des pairs*) and the *chambre des comptes*, emerged from *curia regis* in the thirteenth and fourteenth centuries, obtaining a high status as near-independent corporations in the king's government.[39] The council, slowly losing the character of an *ad hoc* assembly of friends and advisers, consistently was a breeding place of other governmental agencies. From the last years of the fifteenth century onwards, the council itself was progressively divided into more specialised components, a development consolidated by Henry II in 1547. The great officers of the realm, whether or not directly connected to the household, remained connected to the court. The *chancelier* guarded the king's seal and presided over the councils. The *connétable*, originating in the household, became the senior military commander of the realm, the *écuyer* taking over his household responsibilities. The *maréchaux*, under the first Capetians equally officers of the *écurie*, were close associates of the *connétable*, wielding considerable power in military, judicial, and administrative matters. In the council, the chancellor, constable, and marshals, were on a par with the household's senior officers, the steward and chamberlain. In the fifteenth century, the steward, now *grand maître d'hôtel*, in addition to his responsibility for the services for the king's table, had become the senior officer of the household.

In the fourteenth century, the *hôtels* of the king, his spouse, and their children together numbered between 500 and 800 persons, a number that would decline

[34] The *grand queux*, or head of the king's kitchens, is mentioned as the predecessor of the *tranchant*, the *échanson* was seen as the *bouteiller*'s successor.

[35] Potter, *History of France*, p. 63: in 1483 the *menus plaisirs du roi* were instituted; in 1520 a *trésorier de l'hôtel* emerged, towards the end of Francis I's reign a *trésorier de la maison*.

[36] Bernard Barbiche, *Les institutions de la monarchie française à l'époque moderne* (Paris 1999), pp. 364–368.

[37] Potter, *History of France*, p. 64. [38] *Ibid.*, p. 72.

[39] E. Bournazel, 'Curia Regis, IV, Frankreich', in *LMA*, III, pp. 378–381; E. Lalou, 'Chambre des comptes', in *LMA*, II, pp. 1673–1675; Lalou, 'Chambre aux deniers', in *LMA*, II, pp. 1675–1676; F. Autrand, 'Parlement', in *LMA*, VI, pp. 1731–1733.

during the troubles of the first half of the fifteenth century.[40] Indeed, in the fifteenth century the Burgundian court numerically exceeded its French model: in 1426–1427 it was attended by *c.* 400 persons, a number that had risen to 900 by 1458–1459. Anne de Bretagne seems to have been the first queen with a sizeable independent household, numbering, in 1496, 325 persons of whom 53 were women.[41] Expansion entailed changes in the structure of the court. A system of job sharing allowing court office to be held *par quartier* or *par semestre*, made possible the rapid expansion of the Burgundian court.[42] From the later fifteenth century onwards, the French court adopted several Burgundian innovations, and *service par terme* became the standard for many offices. Under Francis I, the household expanded, the king's *maison* alone numbering a little more than 600. The king allowed several honorary offices and the kitchen (*cuisine de bouche et commun*) to expand, but soon tried to prevent further growth. In 1515 Francis I created the *gentilshommes de la chambre*, in addition to the *valets de la chambre*, an innovation soon copied by the English King Henry VIII.[43] The *gentilshommes* tripled from 21 to 64 during his reign, but their rise coincided with the disappearance of *chambellans* and the *enfants d'honneur*. We find *chambellans* as well as various types of *gentilshommes* for the chamber under later Valois rulers, however; and while both young princes and *enfants* were absent in the later sixteenth century, *enfants d'honneur* would again attend seventeenth-century royal princes.[44] Francis limited access to the table to reduce costs; household salaries remained stable throughout the late fifteenth and early sixteenth centuries. Between 1523 and 1549, nevertheless, the budget of the king's household rose from 287,500 to 616,298 lt. This figure did not include the rising costs for other households: Queen Eleonora of Austria's *maison* was near 400 persons including *c.* 100 women by the end of Francis I's reign; in 1535 *dauphin* Henry's *maison* numbered 300, roughly half of his father's household. From the reign of Francis II rapid growth of the various *maisons* was evident; the king's *maison* reached a number of 1,049 in 1560. The ensuing period of turmoil was to lead to further expansion, and to the attempts to establish a new order for the court by Henry III in 1578 and 1585.

40 E. Lalou, 'Hotel du roi', in *LMA*, V, pp. 140–141; Lalou mentions a budget of 150,000 in the late thirteenth century, doubled to 300,000 in the early fourteenth century. Also see Lalou's 'Les ordonnances de l'hôtel des derniers Capétiens directs', in *Höfe und Hofordnungen*, ed. Kruse and Paravicini, pp. 91–101; Potter, *History of France*, p. 65, suggests 366 in 1495–6, with 343 for the queen's *maison*, totalling *c.* 720; Solnon, *Cour de France*, p. 46, notes 366 for the king's *maison* in 1495, 540 in 1523, 622 in 1535; Le Roux, *Faveur du roi*, p. 722, gives a table for the inner *maison* from the 1490s to 1650, including these figures.

41 Monique Chatenet, 'Les logis des femmes à la cour des derniers Valois', in *Frauenzimmer*, ed. Hirschbiegel and Paravicini, pp. 175–192, numbers at pp. 177–178.

42 Kruse on Burgundy in Kruse and Paravicini, eds., *Höfe und Hofordnungen*, pp. 149–153; Paravicini, 'Court of the Dukes of Burgundy', in *Princes, Patronage, and the Nobility*, ed. Asch and Birke, pp. 76–79.

43 Henry VIII keenly watched the French court, and adopted some of its features: he instituted the *gentilshommes de la chambre* in England; and a parallel of the *grand maître* for a short period as well; see Solnon, *Cour de France*, p. 45.

44 See the numbers in Potter, *History of France*, pp. 66–69, table 1; Le Roux, *Faveur du roi*, pp. 722–725; Chatenet, 'Logis des femmes', in *Frauenzimmer*, ed. Hirschbiegel and Paravicini, p. 178.

A 'HABSBURG COURT' BEFORE 1500?

Notwithstanding its irregular curve of development, the French court was an entity with a clearly recognisable organisation retaining basic characteristics from the thirteenth century to its demise. The Habsburg court of the early modern age, on the other hand, was the progeny of various courts at the same time. In the fifteenth century, the Habsburg patrimony was divided among three Habsburg *Landesfürsten* independently governing their territories. The connection of the Habsburgs with the royal or imperial court of the empire, originating in the reign of Habsburg King Rudolf I (1273–1291), became lasting only in the course of the fifteenth century. Duke Frederick V of *Innerösterreich* (Inner Austria) elected king in 1440, in 1453 was crowned emperor by the pope – an honour he would share only with one other Habsburg dynast: Charles V, crowned in 1530 in Bologna. As Emperor Frederick III (1453–1493), he was the first of a line of Habsburg emperors interrupted only by the misfired Wittelsbach experiment of 1742–1745, and continuing in the Habsburg-Lorraine line until the end of the Holy Roman Empire and its Austrian successor-empire. The fifteenth-century Habsburg court was not automatically synonymous with the royal or imperial court, nor did Frederick III match the resplendent courts of some of his predecessors, such as Charles IV of Luxemburg's (1347–1378) Prague court. During the imperial reigns of Frederick III, Maximilian I (1493–1519), Charles V (1519–1556), and Ferdinand I (1556–1564), the subsequent unification, consolidation, expansion, and redivision of Habsburg dynastic power brought together a bewildering variety of courtly legacies. Leaving aside the Burgundian, Flemish, and Spanish connections, we still need to differentiate between the legacies of the imperial court, and the Habsburgs' territorial households.

The empire was of prime importance for a dynasty that held the imperial status as a near-monopoly during the early modern age. In the Ottonian period (936–1024) four offices had emerged at the royal court that were to become typical for many courts in the empire: *Truchseß* (*dapifer*, seneschal), *Marschall* (marshal), *Mundschenk* (*pincerna*, cupbearer), and *Kämmerer* (chamberlain). These *Erzämter* of the empire, closely matching the four offices of the early Capetians, were later vested in the imperial electors: Bohemia (cupbearer), Brandenburg (chamberlain), the Palatine (seneschal), Saxony (marshal).[45] The worldly electors would exercise these functions only during the great ceremonies of the empire, when they formed the *curia maior*, leaving the parallel everyday tasks in the *curia minor* to lesser-ranking substitutes.[46] Similarly, the archbishop

45 After 1623, Bavaria held the title of arch-seneschal; in the Westphalian settlement, the *Erzämter* were reshuffled, and the later addition of the ninth electorate again led to changes, the Elector-Palatine obtaining the *Erzschatzmeisteramt* in 1652, the new elector of Hanover first the *Erzbanneramt* in 1692, then in 1778 the *Erzschatzmeisteramt*.

46 See the discussion by Gisela Drossbach, 'Sciencia de regimine domus regie: Der Hof zwischen Ideal und Wirklichkeit in der "Yconomica" Konrads von Megenberg', in *Höfe und Hofordnungen*, ed. Kruse and Paravicini,

of Mainz held the charge of *Erzkanzler*. In addition to the chancellery, a chapel was connected to the court; before the struggles with the papacy reduced the emperor's rights to nominate bishops, it functioned as a reservoir for episcopal nominees in the empire. Together, the electors ideally formed the supreme council of the empire, more or less like the French *cour des pairs*. Namesakes of the four officers emerged on the level of the various territories within the empire, where they quickly attained honorific status, and became hereditary dynastic assets, *Landeserbämter*. The substitutes of these *Erz-* and *Erbämter* at court formed the ruler's day-to-day household. Thus, the court offices of the great feudatories were in practice performed first by dynasties of unfree *ministeriales* quickly rising to noble status, and finally taken over by yet another group executing these tasks in exchange for remuneration.

Ordinances predating the late fifteenth century are available only for the Habsburg Tyrolean court; they offer an indirect reflection of the workings of the contemporary court of Frederick III at best. Maximilian's and Ferdinand's ordinances give us more substantial evidence.[47] In addition to the four traditional offices – seneschal, marshal, cupbearer, and chamberlain – a *Kanzler* (chancellor), and a *Kaplan* (Chaplain), a *Hofmeister* (steward) had been active at the Habsburg court since 1293. The steward, in imitation of his namesake, responsible for the management of abbeys and their domains, initially controlled the household's logistics, but like the French *maître d'hôtel*, he was quickly granted more general and governmental responsibilities.[48] As in the French case, the rise of the steward may plausibly be connected to the increasing significance of controlling the ruler's hospitality. An Innsbruck ordinance suggested that the fanfare of trumpets announcing dinner in the princely hall attracted a crowd eager to profit from the occasion.[49] The range of officers responsible for financial management, *Schatzmeister*, *Pfennigmeister*, *Contralor* (instituted in 1502), book-keepers and secretaries, in addition to the repeated reforms of *Schatzkammer* or from 1527 onwards the *Hofkammer*, again underline the importance of budgets and accounting.

The *Truchseß* or seneschal, originally an agent of royal power, was now understood as honorary servant for the table (a change of function complicating the translation of this title); with his fellow officers, the cupbearer and the less

pp. 23–35; see also Tillet's discussion of the four offices, *Recueil des Roys*, II, 19; I, 273–274; he explicitly compares the Capetian and Ottonian offices, likening the *connétable* to the *Marschall*, the seneschal to the *Truchseß*.

47 Bojcov, 'Sitten und Verhaltensformen', pp. 243–283, particularly the lists on pp. 253–258 and pp. 263, 266. Maximilian maintained the basic structure of the Innsbruck court, see Paul-Joachim Heinig, 'Theorie und Praxis der "höfischen Ordnung" unter Friedrich III. und Maximilian', in *Höfe und Hofordnungen*, ed. Kruse and Paravicini, pp. 223–242, here at p. 230, n. 25.

48 Ivan Zolger, *Der Hofstaat des Hauses Österreich*, Wiener staatswissenschaftliche Studien 14 (Vienna and Leipzig 1917), pp. 16–20; Rösener, 'Hofämter'; Gerhard Seeliger, *Das deutsche Hofmeisteramt im spaeteren Mittelalter* (Innsbruck 1865), with *Ordnung* on pp. 134–135.

49 Bocjov, 'Sitten und Verhaltensformen', p. 282; compare J. Adamson, 'The Tudor and Stuart Courts 1509–1714', in *The Princely Courts of Europe*, pp. 94–117, at pp. 99, 116, on the wide hospitality in the hall, abolished in the 1660s.

antique *Fürschneider* (carver), he now stood in the shadow of the *Hofmeister*. The concrete tasks of these three officers for the table, moreover, had been taken over by subordinates: the *Küchenmeister*, *Speisenmeister*, and *Kellermeister* (masters of kitchen, provisions, and cellar). Of the four traditional offices, only the marshal arguably had been able to withstand the rise of the steward; the ranking of these two officers remained ambivalent into the sixteenth century. Travel required the court to be mounted, and its servants were given horses as they were provided with food and shelter. Thus, we can assess their rank by the number of horses they were given: Maximilian's *Hofstaat* of 1519 granted the first place to the marshal, with eighteen horses; the steward was listed only in the council, without any indication of the number of horses he was granted. Ferdinand's 1527 and 1537 ordinances, however, explicitly stated that the steward 'sol die erst person bei kgl. Mt. Geacht werden'. The 1527 ordinance, moreover, listed twelve horses for the steward, and only eight for the marshal.[50] The treasurer (*Schatzmeister*) and the chamberlain (*Oberstkämmerer*) were similarly recompensed, whereas the master of the stables (*Oberststallmeister*) could expect eight horses only if he were a *Graf* or *Herr* – a simple *Ritter* would get six. A range of other dignitaries immediately followed: the *Stabelmeister* (the steward's deputy, or master of the baton) with six or alternatively five; the cupbearer, carver, *Truchseß*, and *Pfennigmeister* five; the *Hofräte* or councillors five or alternatively four. The allowances for the chancellor and the chaplain – the first undoubtedly, the latter probably an important member of the *Hofstaat* – are not explicitly mentioned.[51] The lists show that remuneration was partly determined by the office, partly by the rank of the incumbent.[52]

The 1518 reform of the *Hofrat* (council), instituted by Maximilian in 1498, stipulated the provenance of the eighteen councillors: the Empire (5), Lower Austria (5), Tyrol (2), Upper Austria (2); the marshal, steward, chancellor, and treasurer were permanent members. Moreover, both *adel und doctores* were to be represented.[53] The energetic emperor added a 'Burgundian-Austrian' chancellery to the imperial *römische Kanzlei* headed by the archbishop of Mainz, and restructured the institutions responsible for the finances of his

50 Thomas Fellner and Heinrich Kretschmayr, eds., *Die österreichische Zentralverwaltung. I. Abteilung Von Maximilian I. Bis zur Vereinigung der Österreichischen und Böhmischen Hofkanzlei (1749)*, 3 vols. (Vienna 1907) (*ÖZV*), I, 2, pp. 100–116 (ordinance 1527); pp. 116–126 (ordinance 1527); pp. 139–147 (*Hofstaat* Maximilian 1519); see pp. 102, 105, 139, 142. Note, however, that Ferdinand's court was not the court of the emperor.

51 *ÖZV*, I, 2: on p. 100 von Trient is listed as president of the *geheime Rat*; on p. 117 as chancellor; on p. 100 with the addition 'soll halten phert nach kgl. Mt. Wolgevallen'.

52 *ÖZV*, I, 2, pp. 100–116 (ordinance 1527); for the *Truchseß*, *Schenk*, and *Fürschneider*, it was taken for granted that they were either Graf or Herr, underlining the increasingly honorary character of these offices. See also the allowances for the ranks among the *Räte*, in the 1518 Innsbrucker Libell, *ÖZV*, I, 2, pp. 84–91, here p. 84. See the major study by Heinz Noflatscher, *Räte und Herrscher. Politische Eliten an den Habsburgerhöfen der österreichischen Länder 1480–1530*, Veröffentlichungen des Instituts für europäische Geschichte 161 (Mainz 1999).

53 Innsbrucker Libell, *ÖZV*, I, 2, pp. 84–91, here at p. 84: 'adel und doctores'; later the *Herren-, Ritter, und Gelehrten Bänke* would characterise many assemblies. Compare the arrangements for the *Hofrat* in Ferdinand I's 1537 ordinance, *ÖZV*, I, 2, pp. 124–126, with only four councillors from the empire, and none for Tyrol.

dominions.[54] The balance between institutions pertaining to the empire (*Reich*), and institutions devoted to the governance of the Habsburg hereditary lands (*Hof*), was to remain a complicating factor for the emperors until the Holy Roman Empire imploded under the impact of Napoleon. The competences of imperial institutions based at the Habsburg court and their rivals elsewhere in the empire – most notably the *Reichshofrat* and the *Reichskammergericht* – were far from clear, and were first and foremost a symptom of the renewed competition between the emperor and princes of the empire.[55] Maximilian's court represented a recent and tentative fusion of various territories, and the expansion of his rule did not foster consolidation. When in 1519–1521, Charles and Ferdinand were sorting out their responsibilities, and when after 1526 Ferdinand acceded to the thrones of Hungary[56] and Bohemia, the situation became even more opaque. Ferdinand truly ruled as emperor only in his last eight years, after the abdication of Charles in 1556 and his coronation in 1558. Undoubtedly, this had important consequences for the nature of Ferdinand's court and government. The very success of the dynasty stretched its dominion beyond a level that could be controlled by one ruler, and the less than clear family settlement, in combination with the fundamental impact of religious schism, postponed for more than a generation the fulfilment of Maximilian's administrative reforms.

While the court of the Habsburg dukes of Tyrol in the fifteenth century may not have matched Burgundian refinement, numerically it was far from negligible. Assembling 400 people during festivities halfway through the century, and reaching a structural level of 500 under Maximilian's rule towards the end of the century, it was among the largest courts of the empire.[57] Emperor Frederick III's Wiener Neustadt court was probably slightly larger, numbering a little less than 600. When Maximilian died travelling in 1519, he was accompanied by 350 persons; in Innsbruck another 170 had stayed behind. Thus, the emperor's court before the advent of Charles V seems to have numbered 600 persons at most.[58] Rulers were expected to pay the household from their domanial revenues, but this was clearly impossible, forcing the Habsburgs to ask the estates assemblies for more support, or to reduce costs. When the Lower Austrian estates granted

[54] *ÖZV*, I, 2, *Hofordnung* 1498, no. 4, pp. 6–16; *Kanzleiordnungen*, 1498, nos. 7–8, pp. 48–54; Innsbrucker Libell 1518, no. 10, pp. 84–91.

[55] The fusion of the chancelleries: *ÖZV*, I, 2, no. 10, pp. 84–91 (1518), here at p. 87; also see Paul-Joachim Heinig, 'How Large was the Court of Emperor Frederick III?' in *Princes, Patronage, and the Nobility*, ed. Asch and Birke, p. 147.

[56] On Hungary see Géza Pálffy, 'Der Wiener Hof und die ungarischen Stände im 16. Jahrhundert', *MIÖG* 109 (2001), pp. 346–381, underlining that the Hungarian defence against Ottoman incursions was possible only thanks to Habsburg financial support.

[57] Michael Bojcov, 'Sitten und Verhaltensformen am Innsbrucker Hof des 15. Jahrhunderts im Spiegel der Hofordnungen', in *Höfe und Hofordnungen*, ed. Kruse and Paravicini, pp. 255–256 and n. 82; 400 attended the Tyrol court during festivities.

[58] Heinig, 'How Large was the Court of Emperor Frederick III?' pp. 149–151 and n. 21, gives fewer than 600 for Frederick; Peter Moraw, 'The Court of the German King and of the Emperor at the End of the Middle Ages, 1440–1519', in *Princes, Patronage, and the Nobility*, ed. Asch and Birke, p. 107.

Maximilian a subsidy of 400,000 florins for four years in 1515, two-thirds of this sum was earmarked to restore the solvency of the *Kammergut*.[59] Bearing in mind that paying for the bare minimum of feeding the *Hofgesinde*'s *c*. 600 horses amounted to at least 72,000 florins a year, prospects were decidedly bleak.[60] The expenses of Habsburg court – that is household and administration, but not the army, to be paid from the estates' contributions and controlled after 1556 by the *Hofkriegsrat* – would consistently overstretch the financial capabilities of the domains. Thus, the support of the estates, and of individual financiers, remained indispensable.[61] Whereas Charles V's multinational wandering court may have numbered between 1,000 and 2,000, and his son Philip II's (1556–1598) court with *c*. 2,500 was arguably the largest court in Christendom, Ferdinand I's more firmly rooted Viennese court initially did not match the levels of his predecessors' courts, remaining below 400 in his early years.[62]

STRUCTURES AND PARALLELS

The parallels in the development of the French court and the various predecessors of the Austrian Habsburg court are unambiguous. The same 'four great officers' – seneschal, marshal, chamberlain, cupbearer – emerged in the post-Carolingian epoch. In both realms, these offices existed on different levels: the great feudatories performed their tasks on ceremonial highpoints; substitutes served daily at the ruler's court, and other variants of the same offices served in the regions of both realms. In the last decade of the thirteenth century the steward made his entry at both courts, controlling the household, and gradually pushing aside the day-to-day incumbents of the four offices. The personal bond with the ruler, and the personal nature of service, predominated, and the ascendancy of the *maître d'hôtel* or *Hofmeister*, responsible for the ruler's table should not surprise us. Jean du Tillet, discussing the pre-eminence of the four great officers in France and in the empire, noted that 'ceux chargez de ce qui concerne la personne de l'Empereur, precedent ceux qui n'ont charge que des affaires'.[63] While du Tillet referred to an earlier phase, his message was still highly relevant in the sixteenth and seventeenth centuries.

[59] Zolger, *Hofstaat des Hauses Österreich*, pp. 34–35.

[60] Alternatively 90,000: compare the allowances mentioned in the Innsbrucker Libell, *ÖZV*, I, 2, p. 85: 100 Gulden rheinisch as '*lifergelt*' and an additional 50 Gulden as '*sold*', i.e. 150 per horse per year; and Ferdinand's ordinance of 1527, no. 12 in *ÖZV*, I, 2, on p. 115: 10 Gulden a month for a horse, i.e. 120 a year; this last number is repeated in Heinig, 'How Large was the Court of Emperor Frederick III?', p. 151, and Heinig, *Kaiser Friedrich III. (1440–1493). Hof, Regierung und Politik* (Cologne 1997).

[61] See the perceptive discussion of the court's financial Achilles' heel in Paula Sutter Fichtner, 'Habsburg Household or Habsburg Government? A Sixteenth-Century Administrative Dilemma', *Austrian History Yearbook* 26 (1995), pp. 45–60.

[62] Alfred Kohler 'Karl V', in *Die Kaiser der Neuzeit 1519–1918. Heiliges Römisches Reich, Österreich, Deutschland*, ed. A. Schindling and W. Ziegler (Munich 1990), pp. 33–54, here at p. 40; for Ferdinand, see Spielman, *City & the Crown*, p. 59 (400); and Ehalt, *Ausdrucksformen*, p. 57 (286 for 1537 without guards or the queen's household).

[63] Du Tillet, *Recueil des Roys*, p. 273.

Table 1. *The four traditional offices*

Pincerna/buticularius	Butler/Cupbearer	Schenk	Bouteiller/Echanson
Dapifer	Seneschal	Truchseß	Sénéchal
Comes Stabuli	Constable	Marschall	Connétable
Camerarius/Cubicularius	Chamberlain	Kämmerer	Chambrier/Chambellan

Table 2. *Noble table servants after the rise of the steward*

–	Truchseß
pannetier	Pannathier (incidentally)
échanson	Mundschenk
écuyer tranchant	Vorschneider/Fürschneider

The personal bond was the basis of high court office, yet court dignitaries were not necessarily the king's friends, nor were they always in his proximity, as the various levels of incumbency of the great court offices indicate. Honour and proximity, honorific and actual service, stand in a curious and changeable relationship. Would the great feudatories truly serve near the king's bed, spending the night at his feet when the queen was absent, or alternatively attending to the king's close stool? Even if they were willing the ruler might think it ill-advised to rely on them, as their intimidating accumulation of dynastic power might dispose them to abuse their proximity. Usually, their lesser substitutes performed such tasks, or lower servants the latter employed to do so. Yet the closeness these tasks inevitably entailed could allow lesser-ranking servants to reach high status in a short time span. The ruler could choose to confer particularly delicate tasks and responsibilities on such trusted companions. Whether concentrated in the *chambre*, as in the case of Francis I, or in other segments of the household, such groups more often than not formed a pool of candidates for high-ranking offices and missions.[64] The upward movement of favourites and intimates in the personal environment of the king gave a powerful impetus to change at court.[65] New offices were created for them, sometimes overlapping existing ones. Such earlier charges would as a rule be suppressed only when the place became vacant by the death of the incumbent and his dynasty; or they would be filled with lesser persons, and slowly recede into insignificance. A multi-layered structure of offices with overlapping and changing duties was the consequence of this practice of *laisser végéter*; the servants in the chamber, *chambrier*, *chambellans*, *gentilshommes de la chambre*, and *valets de la chambre* may serve as an example.

[64] See Potter, *History of France*, pp. 76–83, in addition to the *gentilshommes de la chambre* many of whom were charged with important missions, Potter mentions the *maîtres d'hôtel* as a reservoir for mostly practical services.

[65] See Le Roux's massive study of favourites and faction in the late sixteenth century, *Faveur du roi*.

If, on the other hand, trusted household officers were consistently charged with high military, diplomatic, and political commissions, they would not be able to attend to the ruler's needs, leaving others to profit from his proximity – the sequence of *connétable*, *maréchaux*, and *écuyer* may serve as illustration here. Moreover, as their distance from the household increased, they were likely to turn from agents of royal power into guardians of their own dynastic interests. At the Habsburg court, the imperial (*Erzämter*) and regional (*Landeserbämter*) levels of high court office remained intact, but their functioning was mainly limited to special occasions, and their day-to-day substitutes had risen to social prominence. In France, supreme office at court did retain a strong bond with senior princely dynasties, but at court these usually were seconded by deputies, as the habitual range of prefixes for high offices, *grand- premier- ordinaire-*, indicates.

The household was not only a supreme dynastic establishment among other noble houses; it shows many parallels with the army, also a predominantly male peripatetic body, partly overlapping in personnel: periodic mustering, billeting by quartermasters and maintenance of discipline by provosts were familiar for both. It resembled an abbey in its train of domestic activities and its structures for management of domanial finances. In its habitual urban environment, the court operated as the principal corporation among other corporations. Members of the court, the king's *commensaux* or the Habsburg *Hofgesinde*, were subject to no other justice than that of the *prévôt de l'hôtel* or the *Hofmarschall* as edicts would make clear to the *Chatelet de Paris* and Viennese authorities.[66] They enjoyed a variable set of immunities and privileges, and were a marked presence in the environment where they chose to reside. French court officers, moreover, ideally served as patrons for Parisian *métiers* matching their household tasks: thus, the *panetier* oversaw the bakers, the *échanson* the wine merchants and taverners, while a range of crafts connected with garments was controlled by the *chambrier*.[67]

The court on the eve of the early modern age retained fluid characteristics. Domestic service, household management, honorary service, and executive or governmental duties were communicating vessels. Nor can we sharply differentiate between common and noble service at court, 'below' and 'above' stairs;

[66] See, for example, the materials on the jurisdiction of the *prévôté* versus the Chatelet de Paris in BN Clair 828, pp. 1145–1158, 1161–1167, 1261–1263 (now against the bailiff of Versailles), 1317–1318 (as late as 1722). HHStA, OMaA I, K I (1564–1712), and K 519 (1656–1689) contain many reports on the relations with Vienna, disturbed by the *Gefreyte hoffhandlsleuthe*, and other members of the *Hofgesinde*, who were subject only to the *Obersthofmarschall Gericht*, see, for example, a 27 June 1667 decree and a *Hoffhandlsleuth Ordnung* in K 519. Compare Khevenhüller, *Tagebuch*, II, p. 394, n. 69, reporting a change in the jurisdiction of the *Obersthofmarschall*.

[67] Du Tillet, *Recueil des Roys*, pp. 287, 290–292. Anselme, *Histoire de la Maison Royale*, VIII, pp. 680–682, includes an 'edit du roy. Pour la suppression de la jurisdiction de la panneterie donné à Fontainebleau au mois d'Août 1711': the *grand pannetier*, the duc de Brissac, was compensated for the loss of income, generated by rights *maîtres et apprentis* had to pay upon reception. The *maître de la garderobe* took over the *chambrier*'s patronage.

the boundaries were as fragile as they were volatile. Yet written procedures were becoming stronger in the sixteenth century. Court ordinances stressed the need to make inventories of various sorts, urged the major officers to carefully check the presence of the *Hofgesinde*, demanded written records of all financial transactions, and laid down rules for precedence at court. These requests and rules, far from novel, now indeed may have helped to solidify practices at court. Ferdinand I's 1527 and 1537 ordinances served as points of reference for the Austrian Habsburg court throughout the sixteenth, seventeenth, and eighteenth centuries. The author of the only comprehensive study of the Habsburg court, a work published in 1917, could still see Ferdinand I as the founding father of 'his' court.[68] Francis I and Henry II consolidated the French court, and Henry III's great ordinances of 1578 and 1585 fulfilled a role parallel to those of Ferdinand I.[69] Thus, in the course of the sixteenth century the constellation of senior officers at both courts reached the form it would roughly maintain in the following centuries, although their hierarchies were subject to fluctuation, and new offices were created within the established structures of the staffs.

At both courts the staffs consolidating in the sixteenth century clearly reflect the routines of table, chamber, stable, hunt, and chapel, but neither the offices nor their status match perfectly. A high steward or maiordomo (*grand maître de l'hôtel de France*; *Obersthofmeister*) catering for the ruler's table, held responsibility for the kitchen, the cellar, provisioning, and the stock of costly tableware. The steward combined the senior position in the household with a voice in the council, and he commanded a vast range of subordinates. In the upper echelons of his staff, we find his senior deputy (*premier maître d'hôtel*; *Oberststabelmeister*) with their numerous assistants (*maîtres d'hôtel*; *Tafeldiener*), and the familiar triad of table servants (*panetier, échanson, écuyer tranchant*; *Fürschneider, Mundschenk, Truchseß*, sometimes *Pannathier*). In France, the senior incumbents of these three honorary charges for table service were labelled *premier*, later *grand*; in Vienna we only find the tripartite functional division in the lists, closely resembling that of the *gentilshommes servants*. After the high-ranking *Obersilberkämmerer* and his deputy, came the master of the *Küchelparthey* (kitchen) overseeing a variety of cooks, carriers, and boys, the *Kellerparthey* (cellar), the *Lichtkammer* (lighting), and the *Zehrgaden* (kitchen garden). The French *sept offices*, roughly the equivalent of these Habsburg staffs, were still divided between the services catering for the king's table, or *bouche*, and those responsible for the tables of the *commensaux* or *commun*. Controllers and treasurers oversaw provisioning and payments.

[68] Zolger, *Der Hofstaat des Hauses Österreich*.

[69] See Ferdinand's 1527 and 1537 ordinances in *ÖZV*, I, 2, no. 12, pp. 100–126; Henry III's 1585 ordinance is printed in Cimber and Danjou, *Archives curieuses de l'histoire de France*, serie I, vol. X (Paris 1836), pp. 301–358; manuscript copies of the 1578 and 1585 ordinances can be found in AN KK 544 and BN MS naf 7225 (the equivalent of BN Brienne 256). Many other volumes include selections from these texts.

A chamberlain (*grand chambellan*; *Oberstkämmerer*) controlled access to the 'private sphere' of the ruler, and guarded the objects and treasures in the chamber; both the French and the Habsburg chamberlains initially took part in financial management. With the development of impositions and taxes, this increasingly complicated burden was conferred on others. In France the chamberlain, supreme officer of the chamber after 1545, was assisted in his tasks by various *chambellans* and *gentilshommes*, among whom the *premiers gentilshommes* and the *maîtres de la garderobe* served as senior officers. The structure of the French chamber was subject to frequent redefinitions until it stabilised in the early seventeenth century.[70] In Vienna, no such confusion existed; we find only the ranks of *Kämmerer* and *Kammerdiener*. The latter were a notably less prestigious parallel to the French *premiers valets* of chamber and wardrobe whose coveted position was followed by *valets ordinaires* and *autres valets* of hazy responsibilities.[71]

In addition to the staffs of these two senior domestic offices, we find a marshal, master of the stables, or master of the horse who oversaw the stables, and arranged the frequent transports of the court. The marshal traditionally held jurisdiction over courtiers and foreign visitors, maintained peace at court (*Burgfrieden*), was responsible for quartering, and could be expected to lead the army into battle. In France, these duties were divided among a range of officers; the *grand écuyer* overseeing the stables and the pages; the *prévôt de l'hôtel*, with his guards wielding disciplinary and judicial powers over the *maison* and controlling its purveyors, and the *maréchal des logis* (the Carolingian *mansionarius*) taking care of the court's quartering. The *connétable* and the *maréchaux*, commanding, provisioning, and financing the army, were not closely connected to the household. At the Austrian Habsburg court, the *Obersthofmarschall* retained judicial and disciplinary powers over courtiers, foreigners, and diplomats; he also oversaw the quartering of the court. The *Marschall* was second-in-rank, and replaced the steward when necessary. Transport and the supervision of the stables with their *Edelknaben* were conferred on the *Oberststallmeister*, a somewhat less prestigious counterpart of the French *grand écuyer*.

[70] See Potter, *History of France*, pp. 66–69; Le Roux, *Faveur du roi*, pp. 722–725 and pp. 519–522 for the 45 *gentilshommes ordinaires* created by Henry III in December 1584. Only the *grand chambellan*, four *premiers gentilshommes*, and 24–26 *gentilshommes ordinaires* can still be found in seventeenth-century *états*. See BN Clair 837, pp. 3252–3253, for Henry IV's chamber staff, with the *grand chambellan*, a *chambellan ordinaire*, and two *premiers gentilshommes*, and the reflection of later practice in Loyseau, *Cinq Livres*, p. 229; Eugène Griselle, *Etat de la Maison du Roi Louis XIII . . . comprenant les années 1601 à 1665* (Paris 1912), p. 10. The *chambellans* and other varieties of the *gentilshommes* in the chamber are absent in the seventeenth-century *maison du roi*. BN Clair 1216, fols. 73r–74r: 1627–1628 'Estats de payement des gages des officiers . . . frère unique du roi'; Gaston d'Orléans, however, still includes a variety of *chambellans* and *gentilshommes*.

[71] Yet see the history of a *Kammerdiener* reaching and abusing favour at Rudolf's court: Friedrich Hurter, *Philip Lang, Kammerdiener Kaiser Rudolfs II. Eine Criminalgeschichte aus dem Anfang des siebenzehnten Jahrhunderts* (Schaffhausen 1851); Lang apparently was something like a *premier valet* turned into favourite and bully. Compare nuncio Carafa's report in Friedrich Hurter, *Friedensbestrebungen Kaiser Ferdinand's II. Nebst des Apostolischen Nuntius Carl Carafa Bericht über Ferdinand's Lebensweise, Familie, Hof, Räthe und Politik* (Vienna 1860), pp. 212–280; pp. 238–239 mention twelve *Kammerdiener* as 'Edelleute geringern Ranges' – usually we find neither *premiers valets* nor noble titles for the lower servants in the chamber.

A chaplain or almoner (*grand aumônier*; *Obersthofkaplan*) headed the chapel, administering to the spiritual needs of the court. Surprisingly, we find the chaplain in a position subservient to the *Obersthofmeister* at the Habsburg court, whereas his French compeer had his own staff and, following Burgundian practice, this *maison ecclésiastique* was listed at the head of the *états*. The rank of the incumbents reflected this divergence, as the *grand aumônier* was invariably of high noble stock, the *Hofkaplan* of indifferent background. The chapel included instrumentalists and choristers, though sturdier musical accompaniment for outdoor ceremonies was provided by the drums and trumpets of the stables, and in France other musicians served in the *chambre*. The staffs of huntsmen and guards, overlapping in the upper ranks of *grand veneur–Oberstjägermeister* and *Oberstfalkenmeister–grand fauconnier*, were more extensive and variegated in France. The mounted archers and infantry guards in Vienna, *Hartschieren und Trabanten*, can be likened to the 'gardes du dedans du Louvre', the *gardes de la porte*, *gardes du corps*, and Swiss guards in France. They protected the ruler, and took part in processions and ceremonies. The captains of these companies formed the lower echelons of the supreme layer of court offices.

Both courts expanded in the course of the following centuries, and most services became more diverse and specialised. The structures outlined above remained basically unaltered, and only in the position of the chapel and the incongruence of the *Marschall* with either the *prévôt de l'hôtel* or *maréchal des logis*, did they fundamentally differ. The household, serving the ruler's daily needs, ideally represented and strengthened his bonds with a variety of groups in the realm. The cohesion of this constellation was severely tested by a range of developments. In France, new men in government, using their financial and legal expertise to gain a foothold at court, secured ennoblement and influence. Sword nobles vehemently attacked the 'usurpations' of these new rivals, stressing their age-old rights. In the German lands, nobles were less averse to the unchivalrous forms of education necessary to retain their dominance in government; nor did they cultivate an overall antipathy towards the administrative specialists – indeed, no robe nobility in the French style developed here, and the institutional structures slowly evolving never neatly fitted the categories of rank and lineage. More incisive than the long-term development of government by paper and its socio-political consequences, however, was the success of the Protestant creed. Halfway through the century, Calvinism was developing into a major force, and nobles figured prominently among its converts in France as well as in Hungary and to a lesser extent in the Austrian Habsburg lands. Thus, the ruler and his greatest nobles, close but rarely wholly comfortable, had to overcome two major obstacles: the rise of non-noble service elites and the exacerbation of religious discord.

Could rulers use their households to pacify noble dissent and reward loyal support? Did they restructure their courts in the process? During this turbulent phase, lasting roughly from the late sixteenth century to the second half of the seventeenth century, the courts in France and the Austrian Habsburg lands assumed some of their defining characteristics. The constellation of noble dynasties around the court, profiting from their hold on political power and from access to the ruler's graces, was frequently reshuffled by the hazards of rebellion and warfare. The families emerging successfully from this trial would hold sway until the end of the *ancien régime*. How did numbers, costs, and hierarchies of the household develop in these alternating phases of crisis and compromise?

PART II

Contours

CHAPTER 3

Numbers and costs

ETATS AND *VERZEICHNISSE*

For neither of these courts is a reliable sequence of lists available before the eighteenth century: we have well-documented instances, but no comprehensive picture. The available material, moreover, is often distorted as well as incomplete, because the specific reasons which prompted the household's administrators to record numbers to a large extent determined the results. Were the compilers concerned mainly to present an impressive array of court servants paid and unpaid, maximising their numbers? Or did they list the bare minimum of those actually paid for specific services, leaving aside unpaid honorary servants, and frequently the stables and the hunt as well, if these had separate budgets? Would they include the personal secretaries and dependents of higher officers, not necessarily paid from the ruler's coffers? An acceptable level of precision can be achieved only when we combine numbers of the generally inexact overviews with the more detailed and reliable, though mostly incomplete lists used as a basis for the payment of *gages*, or the registers of such payments. *Quartierbücher*, containing the names of courtiers and the quarters where they were billeted, may allow a similar level of precision. To date this laborious task has been performed systematically only for the exceptionally well-documented Burgundian court.[1]

By the mid-seventeenth century, the French *états*, including lists of officers and short descriptions of their rank and tasks, had found their way to the printer. Not only did the process of printing suggest more clearly defined sections for households and administrative services; it allowed the lists to reach wider audiences, and may have changed their character in the process. The manuscript overviews were inward-looking instruments intended to manage an

[1] For Burgundy see Holger Kruse, *Hof, Amt und Gagen: die täglichen Gagenlisten des burgundischen Hofes (1430–1467) und der erste Hofstaat Karls des Kühnen (1456)*, Pariser Historische Studien 44 (Bonn 1996), and Kruse, 'Die Hofordnungen Herzogs Philipps des Guten von Burgund', in *Höfe und Hofordnungen*, ed. Kruse and Paravicini, pp. 141–165; for France, see Boucher's early and important 'Evolution', and for the Austrian Habsburgs see Jaroslava Hausenblasová, 'Seznamy dvoranu císare rudolfka II. Z let 1580, 1584 a 1589', in *Paginae Historiae. Sborník Státino Ustredniho archivu v Praze* 4 (Prague 1996), pp. 39–151, and her forthcoming edition of *Hofstaatverzeichnisse 1576–1612*; Stefan Sienell, 'Die Wiener Hofstaate zur Zeit Leopolds I.', in *Hofgesellschaft und Höflinge*, ed. Malettke and Grell, pp. 89–111.

unwieldy household, and usually devoted primarily to balancing the budget. These documents reached a small internal audience. In the 1650s the first short and incomplete *états* were printed, in a haphazard rhythm. From 1661 until 1698, Nicolas Besongne, *clerc de chapelle*, *chapelain*, and *aumônier du roi*, edited a more systematic and comprehensive *Etat* every one to three years; after 1699 when his *survivancier* for the charge of chaplain, Louis Trabouillet, took over the task, the *états* were published with an interval of four to six years. After 1727, this cadence further slowed down; only for 1736 and 1749 do we find full *états*. These steadily swelling volumes not only included all major persons and institutions of the French commonwealth but also offered an outline of ranks and ceremonies at court.[2] Dynasty, household, government, army, and regional administration appeared in different sections in the later volumes. From the last years of the seventeenth century onwards, moreover, an *almanach royal* was published annually. The ill-assorted information offered in the *almanach* did not match the relative precision of the *états*, yet in the course of the eighteenth century a short overview of the court's major officers was included.[3] These publications were hardly as deliberate and explicit vehicles of royal representation as the descriptions of court spectacle in the *Mercure* and the *Gazette*, or Félibien's lavishly illustrated volumes; yet they certainly helped to convey the image of the court to an audience that reached beyond the palace precinct and the borders of the realm.[4] This may have strengthened their tendency to present an ideal situation.

In Vienna a parallel development followed almost half a century later. For the later seventeenth century, we find a variety of *Hofstaatsverzeichnisse*, generated by

[2] See, for example, Jean Pinson de la Martinière, *Estat de la France, comme elle estoit gouvernée en l'an 1648* (Paris 1649); *Estat et gouvernement de France* (Amsterdam 1653); N. Du Verdier, *Le vray et nouveau estat de la France* . . . (Paris 1656); then the sequence edited by N. Besongne, for example, *L'Estat de la France* . . . (Paris 1663); *L'Etat de la France*, 2 vols. (Paris 1669); *Etat de la France, où l'on voit tous les princes, ducs & pairs, maréchaux de France & autres officiers de la couronne*, 2 vols. (Paris 1672); *Etat de la France, où l'on voit tous les princes, ducs et pairs* . . . , 2 vols. (Paris 1677); Ange de Sainte-Rosalie (François Raffard), *L'Etat de la France, où l'on vois tous les princes, ducs & pairs, marêchaux de France* . . . , 2 vols. (Paris 1682); *L'Etat de la France, ou l'on voit tous les princes, ducs & pairs, maréchaux de France & autres officiers de la Couronne*, 3 vols. (Paris 1687); L. Trabouillet, *L'Etat de la France contenant tous les princes, ducs & pairs, & maréchaux de la France* . . . , 3 vols. (Paris 1712); Ange de Sainte-Rosalie, *L'Etat de la France, contenant tous les princes, ducs & pairs, maréchaux de France*, 4 vols. (Paris 1722); Boucher, 'Evolution', pp. 360–361, discusses the series; the 'avertissement' of the 1722 *Etat de la France*, pp. x–xi, provides details about the preceding editions, reiterated and updated in the last printed *Etat de la France*, 4 vols., published in 1749, I, p. xi. See the printed BN *Catalogue de l'histoire de France* (Paris 1968), IV, pp. 606–622, Lc26, 'annuaires administratifs'.

[3] See the series in the AN salle de lecture: *Almanac ou calendrier pour l'année Mil Six Cens quatrevints-dix-neuf: exactement supputé sur le méridien de paris. Où sont marquez les Eclypses, le lever & le coucher du soleil, le mouvement de la lune, les jours des foires, le journal du palais, la demeure des messagers, le depart des couriers, le tariff des monnoies & la liste des bureaux de messieurs des finances, & leurs departments* (Paris 1699). These volumes can be compared to the Viennese *Schematismen*, yet in the first decades they do not give information about the *maison du roi*; only from 1726 onwards do we find the new queen's *maison* (p. 96) and from 1729 onwards the *maison du roi* (pp. 106–107). The overviews of *c.* one page per *maison* increase slightly, but give only the structure of the establishment, and the major charges. For 1789, the aggregate of *maisons* within the dynasty fills pp. 124–148. Compare the diminutive in-16 volumes of the *Calendrier de la cour tiré des éphémérides pour l'annee mil sept cent quatre vingt six. . . . Imprimé pour la famille royale et maison de sa majesté* published from 1701 to 1791, containing even less detail on the *maisons* – but adding the birthdays of courtiers and rulers.

[4] The volumes predating 1749 given in n. 2 are all available in Dutch libraries, an indication of the more extensive audiences reached by the printed *états*.

travel, ceremonial occasions, or pertaining to specific sections of the court, and only incidentally printed. In the more comprehensive lists administrative institutions and councils governing the various levels of the Habsburg commonwealth were given in a curious admixture with the household. The *Teutsch-Österreichisch Aussgelegter Adler oder unvorgreifflicher Kurtzer entwurf Kaysserlichen Hoff...*, a series of manuscript volumes devoted to the emperor's finances, gave the domanial revenue of various regions, and included households, councils, and the army in their computations.[5] Only with the *Staats- und Standskalender*, published annually from the third decade of the eighteenth century after a less regular start in 1701, do we find more or less reliable consecutive printed lists.[6] These initially small, but steadily growing volumes, known as *Schematismen*, proudly presented an alphabetically ordered register concentrating on Vienna and its corporations, yet they included a separate section with the *Hofstaat* of the emperor and his relatives.[7] From *c.* 1715 onwards, a calendar, *Zum Gebrauch der Kayserlichen Hof-Statt*, was published separately.[8] In the early years of the nineteenth century the *Schematismen*, or *Staats- und Standskalender* were unequivocally divided into *Hofstaat* and *Staat* respectively. The army had its own printed *Schematismus* from the 1790s onwards.[9] Thus, only in the course of the eighteenth century did the emerging separation of household, government, and army attain the printed confirmation it had obtained in France in the later seventeenth century.

FRINGES OF THE HOUSEHOLD

We can define the court in many ways, and each definition will lead to a different assessment of its numerical development. The medieval differentiation between the *curia maior*, bringing together the great feudatories, and the *curia minor*, those daily serving the ruler, suggests a divide between permanently attending

[5] For example, ÖNB cod. 14113, 14209; AVA Harrach Handschriften no. 145; HHStA Handschriften Weiß 1032; Handschriften Blau 386. In the Vienna HKA the HZAB, accounting for payments to the *Hofgesinde*, rarely fitting the general data in the overviews, can help to establish a more detailed view.

[6] See recently Volker Bauer, *Repertorium territorialer Amtskalender und Amtshandbücher im Alten Reich. Adreß-, Hof-, Staatskalender und Staatshandbücher des 18. Jahrhunderts*, vol. II, Heutiges Bayern, Österreich, Liechtenstein. Ius Commune, Sonderheft 123 (Frankfurt 1999).

[7] *Kayserlicher und Königlicher, wie auch Erz-herzoglicher und dero Residenzstadt Wienn Staats- und Standskalender / auff das Jahr MDCCII. Mit einem noch nie dergleichen gesehenen Schematismo geziert*; other *Schematismen* for 1704, 1706–1708, 1709–1710, etc., are available in the ÖNB, Katalogsaal, 393.866–A.kat or microfilm 4478, 1704 and 1706–1708 in the ÖNB Portraitsammlung 6079. Only from the 1720s do these volumes offer a more or less continuous coverage.

[8] See HHStA Bibliothek 38 K 2: *Kayserlicher Hof- und Ehren-Kalender / Auf das Jahr nach unsers seeligmachers Jesu Christi Geburt* [*1715* etc.] *Zum Gebrauch der Kayserlichen Hof-Statt / Land-Ständen und Regierungen eingerichtet / und in solche Form gebracht. Die constellation, Witterung / und festtage seynd mit sonderlichen Fleiß nach dem Oesterreichischen Horizont gestellet. Dardey* [*sic*] *auch alle Galla-Täg / Toson* [*sic*] *vespern / und andere hof-fest ordentlich bey jedem Monath angezeichnet*; and the *Kaiserl. auch Kaiserl. Königl. Hof Kalender auf das Jahr nach der gnadenreiche Geburt unsers Seligmachers Jesu Christi 1806. Zum Gebrauche des Kaiserl. auch Kaiserl. Königl. Hofes* (Vienna 1806): ÖNB 393.537–B.Kat of A 120 a 13.

[9] The 1807 *Staats- und Standeskalender* was organised in two parts: *Hofstaat* and *Staat*. The army *schematismus*: *Oestreichischer Miliz-Almanach für das Jahr 1790 nro I (*Nürnberg and Vienna 1790): ÖNB 392.994–A.Kat, A 120 a 12.

servants and incidentally serving dignitaries. Are we interested in the numbers of those in fact attending court, or of those who could choose to do so? Among those daily serving the ruler, do we include all hierarchical levels, and all conceivable sectors of the court? For many among them, the label 'courtier' surely is hardly appropriate. These and other questions need to be addressed before turning to the analysis of the courts' numerical development.

Older lists and ordinances make emphatically clear that the household was only the inner core of an environment including governmental agents and agencies. The chancellor was as characteristic for the medieval court as the treasurer, or a council of grandees with judicial and executive powers. Secretaries and clerks slowly became indispensable parts of the administrative machinery. Whatever the exact relationships of household and government, it is evident that we cannot unequivocally draw the line between them. Contemporary definitions presented the central agencies of government as a component of the 'wider' court, and visitors could choose to include them in their estimates of the numbers residing there. Indeed, an assessment of parallel or divergent development of the numerical strength in these two spheres may help to clarify their interaction.

In other ways as well, the ruler's household was only the nucleus of a wider environment. It frequently formed but the most conspicuous component in a constellation of dynastic households. Such establishments could be physically separated from his court when siblings ruled parts of the realm as stadholders: Maximilian II's brothers Karl and Ferdinand ruled in Graz and Innsbruck. Until the extinction of the Tyrolean Habsburg lineage in 1665, Tyrol was ruled from Innsbruck. When the ideals of primogeniture and the 'indivisibility' of sovereignty made it increasingly unwelcome to grant appanages to agnates, it remained habitual for them to have their own households and palaces. Spouses brought their cortèges and transformed them into sizeable establishments, including a parallel hierarchy of women in the upper echelons.[10] A queen or empress would gain an even more important position after the death of her husband, particularly in the first years of the new reign, before the young ruler married. The dowager's household, absorbing many of the deceased ruler's servants, could outshine the 'young court'. Children and grandchildren were habitually granted a personal following when they reached adolescence. Births and deaths could change the constellation of dynastic households within the court overnight, causing the aggregate numbers of such households to vary greatly within a short time span. Charles VI, returning to Vienna in 1711, had to provide for his deceased brother Joseph's establishment, for the households of two dowager-empresses, for his empress, for those forming his Spanish household, and for the small establishment left in Vienna upon his earlier departure to Spain.

[10] See, for example, Catherine Wilkinson-Zerner, 'Women's Quarters in Spanish Royal Palaces', in *Architecture et vie sociale. L'Organisation intérieure des grandes demeures à la fin du moyen âge et à la renaissance. Actes du colloque tenu à Tours du 6 au 10 juin 1988*, ed. Jean Guillaume (Paris 1994), pp. 127–136.

Other rulers were relatively free of such pressures. The secondary households, finally, formed an ideal stepping-stone for ambitious yet less well-connected persons: in this less exposed environment they could build up their networks before jumping to the generally more prestigious and lucrative charges in the ruler's court. We should take notice of the cultural and political relevance of these important satellite-courts, and include them in our conjectures about the court's expansion.

Administrators were at or near court; the ruler's closest relatives had significant personal establishments, and were expected to remain in contact with the ruler – long absences were read as an ominous sign. By definition, however, a substantial number of court officers were hardly as assiduous as the administrators, nor was their absence upsetting. The overviews notably include honorary officers such as chamberlains, esquires (*écuyers*), *maîtres d'hôtel*, *gentilshommes servants*, almoners, ladies-in-waiting, or secretaries, who enjoyed the right to attend court and were theoretically expected to actively perform their tasks following a rota system. Most honorary servants attended court only in alternation, and for shorter periods: weeks, quarters, semesters, or years. A certain measure of actual service was usually stipulated, but these charges could be held simply as an honorific privilege, granting immunities and various rights to the incumbents.[11] At the Habsburg court, brief periods of active service alternating with longer absences were relevant only for the typical honorary officers, the *Kämmerer*: most others were expected to remain at their post throughout the year. The divide between honorary and 'actual' service was relatively clear-cut. The French court, however, had adopted service *par terme* on a large scale, and it ranged from the highest to the lowest levels of the courtly hierarchy – a fact indicating the significance of the lower echelons. Whereas the structural use of *service par terme* or the proliferation of specific honorary offices suggests that the number of charges was smaller than the number of those holding these charges in alternation, the frequent concentration of several offices in one person or family complicates the matter. In Vienna, for example, noble courtiers were always chamberlain in addition to their other charges, and frequently councillor; in addition we often find their names in the regional and central administrative institutions close to the household. In France the accumulation of offices, repeatedly forbidden, remained endemic, and incidentally extended to the highest offices. Counting persons and counting charges lead to different results, and the incongruity between these results can only be solved when we know the names of all courtiers. Honorary office shares some characteristics with the great orders of chivalry – like *service par terme* a feat typical of the Burgundian court. For orders as well as for honorary office, membership itself was a special privilege, and the bond

[11] See, for example, the 'autres sécrétaires' mentioned Gaston d'Orléans'1628 household in BN Clair 1216 with the addition 'pour jouir des privileges' (fol. 92r).

it created was not necessarily contingent upon frequent contact. Surely, these distant courtiers belonged to the court – they were one of its vital components. Yet we cannot collectively add them to the numbers attending court.

We find a multifaceted group of artisans, servants, and purveyors, ranging from painters or jewellers of great repute to practitioners of less conspicuous crafts, in the overviews. Some of these had a recognised position in the courtly environment; others may have sought entry into the household even when their dealings with it were infrequent. As members of the ruler's *familia*, they gained exemption from regular taxes and jurisdiction – a position opening lucrative vistas. It is difficult to assess the number of such sinecures, nor is it always clear whether the overviews include the lowest servants of the household. As long as the overviews were primarily a means to balance the budget, they would necessarily include all those paid on a regular basis; when they tended to develop into representative lists of the court, they were more likely to omit the lower servants, or include them in general terms only.[12]

Seasonal variations further complicate the computation of numbers resident at court. In the early modern age, most courts spent the winter months in their major residence, while sojourning in a sequence of hunting lodges from spring to autumn. Most of these secondary palaces were not equipped to lodge the same number of people as the winter residence. The ruler was served by a reduced establishment, and only a small number of visitors could be accommodated. The pleasures of hunting and the advantage of easy access to the ruler made these outings quite attractive, but they were necessarily limited to a relatively small group of companions. The close link between noble rank and military valour secured yet another parallel seasonal variation. In the campaigning season during the warmer months, when the horses could feed off the land, wars caused the absence of many courtiers. Guard regiments could figure as elite units in the regular army, further depleting the ranks at court. Indeed, the expansion of the guards and other military units at court could blur the border between the court and the army, and unduly inflate the numbers of the court.

Finally, a politically effective court by definition was a point of contact, a meeting place for a heterogeneous assemblage of high-ranking visitors, foreign representatives, petitioners, seekers of adventure and employment, and tourists grand or small. Spouses, relatives, and dependants of the higher charges were probably regular guests at court, but we find them on the payrolls only when they themselves obtained a *charge*. More importantly, jousts, hunting parties, and festivities would attract crowds to the court, an assemblage of mostly noble persons eligible for court attendance, yet not usually to be found there. The *états* and *Verzeichnisse*, outlining the household and its administrative fringes,

12 See Boucher, 'Evolution', p. 374: the *état d'écurie* lists 250 *officiers* whereas Besongne's 1694 *état* listed 444 persons, while hinting at 'quantité d'autres'; Reytier, in *Les écuries royales*, pp. 75–76, contrasts the low numbers of *officiers* in the regular *états* of the stables with the higher numbers of servants recorded in other series.

unfortunately do not allow us to reconstruct this most evasive yet crucial dimension – though they often include lists of diplomats residing at court. Contemporaries, on the other hand, impressed by the bustle of passers-by crowding the court, may have overestimated their numbers. Primi Visconti, a regular visitor at the French court from 1673 until 1681, argued that courtiers and servants together numbered at least 7,000, without counting the soldiers at court, numbers exceeding the modest evaluation given below. Can we simply discard such frequent high estimates, or did these observers rightly assess categories we do not find in our sources, but of undisputed relevance for the court?[13]

FRANCE

In the reign of Francis II, the aggregate of services headed by the *grand aumônier*, the *grand maître*, the *grand chambellan*, and the *capitaine de la porte* (together the 'inner' *maison*) surpassed the limit of 1,000 members.[14] Adding the establishments for hunting, the stables, the guards, and judicial officers of the *prévoté*, we may accept a number of *c.* 1,700; yet the *maisons* of the queen-mother and queen together added another 700–800, suggesting a grand total for the 'wider' court of *c.* 2,500. Henry III, far from initiating the court's expansion, followed in the footsteps of his predecessors. Yet while only *c.* 500 nobles had held charges in Charles IX's *maison*, this number doubled for the years 1575–1586. The share of nobles in the *maison* rose from *c.* 25 per cent to *c.* 44 per cent. The rise was the consequence mostly of proliferation of the charge of *gentilshomme ordinaire de la chambre*, reaching of 380 in 1583 alone, and many more for the entire decade. In January 1585, Henry reduced the gentlemen of the chamber to 45 per quarter, or a total of 184, but this move occurred shortly after his creation of a new group of *gentilshommes ordinaires* intended as a new body of 45 devoted clients willing to protect and serve the king. These measures, alternatively enticing nobles to the court and protecting his environment, were not the only reason for the court's expansion.[15] Henry grudgingly appeased the rush of other petitioners, but he tried to limit the scope and the consequences of the expansion. Thus, in 1584 he added 216 officers *sans gages* to his establishment: they would benefit from the privileges attached to court charges, such as the exemption from the *tailles* and other burdens, but could not expect further remuneration.[16] In the 1580s the inner *maison*, excluding

[13] J.-F. Solnon, ed., *Mémoires de Primi Visconti sur la cour de Louis XIV, 1673–1681* (Paris 1988), p. 145; Benvenuto Cellini and Venetian ambassadors cited in Solnon, *Cour de France*, p. 21; compare the extremely high estimates given in Bauer, *Höfische Gesellschaft*, p. 65.

[14] BN Clair 836, an overview of the *maisons* from Henry II until Henry III, given as lists containing numbers for entire reigns, suggests a relative stability in Charles IX years, just below the 1,000 level, an uncertain computation confirmed generally by Le Roux's depiction of Charles' reign in *Faveur du Roi*.

[15] See Le Roux's analysis in *Faveur du roi*, pp. 192–198, 519–522, from which these figures and interpretations are taken. BN Clair 836, pp. 3019–3221, lists all officers for Henry III's reign, with the hypothetical totals hovering between *c.* 1,491 and 1,835. The list clearly shows increasing numbers, and indicates changes mostly in chamber and wardrobe, suggesting a total of at least 1,500 for the inner *maison*.

[16] Solnon, *Cour de France*, pp. 47–48.

these 216 officers, still hovered between 1,000 and 1,100; with the *écuries*, the hunt, the *prévoté*, the guards, the queen's *maison*, and the queen-mother's establishment of 668 persons, the wider court must have included more than 3,000 persons.[17] The king's restive brother, François de Valois, duke of Alençon and Anjou, moreover, assembled a personal following rivalling the king's *maison*: starting from a moderate 277 in 1572, it rose from 415 to 942 in 1576 after the peace of Beaulieu; in 1578 it numbered 1,123. Anjou, keen on his sovereign status, even employed a *sécrétaire d'état* and a *conducteur des ambassadeurs*, offices recently developed to further both the administrative competence and the international representation of the court.[18] The constellation of households around the court, including those of the Guise *grands maîtres de France*, reached a temporary peak in the political-religious crisis of the later sixteenth century. It was to be neither the last nor the most extensive explosion of the court.

Henry IV undoubtedly intended to shed some of his predecessor's domestic officers. Yet his *maison* never counted fewer than a thousand members.[19] On the contrary, it soon became obvious that the first Bourbon was subject to the same pressures as the last Valois. Thus the *aumôniers sans gages* rose from 31 in 1591 to 174 in 1599; the *maîtres d'hôtel* from 10 in 1590 to 22 in 1599; the *gentilshommes servants* from 32 in 1590 to 77 around 1600; *valets de chambre* from 46 to 67 in the same period. Most striking was the proliferation of secretaries of various kinds, surpassing 300 by 1600.[20] Nor was the inner *maison* the only sector of expansion: in 1596, we find 562 persons in the king's hunting services, including 132 *gentilshommes de la vénerie* instead of the habitual *c.* 14, whereas a 1605 *état* for the *écuries* listed more than 600 persons both for the hunt and the stables, roughly twice as many as in the years of Henry III.[21] Henry IV had to appease former *ligueurs*, and sought to content them by resorting to the expedient of doubling the senior charges, to be held by representatives of both religious parties.[22] The 'wider' court, including the household of Marie de Medici (*c.* 465 in 1609),[23] may only have been reduced thanks to the temporary absence of other major *maisons*.

17 See Chatenet, 'Logis des femmes', in *Frauenzimmer*, ed. Hirschbiegel and Paravicini, p. 178, for Catherine de Medici's household; Jacqueline Boucher, *La cour de Henri III* (Rennes 1986), p. 40, mentions 666.

18 Jacqueline Boucher, 'Autour de François, duc d'Alençon et d'Anjou, un parti d'opposition à Charles IX et Henri III', in *Henri III et son temps. Actes du colloque international du Centre de la renaissance de Tours, octobre 1989*, ed. Robert Sauzet (Paris 1992), pp. 121–129, here at p. 127. See for 1572 BN Clair 1216, fols. 112–120: 'Duc d'Alencon janvier 1572'.

19 Henry IV did reduce the *gentilshommes ordinaires* from 48 to 24, see Besongne's *Etat* of 1687, I, pp. 177–178: 'Les Gentils-Hommes ordinaires de la Maison de Roy. Ils furent créés par Henry III. au nombre de quarante-huit, Henry le Grand les réduisit à la moitié.'

20 BN Clair 837, pp. 3225–3349.

21 Boucher, 'Evolution', pp. 373 and 375. On Henry IV's *vautrait* and short-lived *grand vautrayer*, see Salvadori, *Chasse*, pp. 194–195.

22 See Le Roux, *Faveur du roi*, and his conference paper Marburg 28–30 September 2000: 'La Religion des courtisans dans la France de la Renaisssance', in *Hofgesellschaft und Höflinge*, ed. Malettke and Grell, pp. 507–524. In the discussion following his paper, Le Roux mentioned the doubling of charges by Henry IV.

23 Solnon, *Cour de France*, p. 169, gives the 465 for 1609, a figure supported by BN Clair 837, pp. 3355–3426, a list for the entire period 1601–1632 suggesting an aggregate of *c.* 513.

After Henry IV's violent death, the merging of his *maison* with the establishment of the *dauphin* Louis caused a substantial yet short-lived expansion of the inner *maison*, reaching 1,780 in 1612. The *écuries* reached their apex in 1623, with 750 persons. In 1624–1625, however, Louis XIII, seconded by Richelieu who had ascended to power early in 1624, dared to confront his elites with truly far-reaching reductions: he cut the number of *aumôniers* from 252 to 10, and the *sécrétaires de la chambre* from 316 to 11.[24] In 1631 Louis XIII divided the reduced staff of the *écuries* into 208 officers with remuneration and 205 others *sans gages*. Yet he went further, decreeing that officers not included in the annual *états de paiement* for the *cour des aides*, officers paid less than 20 *écus*, and officers not serving on a regular basis were to be excluded from the privileges usually enjoyed by the *officiers domestiques*.[25] In 1641, the king tried to save money by limiting the exemptions previously granted to *officiers domestiques*, again most notably the exemption from the *tailles*.

None of these bold measures lasted, and their consequences were limited. The *aumôniers* and the *sécrétaires* did not reach their previous high levels, but the numbers of *maîtres d'hôtel* and the *gentilshommes servants* remained high, and further increased in the 1630s. The *maîtres* expanded from 114 to 233; the *gentilshommes* from 133 to 170 – yet the *états* faithfully repeated the necessity to reduce them to 12 and 24 or 36 respectively, 'vacation avenant'.[26] In the stables, the *écuyers*, *autres écuyers*, and *écuyers cavalcadours* numbered 111 in the 1640s.[27] Less elevated charges, such as the *peintres gens de metier* or the *portiers*, also were subject to inflation. Similar inflation occurred in other households. The household of Gaston d'Orléans, barely twenty years of age, numbered 542 persons in 1628 – this represented a rise of *c.* 50 persons in the *c.* 17 months since an earlier 1627 *état*, notwithstanding the reductions decreed there.[28] Many of the officers listed in the king's brother's *état*, however, did not receive payment, though they could profit from the habitual privileges. All attempts to rein in the expansion of the households came to naught in the troubled years of Anne of Austria's regency. In 1645 the *maison* had surpassed 1,600; it would be near the

[24] Boucher, 'Evolution', p. 367, for the 1612 aggregate and p. 373 for the *écuries*; Eugène Griselle, *Ecurie, Vénerie, Fauconnerie et louveterie du roi Louis XIII* (Paris 1912) provides a list of expenditure for the *écuries* in 1631 and a short overview for 1641, likewise for the *vénerie* and *fauconnerie* in 1641. See Louis XIII's 1625 *règlement* in several manuscript collections, for example, BN naf 2004 fols. 291–296.

[25] The Estates General of Blois (1579) demanded the minimum of 20 *écus*, a measure reiterated in 1614, though with the exception of the staff of the *sept offices*. See the discussion of the 'privilèges des commensaux de la maison du roi et des autres maisons royales' in the various *états*, for example Besongne's *état* of 1669, I, pp. 315–326, or *état* of 1687, I, pp. 582–594. See Loyseau, *Cinq livres*, pp. 228, 235, on the ordinances of Orléans and Blois; and F. Isambert, *Recueil général des anciennes lois françaises depuis l'an 420, jusqu'à la révolution de 1789* (Paris 1829), XIV, no. 103, pp. 380–463, for the text of the *ordonnance de Blois*, with the relevant articles on pp. 438–439.

[26] See AN Z 1a 472 *états* 1535–1642 (copies made by Amelot in 1777), the 1631 *état* on fols. 84–123, the 1642 *état* on fols. 362–406, on fols. 265–306v there is a 1638 *état de paiement* similar to that in BN Clair 814, pp. 1 82. Boucher, 'Evolution', p. 366, mentions the inflation, and provides parallel numbers, including those for 1650 given below.

[27] See AN O 1 872, 'Grand Ecuyer – Personnel – Etats Généraux', listing 20 for 1553, 111 for 1646–48. The 1664 *état* in this collection stipulated 13 *écuyers*, and one *premier écuyer* of the *grande écurie*.

[28] BN Clair 1216, June 1628, fols. 72–94; February 1627, fols. 95–111. Many of the officers were listed without payment, 'pour jouir des privileges'.

mark of 2,000 in 1650. In that year the *maîtres d'hôtel* alone numbered 321 and the *gens de métiers* 309. Nor did the new officers have to content themselves with a secondary status: they received remuneration (at least in theory) and enjoyed the habitual exemptions, re-established in 1643.[29]

Inflation of offices had developed into an unstoppable phenomenon; it may not be a coincidence that the 1650s are particularly poorly documented. Pinson de la Martinière, listing more than 170 *gentilshommes servants* in his 1653 *état*, noted that 'le nombre des officiers du roy accroist de jour en jour'.[30] Looking back from the early 1720s, the editor of another *état* stated:

> Au commencement du règne de Louis XIV. un si grand nombre de personnes avoient le titre de Maître d'Hôtel du Roy, que l'Etat de la France, imprimé en 1649, en mettoit cent septante, employez avec des gages. Deux autres états de 1653. & de 1660. en nommoient trois cens dix-huit : mais en même-temps on avertissoit qu'il n'y en avoit jamais que trois qui servoient par quartier, au choix du Grand Maître, ce qui faisoit douze par an, & que ce grand nombre seroit enfin réduit à douze, vacation avenant.[31]

Indeed, during the *Fronde* the royal *maisons* reached levels that were unprecedented – and they were to remain without parallel. A reduction of the honorary officers was decreed in April 1654, but it took another decade to redress the inflation of the preceding period.[32] Louis XIV, announcing further reductions in a declaration of May 1664, proved able to stabilise the *maison* at far lower levels.[33] In the early 1660s, for the first time in more than a century the household was below 1,000 members, with the *maîtres d'hôtel* and *gentilshommes servants* at their customary levels of 12 and 36. From the late 1670s to the triumphant early 1680s the inner *maison* of Louis XIV expanded to *c.* 1,100–1,200 officers; after 1689, however, the core services of the *maison* – chapel, chamber and wardrobe, table, *gardes de la porte*, and *marechaux des logis* – together were consistently below 900.

Jacqueline Boucher, the source of many of the figures cited in this chapter, has provided a lucid analysis that makes this great contraction a somewhat less stunning achievement. Louis XIV systematically followed an expedient earlier

29 See the 26 November 1643 edict in the *Code des commensaux ou recueil general des edits, declarations, ordonnances, lettres patentes, arrests, & reglemens: portant etablissement & confirmation des privileges, franchises, libertez, immunitez, exemptions, rangs, préséances, & droits honorifiques des officiers-domestiques & commensaux de la maison du roy, des maisons royales, & de leurs veuves* (Paris 1720).

30 *Estat et gouvernement de France* (Amsterdam 1653), p. 48.

31 *Etat de la France* (Paris 1722), I, pp. 191–192; yet compare BN MS f 22713, an ongoing *état* for 1661–1683, citing low numbers of *gentilshommes servants* and *maîtres d'hôtel* as early as 1658, fols. 40–80.

32 *Etat de la France* (Paris 1687), I, p. 47, and AN O 1 756, pp. 306–308.

33 See AN O 1 715, an *état* for 1664 giving only functions and numbers, no names, and interspersed with several edicts regarding the reductions, notably 30 May 1664, 10 November 1664, 27 August 1666 and, for the queen's *maison*, 9 December 1670. Compare the 1664 'model'-*état* for the *grande écurie* in O 1 872. See the major edict in F. Isambert, *Recueil général des anciennes lois françaises depuis l'an 420, jusqu'à la révolution de 1789*, 28 vols. (Paris 1820–1830), here at XVIII, no. 433, p. 37, préambule of the declaration, stressing the king's financial motive and the advantages for other 'contribuables' for the tailles, i.e. the reduction of the number of tax-exemptions as to reduce the burden for other taxpayers.

tried out by his father: his effort partly was a reduction not of the numbers of those serving at court, but of those holding the privileged status of *officier domestique*. In 1661 he decreed that roughly half of the 600-odd officers and servants of the *écuries* would be paid 'selon ce que le roi ordonnerait', a decision that entailed loss of privileged status for them, as earlier decrees had made that contingent upon a stable remuneration of at least 20 *écus*. Undoubtedly, many of those demoted were still employed at court, but we no longer find them among the *officiers domestiques*.[34] *Etats* concentrating on the *officiers* would not include the lower fringes of commissioned labour. This explains why we find a staff of only slightly more than 250 for the *écuries* in various handwritten *états*, whereas the printed 1694 Besongne *état* listed 444, and alluded to 'quantité d'autres'.[35] A recent estimate based on archival sources argues that before the reform of 1787, the two *écuries* and the king's *haras* together in addition to *c.* 270 *officiers domestiques* employed a staff of more than 1,200 liveried servants, with another *c.* 500 sundry *valets* and *garçons* totalling *c.* 2,000. Other examples indicate that the *états* are not always complete or reliable. Whereas most sources give 496 *gardes du corps*, Dangeau listed 1,680 for 1690 and 1,656 in 1699, after an attempt to reduce the numbers.[36]

Surely this does not indicate that Louis XIV's reductions were first and foremost a cosmetic operation, but it shows a parallel process that was as important as the reductions themselves. 'Above stairs' and 'below stairs' were redefined in the course of Louis' reign. He limited the number of honorary noble servants but consolidated their status by confirming their privileges and protecting their offices against creditors.[37] At the same time, however, he allowed the number of those running the day-to-day machinery of the court to grow or decline according to the pace of their activities – but without the supreme status and resources available to their social superiors above stairs. Lower officers in the *sept offices* – the early modern counterpart of the medieval *six métiers*: the *gobelet* (or *paneterie-bouche* and *echansonnerie-bouche*), *cuisine-bouche*, *paneterie-commun*, *échansonnerie-commun*, *cuisine-commun*, *fruiterie*, and *fourrière* – catering for the tables of king (*bouche*), *grand maître* and *chambellan* (*petit-commun*), and

34 Compare the similar operations after the reform of *bouche* and *commun* in 1780, or the habit of employing staff on the basis of a revokable *commission* in hunt, stables, and musical establishment.

35 Reytier, 'Ecuries de Versailles', in *Les écuries royales*, p. 76, mentions 319 offices held by the *grand écuyer* in 1640, and charts a decline to 261 in 1695, matching the 254 cited for 1699 in BN Clair 814, with a very moderate increase to 272 in 1735 and 273 in 1775. More importantly, he indicates that while numbers of *officiers* declined, the less privileged staff remained at a high level, and the staffs did not change much from the early seventeenth century onwards to the 1787. The printed *états* (e.g., 1663, pp. 98–99) habitually include the following formula: 'Quoiqu'il ait un grand nombre d'ecuyers, on ne voit ordinairement servir que ceux-cy, qui instruisent les pages & c. aux gages de 400. l. & 4.ou 500. l. de livrées . . . Les autres servent quand ils sont mandés, & que le service le requiert.'

36 Boucher, 'Evolution', pp. 377–378; BN Clair 814 *gardes du corps* on pp. 327–332, total of 492 on pp. 397–398; *Journal du marquis de Dangeau*, ed. E. Soulié and L. Dussieux (Paris 1854–1860), III (3 March 1690) p. 72, and VII (16 December 1699), p. 211.

37 See relevant edicts in the *Code des commensaux*, for example the 1664 reduction on pp. 135–137; a 1678 confirmation on pp. 204–206.

household (*grand commun*) did expand slowly from *c.* 232 in 1560 to 341 in 1713 and *c.* 400 in 1754. This development, as that of the *prévoté* roughly tripling between 1560 and 1713, reflected the diversification and growth of tasks.[38] Those among the lower servants who did retain their *charge* and status as domestic officer could hope to be promoted into hereditary nobility: the *code des commensaux*, a compilation of decrees pertaining to the king's domestic officers published in 1720, includes a sequence of *arrêts* allowing ushers, valets, and garçons 'de prendre la qualité d'écuyer', conferring noble status.[39]

A detailed 1699 memoir outlining the 'officiers des maisons royales' gives 886 for the *maison du roi*. This number includes the highest charges, the 40-odd *maison ecclésiastique* of the *grand aumônier*, the high steward's staff with the *c.* 400 *bouche et commun* and 53 honorary table servants, the staffs of chamber and wardrobe just below 200, the *capitaine de la porte* with his four lieutenants and 50 guards, another *c.* 60 serving the *grand maréchal des logis*, and several smaller services. In addition, 191 sundry staff connected to chapel, chamber, and wardrobe were listed, rendering a total of 1,077 officers. The court employed 55 persons in the *Sainte Chapelle*; 340 persons were listed for the hunt; 254 for the *écuries*; and 131 for the *prévoté*. To the services for the hunt we may add the range of *capitaineries* totalling 263 men. The king's establishment, without the *maison militaire* or the *maisons* of his relatives, numbered, 2,120 *officiers domestiques*, but its activities were undoubtedly supported by a larger group of servants without the privileges of the *commensaux*, most notably in the stables, the hunt, the musical establishment, and the services connected to the *bâtiments du roi*.

The guards at court complicate the picture. In addition to the *gardes de la porte* and the provost's guards included in the 2,120 suggested here, the memoir lists 496 *gardes du corps*, 128 *Suisses*, 114 *gentilshommes*, 250 *chevaux legers*, 250 *gendarmes*, and 159 officers for the *artillerie* and the *connétablie*: an aggregate of 1,393 men. By the 1690s, however, the *maison militaire* had developed into a large-scale establishment, numbering 10,050 men around a smaller core of 2,690 consisting of the *gardes du dedans* and *gardes du dehors du Louvre*.[40] Apart from the guards of the *capitaine de la porte* included in the *maison étroite*, the provost's guards maintaining order at court, the *cent suisses*, the *gentilshommes à bec de*

[38] Boucher, 'Evolution', pp. 368–369, 377. In 1664–1667 Louis created a 'petit-commun' catering for the tables of *grand-maître* and *grand chambellan*. Note that Boucher's numbers exclude the honorary *huissiers*, and *maîtres d'hôtel*; the number for 1754 is taken from AN Z 1a 480, fols. 1–73, with the *controleurs clercs d'office*, the *huissiers de salle*, and the *fourrière* the total is 422.

[39] *Code des commensaux*, pp. 369–377.

[40] The 1699 memoir includes 114 *gentilshommes*; Boucher, 'Evolution', indicates two companies of *gentilshommes à bec de corbin*, each of them 114; on the other hand André Corvisier, 'Maison militaire du Roi', in *DGS*, pp. 942–944, here p. 943, notes that the *gentilshommes* had been abolished in 1688. The printed *Etat* of 1722, II, p. 10, still lists the *gentilshommes*. In the same volume, on p. 186, more explanation is given: both companies had been abolished by Louis XIII in 1629, but were restored in 1649. Louis XIV in 1688 abolished one of the two companies, whereas only in 1723 did the last company disappear. The overview of the court guards in the printed 1749 *état*, II, following p. 11, notes succinctly that: 'Il y avoit encore: les Cent gentilshommes au Bec de Corbin qui ont été supprimez'.

corbin (until their abolition), and the four companies of *gardes du corps*, it is far from clear whether we should see any of the military units as belonging to the court. Drawing lines here is arbitrary, but it does not seem unreasonable to follow the example of the 1699 memoir, leaving out the regiments of the *gardes Françaises* and *gardes Suisses*, and the companies of *mousquetaires*. The captains of the latter, however, were included in the diminutive and thus exclusive *états* of the *almanach royal*, and all senior officers in the *maison militaire* must have been close to the court. The expansion of the *maison militaire* and the frequently confirmed privileged status of its officers show the Sun King's eagerness to reinforce the ties between the French nobility and military service.[41]

Another small but relevant exception to the rule of stabilisation or reduction can be found in the pages at court. While the *pages de la chambre* consistently numbered 24, the number of pages in the *écuries* tended to expand. Besongne noted in his 1687 *état* that for the pages of the *grande écurie*: 'Il n'y a fonds que pour dix-neuf, quoiqu'il s'en trouve beaucoup au dessus de ce nombre'.[42] Indeed, in the early 1660s we find *c.* 70 pages in the *grande écurie*, slowly declining to *c.* 40 towards the end of Louis XIV's reign. A *règlement* for the *grande écurie* issued in 1722 noted that in the previous reign the number of pages had usually attained 50 or 60, but was fixed at 42 in 1720.[43] The pages in the *petite écurie* rose from *c.* 20 to *c.* 30, but had again reached their initial level by the 1720s. Félix d'Hézecques, one of Louis XVI's *pages de la chambre*, upon his arrival in Versailles noted an aggregate of 158 pages, including 58 for the *grande écurie*, 40 for the *petite écurie*, and 26 for the *chambre*.[44] Louis XIV's preference for a *noblesse militaire* may explain the development both of the *maison militaire* and the pages. Pages, residing at court for three or four years, were expected to pursue a military career thereafter, often in one of the court's elite units. After 1643 the pedigree of the pages of both *écuries* was to be examined by the *généalogiste* [*des pages*] *du roi*, an office long vested in the d'Hozier family.[45]

1699 was exceptional in one respect: we find no establishments for a queen or queen-mother. In the year of her death, 1666, the queen-mother Anne of Austria

[41] See Guy Rowlands, 'Louis XIV, Aristocratic Power and the Elite Units of the French Army', *FH* 13, 3 (1999), pp. 303–331.

[42] Besonge, *Etat* 1687, I, p. 265. The pages of the *grande écurie* expanded in the 1650s and 1660s, reaching 70 in 1663 (*état* of 1663, p. 100), later slowly declining from 55 (*état* 1669, I, p. 130), to 54 (*état* of 1672, I, p. 138), 50 (*état* of 1677, I, pp. 145–147), and finally 36 (*état* of 1687, I, pp. 263–265), then expanding again to 46 (*état* of 1712, I, pp. 558–560) and finally reaching 41 in 1722 (*état* of 1722, II, pp. 206–208). In the *petite écurie*, the pages gradually expanded from 20 to 30 (*état* of 1672, I, p. 155; 20; *état* of 1712, I, pp. 288–290: 32), falling back to 20 in the 1722 *état* (II, pp. 241–242). Compare Charles Dreyss, ed., *Mémoires de Louis XIV pour l'instruction du Dauphin*. 2 vols. (Paris 1860), I, p. 170, where the king mentions the increasing numbers of the pages in the *grande écurie*.

[43] AN O 1 970, 104 (draft) and 105, p. 1.

[44] Félix d'Hézecques, *Souvenirs d'un page de la cour de Louis XVI* (Paris 1998), pp. 112–114: the pages of the chamber were reduced to eight (permanently serving) in 1784; the *écuries* were fused in 1787 allowing for a total of 50 pages, including the pages of the *vénerie*.

[45] See examples of documents in AN O 1 970 signed by d'Hozier, and in O 1 976, a sequence of printed 'extraits de l'armorial général de la France'; Frédéric d'Agay, 'Pages', in *DGS*, p. 1137.

had had an establishment of *c.* 525: like the habitual queen's *maison*, it was a replica of the king's, including a *c.* 50 person female establishment, additional male servants for council, chamber, and wardrobe, a full service for *bouche et commun* and *fourrière*, an *écurie*, and musicians – yet with few guards and no hunt. Anne's sizeable establishment as queen-mother was to be the last of the *ancien régime*.[46] Queen Maria Teresa was served by *c.* 643 persons in 1660, but her following had dwindled to 538 in 1676.[47] After her death in 1683 only the *maison* of the Bavarian *dauphine* could serve as an alternative female focus for the court's activities, and she died in 1690. In 1697 the court finally welcomed a new high-ranking princess: Marie-Adélaide de Savoie (1685–1712). The king hand-picked the establishment for the *dauphine*: 'le roi a écrit de sa main toutes les charges qu'il a données, qui sont presques toutes pour les domestiques qui l'approchent de plus près'.[48] Less than two years later, in 1699, the *dauphine*'s *maison* included 443 persons, yet her spouse, the duc de Bourgogne (1682–1712) did not have a substantial household. Nor did *Monseigneur*, Louis XIV's son and the French *dauphin*: he was served by his father's *maison*, and had to content himself with a limited following taking care of his education and health, as well as a prestigious establishment for hunting, and a group of noble companions, *gentilshommes d'honneur* or *menins*. As a boy, the future Louis XIII had still been served by a small yet more or less complete establishment reflecting the structure of the royal court. Later *dauphins* had no autonomous establishment, and would be served largely by their fathers' staffs.[49] In the overviews, we find an

46 BN Clair 814, Anne of Austria's *maison* in 1666 on pp. 83–115: with 51 women in her staff, and a *garde des cabinets* Marie de la Haye, the proportion of women was near 10 per cent.

47 See BN Clair 814, pp. 679–710, where *c.* 643 persons are listed for Maria Teresa's following in 1660; we find only *c.* 30 women, and the high numbers can be explained mostly by the proliferation of *maîtres des requêtes* and secretaries in the queen's council; their numbers were reduced to 12 and 14 respectively in 1676, yet notwithstanding the fact that five Spanish *femmes de chambre* had returned to Spain, we find *c.* 50 women in 1676 instead of the *c.* 30 in 1660; see AN O 1 3715 opening with an 'Abrégé des Estats de la maison de la reyne et des attributs aux officiers chacun en particulier' (1676; unpaginated, 50 pages). The services in the queens' establishment remained basically unaltered; numbers were lower in the eighteenth century, around 430, rising to around 500 in Marie-Antoinette's reign.

48 See, in AN O 1 3715, an 'Abbregé de tous les estats de la maison de Madame la Duchesse de Bourgogne & des attributs aux officiers chacun en particulier' (1698), with later additions and estimated value of offices added in the margin; for most senior charges, except the *sécrétaire des commandemens*, we find the addition 'la charge appartient à madame'; Dangeau, *Journal*, VI, pp. 218–220 (29/31 October 1697), by the 29th, 250 venal charges had been filled, representing a value of 2,000,000. Dangeau, *Journal*, XIII, p. 295 (9 December 1710); *Mémoires du marquis de Sourches sur le règne de Louis XIV*, ed. Gabriel-Jules de Cosnac (Paris 1882–1893), XII, p. 411 (12 December 1710), mentions the Duchesse's rights to govern her own *maison* after 1710, cited in Solnon, *Cour de France*, pp. 319–320 and nn. 10–11. Solnon contrasts this sharply with Louis XIV's attitude towards other royal establishments, notably that of Monsieur, yet several lateral remarks in Dangeau's *Journal* – for example I, p. 25 (12 June 1684) or I, p. 114 (29–30 January 1685) – indicate that Monsieur too, could to choose his own servants, with nominations subject to the king's endorsement for the highest charges only. Sourches, *Mémoires*, I, pp. 426–427, mentions Conti's choice of *grands officiers* for his *maison*, adding that one of them was hardly 'agréable au roi'. Even the king's endorsement may have been an informal matter, important for one's position and goodwill at court, but not subject to any rules.

49 Marcel Marion, *Dictionnaire des institutions de la France aux XVIIe et XVIIIe siècles* (Paris 1923; repr. 1979), pp. 362–364; Barbiche, *Institutions*, pp. 27–28; Bluche, 'Dauphin', in *DGS*, p. 448, suggests that it was almost impossible for the *dauphin* to escape from the opposed charges of either being too lazy, or being too active and threatening; and for the king to either educate a rival or be succeeded by an inexperienced son. Monseigneur

'education' for young princes, and a set of personal servants and after 1680 *menins* for adolescents. Louis XIV's younger brother Philippe d'Orléans or *Monsieur* (1640–1701), however, did have an impressive household of 830 officers in 1699. His second spouse, Elisabeth Charlotte von der Pfalz or *Madame* (1652–1722), was served by another 242 officers. Together, the secondary establishments of the royal family employed 1,589 officers in 1699.[50] The Condé, holding the office of *grand maître*, had their own household in Chantilly, numbering 274 in 1699 – the memoir adds that it had seriously been reduced after the death of the grand Condé in 1686.[51]

The proportion of women was far higher in the female royal households with their *filles* or *dames*, and *femmes de chambres*, than in those of their male counterparts; thus, the number of well-established princesses greatly influenced the number of office-holding women at court. The sixteenth-century establishments of French queens had usually included *c.* 20–25 per cent women.[52] In the 1666 household of Anne of Austria, or the 1660 and 1676 establishments of Louis XIV's queen, however, the women did not even reach 10 per cent, and later lists indicate the same or smaller proportions.[53] As salaried officials, women remained a small minority at court. Probably we can say the same for foreigners. The household had been a cosmopolitan environment in the early sixteenth century, with a notable Italian influence. The share of 'foreigners' in the king's household increased until the third quarter of the century, but the tendency reversed around 1560, leading to an increasing preponderance of French courtiers in the early seventeenth century. The share of foreigners in queens' households remained more important, though finally we find the same tendency here. In the troubled first twenty years of the seventeenth century, notably the regency of Marie de Medici, and the rise to favour of the Concinis, Italian presence again was more marked. It dwindled in the course of the century: notwithstanding Mazarin, Anne of Austria, Louis XIV's short-lived Spanish queen, and other

did have an extensive establishment for the hunt, at times eclipsing that of his father. Moreover, the numbers and the status of his staffs increased slowly, when he commanded the army of the Rhine in 1688, Dangeau, *Journal*, II, pp. 171–172 (22/23 September 1688) noted: 'On double la service de la maison de Monseigneur: deux maîtres d'hôtel, quatre contrôleurs, etc.' The overview of the young Louis XIII's establishment in BN Clair 837, pp. 3429–3446, 'officiers domestiques de la maison de Mgr le Dauphin 1601–1610', includes a kitchen staff and suggests that his *maison* would reach more important proportions than later prac-tice indicates, a notion supported by the numbers for 1612 cited in Boucher, 'Evolution', p. 367.

50 BN Clair 814, pp. 397–398, this overview included another establishment for the duchesse de Chartres of 74 persons.

51 See the more detailed date on Condé's *maison* in the pathbreaking study by Béguin, *Les Princes de Condé*, on p. 161 giving a remarkable figure of 546 for 1660, 273 for 1664, and *c.* 180 under Henry-Jules after 1686, substantially lower than the 274 given in the 1699 memoir on pp. 390–393. AN O 1 715, pp. 95–101, lists 263 for Condé's *maison* in 1664, more or less matching Béguin's numbers.

52 Boucher, *Cour de Henri III*, p. 40, gives 20–25 per cent of women in two female households, as does Chatenet, 'Logis des femmes', in *Frauenzimmer*, ed. Hirschbiegel and Paravicini, pp. 177–178; Ruth Kleinman, 'Household of Anne of Austria', p. 518, stresses that among those personally attending the queen, only one man served, the gentleman of honour. Compare the lists in Griselle, *Etat de la maison du roi Louis XIII*, including the households of queens, with male and female servants.

53 AN O 1 3715, BN Clair, pp. 83–115, for Anne of Austria, fols. 679–710 for Maria Teresa.

foreign princesses, the French nation became increasingly dominant at court. The 1676 *état* for the Maria Teresa notes in the margin that three years earlier, the last Spanish women had been sent back to Spain.[54] Artists long retained their international and predominantly Italian outlook, visitors and diplomats from every conceivable nation frequented the court, but French personnel came to dominate the household staffs, above and below stairs.[55]

On the basis of the 1699 memoir, we arrive at a reliable total of *c.* 5,102 *officers domestiques* in the various *maisons* together forming the royal court, with the guards: 1,077 in the inner *maison*, 55 persons serving in the Sainte Chapelle, another 725 persons for the services of hunt, stables, and *prévoté*; a further 1,524 as the nucleus of the *maison militaire*, 1,589 persons in the other establishments of the royal family. Around 1700, the inner *maison* was close to what it had been in the first years of the prolonged political and religious crisis after Henry II's death. The king's inner household would not stray far from these levels: the 1729 *maison du roi* numbered 896 persons, ten more than Louis XIV's *maison* in 1699. This number was only marginally lower than ten years later, whereas in 1755 it had risen to 921 persons. Two decades later, just before the first phase of reform, the *maison* again stood at 879. With 260–270 persons, the stables remained on Louis XIV's reform levels as well.[56] The *maison militaire*, strengthened in the later seventeenth century, remained stable until the 1770s. Only the establishments for hunting, curtailed in 1705, showed a persistent tendency to expand.[57] A 1715 *état* had listed *c.* 230 persons in addition to 272 for the *capitaineries*, yet the 1749 printed *état* numbered 309 for the hunt, and an even higher number for the *capitaineries*. A 1737 reform had sought to reduce numbers – again partly by changing *officiers domestiques* into employees 'par commission & à la volonté de M. le grand veneur, & la plupart sans gages fixes'.[58] The expansion of the services for hunting coincided with the development of services for *eaux et forêts*, and thus cannot only be seen in terms of courtiers and their entertainment. Parallel to the development of the service for forestry, the staffs for building and music expanded and became increasingly professionalised. These services were

[54] See the 50-page unpaginated *état* for 1676, to be found in AN O 1 3715 (the remark cited follows the list of French *femmes de chambre*).

[55] Jean-François Dubost, *La France Italienne XVIe–XVIIe siècle* (Paris 1997), pp. 270–278; and 'Les étrangers à la cour de France: de la polémique à l'évolution numérique 1515–1630', in *Hofgesellschaft und Höflinge*, ed. Malettke and Grell, pp. 55–66.

[56] See, for example, AN Z 1a 478, 1729, fols. 1–46; 1737, fols. 232–299; Z 1a 480, 1754, fols. 1–73; 1755, fols. 74–136; 1756, fols. 137–204; 1757, fols. 205–249; 1758, fols. 250–295; 1759, fols. 96–348; see AN O 1 730 for the years 1760–1773, with an aggregate of 879 for the last year. The *écuries* reflect the same pattern, see AN O 1 872 for 1553–1695, and Z 1a 489 for 1695–1761, with 263 for 1695, 274 for 1734, 271 for 1752, and 264 for 1761; compare Reytier's data in *Les écuries royales*, pp. 75–76. The *vénerie*, however, reduced in the last decade of the Sun King, expanded in the early eighteenth century.

[57] Louis XIV severely cut the *louveterie* in 1705, see Boucher, 'Evolution', pp. 374–376.

[58] For 1715, BN Clair 830, pp. 285–326; for 1737 and 1749 the printed 1749 *état*, II, pp. 264–289, quote at p. 267, and the *capitaineries* in I, pp. 399–471, listed under the staff of the *maisons royales*.

increasingly distant from the court, as many among their staff were employed on the basis of commission only, and would remain distant from court life.[59] The other households within the dynasty followed the general pattern: they retained their importance but tended to decline somewhat. There was no great queen-mother's household after the death of Anne of Austria; the queen's household hovered between 425 and 500.[60] Smaller female households proliferated in the second half of the eighteenth century; as did those of the princes of the blood. These were paid by the king, and we find them listed in the *almanach royal*.[61] The number of such households, however, would always be determined by demography rather than by policy.

Elite guards of the court were reduced in the comte de Saint-Germain's 1776 army reform; this proved to be the first of a series of reforms, and soon the household itself would be a major target.[62] In 1780, Louis XVI reorganised the services for *bouche* and *commun*, leaving only 21 *officiers domestiques*, and a much-reduced establishment of employees without formal office for the court's tables; at the same time the 36 *gentilshommes servants* were reduced to 18.[63] Accounting procedures for court staffs were simplified, and subjected to the scrutiny of one central treasurer. There were attempts to fuse the establishments for king and queen, but the queen's household initially withstood the challenge: in 1781, with 184 persons, her *bouche* and *commun* were larger than the king's truncated services. In 1786, the king's *maison étroite* stood at 427, roughly half of its previous level, but more was to follow. A further measure decreed in

59 *Etat* 1749, I, pp. 81–90, for the *chapelle-musique*; I, pp. 395–471, for the *bâtiments* and *maisons royales*. Compare Benoît, *Versailles et les musiciens du roi*, and Newton, *Espace du roi*.

60 An O 1 3742 *maison de la reine Marie Leczynska* 1725–1777: 429 in 1725; 434 in 1743 (with 29 and 30 women respectively); slightly higher numbers for Marie-Antoinette, for example, AN O 1 3794 *maisons reines, princes*: 501 persons for her 1781 household.

61 The *Almanach Royal* for 1789 (pp. 124–148) lists: *maisons* for roi; reine; 'education' de Mgr le Dauphin; 'education' des enfants de France; monsieur; madame; comte d'Artois; comtesse d'Artois; madame Elisabeth; madame Adelaide; madame Victoire; mgr le duc d'Orleans. In reforms following 1780, a fusion of the king's and queen's establishments was apparently considered, but it came to naught, see AN O 1 747, no. 30.

62 *Mémoires de M. Le baron de Besenval, Lieutenant-Général des armées du roi, sous Louis XV et Louis XVI . . . écrits par lui-même*, 4 vols. (Paris 1805–1806), II, pp. 246–263, on p. 249: 'Les gens à charges, les chefs des corps priviligiés, mirent toutes intrigues et tous moyens en usage, pour ne souffrir aucune diminution, ni être privés d'aucune prérogative; ils furent tous merveilleusement secondés par M. de Maurepas, qui, selon sa coutume ordinaire, approuvant tout système de réforme, étoit le premier à en empêcher l'exécution'; William Doyle, *Venality: The Sale of Offices in Eighteenth-century France* (Oxford 1996), pp. 134–136, 138, 146–147; Solnon, *Cour de France*, pp. 503–527.

63 See AN O 1 731, 'états generaux annuels des officiers de la maison du roi 1774–1786': for example, the 21 *bouche* and *commun* staff in 1786; we find the lesser employees listed in quarter-rolls in O 1 781 'état d'appointements du personnel de la Bouche 1780–1792': 105 for October 1780, 118 for April 1784, 125 for January 1788. Compare the *c.* 422 *bouche* and *commun* of 1754 in Z 1 A 480, fols. 1–73, or the 394 for 1779 in O 1 731, and the queen's 184-person establishment for the table in 1781, AN O 1 3794. Compare also Veri, *Journal de l'abbé de Véri publié avec une préface et des notes par le baron Jehan de Witte*, 2 vols. (Paris s.d.), II, pp. 294–297 and 352–353, who is sceptical about Necker's motives and the success of the reform, as well as critical of the court's grandees. See *Correspondence secrète entre Marie-Thérèse et le Cte de Mercy-Argenteau*, III, p. 398 (Marie-Antoinette to Maria Theresa, 15 February 1780), about the edict of 29 January 1780; p. 422 (Mercy to Maria Theresa, 17 April 1780) about the opposition of Artois.

August 1787 abolished *fauconnerie*, *louveterie*, and *vautrait*, while at the same time merging the two *écuries* – in 1789, finally, the queen's *écurie* was fused with this establishment.[64] Likewise in 1787, the court guards were further truncated and honorary officers were reduced by turning quarters into semesters. The archives of the *maison du roi* reach an impressive density in the years 1780–1790, reflecting the cumbersome process of reform and the vehement protests against it. The revolution brought the dissolution of an institution that had seen its numbers reduced, structures changed, and status diminished in the preceding decade.

The expansion, consolidation, and reduction of the household were matched by parallel developments in the central administrative agencies. The venality of offices, pervading most domains of royal administration, inextricably entwined financial and administrative objectives, and complicated the creation of a loyal and effective bureaucracy. In the course of the seventeenth century, the rise of the *commissaires* carrying revocable commissions instead of semi-hereditary offices, and the *commis* doing the paperwork in the ministerial departments improved this situation. Throughout the early modern age, however, their numbers remained small. The central services for the *sécrétaires d'état*, the *contrôleur général*, and the *chancelier* expanded in the reigns of Louis XIV and Louis XV, to be slightly reduced in the reign of Louis XVI. In the years immediately preceding the French Revolution, the personnel of the six central departments – the four secretaries, the *contrôle général*, and the *grande chancellerie* – numbered fewer than 700.[65] Other agents of central government may be added, but they usually form corporations of venal offices; thus the *grande chancellerie* included 300 *sécrétaires du roi*, and the work both in the chancellery and in the councils was partly done by the 67 *maîtres des requêtes*.[66] The 'true' royal councillors, or *conseillers d'état*, remained a small group: reduced from 120 in 1644 to 30 in 1673; they numbered 32 in 1787 – yet multitudes bore the empty title of *conseiller du roi*.[67] Intendancies would have a staff of 10–15; the more autonomous regional corporative counterparts of royal government were far more numerous. The numerically most impressive institution apart from the army undoubtedly was the *ferme générale*. Collecting indirect taxes and a variety of rights for the *contrôle général* (amounting to more than 40 per cent of revenue in the eighteenth century) in 1774 it employed 30,000 persons in the provinces, and another 700 in

64 AN O 1 731 for the 1774–1786 *états*; AN O 1 3794, no. 203: 'réunion de l'écurie de la reine à celle de sa majesté donne lieu à la réforme de [80 gens de livrée]' (31 December 1789).

65 Barbiche, *Institutions*, pp. 86, 126.

66 J. F. Bosher, *French Finances, 1770–1795: From Business to Bureaucracy* (Cambridge 1970), p. 49, gives 256 for the *contrôle général*; Barbiche, *Institutions*, pp. 86, 123, 126, 163, 265, 283, gives numbers for most departments, and an estimate of 670 for the aggregate of services. Compare Emmanuel Le Roy Ladurie 'Etat', in *DAR*, pp. 506–508, inferring the rise of the administrative monarchy from the tenfold increase of officers between François I's 5,000 and the 50,000 *officiers* in the early years of Louis XIV; among these high numbers, however, the heart of the 'monarchie administrative' occupied a small place.

67 See Olivier Poncet, 'Conseils du Roi', in *DAR*, pp. 320–325.

Paris. The core of the royal bureaucracy, however, did not surpass the levels of the inner *maison du roi*, and remained far below the aggregate of households and services connected to the court.

The expenses for the court can roughly be traced from the seventeenth century onwards, both in absolute figures and as a proportion of the total expenditures. For the seventeenth century the materials assembled by Jean-Ronald Malet as *premier commis* of *contrôleur général des finances* Desmarets (1708–1715), offer an excellent source; for the eighteenth century the *états de prévoyance*, predecessors of Jacques Necker's famous 1781 *Compte rendu*, provide a more limited basis.[68] The alternation of war and peace dominated the budget: peace allowed the 'civil' expenses to expand; war demanded an all-out financial effort. The military effort generated extraordinary expenditures, partly to be met by extraordinary revenues such as the *capitation* of 1695, the *dixième* of 1710, the *vingtièmes* of 1749, 1756, and 1759, or later additional loans. Nevertheless, warfare invariably put other budgets under pressure. The absolute levels of household expenses tended to decline in periods of military struggle, and their share in the overall budgets including the extraordinary spending was much smaller as a consequence of huge military expenditures. Peace and war, partly overlapping with ordinary-extraordinary financing, heavily influence the proportion of court expenses in the state budgets.

We can identify the household's major pursuits in Malet's lists. Throughout the seventeenth century, the *chambre aux deniers*, responsible for the tables at court and for provisioning, took an important share of the expenses for the royal household proper, rising from an average 25 per cent in the years 1600–1656 to an average 36 per cent for 1662–1695; courtiers' wages declined from a moderate 15 per cent to 12 per cent in the second half of the century – we should note, however, that the *chambre aux deniers* also paid a variety of rights to courtiers.

[68] See the recent edition of Malet's work in *Jean-Roland Malet premier historien des finances de la monarchie française*, ed. Margaret and Richard Bonney (Paris 1993), with useful introduction, analysis, 67 tables and 98 figures. Tables 6, 13, 20, 43, 66, and figures 6, 7, 37, 44, 51, 74, 97, as well as the analysis on pp. 31–37, 55–57 are of particular relevance for the court, and form the basis of my spreadsheets available at http://www.le.ac.uk/hi/bon/ESFDB/index.html; see Richard Bonney, 'France, 1494–1815', in his *The Rise of the Fiscal State in Europe, c. 1200–1815* (Oxford 1999), pp. 123–176, here at pp. 130–132. For the eighteenth century, see Michel Morineau, 'Budgets de l'Etat et gestion des finances royales au XVIIIe siècle', *Revue Historique* 104 (1980), pp. 288–336. For the early decades, F. Véron de Forbonnais, *Recherches et considérations sur les finances de France depuis l'année 1595 jusqu'à l'année 1721*, 2 vols. (Basle 1758). These materials, covering the late seventeenth and early eighteenth centuries, are available at the European State Finance Database (ESFDB) http://www.le.ac.uk/hi/bon/ESFDB/index.html. For the second half of the eighteenth century see Mathon de la Cour, *Collection de Comptes rendus, pièces authentiques, états et tableaux, convernant les finances de France depuis 1758 jusqu'en 1787* (Lausanne 1788), pp. i–xii, pp. 1–232, in a BN Tolbiac copy bound in one volume with Etienne-Charles Loménie de Brienne, *Compte rendu au roi Au moi de Mars 1788, et publié par ses ordres* (Paris 1788), pp. i–xiv, pp. 1–183; Pierre Clément, *Lettres . . . de Colbert*, II (Paris 1863), pp. 771–784, lists *recettes* and *depenses* for 1680, expenditure for the *maison du roi* and connected costs on pp. 781–782. Compare the contrasting views on the 1781 *compte rendu*, and more generally Necker, in Robert D. Harris, *Necker: Reform Statesman of the Ancien Régime* (Berkeley, Los Angeles, and London 1979), and John Hardman, *Louis XVI* (New Haven and London 1993).

Typically, the costs for travel declined from 25 per cent in the first half of the century to 16 per cent in the second half, whereas the costs for ceremony mostly paid through the *argenterie* rose from 9 per cent to 23 per cent. The share of the *écuries* rose from 11 per cent to 13 per cent; expenses for festivities remained stable at 7 per cent; the hunt rose from 5 per cent to 7 per cent.[69]

Expenses for several items in the household budget fluctuated wildly. Great ceremonies or longer travel could cause sharp peaks and sometimes necessitated extraordinary financing – as did for example the *sacre* of Louis XV in 1722, his marriage in 1725, the 1739 marriage of Louis XV's eldest daughter, or the frequent dynastic deaths to be mourned at court.[70] The 1775 *compte rendu* listed 6,000,000 lt for 'dépenses imprévues' stating that these 'comprennent les frais de baptême & de mariage des enfans de France & des princes du sang, les pompes funèbres & autres dépenses de même nature . . .'[71] Individual indulgence added its share: in 1775 Marie-Antoinette purchased from her own *cassette* a *girandole* of diamonds worth 460,000 lt – almost four times the budget for *pierreries* in that year, and nearly as much as the sum spent on *offrandes et aumônes*. The king, moreover, had given her 300,000 lt worth of jewellery in the preceding year. Mercy-Argenteau, the Austrian ambassador in France and confidant of Maria Theresa, told the empress that her daughter proved impervious to his admonitions; the indignant mother replied that she herself had not spent more than 2,000 fl on jewellery in her entire life.[72] Even without extravagance or exceptional circumstances, the budget was never stable. A memoir from the 1780s criticising disorders in the financial procedures of the *maison* avowed that: 'en effet, les dépenses de la maison du roi peuvent eprouver d'une année à l'autre des differences de plusieurs millions, sans qu'il y ait de mauvais ordre ou d'abus dans les differentes administrations qui la composent'.[73]

The main components of the household budget, controlled by the *ordonnateur* or relevant court dignitary, assisted by his intendants, controllers, and treasurers, were reviewed in the same memoir.[74] The costs for the king's tables, overseen by the *grand maître* and the *bureau* were paid by the *chambre aux deniers*. The serving *premier gentilhomme de la chambre*, with his intendants and controllers, was responsible for the separate budget of the *menus plaisirs*, *argenterie*, and *chambre*:

69 See my spreadsheets at the ESFDB; other relevant databases on the same site, for example, expenditure on Versailles, 1660s–1715.

70 Morineau, 'Budgets', p. 295, n. 14, citing manuscript no. 152 from the Bibliothèque du Sénat.

71 *Collection des comptes rendus*, the 1775 numbers and explanations on pp. 141–165.

72 *Correspondence secrète entre Marie-Thérèse et le Cte de Mercy-Argenteau, avec les lettres de Marie-Thérèse et de Marie-Antoinette*, ed. Alfred Arneth and M. A. Geffroy, 3 vols. (Paris 1874–75), II, p. 418 (Mercy to Maria Theresa, 19 January 1776), pp. 422–423 (Maria Theresa to Mercy 12 February 1776); compare III, p. 35 (18 March 1777) Mercy's complaints to Maria Theresa that the queen had a costly 'gout immodéré' for 'jeux de hasard': the king's special support for her old playing debts did not even cover the current costs of playing at court.

73 AN O 1 749, no. 40 (unpaginated), in the section proposing the establishment of a single general treasurer for the whole budget.

74 AN O 1 749 no. 40, a memoir written after 1787, in defence of Necker's budget cuts, warning the king against the displeased *grands*. Compare the various treasurers cited in the 1661–1683 *état* BN MS f 22713, fols. 81v.

the *chambre* covering sundry expenses for the chamber, the *argenterie* religious ceremonies, and the *menus plaisirs* court festivities or theatre. Connected to this budget, but not controlled by the *premier gentilhomme*, was the *garde-meuble*, taking care of the castles' furnishings. Together, *garde-meuble* and *menus-plaisirs* were paid by a *trésorier particulier*. The *grand écuyer* ordained the expenses for the *grande écurie*, checked by intendants, and paid by yet another treasurer. The *premier écuyer* reported the expenses of the *petite écurie* in a short *état*, directly to the king, as did the *grand veneur* for the *vénerie* – the *trésorier de la vénerie*, however, had to report to the *chambre*. Other establishments for hunting had become less relevant in the later eighteenth century, and had fixed budgets. Building and maintenance of the castles were concentrated in the service for the *bâtiments*, under its own director and treasurer, only in part coming under the *maison du roi* and its secretary. The officers' *gages ordinaires* – a 'partie peu considerable' of the budget, the memoir significantly adds – were paid by the *trésorier général* of the *maison*, and recorded in *états*. The remaining range of expenses, including gratifications, pensions, and the maintenance of other households within the *sang royal*, were covered directly by the 'trésor royal sur des états ou ordonnances expédiés par le ministre de la maison du roi'. Necker's reforms of 1780 limited the authority of the great court dignitaries over their budgets, abolished the proliferation of *trésoriers particuliers*, and instituted a central treasurer to replace them – measures providing the groundwork for later reductions.

The king's household was only the core of a wider range of court expenditures: in addition, we should always take into account the distribution of pensions or other rewards, the expenditure for the secondary households within the dynasty, the costs for the building and maintenance of royal palaces, and, finally, the military units attached to the court. All were variable, but not to the same extent. Secondary households were dictated mostly by the erratic rhythm of dynastic demography; building costs fluctuated more than any other part of court outlay. The construction of Versailles was concentrated in the intermission of Louis XIV's great wars between 1678 and 1690: it peaked in the early 1680s. The table below gives an impression of the proportional costs of major components in the court's budget. It shows that the costs for the king's household were usually on a par with the costs for pensions, and indicates the peak of building activities in Louis XIV's reign.

In Henry IV's reign, the aggregate of costs related to the court frequently represented around 25 per cent of the total ordinary and extraordinary expenditures; in 1618 it peaked at 38 per cent. In the course of the Thirty Years' War, the share of the court in total expenditure dropped to less than 10 per cent, in the critical years following 1648 it hovered between 5 per cent and 8 per cent – in these very years, we should note, the numbers of the court soared. In 1662, the court again consumed 38 per cent of the total expenditure, and it would

Table 3a. *Breakdown of French court expenditure 1600–1656 (in Livres Tournois)*[a]

Component parts	Average annual expenditure	Share in total (%)	Highest annual expenditure		Lowest annual expenditure	
King's household	2,996,780	(36%)	4,600,057	(1619)	1,677,082	(1604)
Pensions	3,044,255	(36%)	5,452,586	(1620)	1,443,062	(1625)
Secondary households	1,605,361	(19%)	3,353,982	(1644)	105,400	(1611)
Building	451,551	(5%)	1,358,137	(1634)	10,435	(1649)
Military	256,018	(3%)	375,253	(1619)	201,871	(1604)
Totals	8,353,965	(100%)	11,959,290	(1620)	4,959,899	(1605)

Table 3b. *Breakdown of French court expenditure 1662–1695 (in Livres Tournois)*

Component parts	Average annual expenditure	Share in total (%)	Highest annual expenditure		Lowest annual expenditure	
King's household	5,103,035	(27%)	7,370,968	(1662)	3,733,643	(1666)
Pensions	4,796,122	(25%)	7,416,186	(1694)	2,578,049	(1670)
Secondary households	2,782,308	(15%)	5,401,069	(1662)	1,662,810	(1669)
Building	4,704,464	(25%)	15,340,901	(1685)	1,456,438	(1693)
Military	1,533,814	(8%)	5,352,481	(1662)	418,675	(1677)
Totals	18,808,038	(100%)	30,364,627	(1685)	13,604,106	(1673)

[a] See my spreadsheets based on Bonney, *Malet* at http://www.le.ac.uk/hi/bon/ESFDB/index.html, Compare Bonney, *Malet*, figs. 6 and 7, and the percentages cited on pp. 37, 57; see the reworking of Malet's material in William Beik, *Louis XIV and Absolutism. A Brief Study with Documents* (Boston and New York 2000), pp. 96–107, particularly Tables 4 and 5 on pp. 104–106; Verlet, *Versailles*, pp. 138–143, chart on p. 141, for the costs of royal palaces, peaking in the relatively peaceful 1680s. See A. M. de Boislisle, *Correspondence des contrôleurs généraux des finances avec les intendants des provinces* (Paris 1897), III, pp. 624, 662–672 for a comparison of expenses in 1683 and 1715, and a more detailed breakdown, including pensions, for 1708–1709.

remain close to 25 per cent for almost a decade. Warfare led to more moderate percentages, but only in the 1690s would the share of the court fall below the 10 per cent mark. In the course of the War of Spanish Succession, they would decline to less than 5 per cent.[75] On average, total costs of the household represented *c.* 18 per cent of total expenditures, ordinary and extraordinary, throughout the seventeenth century.

[75] See Bonney, *Malet*, p. 62, fig. 25.

Table 4. *French court and other expenditure, eighteenth century (in Livres Tournois)*[a]

Expenditure	1726	1741	1751	1752	1768	1775	1781	1788
Households	31,000,000	30,154,000	26,000,000	28,200,000	34,000,000	43,000,000	41,421,000	42,000,000
Pensions	14,000,000	11,944,000	18,900,000	13,300,000	8,000,000	33,000,000	29,379,000	47,800,000
Others	137,300,000	–	211,400,000	272,500,000	307,119,284	335,400,000	183,154,000	543,300,000
Total expenditure	182,300,000	–	256,300,000	313,800,000	349,119,284	411,400,000	253,954,000	633,100,000
Expenditure	1726	1741	1751	1752	1768	1775	1781	1788
Households	17.0%	–	10.0%	8.9%	9.7%	10.4%	16.3%	6.6%
Pensions	7.6%	–	7.3%	4.2%	2.2%	8.0%	11.5%	7.5%
Others	75.3%		82.5%	86.8%	88.0%	81.5%	72.1%	85.8%
Total expenditure	100%	100%	100%	100%	100%	100%	100%	100%

[a] I cannot exactly verify the components listed here under 'households' and 'pensions and gages' respectively; it is not clear, for instance, whether Morineau included buildings, or the *maison militaire*, in the household costs. Morineau, 'Budgets', table on p. 315 for 1726, 1751, 1775, 1788; p. 293 for the *trésor royal* in 1741; Mathon de la Cour, *Collection de Comptes rendus*, pp. 141–165, gives comparable costs for the households in 1775 (48,493,910 or 11.7 per cent of the total expenditures of 414.445,163), though not for the pensions and *gages*. See James C. Riley, *The Seven Years War and the Old Regime in France: The Economic and Financial Toll* (Princeton 1986), pp. 55–59, for the 1752 expenditures, providing 243.6 million lt as total ordinary expenditures, 313.8 million lt total extraordinary and ordinary expenditures. Joël Félix (Reading) kindly provided a transcription of AN K 885, 4: 'Rapport de la situation des finances, janvier 1768, par M. de Laverdy, contrôleur-général des finances', with a general overview (p. 102), and a specification of costs for *finances*, *maison civile* and *maison militaire* (pp. 106–108). Under finances, we find the *bâtiments*, pensions for princes, *gages du conseil*, academies, library, garden in Paris (together 1,200,000), and travel: mostly court-related expenditure. Other expenses are listed in deductions from the income of the *pays d'états* (pp. 95–97) with substantial payments to Orléans, Condé, Conti and others. The categories chosen by Laverdy substantially differ from those found in Mathon de la Cour and Necker, which complicates comparison. Jacques Necker, *Compte rendu* (1781), p. 118, for the 1781 ordinary revenues and expenses; compare Necker, *De l'administration des finances de la France*, 3 vols. (1784), II, pp. 390–398, for the pensions, pp. 442–464 for the *maisons* and related costs, and the overview on pp. 517–518 with 67,572,000 lt court expenditure in a total budget of 610,000,000 – or 11 per cent. See other overviews of court costs in Mathon de la Cour, *Collection de Comptes rendus*, pp. 3–10 (1758: 28.6 for the households); pp. 50–52 (1764: 27 – including 'finance'); p. 53 (1768: 31.5 – now including the *troupes de la maison du roi*); pp. 88–89 (1773: 26 – including 'finance'); p. 111 (1774: 32 – including the *maisons* of Provence and Artois); only for 1775 (pp. 141–165) and 1787 (pp. 203–223) is there a full breakdown of costs, compare the *Compte rendu* for 1788, p. 94.

It is more difficult to find detailed information for the eighteenth century, and the materials do not allow the same precision as did Malet's annual overviews. Table 4 presents figures that should be treated with circumspection: they have been gleaned from a variety of works, and will hide different interpretations and computations. This is evident in the case of 1781, where I used Necker's *Compte rendu*. Necker chose to list only ordinary expenditures, reducing the deficit, but unduly inflating the share of the court in total expenditures.

In years of peace through most of the eighteenth century the expenditure for the households remained close to 10 per cent, with a somewhat smaller share for pensions and *gages*. Household costs rose at a slower pace than did the entire budget, and higher absolute figures can be explained mostly by inflation.[76] Although the figures listed here for pensions and *gages* are far from reliable, it is remarkable that they seem to expand rapidly in the 1770s, in absolute figures as well as in proportion to other household-related costs.[77] From Necker's 1781 *Compte rendu* to the last years of the *ancien régime*, pensions remained high, whereas other household costs had dramatically been reduced.

It is difficult to assess the courtiers' share in pensions and *gages du conseil*. We find *gages du conseil* listed as income for many court dignitaries in the *états*, yet neither pensions nor *gages* were ever wholly consumed by courtiers. A breakdown of the pensions in 1787, the midst of a period of active reform, shows that the *maison du roi* consumed 4,000,000 lt – a quarter of the 16,000,000 distributed by the secretary for war, and one-seventh of the entire budget for pensions. The departmental differentiation, however, is misleading: dynasties of *grands officiers* at court were well-represented in army and diplomacy alike, receiving supplementary bonuses through these ministries. Likewise, the ministers consuming by far the largest part of the *gages du conseil* in 1787 were now recruited partly among court nobles.[78] Court dignitaries and princes of the blood undoubtedly were among the major beneficiaries of the regime. The princes and princesses loom large in the budgets of Louis XVI's reign: their costly and numerous establishments were paid from the king's coffers. The households of the queen and the *famille royale* followed the reforms in the *maison du roi* only hesitantly.

Only with ample and consistent material, can we establish a clear-cut dividing-line between court-related expenses and other categories. The sources do not allow that level of precision. The available sources for the eighteenth century,

[76] Morineau, 'Budgets', p. 318: the rise of 31 to 42 million between 1726 and 1788 reflects a 'progression par 1,4 inférieure à celle du budget ordinaire'. Morineau's conclusion on p. 318 compares the rising expenses for war with the steady or proportionately declining costs for the *maisons*.

[77] Morineau, 'Budgets', p. 315, combines pensions and *gages* without further explanation; the pensions cited in Mathon de la Cour, *Collection de Comptes rendus*, pp. 3–10, 50–52, 53, 88–89, 111, are substantially lower, yet the categories differ from year to year.

[78] See a breakdown of pensions for the princes in 1775 in *Collection de Comptes rendus*, pp. 141–165, specifications of pensions per department in 1787 on p. 204, *gages de conseil* in 1787 on p. 214; compare Necker, *De l'administration des finances de la France*, II, pp. 390–398; AN O 1 656, nos. 18–24; pp. 171–173 chart the phases of reform of the pensions in 1779, 1785, 1787.

moreover, are internally inconsistent and difficult to interpret. Therefore, we cannot comfortably deduce any long-term trend in court expenditure from the seventeenth century into the 1780s. For my current purposes, a broad yet well-founded indication may suffice. Throughout the seventeenth and eighteenth centuries, we should allow for an average spending on the court and court-related activities of 15–20 per cent of ordinary and extraordinary expenditure. In varying proportions, it consistently remained the third category of expenditure, following the costs of warfare and debt service.

THE AUSTRIAN HABSBURGS

For the French court a wealth of published material helps to ascertain numbers and costs; parallel studies for the Austrian Habsburg have yet to be published. The available manuscript sources do not allow us to study in full detail the numerical development of the household throughout the seventeenth century, but they roughly indicate absolute numbers and variations in composition – a basis sufficient for the comparison of developments in France and Austria. From the last decades of the seventeenth century onwards, there is more information: we can compare the household staffs of Leopold and Louis with some detail.[79]

In 1554, Ferdinand I's *Hofstaat* numbered around 550 persons, the establishment of his son Maximilian 325, and of the latter's spouse Maria 90: together *c.* 965 persons.[80] The household of Maximilian II (1564–1576) may have expanded somewhat, and it surely matched that of his earlier namesake. In the last decades of Rudolf II's reign (1576–1612) an inflation occurred that resembled the

[79] Spielman, *The City & the Crown*, p. 59, mentions 400 in the beginning of the reign of Ferdinand I; Ehalt, *Ausdrucksformen absolutistischer Herrschaft*, p. 57, mentions 286 for 1537, not counting the guards and the queen's household; Paula S. Fichtner, 'To Rule Is Not To Govern: The Diary of Maximilian II', in *The Mirror of History: Essays in Honor of Fritz Fellner*, ed. Solomon Wank and Heidrun Maschl *et al*. (Santa Barbara and Oxford 1988), p. 262, n. 30, suggests 500 during the reign of Maximilian II; Evans, 'The Dynasty as a Political Institution', in *The Courts of Europe*, ed. Dickens, p. 123, mentions 600 persons for the court of Ferdinand II in 1636. See the research project by Mark Hengerer, 'Adelsintegration am Kaiserhof 1620 bis 1665', in *MRK* 10, 1 (2000), pp. 21–32; the forthcoming dissertation by Hengerer will probably provide more information about the first half of the seventeenth century. Two important projects are now under way in Vienna, the first a prosopographical study of the court nobles and their clients *c.* 1630–1660 (see http://www.univie.ac.at/Geschichte/wienerhof/), the second an institutional and socially more comprehensive study of the dynastic establishments in Leopold's reign, supervised by Leopold Auer (HHStA). Sources are probably sufficient to chart the numerical development of the Austrian Habsburg court. Manuscript *Hofstaatsverzeichnisse* can be found in HHStA OMeA Sr 181–189 and in many other sources, for example HHStA Handschriften Blau 386, pp. 66–98 (1696 and 1679); Handschriften Weiß 1032 (*c.* 1688); ÖNB cod. 14071 (*c.* 1675), 14725 (1677–1680), 12388 (1678); 14209 (1692–1694), 14443 (1690); AVA Harrach, Handschriften 145 (1676–1677), Harrach Historica 796, an undated late seventeenth-century (shortly after the birth of Charles?) 'Lista' of the *Oberstofmeisteramt*. For the eighteenth century, we can consult the printed *Schematismen*, for example the first: *Kayserlicher und Königlicher, wie auch Erz-herzoglicher und dero Residenzstadt Wienn Staats- und Standskalender / auff das Jahr MDCCII. Mit einem noch nie dergleichen gesehenen Schematismo geziert*, and 1704, 1706–1708, 1709–1710 etc., available in the ÖNB, Katalogsaal, 393.866–A.kat or on microfilm 4478, 1704 and 1706–1708 in the ÖNB Portraitsammlung 6079.

[80] Christopher F. Laferl, '"En tierra ajena" Spanier in Wien zur Zeit Ferdinands I. (1522–1564)', *WRGB* 52, 1 (1997), pp. 1–14, gives details for the *Hofstaat* based on HHStA OMeA Sr 182/33 and 182/40; *ÖZV*, I, 1, pp. 75–76, gives 300,000 fl for Ferdinand's household and administrative gremia, and another 230,000 for his sons' establishments, to be paid from the aggregate 'ordinari' revenue of 1,000,000 fl, whereas the troops in Hungary and near the Italian territories alone demanded a yearly payment of 550,000 fl.

situation in France during the religious crisis. The court expanded from *c.* 700 in the early 1580s to 1,100–1,200 in 1611.[81] In 1611, we find 131 *Tafeldiener*, the aggregate of *Mundschenken, Truchsessen, Panetiers*, and *Fürschneider*, 134 *Hofdiener mit Pferden*, and 38 *Kämmerer*, all honorary charges held by nobles. This reflected a doubling of these groups since the 1580s, in the case of the *Kämmerer* a tripling.[82] In the non-noble section of the court the number of the guards, at 205, was high in proportion to the modest numbers of servants in chamber and kitchen, but this was the habitual situation throughout Rudolf's reign. The *Beschreibung des gantzen Burgundischen Hoffstatts*, an early seventeenth-century manuscript giving wages, instructions, and oaths for court officers, in addition to a variety of rules mainly connected to financial matters, explicitly discussed this marked increase in the number of *Hofdiener* (court servants). Before being accepted as *Truchseß*, carver, cupbearer, or chamberlain, the text argues, nobles were expected to serve as generic *Hofdiener* for a few months. While qualifying for higher office by serving at court, they strengthened its splendour and reputation. The number of these servants, receiving a monthly fee of 20–40 *Gulden*, expanded rapidly from *c.* 20 to 'bis in hundert'. Moreover, many 'übel qualificirte personen' were admitted, more often than not the followers of the frequently changing incumbency of the highest court office. *Obersthofmeisters* rewarded their loyal followers by granting them places as servants, frequently for the remuneration only, and even if the person thus rewarded already held court office. This inflation had two serious consequences: financial problems and a bad reputation. The fact that wages could not be paid properly allegedly led to a 'terrible revolt of the household'. Moreover, the nobles for whom the charge was intended now had reason to look down on their co-servants, or even avoid service at court altogether.

Matthias (1612–1619), the text argues, put an end to the situation by sending away many of the servants; after Rudolf's death, moreover, the new emperor decreed that in the future, nobody would be allowed to receive payment for more than one court office – a measure calling to mind the decision of the Estates of Orléans (1560) forbidding the accumulation of offices in one hand,

[81] See Hausenblasová, 'Seznamy dvoranu císare rudolfka II', with the edition of the 1580 *Verzeichnis* on pp. 45–70; 1584, pp. 70–88; 1589, pp. 88–110; Hausenblasová, 'Nationalitäts- und Sozialstruktur des Hofes Rudolfs II. Im Prager Milieu an der Wende vom 16. zum 17. Jahrhundert', in *Berichte und Beiträge des Geisteswissenschaftliches Zentrums Geschichte und Kultur Ostmittleuropas e.V. 1999. Öffentliche Vorträge 1998–1999* (Leipzig 1999), pp. 20–37, with an analysis of the *c.* 1,100-person 1611 *Verzeichnis*; and Hausenblasová, 'Die "Höflinge" des Kaisers Rudolf II. – Beitrag zur Begriffsbestimmung', in *Rudolf II, Prague, and the World. Papers from the International Conference, Prague, 2–4 September, 1997*, ed. Lubomir Konecny, Beket Bukovinska, and Ivan Muchka (Prague 1998), pp. 239–243, p. 242, n. 9, suggests 700 for 1576, more than 1,200 for 1612.

[82] Hausenblasová, 'Seznamy dvoranu císare rudolfka II', honorary noble *Tafeldiener*, 1580, pp. 47–51: 75; 1584, pp. 71–73: 72; 1589, pp. 91–93: 85; *Hofdiener*: 1580, pp. 52–54: 45; 1584, p. 74: 36; 1589, pp. 94–95: 48; *Kämmerer*: 1580, p. 64: 13; 1584, pp. 83–84: 16; 1589, p. 105: 12. The 1584 decrease in *Tafel-* and *Hofdiener* may be connected to Rudolf's move to Prague. See Hausenblasová, 'Nationalitäts- und Sozialstruktur des Hofes Rudolfs II', p. 36, for a table (noble, non-noble, nations) with the aggregates of the 1611 *Verzeichnis*.

and probably just as futile.[83] Early in 1615 Matthias indeed attempted to reform the *Hofstaat* and its budget, laying down maximum numbers for the honorary court officers. The *Hofstaatsverzeichnisse* generated in the process suggest that the aggregate of household and councils – though without hunt and falconry (*c.* 25 persons in Rudolf's *Verzeichnisse*), or other households within the dynasty – now numbered *c.* 785 persons. Comparing the data for 1615 and 1616 in the *Hofzahlamtsbücher*, or registers of the court's paymaster's office, we note declining expenses for wages and pensions, and a substantially larger amount reserved for the payment of debts in the latter year.[84] This may indicate either a partial success of the measures, or simply persisting financial crisis.

When from 1617 onwards Ferdinand of Styria (1619–1637) slowly took over Matthias' responsibilities, his rise to power coincided with the onset of what was to become the Thirty Years' War. A determined supporter of the Catholic cause, Ferdinand defeated the Protestant challenge in Bohemia and in the Austrian Lands, and reorganised the government of his realm along more monarchical lines. Were the numbers of Ferdinand II's court influenced by the process of remoulding the bond of the dynasty with the major nobles, which had been seriously undermined by religious dissent? Most services and staffs within the household will not have strayed much from the 1615 standard, but honorary court office again tended to expand. The honorary table servants surpassed the levels agreed upon in 1615, an undated overview from the years of Ferdinand II or Ferdinand III gives 19 cupbearers instead of 4, and 26 *Truchsesse* instead of 12. In a *Hofstaat* covering Ferdinand III's whole reign, a total of 79 cupbearers, 19 carvers, and 94 *Truchsesse* was listed.[85] Slowly, however, these honorary table servants were pushed aside by the *Kämmerer*, or chamberlains. In the sixteenth century we find only 3–10 chamberlains, and a slightly lower number of *Kammerdiener* (chamber servants); in Rudolf's years the chamberlains number 12–13, the chamber servants 4–5. Yet in Ferdinand II's reign their numbers rose markedly. In his 1629 report, papal nuncio Carafa suggested that Ferdinand in the first decade of his rule had elevated hundreds of *Cavaliere* to the rank of chamberlain as a reward for their loyal service in the army, or simply out of *Gutmüthigkeit*. At the time of

83 'Beschreibung des Gantzen Burgundischen Hoffstatts, wie derselbe bey dem Hause von Oesterreich in Brauch gewesen nach den vier obersten Hofämtern', ÖNB cod. 14676, fols. 29–30. The November 1615 'Resolution über die Reformation der Kaiserlichen Hofstaat' in HHStA OMeA Sr 184, fols. 53–77, offers a parallel tract, written from the perspective of the *Hofkammer*; on fols. 74v–75r the expansion of the *Hofstaat* and the *Besoldungen* are discussed. See the remarks by Hengerer about numerous court servants in Ferdinand I's reign, 'Adelsintegration am Kaiserhof', p. 25. See Loyseau, *Cinq livres*, pp. 228, 235 for the ordinances of Orléans and Blois.

84 On the reform HHStA, OMeA Sr 184, no. 75, with the *Verzeichnis*. 75/6, see also the *Verzeichnis* in 184, no. 76, with several notes in the margin giving maximum numbers. Compare HKA HZAB 1615/64 fols. 104r, 141v, 46r; 1616/65, fols. 49r, 64r, 252v. Revenues listed for 1615/64, fol. 144r were much higher than those for 1616/65, fol. 88r.

85 HHStA, OMeA Sr 184, no. 84; OMeA Sr 186 (fols. 8v–311), compare HHStA OMeA Sr 187 Hofstaat Ferdinand III. 87 *Mundschenken* (fols. 27–29, 32–33): 19 *Fürschneider* (fols. 30–31), 95 *Truchseßen* (fols. 36–42), an aggregate of 201 table servants for the entire reign, probably never more than 130 at any particular time.

Carafa's report, however, the chamberlains' key was more difficult to obtain. The emperor, moreover, had selected six German and six Italian chamberlains to perform actual services at court, leaving the others a mere title. Several decades later, by the time of Ferdinand III's death, the total of ordinary and extraordinary, or serving and titular, chamberlains, stood at *c.* 150.[86] In the course of the seventeenth century, the chamberlains took over the role of the *Hofdiener* and the honorary officers of the table, all more numerous in the sixteenth century. Indeed, the chamberlains were the nearest Austrian Habsburg equivalent to the rapidly expanding honorary officers at the Louis XIII's court – *maîtres d'hôtel* and *gentilshommes servants*.[87] Whereas the four *gentilshommes de la chambre* had in France become a perquisite for the finest families only, in Austria in the long run any noble family that valued its connections with the court would try to get its sons accepted as *Kämmerer*.

Throughout the first two-thirds of the century, the aggregate of the six major staffs – steward with guards and chapel, chamberlain without honorary chamberlains, marshal, master of the stables, master of falconry, master of the hunt – probably remained below 800 persons, not counting councils, chancelleries, or other *Hofstaaten*. The paucity of sources makes it difficult to chart the numerical variations in great detail. Nor is the available material always in harmony. Papal nuncio Carafa noted that Ferdinand II employed 150 hunters and *Büchsenspänner*, in addition to regional staffs for hunting. In the later overviews however, we only find a *c.* 55-person staff for the *Jägermeister*.[88] It is quite likely that the court in Leopold's difficult first years was smaller than that of

[86] *ÖZV*, I, 2, p. 159: 3 *Kämmerer* and 3 *Kammerdiener* (1539–1541); p. 186: 5 and 3 (1563–1564); p. 197: 11 *Kämmerer*, 6 *Kammerdiener*, and 6 *Buben* or boys (1576); Hausenblasova, 'Seznamy dvoranu císare rudolfka II', p. 64, 1580: 13 *Kämmerer* and 5 *Kammerdiener*; pp. 83–84 for 1584: 16 *Kämmerer* and 4 *Kammerdiener*; p. 105 for 1589: 12 *Kämmerer* and 4 *Kammerdiener*; for 1637 no number is given in *ÖZV*; the 1637 Status Particularis Regiminis as presented on the web-page of 'Der Wiener Hof und sein Klientel- und Patronagesystem', www.univie.ac.at/wienerhof/, includes 32 ordinary and 62 extraordinary *Kämmerer*, a total of 94; *ÖZV*, I, 2, p. 229, notes 148 *Kämmerer* for 1655; compare the unspecified 29 'Diener' in *ÖZV*, I, 2, pp. 153–154 (1527–1528) surely a group comparable to the later *Kämmerer*. HHStA OMeA Sr 184, no. 83, fols. 1–3, gives 76 'würckliche Kämmerer' for 1649; HHStA OMeA Sr 186, fols. 121r–138r, gives an aggregate of 222 *Kämmerer* for the whole reign of Ferdinand III; HHStA OMeA Sr 187 Hofstaat Ferdinand III: 229 *Ordinarii Kämmerer* (fols. 190–194, 261–270) for the entire reign of Ferdinand III – the numbers do not reflect the aggregate of the *Kämmerer* at any particular moment, as they include deceased servants; 2/3 may reflect a plausible maximum, that is *c.* 150 matching the 148 given in *ÖZV* and the 1655 *Verzeichnis* on www.univie.ac.at/wienerhof/; Hengerer, 'Adelsintegration', p. 25, n. 16, suggests 'mehrere hundert' for Ferdinand II and 'etwa 200' for the last year of Ferdinand III, a high estimate. Compare Mark Hengerer, 'Hofzeremoniell, Organisation und Grundmuster sozialer Differenzierung am Wiener Hof im 17. Jahrhundert', in *Hofgesellschaft und Höflinge*, ed. Malettke and Grell, pp. 337–368, at p. 344, n. 28, citing 700 *Kämmerer* in Ferdinand II's reign, a number possibly matching Carafa's statements about Ferdinand's liberal use of the title. Carafa's 'Bericht' is printed in Hurter, *Friedensbestrebungen*, pp. 212 ff., remarks cited on pp. 237–238.

[87] In Vienna there was no equivalent for the *maîtres d'hôtel*, but the *gentilshommes servants* fit the traditional three honorary officers serving the emperor's tables (we frequently find the French–Burgundian–Spanish *panetier* or *panathier* in the Habsburg *Verzeichnisse* in addition to the other three offices of the table). The *premier maître d'hôtel* can well be compared with the *Stabelmeister*, the *Obersthofmeister*'s senior deputy for the service of the table.

[88] Carafa in Hurter, *Friedensbestrebungen*, p. 221, for the later *Verzeichnisse*, see below. Hunt and falconry were frequently omitted in the overviews of the court.

Ferdinand III in its last years: the *Hofzahlamtsbücher* indicate a decrease for most categories of household expenditure. We cannot further verify this possibility, because no reliable and complete *Hofstaatsverzeichnisse* are available for the 1650s and 1660s.[89] The more copious series of manuscript *Verzeichnisse* of the 1670s indicate that Leopold's household staffs, without the honorary chamberlains or other establishments within the dynasty, numbered between 800 and 900 persons. Towards the end of his reign, they surpassed the 1,000 level; further expansion occurred in Charles VI's reign, and in the latter's last years the core staffs exceeded 1,500. Warfare and the temporary loss of the imperial throne to the Wittelsbach dynasty complicated the beginning of Maria Theresa's reign; her court in the 1740s was decidedly less impressive than had been her father's establishment in 1739. In 1760, however, her household staffs and guards approached pre-1740 levels; the 1760 *Schematismus* lists 1374 persons as employed at court without the chamberlains' list, and a 1763 state inventory notes 1,478 persons.[90] By 1780 the six staffs and the guards reached a temporary peak above the 2,000 level.[91] In Joseph II's reign, numbers declined, yet always remained at levels higher than those of the Leopoldine age. The share of each of the staffs in these aggregates was variable, as a further breakdown shows.

In the 1670s we find roughly 180 persons in the *Obersthofmeister*'s staff, including the services for kitchen, cellar, illumination, but also the chapel and its 40-odd musicians. With 10–15 members, the ecclesiastical establishment within the steward's staff initially was remarkably small; the preacher, chaplain, and almoner, moreover, were not noble, and surely not on a par with the great court dignitaries. In addition came the mounted guards (*Hartschieren*) and the infantry guards (*Trabanten*), who together numbered *c.* 220. The first printed overviews suggest that towards the end of Leopold's reign, the *Obersthofmeister*'s staff was increasing, reaching a level of more than 300 in the year of his death.[92] Indeed, during Charles VI's reign growth continued, with the chapel reaching 160 in 1739, and other services *c.* 210 – the guards with 234 only marginally surpassed

[89] The *Hofstaat* in HHStA OMeA 185, no. 85 is wrongly dated 1659: it dates from the late 1670s, as do most available overviews.

[90] *Schematismus*, 1760; Dickson, *Finance and Government*, I, pp. 308–309 and fn. 48, discussing Oberleitner's work on the 1763 Inventory and other contemporary estimates; Dickson, 'Monarchy and Bureaucracy', p. 340, elaborates these numbers, giving 1,500 both for the households (minus guards?) and for the central bureaucracy towards the end of Maria Theresa's reign.

[91] G. E. Rinck, *Leopold des Grossen Röm. Kaysers wunderwürdiges Leben und Thaten aus geheimen Nachrichte eröffnet* (Cologne 1713) gives an incomplete list; when we add the musicians it reaches *c.* 950, but his figures for the *Stallparthey* are low when we compare them to previous and later manuscript overviews, for example the detailed 1711 list in ÖNB cod. 14848, giving 436 persons; Johann Basilius Küchelbecker, *Allerneueste Nachricht vom Römisch-Kayserl. Hofe* (Hanover 1732), gives 1,332 for the staffs; the 1739 *Schematismus* lists up to 1,569 persons; the 1748 *Schematismus* 1,128 persons; the 1760 Schematismus 1,374; the 1780 *Schematismus* 2,046; the 1791 *Schematismus* 1,461; and finally the volume for 1820, 2,542 – all figures given here concern the *Hofstaat* in the most restricted sense, i.e. the 'six staffs': steward (with guards and musicians), chamberlain (without chamberlains' list), marshal, master of the stables, master of the hunt and falconry, without councils or other households. Vehse, *Geschichte der deutschen Höfe* XIV, 2. Abtheilung 8, pp. 69–77, gives 2,400 for the end of Maria Theresa's reign on p. 69, with an estimated cost of 4,300,000 Gulden.

[92] *Schematismus* 1704, pp. 161–171; Rinck, *Leopold*, pp. 201–204.

previous levels. By the 1760s, Maria Theresa's staff had recovered from its temporary setback, and almost matched Charles VI's levels; the *Obersthofmeister*, now seconded by the newly introduced *anderter Hofmeister*, supervised a staff of 258, with a smaller chapel of 73, and a new assemblage of *c.* 243 guards, including a French-style Swiss guard. The Swiss guard was abolished after Francis Stephen's death, but its name stuck to the *Schweizerhof*, one of the inner courtyards of the Hofburg. In another twenty years, the guards had tripled to 727, one of the noteworthy innovations of Maria Theresa's and Joseph's court. In addition to the traditional *Hartschieren und Trabanten*, in the 1780s we find the *Arcieren Leibgarde*, the *Königliche Ungarische Adelige Leibgarde*, a *Leibgarde zu Fuß*, a Milanese detachment, *gardes de palais*, and a *Schloßgarde*. Frequently, officers in the old guards doubled as officers in the newly instituted guards, and finally the establishments were merged, yet the new structures of the elite guards and their concomitant growth indicate a significant shift.[93]

The *Oberstkämmerer*'s staff also expanded, but in a different cadence. Consistently between 60 and 70 in the decades around 1700, it was well past 100 towards the end of Charles VI's reign; there was no notable decline in Maria Theresa's first years, and by 1780 it stood at 263. These figures do not include the volatile group of honorary *Kämmerer*, numbering at least 300 from the 1670s onwards, but more often reaching higher levels. Most of these chamberlains were labelled 'true' or *würckliche Kämmerer*, indicating that they were indeed expected to serve the emperor, and demarcating them from the smaller group of *titulares*, holding the honour without the obligation to serve. The compiler of a 1679 *Verzeichnis* stoically remarked that the 'true' chamberlains: 'sind gemeiniglich jetziger zeit bey nah 500 an der Zahl, und ist fast kein adelich haus im Kays. Erblanden so nicht den schlüssel . . . empfangen.[94] The chamberlain's symbolic golden key to the emperor's chambers offered the habitual entry into the courtly hierarchy, establishing the holder's seniority vis-à-vis others in the hierarchy. For those interested in securing their status at court, it was necessary to obtain an early nomination, but the inflation of the honour made it less effective an instrument of discrimination. The number of chamberlains followed the

93 See the printed *Schematismen* for the various new guards; further analysis of the shift in Michael Hochedlinger, 'Mars Ennobled: The Ascent of the Military and the Creation of a Military Nobility in Mid-Eighteenth-Century Austria', *German History* 17, 2 (1992), pp. 141–176.

94 HHStA, HS Blau 386, pp. 78 ff. See the parallel quote about the rank of chamberlain in Hengerer, 'Adelsintegration', p. 31: 'Es sey keine ehre ihn zu haben / aber wohl eine schande ihn nicht zu haben'. Rinck, *Leopold*, gives a detailed list for the *Hofstaat* in 1705, containing 423 *Kämmerer*; Küchelbecker, *Allerneueste Nachricht*, pp. 176–186, lists 234 *Kämmerer*; Johann Georg Keyszler, *Nieuwe Reizen door Duitschland, Bohemen, Hongarije . . . Uit het Hoogduitsch vertaalt*, 4 vols. (Amsterdam 1753–1755), III, p. 322, notes 226 *Kämmerer* for 1731; Pöllnitz, *Mémoires*, I, p. 279, remarks that Bohemian nobles tried to become *Kämmerer* mainly to obtain *préséance* for their spouses, while they were hardly interested in pursuing their role at court. See Ferdinand III's March 1637 instruction for the *Oberstkämmerer* and the rules for his deputies in HHStA, Familienakten III K 100, and the similar March 1651 Kammerherreninstruktion in HHStA, OMeA Sr. K 73 (each of these *c.* 5 unnumbered folios). Of the three declining honorary table servants, only the *Truchsessen* maintained their position at court, becoming numerous in the eighteenth century, when carvers and cupbearers were almost absent.

rhythm of deaths and promotions; new rulers could choose to adopt their predecessors' chamberlains, but usually started with a smaller group, adding their own nominees on major occasions of the monarchy: marriages, coronations or *Erbhuldigungen*.[95] Thus numbers were quite variable, but they remained high, and the *Schematismen* stopped listing them for this reason. Vehse gave an unsubstantiated number of 1,500 for the end of Maria Theresa's reign; a multi-page list in the 1820 *Schematismus* comes near that number.

Küchelbecker reports that in 1729 four *Kämmerer* served at the same time, in two alternating pairs, each of these serving two weeks in *Vordienst* (preliminary duty) then two weeks in *Hauptdienst* (main duty). After two weeks *Hauptdienst*, one pair of *Kämmerer* could leave while the other pair took over the *Hauptdienst*, making room for another pair in the *Vordienst*. The chamberlains served for four weeks: this allows us to expect that at least 52 among the long lists of 'würckliche' chamberlains actually served in one year – yet it is far from clear whether this reflected preceding practice, and how the system operated.[96] Seventeenth-century ordinances stipulated longer service, ideally for two or three years; yet in the same articles provisos were made for those who could for legitimate reasons not serve as long as that – the office would not be withheld from them. Those indeed willing to serve for a longer period were granted an annual leave: six weeks for unmarried, eight weeks for married chamberlains.[97] In 1781, Joseph II changed the rules for chamberlains' service, appointing 36 *Dienstkämmerer*, each of whom had to serve during one week twice a year.[98]

Throughout the seventeenth century the *Obersthofmarschall* had to carry out his important tasks with fewer than 20 subordinates – including the quartermaster's small staff, sometimes listed under the *Obersthofmeister*'s department.

[95] See the interesting passage in Khevenhüller, *Tagebuch*, II, pp. 43–45 (April 1745): Khevenhüller, then *Oberstkämmerer*, discusses the marked lack of enthusiasm of the *Fürsten* who had obtained the status of chamberlain in Charles VI's years to continue active service, or to apply for it. The situation was improved only when Maria Theresa decided that those without *Hoffbedienung* or function at court would receive no special treatment or distinctions. Thereafter, the princely chamberlains did obtain special privileges to soften the measure.

[96] Küchelbecker, *Allerneueste Nachricht*, p. 176, compare with ÖNB cod. 14443 (1690), fol. 81: 'diese cammerherren bedienen Ihro Kays. Maj. wochentlich par und par ein alter und ein junger, und sie gehen zum dienst am sontag, und werden also von sontag zu sontag abgelöst'. It is not clear whether two pairs are serving, or only one, of a younger and an older chamberlain, yet because of the shorter service (one week) stipulated here, the number of persons involved would be higher than in Küchelbecker's version. The same text can be found in ÖNB cod. ser. n. 1849, fol. 9r, with the addition that one of the *Kämmerer* serves as cupbearer, the other as carver – explaining the decline of these offices in Leopold's years, and the notice that chamberlains pledge their oath of loyalty to the Oberstkämmerer. In the *Schematismen*, for example 1760, pp. 392–393; 1780, p. 373, we find a slightly diverging standard text describing the chamberlains, nobles from all parts of the monarchy: 'die Ihre kays. Königl. Majestäten beyderseits in der gewöhnlichen Hof-Kleydung zwey und zwey acht Tage in dem Vordienst, und acht Tage in dem Hauptdienst, nebst zweyen durch acht Tage im Vordienst solcher Gestalten bedienen, daß allezeit 6. Cammerer bey Hof sich befinden', suggesting service of 32 days, and 6 chamberlains at court. Compare Carafa in Hurter, *Friedensbestrebungen*, on p. 238, mentioning that only two chamberlains together served the emperor.

[97] 1637 Instruction for the Oberstkämmerer Hans Rudolf count of Puchaim in HHStA, Familienakten III K 100, articles 2 and 3; Kammerherreninstruktion in HHStA, OMeA Sr. K 73, articles 2 and 3.

[98] ÖNB cod. 12957, ceremoniale 1781, 'instruction für die von S. K.K.M. ausgewählten 36 Dienstkammerherren' (fols. 1–4).

The marshal's establishment expanded slowly in the eighteenth century, reaching *c.* 35 in 1729, but never surpassing 40 persons.[99] The *Oberststallmeister*'s staff counted *c.* 275 persons towards the end of the seventeenth century, including 18–20 pages or *Edelknaben*. It expanded more rapidly than the other staffs: a detailed overview of 1711, including pensioners, added up to almost 500. While this may reflect an exceptional situation, or an unusual computation, Küchelbecker's 1729 lists gives an even higher total of *c.* 550, a number confirmed in the 1739 *Schematismus*. Throughout the reigns of Leopold and Charles, this staff steadily expanded, a process undiluted by multitudes of honorary officers – an exception the *Stallparthey* shared only with the musical establishment and the services of kitchen and cellar in the *Obersthofmeister*'s staff. Halfway through the eighteenth century, the numbers of the *Stall* tended to decrease, and its share in the expanding household fell more sharply. Even the moderate number of pages was reduced from 18 to 12.

In the 1670s the *Jägermeister* employed a little fewer than 60 persons, and the *Falkenmeister* around 30. In the early eighteenth century, these numbers had risen to 100 and 35 respectively, and growth continued in the course of Charles VI's reign. The *Jägermeister*'s staff reached 161 as it assumed responsibility for forestry as well; with the falconry the establishment for hunting had a staff of more than 200 in the 1730s.[100] In Maria Theresa's early years numbers sharply dropped, but then rose steadily into the 1780s to reach a level of 235, slightly higher than that of the 1730s – in addition to the regular establishments for hunt and falconry, the 1780 *Schematismus* included a *vénerie*. Numbers stabilised just below the 200 level, but forestry was becoming increasingly prominent within the staff, and the falconry disappeared in the 1790s.[101] Several other staffs connected to the court expanded and became professionalised in the course of the eighteenth century, – the *Hofbau-amt* or service for building more than doubled from 42 in 1748 to 102 in 1780 – but such staffs operated in the margin of the traditional household, and are not included in the preceding figures.

Nor are the establishments of empresses, archdukes, and archduchesses. New empresses may have travelled with a 300–400-person entourage to Vienna, but

[99] Küchelbecker, *Allerneueste Nachricht*, pp. 190–191.

[100] ÖNB cod. 12388 (1678), fols. 31–32, lists 57 for the *Jägermeister*, adding only the *Falkenmeister*; ÖNB cod. 14443 (1690), fols. 97–103, gives 59 for the *Jägerey*, and mentions only the expenses of the *Fälcknerey*, *c.* three-quarters of the *Jägerey*. The *Falkenmeister*'s staff probably included *c.* 20–25 persons, as the costs of falconry seem to have been higher than those of the other forms of hunting. Rinck, *Leopold*, p. 220, for 1705 lists 57 and 28 respectively, and Küchelbecker, *Allerneueste Nachricht*, pp. 195–197, for 1729 gives 161 for the hunt (now including forestry) and 44 for the falconry – adding that the latter was proportionately much more expensive. Thus, Rinck's figures can be accepted as reflecting later seventeenth-century practice. Oskar von Mitis, *Jagd und Schützen am Hofe Karls VI.* (Vienna 1912), p. 51, mentions 100 and 35 respectively for Joseph I's *Jägerey* and *Fälcknerey*, 115 and 40 for Charles VI's.

[101] Vehse's numbers for the end of Maria Theresa's reign (*Geschichte der deutschen Höfe*, II, 8, p. 75), 151 and 41 for hunt and falconry, fit well Küchelbecker's. Other data from the *Schematismen*, 1748, 1760, 1780, 1791; in 1793, the Falconry was abolished, see Mitis, *Jagd und Schützen*, p. 40.

soon afterwards it would dwindle to a mere 60–100 persons.[102] More or less like the French *dauphins* from Louis XIV onwards, the empresses did not have a fully independent *Hofstaat*, as they were partly catered for by the emperors' staff. Interestingly, the dowager-empress' *Hofstaat* was far more important. It could function more independently than the ruling empress' *Hofstaat*; and probably helped to solve the problem of the staff left over from the previous reign, who in any case were entitled to some support. The two Eleonora Gonzagas long outlived their imperial husbands, Ferdinand II and Ferdinand III respectively; with *c.* 250 persons, their well-funded and much-admired establishments were notable presences in Vienna. In the eighteenth century, Leopold's widow Eleonora Magdalena assembled a *Hofstaat* of *c.* 365 members, and patronised the female *Stern-Creuz-Orden*, established in 1668 by her predecessor Eleonora II Gonzaga. Amalia-Wilhelmine, Joseph's widow, maintained a similar establishment from Eleonora Magdalena's death in 1720 until her own death in 1742, as would Charles' empress Elisabeth-Christine until her death in 1750.[103] The female establishments did somewhat increase the proportion of women at court: ruling empresses habitually employed slightly more women than men in their 70–80 person establishments. In the larger establishments of dowager-empresses, this proportion was markedly less, closer to the 10 per cent to be found in the *états* of French queens. *Hofdamen*, moreover, would stay at court maybe for a year, but rarely for protracted periods; only the Spanish or Italian ladies around the empress tended to hold their positions. The service of noble ladies usually

102 HHStA OMeA Sr 184, no. 81 gives 96 for empress Maria's *Hofstaat* in 1639. HKA HZAB 1655/101 list 70 persons (41 women and 29 men) in the *Hofstaat* of Eleonora II Gonzaga. Leopold's first bride, Margarita Teresa, did not match the splendour of her elder half-sister, Louis XIV's queen, when she came to Vienna, a 1666 printed 'relacion' listing those accompanying her from Madrid to Vienna in HHStA ÄZA 7 gives a total of 306, excluding the *cavallieri's* own officers and servants. It is not stipulated which of them would return after having escorted the new empress to Vienna, though the fact that some of them did return is clearly stated on fol. 471, and confirmed by the list in HHStA OMeA Sr 184, no. 86, listing 86 persons, matched by the 83 (43 women, 40 men) listed in HKA HZAB 1169/112; the new empress' contingent, however, did cause distress in Vienna, see Spielman, *City & the Crown*, pp. 96, 99, 119–120, and the unpublished dissertation by Claudia Ham, 'Die Verkauften Bräute. Studien zu den Hochzeiten zwischen Österreichischen und Spanischen Habsburgern im 17. Jahrhundert' (Vienna 1995). Claudia Felicitas undertook her voyage from Innsbruck to Graz in September 1673 accompanied by 388 persons (and 458 horses), see her *Hofstaatsverzeichnis* in HHStA, ÄZA K 9, but it seems unlikely that her *Hofstaat* maintained such proportions later: in ÖNB cod. 14071, fol. 17, the number is 71. In HHStA, Sr. 184, no. 85 (1677–1678, unnumbered) we find 58 persons in Eleonora Magdalena's *Hofstaat*; 68 are given for her establishment in 1678, ÖNB cod. 12388, fols. 28–29; 78 for 1679 in HHStA HS Blau 386, fol. 85, for 1690 a lower number, 61, is given in ÖNB cod. 14443, fols. 103–104, confirmed by HKA HZAB 1690/135, fols. 231–240, noting 65 (38 women, 27 men). Compare Küchelbecker, *Allerneueste Nachricht*, pp. 198–20, for empress Elisabeth-Christine's 81-person *Hofstaat* in 1729; after 1740, there was no separate *Hofstaat* for the ruling empress, as Maria Theresa and Francis Stephen had one establishment.

103 See HHStA ÄZA K 3/18 for the 1651 *Hofstaat* of Eleonora I Gonzaga; ÖNB cod 14071, fol. 73, for the 252 *Hofstaat* of Eleonora-Gonzage, and ÖNB cod 12388 (1678), fols. 28–30, for her 205 *Hofstaat*. Whereas the 1704 *Schematismus* on pp. 193–196 mentions only *c.* 60 persons for empress Eleonora Magadalena, in the unnumbered pages after p. 202 of the 1709–1710 *Schematismus* we find *c.* 365 for dowager-empress Eleonora Magdalena, a number repeated, though with slightly varying categories, for Amalia-Wilhelmine on pp. xxxiii–xlii of the 1721 *Schematismus*. Immediately following the dowager-empresses' lists we find the Creuz-Orden. Küchelbecker, *Allerneueste Nachricht*, pp. 204–212, gives 362 persons in Amalia-Wilhelmine's *Hofstaat*.

represented a relatively short phase in their lives, the introduction into the world of the court – as it did for the *Edelknaben*, or for the *Kämmerer*.[104]

The emperor's household was predominantly male; we usually find only a handful of women, three washerwomen, and several *musicallische Weibspersohnen* in the chapel.[105] No full-scale Habsburg male establishments existed in Vienna apart from the emperor's, though we routinely find smaller households for the *junge Herrschaften*, as the archdukes and archduchesses were called. Indeed, shortly before his election as King of the Romans in 1690, young Joseph's *Hofstaat* numbered 49 persons, notably male companions not unlike the *dauphin*'s *menins*, headed by several prominent *Kämmerer*. In the 1690s, his establishment developed into a small replica of Leopold's court, the earlier chamberlains filling the major positions. It numbered around 200 persons towards the end of 1694, more than 400 with a separate 58-person establishment for his queen in 1704.[106] After the ominous days of Rudolf and Matthias, brothers tended to be less conspicuous in Vienna than in Paris. They were comfortably established prelates, stadholders in the Tyrol or in the Low Countries, and we do not usually find their establishments in Vienna. Even when they resided there, they rarely were as disturbing a factor as Gaston d'Orléans had been. Ferdinand III's younger brother Leopold-William (1614–1662), returning to Vienna after serving as stadtholder in the Spanish Netherlands in 1656, did have a sizeable establishment counting *c.* 270 persons, as well as a famous musical chapel and a conspicuous collection of paintings. After the death of Ferdinand III in 1657, moreover, Leopold-William's presence in Vienna somewhat disturbed young Leopold's chances for the imperial election.[107] Likewise, if Joseph I had not died prematurely, but Charles' Spanish adventure had still ended in the same débâcle, the latter could have made himself a nuisance in Vienna, though a suitably splendid appanage could conceivably have been found for him in the Italian territories or in the Austrian Netherlands.

From 1637 to 1742, the most typical and important secondary establishment within the dynasty was that of the dowager-empress: partly a continuation of the deceased emperor's establishment as far as it was not *confirmirt* by the new

[104] See Beatrix Bastl, 'Das Österreichische Frauenzimmer. Zum Beruf der Hofdame in der Frühen Neuzeit', in *Frauenzimmer*, ed. Hirschbiegel and Paravicini, pp. 355–375, with the 'Ausstattung' of a *Hofdame* printed on pp. 272–275, and her 'Das Österreichische Frauenzimmer. Zur Rolle der Frau im höfischen Fest- und Hofleben 15. bis 17. Jahrhundert', *Opera Historica* 8 (2000), pp. 79–105.

[105] See, for example, HKA, HZAB 1640/86 eight women in the chapel, fols. 85v–86v; HZAB 1662/107, three women, fols. 236v–237r.

[106] For an early 1685 list of 35 persons, see HHStA OMeA Sr 188; for the 49 persons listed after Joseph's coronation in 1690, see ÖNB cod. 14443; more rapid expansion occurred in 1694 charted in the HHStA OMeA Prot 5 1690–1699: 23 April 1694, fols. 257–266 (fol. 264: 134 persons) further accretions on fols. 295–300 (20 July 1694); fol. 301 (23 July 1694); fol. 323 (12 September 1694); ÄZA K 17 lists 226; for the 400 *Hofstaat* see *Schematismus* 1704, pp. 196–206; OMeA Sr 189 gives a detailed list of Joseph's staff until 1705, but does not include the remarkably expanded numbers given in the 1704 *Schematismus*.

[107] See Sienell, 'Die Wiener Hofstaate zur Zeit Leopolds I.', in *Hofgesellschaft und Höflinge*, ed. Malettke and Grell, pp. 95–96; on Leopold William see Renate Schreiber, 'Erzherzog Leopold Wilhelm', unpublished dissertation (Vienna 2001).

emperor, at the same time providing for his pensioners and allowing more freedom in the selection of his own *Hofstaat*. The emperors were involved mainly in the details of nominations in other households with a view to limiting the number of people to be provided for – though we may expect them to have expressed an interest in the selection of major officers. After the death of Amalia-Wilhelmine, there were no great independent establishments in Vienna within the dynasty. Maria Theresa and emperor Francis Stephen had one establishment, though they maintained two *Obersthofmeisters* and an *Obersthofmeisterin*. After the death of Francis Stephen in 1765, the households of Joseph and Maria Theresa were merged, a process entailing the temporary duplication of senior charges. In 1766 we find the *erster Obersthofmeister*, another *Mit-erster Obershofmeister*, the *anderter Obersthofmeister*, an *Obersthofmeisterin*, a 'Bey der Römischen Kayserin Majestät Obristhofmeisterin', and two *Oberststallmeisters* – surely an awkward expedient dictated by consideration for the court dignitaries. In addition to this new unitary *Hofstaat*, only small staffs for the *junge Herrschaften* remained.[108]

The household included personnel from most of the territories connected to Habsburg rule, yet it did not stop there. Rudolf's Spanish experiences, and the world of artists assembled around him, gave his court a markedly cosmopolitan reputation, yet 70 per cent of the *Hofstaat* carried a German name.[109] The international hotch-potch of generals in the Thirty Years' War left its imprint on the landed elites in Bohemia and the Austrian lands, and indirectly on the household staffs. For the honorary officers a measure of 'representation' of all territories had become a principle.[110] Major families from the hereditary lands were habitually included; before the recovery of Hungary from the Ottomans, Hungarians represented a small minority, nor would their numbers rapidly rise in the eighteenth century.[111] Bohemians were well represented, particularly in the highest charges. The empire was steadily represented, in higher offices, in the household as well as in the various administrative institutions – most obviously those responsible for imperial affairs. For the lower echelons names are

[108] See HHStA ÄZA K 70: 13 September 1765 Vereinigung der Hofstaaten *c.* 11 fol., and Maria Theresa's and Joseph's letters; offices as cited are given in the 1767 *Schematismus*. Compare the discussions of this change in Khevenhüller, *Tagebuch*, VI, pp. 140–143 (11–15 September 1765). Khevenhüller lost his office as *Oberstkämmerer* to Salm, and became *Mit-erster Obersthofmeister*. Compare Khevenhüller, *Tagebuch*, VI, pp. 140–143 (September 1765).

[109] See Jaroslava Hausenblasová, 'Nationalitäts- und Sozialstruktur des Hofes Rudolfs II. im Prager Milieu an der Wende vom 16. zum 17. Jahrhundert', in *Berichte und Beiträge des Geisteswissenschaftliches Zentrums geschichte und Kultur Ostmittleuropas e. V. 1999. Öffentliche Vorträge 1998–1999* (Leipzig 1999), pp. 20–37, Table on p. 36.

[110] See the standard description of the *Kämmerer*: members of the finest families from all territories, for example in *Schematismus* 1760, pp. 392–393.

[111] See in general Géza Pállfy, 'Der Wiener Hof und die ungarischen Stände im 16. Jahrhundert', *MIÖG* 109 (2001) – the author kindly gave me several important articles in typescript before publication. He tends to see continuity more than change after 1711 or 1740; generally only few Hungarians were active at court in Vienna, and those who were able to secure a foothold at court often came from a limited group of major families, and profited from their office at court by strengthening their position in Hungary. Forthcoming work by Dr Pálffy will shed light on these as well as other aspects of the relationship between Hungary and the Viennese court in the sixteenth and seventeenth centuries.

frequently omitted in the *Verzeichnisse*, nor are German names invariably helpful as an indication of origins. The presence of Italians and Spaniards remains evident throughout the seventeenth and early eighteenth centuries, particularly in the chapel musical and spiritual, among other musicians and specialised artisans, but also more incidentally in other services. The *Hofstaat* of seventeenth-century empresses was more strongly Italian and Spanish than was the emperors' establishment. Charles VI's Spanish adventure, and the Italian territories gained in compensation after the loss of the Spanish Succession, combined to strengthen the Iberian-Italian influences at court in Charles' reign. The later eighteenth-century court changed its orientation, increasingly conforming to the dominant French court style, while at the same time it adhered to traditional methods in strengthening its ties with the territories by incorporating them into household office.

The reigns of Ferdinand III, Leopold I, Joseph I, Charles VI, and Maria Theresa coincided with a long phase of growth of the Habsburg court, interrupted by troublesome successions halfway through both centuries, and truly rapid only in the recurring expansion of honorary office. The forms of honorary office changed, but the principle ruled supreme from the seventeenth century onwards. We do not find honorary *Hofdiener* in the later seventeenth-century *Verzeichnisse*; halfway through the eighteenth century, carvers and cupbearers disappeared, and the *Truchseß* only barely survived into the nineteenth century. Maria Theresa had to take measures to restore this charge and dignified service for the table at court. She achieved this by ruling that nobles had to apply for a position of *Truchseß* before being admitted to the status of councillor.[112] Other typically honorary offices, such as the traditional *Landeserbämter*, likewise were carefully maintained. Each of the important constituent parts of the Habsburg heritage had such offices, and Maria Theresa still thought it well advised to institute them when she acquired Galicia.[113] In addition to the ubiquitous *Kämmerer*, ideally from all parts of the monarchy, *Schematismen* for Maria Theresa's years list the *Ungarische aulae familiares*, specifically demonstrating the bond between the Hungarian elite and the Habsburgs.[114] The newly instituted Hungarian *Leibgarde* and the Milanese detachment served the same

112 Khevenhüller, *Tagebuch*, IV, pp. 57–58 (25 December 1756); see the lists of these honorary officers actually serving the empress' table around 1760 in HHStA OMeA Sr 184, no. 98: *Stabelmeister*, *Mundschenken*, *Truchseßen*, incidentally *Vorschneider*.

113 Though not in the traditional hereditary form, see Zolger, *Hofstaat*, pp. 13–14; Werner Rösener, 'Hofämter an mittelalterlichen Fürstenhöfen', *Deutsches Archiv für Erforschung des Mittelalters* 45 (1989), pp. 485–550. Du Tillet, *Recueil des Roys*, pp. 283, 285, 296, notes regional hereditary offices for Champagne, Bretagne, Berry, and Auvergne, though these seem to have led a somnolent existence.

114 See also HHStA ÄZA K 89 (1776–1779): 13 January 1777 'Note des ungarischen Hofkanzlers Esterhazy über die Ertheilung des Würde eines familiaris aulae an Gabriel Bazanyi, Assessor des Gerichtstafel des Biharer Komitats', similar notes follow on 14 February 1777, 17 October 1777, and 27 November 1778; other candidates were proposed by the Hungarian *Hofvizekanzler* Pálffy: 16 July 1779; 24 September 1779; 29 October 1779.

purposes. Joseph II's reforms, and revolutionary warfare, temporarily stopped the process, but it continued into the nineteenth century.

In the seventeenth century central administrative institutions did not keep up with the growth of the court. The intricate structures of the monarchy make it difficult to unequivocally identify these agencies. The *Österreichische Hofkanzlei*, founded in 1620 by Ferdinand II as an institution functioning independently alongside the older *Reichshofkanzlei*, and two other sixteenth-century institutions, the *Hofkammer* overseeing finances, and the *Hofkriegsrat* responsible for warfare, need to be included. Can we say the same for the *Reichshofrat* and *Reichshofkanzlei*, with their unmistakable orientation on the Holy Roman Empire? The dominant impact of the imperial title for the Habsburg court and the politically relevant litigations of the *Reichshofrat* make inclusion necessary. The important Bohemian chancellery and its less significant Hungarian counterpart, though located in Vienna since the 1620s, had a regional focus, and I will omit them here. *Verzeichnisse*, finally, habitually include the Vienna-based institutions for Lower Austria, a choice that cannot be followed here.

Verzeichnisse of the late 1670s give 25–30 councillors for the *geheime Rat*, 6–8 of whom were member of the *Konferenz*, or inner council; the *Hofkanzlei* employed 15 secretaries, *referendarii* and *expeditores* in addition to its director, the chancellor, who doubled as a conference minister. Another 18 may be added for the separate Inner- and Upper-Austrian chancelleries operating within its compass until 1720.[115] The *Reichshofrat* included *c.* 25 persons, supported by a chancellery of 34. The *Hofkammer* with a council of 19, was assisted by a staff of *c.* 48 (including the *Buchhalterey*); the 10 councillors of the *Hofkriegsrat* employed another 31 persons. Together these councils and chancelleries numbered *c.* 225 – no match for the household staffs. The aggregate of councillors, secretaries, and other staffs in the central administrative gremia around the imperial court rose to slightly more than 400 in Leopold's last years. By 1705, expansion of the councils was evident: *geheime Räte* now numbered 164, and *Hofkammerräte* 73, yet these charges were largely honorary, and cost money without bringing benefit to the services.[116] The inflation of honorary offices in the administration closely matched that in the household, for councillors and chamberlains alike, the labels 'true' and 'titular' were used. In 1729, Küchelbecker declined

[115] See, for example, ÖNB, cod. 14209, fols. 68v–69v; my thanks go to Stefan Sienell for this reference, and his information on the chancelleries.

[116] Compare the doubts expressed earlier on the subject of expanding numbers of councillors by Leopold to his ambassador in Spain, Count Pötting: *Privatbriefe Kaiser Leopold I an den Grafen F. E. Pötting 1662–1673*, ed. A. F. Pribram and M. Landwehr von Pragenau, 2 vols. Fontes Rerum Austriacarum LVI–LVII (Vienna 1903–1904), I, 156–157 (2 September 1665); Rinck, *Leopold*, pp. 222–233, including 164 *würckliche geheime Räthe* and 4 *titulares*; the 1702 *Schematismus* gives 139 'true' councillors, and 5 *titulares*; Küchelbecker, *Allerneueste Nachricht*, cap. IX, pp. 299–338; see HHStA OMeA 184, no. 53a, for the 325 'true' and 33 'titular' councillors in 1767. Brigitte Holl, *Hofkammerpräsident Gundaker Thomas Graf Starhemberg und die österreichische Finanzpolitik der Barockzeit (1703–1715)*, Archiv für österreichische Geschichte 132 (Vienna 1976), pp. 200, 352: a decision of 1 September 1705 reduced the 73 to 31, yet in 1717 we again find 67 *Hofkammerräthe*; see also Dickson, *Finance and Government*, I, p. 219.

to list the councillors, giving only the names of the 48 who could plausibly expect to be asked to take part in the deliberations of the *Konferenz* (the inner council of government) or any of its less permanent variants (usually not admitting more than six councillors at any time). Moreover, he stressed that unpaid *titulares*, holding only the *Praedicata* or the *Expectanz* of a function, were more prevalent in the bureaucracy than in the household.[117] Omitting the expansion of the councillors, we still find that the various institutions expanded at a leisurely pace, somewhat more quickly only in the financial administration, the *Hofkammer* reaching 159, including 57 councillors, in 1702.[118] Important changes were to follow during and immediately after the War of Spanish Succession. From 1716, a *Finanz Conferenz* and the *Ministerial Banco Deputation* were added to the *Hofkammer* – changes reflecting the need to improve credit and accounting. Following the war, new councils for Spain (later Italy) and the Austrian Low Countries were instituted. In the course of Charles' reign, the administrative staffs expanded steadily, but they never approached the numbers of the household.[119] Only with the great reform of 1749 did this change. Regional agents of government, particularly those connected to taxation, did seem to have reached far more impressive numbers: Küchelbecker cites 40,000 *Cammer-Officianten und Bedienten*, an estimate topping the staff of the French *ferme générale*.[120]

Haugwitz's reforms, and the continuation of administrative reform under Maria Theresa and Joseph greatly increased the numbers of salaried officials of government, as well as the pace of law-making. Peacetime ordinary net revenue, somewhat improved in Charles's reign, increased sharply after the Theresian reforms – from *c.* 20 million fl in 1717 it rose to *c.* 55 million fl in 1782, testifying to the success of reform.[121] The institutions created in 1749, and their reshuffling in later years, have been traced elsewhere, and need not concern us here.[122] By 1763 these more effective and specialised institutions of central government stood at 905, by 1781 they reached 1,626, in 1789 they had climbed to 1,724, in 1796 to 1,888. In the decades after 1740 the household was at a low ebb, while the rejuvenated bureaucracy thrived. Both sectors expanded in the 1770s, the household with guards maintaining the upper hand until the end of Maria Theresa's reign. Joseph II's reforms did not hit the court as severely as may

117 Küchelbecker, *Allerneueste Nachricht*, p. 160.

118 *Schematismus* 1702, giving another 18 for the *Hofbuchhalterei*.

119 *ÖZV*, I, 2, p. 237, gives 167 for the *Hofkammer*, and 61 for the *Hofkriegsrat* after the War of Spanish Succession, and suggests further growth; see the lists in HKA, HZAB 1715–1720/158, giving 418 persons for *Hofkammer*, *Hofkriegsrat*, and chancelleries.

120 Küchelbecker, *Allerneueste Nachricht*, p. 322.

121 Dickson, *Finance and Government*, II, appendix, Table 3.1; cf. Bérenger's positive assessment of finances in Charles VI's years, 'finances de l'Autriche', p. 227.

122 See Dickson, *Finance and Government*, I, p. 213, Table 9.1: institutions in 1740, 1749, 1762; and his 'Monarchy and Bureaucracy', p. 326, for developments in 1781–1796.

have been expected: the household with guards counted *c.* 1,676 in 1789, and had again risen to 1,881 in 1796 – almost exactly matching the institutions of central government, 1,888 in the same year.[123] Comparing the numbers of *c.* 1700, 1750, and 1800, however, it is evident that the connections of household, government, and army had undergone fundamental changes in the second half of the eighteenth century.

We can easily recognise the staffs of the emperor's household in the categories of civil expenditure recorded in the *Hofzahlamtsbücher.* In the seventeenth century, provisions for kitchen and cellar together demanded an average 26 per cent of the budget for the household proper; fodder and other necessities for horses and transport took 20 per cent, the chapel almost 10 per cent. Hunting and falconry, illumination and furnishings in the chamber consistently figure in the accounts with smaller shares. The ordinary wages (*Besoldungen*) in the staffs, councils, and chancelleries form another major category in the expenditure of the household proper; they were long supplemented by payments for cloths, fuel, sustenance; support for aged servants, for their widows. The remainder of establishments of previous rulers and the upkeep of other households within the dynasty form another habitual item in the records. Gratuities, minuscule to gigantic, for courtiers and servants at all levels of the hierarchy, are recorded under a range of headings. In the monthly specifications of the ruler's secret expenses, or *geheime Cammer*, we find a variety of payments made to the ruler mostly for unspecified purposes, but also rewards for courtiers, and incidental costs for court ceremonies.[124] In addition to this aggregate of costs connected to the court, civil expenditure included embassies and couriers, the post office, expenses necessary to secure the extraction of revenues, debt service, and the inevitable *extraordinaria*. In a simplified form we find the same categories in instructions for the *Hofkammer*, frequently added to the manuscript *Verzeichnisse* of the 1670s.[125] For the first half of the seventeenth century, the heading *Besoldungen*, or wages, included pay for councils and chancelleries as well as for the household; from the second half of the century the wages and expenses of the administrative institutions are specified.

We cannot determine without detailed further analysis of the pensions or secret costs in the *Hofzahlamtsbücher* which part of them may be seen as pertaining to the court; yet until the reforms of Maria Theresa it surely was a major share,

[123] Dickson, 'Monarchy and Bureaucracy', pp. 326 (tables of internal government), 335 (numbers cited), 336 (table of central departments), 340. Compare the figures from the *schematismen* given above. Yet note the extremely low spending on the court in 1784, see Dickson, *Finance and Government*, II, p. 386, Table 3.10.

[124] See, for example, HKA, HZAB 1675/119, fols. 77–97; Geheime cammer, no. 31, fol. 81r: costs connected to the Maundy Thursday pedilavium; no. 75, fol. 87v: a diamant ring for Montecucoli; no. 108, fol. 92v: 30,000 fl for the imperial *Cammerzahlmeister*. It is frequently unclear whether such sums are connected either to earlier financial services of courtiers, or were simply a reward for loyal service.

[125] For example, in ÖNB cod. 8025 (dated 1658, but giving the same figures as the following late 1670s *Verzeichnisse*), fols. 4v–8v; Cod 14233 fols. 86v–87r; Ser n. 1849; AVA Harrach, MS 145.

and only under Joseph was the payment of pensions dramatically altered.[126] The *extraordinaria* frequently list expenses for mourning at court, or other court-related outlay, but usually include a variety of other costs, not even necessarily civil.[127] The *Hofzahlamtsbücher* did not list all court-related expenditure: thus we do not find the costs of Joseph I's expanding *Hofstaat* in this invaluable source after 1694, nor do they seem to be taken into account elsewhere. Within the various categories of court expenses, variations are huge, and not always easy to explain without contextual detail. Journeys to the urban centres of monarchy and empire for coronations of *Erbhuldigungen*; visits of electors or other princes, and various other randomly occurring occasions made great outlay inevitable. The *Küchenmeister* in 1685 explained the huge increase in expenses by pointing to the visit of the Bavarian elector.[128] As in France, the volatility of expenditures, and the concomitant division between ordinary and extraordinary finances further complicate the situation. Warfare necessitated extraordinary taxes, such as the notorious *Türkensteuer*; yet imperial coronations or weddings could likewise be financed by extraordinary revenues – gifts or *Vermögenssteuer*. For Leopold's imperial coronation, the estates contributed an extra 307,000 fl; for his first marriage in 1666 they supplemented an initial *Verehrung* with another gift of 939,000 fl.[129] The emperor's desires and tastes, most frequently for court opera, or for splendid jewellery, could wreak havoc in a budget always on the verge of collapsing.[130] Leopold I's bridal jewellery for his first Spanish bride cost the emperor ten times as much as the construction of the *Mariensäule am Hof*; in 1705 Joseph I, to the distress of his *Hofkammerpresident* Gundaker Thomas Starhemberg, acquired a diamond for 240,000 fl – substantially more than the

[126] Maria Theresa's largesse is stressed in Hans Wagner's detailed article based on the HKA Kammerzahlamt: 'Royal Graces and Legal Claims: The Pension Payments of Maria Theresa and their Withdrawal by Joseph II', in *Intellectual and Social Developments in the Habsburg Empire from Maria Theresa to World War I. Essays Dedicated to Robert A. Kann*, ed. Stanley Winters, and Joseph Held, East European Monographs 11 (New York and London 1973), pp. 5–29. Courtiers and court servants, Wagner's data suggest, were still conspicuous among the beneficiaries.

[127] *Cammerclagen*, and provisions paid to servants for clothes of mourning, are included in the *extra-ordinaria* of, for example, HKA HZAB 190/135, 1693/138; yet HKA HZAB 1706/148 and HZAB 1713/155 include huge payments to Barcelona; we usually find the 'Behaimbische zuraittungsposten' in the *extraordinaria*. The 12,200 Gulden Rheinisch granted to Gualdo Priorato 'Kaijs. Historico' for writing his history of Leopold I are likwise to be found in this category, see HZAB 1669/112, fols. 257r. Without further analysis we cannot add the *extraordinaria* to court expenses.

[128] HKA, HZAB 1685/130, fol. 69r–v.

[129] Franz Hadamowsky, *Barocktheater am Wiener Kaiserhof. Mit einem Spielplan (1625–1740)* (Vienna 1955), p. 35, citing HKA HZAB 1666, fol. 440.

[130] Adam Wolf, *Die Hofkammer unter Leopold I* (oktoberhefte des Jahrganges 1853 der Sitzungsberichte der Philos.-histor. Classe der kais. Akademie der Wissenschaften, XI. Band, pp. 440 ff., but separately published pp. 1–47), p. 19, on the gifts of the estates for coronations; Franz von Mensi, *Die Finanzen Österreichs von 1701 bis 1740 nach archivalischen Quellen dargestellt* (Vienna 1890), pp. 29–31, on *Vermögenssteuer*; n. 2 on p. 561: 'Wenn wir unter "Staatsbankerott" schon die momentane Zahlungsunfähigkeit des Staates verstehen, d.h. Die Unmöglichkeit, jede fällige Zahlung termingemäss zu leisten, so bietet Österreich in der ersten Hälfte des vorigen Jahrhunderts allerdings, von kurzen Unterbrechungen abgesehen, das Bild des fortgesetzten Bankerottes. In dieser Beziehung unterscheiden sich die einzelnen Perioden mehr quantitativ als qualitativ.'

entire annual budget for the court's kitchen.[131] Finally, emperors could reward loyal service, usually compensated by meagre ordinary wages that frequently went unpaid, by dispensing sums wholly incommensurate with their limited budgetary leeway.[132]

Many questions remain. A tripling of expenses for kitchen and cellar occurred between 1615 and 1622, immediately followed by a 2.5 increase from 1622 to 1624. The collapse of 1615–1620, and the rapid inflation of the early 1620s, may partly explain this phenomenon, also visible in expenses for the *Fuettermaister*.[133] Yet whereas the latter's expenses soon dwindled after the peak of 1624, the costs for kitchen and cellar remained high in the reigns of both Ferdinand II and Ferdinand III – the levels in the latter's last years would be reached again only in the early eighteenth century. These high figures may indicate a wider hospitality at court, coinciding with the proliferation of chamberlains in Ferdinand II's early years, and the steady growth of their numbers in Ferdinand III's reign. The development of the court's numbers and costs was frequently disturbed by warfare and succession crisis. The figures in the *Hofzahlamtsbücher* more forcefully suggest a decline in Leopold's first decades than any lasting reduction of the court's hospitality during the Thirty Years' War.[134] This makes the expansion in Leopold's last decades, and its prolongation in Charles' years, even more noteworthy. Maria Theresa's reign shows the same dynamics of decline and restoration, though her initiatives led not only to a recovery of the household, but simultaneously to a structural change of the court's style and the competence of the administration.

Assessing the proportion of court spending in the state budget is exceedingly difficult for the Austrian Habsburgs, as there was no such thing as a state budget. Dickson, examining the eighteenth-century situation with great acuity, warns against easy conclusions about opaque materials; his warning surely is even more relevant for the preceding centuries.[135] The accounting of civil expenses

[131] Friedrich Polleroß, 'Zur Repräsentation der Habsburger in der bildenden Kunst', in *Welt des Barock*, ed. Elisabeth Kovacs and Rupert Feuchtmüller (Vienna 1986), pp. 87–104, here at p. 91; Holl, *Starhemberg*, p. 209; see the budget for the *Küchen* in HKA HZAB 1704/146: 158,000 and 1706/148: 215,400.

[132] For example, Joseph I's 300,000 fl gift to Eugene in 1710, to which Charles VI later added another 100,000, see Holl, *Starhemberg*, pp. 208, 347 and other examples throughout the book.

[133] On confiscations, *Münzrecht*, and inflation, see the explanations in Schwarz, *Imperial Privy Council*, p. 194.

[134] The figures cited somewhat loosely in Holl, *Starhemberg*, p. 81 and n. 9, p. 197 and n. 5, support the decline after Ferdinand, and the rise in Leopold's later years: for Ferdinand III's last years 1,723,436 fl; for the beginning of Leopold's rule 1,372,401 (a high estimate, given the results presented here) and for his later years 2,866,908 or 2,864,908; 1,215,865 for 1672 (Mikoletzky) and 1,806,940 for 1705 (Mensi). Wolf, on p. 14, gives 1,013,000 court-related expenses for 1670, yet on p. 16 he gives a wholly different indication, followed on p. 31 by a low estimate of the average *Gesamthofausgaben*: 450,000–600,000, correct only until the early 1690s and excluding pensions and other households. Wolf's data for 1670 more or less match Bérenger's Table in 'Finances de l'Autriche', p. 228, with the military expenditure he cites, 1,375,440, the percentage of court-related expenditure for 1670 would amount to *c.* 68 per cent of the civil budget I (using the *c.* 1,504,600 in Wolf, not Bérenger's 1,400,000) and of total expenditure (2,880,040).

[135] See Dickson, *Finance and Government*, II, appendix C, pp. 360–364.

and revenues was separated from the military budgets; the civil budget was administered by the *Hofzahlmeister* (court paymaster) the military budget by the *Kriegszahlmeister* (war paymaster). Financial responsibilities were divided between the *Hofkammer* and the *Hofkriegsrat*, the latter administering the contributions from the various diets to finance military expenditure. Financial accounting was even less orderly than in France, and we recognise Necker's worries about the proliferation of treasurers in a 1714 complaint of *Hofkammerpräsident* Starhemberg, bemoaning that the administration counted 'fast so viel Zahlmaister wie Amtleute'.[136]

The *Hofzahlamtsbücher* in the *Hofkammerarchiv* listing civil revenue and expenditure, usually include substantial payments to the *Kriegszahlmeister*'s office, debt service connected to warfare, and sometimes payments for weaponry or fortifications. By deducting the military expenses in the civil budget we obtain a total of civil expenditure. The court usually was its major item, with a share varying between 26 per cent and 81 per cent in a selection of 24 years between 1615 and 1714 – an average of 53 per cent.[137] In the first half of the eighteenth century, civil revenues rose and the less rapidly rising costs of the household and pensions varied from 25 per cent to 47 per cent of civil expenditures.[138] Sources on military expenditure are scant, and for most of the early modern period, we cannot confidently determine the proportion of households and pensions in a fictional 'general' budget. The available materials indicate extreme variability, with the costs of the court and pensions ranging from less than 3 per cent in the war year 1704, to a peak of 31 per cent in 1651 – the first year with full payment of wages after a protracted war, and the very year a major restoration of the court was initiated.

In the first half of the seventeenth century household expenditures and pensions together remained below 500,000 fl in most years. In 1651 and 1653 expenditures rose to more than 1.2 and 1.3 million respectively, but by 1655 they had dropped to less than 800,000 fl. The average expenditure for selected years from 1610 to 1655 was 680,993 fl, or around 19 per cent of civil and military expenditure combined. From 1662 to 1693 average court expenditure rose to 1,116,717 fl, now representing 13 per cent of total expenditure. It further increased to an average 1,854,885 fl for the years 1697–1714, peaking in 1714 with 2,788,596 fl. In these years, however, military expenditure steeply rose, and the share of the court in the overall expenditures declined to *c.* 8 per cent. An average of 13 per cent emerges for all years where information on military expenditure was available

136 Holl, *Starhemberg*, p. 342.

137 See my spreadsheets based on the HZAB at http://www.le.ac.uk/hi/bon/ESFDB/index.html. In deducting the payments to the *Kriegszahlamt* and the *Proviandamt* from the total expenditure in the HZAB, we may still leave a varying margin of military expenses in the civil budget, included in the *extraordinaria* and the payment of debts – studying the breakdown of the totals given for these in the HZAB was infeasible for my book.

138 Mensi, *Finanzen Oesterreichs*, Tables on pp. 746–747.

in the period 1610–1714.[139] In the eighteenth century percentages ranged from a substantial 14.6 per cent in 1729 to a modest 4.2 per cent in 1784 – when Joseph II's reforms were in full swing. With an average of 9.5 per cent, the share of the court in the budget had declined somewhat; yet this apparent decline was not reflected in the absolute costs of the court: it can be explained mostly by the growing costs of salaries for the administrative staffs, usually surpassing the costs of the household in the second half of the century.[140]

The emperor's household always represented a larger share of aggregate court expenditure than did other recurring items. As in the French case, pensions were substantial. The costs for secondary households, however, were relatively low: only in the years after 1700, with the subsequent deaths of Leopold and Joseph, and an accumulation of dowager-empresses, did they represent a share comparable with the French situation. Building activities may not have been covered by my selection of years, and the relevant costs may be hidden in other sources. Nevertheless, it is clear that the Habsburgs did not engage in major efforts in the grand style of Versailles. Nor did they employ large numbers of soldiers around court. In the eighteenth century, the share of pensions as well as that of the other households in the overall court costs further declined in Vienna.[141] The contrast between Versailles and Vienna becomes fully clear only if we connect the total outlay of these two courts. While it is problematical to establish a reliable basis for comparison of *livres Tournois* (lt) and *Gulden Rheinisch* (fl), the changing silver content of these moneys of account in the course of the seventeenth century suggests we can roughly double the Habsburg amounts in fl to compare them with the French amounts in lt. If we do so, a striking discrepancy emerges: in the seventeenth century, total Habsburg budgets seem to have amounted to less than one-sixth of total Bourbon budgets. While Habsburg revenues and expenditures rose markedly after the reforms of 1749,

139 See my overview at http://www.le.ac.uk/hi/bon/ESFDB/index.html, with HZAB date for the years 1610, 1615, 1616, 1622, 1631, 1633, 1640, 1647, 1651, 1653, 1655, 1662, 1669, 1675, 1686, 1690, 1693, 1697, 1699, 1710, 1704, 1706, 1710, 1713, 1714. Information on military expenditure, allowing me to provide tentative percentages, was found for 1610, 1622, 1651, 1655, 1662, 1669, 1675, 1686, 1690,1693, 1699, 1704, 1706, 1710, 1714. For 1610 and 1623, I rely on the data kindly provided by Géza Pálffy; see also his *Gemeinsam gegen die Osmanen. Ausbau und Funktion der Grenzfestungen in Ungarn im 16. und 17. Jahr-hundert* (Budapest and Vienna 2001), Kat.-Nr. II-9a: pp. 13–14. Note that I use military expenditure for 1623 whereas I list court expenditure in 1622. For other years I have used the data provided by Jean Bérenger, *Finances et Absolutisme Autrichien dans la seconde moitié du XVIIe siècle* (Paris 1975), pp. 293–294, and his 'A propos d'un ouvrage récent: les finances de l'autriche à l'époque baroque (1650–1740)', *Histoire, economie et société*, 3, 2 (1984), pp. 221–245, at p. 228. Again, the years of court and military expenditure do not always match, nor is the latter always established beyond doubt: the percentages may serve as an indication only.

140 Dickson, *Finance and Government*, II, pp. 385–387, Table 3.10, including pensions and court for 1729 (14.6 per cent), 1749 (8.6 per cent), 1752 (6.1 per cent), 1754 (8.9 per cent), 1763 (10.1 per cent), 1767 (8.9 per cent), 1768 (8.5 per cent), 1769 (8.3 per cent), 1770 (11.2 per cent), 1771 (9.7 per cent), 1772 (9.7 per cent), 1773 (11.3 per cent), 1774 (10.3 per cent), 1775 (11.2 per cent), 1778 (10.7 per cent), 1784 (4.2 per cent).

141 See Dickson, *Finance and Government*, II, pp. 385–387, Table 3.10. As Dickson did not include the other households as a separate category, the percentages cannot easily be compared, nor is it likely that the categories used by me and by Dickson are similar. The general development, however, seems well-attested. See Morineau, 'Budgets', pp. 314–315, and the other sources cited above for French costs in the eighteenth century.

Table 5a. *Average, minimum, and maximum expenditure on the main household, secondary households, and pensions at the Habsburg court 1610–1714 in Gulden Rheinisch (years in brackets)*[a]

	1610–1655			1662–1693			1697–1714		
	Average	Maximum	Minimum	Average	Maximum	Minimum	Average	Maximum	Minimum
Main household	458,275	731,734 (1653)	271,097 (1610)	518,025	670,757 (1690)	353,869 (1662)	920,789	1,606,571 (1714)	620,068 (1704)
Secondary households	35,328	105,020 (1640)	0	108,884	206,259 (1669)	62,877 (1675)	300,930	838,403 (1713)	28,322 (1710)
Pensions	187,390	531,341 (1653)	19,959 (1610)	489,808	656,025 (1675)	383,473 (1693)	633,166	783,487 (1706)	352,303 (1704)
Total expenditure	680,993	1,319,651 (1653)	303,372 (1610)	1,116,717	1,291,598 (1690)	898,230 (1662)	1,854,885	2,788,596 (1714)	1,004,385 (1704)

Table 5b. *The share of expenditures on the main household, secondary households, and pensions in total Habsburg court expenditure 1610–1714*

Component	1610–1655	1662–1693	1697–1714
Main household	67%	46%	50%
Secondary households	5%	10%	16%
Pensions	28%	44%	34%
Total:	100%	100%	100%

[a] See my materials at the European State Finance Database (ESFDB) http://www.le.ac.uk/hi/bon/ESFDB/index.html.

they never came close to the higher French budgets. In 1775, for example, the Habsburgs spent 46,780,374 fl; taking into account the changed values of lt and fl, this represented *c.* 30 per cent of French expenditure (411,400,000 lt). Thus, the percentages given above should be evaluated with this in mind: Habsburg court expenditure as expressed in percentages of a total budget represented a share of a budget slowly expanding from *c.* 15 per cent to *c.* 30 per cent of the French budget.[142]

My tentative discussion of budgets and court expenditure sidesteps many thorny complications inherent in this subject, and cannot be seen as more than a crude attempt to indicate major differences. Yet the conclusions pertaining to the court itself are relevant and appear well-founded. With other matters pertaining to numbers and costs, they will be considered in the conclusion of the next chapter.

142 Silver contents of the lt can be found in Nathalis de Wailly, *Mémoire sur les variations de la livre Tournois depuis le règne de Saint-Louis jusqu' à l'établissement de la monnaie décimale* Extrait des Mémoires de l'Académie des Inscriptions et des Belles Lettres, XXI, 2ème partie (Paris 1857) – they are available on the ESFDB website; compare George Frêche and Geneviève Frêche, *Les prix des grains des vins et des légumes à Toulouse (1486–1868) Extraits des Mercuriales suivis d'une bibliographie d'histoire des prix* (Paris 1967), pp. 127, 131, for the silver contents of Livres Tournois, mostly, but not entirely conforming to the range given in the ESFDB. For the fl silver contents are given in Alfred Pribram, Rudolf Geyer, and Franz Koran, eds., *Materialien zur geschichte der Preise und Löhne in Österreich* (Vienna 1938), I, pp. 28–29. These data would allow a more precise approach, based on the changing relationship of lt and fl, hovering between 1 fl = 1.7 lt and 1 fl = 2.3 lt between 1550 and 1715, with the Gulden relatively stronger in the eighteenth century, from 1727 to 1747 1 fl = 2.83 lt, from 1750 to 1790 1 fl = 2.63 lt.

CHAPTER 4

Status and income

The major charges in the household were held by nobles, yet as a community of people living and working together, the court was never an exclusively or even primarily noble domain. What were the functional hierarchies among the various levels of servants and courtiers, and how were these reflected in remuneration? Hierarchies were hotly debated at court in the sixteenth, seventeenth, and eighteenth centuries, and many attempts were made to spell out the position of courtiers and servants at court. Ceremony, always the testing ground for hierarchical conflict, will be discussed in a separate chapter; here, I will focus on the hierarchies among the staffs and their superiors, and the level of autonomy of the staffs. Finally, I will discuss the forms of remuneration, and give an overview of the ordinary wages, usually only a minor part of the material benefits of service at court.

FUNCTIONAL HIERARCHIES

In France, writers such as Jean du Tillet and Charles Loyseau, defining which court charges were to be held by nobles only, and which offices secured entry into the hereditary nobility, did their best to create order from chaos. For the highest echelons their task was relatively simple. First came the *grands officiers de la couronne*, the supreme dignitaries of the realm. Henry III confirmed the status of chancellor, constable, marshals, steward, and chamberlain in 1582, by collectively making them *grands officiers de la couronne* together with the *amiral*. The *grand écuyer* attained the same supreme status in 1589; the *grand maître de l'artillerie* in 1601.[1] The *grand aumônier*, heading the *maison ecclésiastique* in the household, was not unanimously granted this supreme rank, but he indisputably

[1] The ancient office of *connétable* was abolished in 1626, together with that of the *amiral*. Louis XIV restored the admiralty and its elevated rank in 1669, in favour of the comte de Vermandois, his illegitimate son. The admiralty, held by the comte de Toulouse and his descendants, the Bourbon-Penthièvre, would remain in the hands of *fils légitimés* until the end of the *ancien régime*. The office of *colonel général de l'infanterie*, created in 1584 for Henry III's favourite the duc d'Epernon, was abolished in 1661 after the death of the incumbent (to be restored for Condé in 1780). Boucher, *Cour de Henri III*, p. 60, mentions 1589 as the date of elevation of the *grand écuyer*; compare Solnon in *DGS*, p. 1109.

belonged to the next category of great household dignitaries, the *commensaux du premier ordre*.[2]

The *commensaux du premier ordre* were noble officers ideally heading autonomous staffs and swearing loyalty to the king in person, such as the *grand prévôt de France*[3] or the *grand veneur*, or officers heading semi-autonomous departments within staffs, such as the *capitaine de la porte*, or the *grand fauconnier* and *grand louvetier*.[4] There was some mobility: Henry III promoted the *grand maréchal des logis* to this rank, and in 1585 did likewise for the new office of *grand maître des cérémonies*. In 1669 Louis XIV created the senior office of *grand maître de la garderobe*, a charge earlier shared by two or four officers.[5] By that time, however, the label had lost relevance for ranking at court: the highest group below the *grands officiers de la couronne* consisted basically of the senior charges taking orders from the king directly. This upper layer was typically indicated by the label *grand*, yet their noble substitutes and daily stand-ins, labelled *premier* and *ordinaire* respectively, could complicate the hierarchy, nor were criteria ever wholly clear.

In the high steward's staff, the *grand échanson*, *grand panetier*, and *grand écuyer tranchant* were included among the *commensaux du premier ordre*, yet they were the *grand maître*'s honorary deputies, and did not have their own staffs. The *premier maître de l'hôtel*, and his proxy, the *maître d'hôtel ordinaire*, frequently fulfilling the high steward's tasks, fitted uneasily into this hierarchy, and tended to encroach upon the rights of the three traditional table servants. The *grand maître des cérémonies* swore loyalty to the high steward, and had only a diminutive staff. Other staffs show similar complications. The *premier écuyer* heading the *petite écurie*, established in 1582 alongside the *grande écurie* to accommodate the court's newly developed taste for carriages, did not unequivocally belong to the first order. He stood uncomfortably between two positions: deputy to the greater dignitary, such as the *premier maître d'hôtel* and the *premier aumônier*, and head of his own staff. Another *premier écuyer*, commanding in the *grande écurie*, was created in the course of the seventeenth century, further confusing the hierarchy.[6]

[2] Père Anselme did grant the grand almoner this rank, see *Histoire généalogique et chronologique*, VIII, p. 223.

[3] In 1578, Henry III had turned the *grand prévôt de l'hôtel* into *grand prévôt de France*, a promotion parallel to that of the *grand maître des cérémonies*, possibly part of the measures taken by Henry to secure support against the ambitions of Henry de Guise, his *grand maître*. On the promotion, and the first incumbent, François du Plessis-Richelieu, the cardinal-minister's father, see Le Roux, *Faveur du roi*, pp. 186–188, on Guillaume Pot and his new charge, *ibid*, pp. 184–185.

[4] And the short-lived *grand vautrayeur* added by Henry IV, heading a staff of 14 persons, see Salvadori, *Chasse*, p. 195.

[5] See BN MS f 7859 fol. 220v: 'reglement des fonctions de Grand Mtre et Mtre de la Garderobe du 26 novembre 1669'. The charge was initially held by Chaumont de Guitry (Dangeau writes: Quitri); Soyecourt, *maître de la garderobe*, was allowed to purchase the office of *grand veneur* in compensation. From October 1672, François VII de la Rochefoucauld was *grand maître de la garderobe*, and the office would remain vested in this house – his son sold the office of *grand veneur* held by the duke since 1679, upon his father's death. See Sourches, *Mémoires*, I, p. 196, n. 3, on Guitry and Soyecourt.

[6] In AN O 1 872 we find the first explicit reference to the *premier écuyer* of the *grande écurie* only in the 1664 *état*; compare O 1 120, fol. 75: the 'creation de la charge de premier ecuyer de la grande ecurie' on 31 March

The *petite écurie*, moreover, was in several respects tied to the steward, the *premier écuyer* never pledged loyalty to the *grand écuyer*, and his staff was listed partly in the inner *maison*, partly in the separate *états* for the *écuries*. In the regency M. le Duc, Condé high steward, and soon Louis XV's first minister, also obtained sole responsibility for the budget of the *petite écurie*.[7] In the chamber, we find a striking accumulation of high court officers: the *grand chambellan* was assisted not only by the *premiers gentilshommes de la chambre*, four since 1618; after 1669 the *grand maître de la garderobe* and his two *maîtres* strengthened the semi-independence of the wardrobe.[8] The serving *gentilshommes*, moreover, took the oaths of the personnel of the chamber.

Even more diffuse was the next category of *commensaux du deuxième ordre*: typically the noble office to be held by many persons at the same time, such as *maîtres d'hôtel, gentilshommes servants, gentilshommes à bec de corbin, écuyers* in the *écurie* or *cuisine, archers des gardes du corps, gentilshommes de la vénerie, gentilshommes ordinaires.* In this league we may also place the *aumôniers* of the chapel, never wholly commensurate with worldly hierarchies, they were frequently of high birth, and candidates for bishoprics. Yet the same broad category also included a variety of other offices not necessarily held by nobles such as valets of the chamber and the wardrobe, *maîtres des requêtes*, secretaries, ushers, *portmanteaux*. Indeed, the ordinance of Blois (1579), reserving the upper ranks at court for the nobility, implicitly shows that many of these charges were routinely available for *roturiers*.[9]

Theoretically below this predominantly noble layer, but in practice often occupying an influential position at court, we find specialists such as medical doctors, apothecaries, surgeons, instrument-makers, mathematicians, distillers, librarians, historians, poets, theatre engineers, musicians, jewellers, goldsmiths, joiners, and the like. Their special skills frequently entailed proximity to the ruler, and allowed them to break through accepted hierarchies. Less highly skilled artisans were situated among the lower servants, kitchen boys, errand-runners, labourers, and artisans together forming the *commensaux du troisième ordre*: a

1773 following the abolition of the charge after the death of Sainte-Maure in 1763. Reytier, *Les écuries royales*, pp. 61–65, discusses the hierarchies among the *écuyers*, and lists them from the later seventeenth century onwards, on pp. 90–95.

7 On the *serment*, see below; on M. le Duc and the budget, see Blanquie, 'Dans la main', pp. 244–245.

8 The *gentilshommes de la chambre* were created by Francis I in 1515 in addition to the valets; after the abolition of the charge of *chambrier* in 1544–1545 two *premiers gentilshommes* came to the fore. From the reign of Louis XIII onwards four *premiers gentilshommes* served each for one year in alternation; in Henry III's 1585 *règlement* as printed in *AC*, p. 322, we find a reference to the *premier gentilhomme en quartier*; see the repeated overviews of the tasks and privileges of the *grand chambellan* and the *premiers gentilshommes* in AN, O 1 820, no. 8, more particularly on the *premiers gentilshommes* in O 1 822. Le Roux, *Faveur du roi*, discusses the various types of *gentilshommes* and *chambellans*, including the trusted favourites and semi-bodyguard of 45 gentlemen (pp. 519–522), of which we find a remnant of 26 *gentilshommes ordinaires* in the seventeenth-century *états*. Voltaire held this honorific charge in the eighteenth century. These *gentilshommes* were hardly relevant for chamber routines.

9 Loyseau, *Cinq livres*, p. 228; F. Isambert, *Recueil général des anciennes lois françaises depuis l'an 420, jusqu'à la révolution de 1789* (Paris 1829), XIV, no. 103, pp. 380–463, for the *ordonnance de Blois*, with the relevant articles on pp. 438–439.

numerous, colourful, and distinctly non-noble bunch that nevertheless enjoyed the privileges of the *commensaux*. In the *sept offices*, *chefs*, *écuyers de cuisine*, or *sommeliers* commanded their *aides* and *sommiers*, assisted by a legion of *hâteurs*, *potagers*, and *galopins*. Anywhere in the household we find *lacquais*, *huissiers*, and *valets*; *marchands*, *artisans*, and *gens de métier* proliferated in the *fourrière* as well as in the wardrobe. This third layer of the hierarchy, providing the actual instead of the honorary services in the household, was far more numerous than the other two layers. The inflation of honorary office could temporarily shift this balance, and Louis XIV's redefinition of court office may have changed it more permanently: from a numerical perspective, however, it is never justified to picture the household as a gathering of nobles.

Loyseau also suggested another method to discriminate among those serving at court: *officiers domestiques* held *charges* that conferred rights which could not simply be taken away; others held only *commissions*, performing their tasks as simple employees. This hierarchy did not fit the three orders of *commensaux*, and neither of the divisions can truly convey the dynamics of the court. Indeed, there was much movement between the groups. Privileges of the *commensaux* were frequently withdrawn, granted again, or redefined.[10] Only in the course of the reign of Louis XIV was the notion of a privileged upper layer of *officiers domestiques* versus a less distinct and less privileged group of servants more structurally founded in practice. A series of edicts around 1700 granted valets, ushers, and *garçons* of the king's chamber and wardrobe the quality of *écuyer*, whereas other lower servants as well as specialised staff in the stables and the establishments for music or hunting had lost their status of *officiers domestiques* in the preceding phase of reforms, henceforth carrying out their tasks on the basis of commission. This redrawing of the borders between privileged court staff and commissioned labour cosmetically purged the ranks of the *commensaux*. The numbers, activities, and status of the groups serving at court without the benefit of a *charge*, and without the privileges of the *commensaux*, are more difficult to chart than those of the emerging upper structure of court servants.[11]

The secondary establishments within the dynasty, including those of the *princes du sang*, basically followed the same tripartite division, and the same development over time. Their male officers, however, rarely attained quite the same status as their peers in the central household, and the *grands officiers* were conspicuously lacking – this supreme level remained limited to the king's

[10] See the sections discussing the privileges of court servants in the printed *états*, for example Besongne, *Etat* 1669, pp. 315–326; *Etat* 1687, I, pp. 582–594; Loyseau, *Cinq livres*, pp. 227–235, and a printed volume specifically devoted to these rights, the 1720 *Code des commensaux*.

[11] See these edicts in the *Code des commensaux*, pp. 369–377; compare remarks about staff hired on the basis of commission, and not usually listed in the overviews of *officiers* in the last printed *état* of 1749, I, pp. 81–90 the chapel, and pp. 308–320 *musique de chambre*, pp. 395–399 for the *bâtimens*, and in II, p. 267, on staff in the *vénerie*: 'tous lesquels Officiers susdits ne sont que par & à la volonté de M. Le grand veneur, & la plupart sans gages fixes'. As only officiers received *gages ordinaires*, these additional persons were not necessarily listed in the enumerations of staff and their *gages*; compare the careful research of Reytier, in *Les écuries royales*, pp. 61–95.

household. For women, female households offered prestigious charges and chances not available in the *maison du roi*. In the queen's household, the *surintendante* and the *chevalier d'honneur* occupied somewhat comparable positions, acting as supreme officers for female and male staff respectively – as did the *Obersthofmeisterin* and the *Obersthofmeister* in the empress' establishment. With the *gouvernante des enfants de France*, the only female charge swearing loyalty to the king in person,[12] the *surintendante* and the two other senior noble women in the queen's establishment, the *première dame d'honneur* and the *dame d'atour*, were the highest ranking female officers at court. Ladies-in-waiting, previously styled *dames* or *filles d'honneur*, were christened *dames du palais* in 1674; twelve *dames* would henceforth serve the queen.[13] Such ladies enjoyed high rank, particularly those serving the queen, but also ladies in lesser establishments. The *première femme de chambre* was of some importance; other *femmes* and *lavandières* were clearly below her level. The *surintendante* was abolished after the death of Madame de Clermont in 1741, but reinstituted for Marie-Antoinette's friend the princesse de Lamballe in 1775.[14] The interval had blotted out previous practice, and no extensive written instructions existed. Mercy, the empress' ambassador to France, typically noted that:

> d'après les recherches faites sur la nature de cette place, il s'est trouvé que jusqu'à ces derniers temps, rien n'avait été bien fixé ni déterminé, soit sur la quotité des appointements d'une surintendante, soit sur le degré d'autorité qu'elle a à exercer sur la maison de la reine.

All officers serving the wider *famille royale* enjoyed the privileges of the king's *commensaux*, as did the staffs taking care of unoccupied *maisons royales*, and many among the purveyors and artisans loosely tied to the court.

The *officiers domestiques* in France did not seriously challenge the *grand maître*'s seniority. Among them, only the *grand chambellan* and the *grand écuyer*, usually presented as the second and third in rank respectively, shared the high steward's status as *grand officier de la couronne*. The *grand aumônier*, in charge of the *maison ecclésiastique*, and the *grand veneur*, most prestigious officer of the hunt, came next. The *grand fauconnier*, *grand louvetier*, *grand maître de la garderobe*, *grand*

12 *Mémoires du duc de Luynes sur la cour de Louis XV*, ed. L. Dussieux and Eud. Soulié (Paris 1860–1865), XIII, p. 133 (January 1754); *Journal inédit du duc de Croÿ, 1718–1784*, ed. Grouchy, Cottin, 4 vols. (Paris 1906–1907), II, p. 277, Mme de Guéménée's *serment* and Croÿ's comments.

13 See the articles 'dames d'honneur' and 'filles de la reine' by the chevalier de Jaucourt in the *Encyclopédie*.

14 Marie-Anne de Bourbon-Condé, Mademoiselle de Clermont, see Luynes, *Mémoires*, X, p. 205, February 1750; the *Almanach Royal* does not list a *surintendante* until the reign of Marie-Antoinette. *Journal de l'abbé de Véri*, I, p. 358, recounts that in the autumn of 1775 the queen resurrected the office of *surintendante* for the princesse de Lamballe, which provoked her *dame d'honneur*, the comtesse de Noailles, to resign. See the more extensive and critical discussions of this measure in *Correspondence secrète entre Marie-Thérèse et le Cte de Mercy-Argenteau, avec les lettres de Marie-Thérèse et de Marie-Antoinette*, ed. Alfred Arneth and M. A. Geffroy, 3 vols. (Paris 1874–75), II, pp. 275 and 359 (18 December 1774; 17 July 1775: Mercy to Maria Theresa); p. 363 (13 July 1775: Marie-Antoinette to Rosenberg, Chamberlain in Vienna).

prévôt, *grand maréchal des logis* and *premiers gentilshommes* closely followed the status of these five charges; among them, ranking was less clear. The stewards' carefully guarded rights did not extend to the other staffs: each of the supreme officers enjoyed rights of nomination for his own staff. Chapel, chamber, stables, and hunt represented the domains of their supreme officers, who invariably pledged loyalty to the king in person. The oath to the king symbolised the immediate relationship with him, a proximity conferring substantial autonomy. Comparing several tracts listing those entitled to swear loyalty 'entre les mains de Sa Majesté' we find that several officers initially swearing loyalty to the senior officer of their staff later obtained this right. This indicated the ascent of the *capitaine de la porte*, the *grand maréchal des logis*, and the *premier écuyer*; it potentially undermined the position of their superior, the high steward or alternatively the *grand écuyer*.[15] Conversely, these deputies could themselves be bypassed by their senior assistants: the *écuyer ordinaire* and the *lieutenants de la porte* swore loyalty to the high steward. The *grand chambellan* was surrounded by officers who swore their oaths directly to the king: the four *gentilshommes*, the *grand maître* and *maîtres de la garderobe*: contentions among the superiors of this top-heavy staff were inevitable. The *premiers gentilshommes*, moreover, received the oaths of the chamber staff, signed the certificates for offices, and ordained the budgets connected to chamber, *argenterie*, and *menus-plaisirs* – leaving the chamberlain with an undisputed, but somewhat vacant supremacy.[16] Sharp conflict threatened when the supreme officers felt that officers they perceived as deputies acted too independently, especially in their communication with the king; the slightest ambiguity could lead to serious trouble. In 1671 the *grand veneur* complained that the *grand louvetier* disturbed his hunting parties, and demanded that he be forbidden to pursue wolves during the *chasse aux cerfs* – a conflict thinly veiling the *veneur*'s attempt to assert his supremacy. In the years following Louis XIV's death the tension inherent in the relationship

[15] It remains opaque when and how these changes were affected, but they are suggested by the following sources. Lists of those swearing loyalty to the king include: BN Clair 814, p. 435, Besongne's *Etat* of 1687, I, pp. 214–218; lists of those swearing loyalty to the *grand maître* are: O 1 755, pp. 37–43 and pp. 113–115; in the last pages, we find the notice that the *grand maréchal des logis* previously swore loyalty to the high steward, but with his acquiescence had ceased to do so since: and here follows a long blank. Dangeau, *Journal*, II, p. 71 (28 November 1687): 'M. de la Chaise prêta le serment de capitaine de la porte, charge qu'il a achetée de M. de Saint-Vallier. Il n'y a pas longtemps que cette charge-là prête serment entre les mains du roi; elle le pretoit entre les mains du grand-maître de la maison. Le roi lui a donné 100,000 francs pour lui aider à la payer, et un brevet de retenue de 200,000.' The *premier écuyer* is not in the BN Clair 814, p. 435, list of those swearing loyalty to the king; Besonge's 1687 *état* lists him on p. 215; yet we do not find him in the O 1 755 lists of those swearing loyalty to the high steward, as did his deputy the *écuyer ordinaire* and the other *écuyers* of the *petite écurie*.

[16] See, for example, the specific descriptions in 1749 *Etat de France*, I, p. 235; discussion of the changing balance between *gentilshommes* and *chambellan* in BN Clair 827, fols. 53r–54v; compare the contradictions in the sources about the oaths of loyalty of the staff in *chambre* and *garderobe*, with the *grand maître de la garderobe* and the *premiers gentilshommes* rivalling the supreme authority of the chamberlain, Du Verdier, *Estat* (1656), pp. 130–131, 146–149; AN O 1 820, and more particularly the instructions for the *premier gentilhomme* in O 1 822, pp. 1–6. Le Roux, *Faveur du roi*, p. 51, states that the officers in the chamber pledged their oath to the *premier gentilhomme*, supporting the interpretation offered in O 1 822. Dangeau, *Journal*, II, p. 123 (25 March 1688), gives an example of a contestation between the acting *premier gentilhomme de la chambre* and the *grand maître de la garderobe*.

between the *grand écuyer* and the *prémier écuyer* burst into open conflict, and turned into a protracted fight. In 1728 *M. le Grand* even published his grievances in a printed tract, asserting that the *petite écurie* was a subdepartment of his staff, and *M. le Premier* his subordinate.[17]

Heading the most numerous establishment within the household, the high steward could choose to fill it with his supporters. Henry III's 1574 instruction for his Guise *grand maître* stressed that all nominations were contingent upon his royal approval, a desire reiterated in the more extensive 1585 *règlement* and later by other rulers.[18] Such repeated rulings show that courtiers used their patronage to strengthen their power. Henry's decision to create a *petite écurie* in 1582 and his institution of the office of *grand maître des cérémonies* in 1585 for his loyal follower Guillaume Pot, sieur de Rhodes, can be seen as countermoves, limiting the Guise empire over senior court charges.[19] Both new officers, however, apparently pledged their oath of loyalty to the high steward, not to the king himself. The patronage of high stewards, token of their supreme charge, remained substantial. With his 'treason', the *Grand Condé* temporarily forfeited his rights, and his successors did not fully regain them: 24 of the 36 *gentilshommes servants*, and 8 of the 12 *maîtres d'hôtel* were now appointed by the king himself; the royal charges, moreover, were evaluated higher than those in the high steward's gift.[20] This measure, painful as it may have been, hardly terminated the high steward's patronage. He signed the *certificats* for the *provisions d'offices* in the seven offices catering for the court's tables, though the king himself held the charges in the *gobelet* and the *cuisine-bouche*.[21] We find records of the offices within the stewards' rights of nomination throughout the seventeenth and eighteenth centuries: more than 250 charges in the *sept offices* alone halfway through the seventeenth century, within the total of 459 'sous la charge du grand maître'. The high steward had patronage over 320 officers and servants in 1752 with another 99 appointed by the king, but under the high steward's control. The

[17] See Reytier, in *Les écuries royales*, pp. 63–64; AN O 1 858 on the 1728 Armagnac–Beringhen row, including printed tracts, and AN O 1 15, fol. 410r–v and fol. 463r–v: 'Reglement sur les differends des grand veneur et grand louvetier, Soyecourt and Heudicourt' (2 November 1671), and more extensive material in BN Clair 830, pp. 107–149; a relevant instance in the queen's household: the conflict between comtesse de Soissons, the queen's *surintendante* and duchesse de Navailles, her *dame d'honneur*, in BN Baluze 182, fol. 63r–v: 'Règlement pour la surintendante de la maison de la reine' (14 May 1661), and BN Clair 814, fols. 675–678; Below, in chapter 6, the quarrel of Sainctot and Blainville, *maître* and *grand maître des cérémonies*, will be discussed, a comparable difficulty, yet on a lower hierarchical level.

[18] AN KK 1431, pp. 13/313–37/319 (double pagination), gives the 1574 rules; AN KK 544 and the *AC* the 1585 règlement. Compare Louis XIV's edict of 1653, see Boucher, 'Evolution', pp. 363–365.

[19] See the detailed analysis of the Guise empire at Henry's court in Le Roux, *Faveur du Roi*.

[20] On Condé and the rights of his successors, see Dangeau, *Journal*, I, 'appendice à l'année 1684', p. 98, the number of *gentilshommes* stipulated here is 9, whereas O 1 751, no. 76, gives 12, the same reduction to one-third as in the case of the *maîtres d'hôtel*. Dangeau, *Journal*, I, p. 168 (8 May 1685), upon the death of Mortfontaine, one of the four *maîtres d'hôtel* in the high steward's gift, notes that the filling of this vacancy would bring M. le Duc at least 20,000 écus.

[21] See Clément, *Lettres . . . de Colbert*, III (Paris 1865); Colbert's instruction for Seignelay, 1671, pp. 46–64, with rules for the *maison* on pp. 47–49: 'sermens-provisions-certificats'. The *grand officier* signing the certificate had patronage over an office, the oath itself was not sufficient.

same 1752 overview notes that 120 officers swore their oath of loyalty to the high steward, and adds that he could distribute pensions and rewards.[22] A 1733–1734 compilation of rules for household services was aptly titled 'Code des officiers du roy ou recueil des règlements generaux de nos roys, et de nos seigneurs les grands maîtres de France'.[23]

In the fifteenth century, the household was in theory dismissed upon the death of the king; in the sixteenth century the death of a ruler could still rapidly change the face of the court, as the new king would sooner or later install his friends and supporters in the highest offices. Thus Loyseau's contention that 'les officiers de la maison du roy sont transferez au successeurs dès l'instant de la mort du predecesseur' was closer to seventeenth-century practice, when service at all levels of the household showed remarkable continuity.[24] Nevertheless, a 1653 edict stressed that great court offices remained the gift of the king: he could oust his greatest servants from office, and their charges reverted to the throne upon the death of the incumbent officer.[25] Among the *grands officiers* only the chancellor was appointed for life: others could be dismissed when they lost favour.[26] The Condé, high stewards since 1643, lost their supreme office during the *Fronde*, regaining it with the peace of the Pyrenees (1659). The *Grand Condé* held the *survivance*, leaving the charge to his son Henri-Jules. The eldest son of the Bouillon *grand chambellan*, Turenne, Saint-Simon suggests, saw his *survivance* threatened; his uncle, the *grand aumônier* cardinal of Bouillon more than once roused the king's anger; he was temporarily exiled in 1685, and finally lost his charge in 1700.[27] It passed to the Rohan in 1713, who held the office for much of the eighteenth century, but would lose it in the affair of the *collier*. A La

[22] See O 1 755 Maison du Roy, 1686, pp. 37–43, for the officers pledging loyalty to the high steward and the number of 250 within his nomination ('desquels M. le Grand Maître dispose'); pp. 116–118 for a list of 459 officers 'sous la charge du Grand Maître, with another 47 without charge or on pp. 123–124; AN O 1 751, especially nos. 69, 76, 80 give the situation in respect of 1740 and 1752 figures from 76; also see AN O 1 762, 'état général des officiers de la maison du roy qui sont sous la charge du Gr Mtre' (*c.* 1660–1816). See Christophe Blanquie, 'Dans la main du Grand maître. Les offices de la maison du roi, 1643–1720', *Histoire & Mesure* 13, 3–4 (1998), pp. 243–288, a well-informed article with statistics on the *casuels* and officers within the high steward's gift, kindly sent to me by Nicolas le Roux.

[23] AN KK 547, 548, and O 1 756.

[24] In 1515, 1547, 1559, 1574 and repeatedly in Henry III's reign, see Le Roux, *Faveur du roi*, pp. 36–37, 50 (with Loyseau's remark). *Mémoires de l'Abbé de Choisy*, ed. Georges Mongrédien (Paris 1966), pp. 135–136, on Henry IV; compare Loyseau, *Cinq livres*, pp. 225–226, stressing the same point.

[25] *Code des commensaux*, pp. 109–111 (July 1653).

[26] The *chancelier* held his office for life, though he could voluntarily retire; the *garde des sceaux* would replace a disgraced *chancelier* still formally holding his office.

[27] The Bouillon obtained the charge of *Grand Chambellan* upon the resignation of the duc de Guise in 1658; they held the government of Auvergne since 1662. See Dangeau, *Journal*, I, p. 75 (30 November 1684): 'Après le petit coucher, le roi appella M. de Turenne, et lui fit une forte réprimande sur ce quíl le servoit peu respectueusement.' Saint Simon adds: 'M. de Turenne, fils aînée de M. de Bouillon et Grand Chambellan en survivance, profita mal de cette correction, et se fit enfin exiler. Un matin en donnant la chemise au roi, il ne prit pas la peine d'ôter des gants à frange, de laquelle il donna par le nez au roi fort rudement, qui le trouva aussi mauvais qu'il est aisé de le croire.' Turenne died in the battle of Steinkerque in 1692. See the Cardinal's first problems cited in *Journal*, I, p. 201, and Sourches, *Mémoires*, I, p. 274, when he was sent away from the king's table; and his disgrace in September 1700 *Journal*, VII, p. 373. See Oroux, *Histoire ecclésiastique de la cour de France. Où l'on trouve tout ce qui concerne l'histoire de la chapelle & des principaux officiers ecclésiastiques de nos rois*, 2 vols. (Paris 1776–7), II, pp. 527–528: 'Aux nôces de Madame la Duchesse le Cardinal de Bouillon, dit Mademoiselle de

Rochefoucauld master of the wardrobe was exiled after Louis XV's embarrassing 1744 Metz illness and subsequent apologies for his extramarital adventures, but his family would hold on to the office. Around 1700 the highest charges at court were in practice becoming the near-hereditary property of princely and ducal dynasties: Condé for the high steward, Bouillon for the chamberlain, Lorraine-Guise for the master of the stables, Rohan for the grand almoner – an office never wholly hereditary for obvious reasons, La Rochefoucauld for the master of the wardrobe, and the Penthièvre descendants of Louis XIV's *bâtard* Toulouse for the *grand veneur*.[28] This extremely exclusive circle of dynasties widened for the first order of the *commensaux*, predominantly recruited from the *ducs et pairs*, but broadened much more substantially only for the next layers. Office throughout the household tended to become hereditary, with *survivances* securing its status as family heirloom – and capital investments.[29] Thus, tenure of office usually was long, often life-long, but frequently it was combined with other occupations and activities – for higher charges, most notably in the army and in provincial governments.[30] Offices could change hands, either because of the absence of male heirs, or as a consequence of the acquisition of other offices. Neither Louis XV nor Louis XVI liked the entrenched custom of the *survivances*, but only incidentally did they break with it.[31] The lively trade in offices, particularly the transactions for the higher offices needing the king's endorsement, was noted carefully by Dangeau, whose daily entries allow us to establish a table of the 'commercial value' of offices. *Brevets de retenue* representing the mortgageable value of offices were listed in the *états*, and we find several overviews of *brevets* in the records.[32]

Montpensier, voulut manger à la table du roi, apparamment parce que les princes légitimés y mangeoient pour la première fois. Cet honneur ne lui fut pas seulement refusé: il eut ordre de sortir de la cour & de se retier dans ses abbayes.' For more detail on the king's turbulent relations with the Bouillon see Saint-Simon, *Mémoires*, ed. A. de Boislisle (Paris 1879–1930), I, p. 96; II, pp. 126, 204–205; VII, pp. 157, 198; XVII, pp. 414–415; XX, pp. 27, 46–61, with a discussion between the *chambellan* and the king on the cardinal's faults on p. 51; see also XXVI, pp. 139–154, a biography of the unlucky grand almoner. Compare Boucher, 'Evolution', p. 364, citing Dangeau, *Journal*, I, p. 98, for Condé and VII, pp. 369–375, for the grand almoner.

28 On the descendants of the comte de Toulouse, see Jean Duma, *Les Bourbons-Penthièvre (1678–1793): Une nébuleuse aristocratique au xviiie siècle* (Paris 1995); see Béguin, *Les Princes de Condé*, on Henry II's successful efforts to strengthen his family by allying with the monarchy, and notably Richelieu, after 1626. He obtained the high stewardship from the cadet line of the Soissons in 1641. After the troubles of the *Fronde*, Louis II regained it but held the *survivance*, leaving the office to his son Henri-Jules. Béguin's fine study focuses on the independent network or 'nébuleuse' of the Condé, and only marginally included Henry Jules' functioning as *grand maître*, or the patronage coming with the office.

29 BN Clair 828, fols. 1247–1249, gives the edict of 1653 and its repetition in 1678, confirming the courtiers' privileges, protecting them against creditors etc. Compare the quarrels reported by Besenval, *Mémoires*, II pp. 20–25, upon Choiseul's disgrace as *sécrétaire d'état* in December 1770: could he be ousted from his charge of *colonel-général des Suisses et Grisons*? In the end, the charge was indeed taken away from him, but he was richly compensated. The discussion and the compensation stress the strength of office-holding.

30 Horowski, 'Obersten Chargen', stresses the preponderance of dynasties of courtiers in the army and in regional government.

31 See, for example *Journal de l'abbé de Véri*, II, pp. 215–216 (17 June 1779), n. 34 on p. 436: Louis XVI refusing the *survivance* of a guard captaincy to Lorges, his former *menin*, because the duke was too young, and he wanted to abolish 'l'usage des survivances'.

32 See *brevets d'assurance* in AN O 1 711 (1717–1789); O 1 712 (1750–1778); O 1 747, nos. 122 and 123: 'brevets d'assurance de la maison du roi', 122 for 1781. See the *brevets* listed below.

Early in the seventeenth century, Loyseau deplored the habit of *chefs* – at all levels of the household – to augment their income by marketing the charges under their supervision upon vacancy, or by benefiting from the pecuniary rights connected to the mutation of office; his complaint was more vehemently reiterated by late eighteenth-century critics.[33] Dangeau indicates that the level of patronage of the senior charges over their staffs with its attendant financial advantages, was an important factor in the estimation of the value of court office.[34] While Louis XIV confirmed the privileges of his courtiers, he emphatically made clear that he himself wanted to oversee the distribution of graces, strictly forbidding uncontrolled expansion of the household staffs. A minor deviation from this course occurred in 1673, when Louis granted his *grand maître de la garderobe*, François de la Rochefoucauld, the right to confer at his discretion the status of *officier domestique* upon artisans and merchants attached to his staff. The number of those thus recompensed had risen to 230 in 1683–1684, and the Sun King understandably judged it wise to reduce them to 26 in 1689.[35] Yet within the limits decreed by his reductions of the household, and with the proviso that his *agrément* was necessary for transactions with important offices, he acknowledged the responsibility of his *grands officiers* for their staffs and budgets.[36] The *grand écuyer* enjoyed the patronage over *c.* 275 charges in both *écuries* and the *haras*; other senior charges likewise controlled offices and budgets.

In the eighteenth century, the control of the *grands officiers* over their staffs and budgets was not seriously challenged until the reforms of the 1770s and 1780s. After the comte de Saint-Germain's reductions in the army, complaints about the costs of the household, exacerbated by many forms of semi-legitimate and illegitimate self-enrichment, were widespread.[37] Reform seemed unavoidable, but it was notoriously difficult to overcome the opposition of the court dignitaries to any infringement upon their rights. Chrétien-Guillaume de Lamoignon de Malesherbes, during his short service as *sécrétaire d'état* for the

[33] Loyseau, *Cinq livres*, pp. 231–234; *Journal de l'abbé de Véri*, II, 294–298, a discussion of the abuses in the context of Necker's 1780 reform. Doyle, *Venality*, pp. 65–66, cites Véri's complaints and provides a general analysis of venality.

[34] See, for example, Dangeau, *Journal*, II, p. 132 (20 April 1688): 'M. des Marets, grand fauconnier de France, est mort . . . , il y a 250,000 livres de brevet de retenue, elle vaut 11,000 francs de réglé, et on estime les casuels à 15,000 livres par an, parce qu'il y a beaucoup de charges qui dépendent de lui, et qu'il vend lorsqu'elles viennent à vaquer.'

[35] See Boucher, 'Evolution', pp. 363–365, for the temporary slackening in La Rochefoucauld's case, see BN MS f 22713, for the new charge of *grand maître de la Garderobe*, fol. 184r: 'par un brevet mai 73 le roi donne pouvoir au Grand Me de la Garderobe [after 21 October 1672 François de la Rochefoucauld] de choisir deux artisans de chaque metier pour servir à la garderobe, qui jouissent du privilege de commensaux et ont 60 lt de gages, il y en a plus de deux cens'; compare AN Z 1a 475, fol. 151.

[36] See the 1749 *Etat de France* for frequent statements of this practice, with several marked exceptions, such as the places among the *gardes du corps* (II, p. 27), taken away from captains in September 1664, a measure compensated by annual payment of 14,000 lt.

[37] See AN O 1 749, nos. 1–5, on the preceding years, no. 5 (February 1774) ending with the remarkable statement: 'Il est difficile d'imaginer qu'un aussi grand nombre de personnes prises dans la classe honnête et de société et qui ont toute une fortune personnelle soient une troupe de briguans qui s'accordens pour voler ou laisser voler le roy'.

maison du roi (1775–1776), tried to convince Louis XVI of the need to take away financial responsibility from his friends in high court office, conferring it upon employees less exalted and thus more easily chastened. This was a *sine qua non* for reform, he argued, as the king: 'ne fera point à son ami l'affront de lui ôter sa charge parcequ'il est un mauvais éconôme.'[38] When a few years later Necker successfully introduced reforms taking away financial responsibilities from the senior officers, this engendered a bout of feverish activity at court.[39] A 1787 reassessment of Necker's explains the attitude of the *ordonnateurs* of the court staffs; they:

ne se prêtoient jamais volontiers aux retranchements, parcequ'ils avoient un interret direct à les éviter. Cet Interrêt prevenoit de ce que la pluspart avoient des casuels qu'ils ne pouvoient faire valoir qu'autant qu'ils toléroient des abus anciens et passés en usage; et sans lesquels les charges à vendre auroient diminués de valeur; d'ailleurs la facilité d'accorder des graces à leurs créatures, de se procurer à eux mêmes et à leurs subordonnés des agréments et des commodités etoit une cause journalière de progressions dans les dépenses.[40]

The *grand maître* and the *grand écuyer* led their fellow courtiers in presenting an *état* of their annual income from the *casuels*, henceforth to be supplemented by the king.[41] Reportedly, this was not the only compensation they exacted for the reduction of their independence. In 1780, the reform year, Condé swore loyalty to the king as *colonel-général de l'infanterie*, a charge created for Epernon in 1584, and abolished in 1661 after the death of the incumbent. Croÿ, explicitly connecting the prestigious nomination to the preceding reforms, philosophically commented that at court 'on ôte toujours d'un coté, pour mettre de l'autre . . .'.[42]

The established hierarchy among the *grands offices* was constantly disturbed by minor conflict, yet in only one case did this lead to a change both fundamental and lasting. The most marked and contested rise of any group at court was that of the new charges connected to finance and administration. In the staff of the *grand maître*, the *bureau* with its various well-paid *contrôleurs* trying to control and limit expenses, became more prominent. Yet its success was overshadowed by the rise of administrators operating at court, outside of

[38] AN O 1 749, no. 51 (1775).

[39] See *Journal de l'abbé de Véri*, II, pp. 352–353, expressing his doubts about Necker's motives as well as the longevity of the reform: 'l'abus ne tardera pas de se glisser de nouveau sans qu'il puisse s'en préserver'.

[40] AN O 1 749, no. 40, an assessment of the reforms, and a defence of Necker, written in 1787 or slightly later.

[41] See AN O 1 748, no. 67: 'l'édit du mois de janvier 1780, a réuni aux parties casuelles de sa majesté toutes les charges et offices de sa maison. Le Roy, dans le préambule du même edit, s'est reserve d'examiner quelle dédomagement pouroit être dû aux grands officiers pour la privation qu'ils éprouvent de ce casuel', lengthy discussions, both preceding and following the reform in nos. 15, 19, 40, 41 and AN O 1 749 1–5, 38–40, 51. AN O 1 751, no. 67, gives a 90,000 lt. *indemnité annuelle* for Condé; for the same amount in an acerbic assessment of the reform including an overview of indemnities see AN O 1 793 98 *bis*.

[42] *Journal inédit du duc de Croÿ*, IV, p. 214 (9 April 1780); *Journal de l'abbé de Véri*, II, p. 298: note that Condé swore his oath for the resuscitated dignity a week after the reform decrees became active.

the great staffs. The *contrôleur général des finances*, of much more recent stock than the *chancelier*, monitored the king's expenses. Under the vigilant eye of Jean-Baptiste Colbert the charge acquired truly ministerial standing, usurping many of the chancellor's duties and rights. Near-ministerial figures had emerged from the wider circle of honorary *sécrétaires du roi* as well.[43] In 1547, Henry II established four *sécrétaires*, charging them with the responsibility for various regions and other special tasks, such as war or foreign affairs. To correct the imbalance with the more solemnly named Spanish 'minister of state' during the peace negotiations of Cateau-Cambrésis (1559), de l'Aubespine acquired the title *sécrétaire d'état*, and his colleagues followed suit. From 1570, one of the secretaries held responsibility for the *maison du roi* as well. Henry III, in 1588, allowed the secretaries to pledge their oath to the king in person instead of to the *chancelier*. The four *sécrétaires d'état* were the equivalent of ministers, heading their departments, and working with the king in person. Yet they were not automatically and functionally members of the king's inner council, nor were they invariably styled ministers of state. Loyseau equated the secretaries of state to the *officiers de la couronne*, and towards the end of the century, their status at court was not far removed from that of the dukes – their dynasties married among ducal families, and were integrated in the higher offices at court and in the army. Courtenvaux, Louvois' son obtained the *survivance* for the captaincy of the *cent suisses* in 1688.[44] From 1723, when Colbert de Croissy was granted the charge of *capitaine de la porte*, onwards, scions of the two major ministerial dynasties of the late seventeenth century would hold these prestigious and most traditional of military charges within the *maison* until the end of the *ancien régime*. In Louis XIV's days ministers established a *de facto* advantage, more frequently connected to domestic office: when they carried important messages, we find them directly approaching the king even before his *lever*, preceding the *premier gentilhomme de la chambre*. Moreover, senior ministers spent more time in private quarters with the king than did most high-ranking courtiers.[45]

Contrôleurs, councillors, and secretaries of state operated mostly within the same space as the household officers. In the sixteenth and early seventeenth centuries they worked together in councils, and must have shared many daily

[43] Only the secretary for foreign affairs entered the *conseil d'en haut* as a consequence of his function. See François Bluche, 'Sécrétaires d'Etat', in *DGS*, pp. 1427–1428, and pp. 1428–1431 for other relevant articles.

[44] Dangeau, *Journal*, II, p. 117 (7 March 1688); Sourches, *Mémoires*, II, p. 147.

[45] See, for example, Dangeau, *Journal*, II, p. 193 (21 October 1688): 'M. de Louvois est venu ce matin au leve du roi avant même que le prémier gentilhomme de la chambre fut entré'; II, p. 210 (14 November 1688): 'M. de Barbézieux entra chez le roi à son lever, avant le premier gentilhomme de la chambre, et lui donna des lettres de monseigneur qui lui mande que la ville de Manheim s'est rendue'; II, p. 234 (23 December 1688): Seignelay enters while the king was still in bed, reporting on Lauzun's mission to save the English Stuarts. See Clément, *Lettres . . . de Colbert*, III (Paris 1865), pp. 71–74, a 1671 *mémoire* by Seignelay commented in the margin by Colbert, urging him to attend the king's *lever* or Mass daily. Yet compare Horowski, 'obersten Chargen', p. 42 and n. 36, for the more dominant role of the serving *premier gentilhomme* in the eighteenth century, determining ministers' access to the king, and Hardman, *Louis XVI*, pp. 33–34 and 150–151, for the rather limited access of ministers when the king sojourned in hunting lodges.

routines.[46] When in the 1660s membership of the councils was restricted, contacts between *sécrétaires* and courtiers undoubtedly persisted.[47] The four secretaries were still habitually included in the *maison du roi* as *sécrétaires de la chambre du roi*, but in the printed *états* they were more extensively described in the subsequent overview of the government as heads of their respective departments. After the installation of the court in Versailles (1682), the *sécrétaires d'état* came to occupy the *aile des ministres*, separated from the main palace yet in its immediate vicinity – neatly reflecting their semi-detached position vis-à-vis the household.[48]

The rapid and lasting promotion of the secretaries of state, especially noteworthy for the great dynasties of *robe de conseil*, was much lamented in the later seventeenth century. In the course of the eighteenth century, their well-established status, never wholly on a par with the highest court dignitaries, does not seem to have risen further. Indisputably, the ministers were a force to be reckoned with even for the most prestigious courtiers. Courtiers' interests were dependent upon the war minister who controlled noble careers in the army, and upon the controller-general who could influence the payment of pensions. In the case of the *sécrétaire d'état* holding responsibility for the *maison*, the court dignitaries could choose to adopt a defiant stance. Malesherbes, in the *mémoire* cited earlier, stated that the *sécrétaire d'état* could not address the *grands officiers* in firm language, as they received their orders from the king in person, and frequently treated the minister as a mere administrator – when one of Malesherbes' *commis* wanted to ascertain the number of horses in the *grande écurie*, his innocent action led to an outcry and accusations of intolerable espionage.[49] In matters less close to their own domain, courtiers had to respect the leading role of ministers. The secretary responsible for the household also had Paris in his portfolio, and could not be challenged there. His position as manager of the household, moreover, was strengthened by Necker's 1780 reforms.

Ministerial dynasties obtained court offices, but under Louis XIV, ministerial status and membership of the council were rarely granted to sword nobles – Beauvillier, and to a lesser extent Chevreuse, being the major exceptions. Leaving aside the atypical experiment of the *polysynodie* in Philippe d'Orléans' regency, with a strong *épée* presence, it is still evident that sword nobles figure more frequently as ministers of state in the eighteenth century – the title indicated status as important adviser, without necessarily serving as secretary of state; nor were all secretaries of state granted this title. A small group of high nobles would finally serve as secretary of state in the second half of the eighteenth

[46] Boucher, *Cour de Henri III*, p. 52, presents an overview of 'a week in the life of Henri III', closely matching the 1585 *règlement* as printed in *AC*, I, 10, pp. 301–358, more particularly at pp. 315–332.

[47] Parallel to the reduction of the household, Louis reduced the number of *conseillers*: in 1644 we find 120 councillors, after 1673 only 30 councillors remained. All royal officers, however, bore the empty title *Conseiller du Roi*, see Olivier Poncet, 'Conseils du Roi', in *DAR*, pp. 320–325.

[48] Newton, *Espace du Roi*, pp. 415–417.

[49] AN O 1 749, no. 51.

century, characteristically taking responsibility for war and foreign affairs. Yet they approached these desirable high offices from their own field of activities. The office of secretary of state usually stood at the apex of a robe *cursus honorum* clearly separated from the habitual careers of court nobles. While the idea to serve as *maîtres des requête* or *premier commis* would be alien to major *épée* families, they could perceive ministerial responsibilities as an attractive corollary to their careers in army, diplomacy, regional government, court service. Thus among the dynasties of nobles prominent at court, we find Noailles serving as a minister of state 1743–1756, Soubise, serving as minister of state 1759–1787, Choiseul holding various secretarial portfolios from 1758 to 1770, and Aiguillon serving as secretary 1771–1774. To these familiar names, others may be added.[50]

At the Austrian Habsburg court, the four major offices, steward, marshal, chamberlain, and master of the stables, were consolidating a collective supremacy by the later sixteenth century. The marshal, under Maximilian I arguably the senior household officer, did not keep pace with the others. His staff remained small, and he himself did not retain a noticeable role in the vicinity of the ruler – table, chamber, and stables were looked after by his three colleagues. While the steward strengthened his primacy among the four officers, the marshal had trouble safeguarding his place as the second-in-rank. Ferdinand III's 1637 instruction for the marshal stipulated that in case of the steward's illness or protracted absence, the marshal would take charge of his 'Ambt und Handlung'.[51] Soon, however, the chamberlain, with the rapidly expanding trail of honorary chamberlains swearing loyalty to him, would be breathing down the marshal's neck. Towards the end of the seventeenth century, the *Verzeichnisse* do not necessarily mention him before the chamberlain. Incidentally, they even included the *Quartieramt*, usually in the marshal's staff, in the *Obersthofmeisteramt*.[52] Finally, in the printed *Schematismen*, we find the marshal habitually listed after the chamberlain, a sequence explicitly confirmed by Rinck in 1705 and by Küchelbecker in 1729. When in 1746 Maria Theresa asked her *Oberstkämmerer* (and later *Obersthofmeister*) Johann Joseph Khevenhüller-Metsch to take on an honorific task for the absent high steward, Khevenhüller convinced her that the marshal customarily ('nach alter etiquette') acted as the steward's deputy, a recommendation she adopted. The marshal retained this right throughout the eighteenth century.[53]

50 For these paragraphs, I rely heavily on the advice of Leonhard Horowski; his forthcoming study of the careers of French court-related noble families will provide detailed information on this vital matter.

51 HHStA, OMaA I, K. 1 (1564–1712), instruction 1637 (Ferdinand III), point 18.

52 The late seventeenth-century 'Lista' of the *Obersthofmeisteramt* in AVA Harrach Historica 796 includes the *Quartieramt*; see a similar remark by Hengerer, 'Adelsintegration', p. 23, n. 10; Carafa's 1629 report in Hurter, *Friedensbestrebungen*, pp. 236–237, includes the marshal in the high steward's staff, but pictures him as one of the most important officers of the court, with 'großes Ansehen, reiches Einkommen, ausgedehnte Gewalt'.

53 Khevenhüller, *Tagebuch*, II, p. 101 (July 1746): 'Den 13. befahle die Kaiserin mir, in Abwesenheit des Obrist Hoffmeisters Graffen Sinzendorff, dem neu resolvirten hungarischen Canzlern Graffen Nadasdy seine beschehene Benennung schrifftlich nach Pressburg zu notificiren; weillen aber nach alter Etiquette den Obrist

The master of the stables may have watched the shifting balance between the marshal and the chamberlain with keen interest, as two factors explaining the rise of the chamberlain worked in his favour as well: he had a far greater and more evidently autonomous staff than the marshal, and his tasks more frequently gave him access to the emperor. An unsigned manuscript, probably written towards the end of the seventeenth century, outlines the reasons why the master of the stables should in the future precede the marshal. The author pointed to the Burgundian heritage where the *Stallmeister* allegedly had precedence; denied the marshal his own staff, placing it within the purview of the steward; and contrasted the *Stallmeister*'s personal attendance upon the emperor outside of the palace with the less personal and thus less elevated jurisdictional powers of the marshal. Finally, he shrewdly turned one of the marshal's major assets – his position in ceremonies pertaining to the empire, carrying the sword – into a disadvantage: didn't the marshal perform this task as the substitute of the *Erzmarschall*, the elector of Saxony? How could a *Vice-Ampt* take precedence over a *Haupt-Ampt* such as that of the *Stallmeister*?[54] In spite of the attempts to unsaddle the marshal, he was able to cling to his rank.

Conflict between the staffs, or between the chiefs and deputies within the staffs, was far less frequent than in France. The functional hierarchy was only incidentally contested, and conflict was prevented or tempered by the generally effective ranking of privy councillors (*Geheime Räthe*) and chamberlains according to their date of nomination – with the councillors always preceding the chamberlains.[55] The steward clearly served as the supreme court officer, and the marshal remained responsible for order and justice at court, in close conjunction with the steward. As in France, the staffs of chamberlain and master of the stables enjoyed considerable autonomy, and they looked directly to the emperor.[56] With the steward and the marshal, they pledged loyalty to the emperor in person. Oaths of most higher officers seem to have been pledged to the heads of the staffs: the *Wienerisches Diarium* reports the oath only of *geheime Räthe* and *hohe ministri* to the emperor (or when relevant the empress) in person; chamberlains pledged loyalty to the *Oberstkämmerer*.[57]

Hoffmeister nicht der Obrist Cämmerer, sondern der Obrist Hoffmarschall zu suppliren pflegt, nahm ich die Freiheit disen Umstand I.M. zu erinnern, welche mich zu zwei Mahlen befragte, ob ich dessen sicher seie und, nachdeme ich es bekräfftiget, sodann erst meinem Schwagern den Befehl dieser Notification halber ertheilet.'

54 'Motiva, warumb der Oberstallmeister . . .' HHStA, OMeA, Sr. 73, fols. 357–359.

55 Zolger, *Hofstaat*, pp. 53, 149, adding that the *Truchsessen* followed the *Kämmerer*. Moser, *Teutsches Hofrecht*, II, p. 235, a variety of references in HHStA ÄZA and ZA Prot. See chapter 6 on ceremony.

56 See in AVA Harrach historica 797 the highly interesting review of the court's major officers and procedures 'Guettachten wegen der hoffordnung über des obristen hoffmaisters Instruction', explicitly in points 1, 2, 5; but also the remarks recurring throughout the text, stressing the autonomy of *Oberstkämmerer* and *Stallmeister*, matching the positions of the *chambellan* and *écuyer* in France.

57 See reports of oaths in the *Wienerisches Diarium*, for example, 3 August 1704 and 10 April 1728 for a *geheime Rath*; 4 August 1704 for the empress' *Obersthofmeister* both swearing loyalty to the emperor; 2 January 1728 the *Hartschierenhauptmann* swearing loyalty to the *Obersthofmeister*; 18 May 1729, a chamberlain swearing loyalty to the *Oberstkämmerer*.

After the four supreme officers came the *Oberstjägermeister* and the *Oberstfalkenmeister*, the latter traditionally senior, but demoted *de facto* by the declining vogue for falconry in the course of the eighteenth century. The captains of the *Hartschieren* and *Trabanten*, later supplanted by Maria Theresa's new guards, belonged to the highest echelon, but they were listed under the steward's staff, as was the chapel. The captains, moreover, swore their oath to the *Obersthofmeister*, and proved unable to strengthen their autonomy.[58] They clearly did not match the rank of their French counterparts, who swore loyalty to the king in person and were frequently reckoned among his intimates. Like the French *commensaux du premier ordre*, each of these supreme officers headed his own establishment. The emperor in theory had full control over the nomination of court officers in all staffs; in practice, the four senior court dignitaries, and the heads of guards and hunting, were able to further the interests of their dependents by employing them at court, but such proceedings never became a formally vested right. Nor do we find any dynastic monopolisation of these four supreme officers, or the four others immediately below them.

An exclusive group of families – among them the Lamberg, Harrach, Schwarzenberg, Liechtenstein, Dietrichstein, Trautson, Sinzendorf, Starhemberg, Mollart, Waldstein, Mansfeld – dominate the offices at court, but they had to follow the habitual *cursus honorum*, starting as a simple chamberlain, frequently holding lower charges and fulfilling diplomatic missions before reaching the highest charges.[59] These, moreover, never became attached to a single dynasty: progression through the ranks and, most of all, the emperor's choice remained the determining factors. In sharp contrast with French practice, moreover, the *Hofstaat* of the ruling emperor was dismissed upon his death – the *Reichsvizekanzler*, theoretically the deputy of the Elector of Mainz, imperial *Erzkanzler*, formed the only exception.[60] After the death of an emperor, lengthy deliberations took place to decide which servants would be maintained, or *confirmirt*, and which would be transferred to the new and expanded establishment of the dowager-empress. For the unlucky, provisions and pensions were made available – they can be found in the court's expenses decades after the death of the relevant emperor or empress. Interestingly, the senior court officers were all dismissed, allowing the new emperor a fresh start, usually bringing in the servants and intimates of his own *Hofstaat*.[61]

[58] See HHStA Hofakten des Ministeriums des Inneren, K 14 (1650–1699), documents on the 'Ernennung von Garde Hauptleuten' (14 August 1677–23 May 1686): the captains and lieutenants swore their oath to the high steward, and could not autonomously fill senior vacancies of their staffs; Leopold confirmed the steward's rights, see 1684, fol. 236r; 1685, fol. 242r–v. Compare the steward's rights in the chancelleries, for oaths and nominations, mostly confirmed by Leopold I on fols. 24–31, 33–36 (1693).

[59] See Klaus Müller, *Das kaiserliche Gesandtschaftswesen im Jahrhundert nach dem Westfälischen Frieden*, Bonner Historische Forschungen 42 (Bonn 1976), particularly chapter 6, for illuminating detail about the diplomats' careers, and their notion of court office as the supreme reward for strenuous service in diplomacy.

[60] Compare the French *chancelier*.

[61] OMeA Prot 6 1700–1709 *Referate* after Leopold I's death, discussing the creation of his dowager's establishment, the servants to be *confirmirt* or taken over by Joseph I, and the compensations to be paid for those for whom

Within the life-span of an emperor, high office was not necessarily held as long as the incumbent lived: court dignitaries themselves could resign, or at least ask the emperor to grant them this favour. The end of high office was less predominantly connected with disfavour, dismissal, and exile than it was in France, where life tenure was the rule. High court office never became an 'office' in the French sense, nor was it ever formally venal. A tendency towards the French system of *brevets d'assurance* may have been developing. August Christoph Count Wackerbarth, the Saxon envoy, in 1709 reported that count Trautson, *Oberstkämmerer*, had the 'Versicherung' for the high steward's charge at that time still held by the elderly prince Salm; Khevenhüller-Metsch mentions the 'Versicherungsbillet' Count Franz Rosenberg had obtained for the charge of *Oberstkämmerer* during the incumbency of the elderly Fürst Heinrich Auersperg.[62] Explicitly hereditary offices were connected to the various components of the monarchy, and to the empire, but these *Erzämter* and *Landeserbämter*, prestigious for the incumbents as well as important for the cohesion of the monarchy, were less relevant for the household. Possibly, the feudal traditions helped to prevent high household offices at the Habsburg court from turning into family heirlooms. The oath of loyalty was strictly personal and had to be renewed when a new emperor came to the throne, for court officers as well as for those who held imperial fiefs. While this would basically hold true for France as well, Habsburgs were never wholly certain to be elected emperor. Thus, if they styled their household as the imperial household, it was difficult to grant the dynasties serving them a lasting right to their offices. Formally, the household in Vienna could be perceived as only the *curia minor* of the emperor, with the territorial princes of the empire serving as his *curia maior*. In practice at court, however, such distinctions lost relevance and the imperial title was used loosely to indicate the incumbent Habsburg in all his capacities.

The deputies to the four major officers would be of high noble rank as well, such as the *Stabelmeister*, *Küchenmeister*, *Silbercammerer*, and *Untersilbercammerer* in the steward's staff. In 1740 the *anderter* or *zweiter Hofmeister* was added, who did not seem to have changed either the *Obersthofmeister*'s pre-eminence, or the balance among the highest charges: the new office may simply have been the consequence of the decision to abolish the separate establishments for empress

no accommodation in one of the establishments could be provided, and pensions to be distributed among loyal servants, see fols. 515–520, 572–587, 613–628; OMeA Prot 7 comparable proceedings after Joseph's death: fols. 125v–129. Joseph paid off the high steward (50,000), chamberlain (50,000) and master of the stables (40,000), see the *Gnadengaben* in HKA HZAB 1706/148, fol. 261v; Charles did likewise in 1711, with the same amounts, suggesting that this was accepted practice, see HZAB 1713/155, fols. 429–431. Pecar, 'Ökonomie der Ehre', p. 137, notes that Charles went on paying the *Besoldung* for Trautson and Starhemberg as compensation for their loss of office upon Joseph's death.

62 The envoy's report was printed in Katrin Keller, 'Der Wiener Hof von außen. Beobachtungen zur Reflexion des Kaiserhofes im Reich im 17. und 18. Jh.', *Frühneuzeit Info* 12 (2001), pp. 21–31. Khevenhüller, *Tagebuch*, VII, pp. 48–49, and on p. 167 (1 June 1773): Rosenberg's 'in petto vorbehaltener Destination zum Obrist-cämmerer-Ammt'.

and emperor.[63] Nobility was the defining characteristic of all honorary officers within the household: cupbearers, carvers, *Truchsessen*, and chamberlains (only the last two categories persisted into the nineteenth century). In addition to the deputies of the great officers they may be seen as holding the rank of the *commensaux du deuxième ordre*.[64] Ferdinand III noted in his instructions for the chamberlains that nobody should carry the ruler's key who could not boast of his 'uralten Geschlecht und Herkommens', preferably in combination with a title and wealth.[65] Situated below these almost exclusively noble highest echelons, but above the non-noble servants at court, a multifaceted group of specialists complicates a clear-cut above-stairs/below-stairs division. In the chamber, for instance, *Leibmedici* and apothecary, a *Schatzmeister*, a jeweller, stonecutter, painter, and the confessor stand between the noble *Kämmerer* and the non-noble *Kammerdiener* or *Türhüter*; and their arts could help them to reach higher status than most *Kämmerer* could aspire to. The standing Habsburg predilection for music and theatre secured a favourable environment for musicians, playwrights, and theatre engineers whose talents were duly honoured. In Charles VI's reign, the musical establishment was crowned with its own noble court officer, the director or *Musikgraf*, operating as the *Obersthofmeister*'s deputy for this expanding sector. The *Obersthofmeisteramt* included not only the musical chapel, but also its ecclesiastical counterpart, non-noble yet clearly set apart by the priestly status of its members. The librarian, architect, secretaries, and the *Hofcontralor* (or controller of expenses for the kitchen and its dependencies); the provost and quartermaster in the marshal's staff; *Hofmeister*, *Praeceptor*, and teachers for the *Edelknaben* in the *Stallmeister*'s staff may be added.[66]

Parallel to the *commensaux du troisième ordre* we find a variety of lower servants: *Diener*, ushers, writers, *Heizer*, *Jungen*, and *Gehilfe* of all sorts; huge numbers of lackeys, coachmen, and *Pferdeknechte* in the stables, the ordinary guards, and such diverse persons as the *Zwergendiener* or the *Stiefelwischer*. In the female establishments, below the noble echelons of *Hofdames* and *Kammerfreylen*, we may find a curious ladder of *Kammerdienerinnen*, a *Kammerzwergin*, *Kammerweiber*, and *Kammerdienerin-Menschen*.[67] The below-stairs element was far more

[63] See Dickson, *Finance and Government*, I, p. 209, n. 2, summing up the curious alternation of *Hofmeister*. In the *schematismen*, we find the 'anderter Hofmeister' without a clear following; nor does the September 1772 discussion of *erster Obersthofmeister* Khevenhüller's prerogatives in HHStA ZA Prot 70, fols. 159r–170r, clarify the position of his subservient counterpart. Somewhat more information is given in the 11 September 1765 letter on the fusion of the establishments of Maria Theresa and Joseph, where functions for a '2do-loco erster Obersthofmeister' are outlined, and a 'zweyter Obriststallmeister' is indicated, and a 14 September Handbillet changing the nominations.

[64] Hausenblasová, 'Nationalitäts- und Sozialstruktur', p. 36, gives 35 per cent nobles in Rudolf's *Hofstaat* – dominant in the honorary offices, vulnerable to inflation. A lower percentage of nobles must actually have served at court on a day-to-day basis.

[65] 1637 Oberstkämmerer's Instruction in HHStA, Familienakten III K 100, article 1; Kammerherreninstruktion in HHStA, OMeA Sr. K 73, article 1.

[66] The enumeration is indicative only, the *Tapezierer*, *Kammerfurier*, *Futtermeister*, etc. follow the major deputies; high pay for other lower charges, such as the *Oberroßbereiter* in the *Stall*, indicate a privileged position.

[67] See Sienell, 'Wiener Hofstaate', in *Hofgesellschaft und Höflinge*, ed. Malettke and Grell, pp. 104–105.

numerous than their above-stairs colleagues, with the exception of the honorary chamberlains. The continuity in these lower echelons of the household is at least as remarkable as that in the upper echelons: charges long remained vested within the same families. The household represented a lasting focus for networks of families at all levels of society. They cherished the rights and exemptions shared by all members of the *Hofgesinde*, demarcating them from the other inhabitants of Vienna. These did not change much throughout the centuries, and frequently caused problems with the city authorities.[68]

While the *Obersthofmeister* oversaw the spheres both of administration and household, a certain level of separation was visible, as the presidents of the main chanceries or councils, and the *geheime Räte* themselves, pledged loyalty to the emperor directly, not to his highest court officer.[69] Institutions controlling judicial procedures, finances, and the army were run by specialists in these fields, frequently recruited among the same noble families mentioned earlier. Senior courtiers doubled as *geheime Räte*; on a lower level of the hierarchy councillors in the *Hofkammer* represented a similar mixture. A consistently expanding number of secretaries can be found in the *Verzeichnisse*; many of them were much more than scribes, and took a major part in the written groundwork of decision-making, for matters related to the household as well as for other concerns.[70] The *Obersthofmeister* long chaired sessions of the *geheime Rat* and usually took part in the sessions of smaller committees of Leopold's later reign, or from 1708 onwards in the permanent conference. Into the reign of Maria Theresa, he had a position in the machinery of decision-making, though by that time his responsibilities in government were far more restricted than in previous reigns.[71]

The *Hofkanzler*, strengthening his position vis-à-vis his imperial colleague, the *Reichsvizekanzler*, had, since the 1620s, become a driving force in the government of the Habsburg dominions. He did not initially enjoy the same status as the venerable French chancellor: yet it waxed steadily and finally matched that of the French *sécrétaires d'état*. The first two chancellors in the seventeenth century, Verda and Prickelmayr, were of modest origins, but acquired nobility through their service, as would later chancellors Hocher, Strattmann, and Seilern. Yet a Sinzendorf count succeeded Prickelmayr, and Count Bucelleni came between Strattmann and Seilern; they themselves, moreover, acquired the title of count during their incumbencies, and found good marriage alliances. From then on,

68 Spielman, *Crown & the City*, on the abuse of tax exemptions, problems with quartering; see various tracts and measures on 'Befreyte Hoffhandlsleuthen und Handwerckers', in HHStA OMaA K 519 (1656–1689).

69 AVA Harrach Historica 797, point 2 of the 'Guettachten'.

70 See details and biographical data on the secretaries in Stefan Sienell, *Die geheime Konferenz* and his 'Die kaiserlichen Beratungsgremien und die spanische Erbfolgefrage 1699/1700)', *MÖStA* 47 (1999), pp. 117–145.

71 Dickson, *Finance and Government*, I, pp. 207–256, see Tables 9.1 and 9.2, the second giving the sessions of the Konferenz attended by *Oberstkämmerer* Khevenhüller – the conference, however, no longer was the centre of decision-making.

the charge was held by nobles, and the chancellor soon was on a par with the highest court charges, balancing his more extensive political role against their rank. Interestingly, Philip Ludwig Count Sinzendorf, successor in office to the *erster Hofkanzler* Seilern and member of one of the prominent families cited earlier, made every effort to become *Obersthofmeister* in 1721 as well as in 1724, still clearly perceiving this as a promotion.[72] In 1724 the charge went to another Sinzendorf – Sigmund Rudolf Count von Sinzendorf-Thannhausen – but the example shows that traditional hierarchies remained strong.[73]

Khevenhüller-Metsch's notices frequently indicate tensions between the high steward, marshal, and the various institutions of government. Ongoing reform made the competences and responsibilities among the 'Dicasterien', and between their leaders and the court dignitaries, increasingly unclear. Whereas the latter had lost some of their immediate political influence, their supremacy in the public representation of dynasty and government was confirmed by Maria Theresa. The steward's public role in the presentation and installation of his colleagues when they pledged their oath to the ruler underlines this.[74] Notwithstanding the complaints of the incumbents, there was no straightforward decline in the power and responsibilities of the court offices: the marshal's legal rights and duties had been severely restricted by the 1749 reforms, yet in 1763 they were restored.[75] A lengthy 1772 enumeration of the rights of the *Obersthofmeister* unequivocally emphasized his superiority over all other servants of the *allerhöchsten Herrschaften*.[76] When shortly after Francis Stephen's death Maria Theresa wrote several tracts to advise her children on their future responsibilities, and more

72 From 1705 to 1715, the charge was divided in two, the *erster* and *zweiter Hofkanzler*; in 1715 the double chancellorship, and after 1720, when the subdepartments for Inner and Upper Austria disappeared, the two chancellors formed 'departments', the first chancellor's for foreign and family affairs, the second or *anderter* chancellor's for provincial administration and judicial matters. In 1742, the first chancellor responsible for foreign affairs became *Staatskanzler*, the second Austrian chancellor – the latter assisted by a vice-chancellor. See Dickson, *Finances and Government*, I, pp. 217–218.

73 See Theo Gehling, *Ein Europäischer Diplomat am Kaiserhof zu Wien. François Louis de Pesme, seigneur de Saint-Saphorin, als englischer Resident am Wiener Hof 1718–1727*, Bonner Historische Forschungen 25 (Bonn 1964), p. 74. The 1724 Sinzendorf example was brought to my attention by Andreas Pecar (Rostock).

74 Khevenhüller, *Tagebuch*, VI, pp. 29–30, steward and *Oberstkanzler* (24 June 1770); p. 37 (1 August 1770), conflicts between *Reichshofrath*, *Reichskanzlei*, and *Obersthofmeisteramt*; compare p. 47 (1 November 1770), Khevenhüller, now steward, and gaining the upper hand, explained the steward's supremacy in such affairs with the following remark (p. 47): 'dessen Ursprung vermuthlich noch von jenen alten Zeiten herzuhollen, da die Regierung das vornemmste Dicasterium und noch keine Canzlei vorhanden gewesen'.

75 HHStA, Hofakten des Ministeriums des Inneren K 16, 12–30 April 1763, and an addition from 1765: 'Decret des Obersthofmeisteramtes über die Wiederherstellung der Gerichtsbarkeit des Obersthofmarschalls'; see Khevenhüller, *Tagebuch*, VI, p. 11n. and pp. 220–225, n. 24. Yet compare complaints of the incumbent about the decline of their charge, for example HHStA Hofakten des Ministeriums des Inneren K 14, fols. 33–36 (21 July 1693), with Dietrichstein complaining about the usurpations of the chancelleries, who sought 'das Obristhofmeisteramt zu diminuiren, und derselben die wenige apparenz der Ehr so er noch hat auch völlig wegzunehmen . . .', fol. 34r; or Khevenhüller, *Tagebuch*, VI, p. 141, stressing that the steward had lost status since Anton Florian von Liechtenstein's days, and citing the precedence of Prince Eugène in the council.

76 See HHStA ZA Prot 70 for a discussion of the *Obersthofmeister*'s prerogatives in 1772, fols. 159r–170r; his precedence over *geheime Räthe* and *Conferenz-Ministri* is noted on fols. 160v–161r: he preceded councillors with earlier nominations, and presided meetings of the council or conference in absence of the *allerhöchsten Herrschaften*; Rudolf Sigmund von Sinzendorf (i.e. Sigmund Rudolf von Sinzendorf-Thannhausen) is cited as an example.

particularly the court, she noted that: 'si vous voulés être bien servi, et avoir de bons domestiques, il faut soutenir les chefs, et laisser tout aller par leur canal'.[77] The differentiation between household and administration occurred gradually, and the lasting proximity of the supreme incumbents in both spheres prevented the intense contestations that accompanied this process in France – though the results, finally, may not have been profoundly different.[78]

INCOME

The regular wages for service at court were moderate at best; these *gages ordinaires* or *ordinari Besoldungen* in most cases did not stray far from the levels reached in the early seventeenth century, representing an ever-diminishing real value. Throughout the seventeenth century, wages never were a major category in the French budget. On average, they represented 15 per cent of the total expenses for the king's household in the years 1600–1656, 12 per cent in 1662–1695 – substantially less than the court's table, with 25 per cent and 36 per cent respectively. The *gages ordinaires* indeed were a 'partie peu considerable' of the budget, particularly if we keep in mind the fact that the pensions and special rewards together were roughly on the same level as the total costs for the king's household for most of the seventeenth century. If anything, these tendencies became more marked in the eighteenth century.[79] In Vienna, with its more restricted financial potential, and usually more moderate *Gnadengaben*, the wages of the various staffs were a major item in the budget, yet it decreased in proportion to other expenses. The *Hofgesinde* could hardly expect to be paid punctually: the emperor consistently borrowed time and money by postponing and reducing payment. Outstanding payments could hence be treated as the crown's debts: as loans agreed upon more or less unwillingly, and paid back irregularly. Thus, the *Hofzahlamtsbuch* for 1615 explicitly lists the 'Als darlehen beschribne besoldungsausstand'.[80]

77 ÖNB cod. ser. n. 1713, fol. 91r.

78 The lists of highest charges *ÖZV*, I, 1, pp. 275–288; the Tables in Payer von Thurn, *Die kaiserlich-königliche Hofstellen, ihre Chefs und deren Stellvertreter* (1749 May 1–1848 March 15) (Vienna 1902) and Dickson, *Finance and Government*, I, pp. 449–456, and the analysis in Dickson, 'Monarchy and Bureaucracy', pp. 345–351, show the gradual changes and the overall continuity in the composition of the highest echelons of household and government.

79 See the tables based on Malet at http://www.le.ac.uk/hi/bon/ESFDB/index.html; *Maison du Roi* gives the wages the *Chambre aux deniers* paid for the kitchen – yet several officers drew extra payments from the *Chambre aux deniers* as well, so the figures cannot wholly be read as representing salaries and kitchen respectively (see, e.g., Frère Ange, *Etat* (Paris 1722), I, p. 191: 'Ces douze Maîtres d'Hôtel servent trois par quartier, & touchent chacun chez les trésoriers de la maison 450. l. des gages, à la chambre aux deniers 300. l. à la fin de leur quartier, 64. l. pour les jettons: ils ont encore plusieurs autres droits'). There is another complicating factor, as some of the wages were paid within the budgets of the financially independent staffs, and thus not included in this rough computation. The remark cited from AN O 1 749, no. 40, supports the general impression given here.

80 See HKA HZAB 1615/64, fol. 88r; compare Mensi, *Finanzen*, pp. 37, 125, 490–491, 745; Holl, *Starhemberg*, p. 205; more generally John P. Spielman, 'Status as Commodity: The Habsburg Economy of Privilege', in *State and Society in Early Modern Austria*, ed. Charles Ingrao (West-Lafayette 1994), pp. 110–118; Sutter Fichtner, 'Habsburg Household or Habsburg Government?'.

The records of payment in the Vienna *Hofkammerarchiv* list amounts diverging considerably from the lists of officers' wages given in the overviews, and the actual level of paid *Besoldungen* varied from year to year. From the sixteenth into the eighteenth century, payment of wages was frequently in arrears. Yet upheaval such as the 'terrible revolt' of the courtiers reported in the 1615 *gantze Burgundische Hoffstatt* did not recur. Warfare entailed lengthy suspension of payments: *Hofzahlamtsbücher* for war years frequently fail to list any *Besoldungen*. With peace came the renewal of payments. Only in 1651 was the *Hofgesinde* paid for its services in the preceding years – in the same year, a major reform project was initiated to improve standards of ceremony and order at the imperial court.[81] In France, we find similar instances: a *règlement* dating from Marie de Medici's regency mentions complaints of the *domestiques*, and their insolence after vainly demanding their pay.[82] The crises halfway through the century, and the grim financial situation during the great wars 1688–1713, would again lead to postponement of payments – courtiers were even prompted to bring their table silverware to the mint.[83] In a 1764 *compte rendu* we again find unpaid wages and pensions listed as 'arrérages et dettes sans intérêt'.[84]

Even if we forget these recurring problems, it is clear that ordinary wages did not constitute the prime reason for service at court for most courtiers. For the lesser echelons, low wages were compensated by lucrative exemptions. These not only regarded tax payments, but also justice and commercial regulations, allowing those serving the court to make quick money by ignoring common restrictions. Court employment brought more benefits: clothing, food, and fuel were provided, or replaced by money payments. When the ruler's wardrobe was replaced, or after ceremonies, the surplus materials, frequently rich and costly, were granted to the servants – a benefit the supreme officers in France did not find ignoble.[85] Widows, and incapacitated or elderly servants, or those who lost their place after the death of a scion of the dynasty, could expect some support:

[81] For example, HKA HZAB 1624/73: huge expenses for the kitchen, but no wages; 1646/92 only a diminutive post for 'alt ausstendige hofbesoldungen'; 1647/93 we find wages, including high steward Trautmannsdorf's pay for a protracted period of service: July 1644–December 1647; in HZAB 1648/94, 1649/95, and 1650/96 again no wages: only in 1651/97 truly substantial wages, including on fol. 444v a remarkable 34,233 for the *Fälcknerey* (usually between 8,000 and 12,000) for 'Besoldungen en Anforderungen' from 12 February 1643 until 18 December 1651. See chapter 6 for the 1651 reform.

[82] BN MS naf 2004 (previously AN KK 545), fols. 247–249: 'Règlement sur le payement des gages des officiers domestiques du Roy'.

[83] On the silverware, see Elisabeth-Charlotte von Orléans (Madame), *Briefe*, ed. Wilhelm Ludwig Holland, Bibliothek des Literarischen Vereins 88, 107, 122, 132, 144, 157 (Stuttgart 1867–1881), CVII, p. 107 (8 June 1709), p. 108 (15 June 1709), p. 114 (6 July 1709); Sourches, *Mémoires*, III, p. 181 (1 December 1689); XI, pp. 349–350 (6/7 June 1709); Dangeau, *Journal*, III, p. 33 (3 December 1689); XII, pp. 432–433 (6 June 1709); Saint-Simon, *Mémoires*, XVII, pp. 401–413; *Europische Mercurius behelzende al het voornaamste 't geen zo omtrent de zaaken van staat als oorlog, in alle de koningrijken en landen van Europa, en ook zelfs in verscheidene gewesten van d'andere deelen der wereld, is voorgevallen* (Amsterdam 1690–1739), March 1690, p. 211.

[84] Mathon de la Cour, *Collection de comptes rendus, pièces authentiques, états et tableaux, concernant les finances de la France depuis 1758 jusqu'en 1787* (Lausanne 1788), p. 51.

[85] See, for example, Luynes, *Mémoires*, X, pp. 204, 226; for the abuses more particularly XIII, pp. 427–428; *Journal de l'abbé de Véri*, II, p. 107.

small pensions, or easy yet profitable places in the household establishment – caretakers of hunting lodges offer an example.[86] The proximity with the upper ranks of the realm, surely not available for all servants, brought hopes of further advancement and protection. They could intercede to find other places for their clients.

For servants high and low, gratuities generated additional income. Indeed, they were seen not as an extra, but as a right. The French printed 1687 *état* gives an overview of those pledging their oath to the king in person, adding that they had to pay a certain sum to the valets in the chamber, and another unspecified sum to be distributed by the *premiers gentilshommes* to their staff.[87] Creating 100 new hereditary charges of *lieutenants de roi de province* in February 1692, Louis XIV stipulated that these new officers had to pay 150 *pistoles* to his first chamber valets 'pour la prestation de leur serment'.[88] When Louis III de Bourbon took his oath for the *survivance* of the high stewardship, he gave 2,000 *pistoles* to the *premiers valets de chambre*, 400 to the *garçons*.[89] In Vienna, the *Jurament* was only one of the occasions where such payments were standard. For *Belehnungen*, audiences, and *Neujahrsverehrungen* as well, we find neatly specified lists for payments to servants and courtiers, determined mainly by rank and proximity to the occasion. After taking leave from the emperor, for example, the visitor had to pay:

den beeden anticammerthürhütern sechs oder vier Reichsthaller, zwey Ritterstubenthürhüter drey oder zwey, Hartschier sechs oder vier, Trabandten sechs oder vier, Cammertrabanten sechs oder vier, dem Schweitzern untern Thor stehend ein Reichsthaller.[90]

These extras were defended as an age-old vested right, allegedly deriving from the *mancia* of the venerable Burgundian court. Incidentally, we find attempts

86 See the costs for clothes, fuel, and more generally *Unterhaltung* listed in early *Hofzahlamtsbücher*, recapitulated in ÖNB cod. 14027 excerpta Hofzahlamt 1575–1711, mostly for the later sixteenth century. In later *Hofzahlamtsbücher*, the *Provisionen*, *Adiuta*, *Gnadengaben*, *Recompensen*, ranging from diminutive sums of a few Gulden to huge gifts. The demarcation between small sums supporting servants, and important amounts rewarding the service of the higher courtiers emerges more clearly in the course of the seventeenth century. AN O 1 751, no. 78, describes various rights and payments included in the *livrées* and the *ordinaires en nature* for French *commensaux*. AN O 1 653, the register for the king's *cassette* 1783–1792, shows mostly lower amounts, paid to lower servants; previous overviews of pensions, for example, AN O 1 630 (1683–1718), confirm the impression that the whole range of court servants could expect some support, rarely far from the level of their ordinary wages. The 1788 *Compte rendu*, p. 95, describes the *Comptant du roi* or *cassette* as his support for poor, and contrasts it with the pensions, 'affectées sur les départments' given only in case of great services or special consideration. Widows abound both in the lists of payments, and in the staffs for the *maisons royales*, see, for example, the 1749 *Etat*, I, pp. 399–471.

87 Besongne, *Etat* (1687), pp. 214–218; the king received payments too: see the detailed overview in AN O 1 713: 'Répertoire Alphabetique des charges qui pretent serment entre les mains du Roy, avec le montant desdits sermens'.

88 Dangeau, *Journal*, IV, pp. 25, 66. 89 *Ibid.*, I, p. 200.

90 ÖNB cod 14443, fol. 81; compare L. Baur, 'Berichte des Hessen-Darmstädtischen Gesandten Justus Eberhard Passer', *Archiv für Österreichische Geschichte* 37 (1867), pp. 273–409, particularly pp. 308, 312, 330, and similar reports in Vehse, *Geschichte der deutschen Höfe*, VII, pp. 28–29.

to limit excessive growth of the *Trinkgelder*.[91] Upon his accession to the throne, Charles VI sought to prevent the 'shameful abuses' flowing from such practices, but his councillors assured him that he could not abolish these rights without at the same time improving the meagre ordinary wages. A compromise was sought, by limiting the occasions where tips could legitimately be expected, while stipulating that the servants had to conduct themselves with dignity and moderation. Haggling about these benefits is reported before and after Charles' initiative, however, and the compromise left intact the inevitability of the practices.[92]

The intermediate layer of service specialists received relatively high ordinary wages, and they were more readily adapted to merit or changing circumstances. *Virtuosi* in the chapel, or notable artists in any field, were frequently rewarded with incidental bonuses. The Habsburgs, until Maria Theresa, spent huge sums on the musical chapel, and we find its distinguished musicians among the beneficiaries of *Gnadengaben*. Repeated requests for higher *Besoldung* indicate that the musicians and other artists were not invariably well paid. Lodovico Burnacini, succeeding his father as theatre engineer after 1652 and soon surpassing him in celebrity, repeatedly had to ask for more money.[93] In 1710, the emperor owed his architect, J. B. Fischer von Erlach, 4,241 fl 40 kr.[94] In France, artists at court occupied a comparably favourable position, yet the network of pensions and rewards for artists was cast far wider, and less focused on the household staff.[95]

The wages paid to the staff of the Viennese *Bürgerspital* and materials relating to the income of Parisian construction workers allow us to put into perspective the income of courtiers. In Vienna, a simple servant in the *Bürgerspital* annually received 16 fl for his services in the last decades of the seventeenth century, the *Pfister* or baker 52 fl, the clerk 60 fl, the *Oberkellner* 75 fl, the chaplain 104 fl, and the doctor 220 fl. These wages would substantially rise in 1710: the servant's to 21 fl, the baker's to 70 fl, the clerk's to 80 fl, the *Oberkellner*'s to 105 fl, and finally the chaplain's to 204 fl – the last remarkably close to the 200 fl listed for the court chaplain in the same years.[96] To the wages cited here, we should add

91 See HHStA, ÄZA K 26 (fols. 2–14); OMeA Sr K 74, no. 16, Familienakten K 102, repaginated 26 March 1997, fols. 1–13 for detailed lists of fees for oaths, Belehnungen, and the new year; HHStA Familienakten III K 100 contains a 1644 'Verordnung des Hofmarschallamtes betr. ungebührlicher Forderung von Neujahrsgeldern und Trinkgeldern durch Angehörige des Hofstaates und betr. die Regalien bei fürstlichen Belehnungen'.

92 HHStA OMeA Prot 7 (7 October 1712), fols. 323–325; (7 February 1713), fols. 447–454. See Passer, 'Berichte', for example, at pp. 308, 312, 330, other reports in Vehse, *Geschichte der deutschen Höfe*, VII, pp. 28–29.

93 HHStA OMeA Prot 2 (24 February 1665) ask for higher *Besoldung*, granted on 26 March 1665. Lodovico Burnacini had earlier made the same request, see OMeA Prot 1 (18 March 1656), fol. 85. In the *Hofprotokoll*, *Expectanz* (i.e. the promise of an office), *Besoldung*, and *Recompense* figure prominently. See Herbert Haupt, 'Kunst und Kultur in den Kameralzahlamtsbüchern Kaiser Karls VI.: die Jahre 1715 bis 1727', *MÖStA* 12 (1993), pp. 7–186; Hadamowsky, *Barocktheater*, p. 64.

94 Holl, *Starhemberg*, p. 205.

95 See Burke, *Fabrication*; Blanning, *Culture of Power*; Jürgen Voss, 'Mäzenatentum und Ansätze systematischer Kulturpolitik im Frankreich Ludwigs XIV', in *Europäische Hofkultur*, II, ed. Buck *et al.*, pp. 123–132; Goloubeva, *Glorification of Emperor Leopold I.*

96 A. F. Pribram, R. Geyer, and F. Koran, *Materialien zur Geschichte der Preise und Löhne in Österreich* (Vienna 1938), pp. 175, 339–343; Rinck, *Leopold*, p. 202.

provisions for clothes, food, and fuel – but the same held true for the wages of household servants. Around 1645, Parisian masons and stonecutters could expect their annual income to reach *c.* 290 lt, although particularly assiduous workers could come close to 400 lt. The annual income of the day labourers assisting the masons ranged from 130 lt to 200 lt – *c.* 170 lt on average.[97] Towards 1715, their average annual earnings may have risen to *c.* 200 lt; in the years before the revolution, they stood at *c.* 280 lt.[98]

The paymasters and controllers, close to the sources of revenue, were among the best-paid servants. The two *contrôleurs généraux* in the *bureau*, each serving for six months, were listed with 900 lt *gages ordinaires* in the 1663 *état*, but by 1687 received a remarkable 15 to 16,000 lt.[99] The *Hofzahlmeister* in 1615 collected 2,400 fl, more than the senior court charges except for the *Obersthofmeister*'s 4,000 fl.[100] The *premier medecin*'s gages were 3,000 in 1676; at the Habsburg court the *Leibmedici* received a comparable 1,000 fl.[101] Three washerwomen frequently mentioned in Habsburg *Verzeichnisse*, a *Leib- und Mundwäscherin*, a *Taffelwäscherin*, and an *Edelknaben und Officierwäscherin*, collected between 800 and 2,000 fl, an indication that their responsibilities were taken as seriously as those of the doctors.

The ordinary wages of the typical honorary officers were most obviously incommensurate with their rank at court. *Kämmerer* at the Habsburg court were entitled to 480 fl throughout the seventeenth century, and in 1705 Rinck plausibly suggested that: 'keiner solchen zu ziehen verlanget'.[102] After taking their oath to the *Oberstkämmerer* they received the golden key representing their rank, the novices 'wegen desselben thun . . . ihm ein schöne Verehrung, von Silber und Gold, oder ander gallanterie'. The key, the text proceeds, usually was the only remuneration available.[103] Payment of wages to officers in the sectors susceptible to rapid inflation of honours was feasible only when numbers were stabilised.

97 Corinne Beutler, 'Bâtiments et salaires: un Chantier à Saint-Germain-des-Prés de 1644 à 1646', *AESC* 26 (1971), pp. 484–517, at pp. 500–504, 514; compare M. Baulant, 'Le salaire des ouvriers du bâtiment à Paris de 1400 à 1726', *AESC* 26 (1971), pp. 461–483, on p. 474: 'On peut en conclure, pour ces années [1644–45], qu'un bon ouvrier non spécialisé, suffisamment assidu, pouvait gagner 160 à 190 ar an . . .'.

98 Baulant, 'Salaire des ouvriers', pp. 482–483; Y. Durand, 'Recherches sur les salaires des maçons à Paris au XVIIIe siècle', *Revue d'Histoire Economique et Sociale* 44 (1966), pp. 468–480, using the percentages on p. 476.

99 For example, printed *Etat* of 1663, p. 23: 900.l. *gages ordinaires* . . . ; printed Etat of 1669, p. 41: 1,800 *gages ordinaires*. Compare AN Z 1a 475, l'Etat Général des officiers de la maison du Roy. Année 1676 fols. 136–192, here at fol. 163 (we find the *trésoriers généraux* on fols. 188–189 here, receiving substantial wages of 5,800 and 6,000 l.); Besongne, *Etat* 1687, I, p. 71, gives 15 at 16,000.

100 HHStA, OMeA Sr 184, 75/6; the *Contralor* received only 480 fl, the *Hofkammerpräsident* 2,000.

101 AN Z 1a 475, fol. 160; in HHStA, OMeA Sr 186, fol. 145r, it was noted that the *Leibmedici* rose from 800 to 1,000, the same amount is listed in Rinck, *Leopold*, and most of the intermediate *Verzeichnisse* cited earlier.

102 Rinck, *Leopold*, p. 205, compare OMeA Prot 7 (3 April 1713), fols. 515–517: Charles VI wanted to check how many chamberlains and councillors received pay, but found no precise figures were available. The emperor decided that only the chamberlains 'die beständig bei der Hoffstatt zu bleiben Obligo solle' (fol. 517r) should receive pay – yet they were granted 2,000 fl instead of the 480 habitually listed. For the councillors, matters were complicated by the fact that almost all senior court dignitaries received the rank and 2,000 pay of a councillor, whether or not actually serving in the *Konferenz*.

103 ÖNB cod. ser. n. 1849, fol. 9r; compare ÖNB cod. 14443, fol. 81r.

Even when this difficult process worked well, pay was decidedly unimpressive. The numbers of *gentilshommes servants* and *maîtres d'hôtel* remained constant after the 1660s, but their *gages* were low, and tended to decline. The 1687 *état* gives the usual 700 lt for the *gentilshommes*, but adds that 'ils ne touchent que la moitié'.[104] In the *écuries*, the number of *écuyers* showed a slight tendency to expand, yet only the few *écuyers* actually serving seem to have been paid, and the same holds true for the *gentilshommes* in the *vénerie*.[105] Between the honorary officers and the staffs' heads (the *grand* and *premier* officers) stood the permanently serving *maître d'hôtel ordinaire* and the *écuyer ordinaire*: although their rank initially may have been lower than that of the honorary servants, they soon eclipsed them in status and income. In the later eighteenth century the *maître d'hôtel ordinaire* even surpassed his superior: his *brevet d'assurance* was 350,000 lt, whereas that of the *premier maître d'hôtel* was evaluated at 250,000 lt.[106] The honorary officers in Vienna and Versailles did enjoy other privileges, notably the right to eat at their own table at court. The duration stipulated for service, a *quartier* for the French *maîtres* and *gentilshommes*, four weeks for the *Kämmerer* puts the low wages into perspective.[107] Undoubtedly, they tried, and sometimes found, other means to benefit from their honorific charges, but on the basis of the salaries and formalised advantages, we can expect that they had to invest heavily before they could reap any material benefits – if ever they would do so.

Can we say the same for the highest charges at court? Here we have to differentiate more sharply between the two courts under discussion. For all noblemen seeking employment at the Austrian Habsburg court, the nomination as chamberlain was indispensable: their date of entry determined their position at court, and this honorary office was the first step of the *cursus honorum*. No family escaped from this rule. Higher court office would come after a protracted

[104] Besongne, *Etat* 1687, p. 57.

[105] *Etat* (1663), pp. 98–99: after the *écuier ordinaire* with 600 l *gages* and 2,657 l *livrées*: we read about the *écuyers*: Quoiqu'il ait un grand nombre d'ecuyers, on ne voit ordinairement servir que ceux-cy, qui instruisent les pages & c. aux gages de 400. l. & 4.ou 500. l. de livrées, & c. [three names follow] Les autres servent quand ils sont mandés, & que le service le requiert.' Much concrete information on the *écuries* can be found in Edouard de Barthélemy, *Les Grands Ecuyers et la Grande Ecurie de France avant et depuis 1789* (Paris 1868) and Griselle, *Ecurie, Vénerie, Fauconnerie et louveterie du roi Louis XIII* (Paris 1912); for the *vénerie* see the 1749 *Etat de France*, II, pp. 264–289, and BN Clair 830, pp. 691–693, citing Louis XIV's 1706 edict allowing the *gentilshommes* to reside in their own provinces while maintaining their privileges – and the problems this entailed.

[106] AN O 1 747, no. 122.

[107] In the early seventeenth century, however, service was ideally much longer, see the 1637 Instruction for the Oberstkämmerer Hans Rudolf count of Puchaim in HHStA, Familienakten III K 100, articles 2 and 3; Kammerherreninstruktion in HHStA, OMeA Sr K 73, articles 2 and 3. The 480 fl initially must have been the reward for a full year's service. See the standard description of later practice, the two weeks *Vordienst* followed by two weeks *Hauptdienst* for two chamberlains, alternating with two others suggesting a total of four chamberlains serving at court in ÖNB cod. ser. n. 1849 fol. 9r and ÖNB cod. 14443, fol. 81r. In the *Schematismen*, for example, 1760, pp. 392–393; 1780, p. 373, we find a slightly diverging standard text describing the chamberlains, nobles from all parts of the monarchy: 'die Ihre kays. Königl. Majestäten beyderseits in der gewöhnlichen Hof-Kleydung zwey und zwey acht Tage in dem Vordienst, und acht Tage in dem Hauptdienst, nebst zweyen durch acht Tage im Vordienst solcher Gestalten bedienen, daß allezeit 6. Cammerer bey Hof sich befinden', suggesting service of 32 days, and six chamberlains at court.

period of lesser assignments: a diplomatic mission abroad, frequently costly and uncomfortable, usually far away from the distribution of graces, was a major example; councillorships in the *Hofkammer* or *Hofkriegsrat*, local government, and the army presented alternatives.[108] A nomination as *Geheime Rat* was the next step, as it brought superiority over the chamberlains, incidentally this advancement could be topped by promotion into the order of the Golden Fleece. Supreme office at court usually stood at the end of a career, and only rarely at its beginning. It was the reward for a long period of service and high investments, neither necessarily ruinous, nor always lucrative.

The four senior offices came with considerable, though hardly superlative, wages. Most lists from halfway through the seventeenth century onwards give 6,200 fl for the high steward, with another 12,000 for his *Freytaffel* at court. Curiously, Ferdinand III's *Hofstaat* gives an aggregate 6,200 fl, of which 1,200 was for the *Freytaffel*, 2,000 as *Besoldung* for his function as councillor, and 3,000 ordinary wages.[109] Rinck gave 12,700 fl as the chamberlain's remuneration; it varies greatly in manuscript sources, but is always lower, usually near 4,500 fl.[110] The marshal with 3,000 fl or less, the master of the stables and the *Hartschieren Hauptmann* with 2,000 fl stood between these two officers and the rest of the high-ranking courtiers.[111] For most senior courtiers, the wages represented only a small fraction of their massive landed income.[112] Presidents of the various councils tended to receive higher sums than courtiers below the high steward's level. The payment of wages, however, was only a minor reflection of the financial transactions between the emperor and his noble servants. Nobles

108 Müller, *Kaiserliche Gesandtschaftswesen*, particularly chapter 6, gives an excellent impression of the diplomacy as the necessary and not always welcome preliminary to high court office. See also Klaus Müller, 'Habsburgischer Adel um 1700: Die Familie Lamberg', *MÖStA* 32 (1979), pp. 78–108, here at pp. 98–99 the financial consequences of high diplomatic office; and Susanne Claudine Pils, 'Hof/Tratsch. Alltag bei Hof im ausgehenden 17. Jahrhundert', *WRGB* 53 (1998), pp. 77–99, for an illuminating impression of the toil of the spouse of a diplomat, Ferdinand Bonaventura Harrach, in securing her husband's position at court, and their dynastic interests.

109 HHStA OMeA Sr 186; the same breakdown in HKA, HZAB 1675/19, fol. 115v; 6,200 fl as a total in HZAB 1640/86; HZAB 1653/99; HZAB 1686/131; 6,200 and 12,000 in most later *Verzeichnisse*. HZAB 1714/156 gives 12,900 in cash, 21,500 'durch Anweisung' (fols. 198r, 219r); halfway through the eighteenth century OMeA Sr 96: 2,000 fl; Dickson, 'Monarchy and Bureaucracy', p. 335, n. 2, cites 10,800 fl for the *Obersthofmeister* from HZAB 1785-7/177. See the examples in Pecar, 'Ökonomie der Ehre', pp. 121–124. Whereas the French *gages ordinaires* were very stable, the Viennese wages vary substantially, and it is difficult to bring the materials into one overview.

110 HHStA OMeA Sr 186, fol. 120r: 1,750 fl; HKA HZAB 1675/119: 1,750 fl and 3,000 fl; HZAB 1686/131: 4,750 fl; halfway through the eighteenth century: OMeA Sr 94: 2,500 fl; OMeA Sr 96: 2,000 fl.

111 The marshal wages vary: HHStA OMeA Sr 186, fol. 197r, 1,200 fl; HZAB 1653/99, fol. 186, a stunning 24,000, probably showing settlement of loans or outstanding payment; 1,362 in both OMeA Sr 184, no. 85, and ÖNB cod. ser. n. 1849; 2,362 fl in AVA Harrach, Handschriften 145; 3,000 fl both in Rinck, *Leopold*, and in HZAB 1714/156 (fols. 251r, 254r); OMeA Sr 96: 2,000 fl; OMeA Sr 101: 2,400 fl. The *Stallmeister*'s wages, 800 fl in OMeA Sr, no. 75/6, and 1,416 fl in OMeA Sr 186 (fol. 162) were constantly 2,000 fl in the ÖNB Verzeichnisse and Rinck; no HZAB data have been consulted. Compare Pecar, 'Ökonomie der Ehre', p. 357, *Besoldungen* for 1720.

112 Pecar, 'Ökonomie der Ehre', pp. 126–129, stresses convincingly that great financial reserves were necessary for all families seeking high court office, and on pp. 130–134 discusses the assets of court families, noting as an example that landed income represented between 70 per cent and 97 per cent of the wealth of the Liechtenstein in the second half of the seventeenth century.

were among the main creditors of the emperor. Courtiers in particular advanced huge sums to the crown: loans alleviating acute financial crisis, and contributing to specific buildings or festivities could facilitate nomination to high office.[113] Upon the expectation of vacancy of offices it was not unusual for candidates to press their ambitions by offering loans to the crown. In 1694 the vacant charge of *Obersthofmarschal*, finally obtained by Heinrich Mansfeld, led Anton Liechtenstein to offer a 100,000 fl loan, Josef Lamberg a 50,000 fl gift. For charges in the financial administration, such *Amtsdarlehen* were standard practice. The *Hofkammerpräsident* was expected to use his personal credit to smooth the strenuous progress of state finances.[114] Conversely, the ruler's *Gnadengaben* and his *geheime Cammer* or personal expenses, include payments to a changing group of courtiers. It is rarely clear whether these gifts are connected to the courtiers' earlier contributions, or stand as rewards for loyal service. *Obersthofmeister* Johann Ferdinand Portia received 50,000 fl in 1662, *Reichshofratspräsident* Johann Adolph Schwarzenberg 20,000 in 1675; a quick random check of the *Gnadengaben* in any of the *Hofzahlamtsbücher* presents a variable array of gratifications to their peers.[115] After the death of Johann Michael Althann, Charles paid his friend's debts of 300,000 fl, provided his widow Pignatelli with an annual 72,000 fl, and princely rank for her family.[116] Pensions were structurally used to compensate courtiers, because it was easier to withhold such extras than to lower the ordinary wages once they had been raised. In Joseph I's days *Hofkammerpräsident* Starhemberg pleaded against *Besoldungsaugmentum*, preferring incidental and individual rewards.[117]

The extras, relevant for all layers of the *Hofstaat*, were highest for the supreme charges. In 1629 Carafa argued that the marshal, the quartermaster, and their subordinates received many presents from those seeking a better place to live, or conversely from those trying to escape from the burden of quartering courtiers.[118]

113 See Bérenger, *Finances et Absolutisme*, p. 447, for percentages; specific instances of courtiers' financial support in: Bastl and Heiss, 'Hofdamen und Höflinge', p. 201; Katharina Fidler, 'Mäzenatentum und Politik am Wiener Hof: das Beispiel der kaiserin Eleonora Gonzaga-Nevers', *Innsbrucker Historische Studien* 12, 12 (1990), pp. 41–68, at pp. 61–63 on Eleonora Gonzaga as Leopold's sponsor; Mensi, *Finanzen*, pp. 148–153, concentrating on the personnel of the Hofkammer, listing Salaburg, Starhemberg, Breuner, Neidhart, and Hofkammer councillors; James van Horn Melton, 'The Nobility in the Bohemian and Austrian Lands', in *The European Nobilities in the Seventeenth and Eighteenth Centuries: II Northern, Central, and Eastern Europe*, ed. H. M. Scott (London 1995), pp. 110–143, at p. 124 cites other examples.

114 Müller, 'Habsburgischer Adel', p. 101; Bérenger, *Finances et absolutisme*, pp. 421–427; Holl, *Starhemberg*, pp. 93, 96 on Starhemberg's 1703 proposal of a *taxa officiorum*; Mensi, *Finanzen*, pp. 148–153.

115 HZAB 1662/107 Portia, fol. 86v; Schwarzenberg, HZAB 1675/119, fols. 238v–239; see also Gottlieb Graf von Windischgrätz, in the same volume on fol. 240r; HZAB 1686/131: 4,000 fl for *Obersthofmeister* Ferdinand Dietrichstein on fol. 337r; 10,000 in the same volume on fol. 337v for Mansfeld, 6,000 fl for Franz Maximilian Graf von Mollart on fol. 338r–v. See in general Holl, *Starhemberg*, pp. 204–209.

116 Pecar, 'Ökonomie der Ehre', pp. 139–140.

117 Holl, *Starhemberg*, pp. 353–354; see the opposite argument in Etienne-Charles Loménie de Brienne, *Compte rendu au roi au mois de mars 1788, et publié par ses ordres* (Paris 1788) p. 96, arguing that the proliferation of different accounts and paymasters made it more difficult to control expenses, and that one paymaster should pay one well-defined and sufficient salary to the king's servants. See Hans Wagner, 'Royal Graces and Legal Claims' for the continuity of pensions as additional support for court servants in all ranks during Maria Theresa's reign.

118 Carafa in Hurter, *Friedensbestrebungen*, pp. 236–237.

In Joseph I's reign, new chamberlains following their oaths to the *Oberstkämmerer* did not honour him with a token gift, but paid him a standard 200 Kremnitzer Ducats in a 'goldgestückten Beutel'; for all imperial *Belehnungen* the senior charges received 120 fl from the tax office of the imperial Aulic Chancellery. The resulting admixture of ordinary wages, loans, gifts, extras is penetrable only when the transactions in a short period are intensively analysed – not a feasible project for this book. It will present an uneven picture with enormous benefits for some, eternal debts and recurring disappointments for others. Finally, the emperor's *hohe ministri* could expect inducements from diplomats: in 1725 Luis Duque de Ripperda sought to improve the Spanish position by distributing 1,320,255 fl among the emperor's servants at court and in the councils. While this outlay may have been exceptional, the practice was standard.[119] It is clear that the highest charges were perceived as a boost to the 'capital' of major noble houses; the substantial investments necessary for court office opened the way to a range of social and political privileges that could prove quite lucrative.

In France, the nature of offices high and low changes the picture. The *grands offices* were vested in princely and ducal families, and there was no fundamental change in their constellation after the late seventeenth century. *Survivances* secured incumbency, and family demography primarily determined the age from which younger scions would hold office. When fathers died before their sons reached a mature age, the actual services were ideally performed temporarily by other members of the family: the comte de Charolais served as high steward during the minority of Louis-Joseph de Bourbon after M. Le Duc's death in 1740; Julie Louise Constance de Rohan acted as *grand écuyer* during the minority of her son, prince de Lambesc. Venality of offices at lower levels, moreover, constituted a substantial source of income absent for Habsburg court grandees. Yet in other respects, the situation was much the same. The ordinary wages were low, hovering between 3,000 and 3,600 lt for the *grands officiers* of the household, with the exception of a surprisingly low 1,200 lt for the grand almoner and the officers for the hunt. The almoner's *gages* had already been 1,200 lt in 1484 – 1,200 was the basic payment for the highest officers in the early sixteenth century, rising to the 3,000–3,600 level in the second half of the century.[120] In addition to these *gages ordinaires* came more substantial payments, for the right to eat or offer hospitality at court, for *livrées*, for personal secretaries, for *jetons*, and sundry expenses for their staffs – such as the grand master of the wardrobe's 360 lt 'pour la nourriture d'un 4e mulet sur l'etat des menus de la chambre'.[121]

119 Pecar, 'Ökonomie der Ehre', pp. 140–141; generally, Pecar fruitfully uses Bourdieu's model to suggest that the various forms of 'capital' held by noble families were to a certain extent convertible.

120 See sixteenth-century figures in Potter, *History of France*, p. 72; Le Roux, *Faveur du roi*, p. 723.

121 See Dangeau, *Journal*, VI, pp. 269–270 (1 January 1698) for the distribution of the *jetons* on the first day of the New Year.

It is not clear whether these payments were indeed wholly consumed by the expenses that were their *raison d'être*, or partly pocketed by the *chefs* – we may expect to find reimbursements for expenses that were no longer relevant. More important were the individual recompenses: pensions, *gages du conseil*, *gages* for the knights of the king's orders, and a variety of *droits et appointements* clung either to these offices, or to the dynasties holding them. The printed *états* give these various categories, and they can be verified in manuscript sources.[122] Towards the end of the seventeenth century, 10,000 lt represented the minimum income in the upper ranks, with the high steward with nearly 60,000 at the other extreme.[123] The Condé high steward could add to this the income arising from the *casuels*, but we should keep in mind that the total of these categories represented a proportion only of 5–15 per cent of his total revenues, including the government of Burgundy and a sizeable landed income.[124]

These assessments of income indicate low and steady *gages*, combined with slowly increasing levels of other payments. The supplementary *appointements* and the brevets were variable, tied to the status of the incumbent officeholder as much as to his office – the *brevets* of *premiers valets de la chambre*, an officer included here to indicate the upper level of lesser charges, ranged from 40,000 to 150,000 lt. On the whole, the variation of the *brevets* does not show any consistent long-term pattern. Incidental rewards are not listed here, but they could easily exceed several years' income. Praslin, captain of the *gardes du corps* received 126,000 lt in 1609; Bellegarde, was given 153,000 lt in 1610, Luynes received 111,600 lt in 1616 – other substantial payments were granted to them in the years following. These impressive figures should be seen against the background of the total expenses for wages in these critical years, expanding from *c.* 400,000 to *c.* 600,000 lt. Lower staff too benefited, yet on a scale commensurate with their lesser dignity.[125] In Louis XIV's records, we frequently find more moderate recompenses, ranging from *c.* 5,000 and 15,000 lt for higher offices. Yet for special favourites, the king was hardly parsimonious. He built a splendid *chenil* worth at least 600,000 lt for his *grand veneur* and *grand maître de la garderobe*,

[122] The figures printed here are taken from the printed *états* (1663, 1669, 1672, 1677, 1687, 1712, 1722), and verified in BN MS f 7859; other sources are given when relevant. The *états* in AN Z 1a 472–523 are not very helpful, as they usually give the ordinary wages only.

[123] AN O 1 755, pp. 38, 32,800, pp. 109–110: an addition of 24,000 *livrées par augmentation* leads to the total of 56,800, repeated in the printed 1687 *état* and in O 1 751, no. 77. Yet BN MS f 7859, fols. 117–131, gives 68,600, with the payment for *collations* 11,800 instead of 1,200. The 1712 and 1722 *états* add to the standard amount of 56,800 another 120,000 *livres comme prince du Sang*, and 6,000 as governor of Burgundy. BN MS f 7859, fol. 99, for the almoner; fols. 153–172 for the chamberlain; fols. 204–208 for the *écuyer*; fols. 220–221 for the master of the wardrobe; fol. 234–235 for the *grand veneur*; for the chamber more details in O 1 822, where (on p. 3) 33,142 is given as the total income of the serving *premier gentilhomme*, with the suggestion that the three non-serving *gentilshommes* received only 3,300 less.

[124] See Table 4 for the decades around 1700 in Blanquie, 'Dans la main', p. 263.

[125] BN Mélanges Colbert 318, 'Maison, escurie, et Vennerie du Roy, pensions 1606–1656', examples cited from fols. 15–16, 21–22, 45–47.

Table 6. *Wages, supplementary income, and brevets of several important French court offices in Livres Tournois*[a]

Office	Wages	Supplementary income	Brevets
grand aumônier	1,200	14,400	–
grand maître	3,600	56,800	–
1er maître d'hôtel	3,000	24,000	250,000–400,000
grand chambellan	3,600	23,600	800,000
1er gentilshomme de la chambre[b]	3,500	10,500–30,000	365,000–500,000
1er valet de la Chambre	700	6,000	40,000–150,000
grand maître de la Garderobe	3,500	19,600	475,000
maître de la Garderobe	3,400	18,000	450,000
grand écuyer[c]	1,200–3,600	30,000	600–800,000
premier écuyer	3,000	12,125	400,000
grand maréchal des logis	3,000	22,300	300,000–340,000
grand prévôt[d]	10,750	19,750	300,000–390,000
grand veneur	1,200	17,487	230,000–500,000
grand fauconnier	1,200	19,200	150,000–250,000
grand louvetier	1,200	9,700	160,000–200,000
capitaine des gardes du corps[e]	–	14,000	400,000–500,000
capitaine de la Porte	3,000	14,500	200,000–300,000
capitaine des 100 suisses	3,600	20,400	600,000

[a]This Table is based on a variety of sources: manuscript *états* and overviews cited throughout these chapters give *gages ordinaires*, but rarely other forms of income; the printed *états* from the 1660s to 1749 usually provide the same *gages*, while usually providing *livrées*, and a variety of other rights and bonuses. The supplementary income in the Table follows the figures recurring in the *états* over a longer period, i.e. they do not include incidental rewards; nor have *casuels* been included. The *états* only incidentally include *brevets*: eighteenth-century overviews of *brevets* can be found in AN O 1 711 (fols. 1–18 for the major offices) and O 1 712. Dangeau offers further information, for this Table, for example, in *Journal*, II, pp. 71, 132; XV, p. 209. In the literature, comparable incidental data can be found, mostly fitting the figures given here, see, for example, Salvadori, *Chasse*, gives numbers on pp. 250–252, and 26–33 on pp. 418–419 the first with more *brevets* from Sourches, underlining the variability of their levels. Below, I will provide further references only for dubious cases.

[b]For the *premiers gentilshommes*, various sources cite different *gages*, benefits, and *brevets*; the 1687 *état*, p. 100, listing 3,500 *gages ordinaires* and 10,500; the 1712 *état* on p. 190 suggesting a mere 1,200 lt *gages ordinaires*, and 7,480 supplementary income; AN O 1 822, p. 3 (1780), gives *c.* 33,142 including 3,500 lt *gages*; AN O 1 820, no. 8, p. 4, gives 30,000 income and 500,000 *brevet*, no. 9 citing 33,770.18.6 as one years' revenue for Richelieu – O 1 711, fols. 1–18, gives his *brevet* in 1774 at 365,000, rising to 475,000 in 1751.

[c]Griselle, *Ecurie, vénerie, fauconnerie et louveterie du roi Louis XIII*, pp. 1, 14 (1631, 1641) cites 1,200 lt; BN MS f 7859 'Grands Officiers', fols. 204–208, gives as *gages ordinaires* 3,600 lt, a figure repeated in the printed *états*.

[d]See the unclear indication in *Etat de France* (1749), II, p. 100: 'Appointements et frais de justice 10750 l; appointements extraordinaires 6000 l, logement à Paris 3000 l. Il a droit de nommer à toutes les charges quie dépendent de la sienne.'

[e]No *gages* are given in the *états*, only an augmentation of 4,000 lt after September 1664 when Louis XIV took away their right to fill vacancies (*Etat* 1749, II, p. 270); Guy Rowlands (Cambridge) helped me to find more information, and supplied the figure of 14,000 livres from 1664 onwards, suggesting a mistake in the 1749 *état*; for the *brevet*, compare Luynes, *Mémoires*, X, p. 293 (11 July 1750) discussing the death of Harcourt, and Luxembourg's nomination as *capitaine* – without mentioning *gages*, but noting the king's policy to diminish the *brevets* of major officers by 100,000 lt upon vacancies.

the duke of la Rochefoucauld, and his gift of 150,000 lt in the war year 1693 was one among many.[126]

The pensions, relatively high for most of the eighteenth century, showed a tendency to expand, notwithstanding efforts to curtail them. Only incidental and individual boons can explain the aggregate income of Charles Eugène de Lorraine, prince de Lambesc (1751–1825), the *grand écuyer*, whose position at court secured a total 'courtly' income of 137,300 lt, not far removed from his 176,620 lt landed income.[127] Likewise, the princesse de Lamballe, *surintendante* of the queen's *maison*, received a sum of 950,000 for her various services, and the Polignacs, conspicuous favourites of Marie-Antoinette, pocketed an even more impressive sum.[128] Necker understandably wanted to reduce the incidental rewards that led to such formidable takings, and targeted the pensions in the 1780 reforms. By that time, they were distributed along the lines of the departments of the *sécrétaires d'état*; the *compte rendu* for 1787 indicates that the *maison du roi* received 4,000,000 lt – a much larger sum of 16,000,000 lt going to the war ministry. Other members of the dynasty had their own lists of recipients, and were themselves among the most conspicuous beneficiaries. Louis XVI paid the 1,600,000 debt of his brother Artois in 1783.[129]

With their income, pensions, and the substantial benefits generated by the *casuels*, or rights attached to the mutation of offices in their staffs, the dynasties of princely and ducal *grands officiers* had found a place both profitable and prestigious. They could improve it by acting as intermediaries, facilitating nominations through their close contact with the king. La Trémoille, *premier gentilhomme de la chambre*, received 150,000 lt in 1737 for the presentation of a *fermier général*. Luynes somewhat vexedly commented that although the king would at times allow such gratifications, they usually remained secret.[130] Only on an individual basis can we ascertain whether the benefits attached to court office allowed dynasties to strengthen their position, and were sufficient to cover the expenses dictated by rank and lifestyle. For the highest offices, surely the income offered a comfortable basis for conspicuous consumption, though never one consistently able to withstand the assaults of the liberality run wild fashionable among grandees. Ministers, now closer in status to the higher nobles, were likewise expected to offer hospitality on a grand scale, and flaunt their wealth – arguably, the cleavage in wealth, mentality, and political influence lay not

[126] See AN O 1 656; Dangeau, *Journal*, I, p. 116 (3 February 1685); and Salvadori, *Chasse*, p. 251; see Saint-Simon, *Mémoires*, XVII, pp. 329–331: La Rochefoucauld's 'privance' and the king's favours. Rich gifts, however, were not limited to the upper layer of the court: when Bontemps' eldest son married, the king gave him 330,000 lt; see Dangeau, *Journal*, IV, 227 (26 January 1693).

[127] Solnon, *Cour de France*, pp. 490–496, at p. 494 for Lambesc.

[128] Chaussinand-Nogaret, *Noblesse au XVIIIe siècle*, pp. 77–86.

[129] Mathon de la Cour, *Collection de Comptes Rendus*, pensions on p. 204, *gages de conseil* on p. 214, d'Artois, p. 220. For the reform proposals see Necker, *De l'administration des finances de la France*, II, pp. 390–398; AN O 1 656, nos. 18–24; 171–173 various phases of reform, the other dossiers give lists of pensions 1780–1792.

[130] Luynes, *Mémoires*, I, p. 330 (August 1737); see Solnon, *Cour de France*, p. 495.

between these upper echelons, but between lesser nobles and the elites dominating at court.[131]

CONCLUSIONS

The sequences of growth and decline at these courts show important differences. These reflect the diverging timetables of the religious and political crises, and the specific constellation of the empire. The preoccupation with the numbers and costs of the household, to be limited by written procedures and the concomitant increase of secretaries and controllers occupied with the business of accounting characterised many late medieval courts. In France, the alternation between inflation and ineffective reductions, familiar from the Middle Ages, was exacerbated in the century from 1559 to the 1650s. We cannot always state with certainty whether expansion was actually initiated by the ruler himself, or by his senior courtiers, hoping to gain influence and income by swelling the numbers of their followers at court. Surely, both alternatives were possible. Louis XIV halted the process by reducing honorary officers at court, and redefining the status of *officiers domestiques.* His *maison* set the standard for the eighteenth-century court, relatively stable until the reforms of the late 1770s and 1780s. The household never again matched the zenith reached in Anne of Austria's regency. Louis XIV's operation was partially cosmetic: it reduced status and tax privilege more than the numbers actually serving at court. His reform, finally, put a ceiling on the number of charges held by the heads of court staffs and prevented inflation by their initiative. It did not endeavour, however, to take away their rights over staffs and budgets.

At the Austrian Habsburg court, 'imperial' again only after 1556, the beginnings were more moderate, and numerical fluctuations rarely had the dynamism so evident in France. The expansion of Rudolf's last decades, attributed to the personal ambitions of courtiers in one tract, was checked by Matthias' 1615 reforms. The redefinition and expansion of honorary office in the reigns of Ferdinand II and Ferdinand III were not checked by a comprehensive reduction of honorary office in the style of Louis XIV. Instead, we find further inflation of honorary office, coupled with a slower expansion of servants in the staffs gaining pace in the last two decades of Leopold's reign. The growth continued into the 1730s, but was interrupted in the first decades of Maria Theresa's reign. Towards 1780, however, her court was even slightly larger than Charles VI's high Baroque court, though it had a more bureaucratic and military stance, calling

[131] See Chaussinand-Nogaret, *Noblesse au XVIIIe siècle*, p. 82, for the ministers; the contrast between hoberaux and noble plutocrats of mixed origins is one of Chaussinand-Nogaret's major arguments. The social proximity of ministers and high *épée,* however, has not been established beyond doubt, and may only hold true for the most conspicuously successful ministerial dynasties.

to mind the French court of the later seventeenth century. The expansion of the Habsburg household in the eighteenth century, when Europe's major courts tended to stabilise or decrease, can be connected to the increasing competition in the empire. The electors in Munich, Berlin, and Dresden became more ambitious as Charles' succession seemed less secure. The very success of Maria Theresa's reforms enabled her to re-create the court. The challenges survived by the *Monarchia Austriaca* greatly strengthened its place in Europe, as well as its internal structures, but apparently did not diminish the desirability of a conspicuous courtly centre. Joseph II shifted his means and attention in other directions, but the court survived reform and warfare, persisting into the next century.

On one particular point the two courts sharply diverge. In France from the 1650s onwards the numbers of *maîtres d'hôtel*, *gentilshommes servants*, and *conseillers* were reduced. Even in the difficult years around 1700, the high point of venality for offices throughout the realm, no inflation occurred. Venality of offices was never instituted at the Habsburg court; yet from the reign of Ferdinand II onwards the *Kämmerer* were expanding, and towards the end of the century, the *geheime Räthe* followed suit. This divergence in the role of honorary office became structural, and reflects different circumstances and strategies. At the French court the borders between actual and honorary service were diffuse. Only the highest court offices were held on a permanent basis, and the incumbent officers were frequently replaced by their proxies. Elsewhere, *service par terme* on a semester or quarter basis was the rule: 'actual' office thus could be performed for three, four, or six months a year – and for some offices during one year among several years. In Vienna most charges high or low were held by one person permanently executing its functions. The quintessentially honorary officer in Vienna, the chamberlain, however, held office on a basis more ephemeral than *service par terme* – as did other honorary officers in Vienna: the generic *Hofdiener*, the triad of officers connected to the service of the table, and later the privy councillors. The marked role of honorary office in the Habsburg monarchy, carefully restored and consolidated by Maria Theresa after her first difficult years, has no close parallel in France, and it needs further explanation.

We can only address this question if we proceed from the description of the court itself to the various connections it sustained with the elites at large. The chamberlains in Vienna cannot be included in the numbers of those expected to attend court frequently; yet their honorary office established beyond doubt their right to attend court, and confirmed the status of their families. Surely, the pressures that led Henry III or Anne of Austria to expand their households were active in Vienna as well; yet in accepting the inflation while limiting its budgetary consequences, the Habsburgs did find a means that proved quite suitable for promoting the integration of the nobilities of the various territories into the court. In addition to ennoblement and orders of chivalry, this highly inclusive form of court office allowed the emperor not only to create a bond between the territories and the court, but also to turn the hierarchy of court office in Vienna and noble hierarchies in the realm at large into communicating vessels. The first rank of the privy councillors and the second rank of the chamberlains, arranged internally according to seniority, dominated hierarchies at court, and cannot but have influenced hierarchies throughout the components of the Habsburg realm. The integrating role of honorary office in the Habsburg lands would last as long as the monarchy itself.[132]

In France the number of *officiers domestiques* diminished, but their rights and benefits were safeguarded. A tendency to adopt stricter genealogical norms was evident not only at court – witness the institution of the *généalogiste du roi* – but also in the royal orders of chivalry. The order of Saint-Michel was examined in 1661–1664, and thereafter purged of unworthy members – though it would never approach the status of the order of the Holy Ghost.[133] *Faux nobles* were exposed in the provinces too, by commissions probing into their genealogies in an attempt to limit the number of tax exemptions. Louis XIV's reforms instituted a more exclusive notion of court office, establishing the royal household as an inner sanctum to which only the finest families could aspire to belong; he strove to achieve a similar end through opposite means. The household and its trail of honorary servants became smaller, but the exclusive right to be admitted as a page to either the stables or the *chambre*, or to be 'presented' to the ruler, may have acted somewhat like honorary office in Vienna, establishing the court as the centre and yardstick of hierarchies. The presentation, and its concomitant admission to the 'honneurs de la cour', notably the right to enter the king's coach before or after the hunt, became routine in the course of Louis XV's reign. From 1732 onwards, the *petite écurie* kept a register of all male and female nobles presented to the king, and the procedure was formalised by a *règlement* in 1759.[134]

In both realms the aggregate costs for the court – including other households, buildings, and pensions – were consistently the third largest category of expenditure, never eclipsing war or debt service, but exceeding all other forms of civil expenditure. Table 7 shows that court expenditure rose in France as well as in the Habsburg lands; these rising absolute figures need to be put into the perspective of a total budget rising at a higher pace, and inflation. Most markedly, however, the graph underlines that Habsburg expenditure represented only a small portion of French court outlay. Table 8 shows the same materials in a different

[132] Or outlive it, as the peculiar institution of the *Hofrat* in contemporary Austria indicates.

[133] F. Isambert, *Recueil général des anciennes lois françaises* (Paris 1829), XVIII, no. 446, pp. 44–48: 'Statut et ordonnance pour le rétablissement de l'Ordre de Saint-Michel', and various edicts pertaining to the examination of noble lineage, mostly with fiscal motives, in the same volume.

[134] See AN M 608, 11 (6): 'Règlement fait par le roi pour les Aspirans aux honneurs de la Cour et à la Présentation' (Versailles, 31 October 1759), and MM 817 for the lists and further *règlements*.

Table 7. *Bourbon and Habsburg court expenditure 1600–1714 (grams of silver)*[a]

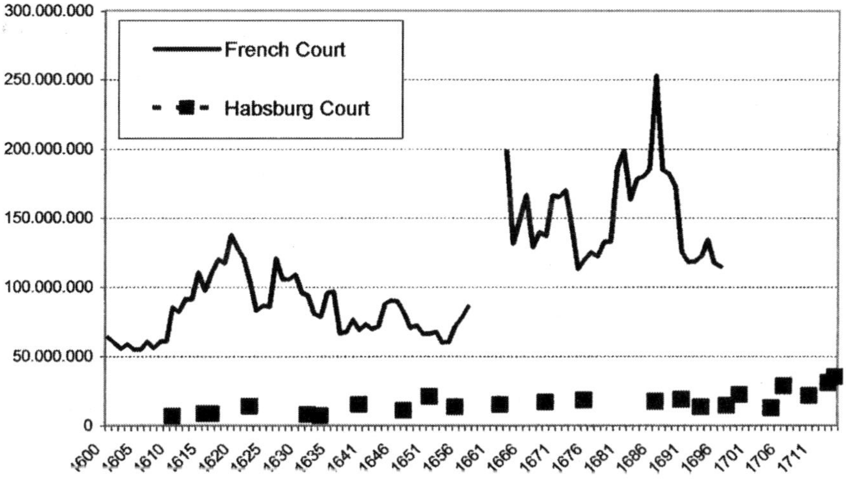

[a]See p. 89, n. 142.

Table 8. *Share of Bourbon and Habsburg court expenditure in total expenditure 1600–1714*

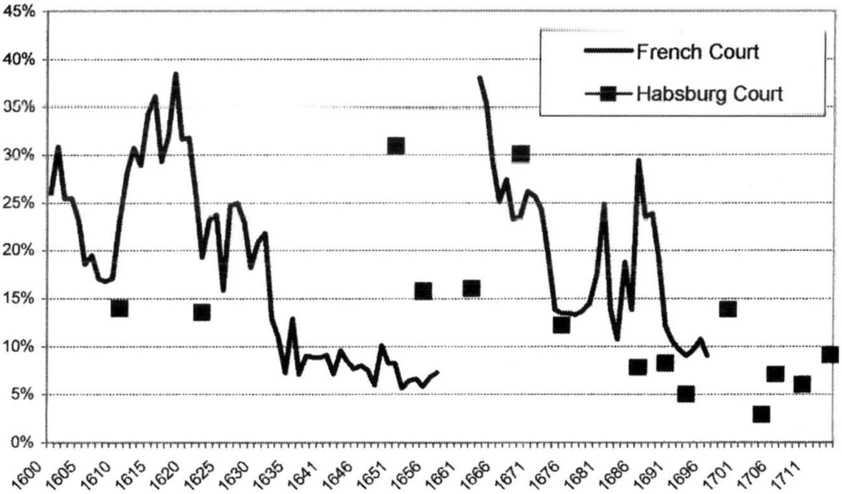

light: the share of court expenditure in the total budget varied greatly in both realms, yet within a roughly similar range, from below 5 per cent to more than 30 per cent.[135] Low percentages can be explained mostly by the incidents of warfare, invariably leading to expansion of the total budget, and frequently to a decline in court expenditure; high percentages point to years of peace with special ceremonial occasions or building projects. On average, court expenditure was around 18 per cent of total expenditure at both courts in the first half of the seventeenth century. In France, it remained close to that level for most the seventeenth century; in the Habsburg lands the share of the court in the total expenditure declined slowly, as the general budget expanded.

In the eighteenth century, the French court probably consumed a somewhat more important share, of a substantially higher budget, than did the Habsburg court. The high costs for military units, sizeable secondary establishments within the royal family, and pensions help to explain the higher French outlays. In Vienna the guards at court expanded in the later eighteenth century. Pensions, however, did not come near the costs of the households: a 1:3 ratio roughly conveys the eighteenth-century practice for peace years. Other households were never as conspicuous or as costly as in France. In the course of the eighteenth century, the king's relatives became, if anything, financially more demanding in France, whereas their share in the Habsburg budgets declined. The marked presence of the French royal family in the budget reflected their conspicuous place in French monarchy, and their frequently defiant stance – it proved more difficult to 'reform' their establishments than the *maison du roi* itself. The rational fusion of households, and the different status and attitude of archdukes, prevented such complications in the Habsburg lands. As in the seventeenth century, war upset peacetime finances, always diminished the share of the court in the budget, and could lead to a decline in absolute figures. Finally, in the 1780s, budget cuts and reforms affected the household both in France and in Austria: expenditures were drastically reduced and court outlay fell below the averages suggested above.

Comparing numbers and costs, several discrepancies strike the eye. The periods of sharp increases in numbers did not always neatly fit with rising costs of wages, provisions, or pensions. Crisis brought not only inflation of office, but also insolvency: rulers may have distributed the expectation instead of the reality of material rewards. Exemptions were easier to distribute, as their negative consequences for state finances were indirect and postponed; the same holds true for the inflation of prestige attached to office. The expansion in Anne of Austria's regency burdened the court of her son with rights and exemptions

[135] The Forbonnais materials on http://www.le.ac.uk/hi/bon/ESFDB/index.html and in Bonney, *Malet*, pp. 55–56 and Table 23, have not been inserted in my graph with percentages, yet they indicate that the share of the court in total expenditure dropped rapidly during the War of Spanish Succession, closely matching the developments in Vienna.

granted to multitudes, and must almost forcibly have led to his reductions. In the interval between Louis' early wars, and the exhausting conflicts of the two decades around 1700, the court's expenditure soared without seriously affecting the numbers of the household. Clearly, the costs of feeding, lodging, and paying the household staffs remained more or less stable, and peaks in expenditure were caused by exceptional outlay, ceremonies and festivities, pensions, or buildings – all somewhat more easily adapted to the dictates of the purse. For the Habsburg court, the huge costs spent on the court's hospitality in the early years of Ferdinand II and throughout most of his successor's reign indicate either an increase in numbers not charted here, or a level of public hospitality no longer habitual in the later seventeenth century. The rise in court expenditure in the early 1650s can be explained by the end of a protracted war and the concomitant restoration of the court, but the decline after the death of the short-lived King of the Romans Ferdinand IV, and Leopold's relatively frugal first years, need more thought. These and many other questions can only be resolved by further research.

The similarities of these households are perhaps more striking than the differences. A small upper echelon of high nobles; a more variegated and much larger group of clerics, nobles, and commoners in a second echelon, notably including the noble honorary servants; finally a broad base of servants for the day-to-day running of the household; mostly male – even in the establishments for female members of the dynasty where the proportion of women exceeded 10 per cent only in the small establishments of ruling empresses. Among the supreme officers, the correspondence was disturbed by the position of the Habsburg marshal, preceding the chamberlain as well as the master of the stables. The gradual weakening of the marshal in Vienna diminished this major difference in the constellations of supreme officers, as it underlined the supremacy of the steward and the chamberlain at both courts. Notwithstanding the rapid expansion of his staff, the Habsburg master of the stables never formally outranked the marshal, and thus was never on a par with the French *grand écuyer*.

Were the highest court dignitaries in Vienna more powerful than their French compeers? The preceding paragraphs indicate that neither the contrast of the temporary eviction of the French *grands* from the council with the more durable political responsibilities of Habsburg court dignitaries nor the fact that the great families in Central Europe frequently wielded power in the estates, and ruled unchallenged over their domains resolves the issue. The unconcealed lucrative patronage of the French *grands officiers* over their staffs, and their hereditary claims to their supreme offices were unknown at the Habsburg court. Nor do we find an equivalent for the pervasive influence of several of these families at the later sixteenth-century court, for their immense prestige and for their recurring leading role in rebellions. Both realms had experienced religious strife and protracted political crisis in the late sixteenth and the early seventeenth centuries, yet after the watershed of 1620, the Habsburg lands endured no great second trial of the bond between ruler and great nobles as expressed in the court. Therefore no reaction such as that of Mazarin and Louis XIV after the *Fronde* occurred. The basis of mutual loyalty was reinforced by the fact that the emperor's more potent rivals were not to be found among his major courtiers, but among the *Landesfürsten* in the empire. Surely, much of the tension that strained the ties between king, vis-à-vis the *princes du sang* and the major noble dynasties in France, was deflected here to these near-sovereign territorial rulers. The strengthening of loyal court nobles, by promoting them to the rank of *Reichsfürsten*, underpinned the emperor's ambitions – just as French kings had fortified their position towards their internal rivals by promoting followers to the rank of *duc et pair*.

After the *Bruderzwist*, junior branches of the dynasty, so prominent in France, were almost absent in the Habsburg lands, a happy coincidence that reduced the threat of conspicuous internal rivals to rare and relatively innocuous instances. The distant but potentially threatening presence of the princes of the empire strengthened the bond between emperor and court dignitaries. Yet the hierarchical distance between the emperor and his noble companions was far larger than that between the French king and his proud servants. Indeed, the charges of high steward, chamberlain, master of the stables, held by princely dynasties cherishing their sovereignty, in status stood between their counterparts at the Habsburg court, and the *Erzämter* of the empire, held by the electors. Marital alliances and ambitious projects of the dynasties closest to royal blood underline their elevated status in Europe, as does their role in ceremonial conflict at court – much more active and assertive than that of their lesser Viennese counterparts. With this in mind, we can readily understand the oft-cited remarks Louis XIV made in his memoirs about the princes and the council; high-handed princely agitation was indeed practically absent in his years. The princely houses and the *légitimés* again came to the fore in the decades after Louis XIV's death, and several among them took an active part in the political turmoil recurring in the second half of the century. Yet they chose a stance more muted than their sixteenth- and early seventeenth-century predecessors. Finally, several princely dynasties were successful in establishing their position in the household, as was a larger and more varied group of mostly ducal *épée* dynasties. Louis XIV's restructuring of the household consolidated the position and wealth of these dynasties holding high court office, and assisted them to form a remarkably durable bastion in the heart of the French state.

PART III

Court life

CHAPTER 5

A calendar of court life

What were the activities of the multifarious company assembled at court? How did the ruler and his retinue spend a year, a week, or a day? Did such routines take on new form in the course of the early modern age? While we can hardly recapture court life in all its detail and verve, we can reconstruct the outlines: a rough timetable and a sequence of recurring activities. *Ancien régime* monarchical government revolved around the person of the ruler; his rhythm of rising, eating, and sleeping provided the setting for most other pursuits. Yet was court life consistently synonymous with this personal agenda? 'Hof wird genennet wo sich der Fürst aufhält', Zedler noted[1] – but should we exclude independent gatherings of the substantial multitude serving the ruler from our definition of court life? Assuredly, an attempt to re-create the activities of all layers and groups at court would be as fascinating as it would be fruitless; only for the ruler do we have sufficient sources. The same ordinances that allow us to reconstruct the staffs and numbers of the court frequently allude to the ruler's schedule and activities, whereas they remain confined to a basic description of major tasks for court dignitaries, and only incidentally give hints about lower servants. The machinery of staffs and servants of the court was permanently active; only when the ruler needed the services of a specific staff, however, did it become a manifest part of court life as reflected in the sources.

Printed descriptions of festivities, travellers' accounts, the emerging periodical press, and other such widely available sources, are heavily tilted towards the public appearances of the court, in the palaces or elsewhere. We may find references to the less visible world of the ruler and his kin in diplomatic correspondence and diaries or memoirs of courtiers, but even they rarely show the ruler fully at his leisure. The courts' self-fashioning, strengthened by their competition and ever more widely disseminated through the medium of print, solidly established a highly ceremonious image of court life. It was strengthened by the late seventeenth- and early eighteenth-century vogue for treatises describing,

[1] Zedler, *Grosses vollständiges Universallexicon*, XIII, p. 405.

legitimating, or criticising the ceremonies of the European court.[2] The simultaneously swelling torrent of scandal-mongering in memoirs and pamphlets did little to correct the image: it helped to create a dichotomy of punctiliousness and debauchery, reflecting the contrast between the courts' public presentation and their tantalisingly inaccessible interiors. This Janus-faced reputation, as old as the court itself, returned with a vengeance after the most splendorous phase of the European court around 1700, and would subsequently dominate the liberal image of court life. Between these exaggerated extremes, however, we will find all shades of human behaviour.

Did ceremony extend its empire throughout the sixteenth, seventeenth, and eighteenth centuries, slowly taking hold of all spheres of activity at court, including those previously untouched by such rules?[3] The printed sources strongly suggest this, and the unpublished ordinances seem to support it as well. Ordinances throughout the centuries contain frequent verbatim repetitions; yet the rules stipulated became increasingly detailed. Reading these texts, it seems likely that court life itself changed – a change either triggered by the instructions, or simply reflected in their minute descriptions. The habitual repetition of phrases does not necessarily indicate that rules went unheeded: the weight of customs and forms in a culture heavily oriented towards the past may account for the repetition. Yet we should discriminate between the processes of putting instructions into writing, elaborating them, finally publishing them in printed form, and the actual implementing of such norms in daily life at court. Nor should we be happy to perpetuate the notion that the ruler's life was subject to an unchanging rhythm, minutely dictating his daily and monthly calendar – a cliché almost unanimously accepted by contemporaries, who readily connected supreme rank with immutable order although such a view was frequently at odds with actual practice at court.[4]

The activities at court do show great consistency over the centuries: devotion and Mass, formal audiences or oaths of officers, reading and signing papers of state, deliberating with courtiers, secretaries, or ministers; banquets and balls;

[2] See the overview and analysis of the ceremonial literature in Milos Vec, *Zeremonialwissenschaft im Fürstenstaat. Studien zur juristischen und politischen Theorie absolutistischer Herrschaftsrepräsentation* (Frankfurt am Main 1998).

[3] See Kruse and Paravicini, eds., *Höfe und Hofordnungen*, and C. M. Woolgar's detailed and admirable study, *The Great Household in Late Medieval England* (New Haven 1999) for changing household routines in the preceding period, and the tendency for meals and other occasions to become more ceremonial in the fifteenth century.

[4] For example, Primi Visconti, *Mémoires*, p. 152; Jean Rousset de Missy and Jean Du Mont, *Le Cérémonial Diplomatique des Cours de l'Europe ou collection des actes, mémoires et relations qui concernent les Dignitez, Titulatures, Honneurs et Prééminences... Et en général tout ce qui a rapport au Cérémonial & à l'Etiquette*, 2 vols. *Supplément* au Corps Universel Diplomatique du Droit des Gens 4–5 (Amsterdam and The Hague 1739), I, p. 682; Johann Christian Lünig, *Theatrum Ceremoniale historico-politicum oder historisch und politischer Schau-Platz aller Ceremonien...*, 3 vols. (Leipzig 1719–1720), I, p. 299. Küchelbecker, *Allerneueste Nachricht*, pp. 219–220, 252; Montesquieu's *pensée* 1842, *Pensées* in *Œuvres Complètes*, p. 1038; Saint-Simon, *Mémoires*, XXVII, p. 143; XXVIII, pp. 148, 340–341; p. 148 quotes the *Parallèle* (p. 87) with the familiar statement: 'Avec un almanach et une montre, on pouvait à trois cents lieues de lui, dire avec justesse ce qu'il faisoit', nuanced on pp. 340–341 by the remark that the king made known his intentions during the *lever*, and thereafter strictly followed his schedule.

games of cards and dice, or ball games; exertions of prowess, marksmanship, and equestrian skills in the festive jousts or carrousels as well as in the frequently changing forms of the hunt – arguably the most time-consuming preoccupation of many a ruler.[5] Musical and theatrical performances, often including courtiers and rulers in the cast, were equally inescapable at court. The frequency and duration of each of these activities was dependent upon the ruler's individual preferences, and it is not at all clear that any structural development overruled such individual variability. Louis XV did not necessarily spend more time on the duties and responsibilities of government than had Henry III, nor was he less enthralled by the hunt – and the same holds true for Charles VI versus Ferdinand I. 'Ceremonialisation' or other structural changes of court life can only be substantiated by examining the aggregate of the court's activities over a longer time-span. This is what I propose to do in the two following chapters.

Alas, the sources are unevenly distributed. Obviously, we have much more detailed information for the late seventeenth and eighteenth centuries than for the preceding ages. Again, the sources for the French court are more abundant than those for the Habsburgs in Vienna. The ordinances promulgated by Henry III include a remarkably detailed overview of his activities, allowing us to connect them to the days of the week and even the hours of the day. His Bourbon successors left no truly comprehensive ordinance; in Louis XIV's years, however, a short outline of charges and domestic rites was available in the printed *états*, and these may have rendered new general ordinances superfluous. Dangeau's *Journal* helps to establish a fairly detailed view of the king's schedule; in his meticulous notes, it is not invariably clear why he explicitly mentions the hour of an activity: possibly because it deviated from established routines. Likewise, he only rarely gives an hour when he adds that the king engaged in an activity 'à son ordinaire'.[6] Why should the indefatigable *Marquis*, moreover, describe details that were self-evident for his world?

For Vienna, the same problem is much more pressing. Instructions for the senior court officers, for the *Kämmerer*, for the *Hofdamen*, or the *Edelknaben* include many hints, yet they habitually refer to the 'gewöhnliche Stunden', or state that certain activities had to be done 'zu rechter zeit', rarely becoming

[5] Salvadori, *Chasse*, pp. 202–215, gives an idea of the frequency of hunting among French monarchs; compare the 'Abschußlisten' and details about frequency etc. in Oskar von Mitis, *Jagd und Schützen*. For gambling and games see Olivier Grussi, *La vie quotidienne des joueurs sous l'ancien régime à Paris et à la cour* (Paris 1985).

[6] Dangeau, *Journal*, I, pp. 87–89: 'Fin de l'année 1684', however, gives a summary of daily routines where such questions are addressed explicitly. Both Dangeau and Sourches, the latter far less preoccupied with the *vie quotidienne* of king and courtiers, often add 'à son ordinaire', or 'à l'ordinaire' to the king's pursuits, instead of explicitly referring to hours or other details. See *Moi, Marie Du Bois. Gentilhomme Vendômois valet de chambre de Louis XIV*, ed. François Lebrun (Rennes 1994), p. 155, waking the *dauphin* 'plus tôt que son heure ordinaire'. Luynes fulfills a comparable role for the reign of Louis XV; his reminiscences tend to be as unaffected as Dangeau's. Sourches (*Mémoires*), less interested in humdrum activities, and more outspoken in his views, is less useful here.

more specific.[7] Nor would they see any reason to describe or explain the everyday habits at court. It is easier to find information about visits of sovereigns, audiences, and festive occasions, but these will not fully match daily routines.[8] The *Schematismen* and the *Hofkalender*, printed only in the eighteenth century, do not offer descriptive sections. Only for the second half of the eighteenth century do we have sources comparable to the French memorialists, notably the diary of Johann Josef Khevenhüller-Metsch, Maria Theresa's *Obersthofmarschall*, *Oberstkämmerer* and finally *erster Obersthofmeister*.[9] Yet by that time, the habits of the Viennese court had markedly changed, showing a mixture of Habsburg traditions, French fashions, and a more national idiom arising in the reforms following the mid-century crisis of the Habsburg dynastic state. Thus, while we have abundant sources for the great public presentations of the dynasty, and sufficient information to outline the recurring patterns of the year throughout the early modern age, the more intimate details of week and day partly elude our examination, and much of what we can establish for Versailles remains shrouded for the Hofburg.

THE LITURGICAL YEAR

At all courts, the liturgical year dictated a basic sequence of annually recurring religious celebrations and feasts.[10] In addition to the major celebrations of All Saints, the Christmas cycle from Advent to Epiphany, the Easter cycle from

[7] HHStA ÄZA K 8 (24 September 1670): instruction for Eleonora Gonzaga's Hofmeisterin, fols. 301–308, 'gewöhnliche Stunden' on fol. 302v; or HHStA ÄZA K 9, 1673–1676, a similar instruction for Margarita Teresa's Obershofmeisterin, adapted for Claudia Felicitas by comments in the margin, fols. 463–469, on fol. 465r we find a reference to hours: *Hofdamen* could not leave court before 10:30 (crossed out), and had to be back before 7.00 (crossed out and changed to 8.00), and in winter before 6.00 (crossed out and changed to 7.00). 'Zu rechter Zeit' on fol. 465v; on 468v: at 6.00, the Hofdames could spend some time in the Audienz Stube with the *cavagliri* before serving the empress' table. A similar text (HHStA OMeA Sr. 367 (1557–1699), no. 16) was edited by Bastl and Heiss, 'Hofdamen und Höflinge', pp. 235–243; see p. 238 for the hours cited above. Compare Johann Weickhard Auersperg's instructions for his daughter, printed in Grete Mecenseffy, *Im Dienste dreier Habsburger. Leben und Wirken des Fürsten Johann Weikhard Auersperg (1615–1677)* (Vienna and Leipzig 1938), pp. 505–508. The instructions for the *chamber* are even less informative in this respect; the March 1651 Kammerherreninstruktion in OMeA Sr K 73 does not refer to the court's timetable, nor do the 20 March 1637 parallel 'Oberstkämmerer Instruktion und Ordnung' in HHStA Familienakten, III, K 100, or the March 1651 Kammerdienerinstruktion in OMeA Sr K 74, no. 11.

[8] For example, see the extracts from the Zeremonialprotokoll (HHStA ZA Prot) in the ältere Zeremonialakten (ÄZA) discussing the frequent exchanges of visits between the electors, emperor, empress and the newly elected king of Bohemia, Ferdinand IV, in Prag, 1652–1653, or the electoral audiences with the empress in ÄZA 3. Such documents can be found for almost any year. See further discussion of these sources below.

[9] Khevenhüller, *Tagebuch*, and Elisabeth Grossegger, ed., *Theater, Feste und Feiern zur Zeit Maria Theresas 1742–1776*, Österreichische Akademie der Wissenschaften Philosophisch-Historische Klasse Sitzungsberichte 476, Veröffentlichungen des Instituts für Publikumsforschung 12 (Vienna 1987). See Dickson, *Finance and Government*, I, pp. 340–341, n. 31, with details of Khevenhüller's career. During most of his short incumbency as *Obersthofmarschal* (November 1742– September 1745) he also was *anderter Hofmeister.*

[10] Adamson, *Princely Courts*, Introduction, pp. 24–47. Woolgar, *Great Household*, pp. 83–110; Küchelbecker, *Allerneueste Nachricht*, chapter VI, gives a month-by-month register of the 'Solennitäten und Andachten' taken from the Hofkalender; divided into 'Gala-Tag' or celebrations of the dynasty's birthdays, 'gewöhnliche Andachten und Solennitäten', and 'Toison-Feste'. His chapter VII describes the 'Divertissemens und Lustbarkeiten': hunting, music, sleighrides, Wirtschaften, etc.

Ash Wednesday to Whitsunday, Trinity, Corpus Christi, and the Marian Feasts (Purification 2 February, Annunciation 25 March, Assumption 15 August, Nativity 8 September), we find smaller celebrations and the feasts of saints. The less than pious rituals of Carnival, occupying a more ambivalent position in the liturgical calendar, enlivened the weeks between Epiphany and Ash Wednesday. The courts' tables inevitably followed the cadence of *jours gras* and *jours maigres*, and the abstention of Lent. Catholic ritual was a potent force at all Catholic courts: devotions and celebrations structured the day as well as the year.[11] While counter-reformatory erudition attempted to strip Catholicism of some of its more colourful paraphernalia, a variety of new devotions was embraced, new orders were founded, and new churches constructed. The ties between religion and rule were strengthened, and as both the Habsburg emperors and the French kings could distribute a wealth of ecclesiastical offices and benefices, the court inevitably was a focus for prelates as well as for administrators and soldiers.

Hierarchies terrestrial and celestial intertwined at court, as the rulers' deference to heavenly powers found its logical extension in the deference of subjects towards superiors.[12] The solemn rituals of the liturgical calendar engaged the ruler and his followers in public worship; marches and processions paraded the hierarchies of a reverent yet proud community.[13] Henry III added his own inventions to the established religious customs, and wanted his court to accompany the pilgrimages and processions dictated by his religious fervour, too high pitched for many of his courtiers. The relics of the *Sainte-Chapelle* were paraded through Paris in an October 1574 procession, in which the king took part, 'tout du long disant son chapelet'. He had prohibited the court's ladies from participating, stating 'qu'il n'y avoit de devotion où elles estoient'.[14] The

[11] Küchelbecker, *Allerneueste Nachricht*, pp. 222–249, gives a detailed calendar of one year at court. For similar calendars and an interesting overview (with bibliography in the notes), see Elisabeth Kovacs, 'Kirchliches Zeremoniell am wiener Hof des 18. Jahrhundert im Wandel von Mentalität und Gesellschaft', *MÖStA* 32 (1979), pp. 109–142, esp. the lists in nn. 61, 69, 84. Kovacs shows the continuity until the first decade of Maria Theresa's rule, and the changes that occurred afterwards. Also see Anna Coreth, *Pietas Austriaca. Ursprung und Entwicklung barocker Frömmigkeit in Österreich* (Vienna 1959); Nicolas Le Roux, *Faveur du roi*, shows the impact of Henry's religious attitudes; *Moi, Marie Du Bois*, shows the density of religious celebrations, at court and in Du Bois' own territories.

[12] Lünig, *Theatrum Ceremoniale*, I, p. 292, saw this as the main cause for ceremony at court: the *Pöbel* needed to see a godly example of orderliness and hierarchy, otherwise it would not be obedient, and copy the bad example of the rulers. Compare the detailed and convincing study by Milos Vec, *Zeremonialwissenschaften*. See Theodore Godefroy's explicit recognition of the religious connotations of ceremony in BI coll. God., 481: fols. 72–73, points 34, 35 and 52 on fol. 73: 34, Respect rendu à la religion. 35, Respect rendu aux ecclésiastiques. 52, Est reservé au roy de baiser les reliques portées au devant des eglises, lorsqu'il passe.

[13] See Denys Godefroy, *Cérémonial François* (Paris 1649), II, pp. 933–987, for the kings' processions.

[14] Godefroy, *Cérémonial François*, II, p. 965; see the 1585 *règlement* in BN Brienne 256 (alternatively BN MS naf 7225), fol. 85, urging the senior charges to attend Masses and Vespers, for all major feasts, and each first Sunday of the month in Notre Dame cathedral, and the variant in *AC*, p. 323. In his paper at the September 2000 Marburg conference Nicolas Le Roux discussed pilgrimages on foot to Orléans and Chartres with grumbling courtiers, see 'La Religion des courtisans dans la France de la Renaisssance', in *Hofgesellschaft und Höflinge*, ed. Malettke and Grell, pp. 507–524, and *Faveur du roi*, pp. 593–602. Compare Saint-Simon, *Mémoires*, XXVIII, pp. 364–371, for devotions in the later years of Louis XIV, the *Saint-Esprit* on p. 367, other processions in the following pages.

institution of the new exclusive order of the *Saint-Esprit* in 1578 was closely connected to Henry III's religious attitudes. Its major celebrations on 1 January (Circumcision), 2 February (Candlemas or *Chandeleur*), and Pentecost would retain their religious connotations, and included a procession to the chapel, in the company of the king.

Henry IV suppressed several of the conspicuous innovations of his Valois predecessor, but we encounter the regular pious customs in his reign, and the convert-king himself patronised a religiously inspired new order of chivalry.[15] Liturgical occasions would retain their conspicuous place in the calendar of the court. French kings and their following would habitually take part in processions on 2 February; Palm Sunday (*Dimanche des Rameaux*); Corpus Christi or *Fête-Dieu*.[16] In a February 1638 declaration, Louis XIII instituted a 15 August procession for the *Sainte Vierge*, probably to celebrate Anne of Austria's unexpected pregnancy. In 1676, Louis XIV reinstated this procession, a measure he repeated in 1700; thereafter we frequently find accounts.[17] On Holy Saturday, and on the vigils of Pentecost, 15 August or 8 September (Assumption or Nativity of our Lady), 1 November (All Saints), and Christmas, French kings were expected to take communion and touch their *malades*[18] – the latter a quality the Habsburg emperors lacked. We find kings touching *malades* on other days too, with numbers varying from a few dozen to more than a thousand.[19] In addition

[15] See *DAR*, p. 939: in 1608 Henry asked the pope's permission to sponsor the new order of Notre-Dame du Mont-Carmel, including both ecclesiastic and lay members and later fused with other orders. Dangeau served as grand-master in Louis XIV's reign, an honour thereafter held by members of the royal family.

[16] These are cited as the 'ordinary' processions in Trabouillet, *Etat*, 1712, I, pp. 40–41 and 311–312. See Henry IV's processions and habitual religious ceremonies in *Cérémonial François*, II, p. 965; BM 2740 (1672–1677), fol. 34, notes the procession 'qui se fait tout les ans le 22.e de Mars en mémoire de la réduction de Paris soûs le regne d'Henry 4.e . . ." BM 2742, fol. 183, again describes the 'procession du 22 mars' now held on 19 March 1689. Yet *Cérémonial François* gives the same procession for earlier years, for example 1531 on II, p. 938, connecting it to the 'reduction de Paris sur les Anglois' on II, p. 978. Compare E. Soulié and E. de Barthélemy, eds., *Journal de Jean Héroard sur l'enfance et la jeunesse de Louis XIII 1601–1628*, 2 vols. (Paris 1868), I, for example, pp. 99 (All Saints), 255–258 (Holy Week). Saint-Simon, *Mémoires*, XXVIII; Luynes, *Mémoires*, frequently cites the processions, for example, I, pp. 166, 275; II, p. 176; IX, pp. 50, 81, 428 indicating continuity.

[17] Saint-Simon, *Mémoires*, XXVIII, p. 367, n. 3; BM 2740 fols. 79–81 'Procession du 15 aout 1676' in Paris, with all the major institutions represented, and for 1683 BM 2742 (1682–1691), fol. 97v, in Versailles, with king and court. In BN MS f 16633, an overview by the master of ceremonies Nicolas de Sainctot, we find on fol. 269 the 15 August 1683 ceremonies in Versailles and in Paris with the major corporations, Sainctot refers back to his longer description in the *registre* for 1675, suggesting that the ceremony had been re-established earlier. On fol. 370 of BN MS f 16633, we find Sainctot's description of the 1684 *procession du Saint-Sacrement* (in Valenciennes); typically, the ceremony was mentioned only because of an ambivalence in the ceremonial proceedings – most recurring liturgical ceremonies went without further comment or description, and thus are less dominant in the sources than they were in practice.

[18] See Luynes, *Mémoires*, I, p. 350, cites these six occasions for communion, listed as the 'six festes' in Henry III's ordinances, only Luynes suggests that the king alternated between Assumption and Nativity.

[19] See Knecht, 'The Court of Francis I', p. 12, for earlier data; Héroard, *Journal*, includes such entries for most feasts, and mentions incidental other instances of the royal touch: see, for example, I, pp. 255–258, 419; II, pp. 120–121 (1,070), 122 (700), 191 (68), 223 (600), 256–257, 292. Sourches and particularly Dangeau faithfully report them; see the instances cited below. Luynes' entries suggest continuity in this respect, yet see his entry for 8 September 1737 Nativity of Our Lady, Luynes, *Mémoires*, I, p. 350 noted: 'Le Roi . . . a touché les malades au pied de l'escalier de marbre, il n'y en avoit qu'un très petit nombre et tous étrangers' – an instance of the 'negative Kommunikation' introduced by Heinz Duchhardt, 'Krönungszüge. Ein Versuch zur "negativen Kommunikation" ', in *Im Spannungsfeld von Recht und Ritual. Soziale Kommunikation in Mittelalter und früher Neuzeit*, ed. H. Duchhardt and G. Melville (Cologne 1997), pp. 291–301.

to the processions of Corpus Christi, the *Saint-Sacrément* was exposed twice a week in the chapel of Versailles in the last decades of Louis XIV's rule.[20]

The king's public devotions had a clearly representative character, as the following description of Louis XIV's devotion on Christmas eve in 1685 suggests:

Les jours que le Roy doit communier, il s'habille en manteau, avec le cordon de l'ordre sur son manteau. Deux huissiers marchens devans luy avec leurs masses. Le Grand Maître et le Maître des Cérémonies s'y doivent trouver et marcher toujours devans le Roy. Le Roy va a midy à la messe, précédé du Capitaine des cens Suisses et suivy immediatemens par le Capitaine des Gardes du Corps.[21]

In the church, the *grand aumônier*, or in his absence the *premier aumônier*, presented the Evangel to the king on his *prie-dieu*.[22] After kissing the holy book, the king was allowed to choose a Hostia, that was subsequently consecrated and put on a *siège pliant* in front of the altar. He proceeded to the altar still accompanied by *huissiers*, *capitaines*, and *maîtres*. The *nappe* or cloth carrying the paten with Hostias was held by two *aumôniers* at the side of the altar, and by two *princes du sang* (or in their absence dukes) at the side of the church. After the king's communion, the bishop offered him the chalice, and subsequently the highest-ranking prince presented him the *serviette*. The king withdrew to his *prie-dieu*, where he attended the rest of the ceremony – with more Divine Offices immediately following afterwards on the major feasts.[23] When present, the *enfants de France* would go through similar motions, attended by the *grand aumônier* or his substitute, whereas the princes had to make do with one of the serving almoners. The ceremony of the royal touch followed after Mass:

Le Roy touche ensuite les malades, le capitaine des gardes leur tien les mains, le premier medecin leur mets la main sur la teste, il est habillé en robe de medecin aussi bien que les autres medecins et chirurgiens qui le suivens. Derrière le Roy marche le premier aumosnier qui distribue a tous les pauvres malades que le roy touche chacun une pièce de quinze sols.[24]

20 For the exposition of the *Saint-Sacrément*, see Trabouillet, *Etat* 1712, pp. 292–293. See, for example, the frequent descriptions of processions and ecclesiastical ceremonies in BN MS f 16633 and BM 2737–2751 (or the old 'cotte' of 1848 a–n): Sainctot's Journal copied and prolonged by Desgranges, a previous commis of Pontchartrain, who had obtained the charge of master of ceremonies in August 1691. The fifteen volumes of this series go from the 1650s to the late 1720s; interestingly, the 1650s do not seem to be covered, a situation matching that of the *états*. The first volume, BM 2737, includes an *avertissement* where Desgranges lists his sources. The descriptions of ecclesiastical ceremonies were mostly connected to dynastic incidents such as baptisms or funerals, to the Parisian corporations, or to the elucidation of ranks at court, the latter, for example, on BN MS f 16633, fol. 216v, connecting the hierarchy of *aumôniers* with the hierarchy of princes for the 'ceremonies du jour des cendres'. We find a variant of this description in Desgranges' copy of Sainctot's journal, BM 2742 (1682–1691), fol. 7; BM 2742 (1682–1691), fols. 185–186, describes various ceremonies in the Holy Week of 1689.

21 BM 2742, fols. 140–141: 'Communion du roy, 24 Decembre 1685. Mr. de Blainville'.

22 Lünig, *Theatrum Ceremoniale*, II, pp. 1016–1017, describes a clash between the *premier aumônier* and a senior cardinal on Maundy Thursday 1718: who would in absence of the *grand aumônier*, perform his tasks in the chapel, the bishop who was *premier aumônier*, or the visiting cardinal? The *premier aumônier* was subsequently granted this honour. Luynes, *Mémoires*, however, notes several conflicts along the same lines, see particularly IX, pp. 63, 73–75.

23 For example, see Dangeau, *Journal*, I, p. 269, for Christmas Eve and Christmas 1685, where he notes that on the 24th the king, *monseigneur* and the *dauphine* attended their 'trois messes' (the first starting at 10.00) and the 25th, 'passèrent presque toute la journée à l'église'.

24 BM 2742, fols. 140–141.

Louis XIV distributed ecclesiastical benefices in the afternoon of these days, attracting a flock of prelates to the court. The celebrations entailed less strictly liturgical ceremonies, such as the rulers' public dining.

A variety of complications could lead rulers to temporarily refrain from practising the royal touch. In addition to the ruler's infirmity, or the threat of contagious diseases, we find a more intriguing cause for its suspension. An eighteenth-century erudite *histoire ecclésiastique* noted that Louis XIV:

> Dans les Pâques de l'an 1680, [il] avoit repris l'usage des sacrémens, dont il s'étoit abstenu durant plusieurs années, au scandale de son peuple, il est vrai, mais préferant la honte d'encourir la blâme publique au crime de profaner les Saint Mystères: il avoit continués depuis de s'en approcher au moins à Pâques, à la Pentecôte, à la Toussaints et à Noël.[25]

If indeed the younger Louis XIV abstained from communion on the greater feasts, he must likewise have refrained from touching his *malades*, otherwise his profanation would have been even worse. Thus, while these rituals were habitually undertaken throughout the seventeenth century, and lasted deep into the eighteenth century, lapses may not have been uncommon.[26]

From Epiphany, the occasion for a joyous banquet celebrating the *fête des Rois*,[27] to Ash Wednesday, masquerades and light-hearted feasts were prominent. The memorialists' entries show that the early months of the year were the preferred season for such divertissements. During Holy Week, however, a crowded

[25] Oroux, *Histoire ecclésiastique*, II, p. 525.

[26] Héroard, *Journal*, II, pp. 237 (17 October 1619), where Louis XIII was unwilling to touch the *malades* who persecuted him even while the Plague was in Paris. He asked his confessor Arnoux to speak to them, and complained that they said that kings could not be infected, and treated him as a *Roi de cartes*. Dangeau and Sourches briefly mention many such occasions, and their notes allow us to conclude that even these venerable ceremonies did not invariably proceed along the lines dictated; see, for example (the selection is random, but can but can be extended ad libitum, both for the habitual ceremonies and for the more exceptional lapses): Sourches, *Mémoires*, IV, p. 464 (9 June): 'Le 9, qui étoit le jour l'octave du Saint-Sacrément, le roi [malade] n'alla pas à la procession, mais Monseigneur et les trois princes ses enfants y allèrent avec la même cérémonie que si le roi y eut été, hormis les gardes du corps, les cent suisses, et les gardes de la prévoté de l'hôtel allèrent attendre Monseigneur à la paroisse et ne l'escortèrent point en revenant, après qu'il eut entendu la grand "messe" '; Sourches, *Mémoires*, VIII, pp. 210–211, no procession on the *fête-dieu* in June 1693: the king visited the army; VIII, pp. 343–344 (10 June 1694): the procession had to do without the king, but *Monsieur* was willing to take over the task; Sourches, *Mémoires*, VIII, pp. 369–370 (1694), Mary's Assumption: 'Le 15, le roi fit ses dévotions, mais il ne toucha pas les malades des écrouelles, avec beaucoup de raison, vu la quantité de maladies populaires qui couraient alors auxquelles les medecins ne trouvoient aucuns remèdes.' Nor did the king distribute benefices, though he took part in the habitual devotions; Sourches, *Mémoires*, VIII, pp. 397–398, All Saints 1694: no *toucher*, now because of Louis' gout; the king did distribute benefices and attend Divine Offices; Sourches, *Mémoires*, VIII, p. 244, Mary's Assumption 1693: no royal touch because the king took quinquina, 'messe à la tribune' in the Versailles' chapel, 'de plain pied' with the king's apartment. Yet he took no communion, and therefore (Sourches argues) no distribution of ecclesiastical benefices took place, much to the regret of the assembled prelates. Luynes' *mémoires* lists many occasions for the royal touch and parallel devotions, incidentally adding 'à l'ordinaire', for example, *Mémoires*, I, p. 154, and also providing explanations when the king did not take communion, or touch the *malades*, suggesting the stability of the custom, see, for example, I, p. 428, when the king was ill. For the temporary disruption of the *toucher* see below; in general on the royal touch see H. Weber, 'Das "Toucher Royal" in Frankreich zur Zeit Heinrichs IV. und Ludwigs XIII', in *European Monarchy*, ed. Duchhardt *et al.*, pp. 155–170; and David Sturdy's 'The Royal Touch in England', in the same volume on pp. 171–184, sceptical about the survival of the tradition into the eighteenth century.

[27] See the descriptions in Sourches, *Mémoires*, III, p. 342 (6 January 1691); AN O 1 822, p. 64: 'Bal de la veille des rois 1708, antichambre pour le buffet; salon pour quatre tables où le roi a mangé'. Each of these tables had 17 *couverts*.

sequence of religious celebrations occupied the court. Notable among these was the Maundy Thursday re-enactment of the Last Supper, or *pedilavium.* This habit, originating in Catholic liturgy and habitually practiced in churches and monasteries, had turned into an obligation for all major ruling houses. The king washed the feet of twelve (or thirteen: both numbers are repeatedly mentioned in the sources) carefully selected poor men or boys. The queen, or the *dauphin*, might choose to do likewise. The humble participants were given a splendid meal, served by the king and his relatives.[28] After the ceremony, they would receive other benefits, like the *malades* touched by the king.[29] Jean Héroard, young Louis XIII's doctor, tells us that when the five-year-old *dauphin* was first expected to perform these rites in his father's name he begged to be excused, stating that the poor 'ont les pieds puants' and adding he would only wash the feet of girls – yet no sovereign could lightly escape from these time-honoured rituals.[30]

The pace as well as the intensity of the household's devotions changed in the course of the eighteenth century. Louis XV's extramarital adventures, starting in the 1730s, prevented him from touching his *malades*, as this rite demanded preliminary confession and communion. From 1739 to 1744 the king refrained from confession and communion, and thereafter he did not practise the royal touch. Louis XVI touched more than 2,400 'écrouelleux vérifiés' after his *sacre* in 1775. Croÿ, no stranger to the routines of the court, commented that:

> A cause de la chaleur, cela puait, et était d'une infection très marquée, de sorte qu'il en fallait bon courage et force au roi pour faire toute cette cérémonie, que je n'aurais pas cru, sans l'avoir vue, si rude et répugnante.[31]

It is possible that Louis XVI took up the tradition that had lapsed in his grandfather's reign, and again touched the *malades* on the great religious feasts, yet

[28] See the description of this 'last supper', *cène*, or *coena* in AN O 1 751, no. 70, where the poor seem almost absent, as only the rank and order of the dignitaries serving them are discussed. Boislisle included Du Peyrat's *Histoire ecclésiastique de la France* (1645) description of the *cène* in the addition to Saint-Simon's *Mémoires*, XXVIII, pp. 542–544. Compare Luynes, *Mémoires*, for example, V, p. 376; IX, p. 377, for a 1744 and 1749 *cène*, with some varying practices, *duchesses* assisting in the queen's *cène*, 'ceux qui se sont présentés' in the king's 1748 and 1749 *cènes*. Usually, only princes served the poor, assisted by court staff.

[29] BM 2740 (1672–1677): fols. 49–50, a description of the *pedilavium* 'la cœne fait à Versailles' on 7 April 1675, with 12 participants and again on fols. 72–74 (1676), now with 13. The princes *étrangers* and the *ducs-pairs* wanted to take part in the ceremony, but the king explicitly restricted it to the royal family. In BM 2742 (1682–1691), fol. 185, we again find the *coene*, *cena*, or *cène* on 7 April 1689 with 13 children. When the king was prevented from performing his ceremonial duty, a close relative would take charge, see, for example, Dangeau, *Journal*, II, p. 130, who notes on 15 April 1688: '*Monseigneur* fit la cérémonie de la cène'. Luynes, *Mémoires*, II, p. 98. See more examples in Lünig, *Theatrum Ceremoniale* for the *pedilavium* II, pp. 996–997, pp. 1013–1014 (emperor and German prince: 12 poor), pp. 1030, 1032 (France: 13 poor) on the *toucher*: II, pp. 1015, 1026–1027, the procession on 15 August: II, p. 1031. In Vienna we also incidentally find the 13, see HHStA, ÄZA K 12 'liste der *dreyzehn* alte Männer die öffentlich gespeist wurden'. Thomas Schäfer, *Die Fusswaschung im monastischen Brauchtum und in der lateinischen Liturgie. Liturgiegeschichtliche Untersuchung* (Beuron 1956), pp. 44–48, 90–91, and 96–97, discussed the varying practices, ranging from a handful to more than 300 persons. On pp. 96–97 Schäfer notes that papal ritual itself prescribed both the *mandatum clericorum*, with 12 clerics, and the *mandatum pauperum*, with 13 poor.

[30] See the remarkable notice in Héroard, *Journal*, I, pp. 255–257 (12 April 1607).

[31] *Journal inédit du duc de Croÿ*, II, pp. 202–204.

courtiers' memoirs as well as the periodical press conspicuously lack references to the practice.[32] Throughout the reigns of Louis XV and Louis XVI, other devotions at court, notably the *cène*, and the processions connected to royal orders or the *fête-dieu*, are described as a matter of course.

While the Austrian Habsburgs in the later sixteenth century may not have matched Henry III's Catholic fervour, they would celebrate the same feasts and processions.[33] Their seventeenth-century successors, moreover, cultivated their counter-reformatory piety even more conspicuously than did their Bourbon rivals. Under Ferdinand II, Ferdinand III, and Leopold I, the sequence of processions and commemorative services became increasingly dense. Every year, the Habsburg *Hofstaat* took part in processions on Palm Sunday, Tenebrae Wednesday (to the Holy Sepulchre in Herrnals), and Pentecost. In the early eighteenth century, Küchelbecker noted nine processions in Whitsun week, most of them including members of the imperial family. Three- six- (or forty hours) and nine-day devotions recurred, often devoted to the cult of Corpus Christi, the adulation of the Hostia – the equivalent of the cult of the *Saint-Sacrément*.[34] Relics were paraded through the streets, and offered for adulation.[35] Miracles were hailed and commemorated. Eleonora II Gonzaga, Ferdinand III's widow, instituted the female *Stern-Creuz Orden* in 1668, having recovered a cherished reliquary from the great fire of the Hofburg, with the golden cross molten, the crystal capsule shattered, but the wooden fragment of the cross untouched. Leopold himself, after having been miraculously saved in 1691, when lightning struck a *Tischl* in his *retirada* or cabinet in Laxenburg, duly honoured the occasion with an annual

32 In 1739, Louis XV broke with the tradition of the royal touch, see Luynes, *Mémoires*, X, pp. 391–392; Michel Antoine, *Louis XV* (Paris 1989), pp. 486–487; Minois, *Confesseur du roi*, p. 498, citing Argenson. Leonhard Horowski brought a conclusive quote to my attention. In 1769 Louis XV, writing to his grandson the duke of Parma, states: 'Il est vray, mon cher petit-fils, que j'ay acquis a mon sacre le don de pouvoir être l'instrument de la grace que Dieu fait de guerrir des écrouelles, mais pour cela il faut que j'y sois [in a state of grace following communion] moy même, et il y a du temps que cela ne m'est arrivé. Nous avons en ce païs cy des remèdes pour guérir de cette maladie. Si vous en voulez je vous en envoirai et la manière de l'administrer'; *Lettres de Louis XV à son petit-fils l'infant Ferdinand de Parme*, ed. Philippe Amiguet (Paris 1938), pp. 135–136. Marc Bloch, *Les Rois thaumaturges. Etude sur le caractère surnaturel attribué à la puissance royale particulièrement en France et en Angleterre* (Paris 1983 [Strasbourg 1924]), pp. 397–405, argues that Louis XVI again touched his *malades* on the great feasts notwithstanding the paucity of documentary evidence. This is possible, but far from certain; D'Hézecques, *Souvenirs d'un page*, pp. 177–194, neatly summarises religious ceremonies but does not mention the royal touch, a subject likely to have attracted his attention. In Louis XV's years, we do find the *cène* or Maundy Thursday ceremonies mentioned 'à l'ordinaire': Luynes, *Mémoires*, for example, XV (1756–1757), p. 25, April 1756; XVI (1757–1758), pp. 15–16, April 1757. Paul Kléber Monod, *The Power of Kings: Monarchy and Religion in Europe 1589–1715* (New Haven and London 1999) suggesting the end of 'the sacred authority of monarchy' by 1715, underestimates a continuity possibly overstated in Bloch's perceptive study.

33 See, for example, *Hans Khevenhüller kaiserlicher Botschafter bei Philipp II Geheimes Tagebuch 1548–1605*, ed. Georg Khevenhüller-Metsch and Günther Probszt-Ohstorff (Graz 1971) (hereinafter Khevenhüller, *Tagebuch*), which contains many short references to the habitual practices, for example, pp. 71 and 199 (Pentecost processions), p. 201 (All Saints); the larger part of the diary is devoted to Khevenhüller's missions in Spain. Papal nuncio Carafa reports the familiar feasts and processions in his 1629 report, see Hurter, *Friedensbestrebungen*, pp. 213–214.

34 See, for example, in HHStA ZA Prot 5, fols. 153–156r (2 August 1694), the description of the order for the carriages taking part in the Corpus Christi procession.

35 Compare Khevenhüller, *Tagebuch*, IV, p. 25 (6/7/8 June 1756), for parallel Whitsunweek devotions.

procession.[36] Other processions honoured victories over the Turks in 1683 (12 September), the French in 1706 (12 May), the 1679 Plague (24 October). This last procession centred on the *Dreifältigkeitssäule* on the Graben; more often the statues and *Ehren-Säule* of the Virgin Mary served as the main focus of Viennese processions.[37] After 1712, the Burgundian order of the Golden Fleece, a more venerable parallel of the French royal order of the *Saint-Esprit*, added its own sequence of celebrations or *Toison Tage* to the *Hofkalender* – most notably its major celebration on St Andrew's feast (30 November).[38]

In the 1680s, Justus Eberhard Passer, envoy from Hessen-Darmstadt, watched a procession going from the Hofburg to the *Michaelerkirche*, to the *Schottenkirche*, and finally to the *Stephanskirche*:

Erstlich gingen derer Cammerherrn, Ambassadeurn und Pottschaffter Ihre Laquayen, Pagen und Bedienten je Zwey Und Zwey. 2.) Die Kayserl. Cammer Trabanten. 3.) Die Kays. Edelknaben je Zwey und Zwey. 4.) Die Cammerherrn in großer Anzahl. 5.) Kays. hohe Ministri. 6.) Uff Beeden Seiten die Kays. Trabanten und Hartschierer. Darauf folgten der Spanische Und Venetianische Pottschafftere, zwischen welchen der Nuncius Apostolicus ginge, nach dißen folgten Ihre Kays. Mt. in einem schwartzen Kleid, und schwartzen Band ufm Hut, eine Bethe [rosary] in der Hand haltend, nach dero ward die regierende Kayserin, und Ertzherz. Prinzessin, durch den Obrist Hofmeister Und Obrist Kammerer geführet; nach dißem folgte das Kayserl. Frauenzimmer, die Kayserl. Wagen Und Wacht.[39]

Nor was the emperor's visible presence confined to such public processions; in church too, he was conspicuously present. Two days later, on Palm Sunday 1682, Passer saw the emperor 'mit der gantzen Hofstatt und Pottschafftern bey den

36 For the Stern-Creuz Orden see Lünig, *Theatrum Ceremoniale*, III, pp. 1161–1163; for Leopold's miracle, see ZA Prot 4: 29 November 1681–December 1691, fols. 590v–592v: 13 May 1691 Laxenburg, the resulting procession was frequently repeated thereafter, see, for example, ZA Prot 5, fol. 79r (17 May 1693). See processions for Vienna's liberation in ZA Prot 5, fol. 94r (13 September 1693), and 157r (12 September 1694). The *Zeremonialprotokoll* and the *Zeremonialakten* will be discussed below; they show the same religious celebrations as Sainctot's registers, with an equally high proportion of the incidents of dynastic demography. On Habsburg piety Petr Mat'a (Prague) presented a paper for the 'Werkstatt Geschichte' of the Vienna academy of sciences, 'Die Habsburger im Fegefeuer. Die Dynastie und die Jenseitsvorstellungen der Barockzeit zwischen Pietas Austriaca und Aberglauben'; for the parallel in the Spanish Netherlands see Luc Duerloo, 'Pietas Albertina.Dynastiek vroomheid en herbouw van het vorstelijk gezag', *Bijdragen en Mededelingen betreffende de Geschiedenis der Nederlanden* 112, 1 (1997), pp. 1–18.

37 We find similar processions in Khevenhüller's *Tagebuch*, see, for example, IV (1756), pp. 6, 39, 42, 47–48.

38 When Bourbon Philip V secured his hold on the Spanish throne, the order of the Golden Fleece continued in two variants: a Spanish-Bourbon and an Austrian Habsburg – or by that time, Habsburgs *tout court*. See discussions about Charles VI's first stately celebrations of the order in HHStA, ÄZA K 24 (22 November 1712): 'Referat einer Conferenz von Toisons Ordens Rittern über das ceremoniel, womit das Andreasfest begangen werden sollte'. Before 1712, we find ceremonies surrounding promotions, but no frequent other festivities of the order in the *Zeremonialakten* and the *Zeremonialprotokoll*. On the order in general, see *La Toison d'Or ou recueil des statuts et ordonnances du noble ordre de la Toison d'Or, leurs confirmations, changemens, additions, ceremonies, immunitez, exemptions, prééminences, . . . depuis l'institution jusques à présent* (Cologne 1689).

39 Passer, 'Berichte', p. 335. Passer's description more or less matches the accounts of Zolger and Vehse. See also on the more famous procession to Hernals, Oswald Redlich, 'Das Tagebuch Esaias Pufendorfs, schwedischen Residenten am Kaiserhofe von 1671 bis 1674', *MIÖG* 37 (1917), pp. 541–597, here at p. 565; Hernals is also mentioned in Brown, *A Brief Account*, p. 150; Küchelbecker, *Allerneueste Nachricht*, p. 239; compare Kovacs, 'Kirchliches Zeremoniell'.

Augustinern 3 mahl in der Kirchen herumb gegangen, und endlich Vorm Altar stehen blieben, alle Palmzweige in den Händen tragend'.[40] In the same years, Edward Brown witnessed a procession on St Stephen's Day to the *Stephansdom* (26 December), where the emperor 'went up to the altar, kneeled, and kissed the plate wheron the Hostia had lain'.[41] In church, the emperor habitually attended 'at the side of the Evangel', at the left of the altar as seen from the church, in a canopied booth, or Oratorio. Prelates, in that case, were not allowed to sit or stand under a canopy.[42]

Carnival, or *Fasching*, made room for a variety of entertainments, notably the *Wirtschaften* or bucolic mock weddings casting the upper layers of the household as characters amusingly contrasting with their day-to-day dignity.[43] This rite of reversal was as much part of the established calendar as the grave devotions that were to follow soon afterwards. During Holy Week, religious observances were ubiquitous. As in France, the sequence of Divine Offices and processions included the *pedilavium*. In Vienna mostly old men were chosen when the emperor himself performed the ceremony; when the ruling empress and the dowager-empress washed the poor, they usually did so for old women. Passer reported several Maundy ceremonies, including one where some of the old men, dazed by food and splendour alike, had to be carried home by the *Trabanten*. In Vienna as in France, the poor were allowed to take their tableware home, or were rewarded in other ways.[44] In 1629 papal nuncio Carafa observed that the old men received a *Goldstück* after the ceremony, a gift repeated every month thereafter. In the course of the eighteenth century, the lists of participants in this ceremony were printed, demonstrating this peculiar mixture of modesty and pre-eminence to a larger public.[45] The *Wienerisches Diarium*, from 1703 onwards faithfully reporting the *Hofstaat*'s public activities, habitually printed annexes with names and ages of the old men and women taking part in the *Fußwaschung*. Shortly after the death of Francis Stephen in 1765, Joseph II proved unwilling to

[40] Passer, 'Berichte', p. 335: The procession described here started at 10.00 in the morning and lasted until 12.30; for similar descriptions, see pp. 335, 336, 348, 370–371, 379.

[41] Brown, *A Brief Account*, p. 152.

[42] For the situation in church see, for example, HHStA ZA Prot 1, fols. 377–381; Passer, 'Berichte', pp. 355–356; Lhotsky, 'Kaiser Karl VI. und sein Hof', pp. 58–59; *Die 'hoechst vergnueglichste Raiss'*, p. 35; on p. 40 the oratorium is mentioned indirectly: the bishop could not have his 'Baldachin' because of the rulers' presence. Luynes, *Mémoires*, I, p. 420, mentions two canopies in the chapel: one for the king, one for the cardinal de Polignac.

[43] Passer, 'Berichte', pp. 278–279; Küchelbecker, *Allerneueste Nachricht*, pp. 257–262; compare the description, on an atypical date, in Khevenhüller, *Tagebuch*, IV, pp. 27–29, 'amusements champêtres' on 14 June 1756.

[44] For instances of the 'grüne Donnerstag Fußwaschung' in Vienna see Passer, 'Berichte', p. 289, and similarly p. 370. Passer further reports that the dowager-empress and the reigning empress did likewise, choosing poor women to undergo the same treatment. In Vienna the same confusion of 12 and 13 occurred, see Carafa's report, where the emperor is said to wash the feet of 13 old men, the empress of 12 old widows: Hurter, *Friedensbestrebungen*, p. 214 (with the reference to the *Goldstück*); HHStA, ÄZA K 12: 'Lista der dreyzehn alte Männer die öffentlich gespeist wurden', whereas the frequent descriptions or lists of the ceremony in the HHStA ÄZA and ZA Prot mostly mention 12. See Khevenhüller, *Tagebuch*, IV (1756), pp. 13–15; (1757), pp. 76–78 for roughly comparable outlines of Holy Week.

[45] See, for example, AVA, Harrach 323, *Obersthofmeisteramt*, fols. 315–316: printed lists of the 12 men for 1703–1705.

take part in the Maundy Thursday rites, but his mother prevailed, forcing her son and co-regent to accept the burden with minor changes. Only in the very last years of Joseph's rule, does the ceremony seem to have been abandoned, but Leopold II restored it in the first year of his rule.[46]

Bourbon piety clearly was no match for the Habsburgs. French diplomats in Vienna were shocked to find themselves exposed to a life they associated more with a monastery than with a sovereign household.[47] Only after the advent of Joseph II did the liturgical calendar with its unending accretions become markedly less dominant. In Joseph's reign, the density of religious ceremonies decreased notably: from the *c.* 68 annual solemn religious observances in his father's reign, to *c.* 32 by 1767, declining to 22 in 1774; furthermore, both dress and forms were simplified.[48] In France and in the Austrian Habsburg territories alike, most great dynastic ceremonies prominently included religious rites, and even the more worldly ceremonies were modelled after Catholic liturgy. Dynastic and military feats were celebrated by *Te Deum* settings, performed throughout the realm.[49] Such occasions, however, were not a stable, recurring part of the courtly calendar: they followed the haphazard rhythm of dynastic demography and military events.

SEASONS, LODGINGS, AND HUNTING

Late medieval rulers and their retinues, moving from battlefield to palace, and from region to region, have rightly been likened to an army. The marshal and the provost had to enforce discipline, and correct abuses; absenteeism was to be checked by quarterly mustering; embezzlement of provisions or the unauthorised use of the ruler's largesse was to be prevented by frequent inspection and accounting, and the expectation of severe punishment upon discovery. Provisioning this roaming band had many of the appurtenances of army logistics.

46 *Wienerisches Diarium enthaltend alle so von Tag zu Tag so wohl in dieser Kayserlichen Residentzstadt Wienn selbsten sich zugetragen*; see ÖNB, 393-052 B-D-E Kat or microfilm 226, for example the Anhang in 1729, no. 31, 16 April, likewise the report in the 14 April 1770 issue, proudly listing the added ages of the male (982) and female (1006) participants. In the later eighteenth century, the *Fußwaschung* is still a recurring item in the documents and protocols, see, for example, Khevenhüller, *Tagebuch*, VI, p. 171 (March 1766), pp. 231–232 (April 1767); HHStA ÄZA K 70 8 (20 March 1765); HHStA ZA Prot 33, fols. 27–28 (1769), with Maria Theresa and Ferdinand; fols. 142–143 (1770) with Joseph II; ZA Prot 34, fols. 20, 133, 242; for the early 1780s ZA Prot 36: fols. 7–8, 327–329; ZA Prot 37, fol. 13 *Fußwaschung* April 1786; no such ceremonies are noted for 1787, 1788, and 1789; fol. 207 reports the *Fußwaschung* under Leopold II on 1 April 1790, and ZA Prot 38, fols. 14, 97 show continuity. Compare other references to the *Fußwaschung* in ÖNB cod. 12958 (1766), fols. 18–19 (the 12 men and women receive 30 Groschen); and ÖNB cod. 12956, fol. 463 (1777).

47 See the statements of the *Mémoires du maréchal duc de Richelieu*, ed. M. F. Barrière, 2 vols. (Paris 1868–1869), I, p. 209. The same letters are cited in in Vehse, *Geschichte der deutschen Höfe*, VI, pp. 287–289. The letters are probably written by the editor of the memoirs, Barrière, but the point is made in many other sources, for example, Freschot, *Remarques historiques*, I, pp. 107–108; Freschot, *Mémoires*, pp. 81–83; Pöllnitz, *Mémoires*, I, pp. 327–328.

48 See Kovacs, 'Kirchliches Zeremoniell', especially the lists in nn. 61, 69, 84. Compare Derek Beales, *Joseph II: In The Shadow of Maria Theresa 1741–1780* (Cambridge 1987), pp. 36–37, 156–159.

49 See Michèle Fogel, *Les cérémonies d'information dans la France du XVIe au XVIIIe siècle* (Paris 1989); references to individual *Te Deum* settings abound in the sources.

In a learned treatise on the history of French royalty, Jean du Tillet noted that the *prévôt de l'hôtel* had under his authority the *filles de ioye suyvantes la cour.*[50] The frequent movement was caused by many different factors, such as the indispensable renewal of the bonds between the young ruler and the components of his realm, or the pervasiveness of warfare in an age which still expected to see the ruler commanding his armies in person. The dictates of hunting were important for movements within a geographically more limited area: the temporary exhaustion of hunting grounds, or the seasonal changes in hunting prey, forced the court to change places. It was a daunting task to maintain a dignified order in such circumstances. Even when travel over longer distances was slowly becoming somewhat more exceptional, or tied mostly to the early stages of the ruler's career, the court retained many traits connected to its itinerant past.

From Ferdinand I's 1527 and 1537 ordinances to the phase of reform in the early 1650s, we see the consolidation of rules for the household that were later reiterated or refined in more particular rulings and instructions. Around 1615 and around 1651, attempts at reform generated a string of texts. The 1615 reform was connected mostly to finances and sought to reduce numbers and costs; the 1651 reform, on the other hand, coincided with renewed payment of wages after a protracted war, and sought to make the court more magnificent, dignified, and orderly.[51] The texts accompanying the reforms tell us mostly about what they sought to redress: inflation of honours, waste, corruption in 1615; the undermining of the court's dignity by 'Zeithero eingeschlichene unordnungen und inconvenientien' in 1651.[52] The reformers of 1651 granted due honour to the *alte guete hoffordnungen*, nor would this attitude change in later decades.[53] Henry III's *règlements* of 1578 and 1585 likewise formed the unchanging nucleus of a corpus of less sweeping additions and restatements. We can find these major ordinances and their more limited and specialised accretions in several volumes, compiled in the early seventeenth century; these volumes contain the texts that were seen as embodying the conventions of the household.

[50] Du Tillet, *Recueil des Roys*, p. 312; see Knecht, *Renaissance Warrior and Patron*, chapter 6, pp. 105–141, on Francis I's court; with a map and descriptions of its progressions in 1532–1534 on pp. 126–130; Potter, *History of France*, pp. 364–365; compare Victor E. Graham and W. McAllister Johnson, eds., *The Royal Tour of France by Charles IX and Catherine de Medici: Festivals and Entries 1564–1566* (Toronto, Buffalo, and London 1979); Jean Boutier, Alain Dewerpe, and Daniel Nordman, *Un tour de France royal: le voyage de Charles IX (1565–1566)* (Paris 1984).

[51] ÖNB cod. 14676; HHStA OMeA Sr K 184, nos. 75–77 (1615), Gundaker von Liechtenstein's proposal for reform are presented in *Fürst und Fürstendiener. Gundaker von Liechtenstein, ein österreichischer Aristokrat des konfessionellen Zeitalters* (Vienna and Munich 1999); they were one of the sources for the 1651 reform, see AVA, Harrach Historica 797, a *Gutachten* of *geheime Rathe* reflecting an interesting dialogue of three *Obersthofmeisters'* practices and ideas: Gundaker von Liechtenstein's reform proposals from the 1620s, Trautmannsdorf's apparent withdrawal or negligence, and Dietrichstein's suggestions. These reforms are closely mirrored in various instructions immediately following the *Gutachten*, for example, HHStA OMeA Sr K 73 Kammerherreninstruktion (2 March 1651), Hofmarschallinstruktion (2 March 1651), and a short Stallmeisterinstruktion (27 February 1651); compare the 2 March Kammerdienerinstruktion in OMeA Sr 74, no. 11.

[52] The quote is from HHStA OMeA Sr K 74, no. 11, a March 1651 Kammerdienerinstruktion, but could come from almost any of the ordinances.

[53] For example, AVA Harrach Historica 797, 'Guettachten wegen der Hoffordnung' (1651), p. 1.

Court ordinances reflect a weariness about familiar and recurring problems; *desordres*, *confusions*; *Unordnungen*, *Confusiones*: these are among the words most frequently recurring in such texts. In the 1585 ordinance, the king stated that: 'qu'à grand peine se recognoist-il plus un seul traict de ceste ancienne probité, dignité, et splendeur qui reluisoit du temps de ses prédécesseurs'.[54] Henry further argued that his court had become a 'lieu de franchise' exempt from regular justice, attracting those who sought to decide their quarrels violently.[55] While Henry was probably right in perceiving a level of disorder exceeding that of the reigns of Francis I or Henry II, his sentiment recurred in most ordinances, lamenting the decline of a largely imaginary past order, and proposing worn remedies. Order remained a cherished yet elusive asset. A 1606 *règlement* for the quartering of the court carefully delineated the rights of the king's following as listed in the *états* versus those of less clearly defined *poursuivants* or the *états* of accompanying princes. We may expect that many sought to benefit from the king's hospitality without being invited, and that the officers responsible for the procedures were not invulnerable to the advantages to be obtained by selective indulgence. The ordinance ominously added that those who obstructed the quartering system, by removing the white cross indicating the quarters for the king's following or by any other mischief, could expect to have their *poing coupé*, whereas blasphemers were to have their *langue percée*. Taverners were asked to report daily the names of their guests to the *prévôt*, to prevent drunkenness in the king's retinue.[56] Habsburg ordinances for the major officers, particularly those for the steward and the court marshal, the latter combining the tasks of the French *maréchal des logis* and *prévôt de l'hôtel*, convey a similar spirit in more moderate form, stressing discipline and the maintenance of the *Policey-Ordnungen*.[57]

Yet courts were becoming more sedentary in the sixteenth and seventeenth centuries, and this helped to make them more orderly. Ferdinand I was hardly a nomadic ruler; after settling in Vienna, he stayed there for most of his days. The unsuccessful Turkish siege of 1529 convinced Ferdinand I to transform Vienna into an impregnable fortress; in 1533 he moved the *Hoflager* there – notwithstanding earlier promises to the Bohemians to choose the more attractive city of Prague as his seat of government.[58] Under Maximilian II this ambivalent situation persisted; he resided in Vienna, without ignoring the Bohemian capital.

54 1585 *règlement* as printed in *AC*, p. 301. 55 *AC*, pp. 307–308.

56 AN KK 1431, 'Règlement fait par le Roy pour les logis de sa cour et suite le septieme jour de juillet, 1606', fols. 129–137, at fols. 133v–136v. On fol. 136, we find that 3 *sols* was the usual payment for a bed 'capable de coucher deux personnes' for the king's followers, or alternatively two *sols* for the queen's *état*. Compare the 1677 and 1682 decrees against theft cited below, BN Clair 828 *prévôté*, pp. 1253–1259.

57 See, for example, the 1561 Hofmarschall's instruction printed in Ferdinand Menčík, 'Beiträge zur Geschichte der Kaiserlichen Hofämter', *AÖG* 87 (Vienna 1899), pp. 447–563, at pp. 495–500, with point 15 on p. 498; HHStA, OMaA I, K 1 (1564–1712), instructions for 1615 (Matthias), 1637 (Ferdinand III), in the latter articles 1, 4, and 15 mainly refer to disorders and their punishment, AVA Harrach Historica 797, Gutachten 1651 (Ferdinand III).

58 Moriz Dreger, *Baugeschichte der K. K. Hofburg in Wien bis zum XIX. Jahrhunderte*, Österreichische Kunsttopographie 14 (Vienna 1914) pp. 89–97; Harry Kühnel, *Die Hofburg zu Wien* (Graz and Cologne 1964), p. 16.

Attracted by Prague's amenities and its location at a greater remove from the Turkish threat, and motivated by financial incentives offered by the Bohemians, Rudolf II departed from the practices of his predecessors by moving the court to Prague in 1582, leaving only a small segment of the administration in Vienna. In 1612, after the accession of Matthias, Vienna regained its position as the first seat of the court. Under Ferdinand II, who came to Vienna as the successful counter-reformatory ruler of Styria, Graz ceased to be the residence of an autonomous branch of the dynasty, yet it retained a prominent role. In 1665, with the extinction of the Tyrolean line of the Habsburgs, Innsbruck shared Graz's fate. Vienna's supremacy was not seriously challenged until the end of Habsburg monarchy. The dispersion of Habsburg hereditary lands, in addition to the imperial diets, elections, and coronations, as well as the ceremonies connected to the royal crowns of Bohemia and Hungary, however, guaranteed that all Habsburgs travelled frequently.[59] Many cities, including Prague, Pressburg and Buda, Graz and Innsbruck, Regensburg, Augsburg, and Frankfurt, retained their place in the imperial, royal, and archducal itineraries of the Habsburgs.

Paris, a city of far greater magnitude than Vienna, had long been an inescapable focus for the court of France. Lyon may vainly have hoped to lure Henry IV away from the Parisian hornet's nest, but no other city could plausibly cherish similar fantasies. When the court resided in Paris, it was the city's major corporation, forming a town within the town. Moreover, Paris permanently harboured the *parlement*, the *chambre des comptes*, and other institutions connected to government. Yet French kings remained quite mobile, shifting from Parisian residences – Louvre, Tuileries, and Palais Royal – to Chambord and other favoured Loire *châteaux*, or alternatively to the castles in the *Ile de France*, such as Saint-Germain-en-Laye, Fontainebleau, or Compiègne – the latter conveniently situated halfway between Paris and Rheims, locus of the king's *sacre*. In his early years, Louis XIV often lodged in Saint-Germain, choosing it as his main residence in 1666 – the castle was renovated and expanded on the eve of his move to Versailles.[60] Only after May 1682, did Versailles, Louis XIV's great project constructed at the site of his father's modest 1623 hunting lodge, obtain undisputed pre-eminence, which lasted until 1789, and was interrupted only by the 1715–1722 Orléans regency. Only in 1746, when Schönbrunn's apartments were expanded to lodge the household, did Maria Theresa's *Lustschloß* reach comparable status. Even at that time, it harboured the court mostly

[59] See a detailed nineteenth-century manuscript overview of Habsburg travel in HHStA Handschriften Weiß 1095: 'Itinerarien von Mitgliedern des Hauses Habsburg'; other works devoted to travel: Hanns Leo Mikoletzky, 'Hofreisen unter Kaiser Karl VI', *MIÖG* 60 (1952), pp. 265–285; Rotraut Miller, 'Die Hofreisen Kaiser Leopold I.', *MIÖG* 75 (1967), pp. 66–103; Wolfgang May, 'Reisen "al incognito". Zur Reisetätigkeit Kaiser Josephs II.', *MIÖG* 93 (1985), pp. 59–91.

[60] Sourches, *Mémoires*, I, pp. 99–101, states that the court fled Saint-Germain because of these works, spending two weeks in Saint-Cloud, Monsieur's residence, in April 1682, immediately preceding the installation in Versailles on 6 May.

during summer, always sharing its position with the venerable Hofburg winter residence.

While more clearly defining their main seat, or at least somewhat limiting their perpetual movement, rulers did not abandon the habit of seasonal changes of location. With the creation of a winter residence, a constellation of secondary palaces and hunting lodges evolved that offered more attractive accommodation in the other seasons: Villars-Cotterêts, Chambord, Fontainebleau, Versailles in its early years, Compiègne, and their more modest Vienna parallels – Neugebäude, Laxenburg, Favorita, Ebersdorf. These secondary palaces were invariably connected to hunting, and the seasonally changing forms of the hunt secured a lasting level of mobility for the court.

In the decades around 1700, the Viennese Hofburg accommodated the court roughly from November to April, a period coinciding with several major celebrations of the liturgical year: Christmas, Carnival and Lent, and Holy Week. In these winter months, sleigh rides in Vienna were the most conspicuous outdoor entertainment. Spring, summer, and autumn surely did not pass without paperwork and pomp, but hunting occupied a more important place in the schedule. In March, the emperor would open the season with a *Fuchsprellen* in the Vienna Prater. Foxes were driven together, caught on strong, taut sheets, tossed into the air, and finally clubbed to death. The Swedish resident Esaias Pufendorf, witnessing a March 1672 *Fuchsprellen*, noted in his dairy that it was truly

> remarquabel, daß der Kaiser selbst mit einem Stocke die Füchse geschlagen und darnach geworfen, wenn sie geprellt waren, und daß er darin die kleinen Jungen und Narren zu Kameraden gehabt, welches mich dünkte etwas alien von der kaiserlichen Gravität zu sein.[61]

In April, a much reduced court accompanied the emperor to Laxenburg, for the *Reiherbeize*, a form of falconry where the heron was the main victim, with crow, duck, hare, and rabbit as accessory prey. Küchelbecker suggested that this pleasant 'Combat zwischen diesen Thieren und Vögeln' diverted the court from day to day until the early summer.[62] In June, the court moved to the Favorita auf der Wieden, where firing at targets was among its diversions. Around 22 July, Mary Magdalen's feast, deer hunts were habitually organised. Great numbers of deer, roe, and occasionally wild boar were chased into a closed area where they would be fired at by the emperor and his relatives, comfortably situated behind a screen. In late August these *gesperrte Jagden* were capped by a peculiar variant, the *Hirschwasserjagd*, shooting the animals after chasing them into a Danube arm. Pursuing deer with hounds in open territory, seen as the 'French' style and

[61] Redlich, 'Das Tagebuch Esaias Pufendorfs', p. 568; compare the *Fuchsprellen* in HHStA ZA Prot 6 (1700–1709), where fol. 452 describes a *Fuchsprellen* 'a privato', presumably without ceremony. See the same forms of hunting in Khevenhüller's *Geheimes Tagebuch*, yet not clearly following the seasonal rhythms outlined here, pp. 39, 60, and more references to parallel practices in Spain: pp. 44, 109, 157, 118, 154, 164, 241, 292.

[62] Küchelbecker, *Allerneueste Nachricht*, p. 253.

labelled *parforce-Jagd*, became quite popular in the eighteenth century, under Charles, a devoted huntsman; the vogue continued under his French-oriented Lorraine successor Francis Stephen.[63] In early autumn, the court could stay in a steadily changing cluster of hunting lodges: among others Ebersdorf, Halbthurn (Féltorony in Hungary, now Halbthurn in Burgenland) or the Favorita. By that time, the boar hunt, following the procedures of the *gesperrte Jagd*, took over. Throughout the year smaller hunting parties near the villages surrounding Vienna would entertain the court; in these pursuits, all members of the dynasty and a varying selection of guests could take part, and women were not necessarily less keen participants than men.[64] Longer voyages, such as Leopold's wanderings around 1680, Charles VI's 1723 and 1732 visits to Prague, or his 1728 *Erbhuldigungen* in the hereditary lands, offered opportunities to test other hunting grounds, notably Brandeis (Brany Hrad) near Prague.[65]

Louis XIV's decision to choose Versailles as the seat of household and government did not turn his court into a static environment. In addition to incidental visits to the palaces of the *famille royale*, the frequent outings to Marly and the Trianon adjacent to Versailles, the *c.* six weeks autumn 'Voyage de Fontainebleau' occupied a permanent place in the court's less itinerant schedule from the 1680s onwards. During these weeks hunting was the favourite pursuit of ministers and courtiers alike.[66] We find falconry, deer hunt, and boar hunt as at the Habsburg court, and a variety of other forms; yet the seasonal sequence was less clear. Dangeau's notes seem to indicate a strong preference for falconry in the early months of the year, but the vogue for falconry dwindled towards the end of the seventeenth century. In the *chasse royale*, or *chasse au cerf*, deer (and incidentally hare or roe) were pursued with hounds, though not driven to the wooden structures of the 'Abschussplatz' common in the *gesperrte Jagd*. Screens or *toiles de chasse* were used for the *chasse au sanglier*, or wild boar.[67] Wolves were energetically pursued by *Monseigneur*, who matched the fervour of his grandfather, Louis XIII. His *louveterie* eclipsed that of his father Louis XIV, and its elegant uniforms were much admired.[68] Indeed, *Monseigneur* was keen on hunting any conceivable species, and courtiers honoured his sylvan preferences by dubbing him *myrtille*, or blueberry.[69] The huge and expanding territories connected to

63 See the descriptions in Mitis, *Jagd und Schützen*; Khevenhüller, *Tagebuch*, IV, pp. 11, 40, 41, 49; and HHStA ZA Prot, for example, no. 34, fol. 200, mention *parforce* hunting.

64 See, for example, Carafa in Hurter, *Friedensbestrebungen*, pp. 217, 221, 225.

65 Compare Dickson's indication of Maria Theresa's travels in *Finance and Government*, I, p. 211.

66 See HHStA Staatenabteilung Frankreich K 26 Bericht (20 November 1699), fol. 56r, where Philip Ludwig Sinzendorf related his problems of reaching Torcy – he had to go to Fontainebleau *incognito*, handing the minister a letter while he was on his way to the hunt – earlier, on 25 August 1699, fol. 21, Sinzendorf had mentioned that at Marly, ministers could not be visited at all. Compare Dangeau, *Journal*, VI, p. 181 (3 September 1697): 'Il fut resolu que le conseil ne viendroit point cette année à Fontainebleau; ce qui donnera beaucoup de logements, dont on a grand besoin'.

67 See the well-illustrated discussion of the 'German' style of hunting, and the development of the *Prunkjagden* in, *Die Lust am Jagen. Jagdsitten und Jagdfeste am Kurpfälzischen Hof im 18. Jahrhundert* (Ubstadt-Weiher 1999).

68 See Salvadori, *Chasse*; Dangeau, *Journal*, II, pp. 122–123 (23 March 1688): Monseigneur distributed '25 justaucorps magnifiques' for his *chasse du Loup* – Louis XIV even asked one for the duc du Maine.

69 Visconti, *Mémoires*, p. 135.

Versailles, including Trianon and Marly, offered enough opportunities for outdoor recreation throughout the year; they constituted a well-stocked domain for hunting that relieved the need to find other hunting grounds. Shooting slowly pushed aside the traditional forms of hunting. The *chasse à courre* retained its popularity in France; in many German territories shooting was more popular in the eighteenth century – Vienna combined the various forms.[70] In the last decades of Louis XIV's reign, longer sojourns to palaces other than Fontainebleau did not recur on an annual basis. In the eighteenth century the autumn voyage to Fontainebleau remained habitual, in addition to sojourns in Compiègne, and shorter stays in various smaller hunting lodges.[71]

Travel, to be sure, was not connected only to hunting. Whereas the first decade of Louis XIV's rule entailed longer visits to many of his provinces, this cadence sharply declined in the 1660s.[72] Until 1693, however, the king frequently visited army camps to muster his troops, and witness their operations, mostly near the north-eastern borders of his realm, and in spring or early summer.[73] Climate and provisioning traditionally brought warfare to a temporary halt in winter, a pause that persisted although innovations in logistics were making it somewhat less imperative. Leopold I, a passionate hunter, was not as keen on soldiers and warfare as his Bourbon rival; his most conspicuous military adventure was his embarrassing flight from Vienna in 1683 – he rushed from Vienna leaving his quarters open and in disarray, encircled by a crowd shouting: 'Ach Ihre Mt. bleiben doch hir, Ach Ihre Mt. verlassen Unß nicht'.[74] The emperor, however, travelled to the various constituent parts of his realms, and to the great centres of the empire for the major ceremonies. The plague more than once forced the court to leave Vienna, and the Ottomans added their share to the movements of the court. Such incidents, however, cannot be seen as part of the recurring calendar of court activities. In Vienna as in Versailles, we may conclude, winter tended to become the 'season' of court life, probably attracting more visitors than the other seasons, and serving as the prime time for ceremony and government, as well as for the light-hearted diversions following Epiphany.

70 Mitis, *Jagd und Schutzen*, pp. 7–8, 56; *Die Lust am Jagen*.

71 Salvadori, *Chasse*, p. 212, notes that Louis XIV visited Compiègne 75 times, and reconstructed the castle; yet it was to become Louis XV's favoured residence in the 1730s. Luynes' entries frequently mention Compiègne and Choisy. Compare John Hardman, *Louis XVI* (New Haven and London 1993), pp. 33–34, for Louis XVI's practices.

72 See Solnon, *Cour de France*, pp. 261–265; and *Moi, Marie Du Bois*, p. 130 (1663): 'Il y avait huit ans que je n'avais été auprès du roi, n'ayant osé le suivre dans ses voyages . . .' and the overview of such travels in n. 2 on the same page.

73 Sourches and Dangeau regularly describe these voyages; Sourches, *Mémoires*, for example, II, pp. 58, 59 (1693) mentions that the king honoured many of his loyal servants in administration, court, and army with a visit, dining or even staying overnight at their *châteaux*; in AN KK 1431, fols. 176–179, we find the same habit, though it is added that the king was usually served by his own staff during such outings.

74 See Passer, 'Berichte', p. 385. The flight from Vienna posed serious problems for the court; see in the ZA Prot 4, fols. 80r–86r: 'Restringierung der Hoffstatt' (24 July 1683) signed Johann Probst, one of the court's secretaries; see Sienell, *Die Geheime Konferenz*, pp. 246–248. The court could only be maintained in a much reduced form; *Kämmerer*, *Räte*, *Cavaglieri*, and other followers of the court had to look after themselves, a solution less acceptable for the numerous *Frauenzimmer* attending the ruling empress and the dowager-empress.

Table 9. *Day and week at the court of Henry III:* Boucher, *Cour de Henri III*, p. 52

	Monday	Tuesday	Wednesday	Thursday	Friday	Saturday	Sunday
Matin	Ouvertures des portes du Louvre à 5 heures Lever du roi, messe privée à 6 heures, grand-messe à 9 heures						
6.00–9.30		conseil des finances		conseil des finances		conseil des finances	
Après dîner	Le roi se retire en son cabinet jusqu' à 2 heures →						
	Chasse	Grand chevaux	Promenade	Paume ou Palle-mail	Promenade	Promenade	Paume ou Palle-mail
	Chez la reine mère collation avec violons					Chez la reine mère collation avec violons	
13.00–16.00	conseil d'Etat	conseil d'Etat	conseil privé	conseil d'Etat	conseil privé	conseil d'Etat	
	Audiences du roi		Audiences du roi			Remise des requêtes au roi	
16.00 18.00	Vêpres → Souper du roi →						
	Musique	Musique	Musique	Bal	Cercle	Cercle	Bal
After 20.00	Coucher du roi →						

DAY AND WEEK AT COURT

Halfway through the fifteenth century, a mechanical clock was installed to assist the tasks of the controller of Henry VII of England's household.[75] Such devices undoubtedly were helpful to coordinate the activities of the expanding households, and from the later fifteenth century, we more frequently find references to the hours of the day in the sources. In addition to the monthly patterns, such information can help us to become more familiar with life at court.

Upon his accession to the throne in 1574, Henry III strove to erect barriers between himself and the court, an attempt that threatened to alienate his grandees. Henry could not implement all his wishes, but his effort generated several texts that grant us a remarkably detailed idea of the intended activities of the last Valois monarch. The 1578 and 1585 ordinances (*règlements généraux*), while mitigating Henry's first initiatives, give a clear overview of his schedule.[76] Jacqueline Boucher has turned the 1585 ordinance into a table of a 'week at court'.[77]

At 5.00 in the morning, the Louvre gates were opened, the king had his *lever*, attended a private Mass at 6.00, and a public *grand'-messe* at 9.00. On Tuesday, Thursday, and Saturday, the council of finances assembled between the two religious services. The king dined around 10.00 and withdrew to his apartment until 14.00.[78] At that time, he engaged in a variety of outdoor recreations, and attended a *collation* in the queen-mother's apartment enlivened by music; alternatively, he could preside over the *conseil d'état* or the *conseil privé*. He gave audiences on Monday and Wednesday and accepted *requêtes* on Saturday afternoon. At 16.00 the king attended Vespers, and at 18.00 he had his *souper*. After supper, the king could take a walk in the company of 'ceulx de sa cour', or

[75] Woolgar, *Great Household*, p. 86, illustration 35.

[76] See Monique Châtenet, 'Henri III et "l'ordre de la cour". Evolution de l'étiquette à travers les règlements généraux de 1578 et 1585', in *Henri III et son temps*, ed. Sauzet, pp. 133–139; David Potter and P. R. Roberts, 'An Englishman's View of the Court of Henri III, 1584–1585: Richard Cook's Description of the Court of France', *FH* 2 (1988), pp. 312–344, and most recently, Le Roux, *Faveur du roi*, pp. 181–186, mentions a printed version of the *règlement* distributed to the courtiers in December 1584 (Calendar of State Papers, XIX, p. 184). The ordinances can be found in AN KK 544, BN MS f 4581–4582 ('règlements des maisons royales et des conseils de Charles IX à Louis XIII', Henry's ordinances in 4581) and BN MS naf 7225 (the equivalent of BN Brienne 256). I have consulted BN naf 7225 (for 1578: fols. 35–84v; 1585: fol. 85ff): a comparable selection of documents, including Catherine de Medici's letter to Charles IX [printed in Hector de la Ferrière, *Lettres de Catherine de Médicis* (Paris 1885), II, pp. 90–95: Au Roy Monsieur mon Fils. This letter is sometimes thought to be addressed to Henry III]. The 1585 *règlement* was published by Cimber and Danjou in the *Archives curieuses de l'histoire de France*, serie I, vol. X (Paris 1836), pp. 301–358. A copy of the 1574 'règlement pour le Grand Maître' is included in AN KK 1431, fols. 31–37 (or alternatively 313–319), only the first folio includes hours, the others contain a demarcation of responsibilities between Henry III and Henry de Guise, his high steward. Together, these documents mostly confirm the overview given by Boucher, *Cour de Henri III*, p. 52.

[77] Table based on Boucher, *Cour de Henri III*, p. 52, and AN KK 1431, fol. 31 (or 313), BN MS naf 7225 (Brienne 256), fols. 43v–50r. Compare Woolgar's overview in *Great Household*, p. 85.

[78] Or alternatively 15.00/16.00, in AN KK 1431, fol. 31 (or 313), it is stated that after dinner the king withdrew to his apartment at 16.00 in summer (1 April–30 September), 15.00 in winter (1 October–31 March). Evening promenades are mentioned on fol. 47r, and audiences for ambassadors in the *après-dinée* of Thursdays and Sundays on fol. 47r, and an extra one-hour audience on Saturday (fol. 46r).

Table 10. *Louis' days in Versailles, 1680s*

8.00–9.00	10–12.30	After 12.30	Around 14.00	*Après dinée*	19.00–21.00	22.00	24.00–0.30
Lever (with oaths and audiences)	councils	Mass	*Diner à petit couvert*	Councils, solitary work, recreations	*Appartements*, ballets, games	*Souper à grand couvert*	End of *coucher*

might enjoy a musical performance, *bal*, or *cercle*. The king's *coucher* took place as early as 20.00.

Henry III would not have been able to invariably follow the rhythm laid down in the ordinances, but the first two Bourbon rulers, repeating the same range of activities, may very well have had less regular habits. Héroard's *Journal* conveys an environment less given to the orderly habits decreed by Henry III. We find the *dauphin* attending his father's *lever* quite late, between 9.00 and 10.00, whereas on other days the king came to visit his son in the early hours.[79] Later, Louis XIII's disturbed nights, nocturnal visits to the queen, and early wanderings are faithfully reported. On the whole, we find that the day of the *roi juste* in his young years started later than Henry III's, yet he was usually active by around 7.00. At 7.30 or 8.00, Héroard's notes tell us, he was in his carriage, and by 8.30, the young king could look back on a range of activities.[80] He often attended Mass around 9.00, had dinner somewhere between 11.00 and 13.00, supped between 18.00 and 19.00 and was usually sleeping – or at least trying to sleep, assisted by the mellow sounds of the lute – by 21.00.[81] The hours for councils and audiences do not emerge clearly from Héroard's notes; we find more entries about hunting, the chapel, meals, and evening entertainments than about the routines of government.[82] The entertainments included Italian comedy, French comedy, and ballets – a combination familiar for parts of Louis XIV's reign. Hunting pursuits, ballets, and festivities frequently altered the hours suggested here. We find the king returning to his apartment at any time between between midnight and 5.00, particularly when he himself had performed as a dancer in the ballet; on other occasions he rose very early to indulge in hunting parties.[83]

Louis XIV's days would start and end later; his activities are well-attested, particularly for the first decades in Versailles, often taken as a *pars pro toto* for the entire reign.[84] In the 1680s Louis XIV rose between 8.00 and 9.00: Besongne notes 8.45 as the habitual time in his 1687 *état*, but Dangeau's *Journal* suggests greater flexibility. After a crowded *lever*, dressing, a shave every two days, devotions, and light *déjeuner* the king was ready for a hard day's work. Audiences and oaths of fidelity would mostly take place in the bedroom, afterwards the king would go to his *cabinet*, issuing orders for the day, and preparing for a long

[79] Héroard, *Journal*, I, pp. 117, 145, 161, for the late *levers* of Henry IV or Marie de Medici.

[80] Héroard, *Journal*, offers invaluable details about Louis XIII's daily habits. Héroard adds the hours for rising, meals, and sleeping frequently, most pages can be cited, for example, I, pp. 211–212, 300, 343; II, pp. 23, 121, 123, 144, 155, 292, 293 etc. The first volume contains many colourful details, but the years 1601–1610 seem less relevant than 1610–1628. Compare the general remarks in Yves-Marie Bercé, 'Heures du Jour', in *DGS*, pp. 718–719.

[81] Héroard, *Journal*, II, p. 121, n. 3.

[82] *Ibid*., pp. 188, 213, 294 give 15.00 as the time for important audiences.

[83] *Ibid*., for example, II, pp. 212, 213, 223, 246, 254.

[84] The following paragraphs are based mainly on Besongne and Dangeau, their remarks are repeated in Luynes. Lünig, *Theatrum Ceremoniale*; Rousset and Du Mont, *Cérémonial diplomatique*, I, pp. 424–434; Visconti, *Mémoires*; Marquis de Saint Maurice, *Lettres sur la cour de Louis XIV*, ed. Jean Lemoine (Paris 1910) and Ezéchiel Spanheim, *Relation de la Cour de France en 1690*, ed. Emile Bourgeois, Annales de l'université de Lyon II 5 (Paris and Lyon 1900) confirm the patterns.

Table 11. *Louis' weeks in Versailles, 1680s*

Monday	Tuesday	Wednesday	Thursday	Friday	Saturday	Sunday
Conseil d'état alternating weekly with *conseil des dépêches* (the latter without the king)	*Conseil des finances*	*Conseil d'état*	*Conseil d'état*	*Conseil de conscience*	*Conseil des finances*	*Conseil d'état*
Evening entertainment: Alternation of *comédie française, comédie italienne, appartement*						

session with one of his councils in the *cabinet*. Having obtained papal permission to celebrate the Mass until 14.00, the king in these years usually attended Mass around 12.30.[85] *Dîner en famille*, usually in relative privacy or *à petit couvert*, would follow between 13.00 and 14.00, in the apartment of the senior female member of the royal family, the queen-mother, queen, or *dauphine*. The *après-dîner* could be devoted to outdoor recreations, to continued work with the councils and with senior ministers, or to various combinations of these pursuits. Hunting, *jeu de paume* or *paille-maille*, promenades or shooting at targets were among the customary recreations in the *après-dîner*, but we find them in the morning hours too, especially when the court was in Marly or Fontainebleau.[86]

Towards the end of the afternoon, there was either *appartement* – a combination of music, various card games, billiards, and collation – French comedy, or Italian comedy. It seems as a rule to have started around 19.00 or 20.00.[87] In Marly, 4 December 1687, Dangeau noted 'la comédie ballet du Bourgeois gentilhomme commença à six heures, afin qu'on put souper plus tôt qu'à l'ordinaire et que tous les domestiques eussent le loisir de manger avant minuit'.[88] Gambling and card games were notoriously popular at court; in Marly particularly, they dominated the afternoon and evening.[89] *Souper*, usually *à grand couvert*, public and dignified, followed either at 21.00 or at 22.00, in the king's antechamber, or in the apartment of the senior female member of the royal family, 'en Famille Roiale'.[90] Dangeau adds that 'le petit coucher étoit ordinairement fini à minuit

85 See Dangeau, *Journal*, II, p. 216 (24 November 1684); XIII, p. 179; Saint-Simon, *Mémoires*, XXVIII, p. 342 (with n. 3) and p. 477 for the papal permission to celebrate Mass at that late hour, and its usurpation by the princes of the blood.

86 Dangeau, *Journal*, see, for example, I, p. 56 (25 September 1684; Chambord, Fontainebleau); II, p. 18 (6 February 1687; Marly).

87 Dangeau, *Journal*, I, pp. 87–88, the overview of Louis XIV's activities gives 19.00, as does II, p. 223 (3 December 1688); other instances give 20.00, for example I, p. 74 (24 November 1684); II, p. 13 (26 January 1687); II, p. 89 (5 January 1688).

88 Dangeau, *Journal*, II, p. 74 (4 December 1687; Marly). In Louis XIV's last years Madame de Maintenon was the undisputed centre, with meals in her apartment, and evening 'petite ou grande musique' too.

89 Dangeau lists among others Blanque; Reversi; Trou-madame; Guerre; Trente et quarante; Pair ou non au portique; Culbas; Ombre. Trabouillet, *Etat* 1712, I, p. 294, gives 'cartes, dez, le trictrac, les échêts, le billiard, le trou-madame, le portique' as the standard entertainments for the appartement. Luynes' *Mémoires* adds cavagnole (II, p. 206), papillon (II, pp. 198–199), piquet, comète (IX, p. 46). Compare Grussi, *Joueurs*.

90 Besongne, *Etat* 1687, p. 223; Dangeau, *Journal*, II, p. 20 (11 February 1687, at 21.00); I, pp. 87–88 (the general overview of 1684), and I, p. 32 (1 July 1684: 22.00).

et demi, au plus tard à une heure'.[91] Shortly before sleeping, the king could listen to the musicians of the chamber, or he fed and patted his cherished dogs. Mardi Gras masquerades or other special feasts could continue much longer. In 1703, Sourches notes, the *mascarade*, starting at 23.00, continued until 5.00 in the morning. The king, however, retired shortly after midnight for a somewhat unusual *coucher*, where the valets of the chamber and wardrobe served *en habit de masque*.[92] On such special occasions a late meal or *medianoche* was served.[93]

When Saint-Simon suggested that with a watch and an almanac he could predict the whereabouts and activities of Louis XIV at any particular time, he referred to the last decades of the reign. Indeed, the life cycle of individual rulers inevitably structured their habits. The younger Louis XIV, with his travels, his less fixed patterns of day and year, his great outdoor festivities, the *galanterie* and impetuosity of his court, has often been contrasted with the older monarch, the centre of an increasingly stable and devout train of life. This familiar contrast may reflect a more general pattern, mostly relevant for longer reigns. The older Sun King's occupations were not as rigidly predetermined as Saint-Simon's dictum suggested, but the variations are minor: more outdoor recreations and gambling in the secondary palaces; more devotion around the great religious feasts; more deliberation with ministers in times of crisis. Undeniably, Louis XIV had a far more settled pattern of activities than his two Bourbon predecessors, and in the first two decades at Versailles, he may have approached in practice what the last Valois had vainly attempted to decree.

Obviously, when the king was ill routines could not continue. Gout troubled Louis XIV as much as it did his fellow monarchs; he experienced several longer periods of illness; and he was frequently encumbered by medical strictures.[94] Louis XIV mostly attended Mass *à la tribune* of his Versailles' chapel – Bluche suggests he did not miss one Mass in his 55-year reign.[95] In addition to the public *grand'-messe* shortly after noon, came daily individual prayer during *lever* and *coucher*. On the eve of religious feasts we also find an early Mass, Vespers in the *après-dîner* and *saluts* or other Divine Offices in the evening hours.[96] On such days religion pushed aside the common evening entertainments, and they were

[91] Dangeau, *Journal*, I, 88; on I, p. 31 (30 June 1684), the marquis notes that the king 'se promena dans les jardins au clair de la lune jusqu'après minuit'. *Moi, Marie Du Bois*, p. 159, notes that the king went to the queen's apartment only towards 2.00 in the morning, after a day of abstention he had eaten meat after 24.00. Du Bois himself had dinner at 11.00, supper at 18.00, see p. 163.

[92] Sourches, *Mémoires*, VIII, pp. 32–33 (20 February 1703). He adds that the masked servants were a novelty.

[93] For example, *Moi, Marie Du Bois*, p. 169, on the king's birthday, 5 September 1671.

[94] Dangeau, *Journal*, November and December 1686: the king's fistula. Sourches frequently mentions gout, or the taking of medicine as explanation for Louis XIV's refraining from his *toucher les malades* on the religious feasts, see above, n. 26.

[95] Saint-Simon, *Mémoires*, XXVIII, p. 364, and his devotional practices on pp. 364–371; Bluche, 'Messe', in *DGS*, pp. 1022–1023; yet compare Oroux's critical remarks cited above.

[96] See Trabouillet, *Etat* 1712, I, pp. 292–293, on the evening devotions, innumerable incidental remarks by Dangeau, *Journal*, for example, II, p. 60 (1 November 1687); II, p. 77 (7 December 1687); II, p. 83 (24 December 1687); II, p. 314 (30 January 1689); XVIII, p. 59 (8 June 1719), *jour de la fête dieu*, with procession to the Tuileries of the Paroisse Saint-Germain l'Auxerrois.

suppressed in times of mourning as well. At all times of the day, senior ministers could visit the king with news, mostly about military exploits – when carrying important messages they could enter the bedchamber even before the first entry of *premiers gentilshommes* and *grand chambellan*.[97]

In his later Versailles years the king often chose not to attend the comedies, and when he incidentally visited the *appartements* it was only to play billiards for an hour or so.[98] In his very last years, following the series of deaths in the royal family, Louis XIV's patterns again changed, he rose later, attended Mass earlier between 9.00 and 10.00, and spent more and more time in Madame de Maintenon's apartment[99] – indeed, after the death of the young *dauphine*, the pivotal position of his morganatic wife was demonstrated more conspicuously, to the utmost distaste of the senior female member of the dynasty, her immensely less influential rival, *Madame*. Luynes' memoirs show that in the eighteenth century, the routines described above still served as a framework, leaving room for multiple variations – I will not discuss them here.[100] Paris was a necessary counterpart to the entertainments offered even in Versailles' glorious first decades: we frequently find Dangeau reporting the return of courtiers from their urban excursions. Around 1700, however, it was regaining its position as the focus for social life.[101] In the eighteenth century, the necklace of dynastic palaces around Paris, luminous as it was, did not outshine its urban centre.

Most activities of the French rulers would have been as familiar for the Viennese Habsburgs as they were for other European dynasties. The isolated references we have about the daily rhythm of the early Habsburgs, limited to hours of councillors, match Henry III's hours.[102] It may well be possible to glean detailed information about the court's daily and weekly routines from early written newspapers, or from correspondence and other private sources, but the ordinances and instructions do not match Henry's meticulous *règlements*, nor can we find

97 Dangeau, *Journal*, II, p. 193 (21 October 1688): 'M. de Louvois est venu ce matin au leve du roi avant même que le prémier gentilhomme de la chambre fut entré' with war news; see also II, p. 210 (14 November 1688): 'M. de Barbézieux entra chez le roi à son lever, avant le premier gentilhomme de la chambre, et lui donna des lettres de monseigneur qui lui mande que la ville de manheim s'est rendue'; or II, p. 234 (23 December 1688): Seignelay tells the king, who was still in bed, about Lauzun and his mission to save the Stuarts. Louis XVI seems to have been far more restrictive towards the ministers, Hardman, *Louis XVI*, pp. 33–34; 151 notes that Necker had to write to the king before being admitted to Marly in June 1789, and suggests that this was usual.

98 See Trabouillet, *Etat* 1712, I, p. 294: 'Tous les soirs en Hyver, ou pour mieux dire, depuis le commencement du mois d'Octobre jusqu'à Pâque Fleuri, il y a Comédie ou Appartemens pour le divertissment de la Cour c'est à dire, un jour Appartemens, le lendemain Comédie Françoise, le troisième, il n'y a rien; le quatrième, Appartemens, et ainsi de suite. Le Roy ne va point aux Comédies, ni aux Appartemens.'

99 See Bryant, 'Françoise d'Aubigné', pp. 243–274; Sourches, *Mémoires*, XIII, p. 272 (11 January 1712) notes Louis' first dinner *à petit couvert* in the apartment of Madame de Maintenon; Dangeau frequently reports this thereafter, for example in *Journal*, XIV, pp. 437, 444, 446; Solnon, *Cour de France*, p. 326.

100 See, for example, Luynes, *Mémoires*, II, 1738, pp. 253, and 271–273, for the Fontainebleau routines.

101 See the 'Calendrier des spectacles sous l'Ancien Régime 1601–1774' at http//foires.net/cal/cal.shtml.

102 See the Innsbrucker Ordnungen studied by Bojcov, 'Sitten und Verhaltensnormen am Innsbrucker Hof', p. 268, where the hours for the Räte are mentioned: 6.00 to 8.00 and if necessary 12.00 to 16.00, compare Maximilian's 1498 rules in *ÖZV*, I, 2, no. 4, p. 8, where the parallel hours were 7.00–9.00 and 12.00–16.00.

an equivalent of Dangeau's notes or the overviews given in the printed *états*.[103] Papal nuncio Carafa noted that Ferdinand II rose early, around 4.00 in the morning, and went to bed around 22.00 'following German practice'. His day opened with devotions: two early Masses, and more to follow on the frequent special occasions in the liturgical calendar. Council meetings took him the rest of the morning hours, and frequently a part of the afternoon; every other, day, council meetings were replaced by hunting, with the emperor more often than not coming home only after nightfall. On council days, the emperor ended his daily work with audiences, reading and signing state papers.[104] Ferdinand may have been an exceptionally early riser: while devotion, council, and hunting remained the basic items of the day, the day tended to start later. An *Edelknabenordnung* urges the pages to rise at 6.00 to pray in their room at 7.00; they had to assemble again for prayer in their room at 20.00, going to bed immediately thereafter. At 21.00, they were expected to sleep, and no lights ought to be seen later.[105] The *Edelknaben* attended the emperor's daily Mass at 8.00, in the Hofburg chapel, in the *Hofkirche*, or in another church in the immediate vicinity of the Hofburg.[106] On other public occasions during the day they were likewise expected to wait upon their lord, thus their schedule may hint at the emperor's habits. The emperors, we may assume, were still early risers; their *Ankleiden* was accompanied only by the chamber's officers and servants, but their instructions do not mention any specific time. In Leopold's time the *Ankleiden* still seems to have been enlivened by jesters and the obligatory *Kammerzwerg*.[107] We find meetings or audiences at 8.30, but with the statement that this was early.[108]

As in the French case, audiences, councils, and deliberation filled the ruler's schedule between Mass and dinner. Yet council meetings were neither as strictly

[103] In the fourth workshop of the 'Arbeitskreises Höfe des Hauses Österreich', Der Habsburger Hof und Prag (5 April 2001), two contributions made clear that the 'geschriebene Zeitungen' and diaries from Rudolf's Spanish sojourn can add more detail: Alena Richterová (Narodni knihovna CR, Praha), 'Die Berichterstattung vom Kaiserhof in den Zeitungen an der Wende vom 16. zum 17. Jahrhunderts'; Karl Rudolf (Österreichisches Historisches Institut, Madrid), 'Madrider und Prager Hof zur Zeit Rudolfs II.'

[104] Carafa, in Hurter, *Friedensbestrebungen*, pp. 213–218.

[105] Menčík, 'Kaiserlichen Hofämter', at pp. 537 and 538. The pages that had to go riding in the early morning had to rise at 4.00 in summer, at 7.00 in winter.

[106] Menčík, 'Kaiserlichen Hofämter', p. 537: 'Ihrer Kay. Mayt. Meess . . . bey den capucinern umb acht Uhr hören . . .'. The connection of the pages with the emperor's activities was in fact quite direct, as they were expected to show up for service at the ruler's table, attend his Mass, etc. Compare the remarks in the 1561 instruction on p. 529 of the same article.

[107] *Kammerzwergen* or their servants and governors are well-attested in the HZAB, see, for example, 1662/107: fols. 251v–252r, Cammerzwergen und Narndiener; 1675/119, fol. 155, Kammerzwergen und Narrendiener; 1699/142, fol. 277r, two dwarfs. Charles VI seemed to have been much attached to his dwarf Hansl or Baron Klein, who accompanied him on his hunting parties, see Mitis, *Jagd und Schutzen*, p. 35; and the 'Relation' of Charles' farewell from Vienna printed in the September 1703 *Wienerisches Diarium*, 1703. Vehse, *Geschichte der deutschen Höfe*, V, pp. 156–162, cites G.-B. Pacichelli, *Memorie de' Viaggi per l'Europa Christiana, scritte à diversi In occasion de' suoi Ministeri dall'abate*, 5 vols. (Naples 1685), ÖNB 48.L.20–24, who is cited too in Rousset, *Ceremonial diplomatique*. In vol. III, pp. 22–23, Pacichelli indeed mentions the dwarfs, though his description seems to point to the dinner, not the *Ankleiden*.

[108] See, for example, HHStA ÄZA K 3 varia fols. 1–49, 2r–27v, here at fol. 25v. The *Beurlaubung* of the elector of Brandenburg.

scheduled nor as regular as at the French court, and the emperor did not invariably attend. Between 1670 and 1673, shortly before *Obersthofmeister* Lobkowitz's fall from power, Leopold did not attend the *geheime Konferenz*, or 'inner council', but studied the *votum* of the council, and subsequently presented his *conclusum*. After 1673 the emperor again attended the council, but from 1688 onwards much work was done in various thematically grouped *ad hoc* committees or *Konferenzen*, and the *geheime Rat* became a vehicle mainly for more ceremonial occasions. Thus, Leopold was again able to study the proposals of his councillors in seclusion, later communicating his decisions to them.[109] Scattered references to dinnertime range from 11.00 to 13.00, but formal dinners seem to have started around 12.30, lasting until *c.* 14.00, or even longer on stately occasions.[110] Shortly after his marriage to his Spanish bride Margarita Teresa, Leopold complained that her Spanish following sought to change the routines of his court, forcing him to wait as long as 13.00 or 14.00 for his dinner – an attempt, he assured his correspondent count Pötting, he would never tolerate.[111] Habitually, dinner was served in the emperor's apartment, where hospitality was more restricted than for supper 'at the empress' side'. In the afternoon, we find the same varied pursuits as at the French court: hunting, music, games, government. Leopold's correspondence with his librarian Lambeck conveys a vivid interest in many a field, and the emperor's fancy for music and composition will also have been

[109] Sienell, *Geheime Konferenz* and 'Kaiserlichen Beratungsgremien'.

[110] Vehse, *Geschichte der deutschen Höfe*, II, 5, p. 159, cites Leopold's letters to his librarian Lambeck including remark about the time of dinner, 11.00; Vehse, II, 6, p. 289, mentions 13.00 for Charles VI's dinner; in the same volume on p. 293 he discusses the late supper or Merende: 'Eine am Wiener Hofe sehr Häufig vorkommende Festlichkeit waren noch die s.g. Merenden: Souper und Ball. Das Souper ward erst zwei Uhr nach Mitternacht aufgetragen und drei uhr begann der Tanz, der bis in den lichten Morgen acht Uhr währte'. See the repeated visits and meals of the electors in Prague on the occasion of Ferdinand IV's election in HHStA ÄZA K 3 Varia, Empfangen, Audienzen, 1: Der Churfürsten Audienz bey der Röm: Kayserin Mayt, fols. 1–5, at fol. 3r states that his guests for the *Nachtmahl* arrived at 19.00; 2: Extract Kay: 'Kön: Hofprotocolli wegen des ceremonialis zwischen Ihro May: den König Ferdinando 4ten und denen Herrn Churfürsten zu Prag, wie auch deroselben Gesandten de anno 1652' (4 October 1652–27 November 1652), fols. 5r–27v, mentions hours for meals mostly between 12.30 and 14.00 (fols. 13v, 14v, 15r, 22r, 23v, 24v); audiences, from 8.30 an early *Beurlaubung*, to the more habitual 10.30 (fols. 19r, 25v); supper from 20.00 to 21.00 and from 21.00 to 23.00 (fols. 14v, 24v); the following extract in the same portfolio, 'Extract aus dem Hoffprothocoll de Anno 1652 wegen des Tractament zwischen Ihr Königl: Maij: Ferd: 4tum Undt denen Herrn Churfürsten zu Praag' (October 1652–May 1653), fols. 1–2; audiences and visits at 10.00, 15.30, 17.00, 18.00. A description of the 1665 Erbhuldigung in the Tyrol, ÄZA K 7, fols. 284–292v) mentions on fol. 288v that the emperor left the festive dinner at *c.* 14.00 to attend a comedy. These disparate references suggest great variability of activities and hours. See also: Ilsebill Barta-Fliedl, Andreas Gugler, and Peter Parenzan, eds., *Tafeln bei Hofe. Zur Geschichte der fürstlichen Tafelkultur. Sammlungsband* 4 (Hamburg 1998); this book is mostly concerned with dining during festive occasions, see p. 53, a meal in the Favorita in August 1719: gegen 21.00 offene Tafel; p. 56: a meal in September 1719 in Dresden, celebrating the same marriage: 14.00–17.00. HHStA OMeA Sr K 184, no. 95 (a 1754 overview of tables at court), lists 12.00–14.00 as the regular hours for dinner, adding that the empress dined alone in her Retirade in the evening.

[111] *Privatbriefe*, I, pp. 264–265 (9 December 1666): 'Übrigens ist mir noch dieses eingefallen, Euch zu berichten, dass die Spanier alles auf Spanisch wollen gehalten haben, und das will mir gar nicht im Kopf gehen. Noch zu dato habe ich auch allezeit erst um 1 oder 2 Uhr geessen, so mir unmöglich wäre in die Läng auszudauern; wird also wohl nicht übel sein, wann die Königin allhier zu verstehen geben wollte. Dass sie keine Neuerung allhier anheben sollten.' Note the indirect communication between the spouses at this stage, going from Leopold to his ambassador in Spain, and conceivably reaching Margarita Teresa via the Spanish ambassador. Compare I, p. 266 (10 December 1666): 'Die hiesigen Mujeres espanolas wollen mein Hof ganz spanisch machen, ich kann ihnen es aber nit angehn lassen'.

indulged both in his solitary hours and in the companionship of family and courtiers. In the hunting lodges, recreations would claim the morning hours as well.[112] Late in the afternoon, or early in the evening, the emperor and empress were available for audiences, though in the sources we find audiences at any conceivable time of the day.

Supper, or *Nachtmahl,* as well was probably slightly earlier than at the French court: guests invited for a stately *Nachtmahl* arrived at 19.00 or 20.00, and usually it was over at 21.00, though we find occasions where it started at that time and lasted until 23.00. Instructions for the *Hofdamen*, some of whom would attend supper in the evening in the empress' apartment, indicate they had to report for service between 18.00 and 19.00, depending on the season – and Claudia Felicitas seems to have changed the hours to 19.00 and 20.00 respectively. The day-to-day supper without special guests, we may assume, usually started around 20.00, and the emperor did not as a rule engage in activities afterwards – incidentally Leopold noted that he went to bed at 22.00.[113] Comedies and Italian operas, either for a highly exclusive company in the form of *Kammerfesten*, or in a more public context, were not as frequent as in Versailles, yet if we add to them balls and other festivities, we might encounter them every month or so, with a much stronger concentration in the early months of the year. Leopold's *Hofstaat* would attend Eleonora II Gonzaga's conspicuous cultural activities, and those organised by the Jesuits.[114] When the court did indulge in festivities, a *Merende* (from the Spanish *merendar*, *merienda*) or 'night meal', was served in the early morning hours to refresh feasters, a parallel of the French *Medianoche*. Such balls and late suppers were particularly prevalent in *Fasching*. Instructions for *Hofdamen* and pages alike explicitly warn against the less official practice of such *Merenden* in the private quarters of courtiers, and urge the courtiers to go to sleep within an hour after the *Nachtmahl*.[115]

Charles VI's habits, as reflected in the *Wienerisches Diarium*, were roughly similar, possibly somewhat more fixed: a steady rhythm of council in the morning, audiences in the afternoon, frequently disrupted by the ubiquitous religious celebrations and hunting parties. Küchelbecker tells us that the *geheime Konferenz* met several times a week, and was usually presided over by the emperor himself – other councils met regularly on fixed days, but were not chaired by the

[112] See Th. G. von Karajan, 'Kaiser Leopold I. und Peter Lambeck', *Almanach der Kaiserlichen Akademie der Wissenschaften* 18 (1868), pp. 103–156; Küchelbecker, *Allerneueste Nachricht*, p. 255, gives the hours for the Laxenburg Reiherbeize: either 6.00 to 10.00 or 15.00 to 18.00.

[113] *Privatbriefe*, I, p. 260 (10 November 1666): 'als ich um 10 Uhr zue Bette gehen wollen'.

[114] Hadamowsky, *Barocktheater*, pp. 20, 26, 27; Herbert Seifert, *Die Oper am wiener Kaiserhof im 17. Jahrhundert* (Tutzing 1985).

[115] HHStA ÄZA K 8 (24 September 1670): instruction for Eleonora Gonzaga's Hofmeisterin, fols. 301–308, fol. 306v no. 29 on the *Merenden*: HHStA OMeA Sr 367 (1557 1699), no. 16, was edited by Bastl and Heiß, 'Hofdamen und Höflinge', p. 237, for the admonitions to go to bed early, as to be able to attend Divine Office in the early morning hours; Mecenseffy, *Im Dienste dreier Habsburger*, pp. 505–508, on p. 508 Auersperg warns his daughter against the 'Kalte merenden'.

emperor.[116] The diary (1742–1776) of Johann Josef Khevenhüller-Metsch shows a marked change in the routines of the court, as Maria Theresa introduced a sequence of entertainments not previously habitual in Vienna:

> Die Dinés bei Hoff continuirten täglich, ausser des Sonntags, welchen Tag der Kaiser mit denen Dames soupirte. Annebens wurde auf der Kaiserin Antrag neuerlich introduciret, daß selber die vier Täge wo kein Concert au Théâtre ware (nemmlich Monntag, Mittwoch, Freitag und Samstag) mit der gewöhnlichen Compagnie von Männern Billard spillte, um täglich des Abends eine Unterhaltung zu haben . . .[117]

This addition of such entertainments to the regular schedule entailed slightly later hours, but left intact the broad outlines sketched above. The advice offered by Maria Theresa in 1765 for the courts of her children underlines both the basic continuity of court life, and the increasing density of social occasions for a gradually widening circle at court.[118]

In Vienna, rulers' schedules followed the same tendency as in France, slowly getting later throughout the centuries. When early instructions mention hours, we still find the seasonal differentiation that occurred in Henry III's ordinances, allowing for longer days in summer.[119] Climate and tradition played a role in the usually earlier hours of sleeping at the Habsburg court, close to 'German' custom as papal nuncio Carafa reported, whereas the French court may have been closer to Mediterranean preferences. From the early sixteenth into the later eighteenth century, the hours of rising and going to bed seem to be set later and later at both courts. Surely, more extensive use was made of lighting, making the dark evening hours available for courtly entertainments. In this respect, the court pioneered a process that was soon to be adopted in Europe's major cities. As a consequence of the lesser relevance of the 'natural' hours of light and darkness, the seasonal differences between winter and summer were also becoming less relevant. It is not unlikely, but difficult to prove, that the daily activities of rulers became increasingly fixed. The contrasting tempers of rulers as well as the changes in the lives of individual rulers prevent easy conclusions.

116 *Wienerisches Diarium*, for example, 2 January 1728; 13 January 1727; 10 April 1728; Küchelbecker, *Allerneueste Nachricht*, pp. 301–302, 307, 313.

117 Khevenhüller, *Tagebuch*, IV (3 March 1756), p. 10; *ibid*., IV, pp. 11, 18, 21, 23, 36, 45, 46 for 'appartements', frequently in the afternoon. On Friday, instead of comedy or concerts, we find card and dice games. See Maria Theresa's schedule and hard work in Dickson, *Finance and Government*, I, p. 210.

118 ÖNB cod ser. n. 1713, fols. 47r–51v; Maria Theresa's 'Instruction pour le ceremoniel aux cours de ses enfans 1765'; fols. 75–82, 'sur la cour'. Compare the lists of dinners and other social occasions in ÖNB cod. 12956, for example fols. 388–389, Ferdinand's dinners in Schönbrunn: July–September 1770. The empress' recommendations fit well the general framework of court life as presented in Khevenhüller's *Tagebuch*.

119 BN MS naf 7225, fol. 46v; HHStA ÄZA K 9, 1673–1676, instruction for Margarita Teresa's *Oberst-hofmeisterin*, adapted for Claudia Felicitas by comments in the margin, fols. 463–469, on fol. 465r we find a reference to hours: Hofdames could not leave court before 10.30 (crossed out), and had to be back before 19.00 in summer (crossed out and changed to 20.00), and before 18.00 in winter (crossed out and changed to 19.00). See Woolgar's overview, *Great Household*, p. 85, with hours roughly comparable to those of Henry III and the habitual summer–winter variations.

FROM INTIMACY TO DISPLAY

Many activities mentioned in this brief outline of year and day at court could either be quite uncomplicated or highly elaborate, secluded or public – nor do these distinctions necessarily overlap. While we find truly private moments even more rarely in Louis XIV's court than in Leopold's, it is easy to see that at both courts events we tend to look upon as private were frequently subject to an elaborate choreography combining the demonstration of sovereign power with the detailed demarcation of the rank of those serving the sovereign.

A small inner nucleus of family, friends, senior court dignitaries, and trusted servants was expected to remain in the vicinity of the ruler even when he was shielded from public attention. Both the practical needs of the household, and the dictate of *repraesentatio maiestatis*, necessitated a widening of this circle. The entry of a larger audience into the court, or conversely the household's frequent public excursions, were matters of great concern. Ordinances invariably attempted to structure access on the basis of rank or function, using the ruler's timetable as well as the spatial arrangements of the palace as their main devices. Spatial and temporal thresholds were set up to prevent outsiders from intruding; guards and ushers barred the way, checking the status of unknown visitors before letting them pass. Ideally, a close fit between the hierarchies of the realm and the various levels of access would be established at court, whether in the palace precincts, in church, in other buildings, during marches, or in open places. Early modern ordinances and instructions as a rule include comprehensive attempts in this direction. The court may indeed be pictured as a series of concentric circles around the ruler, reaching from intimacy and seclusion to distance and display. The continuing movement between these poles was a basic characteristic of all early modern courts.

Most French kings remained loyal to the tradition of openness, and their courts were a bustling and vivacious environment.[120] Was a French king ever truly 'en son particulier', we may ask ourselves, when his eating, sleeping, and excreting were habitually witnessed by others? Without overstating the permanent visibility of the ruler, or confounding our sensitivities with those of another age, it is readily imaginable that not all rulers felt comfortable in such circumstances, particularly when they had reason to look with suspicion on even their closest associates. Henry III's *règlements* implicitly but eloquently convey the burden of open kingship for a ruler averse to such relentless proximity. The 1578 *règlement* strictly forbade courtiers to come to the king's room uninvited; the doors had to be guarded by valets, and after the *coucher*, the king's room was to

[120] See Zeller, *Institutions*, p. 97, quoting from Francis I's edict of 1523: 'entre les rois de France et leurs sujets y a toujours eu plus grande conglutination, de vraye amour, naïfve dévotion, cordiale concorde et intime affection qu'en quelconque autre monarchie ou nation chrestienne'; and the affirmation of these habits by the Venetian ambassador in François II's reign on the same page.

be locked. Courtiers had to keep 'un peu loin' during the king's meals, and only the captain of the guards should stand behind him.[121] More explicitly, the 1585 *règlement* outlined that:

Sa majesté veut que nul ne s'ingère de la servir aux choses qui touchent sa personne, telles qui s'ensuivent, à sçavoir son habiller ou deshabiller, à ses repas, à son desjeuner, collations des après-disnées ou du soir, ny à luy bailler son bonnet, chapeau, ou manteau ny aussi à son botter ou débotter, s'il n'est domestique couché en l'estat de sa maison, et non-seulement ayant quartier, mais estant actuellement en service, si par Sa Majesté n'estoit particulièrement commandé autrement, excepté les princes du sang, cardinaux, autres princes, messieurs les ducs de Joyeuse et d'Espernon, les officiers de la couronne et ceux des affaires de Sa Majesté, deffendant Sadite Majesté à un chacun d'en user autrement.[122]

Henry went on to dictate a detailed system of *entrées*, limiting access to his apartment during the *lever* by erecting temporal as well as spatial thresholds connected to rank. Under no circumstances should anybody address the king unless expressly invited, always staying 'un peu esloigné de Sa Majesté, pour ne la presser point'. During dinner and supper, those invited to speak should do so clearly and audibly, strictly sticking to 'choses de sçavoir et de vertu'; only those joining the king's meal, his guards and servants, could proceed beyond the *barrières* shielding the table. In the evening, the process of withdrawing mirrored the morning procedures. Distance and respect organised according to rank, are prescribed for all conceivable settings; a strong distaste of uninvited physical and verbal contact permeates the whole text.[123]

Henry's prescriptions, many of them assuredly futile, retained their paradigmatic force for later rulers, though they did not necessarily share his sensibilities and their environment may have been more orderly. Louis XIV, reiterating his Valois predecessor's dignified rules, more willingly underwrote the tradition of open kingship. Paradoxically, in his reign we find a fusion of the two elements apparently so deeply opposed in Henry's texts: accessibility and dignity. What in Henry's case had partly been a way out of an uncomfortable predicament, in Louis' hands became a recipe for greater resonance of the court. The multitudes witnessing the dignified pageantry of court life were among its most efficient propagators. Louis XIV explained how courtly magnificence could please his elites, and enthral his peoples at the same time:

121 BN Brienne 256 (MS naf 7225), fols. 43–49, quote on fol. 46.

122 1585 ordinance in *AC*, p. 311. See Le Roux's discussion of the *règlements*, *Faveur du roi*, pp. 177–186.

123 For the quote and the rule that nobody could be covered in the king's presence see *AC*, p. 312; respect for the king's bed and dais, public along the walls of the corridor when the king passes, p. 313; nobody sitting in the king's presence, leaning on his chair or laying a hand on his clothing, service or food, p. 314; a lengthy description of the rooms in the apartment and the persons allowed there, similar to the *entrées*, pp. 315–320; the day's procedures, including *serviette* and other rules for the *dîner*, including the barrières (p. 324), dais and canopy (p. 326), pp. 320–332; the councils, pp. 332–358. See Potter and Roberts, 'An Englishman's View'.

Cette société de plaisirs, qui donne au personnes de la cour une honnête familiarité avec nous, les touche et les charme plus qu'on peut dire. Les peuples, d'un autre coté, se plaisent au spectacle, . . . Par là nous tenons leur esprit et leur cœur, quelquefois plus fortement peut-être, que par les récompenses et les bienfaits; et à l'égard des étrangers, dans un Etat qu'ils voient florissant d'ailleurs et bien réglé, ce qui se consume en ces dépenses qui peuvent passer pour superflues fait sur eux une impression très avantageuse de magnificence, de puissance, de richesse et de grandeur.[124]

The king's long reign may not have been as dignified in its early stages, nor as open in its last years as has been asserted, but the deviations remain limited. On the whole, we see a king highly sensitive to rank and dignity, and devoted to his public role. Nor did he strive to shield his more private actions from his companions. Marie Du Bois, one of Louis XIV's *valets de chambre* in the early years of his personal reign, mentions the king's use of the *chaise percée* or *chaise d'affaires*, in the selected company of the *petit coucher* as a matter of course – and as an ideal opportunity to find the ruler's ear. When a few years later Primi Visconti referred to the same custom, he did so with barely disguised distaste, adding, to Louis XIV's credit, that he mostly went through these procedures 'merely ceremonially'.[125] The king focused ceremony even more strongly on the bedchamber, and declined the opportunity to have a private bedroom in addition to his state bedroom, a decision limiting his privacy.[126] Towards the end of his reign, however, the Sun King sought to spend more time in the company of his family and Madame de Maintenon. The range of private rooms in Versailles' state apartment was not strictly the invention of Louis XV, who followed more actively a predilection evident in the last decades of his great-grandfather's rule.[127]

124 Dreyss, *Mémoires de Louis XIV*, II, p. 568.

125 Primi Visconti, *Mémoires*, p. 61; cf. *Moi, Marie Du Bois*, pp. 133, 135, 141, 143, etc. We find the *portechaise d'affaires* in a list for the *prémières entrées* in the early eighteenth-century court, see O 1 822 pp. 87–90, and O 1 793 (around 1780), no. 105, shows that he had *bouche à la cour*. Compare the memoirs of another *valet de chambre*, De La Porte about the young Louis XIV and his brother: *Mémoires de P. de la Porte, premier valet de chambre de Louis XIV, contenant plusieurs particularités des règnes de Louis XIII et de Louis XIV*, in: *Nouvelle collection des mémoires pour servir à l'histoire de France*, ed. Michaud and Poujoulat (Paris 1850), third series, VIII, pp. 1–57. Compare the details given for the *chaise* during the king's illness in AN O 1 822, pp. 9–10. See Verlet, *Versailles*, p. 160, on the *dauphine*'s giving birth to the duc de Bourgogne reported by Sourches in his entry for 6 August 1682 by Sourches, and Louis XIV's remark addressed to the *dauphine* when she was averse to dance in the evening entertainments: 'madame, je veux qu'il y ait appartement et que vous y dansiez. Nous ne sommes pas comme des particuliers, nous nous devons tout entiers au public.'

126 Hugh Murray-Baillie, 'Etiquette', presents Louis' decision for one central bedroom in the palace, serving both as private and state bedroom, as a regression.

127 Verlet, *Versailles*, shows the importance of *petits cabinets* and other more secluded rooms from the 1690s onwards. Sourches, *Mémoires*, I, p. 351, notes the king's 'fêtes particulières' in his *appartements*; see John Rogister, 'From Louis XV to Louis XVI: Some Thoughts on the Petits Appartements', in *The Art and Architecture of Versailles*, ed. Robert P. Maccubin and David F. Morill, *Eighteenth-Century Life* n.s., 17 (1993), pp. 147–166. Note the levels of access, varying from the open Versailles to the exclusive Trianon and Marly; compare the *Kammerfesten*, *Wirtschaften*, and later also *petits soupers* etc. in Vienna. Louis XV certainly used such favours as a means to secure his pre-eminence among the court nobles, by whom he felt *écrasé*. Many of the special privileges ascribed to Louis XIV were developed or refined in the course of the eighteenth century, by his less secure great-grandson. See on architecture, the apartment, and privacy in Bavaria: Samuel J. Klingensmith, *The Utility of Splendor: Ceremony, Social Life, and Architecture at the Court of Bavaria, 1600–1800* (Chicago 1993).

In Vienna the situation was fundamentally different in at least one respect: the bedroom, one of the focal points of French domestic routine, was not as a rule accessible. Ferdinand I's 1527 ordinance succinctly noted that: 'In irer kgl. Mt. Schlafkamer soll niemand ordinari eingang haben'; a more detailed 1562 instruction reiterated this position, adding that in addition to the highest court officers, the serving *Kämmerer* and the *Kammerdiener*, only those explicitly invited could enter.[128] Entrance into the apartment, and into each of its rooms, was strictly connected to rank or service. In addition to *Ritterstube*, antechamber, *Ratstube*, and the mostly inaccessible *Retirade*, the enfilade of rooms included a second antechamber – in France decreed in theory by Henry III, but truly functioning only from the 1680s onwards. In practice, the restrictions may have been difficult to control, but they sheltered the ruler more than did the French system of *entrées*, regulating access into the heart of the king's apartment.[129]

Levels of access and seclusion differed from court to court, but rulers were to a certain extent able to find refuge from their strenuous public duties. When the sovereign was surrounded only by intimates without serious controversies about their place in the hierarchy, there was room for easier companionship. At the court of the Austrian Habsburgs, such moments were more frequent than in France, yet not all was public at the French court. Primi Visconti noted that Louis XIV knew well how to adapt to different circumstances: 'En public, il est plein de gravité et très différent de ce qu'il est en son particulier . . .'. He goes on to cite an example where the king immediately adapted his posture and deportment when the usher opened the door to admit an unknown public.[130] A more closed environment could help to create more carefree attitudes among courtiers as well. Strict rules for access, the addition of less accessible retirades or cabinets to the apartment, and outdoor diversions or indoor recreations in companionship with intimates, particularly in the smaller palaces, could offer solace. Paradoxically, access to such more private places or activities inevitably attracted courtiers eager for tokens of special favour. While this may have dismayed the ruler when he simply sought shelter, it also enabled him to create new favours *ad infinitum*. The drive to establish safe havens and the consequent possibilities of using these as a means to entice courtiers could turn an initially defensive action into a stratagem that proved quite effective. This impulse was more relevant for the French court with its tradition of open kingship and ever-present multitudes

[128] *ÖZV*, II, p. 108; Menčík, 'Kaiserlichen Hofämter', pp. 3, 17–19.

[129] See HHStA, ÄZA K 26 (fols. 2–14); OMeA Sr K 74, no. 16, Familienakten K 102, repaginated 26 March 1997, fols. 1–124; and HHStA ZA Prot 8 (1713–1715), 6 October 1715 (fols. 266r–271v): 'Allerunterthänigst gehorsambstes Conferenz Gutachten der ordentliche Einrichtung der Kaij. Anticamern betr.'

[130] Primi Visconti, *Mémoires*, p. 28, about Louis XIV: 'En public, il est plein de gravité et très différent de ce qu'il est en son particulier . . . Il sait bien faire le roi en tout'. Primi's presentation of the Sun King, as an invulnerable ruler controlling everything, from his nobles to the weather (p. 167), is as inconsistent as his judgement of the *noblesse d'épée*, either the norm and ideal of all, or the group trampled by the rapid ascent of the all-powerful ministers.

than for the more aloof Habsburg rulers – the latter did not have to resort to new expedients to secure a comfortable level of privacy in their quarters.

How frequent were the incursions of a wider audience into the court, and how close were such outsiders allowed to come? Here, the differences between the Austrian Habsburgs and the Bourbon seem considerable. Küchelbecker made an interesting statement about the Viennese court in Charles VI's reign:

Denn ob mann gleich sehr viel Gala und solenne Feste an solchen zu celibriren pfleget so passiret doch an denenselben weiter nichts, als daß vormittags der Hof sehr zahlreich ist, und ein jedweder in prächtige Kleydung und Equipagien daselbst erscheinet, und daß währender Kayserlicher Tafel eine unvergleichliche Music gehöret wird; des nachmittags ist es bey Hofe gemeiniglich wieder ganz stille, oder es besuchen die kayserlichen, so wohl regierende als verwittibte allerhöchsten Herrschaften einander, und passiren mit solchem Besuch einige Stunden.[131]

If this reflects the situation during festivities, what can we expect about humdrum courtlife? It is improbable that it matched the practice implicitly conveyed in François Hebert's (Versailles' parish priest from 1684 until 1704) description of the courtiers' behaviour during Louis XIV's serious illness and operation in November–December 1686:

... les uns s'appliquant à leurs affaires, les autres s'occupant, ou pour mieux dire, s'amusant au jeu, ceux-ci étant à la promenade, ceux-là se tenant dans les salles et antichambres des appartements, comme il se pratique à la cour pendant que le roi est chez lui ...[132]

Pieter de la Court, a Leiden textile manufacturer visiting Versailles in 1700, noted the 'huge number of courtiers and others' in the *grande galérie*, waiting for the king's Mass to end.[133] Indeed, most visitors report a perpetual hustle and bustle – a situation contrasting sharply with the relative tranquillity of the Viennese court.

The bustle continued when the king was 'chez lui', and it undoubtedly included persons not listed in the *états*. The court was a permanent meeting place; one could go there for entertainment, company, conversation – simultaneously seeking opportunities to see the king, be seen by him, possibly even exchange a few words with him, or more likely to seek the intercession of a senior courtier to obtain advancement or protection. To be 'present' may not necessarily have meant to be 'presented', an honour reserved to those judged worthy of the royal attention because of their loyal service, genealogy, or talents (ideally a combination of these). The presentation was to be systematically organised for the nobility on the basis of genealogy halfway through the eighteenth

[131] Küchelbecker, *Allerneueste Nachricht*, p. 25.

[132] *Mémoires du Curé de Versailles François Hébert 1686–1704*, ed. Georges Girard (Paris 1927), pp. 8–9.

[133] Felix Driessen, ed., *De reizen der de la Courts 1641–1700–1710* (Leiden 1928), p. 53.

century.[134] The French court in Versailles offered an ongoing sequence of entertainments for the elites. The palace included a sizeable number of apartments, for members of the royal family, major court officers, a range of lower servants, and some favourites. Apartments in the auxiliary buildings (*grand commun, écuries, chenil*) added to the numbers of those lodged in the immediate vicinity. While this group of *logeants* necessarily remained limited, probably never reaching more than *c.* 3,000, it added a sense of permanence to court life.[135]

It is not easy to ascertain the limits of the French court's openness.[136] In 1530 Francis I noted the 'grosse fluence des gens qui conversent journellement en nos logis' in an edict prescribing the death penalty for the apparently common thefts from the royal chapel and chamber. In 1677, Louis XIV, judging it necessary to repeat Francis' decree against stealing in the *maisons royales*, once more cited the 'afluence des gens de toutes sortes, faineans & sans aveu qui abordent de toutes parts à notre Cour'. Towards the end of 1682 the edict was reiterated for Versailles.[137] Entry with carriages into the Louvre courtyard was tied to rank, ideally limited to princes, dukes, and *maréchaux de France*, as was the right to be carried there in *chaises*. Yet these rules had repeatedly to be issued as well, and it is unlikely that such spaces were in practice closed to the outside world.[138] In the galleries of the Louvre artisans tied to the household had their *logements*, and exercised their crafts.[139] De la Court, the Dutch traveller cited earlier, compared the Tuileries gardens with a canal fashionable for promenades in his native city Leiden. Domestics were not allowed to enter, nor could 'fiacres' do the tour along the broad alleyways, between the Tuileries and the Louvre yet 'thousands' walked there, and an 'endless queue of coaches' passed through.

134 The 'presentation' and subsequent introduction to the *honneurs de la cour* of nobles – whose ancestry was first scrutinised by the *généalogiste du roi* – was regulated in 1732 and 1759, see Bluche, *Honneurs de la cour*, and in his *DGS* under the same heading. See Salvadori, *Chasse*, pp. 217–220, on the hunt as the most obvious starting point for the new courtier's career: it was during the king's frequent outings that he could hope to be presented, and offered the privilege to sit in the king's carriage. Cf. the formation of the 'appartementsmäßige Noblesse' in Vienna, a process coinciding with the more sociable and the more military character of the Viennese court.

135 Newton, *L'Espace du Roi*, provides a welter of information on the *logements* in the castle, yet no assessment of the overall capacity of the castle and surrounding buildings; see estimates of the *logeants* in Solnon, 'Cour' in *DAR*, p. 356: 3,000 *logeants* in Versailles. *Couvert du Roi*, p. 109, suggests 1,000 rooms in 150 apartments for the *grand commun*, accommodating an estimated 1,500 persons. AN O 1 889 outlines the *logements* for the *Grande Ecurie*.

136 See the quote from the edict in Knecht, 'The Court of Francis I', generally indicating the openness of Francis I's court, on which p. 13 refers to the unconfirmed notion that in the night of the *placards*, 18 October 1534, a *placard* was found on the door of the king's bedchamber.

137 BN Clair 828 *prévôté*, pp. 1253–1259.

138 See, for example BI coll. God. 461, discussing the right of 'entrer en carosse et à cheval en la cour du louvre', compare BN Brienne 256 (or MS naf 7225) 'Roolles des princes et autres qui doivent entrer en carosse en la cour du Louvre', fol. 249ff. There was a renewed attempt to enforce these rules in 1672, see Primi Visconti, *Mémoires*, p. 110, n. 5. For Versailles; BN Clair 814, p. 863, 'Reglement au sujet des chaises a porteurs, a la suite de la cour a Versailles' (10 June 1691).

139 See their *brevets* in AN O 1 1076 1–77, and privileges in BN Clair 828, pp. 1109–1113: 'Privileges accordez aux Ouvriers qui demeurent dans la Gallerie du Louvre' – mostly *valets, peintres, tapissiers, sculpteurs, horlogers, controleurs*.

De la Court visited the palaces, in Paris and elsewhere, and gives the impression that this was routine. Versailles represented a *vaut-le-voyage* for visitors of all sorts. There is no sign whatsoever of the closure of the gardens, reportedly decreed by Louis XIV between 1685 and 1704: travellers report their visit to the gardens and the palace as a matter of course.[140] They could expect to enter the palace, and even approach the inner rooms of the state apartment. De la Court found that only the room where the king was expected to dine was barred to him, as was the *dîner à petit couvert*. He freely roamed through the gardens and courtyards, admired the interior decoration and splendour of many rooms and galleries, and attended several public meals. At the *grand couvert* of Louis XIV's grandsons, he reported the presence of a young Spanish visitor, of 'mediocre standing' engaged in conversation by the duc d'Anjou. Later he witnessed the king's supper *à grand couvert*, with the duchesse de Bourgogne, and likewise the public supper of exiled English royal family in Saint-Germain. James, eating eggs as it was *jour maigre*, inadvertently yellowed his periwig, but nobody in the embarrassed crowd 'dared to inform him'.[141] The environment of the dynastic palaces in France, we may conclude, was relatively open, and Versailles' grandeur structurally invited the attention of foreign tourists as well as French subjects.

In Vienna, we may equally assume the presence in the vicinity of the court of a variegated group of visitors and fortune-seekers, far more numerous than the *Hofgesinde*. Yet the Habsburg rulers did not as a rule cater for elite entertainment, nor did the Hofburg permanently harbour gatherings of relative outsiders. How many persons habitually populated the rooms of the Hofburg? Surely, it could accommodate only a very small segment of the *Hofstaat*, and most courtiers and servants would either be accommodated in Vienna through the marshal's staff, or had to find a place to live themselves.[142] Thus, even the necessary staff did not permanently dwell there. We may expect that serving *Hofdamen* and *Kämmerer* could leave the Hofburg or withdraw to their apartments when their service was not required. Our sources, moreover, frequently mention the 'cavaglieri, cavaglirs, cavallieri' at court, in a generic way discussing them as a visible following for the emperor in his public outings, their closely circumscribed contacts with the *Hofdamen*, or their position in the emperor's apartment. Yet it is not clear whether these were *Kämmerer* and other servants listed in the *Hofstaat*, noble visitors, or grand tourists; probably the word *cavaglieri* simply indicates the highly variable aggregate of all nobles with or without clearly circumscribed

[140] See, for example, Dangeau, *Journal*, I, p. 153 (13 April 1685), for the closure of the gardens: 'Le roi, ne pouvant plus se promener dans ses jardins sans être accablé par la multitude du peuple qui venait de tous les côtés et surtout de Paris, ordonna aux gardes de n'y plus laisser entrer que les gens de la cour et ceux qu'ils mèneroient avec eux. La canaille qui s'y promenoit avoit gaté beaucoup de statues et de vases'; and Dangeau, *Journal*, X, p. 179 (16 November 1704) for the reopening: 'Le roi alla se promener dans ses jardins; il a ordonné qu'on ôtât toutes les grilles qui enferment tous les bosquets, et veux que tous les jardins et toutes les fontaines soient pour le public'.

[141] *Reizen der de la Courts*, pp. 51–56, 60–61.

[142] See Spielman, *City & the Crown*.

charges in the household attending court for whatever reason at any specific moment.[143] On the whole, we seem to miss the sense of the court as a group spending the day in shared activities, whether or not the emperor was present, in addition to the personnel and honorary servants catering for his daily needs. Even when in the course of the eighteenth century the Viennese court adopted the French-style *appartements*, and defined an *appartementsmäßige Noblesse* to be admitted there – a rough parallel to codification of the French presentation – 'court nobles' were not a closely knit group, frequently attending court, but first and foremost the definition of a category entitled to attend.

Paintings suggest the presence of a sizeable and lively company in the great hall of the Prague Hradschin in Rudolf's years, including people waiting to be admitted to any of the rooms adjacent to the hall, and vendors with their booths – was this the exception?[144] In Vienna as in Paris, rules were coined to prevent the proliferation of carriages and horses in the inner courtyards of the Hofburg and other residences, by connecting to rank the right to enter such places with a carriage, as well as the number of horses drawing the carriage. The rapid expansion of the *Kämmerer* almost cost them the privilege of entering the inner courtyard with a carriage: as the *innere Burghof* threatened to become too crowded and confused.[145] Did Viennese citizens stroll through the Hofburg's courtyards? We read no strict prohibitions against walking in these places. Only in the summer of 1711, when the plague threatened Vienna, was there an initiative to keep out unknown persons, by guarding the gates more thoroughly, and introducing a system of badges for court servants.[146] Implicitly, this shows that such precautions were not usually observed. Would visitors enter the palace itself, as they did in France? Travellers routinely discuss the chapel, *Schatzkammer* (treasure room), and other amenities. Purveyors and craftsmen were allowed to enter the palace precincts to perform their duties, but they surely did not form part of the habitual environment. *Edelknaben* and *Frauenzimmer*, or ladies at court, however, were strictly advised not to mix too easily with citizens, and the instructions suggest the ideal of great distance.[147] Undoubtedly, these admonitions served to prevent mischief of either amorous or rowdy nature that

[143] For example, instructions for court ladies, in HHStA ÄZA K 8 (24 September 1670); HHStA ÄZA K 9, 1673–1676 (fol. 468v: at 6.00 the *Hofdamen* could spend some time in the Audienz Stube with the *cavagliri* before serving the empress' table; Bastl and Heiß, 'Hofdamen und Höflinge', pp. 238–239, 242. See 'cavagliri' in AVA Harrach Historica 797, 'Guettachten' p. 5, point 13; Kammerordnung 1715, status under Joseph I, fols. 24r–25r, lists 'cavallieri' for the Ratstube, and the two antechambers, adding different qualifications each time.

[144] See the painting of the great hall in the Hradschin by Aegidius Sadeler, printed in Dickens, *Courts of Europe*, p. 126; my thanks go to Zdenek Hojda for his expert tour of the castle, and his suggestion that the hall served as a waiting room as well as an indoor market for prints, books, and other items.

[145] AVA Harrach Historica 797, 'Guettachten', pp. 21–22, the additions to the *Hofmarschall* instruction seem to imply that *Kämmerer* could not henceforth enter the *innere Burghof* with carriages; yet the instruction written slightly later, in March 1651 in HHStA OMeA Sr K 73, closely reflecting the preceding reforms again grants them this right (point 6, p. 7).

[146] HHStA ÄZA K 25 (from 21 August 1713 to 10 September 1713).

[147] HHStA ÄZA K 8 (24 September 1670); HHStA ÄZA K 9 (1673–1676); HHStA OMeA Sr. 367 (1557–1699), in Bastl and Heiß, 'Hofdamen und Höflinge', pp. 240–241.

could be expected to arise in such contacts, and we should not read them as a description of everyday practice.

The groups witnessing the various public acts of the ruler varied according to the occasion, though surely in Vienna as in Paris many such acts made sense mostly when they were attended by wider audiences. An isolated passage describing the details of homage outlines the acts to be performed by those receiving an imperial fief:

Selbiger so baldt die Ihro May. In das Gesicht bekommen, machen sie eine kniebiegende reverenz, und fallen nach diesem auf beyde knie nieder, alßdann gehen sie etliche schritt biß ohngefehr halbe theil, machen abermahl, wie vorhin ein reverenz, und knien wiederumb nieder, endlich wann sie zu dem untersten staffel [dais] kommen, machen sie abermahl reverenz, und knien letzlich auff den Staffel nieder, so dann der vornehmbste Gesandte die anrede thut, welches hernach Ihr Excell. Reichsvicecanzler beantwortet, und nach diesem das Jurament vorleset, und nach abgelegten jurament, gibt Ihr May. der Kayser ihm den Knopff am Schwerdt zu Küssen, alß dann tretten die gesandten wieder Zurück, knien abermahl auff den staffel, da dann der anderte Gesandte (wann nicht einer allein ist) die dancksagung thut; nach diesem gehen sie abermahl mit reverenz machen und nieder knien wieder zurück, das gesicht aber jederzeit gegen Ihr May. kehrendt.[148]

More interesting than this description of the ceremony, showing a markedly more deferential variant of the habitual forms of audiences, is the *Nota Bene* added by the secretary. As soon as the *Lehenstrager* or his envoy had performed the reverences on bended knee and subsequent kneeling, reaching the dais, the usher (*Cammer-Thürhüter*) allowed in as many people as he could, urging them only not to cause 'großes Gestummel' during the speeches. The emperor himself had decreed this, and gave his reasons:

Daß man alles was hienein will, und hienein kommen kann, passiren lasset, ist die Authorithät Ihro May. des Kaisers, daß alle welt sieht, daß man vor Ihro Kay. May. kniender die lehen empfangen muß.[149]

For such occasions, the interconnectedness of ceremony and publicity is evident. Yet can we consistently and logically relate the level of openness or accessibility to the level of ceremoniousness? Was ceremony mostly limited to moments of public attention? This nut is hard to crack. We know that ordinances give rules for domestic arrangements even if these remained hidden to the eyes of many courtiers and all outsiders. Yet such rules, stressing order, loyalty, and discretion, were hardly comparable to the panoply of representation and rank evident in the

[148] See HHStA, ÄZA K 26 (fols. 2–14), 'Ordnung des Zutritts in die Kaiserl. Antecamera, Rats- u. Ritterstube 8/37-10-1715 (with OMeA SR K 74 no. 16, and Familienakten K. 102, repaginated 26 March 1997, fols. 1–124), fol. 11r–v. The 'Lehenstrager' proceeded from the Ritterstube to the first antechamber, the ceremony was in the second, or 'anderte Antecamera'. The emperor's chair was covered with gold; the *Oberstkämmerer* and the 'Cammer-fourier' led him into the second antechamber.

[149] *Ibid.*, fol. 12r. Compare the short description of a Belehnung in the *Wienerisches Diarium*, 10 April 1728.

great ceremonies of dynasty and state. The same instructions more particularly urge court officers to accompany the ruler *in actis publicis*: public dining, Divine Offices and processions, rides or marches outside the palace precincts. These were the moments the ruler showed himself, and needed his splendorous retinue to demonstrate his pre-eminence.[150]

In the preface of his 1719–1720 three-volume compendium of ceremony, Johann Christian Lünig argued that it was difficult to give straightforward rules for ceremony, as: 'die Zeit und Gelegenheit des Hofes bald ein mehreres, bald ein wenigeres erfordert, und sich kein Souverain dißfalls gerne Ziel und maß setzen lassen will'. The traditions of the various European courts left room for adaptations both to the nature of the occasion, and to the inclinations of the sovereign. Indeed, for most daily activities tradition offered an open framework: the details were truly filled in only for the exceptional and public great moments of dynasty and state. In assessing the relations between ceremony and daily life at court, and between the levels of 'ceremoniousness' of different courts, or the same court in different periods, it is necessary to ascertain the levels of accessibility of the rulers.

Meals, a focal point in any household, may serve as an example here. The order at the courts' tables, the starting point of many early ordinances with their seating arrangements and rules for the 'shifts' of eating, leaving the *Nachessen* or *desserte* of the first tables for the lower echelons of the *Hofstaat*, remained quite relevant for seventeenth- and eighteenth-century courts.[151] Notwithstanding the general tendency for remuneration to replace payment in provisions, many officers in Versailles still had *bouche à la cour*, the right to eat from the king's purse. This right mostly was extended to officers personally serving the king, and to almoners, the confessor, and preachers. The steward held responsibility for tables at court, and had to supervise the rank and number of those attending. Compensation in cash was offered only to those who could present convincing reasons for their absence from the court's tables; frequent unwarranted absences would deprive an officer of his right to eat at court. Two honorific tables held an intermediary position between the king's table and those of lesser officers: the steward and the chamberlain extended the king's hospitality by entertaining visitors at their own tables, catered for by the *petit commun* – established in 1664

150 Actis publicis: Menčík, 'Kaiserlichen Hofämter', and most instructions listed elsewhere for the HHStA, for example, OMaA I, K 1 (1564–1712), instruction for 1637 (Ferdinand) point 11 stipulating that the marshal should take care that all those serving would attend 'offene actus'; negligent members of the 'Hofgesinde' would be punished with 'rodierung' – they would lose their charge. See AVA Harrach Historica 797, 'Guettachten' pp. 6–7, point 13.

151 ÖNB cod. 14676 gives rules for tables and *Nachessen* for most officers; compare the short description in OMeA Sr 74, 14a, a description of the 'Taffeln bei Ferdinand' dated 25 August 1579 fols. 395–396, with a first 24–30 person *Mundtaffel*, and tables for the *Truchseßen*, *Silbercammerer*, *Fürschneider*, *Mundschenken*, *Kuchlmeister*, *Edelknaben*, and finally the servants of the preceding officers; a 12–16 persons table for the *Oberstkammerer* and his staff, with another for 'Kammerdiener, Quardaroba Barbierer, Cammerhaizer und dergleichen Diener', and an 'Officir Taffel' for the *Contralor* and *Kuchl-* and *Kellerschreiber* – served twice daily, for the *früh- und nachtmahl*.

and among the first victims of the 1780 reforms.[152] The steward was joined by the *maître d'hôtel ordinaire*, several *seigneurs de la cour*, and high-ranking guests; he had the right to invite 'qui bon luy semble'. The steward's table, mostly 12 *couverts* for dinner as well as for supper, was served more or less at the same time as the king's table, whether or not the steward was present himself. At the chamberlain's table, as many as 30 guests could be present, a group overlapping with those of the steward's table, and often including ambassadors. These two honorific tables were served neither in the king's absence, nor during sojourns in smaller hunting lodges.

There were five additional tables: the steward's 'second table' for the *maîtres* (42–44 *couverts*); the *aumôniers'* table (11–12 *couverts*), the *table du Serdeau* for the *gentilshommes servants* (16–18 *couverts*), and finally the table for the valets of chamber and wardrobe (20–26 *couverts*). Officers of the guards, controllers, and *gentilshommes ordinaires*; senior ushers, *clercs*, and chaplains ate at these tables. Ambassadors either dined at the chamberlain's table, or had their own prestigious table of 18–20 *couverts*. Incidentally, sources mention separate tables for the confessor and the preachers, and for the personnel of the *sept offices*. In all, between 100–120 officers were entitled to dine at these tables; a 1780 account lists 106 persons actually dining at court, another 28 receiving compensation in cash.[153] In the *chénil* or the *écurie*, moreover, the supreme officers would likewise entertain staff and guests, The queen, whose *bouche* and *commun* counted *c.* 180 persons, had tables for her own establishment, as did the other senior members of the *famille royale*. *Commensaux* without the right to eat at the king's tables received an allotment in food as in other necessities. Moreover, the leftovers of the king's *grand couvert* were distributed among specified numbers of lower officers, and comparable procedures were followed for other tables. This *desserte*, cold and not always palatable, was increasingly disagreeable to the king's own servants, and reportedly gave rise to a thriving market for prepared foods in the *grand commun*.[154]

At the Habsburg court, the emperor's, or *Obersthofmeister*'s, *Freytaffel* was supplemented by tables for chamberlains, *Truchseßen*, *Patres* (ecclesiastics), doctors

[152] Descriptions of the tables at court (and menus, costs) can be found in AN O 1 751, nos. 21–23, 70, and 78 (eighteenth century: most details have been taken from 21 and 70; menus in 22; costs in 23; 78 gives *livrées* for the *commensaux*, including the *ordinaires en nature*, allowances of food following a tripartite division: *fort*, *moyen*, *foible*, and following the rhythm of *jours maigres* and *jours gras*); BN Clair 1220, fols. 79r–80r (late seventeenth century) suggests 12 *couverts* for the chamberlain's table instead of the 30 noted in O 1 751, no. 21); BN MS f 14128 gives the king's tables in 1732, and a variety of menus; AN O1 793, nos. 44, 104, 105, 114, 120 (1774–1783: with numbers of those actually attending, menus, and costs); *couvert du roi* gives information about menus. Le Roux, *Faveur du roi*, p. 193, for Henry III's practices, including a 20-*couvert* table for the *grand maître*; AN KK 1431, fols. 217–226, gives the menu for Henry IV's 1600 marriage, including the tables of all *commensaux*; Luynes, *Mémoires*, V, pp. 143–144 (September 1745), indicates that the chamberlain's table had fallen into desuetude, the *chambellan* receiving financial compensation, his table held by the *premier maître d'hôtel*; the *grand maître's* table was frequently chaired by the *contrôleur de la maison*.

[153] AN O1 793, no. 105: the October quarter of 1780: 86 and 8 for the king *maison*, another 26 and 20 for the tables of his female relatives: the aggregate of table; the theoretical total of the *couverts* listed in no. 114 is 101.

[154] See AN O 1 751, no. 78, for the allotments; *Couvert du Roi*, p. 39, on the food market.

and secretaries, pages, *Kammerdiener*, and the generic *Officir. Verzeichnisse* mention these tables indirectly, by listing the *Taffeldecker*; lists of payments including allowances for the *Obersthofmeister* indicate his share in courtly hospitality. The *Truchseßen* lost their table when their position was taken over by the *Kämmerer*. For the empresses' and archduchesses' female establishments more tables must have existed: a breakdown of those eating at court in June 1754 cites tables for *Kammerfrauen*, *Kammerjungfern*, and female servants. Hospitality must have been offered to high-ranking visitors; for the select few at the table of imperial couple, for others at the *Obersthofmeister's Freytaffel*. Where were these tables located? How many courtiers and visitors habitually dined and supped at court? Such details cannot be gleaned from the *Verzeichnisse* or payrolls, nor do descriptions of festivities help to ascertain them. The 1754 overview of tables, *desserte*, and *Kostgelder* at court mentions a first table of 66 persons, including the imperial family and the highest officers; a second 14-person table for the *Patres*, four others numbering more than 60 persons, and a 15-person *Edelknabentafel*: together more than 155 persons. An even larger group was entitled to consume the leftovers, others received allowances.[155] Yet these isolated figures, following a period of crisis and interruption of court routines, and preceding a protracted phase of change, may well be exceptional.[156]

These meals reflect an intermediate level of publicity: they assembled a noteworthy group of courtiers and servants with high-ranking guests; yet they were not truly a public occasion. The rulers' mealtime, however, would provide recurring opportunities to a larger public to see the sovereign. If the bedchamber remained inaccessible for outsiders – practice at most courts – mealtimes and church attendance were the two most habitual foci for public curiosity. At Louis XIV's Versailles, the public *grand couvert* in the *antichambre* was at least a weekly, more often a daily habit.[157] Louis XIII, Louis XV, and Louis XVI seem to have dined in public roughly twice a week, though the *grand couvert* was more exceptional in the last years of Louis XV's reign.[158] The emperor dined publicly in the *Ritterstube* of the Hofburg on at least four occasions: St Andrew's feast (30 November, when he dined with the knights of the Golden Fleece),

[155] OMeA Sr 184 95 a) 'Verzeichnis der von der Hofküche zu verköstigenden Personen und der Kostgeldempfänger' (1754); OMeA 368 13 (Kammerfrauen Tafel) ÄZA Sr 45/2 20 and 21 (abolition of the Hofkontrollorstafel; Verpactierung der Kais. Edelknaben Tafel). Entries in various *Verzeichnisse* for the *Taffeldecker*: OMeA Sr 186, fols. 85r–91v, with slight variations in most other *Verzeichnisse* cited in III, for example ÖNB cod. ser. n. 1849 (fol. 6v: 'Freylen und Cammerherren; Patres; Secretarius und Musici; Cammerdiener; Edelknaben; Officier'); AVA Harrach Handschrift 145; Harrach Historica 796 Lista (shortly after 1685).

[156] Compare the 1816 printed overview of the diets and allowances for courtiers, in 12 classes indicative of court hierarchies: HHStA OMeA Sr 184, no. 110.

[157] AN KK 1431, fol. 176, also mentions the traditional Christmas *déjeuner* 'dans la grande salle, avec tous les commensaux'.

[158] See Luynes, *Mémoires*, XIII, p. 301 (July 1754) suggesting a routine of at least two *grands couverts* a week for Louis XV when in Versailles; Hardman, *Louis XVI*, p. 176, notes Sundays and Thursdays as the usual occasion for Louis XVI's *grand couvert*.

Christmas, Easter, and Pentecost.[159] When we add the dynastic birthdays, galas, and various incidental occasions, it is clear that such accessible and stately forms of dining were quite frequent.[160] Maria Theresa may have been less given to public dining: in the 1754 overview a gloss in the margin adds that the empress supped alone in her *retirade*. While Khevenhüller's notes show that she readily left a share of the more public burdens of royalty to her husband, they contain frequent references to public dining. In a November 1747 *Winterordnung*, the empress neatly summarised her public duties, announcing:

> ... daß sie disen Winter über alle Sonntäge auf dero Seiten offentlich speisen, vor der Kirchen die gewöhnliche offentliche Audienzien ertheilen, Dienst- und Freitäge Appartement halten, extraordinarie aber alle Sonntäg-, Mittwoch- und Samstäg bei der Obristhofmeisterin sichtbahr sein würden.

The *appartements* were usually followed by a meal with the noble guests; Khevenhüller mentions two tables of *c.* 40 *couverts* each for one such occasion.[161]

Public meals, and particularly the large-scale festive banquets arranged to celebrate special occasions or honour high-ranking guests, were among the most conspicuously public acts of the court. As in the church, ritual cleaning with water basin and napkin underlined the ruler's pre-eminence, and demonstrated the hierarchy of those serving him – or her. A range of roughly comparable rituals developed in the great households of Europe. In seventeenth-century France the *serviettes*, pepper and salt, and carving knives were transported in a 'nef', or boat-shaped container.[162] Serving as the symbol of royal power, the *nef* had to be reverently greeted when the officers of the *bouche du roi* paraded from the

159 Carafa in Hurter, *Friedensbestrebungen*, pp. 218–219, states that Ferdinand II instituted the custom of eating in public on festive occasions in the early 1620s but this must have been a restoration more than an invention. In these pages, Carafa also refers to the habitually more secluded dinner at the emperor's side, the more accessible supper at the empress' side.

160 Passer, 'Berichte', suggests that the emperor dined in public much more often. The fact that the court was travelling, fleeing from the plague in Vienna, and more particularly the coronation festivities of the new empress, who was crowned queen of Hungary, may have been the reason for this. For a detailed treatment of the festival with knights of the Golden Fleece on 30 November 1749, see Raschauer, 'Die kaiserlichen Wohn- und Zeremonialräume'.

161 Quote from Khevenhüller, *Tagebuch*, II, p. 191; for the tables see pp. 225 (May 1748) and 324–325 (May 1749, two tables of 60 and 40 respectively) in the same volume. Compare Ingrid Haslinger, *Küche und Tafelkultur am Kaiserlichen Hofe zu Wien. Zur Geschichte von Hofküche, Hofzuckerbäckerei und Hofsilber- und Tafelkammer* (Bern and Vevey 1993).

162 *Couvert du roi* reports the transport of the cutlery in a flat oblong box, or 'cadenas', as does Rousset, *cérémonial diplomatique*, yet we do not find this in the 1665, 1681, and 1726 ordinances in AN O 1 755, Maison du Roy, 1686, pp. 71–93: 'Prérogatives de la Charge de Grand Maistre', pp. 229–240: 'Reglement pour la maison du Roi du 14 avril 1665', 30 articles; pp. 241–255: 'Reglement pour la maison du Roi du 7 janvier 1681', 41 articles (a section of this *règlement* is printed in the 1722 *état*, pp. 160–176); pp. 311–323, and the more concrete and detailed 'Projet d'ordonnance nouvelle fait en 1681'. See the November 1726 Ordonnance du Roy (56 articles) complementing the 1665 and 1681 ordinances mostly by more extensive rules regarding financial management, in AN O 1 747, no. 6 (unpaginated); articles 29–33 give the procedures for *essai et marche* (with *viande* and *nef*), service and *serviette*. Rousset, *Cérémonial Diplomatique*, gives an extract of these rules, I, pp. 431–434. Compare Saint-Simon, *Mémoires*, XXVIII, pp. 344–349; Dangeau, *Journal*, I, pp. 271–272; Félix d' Hézecques, *Souvenirs d'un page à la cour de Louis XVI* (Paris 1998), p. 197; *Couvert du Roi*, p. 25.

grand commun to the king's antechamber, where his stately meals usually took place. The *nef* was placed on the *table du prêt*, where the acting *gentilhomme servant* offered each item to the *chef du gobelet* for the *essai* or assay, a light touch with a piece of bread subsequently to be tasted by the *chef*, testing food and cutlery alike for poison. At both courts, the hierarchy of servants was adapted to the occasion. The *Obersthofmeister* and the *grand maître* surely were not always present, nor were senior princes and nobles. The substitutes of the two supreme courtiers, the *premier maître d'hôtel* and the *Oberststabelmeister*, were expected to be present, preceding the food with their ceremonial batons; and so were some minor honorary servants. A description of a *souper* on the occasion of the future Louis XIII's baptism well conveys the dignity and splendour:

> Monsieur le Comte de Soissons faisoit sa charge de Grand Maistre, & accompagnoit la viande, marchoient devant luy les Trompettes, qui arrivans devant la table du Roy mettoient le genouïl en terre. Puis marchoient vingt maistres d'hostel du Roy, de la Reyne, de Monsieur de Lorraine, & autres Princes souverains, s'il y en avoit, tous le baston bas, sans rang, trois à trois, puis les deux premiers du Roy & de la Reyne, aussi le baston bas.
>
> Puis Monsieur le Grand Maistre, le baston levé, qui arrivoit iusques auprés du roy pour présenter la viande & alloit et retournoit accompagné de mesme à tous les services; & la viande estoit portées par Princes et Seigneurs.[163]

This particular *souper* was disturbed by a familiar quarrel: the high steward and his elder brother, the prince de Conti, both demanded the right to present the *serviette*. Should it be granted to the steward or to the highest-ranking prince present? Henry III was cited to support the first position; later practice seems to indicate the second.[164] On this occasion, the major princes served as *panetier*, *échanson*, and *écuyer tranchant*; the less elevated regular holders of these honours might serve in person in slightly less dignified settings; but they themselves were more often replaced by the *gentilshommes servants* acting as their substitutes. The number of servants did not invariably render the meal more dignified. Louis XIII, seeking to establish both the numbers and the alternation of such servants for the king's table, deplored the 'confusion que la diversité des temps et changement des Reignes y a aporté'; the frequent rulings, moreover, 'n'auroient en effet n'y pû aporter l'ordre quelle s'en etoit promis'. Even when the officers had punctually obeyed the rules, the argument continues, their very

[163] *Cérémonial François*, II, pp. 176–177, and the charming description of the 14 September 1606 baptism itself in Héroard, *Journal*, I, pp. 211–212; see also pp. 53–56: the meal on the occasion of the marriage of Henry IV and Marie de Medici. AN KK 1431, fols. 227–229, gives the 'ordre de l'assiette' for this festin, listing those present, the various tables, and the servants.

[164] See Héroard, *Journal*, II, pp. 239–240, for a similar quarrel between *grand maître*, the comte de Soissons, and the prince de Condé; solved when Louis XIII asked his brother Gaston to come and present the serviette as *premier prince*. Compare the practice in the chapel, where the *grand aumônier* habitually performed the rites to the king, and in his absence the *premier aumônier* took precedence over other prelates, even when these were senior in ranks or status: see Lünig, *Theatrum Ceremoniale*, II, pp. 1016–1017, for the 1718 ruling.

multitude inevitably brought confusion. Therefore, the king decreed that the *chefs des charges* should not admit new staff, and reiterated the norm that Louis XIV would re-establish more solidly thereafter: three *maîtres d'hôtel* and nine *gentilshommes servants* should serve per quarter.[165]

In Versailles, the public *grand couvert* was served in the king's *antichambre*, or alternatively in the antechamber of the queen or *dauphine*, following the dignified rules elaborated in the 1665, 1681, and 1726 *règlements*. The king often dined alone, and the spectators had to witness his meal uncovered, and standing. Only the king's relatives could join him, more often princesses than princes; only duchesses were allowed to sit on *tabourets* in front of the king's table. When the queen joined the king, she was served by *semblables officiers* – though she had her own *bouche et commun*.[166] Was the king as staunchly devoted to solitary public dining as the habitual reading of Saint-Simon states?[167] Both the *états* and Dangeau's notes suggest that the meal *en famille* was by no means exceptional. Besongne noted in his 1687 *état*:

> le roy dîne ordinairement chés madame la Dauphine: Monseigneur le Dauphin, Madame la Dauphine, Monsieur frère du roy, & Madame, sont d'ordinaire à table avec S. M. J'ay dit Monseigneur le Dauphin, à moins qu'il ne soit à la chasse, comme il arrive assês souvent.

Besongne added that the children of those listed were equally welcome, and that the same rules prevailed for supper.[168] Dangeau gives basically the same

165 Quotes from AN KK 1431, fols. 43–45: copy of the 'Reglement fait par le Roy touchant l'ordre qu'il entend estre gardé par ses maîtres d'hôtel et les gentilshommes servans tant pour cette année que les suivantes', dated 1686 but signed 'Louis et plus bas Loménie', probably from the late thirties.

166 See the general introduction preceding the description of 'festins' in AN KK 1431, fols. 176–179, at fol. 177r, where it is stated that king and queen were served by *semblables officiers*. The author incorrectly explained this divergence from European rules by the fact that only the French queen dined in public. The queen's *bouche* and *commun* were sizeable, see, for example, the 1676 *état* in AN O 1 3715, listing 180 persons, a number remaining stable until the 1780s. Compare various remarks in Luynes, *Mémoires*, I, pp. 360–361, and V, p. 215, outlining responsibilities of the king's and the queen's services on various occasions; on I, p. 400 (November 1737), Luynes reports that the queen's *bouche* served the *grand couvert* of the royal couple, as the king's servants had not yet arrived. These statements clearly indicate that the queen had an independant staff, though they do not indicate whether those serving at her table were male or female.

167 This tends to be the standard description in literature on the court: see *Couvert du Roi*, *Barocke Tafelfreuden*, *Tafeln bei Hofe*, compare the more balanced sources for such suppositions, Saint-Simon, in the Sun King's great portrait, *Mémoires*, XXVIII, pp. 331–335, with the closing statement echoing in the literature: 'Ailleurs qu'à l'armée le roi n'a jamais mangé avec aucun homme, en quelque cas ç'ait été . . .'. Compare Sourches, *Mémoires*, I, p. 274 – on the occasion of the *grand aumônier's* ill-fated attempt to share the king's table.

168 Besongne, *Etat* 1687, I, p. 225, for dinner, p. 233 for supper, and on p. 229: 'Les jours que le roy a couru le cerf avec les dames, il dîne avec elles au retour retour de la chasse dans son cabinet, où il n'entre d'officiers que le grand chambellan, les premiers gentilshommes de la chambre, le premier valet de chambre, le premier maître d'hôtel, & quelques officiers absolument nécessaires pour le service'. Dangeau gives the company of the *dauphine* as the convention for the *dîner* on I, p. 87 (quote), and for the *souper* on I, p. 88; he often includes 'les dames', sometimes more specifically listing the princesses, see, for example, II, p. 18 (6 February 1687) in Marly; II, p. 138 (8 May 1688) in the Trianon without courtiers; II, p. 202 (3 November 1688) on St Hubert in Fontainebleau; and II, p. 20 (11 February 1687). Note that most of these latter instances refer to the hunting lodges or special outings. Compare the parallel remarks about the queen in AN KK 1431, fol. 177, which also notes that great princes, sovereigns, and ambassadors could dine at the king's table, particularly to celebrate treaties and alliances.

account in his generalised overview of 1684, describing the *dîner* in the *dauphine*'s antechamber:

Les gentilshommes servants le servoient. Monseigneur, madame la Dauphine, Monsieur et Madame, mademoiselle et madame de Guise mangeoient avec le roi et quelquesfois les princesses du sang.

The solitary meal was not necessarily more dignified than the *grand couvert* with family members. Yet its over-representation fits the general tendency to distil from all courtly scenes at Versailles an image of unalterable towering dominance.[169]

In Vienna, the *Truchseß*, *Fürschneider*, and *Schenk*, charges held by several persons, performed the duties parallel to those of the *panetier*, *écuyer tranchant*, and *échanson*. Table arrangements for festive occasions neatly reflecting the hierarchy can be found in great quantity, and show that carving and other tasks could be carried out by any senior nobleman. Chamberlains habitually served as cupbearer or carver when the emperor dined in his apartment; *Hofdamen* served the empress during supper in her apartment. *Truchseß*, carver, cupbearer, and pages assisted in the service of public meals, and meals taken outside of the Hofburg.[170] The full range of officers was present only on stately occasions when the sovereign's meal was witnessed by numerous spectators. Such meals were ideally attended by courtiers, the *corps diplomatique*, and many visitors. The emperor and empress and their guests were served on bended knee, by an array of court officers led by the *Oberststabelmeister* followed by the *Oberstsilberkämmerer*, *Truchseßen*, the *Kämmerer*, *Hofdamen*, *Fürschneider*, *Mundschenke*, and *Edelknaben*.[171] Vehse, a nineteenth-century erudite, calculated that any dish went through 24 pairs of hands before it actually reached the emperor.[172] The ambassadors, and all others in attendance, had to remain uncovered and standing, and could only withdraw 'sobald Ihre K.Mt. den ersten Trunk gethan'.[173] The emperor's table was marked by the pan-European insignia of sovereignty:

169 See Greppi, *Notes de voyage du comte Giandemaria envoyé du duc de Parme la cour de Louis XIV (1680)* (Paris, s.d.) p. 8, for a similar description of the royal family dining in public, at Fontainebleau, noting that: 'La conversation est générale selon la coutume adaptée à la cour de France, où tous les gentilshommes, français comme étrangers, peuvent librement assister au banquet royal'.

170 On the *Kämmerer* acting as table servants, see Carafa in Hurter, *Friedensbestrebungen*, on pp. 218, 238, stating that they served the emperor when he dined in private; service during meals is also stipulated in ÖNB cod. ser. n. 1849, fol. 9r; a May 1751 'règlement' for table service in HHStA OMeA Sr 74, 14b, mentions the *Edelknaben* serving the table of the imperial family. See in HHStA ÄZÄ 70, an 18 September 1765 pro memoria outlining responsibilities of *Truchseßen* and *Edelknaben* in the service. The roles of chamberlains and table servants in Vienna more or less match those of the chamber staff versus the *gentilshommes* and *maîtres* in France, for the *petit* and *grand couvert* respectively. Pages, at both courts, served guests, escorted the ruler, and provided lighting.

171 *Küche und Tafelkultur*, pp. 8–19; Pöllnitz, *Memoires*, I, pp. 290–292; Beatrix Bastl and Gernot Heiss, 'Tafeln bei Hof: Die Hochzeitsbankette Kaiser Leopolds I.', *WRGB* 50 (1995), pp. 181–206.

172 Vehse, *Geschichte der deutschen Höfe*, VI, pp. 289–290; *Theater, Feste und Feiern*, p. 226, Khevenhüller notes that for the public dining of 30 January 1765, no ambassadors attended, as the prince and princesses dined with their parents, suggesting that only when the imperial couple dined alone, would ambassadors attend.

173 Passer, 'Berichte', p. 337.

it stood on a dais, or *staffel*, and his chair was crowned by a canopy of state. He would remain covered throughout the meal, taking off his hat only during prayers, or when the empress drank to his health. On Sundays, and during galas, public dining was animated by the court's musicians.

Within the limits of available space, the 'dem Orte und der Feyerlichkeit angemessen Gekleideten' were admitted to the ceremony of public dining.[174] Visitors reporting details of public dining, suggest that they had no problem in being admitted. Brown noted 'three remarkably low dwarfs' during the public dinner on Christmas.[175] Pöllnitz counted 48 dishes, observing that the emperor and empress dined together, but each was served by his or her own *Hofstaat*, and from his or her own kitchen. When the emperor dined in the empress' or dowager-empress' apartment, *Hofdamen* indeed took the role of the chamberlains and pages; yet as only the dowager-empress had her own full establishment, the emperor's apparatus for the preparation and transport of food would necessarily cater for the empress. Dining at either the empress' or the emperor's side reflected a different level of ceremony, and hospitality was quite limited at the emperor's side. Maria Theresa transferred her public meal on a Gala day in November 1746 from her apartment to the emperor's larger antechamber because she feared the throng of spectators in her more confined quarters. The emperor's antechamber, however, was carefully transformed to fit the forms of dining at the empress' side: *Hofdamen* served instead of male servants, and the dais for the table under the canopy was removed. These pains were taken to prevent confusion, as at the emperor's side the ambassadors would be expected to attend standing, and no guests could join the meal.[176] Yet the empress would soon go beyond the limits of traditional exposure to publicity. In January 1765 she decided to allow more people into the *Redoutensaal* to watch the public meal, but it proved difficult to control access: the stream of spectators finally led to such confusion that the sovereigns had to save themselves by withdrawing.[177]

At both courts meals ranged from highly stylised public forms to more private forms without much ceremony. There is a continuum between great state banquets, regular public dining in *Ritterstube* or antechamber, more private dining in *Ratstube* or chamber, a brisk meal in the *Retirade* or cabinet, or on the road, 'en campagna'. We should not overrate the level of ceremony for occasions when the ruler chose to eat in his chamber, or while he was working in his cabinet, 'sur sa serviette'. Dinner habitually was *à petit couvert*, in private and with less pomp, but the stately public supper would take place on an almost daily basis, when illness, mourning, or *jours maigres* did not prevent it.[178] The *petit couvert* was

174 *Küche und Tafelkultur*, p. 14. 175 Brown, *A Brief Account*, p. 152; Passer, 'Berichte', pp. 321, 323, 337.

176 Khevenhüller, *Tagebuch*, II, p. 127 (November 1746), adding that the improvisations caused 'grausam ville Ausstellungen und Glossen'.

177 *Theater, Feste und Feiern*, p. 227.

178 See the frequent references in Dangeau's *Journal* to the dinner *à petit couvert*, except for *bonnes fêtes* in *Journal*, VII, p. 217 (25 December 1699) though the addition *plus guère* suggests that public dinner had been more

prepared in the *petit commun* more conveniently located than the distant *grand commun*, catering for the *grand couvert* and the meals of *commensaux*.[179] The *petit couvert* was served in seclusion by the personnel of *bouche du roi* and the *chambre*. When the king travelled, or visited the army camps, courtiers and military officers were invited to join him.[180] The emperor, on his more frequent travels, brought his ceremonial apparatus and insignia, but willingly adapted to more modest arrangements when limited public visibility allowed this. Khevenhüller, typically, used a French vocabulary to indicate such less ceremonial meals: *à tout petit couvert*.[181]

In the devotions, the hunt, court theatre, balls, parties, and most other courtly pursuits, we find the same continuum from simple to highly ritualised, from secluded to public. Solitary prayer in the relative seclusion of the apartment breathed an atmosphere wholly different than did the ceremony of the royal touch administered to many hundreds, or the processions witnessed by multitudes.[182] Sourches notes 'petites fêtes particulières' in the Sun King's apartment in Versailles' most conspicuously 'public' first decade.[183] The *appartements* came in two sorts: *petits appartements*, for courtiers of recognised dignity, and *grands appartements*, where the serving usher could admit all persons he recognised.[184] For a 1747 *appartement*, Khevenhüller suggests that the temporary presence of outsiders changed the behaviour of intimates: as long as the 'fremmde aus der Statt zugegen waren' the courtiers could not play games.[185] Similarly, small hunting parties with intimates show a striking distance from the meticulously organised and publicly celebrated *Prunkjagden* of the eighteenth-century German court, where hunting blended into an outdoor theatre of sovereignty.[186] The French court did not indulge in similar exploits, but the highly stylised *petits soupers* organised as a corollary to Louis XV's frequent hunts can be seen as an intentional use of 'privacy' more than as an impulse arising from camaraderie. Ballets or comedies could be performed and witnessed by an exclusive group of courtiers, but alternatively they could be put on stage by professional companies,

common earlier; for the evening *grand couvert*, see *Journal*, XII, p. 350; XIV, p. 249; XV, p. 140, cited by Boislisle in Saint-Simon, *Mémoires*, XXVIII, p. 359, n. 2. Compare Saint-Simon's remarks in the overview of Louis XIV's days, *Mémoires*, XXVIII, pp. 344–345; AN KK 1431, fol. 175v, stresses that the grandeur of the king, and the majesty of his state, forbade him to indulge in private dining too frequently. Primi Visconti, *Mémoires*, pp. 27–29, reports a public dinner of the royal family.

179 *Couvert du Roi*, p. 24.

180 See the retrospective remarks on dining in the *Journal inédit du duc de Croÿ*, III, pp. 133–134.

181 Khevenhüller, *Tagebuch*, IV, for example, p. 23 (30 May 1756).

182 The number of malades shows great diversity: from 1,000–1,500 to a mere handful. see the instances in Héroard, Dangeau, Sourches, and Luynes, cited above, nn. 19, 26, and 32.

183 Sourches, *Mémoires*, I, p. 351 (18 January 1686).

184 AN O 1 822, p. 8: 'Le roi ne reçoit aux petits appartemens que les gens de la cour qui aient des noms; mais quand ce sont les grands, l'huissier laisse entrer les personnes qu'il connoit'.

185 Khevenhüller, *Tagebuch*, II, p. 154 (May 1747) (they were mostly present, he adds, between 11.00 and 13.00 or 17.00 and 19.00).

186 Contrast Passer, 'Berichte', pp. 284, 300, and Mitis, *Jagd und Schützen*, with the descriptions in *Die Lust am Jagen. Jagdsitten und Jagdfeste am Kurpfälzischen Hof im 18. Jahrhundert* (Ubstadt-Weiher 1999).

and viewed by a much broader audience. As late as 1752, Khevenhüller deplored the confusion of a *Gala-Tag*, or celebration of a dynastic birthday inviting a somewhat broader audience into the court, with an opera to be performed by nobles (*Kavaliersspiel*) ideally organised as a highly exclusive *Kammerfest*. The nobles, he argued, should have had the good sense to decline this honour for this particular occasion, thus preventing the undesirable admixture of two different domains. Towards the 1770s the circles attending court festivities were widening, and we find a remarkable 5,000 invited guests for the 1770 Belvedere-feast. Nor did Khevenhüller complain in 1773, when a *Kavalierstheater* was given in the public context of the *Stadttheater*.[187]

In conclusion, we may assume that in the later seventeenth century and early eighteenth century the courtyards, halls, and antechambers of the Hofburg were less crowded than their Versailles' counterparts. Nor could the Hofburg harbour more than a small nucleus of members of the dynasty and their most indispensable servants, whereas a privileged layer of those attending the social gatherings at the French court could be accommodated under Versailles' multiple roofs. Until the second half of the eighteenth century the Viennese Habsburg court was connected to specific, more public moments – frequently occurring but hardly permanent. In the city residence, the emperor could long choose to remain more aloof than the Sun King in his not so distant country palace. The notions of 'court life' and 'courtier', therefore, had a different connotation in Vienna than they had in Versailles. The day-to-day routines were partly determined by these diverging tendencies, as the continuing movement between intimacy and display was differently organised at these two courts. The court of the Habsburgs, usually less flamboyant and public than its French counterpart, has frequently been likened to the Spanish court. Yet neither austere dress and the marked religious stance nor the superficial parallels in court organisation offer sufficient basis for this comparison, too readily explained by the inevitable Spanish relatives, travels, and influences. The tendency of courts to aspire to well-organised, aloof, and dignified forms surely goes further than any specific courtly idiom.

In the eighteenth century the ideals of *commodité*, privacy, and family life were becoming stronger in both realms. These tendencies had divergent consequences, and the spirit of reform in the Habsburg domains further changed the

[187] See Khevenhüller, *Tagebuch*, VII, pp. 6–9, and nn. 17–18, pp. 203–219 (Belvedère, 17 April 1770) and 1774–1776, pp. 94, 99–101 and n. 96, pp. 249–251 (Schönbrunn, 11 September 1775); compare the detailed arrangements and groundplans in ÖNB cod. 12956, fol. 36 (17 April 1770); 60 (10 July 1770); 364–380 (11 September 1775). *Theater, Feste und Feiern*, pp. xi, 112–114, 276–277, 307. Compare p. 226, where Khevenhüller describes with some disdain the muddle of the January 1765 *Freibal* in the *Redoutensaal*, admitting 'nicht allein denen sonstigen hierzu qualificirten Personen, sondern überhaupt auch denen vom Handelsstand und Artisten'. On the same page, Khevenhüller notes that the court went to theatre 'in mezzo publico', indicating the middle way in the continuum between private and public. Compare Hadamowsky, *Barocktheater*, pp. 20, 26.

situation. In France, Louis XV, developing a range of more private activities, did not maintain the painstaking loyalty to the public presentation so characteristic for his great-grandfather. Louis XVI, living in a Versailles where many apartments were occupied by members of his extended family, and presiding over a court that was under serious budgetary pressures, followed a middle course. In Vienna, a French-inspired salon-like court life, including an ongoing cycle of concerts, theatre, and *appartements* developed, as elsewhere in the empire.[188] The Viennese court was opening its doors to a public not previously admitted. A measure of convergence between these two courts is evident. The alliance of Marie-Antoinette and Louis XVI gave this process an appropriately paradoxical finale. Marie-Antoinette abolished the French rule that no male guests could attend when female members of the royal family were present: she introduced family-style *soupers* of royals of both sexes with guests. Yet on the other hand she liked to withdraw from her quintessentially public role as queen of France, seeking shelter in private quarters. Her 'attack' on French custom was frowned upon, and her alleged withdrawal would later play a considerable part in the rhetoric of her detractors.[189]

At all times the delicate and changing balance between display and intimacy helped to structure dynastic household routines, alternately inflating its members to superhuman proportions, or sheltering them behind a curtain of hierarchical thresholds. Ceremony helped to achieve both ends.

[188] Khevenhüller, *Tagebuch*, IV, p. 10 (3 March 1756), with repeated references on pp. 11, 18, 21, 23, 36, 45, 46; compare *Theater, Feste und Feiern*, p. 239, entry for 16 July 1765, where the sequence of *appartements* and the 'amusement du jour' is again mentioned. Klingensmith, *Utility of Splendour*, describes a parallel development for Bavaria.

[189] *Journal de l'abbé de Véri*, I, pp. 152–154, and p. 478, n. 71. Véri argues that the rules for dinner parties were changed partly to keep an eye on the king, and prevent him from indulging in hidden pursuits with a band of intimates; compare *Journal inédit du duc de Croÿ*, III, pp. 133–134.

CHAPTER 6

Ceremony and order at court: an unending pursuit

CEREMONIES AND RANKS

What is ceremony, and how did it form court life? This question resounds in the preceding pages, now we should address it more systematically. Recurring occasions for public presentation of power, whether worldly or spiritual, tended to proceed according to detailed conventions. In such conventions, three elements are usually present: the glorification of the ruler, the minute hierarchical demarcation of those attending him, and the restatement of his ties with the commonwealth. *Repraesentatio maiestatis*, the most obvious element in ceremony, was contingent upon the other two, visualising and defining the ruler's relationship with the great officers, princes, and the representatives of regions or corporations. Ceremony, however, was not limited to the courts, nor did it necessarily represent dynastic power. In societies slowly emerging as haphazard constructions of regions, towns, corporations, dynasties, and churches, each component cherished its own forms of collective presentation, often in continuous dialogue with one or more of the other components. Indeed, ceremony states and restates in festive and decorous forms the bond between such potentially agonistic components. In a festive yet dignified way, ceremonies act out social cohesion, and define the mutual relationships by visualising them in a welter of details. Guilds, armies, courts of law, and, most obviously, the church, could be as ceremonious as the royal court.

There is great continuity in the typically ceremonialised instances of dynastic Europe, and it may be helpful to establish several recurring forms of ceremonies. The public acts in the dynastic household, frequently referred to in the preceding outline of activities at court, can be labelled 'domestic ceremony'. These domestic ceremonies amplify routines familiar for any household, at least for the moments such routines were visible to outsiders. Ordinances include rules for the ceremonies of chamber, table, stable, and chapel. Yet ordinances and instructions do not usually include descriptions for behaviour during coronations, or for the ranks and their position during great assemblies.[1] These great ceremonies of dynasty and commonwealth were even more quintessentially public, and not necessarily located at court. They present a continuum starting from 'demographic' dynastic ceremonies such as baptisms, marriages, and funerals, via *sacre* or coronation symbolically re-establishing the new ruler's bond with the realm, to other ceremonies redefining the ties between ruling house and various corporations representing the commonwealth: elections, diets, or estates; urban entries, *Erbhuldigungen* and *Belehnungen*, *lits de justice*, and their many variants. Dynasty and representatives of the realm or its constituent parts were present in all such ceremonies; the urban entry paraded not only the grandeur of the visiting sovereign, but also the long history and great pursuits of the city; coronation and *sacre* not only introduced the new prince, but also reiterated his obligations. Ceremonies connected to the major representative assemblies, to sovereign courts of law, or to the variety of lesser corporations in the realm, show the same two-sidedness. The imperial ceremonies, from diets and elections to *Belehnungen*, conform to this model. A rich legacy of pamphlets and erudite treatises describes such events. I will use dynastic or dynastic state ceremony as shorthand for this whole range.[2]

While both domestic and dynastic ceremonies unsurprisingly included a strong religious component, the ceremonies typically connected to the liturgical year discussed earlier deserve their own category. Equally universal though less ubiquitous were the ceremonies of the orders of chivalry closely connected to the ruling dynasty, with the *Saint-Esprit* and the Golden Fleece as the most prestigious examples in a slowly expanding and broadening range. *Entrevues* and audiences between sovereigns or their representatives gave the conventional forms of meeting, greeting, and escorting special acuteness, and entailed an

[1] See various instructions in AVA Harrach Historica – Österreich – Kaiserliches Haus, 796–797, partly published by Menčík, 'Kaiserlichen Hofämter'; ÖNB cod 14676; short instructions in the Verzeichnisse, i.e. ÖNB cod 14443, pp. 81–88, on the *Kämmerer*; ÖNB cod. 8025 with several short instructions following the lists of staffs; HHStA OMeA Sr 74 Instruktionen Varia contains many instructions for intermediate officers and servants, such as the *Kuchlmeister* (no. 8), *Kuchenschreiber* (9), *Lichtkämmerer* (10), *Kammerdiener* (11) – the latter dating from 2 March 1651, and forming part of the general reform of that year; OMeA Sr K 73 a *Kammerherreninstruktion*. Compare French *règlements* in: AN KK 544; BN MS naf 2004 (previously AN KK 545); BN MS f 4581–4582, BN MS naf 7857, BN Dupuy 218 and 489; BN Brienne 256 (or MS naf 7225), see fol. 38v for the 'restoration and execution' of the older instructions. We find roughly the same documents in BM 2658. AN KK 547–548 and O 1 756 are compilations from the early 1730s, assembling materials from the seventeenth and eighteenth centuries limited to the services within the high steward's purview.

[2] For the historiography of such ceremonies see Alain Boureau's lucid 'Ritualité politique et modernité monarchique. Les usages de l'héritage médiéval', in *L'Etat ou le roi. Les fondations de la modernité monarchique en France (xive–xviie siècles)*, ed. N. Bulst, R. Descimon, and A. Guerreau (Paris 1996), pp. 9–25, and, for example, Ralph E. Giesey, *The Royal Funeral Ceremony in Renaissance France* (Geneva 1960), and 'The King Imagined', in *The French Revolution and the Creation of Modern Political Culture*. I: *The Political Culture of the Old Regime*, ed. K. M. Baker (Oxford and New York 1987), pp. 41–59; Lawrence M. Bryant, *The King and the City in the Parisian Royal Entry Ceremony: Politics, Ritual, and Art in the Renaissance* (Geneva 1986); Sarah Hanley, *The* Lit de Justice *of the Kings of France: Constitutional Ideology in Legend, Ritual and Discourse* (Princeton 1983); Richard A. Jackson, *Vive le Roi! A History of the French Coronation from Charles V to Charles X* (Chapel Hill and London 1984). More recently Fanny Cosandey, *La reine de France. Symbole et pouvoir xve–xviiie siècle* (Paris 2000) filled a gap by discussing the queen's particular position.

ongoing discourse in words and practices, seeking to resolve the problem of hierarchy and rank on a European scale. The consolidation of diplomacy in more permanent embassies during the sixteenth and seventeenth centuries made 'diplomatic ceremony' ever more relevant. Thus, for contemporaries and historians alike, the congress of Westphalia was generally thought to mark a new stage in the development not only of diplomacy, but also of the ceremonial routines at court, as the court offered the setting for most diplomatic encounters.[3] Finally, written formulae for addressing fellow sovereigns and their servants were prescribed in the *Kanzleizeremoniell*.

Ceremony in all these forms served to represent the dignity and supreme rank of the sovereign ruler. His pre-eminence, at court and elsewhere, was ideally visualised by the deferential presence of other members of the dynasty, and scions of the greatest noble houses of the realm. In the early seventeenth century, the erudite author of a compilation of French ceremonies, Theodore Godefroy, listed 64 points illuminating the nature of ceremony starting with an enumeration of what we may somewhat irreverently call 'special effects': colours, apparel, sounds ('sons lugubres'), and symbolic artefacts (sceptre, orb, ring, crown, etc.).[4] Such items figured prominently in *sacres* or coronations.[5] More generally, the colours, magnificence, and quality of clothing, ornaments, and jewellery had to be proportionate to rank, an ideal frequently echoed in sumptuary laws. Trumpets and drums, available through the services connected to the *grande écurie* in France and the *Stallmeister*'s staff in Vienna, were the inescapable accompaniment of any greater ceremony. Processions habitually passed through rows of elite guards with their halberds or similarly ornate weapons, both demonstrating the ruler's power and protecting him against the mob. Worldly ceremony as well as Catholic ritual had a strong impact on the senses, and conveyed the essence of power to an audience less willing or able to be persuaded by learned discourses on sovereignty and *droit divin*.[6] In the margin of these festive and solemn spectacles, the crowds of spectators could hope for entertainment, food, drink, and largesse. Passer, describing the festivities to celebrate the coronation of Leopold's third wife Eleonora of Pfalz Neuburg as queen of Hungary, expressed surprise that 'kein geld ist ausgeworffen, kein Wein gesprungen oder geronnen, keine Ochsen gebraten'; Godefroy noted for the 1606 baptism of the *dauphin* that 'Il fut ietté Largesse de dessus le pulpitre dehors & dedans, de force pieces d'or &

3 Wicquefort, *L'Ambasadeur et ses Fonctions* (Cologne 1690), p. 223; Lünig, *Theatrum Ceremoniale*, I, p. 2. Cf. Vec, *Zeremonialwissenschaft*.

4 BI coll. God. 481: fols. 72–73: 64 points, see the summary in 19 points Denys Godefroy gives of the digressions of the *introducteurs des ambassadeurs* (Berlize and Brûlon) in *Cérémonial François*, II, p. 771.

5 See Croÿ's remarkable description of Louis XVI's *sacre*, including the 'intronisation' in *Journal inédit du duc de Croÿ*, III, p. 186, with the impressed audience as well as the queen crying – the rites evidently had not wholly lost their power.

6 See Dreyss, *Mémoires de Louis XIV*, II, p. 15, for a classic formula on this topic cited below, almost literally echoed in the works cited by Vec, *Zeremonialwissenschaft*.

d'argent', and lists many similar occasions.[7] We may expect that such sideshows added public merriment to solemn display of power, and helped to attract wider audiences.

The upper echelon of the hierarchical pyramid conspicuously demonstrated the divinely ordained order of the realm to all observers. From the French *pairs* and the imperial electors downwards in the hierarchy, all grandees taking part in such proceedings jealously guarded their rank within the larger whole. Even the slightest variation in the delicate balance of rights among officers and staffs could wreak havoc, as the participants might understand it as an attack on their position in the hierarchy – nor was this interpretation necessarily always wrong. The presence of the ruler was not a prerequisite for quarrels, which could ensue in chapel, in councils, during meals, or in any conceivable context where precedence had to be defined among near-equals in the hierarchy. A wider audience inevitably tended to exacerbate such tensions, though the solemn nature of the great ceremonies undoubtedly put a premium on the maintenance of *bienséance*, as disturbances could undercut the proud show of hierarchy. A well-ordered court thus depended upon a commonly accepted table of ranks, granting to all participants the *rangs et séances* they perceived as befitting their status. This harmonious ideal seemed well-nigh unattainable: the hierarchy based on descent could never be solidified into a static system, because it frequently had to make room for foreigners, favourites, and social climbers, whereas on the other hand the power balance among the great houses influenced their attitudes even when their place within the system of ranks was accepted. Diplomats at court, moreover, were professionally committed to ceremonial brinksmanship as they sought to defend and enhance the prestige of their masters.[8]

Nor were the intricacies of ceremony itself always helpful in preventing disputes. Godefroy had put forward in his enumeration that, depending on the circumstances, both the first and the last place in a procession could be more prestigious, or alternatively both left hand and right hand could confer a higher rank.[9] Incidentally, diverging conventions could easily be solved; for Ottomans the left-hand position was habitually the preferred one, whereas in most European countries this would be the right hand. More often, ambivalences only helped

[7] Passer, 'Berichte', p. 321; *Cérémonial François*, II, pp. 8, 13, 20, 42, 54, 122, 150, 176, 177. See *Theatrum Europaeum*, VII (1653), describing the coronation of Ferdinand IV in Regensburg on 18 June, see the 'ausgeworfne Müntze' in illustration 2 and frontispiece.

[8] John C. Rule, 'A Career in the Making: The Education of Jean-Baptiste Colbert, Marquis de Torcy', *FHS* 19 (1996), pp. 967–995, here at pp. 982–983, discussing Croissy's remarks to Torcy: the 'private' virtue of modesty became a vice when serving the king as an envoy, as modesty reflects negatively on the status of the prince one represents. See also Rule, 'The King in his Council: Louis XIV and the Conseil d'en Haut', in *Royal and Republican Sovereignty in Early Modern Europe: Essays in Memory of Ragnhild Hatton*, ed. R. Oresko, G. C. Gibbs, and H. M. Scott (Cambridge 1997), pp. 216–241, and 'Colbert de Torcy, an Emergent Bureaucracy, and the Formulation of French Foreign Policy, 1698–1715', in *Louis XIV and Europe*, ed. Ragnhild Hatton (London and Basingstoke 1976), pp. 261–288.

[9] BI coll. God. 481, fol. 73: points 40–43: 40. 'Ceux qui marchent les premiers sont en rang plus honnorable'. 41. 'Ceux qui marchent les derniers sont en rang plus honnorable'. 42. 'La main droicte est plus honnorable que la gauche'. 43. 'La main gauche est plus honnorable que la droicte'.

to exacerbate the conflicts.[10] In church, the situation was complicated by the fact that there were two conceivable points of orientation: the supreme eye of God and the less-elevated eye of the audience. Rulers mostly attended Mass 'at the side of the Evangel' – from the perspective of the audience at the left side of the altar, yet from the altar on the right hand. How should other dignitaries be oriented towards this dual hierarchical centre? Different solutions could be found, as a commentary of a ceremonial officer during the 1637 funeral service for the duc de Savoye in Nôtre Dame suggests:

> Vis à vis estoit le banc des ambassadeurs, sur lequel estoient le Nonce, l'Ambassadeur de Venise, & moy: Vis à vis estoit le banc des Prélats. Le Nonce faisoit difficulté d'estre de ce costé pource que c'estoit la gauche en entrant; mais ie luy dis que c'estoit le costé de l'Evangile, qui est le lieu le plus honnorable en Italie.[11]

Situational ceremonial rules carried a strong contextual element; the smallest details could cause endless arguments in almost any setting of court life. Lying, sitting, standing; forms of chairs and seating arrangements; doors opening 'à deux battants' or on one side only, the placement of doors, tables, windows, screens, or hearths; the moments of entering, and of speaking covered or uncovered; the forms of address and the style and frequency of reverences; the position from which one greeted a guest, or the number of steps taken to approach, similar questions in seeing out the guest; order and number of visits and revisits – these and innumerable other instances were hotly debated. More problems loomed. Would precedence be determined solely by the status of charges at court, or mostly by the lineage of the incumbents?[12] Would seniority in office prevail over lineage among officers at the same hierarchical level? Did *survivanciers* fully share the status of incumbent officeholders? Such questions were never fully resolved, and produced a highly volatile mixture, inherent in the ingrained hierarchical worldview and ceremony itself. Rulers redefined and clarified their criteria of rank, but could not always implement them. From Pope Julius II's 1504 tentative European 'table of rulers' to the emergence of the internal codifications of rank in northern, central, and eastern Europe in the eighteenth century, we see a permanent endeavour on the part of the rulers to minimise the disruptive consequences of such quarrels – even when they would from time to time exploit them to further their own interests. For any particular moment, we can ascertain the groups and individuals most conspicuously engaged in ceremonial conflict

10 See William Roosen, 'Early Modern Diplomatic Ceremonial: A Systems Approach', *JMH* 52 (1980), pp. 452–476.

11 *Cérémonial François*, II, p. 808, citing one of the *introducteurs des ambassadeurs*; also see the discussions in BI coll. God. 453, on the international variations in the interpretation of the 'côté de l'évangile'.

12 See the quarrels about the *serviette* in chapter 5, or the discussion of the *chemise* in AN O 1 820 (*Grand Chambellan*), p. 38, the 'ordre Henri IV fin de l'an 1601' – after quarrels among the princes, the king decided his *grand chambellan* had to present the *chemise*. In both cases, later practice seemed to reverse Henry IV's preference for the functional rank. Compare another problem in BN Clair 814, p. 861: 'Reglement sur le rang des officiers survivanciers de la maison du roy' (Versailles 15 July 1687) where the king decides that charges actively performed determined precedence.

at court. Just as ceremonial conflict among states can serve as a 'barometer', allowing us to reconstruct international relations as they were perceived by contemporaries by following the ceremonial fluctuations, ceremony at court can help us to keep track of various changes.[13]

Writing roughly a century after Theodore Godefroy, the *Zeremonialwissenschaftler* Gottfried Stieve gave a description of ceremony that ended with aspects close to polished everyday social norms, or *civilité*:

> Generaliter alle dasjenige, was man ratione: 1. Der Stellung des Leibes v.g. Reverentz, Kniebeugung; 2. Der Kleidung, v.g. Trauer-Habit, Burgundische Kleidung; 3. Des Gehens, Sitzen und Stehens, v.g. zu Rechten oder Lincken, it. voran oder hinten nach, zu thun gewohnt oder genöthiget ist.[14]

In the course of the eighteenth century, ceremony and upper-class social mores seemed to become ever closer, with ceremony serving as the equivalent of 'stately'. Hard as it may have been to arrange the great ceremonies, it would clearly be impossible to lay down detailed rules for everyday behaviour. Seventeenth-century sources show a far greater distance between the description of the great ceremonies and the presentation of rules for daily deportment at court and elsewhere, yet the notion of precedence, to be tested in an infinity of concrete situations, was relevant for both.

The connection between ceremony and grand style was hardly new. The idealised image of the Burgundians, outbidding each other in deference, and demonstrating their rank by elevating others, offered a familiar example. Those highest in the hierarchy could prove their consummate manners by granting to their inferiors more than was due to them on the basis of their rank. Conversely, such 'inferiors' could dramatise and overdo their deference, particularly when there was more at stake than a friendly glance. Incidentally, fellow rulers could choose to accentuate their amity by playfully granting each other precedence – the Sun King did so when the English king came as an exile to his court, and when his grandson Philippe d'Anjou suddenly became the king of Spain, thus compensating them for the disadvantages of exile and age respectively.[15] There was much playful convention in the honeyed tongue of the courtier; abject flattery, surely not uncommon, is a category too narrow to describe the phenomenon. Forms of deportment, speech, and writing in the early modern age are characterised by a 'language of fidelity' that could hide a hardnosed determination, looking for the best bargain available.

[13] Roosen, 'Systems Approach'. Julius' list can be found in most ceremonial collections.

[14] Stieve, *Europäisches Hoff-Ceremoniel*, p. 1.

[15] Dangeau, *Journal*, II, pp. 292–294 (January 1689): after exchanging the habitual honours with James, Louis suggested, 'nous vivrons sans façon'. James II, however, was perceived as a far more ceremonious king than his predecessor, see the remarks in Dangeau, *Journal*, I, p. 143 (29 March 1685); and Sourches, *Mémoires*, I, p. 199 (March 1685) about Charles II receiving envoys uncovered and standing, and James II reverting to the dignified practices more generally accepted. On the duc d'Anjou see Breteuil, *Mémoires*, pp. 253–277.

The friendly ruler's finesse, or the subjects' deference, however, was less easily attained among close neighbours in the hierarchy at court. Indeed, near-equals were apt to perceive their relationship as a zero-sum game: the gains of one entailed the other's losses. The promotion of favourites or ministers could strengthen the sense of loyalty among the upper echelons of sword nobles confronted by their rapid ascent, by temporarily creating a common enemy; but when the dust settled they would again find their old rivals, and innumerable instances could arise where precedence was at stake. We frequently find courtiers or diplomats choosing to stay away from courtly events where they knew conflicts over precedence would arise, either because they expected to lose the ensuing battle, or simply because they hated the fuss. The expedients of visiting the court *al' incognito*, or abolishing the rule of ceremony for special occasions or places, were often invoked.

Everyday forms of behaviour at court could cause quarrels that were directly related to rank, but had little connection to the great ceremonies, or even to the ceremonialised domestic routines. No single domain of court life was totally free from such pressures. The persistent problem of protecting one's rank and honour at court connected two spheres we should be careful not to assimilate: ceremony and daily life at court. Ceremony may best be understood as the interplay of three variable fields: ceremonial occasions (i.e. coronations, processions, public dining); forms and rules for such occasions (from 'special effects', insignia of sovereignty, to dress and attire, minute situational details of deportment); and finally the table of ranks (i.e. hierarchies both of nobility and functionality). Court life and ceremony were two extremes within the same continuum: they shared a preoccupation with rank and deportment, but nevertheless remained quite distinct. All fields underwent changes, though the hierarchies were more volatile than the occasions and forms.

At the Habsburg court, a clear standard emerged in the course of the seventeenth century, with councillors preceding chamberlains, and seniority determining the ranking within each of the groups – only the highest court offices, inevitably councillors, would precede their elders. For France, hierarchies were more complicated, and never effectively dominated by court functions. The royal family itself was a multi-layered hierarchical structure, with king and queen; *dauphin* and *dauphine*; *fils et filles de France*; *petits-fils et petites-filles de France* serving as the upper echelon, followed by the *princes et princesses du sang*. The *princes étrangers* and the king's bastards were uncomfortably situated between the princes of the blood and the *ducs et pairs*. Conflicts between the dukes, *princes étrangers*, and *bâtards* were frequent and notorious, as the dukes resented the attempts of these groups to gain equality with the princes, which would entail undisputable precedence over the dukes.

Three series of questions remain to be answered. The first concerns the ways and means rulers sought to make their courts adhere to the ceremonial rules;

the second deals with the pervasiveness of ceremony in late seventeenth- and eighteenth-century court life, and the 'manipulation' of the ceremonial apparatus by rulers; the third looks at alternative forms of representation – it will be discussed in chapter 8.

THE EMERGENT APPARATUS FOR CEREMONY

Whatever the motives of rulers, it is clear that they tried to maintain order at their courts, and more particularly during the great public ceremonies underpinning their rule. In the course of the sixteenth and seventeenth centuries the *mise-en-scène* of the French *sacre* and coronation was increasingly codified, and the same can be said for the assembly of the estates general, or for the *lit de justice* – the sovereign ruler visiting his law court, and enforcing his will. We find pamphlets describing various imperial ceremonies, suggesting a careful arrangement and a great measure of continuity. At several courts a new charge emerged in the sixteenth or seventeenth centuries: the master of ceremonies, who guarded the strict execution of the ceremonies now captured in writing, and sought to prevent conflicts over precedence. The Roman pontiff had long since been served by a master of ceremonies, but this officer was responsible mainly for ecclesiastical routines. Among worldly rulers the vogue for such offices came later, but by the eighteenth century, most great courts would employ them.[16] The late medieval office of herold, the *roy d'armes* or *héraut d'armes*, was connected to the stables and to warfare, occupied with chivalry and ceremony alike; a French herold still formally proclaimed war in 1635, and herolds could occupy a conspicuous place in many a ceremony. Yet the office declined as other forms of announcing and publishing solemn acts came to the fore.[17]

Francis I's court included a master of ceremonies; the incumbent officer, Jean Pot, sieur de Chemaux, was later to be succeeded in his office by a dozen of his descendants.[18] Henry II pursued his father's exploratory steps with more zeal; he

[16] See Lünig, *Theatrum Ceremoniale*, III, chapter XXXII, pp. 1317–1334; Barbara Stollberg-Rilinger and André Krischer, eds., *Das Hofreisejournal des Kurfürsten Clemens August von Köln 1719–1745* (Siegburg 2000), in the introduction, the authors show that the *Kammerfurier*, author of this interesting diary, served as a master of ceremonies, at the Habsburg court his status seems notably lower.

[17] See the description in AN KK 1431, fol. 118/390-121-393: 'Roys d'Armes, Hérauts et largesse'; Lünig, *Theatrum Ceremoniale*, III, pp. 1317–133; the *hérauts* were connected to provinces: Normandie, Guyenne, Valois, Bretagne, Bourgogne, Montjoie. See for the remains of the *hérauts* in the *grand siècle*: Trabouillet's *Etat* for 1712, I, pp. 569–571; or BN Clair 814, a 1718 *état* for the *Ecuries*, pp. 534–535, omitting Valois, Bretagne, Guyenne but including *hérauts* for the provinces Roussillon, Alençon, Charolais, Picardie, Touraine, Saintonge, Lyonnais, Angoulême, and Dauphiné. The *hérauts*, included in the *grand écuyer's* staff, are frequently mentioned in ceremonies, see, for example, Sainctot's register in BN MS f 16633, fol. 34v. Compare Lucien Bély, 'Cérémonies publiques, cérémonial', in *DAR*, pp. 221–223, and Fogel, *Cérémonies de l'information*.

[18] See the remark in BI coll. God. 394, fol. 273: 'Jean Pot, sieur de Chemaux, grand maistre des cérémonies soubs le roy françois I', reiterated in AN KK 1448 fol. 1: 'Sr. de chemault prevost de son ordre et maître des Cérémonies . . .'. Dangeau, *Journal*, I, p. 115 (30 January 1685), gives the number of 12, probably including not only the grand masters, but also the earlier masters of ceremony from this family. Saint-Simon, *Mémoires*, V, p. 19, n. 1, states that six Rhodes grand masters had served French kings between 1585 and 1685, a more precise

elaborated forms for other great ceremonies, and was keen on clarifying the ranks of the participants. In 1548, the king asked Jean du Tillet, senior clerk of the Paris *Parlement*, to compile a volume on great and solemn assemblies, outlining the 'rangs et séances' among princes and officers. Tillet indeed published a *Recueil des Roys de France* in 1577, but this learned and impenetrable study of the roots of French monarchy cannot be said to have offered a practicable handbook for ceremonial matters.[19] In a March 1583 *séance royale* in Saint-Germain-en-Laye with all *cours et corps*, Henry III reiterated his father's desire to establish a 'registre authentique' establishing rank and order – 'pour à l'advenir estre observé', he prudently added.[20] The assembly advised the king to ask his master of ceremonies to compile a new register. Two years later, when Henry III introduced his second, highly elaborate general court ordinance, he elevated Guillaume Pot de Rhodes to grand master of ceremonies. Pot de Rhodes also served as grand master of ceremonies for the king's orders, responsible for the rituals of the new *Ordre du Saint Esprit* – a task not invariably included in his successors' portfolios.[21] In the same year, 1585, Henry III promoted Jérome de Gondy, *commis à recevoir* since the 1570s, to *introducteur des ambassadeurs* – an office later to be held by two officers on a semester basis, and assisted by a secretary.[22]

Charles Loyseau's early seventeenth-century *Traité des droits* clarified the ranks among the senior servants of the French state somewhat more lucidly than did Du Tillet's work, but it did not have the potential to develop into a yardstick for practice at court. Theodore Godefroy, the erudite cited earlier, helped to establish the forms of the great ceremonies by his 1619 compilation of French ceremonies, ranging from the later Middle Ages to his day. His son Denys, *survivancier* of the charge of *historiographe du roi*, would continue his father's work, publishing an extensive two-volume edition in 1649.[23] These overviews were focused heavily on dynastic state ceremonies, almost totally excluding the day-to-day order of court life. Diplomatic ceremony was notably more present

indication than Dangeau's remark. Le Roux, *Faveur du roi*, p. 184, mentions Artus de La Fontaine-Soliers, baron d'Ognon as Pot de Rhodes' predecessor, and adds more information on Jean Pot, sieur de Chemault in n. 3 on p. 184, but without confirming his role as master of ceremonies.

19 *Cérémonial François*, I, *avertissement au lecteur*, fourth text page. Tillet may be compared to Du Haillan, and many similar books most recently analysed by Cosandey, *Reine de France*.

20 Hanley, *Lit de Justice*, pp. 212–214; *Cérémonial François*, *avertissement*, p. vi.

21 BI coll. God. 446, fol. 1: Henry III, 1583: 'la nécessité de faire un recueil des rangs entre les princes, officiers de la couronne & autres grands seigneurs'; fol. 2, 1585: Guillaume Pot, sieur de Rhodes nominated 2 November 1585, in 1603 succeeded by his son Guillaume, in 1616 by the latter's brother François Pot, sieur du maignet. The grand master of ceremonies had to 'scavoir la function de chascun des officiers, et de donner les rangs aux grands . . . '. Guillaume Pot also served as master of ceremonies for the *ordre du Saint-Esprit*, a charge later held by others. The last master of ceremonies from the Rhodes dynasty had to sell his office in 1685 to the fourth son of Jean Baptiste Colbert, the marquis de Blainville.

22 Wicquefort, *L'Ambassadeur et ses Fonctions* (Cologne 1690), p. 198; A. Boppe, *Les introducteurs des Ambassadeurs 1585–1900* (Paris 1901), p. 45. BN Brienne 256 (BN MS naf 7225), fols. 79v–84v, in Henry's 1578 *règlement*: a section where the *maître d'hotel*'s responsibility for the ambassadors' receptions and honourable stay was discussed, suggesting that Gondy's task were not as clearcut as Wicquefort suggested.

23 See the family history of the Godefroy in Godefroy and Ménilglaise, *Les savants Godefroy. Mémoires d'une famille pendant les xvie, xviie & xviiie siècles* (Paris 1873).

in the son's later edition, and ecclesiastical ceremonies form part and parcel of most of the great occasions described in these volumes. In addition to the materials assembled by the Godefroy family, most ceremonial officers created their personal archives of notes and materials. A string of Rhodes grand masters of ceremony served between 1585 and 1685, many of them assembling documents and keeping notes to assist their pursuits.[24] The *introducteurs* did likewise: thus, a written heritage outlining ceremonial practices was developing in the first half of the seventeenth century.

To Henry III's small ceremonial establishment, a deputy master of ceremonies was added early in the seventeenth century: thereafter, the ceremonial staffs, consisting of the grand master (sometimes doubling as the master of ceremonies for the king's orders), the master, the aide for ceremonies, the two *introducteurs* and their assistant, did not fundamentally change.[25] In the late 1660s Louis XIV did add another officer: the *maître des cérémonies ecclésiastiques*. The *états* in the early 1670s show Nicolas Le Madre in this charge, responsible mainly for order in the chapel. This innovation was resented by the masters of ceremonies, who perceived it as a threat to their prominent position in religious celebrations. The office, formally established in 1669, remained vacant from the 1680s: the Sun King succumbed to the pressures of his vested ceremonial officers.[26] The last of the line of Rhodes grand masters sold his office in 1685, after having somewhat disingenuously chased Mlle De Tonnerre, a high-ranking lady at court, and clashed with her male relatives, the maréchal-duc de Luxembourg among

[24] On the Pot family see BN MS f 26289, MS naf 9703; see François Pot's 'Livre des Cérémonies 1616–1620' in BN MS f 3515, the 'table' for ceremonies 1548–1640 in BN MS naf 819 and in the BI coll. God. 400: on fols. 3–8 the table for 'Le Ceremonial de France, ou recueil des ceremonies et rangs observez en France depuis le règne du Roy Henry II en l'an 1548 jusqu'à l'an 1640. Par le sieur de Rodes, et autres (added in different hand: Sainctot) Maistres des Ceremonies'.

[25] It is not fully clear whether the *maître des cérémonies* was immediately established as the new grand master's substitute; thus, the 1585 *règlement* (*AC*, p. 316) gives the phrase: 'le grand maistre des cérémonies ou en son absence celuy qui tiendra son lieu'. From the early years of the seventeenth century, however, we find the masters of ceremony in the *états*. See, for example, AN Z 1 a 472: *états* 1535–1642, 1631, fol. 86v, mentioning after the *grand maître des cérémonies* another 'pour servir en l'absence dud. Maître des ceremonies' (S. Puget de Bellecourt), in 1636, fol. 175, we find S. De Lardenay, Jean-Baptiste Sainctot as 'autre pour servir en absence . . .'.

[26] BN MS f 22713, fol. 174v: 'Maître des cérémonies de la chapelle: cette charge fut créée le 20e dec. 69 avec 1500 lt de gages; Le Madre, après son mort la charge fut supprimé.' Compare Oroux, *Histoire ecclésiastiques*, II, pp. 490–491: 'Louis aimoit beaucoup les cérémonies ecclésiastique, & c'étoit pour lui un plaisir singulier de les voir exactement observées dans sa chapelle. . . . Pour remédier aux fautes qui se commettoient quelquefois dans la célébration du service divin, Sa Majesté demanda un jour à M. le Tellier, si à l'exemple de quantité d'autres églises, on ne pourroit pas établir dans sa chapelle un maître des cérémonies, qui instruisoit en particulier les officiers de l'Autel & les dirigeroit en public. . . . Le sieur Madre, c'est celui que le maître de la chapelle-musique avoit proposé, ayant reçu ces ordres, les exécuta ponctuellement. Il commença le jour de la Toussaints 1669 a exercer publiquement sa commission. Cet essai plut tellement au prince, que le 20 décembre suivant, il créa en faveur du sieur Madre la charge de Maître des Cérémonies Ecclésiastiques de la Chapelle du Roi. On lui attribua quinze cents livres de gages payables par quartier, & mille quatre-vingt-quinze livres pour ses livrées; & pour marque de son office, il devoit porter un bâton d'argent, couvert de velours violet fleurdelisé, sommé d'une couronne royale. Il est rare que les nouvautés soient du goût de tout le monde. Celle-ci éprouva les plus grandes contradictions de la part, tant du grand maître des cérémonies de france, que du maître des cérémonies de l'Ordre du Saint-Esprit, qui craignent apparremment qu'elle ne préjudiciât aux droits de leurs charges. A force de répéter qu'un pareil établissement ne servoit qu'à distraire, & à faire remarquer à tout le monde des fautes auxquelles personne peut-être ne ferait attention, ils vinrent à bout de le faire supprimer.'

them.[27] The Grand Colbert's youngest son, Jules-Armand Colbert, marquis de Blainville, procured the office through the intercession of his elder brother Seignelay, then *sécrétaire d'état* for the *maison du roi*.[28] He would combine the charge with his military pursuits. The senior ceremonial office, created as a new major charge in 1585, was never on a par with the other supreme offices. The grand master of ceremonies had to swear loyalty to the *grand maître*, instead of to the king: this indicated that he had no truly independent staff. With 3,000 lt, the grand master of ceremonies had *gages ordinaires* on the level of the other great officers. While the extras of other *grands officiers* had steadily been rising, yielding total incomes ranging from *c.* 15,000 to 60,000 lt, the grand master of ceremonies' extras paid for marriages, baptisms, *Te Deum* settings etc., only roughly doubled his income. Seignelay's efforts to improve his brother's income led to a moderate rise of 1,000 lt in the *gages ordinaires*: no match for any of the great offices. In 1701 Blainville sold his office to Thomas III de Dreux, marquis de Brézé – prolonging the link between the office and the ministerial families, as Dreux was married to one of Chamillart's daughters. When Dreux's son died in 1754, Luynes noted that the grand masters of ceremonies' charge 'was worth little', and compared it with the more lucrative charge of *prévôt-grand mâitre de l'ordre du Saint-Esprit*, also acquired by Brézé. The Dreux-Brézé lost this charge, but would serve as grand masters of ceremonies until the end of the *ancien régime* – like Blainville, mostly in addition to military command.[29]

The fact that these French grand masters of ceremony, like so many of their fellow-courtiers, actively pursued military careers entailed protracted absences. Therefore, their substitute, the master of ceremonies, was often in charge. The Sainctot family, holding the charge of *maître des cérémonies* from 1635 until 1691, and that of *introducteur des ambassadeurs* from 1691 to 1752, made a singular contribution to the ceremonial archives. Nicolas de Sainctot, first the *aide des cérémonies* helping his father, then the Sun King's master of ceremonies until

[27] For the problems of Rhodes with Mlle. De Tonnerre, see Sourches, *Mémoires*, I, pp. 100–101; Dangeau, *Journal*, I, p. 7. Horowski, 'obersten Chargen', p. 52, n. 63, cites Mme De Sévigné's anger about Rhodes' decision to sever the link of his dynasty with the charge of master of ceremonies.

[28] Jules-Armand Colbert, marquis de Blainville, 1663–1704 (killed in the battle of Hochstädt), grand master of ceremonies from 1685 until 1701; and his elder brother Jean-Baptiste Colbert, marquis de Seignelay (1651–1690), *survivancier* of his father's charges for the *maison* and the navy. See Dangeau, *Journal*, I, pp. 114–115, for Blainville: 'M. de Blainville prêta le serment de la charge de grand maître des cérémonies de France, qu'avoit M. de Rhodes . . . ; il la vend 80,000 écus et un pot de vin, je pense, de 10,000 pistoles; elle vaut 1,000 écus de réglé, et les casuels, bon an mal an, montent peut-être à autant.' Sourches, *Mémoires*, I, p. 177, remarks that the charge was relatively cheap because revenues were low, and it formally depended on the *grand maître*, swearing loyalty to him instead of to the king. Seignelay, Sourches pursues, would try to find more income for his brother.

[29] Dangeau, *Journal*, VIII, p. 61 (20 March 1701): 'M. de Dreux, gendre de M. de Chamillart, achète la charge de grand maître des cérémonies de France, qu'avoit M. de Blainville; il en donne 220,000 livres, et le roi lui donne un brevet de retenue de 40,000 écus. Cette charge ne vaut que 4,000 francs de revenue; les casuels montent encore à peu près autant. Ces casuels sont les mariages, les baptêmes, les pompes funèbres et les *Te Deum*'; Luynes, *Mémoires*, IX, pp. 370, 432; XIII, pp. 161–163 with n. 2 on p. 162 continuing the quote and 3,000 lt gages with extras, 10,000 for the *prévôt-maître* of the king's orders. See the same volume p. 200 (noting the four major offices of the *ordre du Saint-Esprit*: *surintendant des finances* – usually styled *chancelier*, *prévôt-maître des cérémonies*, *trésorier*, *sécrétaire*), p. 217, for the oath of the new provost-grand-master of the king's orders.

1691, and thereafter one of his *introducteurs des ambassadeurs*, left an astonishing number of journals, memoirs, and notes.[30] His digressions on ceremony are ubiquitous in the Parisian libraries and archives; we find several sequences of volumes, organised either on a thematic or on a chronological basis, yet without any clear system. The material is overwhelming and immensely detailed at times, yet it is neither complete nor well-ordered: no systematic archive for the ceremonies of the Sun King's court survives. Under Sainctot's tireless eye, the master of ceremonies became relatively more important, the grand master somewhat less.[31] The master of ceremonies had initially received a mediocre 1,500 *livres*; later *états* give a sum of 2,000 *livres de gages ordinaires*. In the printed *état* of 1687, we find an additional 1,200 lt *gratification*, and another 2,000 lt pension granted to Sainctot personally. Michel Ancel Desgranges, former *premier commis* of Pontchartrain, Seignelay's successor as *sécrétaire d'état* for the *maison*,[32] obtained Sainctot's charge in August 1691, and judged it well-advised to copy his predecessor's journal, later adding his own volumes. In the *avertissement* written in 1723, he listed his sources, allowing us to glimpse the procedures of his charge: he used the two Godefroy editions, the *Mercure François* and *Gazettes*, 37 portfolios of ceremonies,[33] the volumes complied by Sainctot, and the volumes he had added since 1691. Desgranges' son, as could be expected, carried on his father's activities, and the office remained in the family until 1789.[34]

When in 1691 Sainctot sold his office and procured one of the two semesters owned by *introducteur des ambassadeurs* Chabenat de Bonneuil, he secured a marked rise in status. The position of the *introducteurs* was more truly a noble

30 BN Clair 814, the 1638 *Etat* cites as master of ceremonies Jehan Baptiste Sainctot, sieur de Lardenay, as replacement for Loys de Puget. Compare Griselle, *Maison du roi Louis XIII*, p. 11. BI coll. God. frequently mentions the Sainctot, for example God. 400, fol. 3, added to the title page of the table for 'Le Ceremonial de France . . . de l'an 1548 jusqu'à l'an 1640; God. 479 fols. 103–105: 20 September 1642; *Cérémonial françois*, I, p. IV, acknowledges the assistance of the Sainctot brothers, master and aide of ceremonies; a 1656 *Etat Général* included in AN KK 209 lists one Nicolas Sainctot as master of ceremonies, another Sainctot as his aide. AN KK 1448, fol. 5, gives the charge of master of ceremonies (in addition to the grand master) for July 1585, and mentions a Sainctot for 1635. Dangeau, *Journal*, III, p. 423 (27 October 1691), mentions Sainctot's purchase of one semestre of the charge of *Introducteur des Ambassadeurs*: he paid 80,000 *écus* to Bonneuil, and sold his charge for 40,000 *écus* to Des Granges, previously Pontchartrain's *premier commis*. Boislisle notes in Saint-Simon, *Mémoires*, V, p. 5 (1698), n. 6, that Sainctot received two *brevets de retenue* (or *d'assurance*) giving the charge a value of 246,000 livres.

31 AN Z 1a 475 'Etat général du nombre des officiers à la maison du Roy Année 1676', fol. 139v: *grand maître des cérémonies* 3,000 livres, *maître des cérémonies* 2,000 livres; *aide des cérémonies* 600 livres; *conducteurs des ambassadeurs*: 600 livres. Other texts, for example BN Clair 814, p. 294, mention 1,500 for the *maître des cérémonies*. Hanley, *Lit de Justice*, seems to overstate the case when on p. 279 she describes the 'meteoric rise' of the specialised ceremonial staff; the materials she cites in n. 71 on that page do not necessarily say much about the status of the influence of the officers and their indeed impressive written output.

32 Seignelay's successor as *sécrétaire d'état* for the *maison du roi* and the navy, and after 1699 *chancelier*, Louis de Phélypeaux comte de Pontchartrain (1643–1727).

33 Possibly the portfolios that amounted to 50 in 1779, when they were reorganised into 17 cartons, see AN KK 1423–1439; but the materials in AN K 1712, or the various collections in the BN may also be involved, the relationship between these series is far from clear, nor do the various registers help to clarify the situation.

34 See AN K 1712, no. 18: 'lettres et mémoires sur le cérémoniel ou le roi a été sur une estrade, et les princes du sang à ses cotés sur la même estrade' for a very deferential letter by Desgranges, and a haughty answer by the comte de Charolais. Even more markedly than in Saint-Simon's attitude towards Sainctot, we find the irritation of the grandee vis-à-vis the simple officeholder meddling with rank and order.

charge, and did better than the master of ceremonies in other spheres as well. With a surprisingly low pay of 600 lt *gages ordinaires* for his semester, the *introducteur* was on the modest level of the *aide des cérémonies*. Yet the charge of *introducteur* brought in an additional 9,000 *livres d'appointements*, and frequent extras, paid both by the ambassadors and by the king; in the 1750s Dufort de Cheverny estimated his revenues at *c.* 25,000 a year.[35] In 1699, the introductors' aide, a simple *emploi*, was promoted to the charge of *sécrétaire de la chambre à la conduite des ambassadeurs*, and his revenues were tripled.[36] Whereas the changes in the balance between master and grand master of ceremonies may have been due mostly to the superiors' absences, to Sainctot's long service, and to his peculiar style of professional devotion, the advancement of the agents for 'diplomatic ceremony' may be seen as the consequence of the increasing significance of their domain. The reception of diplomats remained a thorny matter, permanently subject to changes in status that had to be recognised in ceremonial forms. It engendered much debate and writing: *introducteurs des ambassadeurs* continued to perform the arduous labours of compilation, notwithstanding the fact that more printed works dealt with ceremony in the early eighteenth century, most of all with the reception and audiences of diplomats.[37]

In the sixteenth century, we find no specialised ceremonial officers at the court in Vienna or Prague. In seventeenth-century *Hofstaatsverzeichnisse*, the court almoner (*elemosinarius*) was also referred to as *ceremonarius*; later we frequently find the phrase 'ceremoniarius, elemosinarius und Oberhofkaplan'. The *ceremoniarius* was not noble, and his 200 fl pay fell far below that of the higher court

[35] BN Clair 814, mémoire 1699, fol. 294, for the traditional 600 livres; BN MS f 22713, fol. 196 (1661–1683), adds the 9,000 *d'appointements*, as does in BN Clair 814, the '1714 Estat de la depens que le roy veut ordonne estre faire par mr jean de turmeny et de nointil garde de son tresor royal pour le payement des appointements, gages . . .', fols. 423–430. Sainctot and Breteuil receiving 9,000 livres. We may add the presents they received from diplomats, see Boppe, *Introducteurs*, pp. 24–26. Cf. the printed *état* for 1712, p. 647. *Etats* for 1663 (pp. 212–213), 1669 (pp. 280–281), 1677 (p. 291) and 1687 (p. 525) listing 600 per semester. Saint-Simon, *Mémoires*, V, p. 5 (1698), n. 6, also adds 9,000 livres 'd'appointements'.

[36] Boucher, 'L'Evolution', p. 364, citing Dangeau, *Journal*, VI, p. 98; VII, p. 90; AN Z 1a 476 and 477 (*états* of 1700 and 1705). This promotion concerned René Girault, serving from 1625 to 1697, the living memory and mainstay of the staff. Girault, or Giraut, was listed in printed *états* of 1663 (pp. 212–213) and 1669 (pp. 280–281) as earning 1,200 livres, serving the whole year: the secretary earned more than the formal officeholder.

[37] See Boppe, *Les introducteurs*, for an overview of the charge and a description of all holders; compare recently Bély, *Société des princes*. Anne de Brûlon's (1634–1659) memoirs can be found in BN MS f 18520 and Bibliothèque de l'Arsenal 5410; Nicolas de Berlize's (1635–1671) memoirs are in BN MS f 18520, with extracts in BA 5410, pp. 421–462; Chabenat de Bonneuil's (1680–1698) memoirs can be found in the Archives du Ministère des Affaires Etrangères (AAE) Fonds France 1835; BA 4230 and 3859; Nicolas de Sainctot (1691–1709) and his notes have been mentioned above; father and son Nicolas Sixte de Sainctot's (1709–1752) collection of memoirs and documents related to the charge of *introducteur* can be found in the fonds cérémonial of the AAE depot, nos. 1817–1859. Louis Nicolas le Tonnelier de Breteuil's (1698–1715) memoirs have been edited by Evelyne Lever, *Mémoires* (Paris 1992); Lever gives more information on Breteuil's memoirs. Eusèbe Felix Chassepoux, marquis de Verneuil's (1747–1757) memoirs in the AAE Fonds France 1852 and BN naf 1111–1115; Jean Nicolas Dufort de Cheverny's (1752–1764) memoirs were published by Crèvecoeur, *Mémoires sur les règnes de Louis XV et Louis XVI et sur la Révolution*, 2 vols. (Paris 1886); finally, Leroi de Séqueville, *sécrétaire à la conduite* from 1761 to 1792, kept a record for the years 1761–1786, see AAE Fonds France 1974–1976. See Vec, *Zeremonialwissenschaft*, for the printed German works, the detailed overview of customs in most European realms by Rousset *Cérémonial Diplomatique* printing many of Sainctot's digressions.

dignitaries. He was responsible for ecclesiastical ceremonies, and thus seems to have been a closer equivalent of the papal officer, or the short-lived French master of ecclesiastical ceremonies, than of the masters of ceremonies in France and elsewhere. Descriptions of great ceremonies, mostly those pertaining to the empire, circulated in print, but compilations and discussions of such recurring events were published much later than in France. In the German territories, the preoccupation with *decorum* and reputation was long seen as an undesirable Italian and French import, better limited to the world of Castiglione and Machiavelli. Religious and philosophical attitudes served as a bulwark against neo-stoicism, *raison d'état* thinking, and counter-reformatory Catholicism. Only in the later seventeenth century, did ceremony acquire a more prominent place among German writers, captivating two or three generations of erudites writing from *c.* 1670 to 1750. Even then, however, splendour and pageantry were deemed legitimate largely because of the dimness and impressionability of the mob: ceremony and courtly splendour were the only way to convince the *Pöbel*. The southern realms in the empire, rapidly returning to the Catholic creed from the later sixteenth century onwards, occupied an intermediate position, not as aloof from the 'welsch' world as the northern, Lutheran or Calvinist parts, but still perceptibly diverging from the attitudes more common in Italy and France.

Whether or not such cultural defences were relevant for practice at court in Vienna with its strong ties to both Spain and Italy is far from clear, but the fact remains that ceremony was not systematically discussed in print. Halfway through the seventeenth century, when in France a specialised staff was active at court and several learned volumes outlining ceremony were available, the Austrian Habsburgs had not instituted any such innovations. The ceremonial records make emphatically clear, however, that the preoccupation with rank and its conspicuous demonstration in ceremony was quite as active in the Habsburg realms as it was in France. We find descriptions and detailed arrangements for various ceremonies from the sixteenth into the eighteenth century, showing an often striking continuity in form and atmosphere. Moreover, the instructions for the great officers invariably included rules with a strong ceremonial component. Whereas in France the specific responsibility for ceremony had been detached from the tasks of the *grand maître de France* – partly because of Henry III's reservations about the incumbent of that powerful charge – the Habsburg *Obersthofmeister* retained it.

Not all went unchanged, however: early in 1651 Ferdinand III judged it necessary to ask a special committee of councillors to propose a remedy for various disorders at court. It was probably no coincidence that 1651 also was the first year with more or less regular payment of wages after the critical last war years: now, an attempt could made to restore and improve the court. The preliminary statements of the committee's *Gutachten* suggest that both the redress of 'disorders that had crept in' as well as the desire to create a grander, truly imperial court, conforming to the practice at other major courts, were important motives. The court had to be put on a more modern footing, adapted to the current needs and standards.[38] Ambassadors' complaints are mentioned several times in the reform proposal, and we find a Saxon resident confirming the reform shortly afterwards:

> Alhier an dem kayserlichen Hofe, ist aniezo eine newe ordnung, wegen der antecamera und kayserlichen ritterstuben gemacht worden, in demevorhero fast menniglich indifferenter in die antecamera hinein geloffen, aniezo aber alle in ein buch verzeichnet werden, welchen der ingressus permittiret ist, und darff kheiner in stifel und sporn hinein khommen, werde mich bemühen, solche ordnung zu erlangen und selbige zu übersenden.[39]

Endless similar efforts had preceded Ferdinand's 1651 initiative, but it had important consequences. Not only did the committee propose a new *Kammerordnung*, it reviewed all major instructions, and suggested the creation of a detailed overview of ceremony, clarifying ranks at court, and stating rules for the reception of sovereigns and their representatives. The decision to assign one of the steward's secretaries to ceremony, instructing him to carefully record major events, was a major step in the *Verschriftlichung* of ceremony.[40] We have no evidence, however, for the existence of a ceremonial handbook; had such a work been produced copies should have survived in the archives. Contemporaries do not mention a printed overview of ceremony and rank at the Habsburg court, and the 1739 Rousset compilation denied the existence of any such work. It is interesting to note that the considerations put forward by the committee resembled Henry II's and Henry III's wish for a register of ranks, establishing precedence at court and in the great ceremonies.

As a result of the committee's report, from 1652 onwards a *Zeremonienamt* was active in the *Obersthofmeisteramt*. Its secretary kept a chronologically organised register of all important ceremonial occasions, the *Zeremonialprotokoll*. This methodical effort allowed the secretary to use his own notes from previous occasions when proposing the arrangements for a new ceremony; the cross-references in the protocol helped him to build a repository of accepted practices that could be consulted when difficulties arose. In the *Zeremonialakten*, the collection of documents relating to ceremony, we often find *Extracte* from the protocol, discussing ceremonial conventions on the basis of a reasoned summary of earlier comparable occasions listed in the protocol. For more complicated matters, *Referate* were written that considered the ceremonial problems at some

38 AVA Harrach historica 797, the 1651 'Guettachten', p. 1, and, for example, p. 22, in the opening phrases on the *Stallmeisterinstruktion*, where it is stated that the current instruction reflected an archducal, not a truly imperial court.

39 Katrin Keller (Vienna) kindly drew my attention to this message, confirming the Viennese reform from an external perspective: from: Hauptstaatsarchiv Dresden, Loc. 8241/1 (Des kursächs. Residentensam kaiserl. Hofe Schreiben 1648–52), Bl. 181 (29 March 1651).

40 AVA Harrach historica 797, the 1651 'Guettachten', see pp. 8, 11.

length. Such longer digressions could be the result of a session of a specific *Konferenz* or committee, instituted to suggest solutions to the emperor. The protocol, and many of the other texts, were typically written *Halbbrüchig*, on one half of the page only to leave room for the emperor's comments.

The *Zeremonienamt* was not headed by an officer explicitly listed in the *Hofstaat*: it fell under the responsibility of the *Obersthofmeister*, and his personal secretary may have been the author of the protocol.[41] The materials themselves are quite close to those assembled and produced by the French masters of ceremony, yet the consistency and continuity of the protocol has no parallel in France. For any major occasion, we can consult the protocol, and may expect to find more related documents in the *Zeremonialakten* – a procedure not unlike that routinely carried out by the secretary in the *ancien régime*.[42] The protocol may have rendered ceremony more methodical; surely, for the greater ceremonies, a settled pattern was within reach. This limited Habsburg apparatus for ceremony was not fundamentally altered in the course of the eighteenth century, though the attitudes of both rulers and public were changing. Indeed, the comments in the margin of the ceremonial notices suggest less close attention to ceremony than is evident in Leopold I's time. 'Placet in toto', was Charles VI's most habitual formula; while Maria Theresa may have adopted an even more aloof perspective, she instructed her children to take ceremony seriously.[43] Joseph II, hardly a friend of ceremony, was well aware of the impact of precedent, and he himself may have consulted the *Zeremonialprotokoll* to trump the ceremonial pretension of Khevenhüller.[44] Only in the early years of the nineteenth century did the court in Vienna adopt an *Oberceremonienmeister* – a French import we may assume. In 1830 we still find a handwritten manual for ceremonial matters.[45]

41 See HHStA ZA Prot 3 October 1674–September 1681, fol. 121 (12 July 1677) we find the name of one of the court's secretaries, Johann Probst, previously Lobkowitz's secretary, as the probable author, as he describes a conflict where he himself had been present.

42 See, for example, works such as Sommer-Mathis, 'Theatrum und Ceremoniale', in *Zeremoniell als höfische Ästhetik*.

43 See her instructions in ÖNB cod. ser. n. 1713, most particularly the German 'Instruction pour le ceremoniel aux cours de ses enfans 1765', fols. 47–51, 75–91. Compare the critical stance in ÖNB cod. 12955–12958 Ceremoniale . . . 1763–1800, a parallel to the *Zeremonialprotokoll*, in 12955, fols. 136r–137v, see the 'Unterthänigst gehorsamte Anfragen' addressed by the *Kammerfourier* Strobl to *Oberstkämmerer* Salm about dress (Campagne oder Mantelkleid) with the additions 'ja', 'wie sonst', 'nein nichts', 'zu fragen' in the margin. On fol. 141r we find the indication, 'Protocollum de Anno 1767': suggesting that this was a parallel of the *Zeremonialprotokoll*. On fol. 147 the 'appartement' in the French meaning of a sociable occasion is mentioned.

44 Khevenhüller, *Tagebuch*, VI, p. 196 (18 August 1766): 'Den 18. waren die exequien . . . jedoch nahme der Kaiser weder heut noch gestern einen fleck vor das Gesicht, indeme aus denen Hof-Prothocollen zu entnehmen ware, daß der Kaiser Joseph bei gleicher Gelegenheit anno 1705 es auch nicht gethan, so diser junge Herr, welcher alles, so einem Cérémonial gleichet, für eine gêne ansiht, alsogleich mit Freuden intimiret hat.' One suspects that Joseph did not really check the ZA Prot, but knew this reply would baffle his punctilious servant.

45 See the appointment of Gundaker Heinrich Grafen von Wurmbrand as *Oberzeremonienmeister* in HHStA Hofakten Min. D. Inneren, K 15 (8 May 1810–24 May 1810), and his successor Friedrich Egon Landgraf zu Fürstenberg, on 8 February 1818. Apparently, even in the 1830s, only a handwritten ceremonial overview existed, see ÖNB cod. ser. n. 4411 'Friedrich Egon Landgraf zu Fürstenberg, Entwurf eines Etiquette-Normals für den Österreichischen Kaiserhof' (1830).

No special officers for the introduction of crowned heads, ambassadors, or envoys were instituted. Senior nobles could meet them at a certain distance, leading them to Vienna; a situation close to French practice, where the *maréchaux* frequently fulfilled this task. In Vienna diplomats and other foreign guests traditionally fell within the responsibility of the *Obersthofmarschall*, who escorted the ambassador in his public entry, and brought him to his public audience: Khevenhüller explicitly likened the marshal to the French *introducteur des ambassadors*. Ambassadors and envoys had to deal with the *Oberstkämmerer* – or alternatively with the dowager-empress' *Obersthofmeister* – to obtain a first audience and present their credentials to the emperor. An *Audienzkommissar*, usually a chamberlain, could be appointed *ad hoc* for any particular ambassador, accompanying him from his quarters to the Hofburg in a special *Audienzwagen*, escorting him to the audience first with the *Obersthofmarschall*, then the *Obersthofmeister*, and finally the *Oberstkämmerer*: as the *trait d'union* between the various participating dignitaries, he seems much closer to the French *introducteur* than was the marshal. It is not clear whether such commissaries were regularly appointed, or only for special occasions: there are no indications, however, that the task was ever turned into an office. Frequently, we find a variety of high-ranking courtiers, including the *Silberkämmerer*, taking part in the procedures of receiving and escorting high-ranking guests.[46] As in France rules for receiving ambassadors were becoming increasingly detailed, though never fully codified, as the problems of precedence encountered by diplomats at the courts of Europe frequently necessitated the adaptation of conventions. Thus, the way Habsburg diplomats were received in France immediately influenced the honours their French compeers could expect in Vienna.

THE CEREMONIAL COURT

The court in Vienna, reputedly one of the most ceremonial courts in early modern Europe, did not employ a senior officer exclusively responsible for ceremony, nor did it produce any printed digests of its ceremonial rules. The *Hofkalender* and the *Schematismen* did not include explanations of charges and ceremonies, as would the French *états*. The unpublished ceremonial materials, however, are preserved in a state that allows us to assess and repeat the procedures of the secretaries. The volume and the style of their work convey the significance

46 See Khevenhüller, *Tagebuch*, II, p. 116 (6 October 1746): 'Eodem hatte der päbstliche Nuntius seinen offentlichen Einzug mit gewöhnlichen Gepräng, worbei dann mein Schwager zum erstenmahl die dem Obrist Hoff Marschall Amt anklebende Charge d'introducteur des ambassadeurs verrichtete'; see ambassador Richelieu's 1725–1726 description of arrival, private audiences (emperor and empresses), *entrée*, and public audience in AN KK 1394, with a reference on p. 249 to 'Cte de Sartago chambellan de L'empereur commissaire nommé pour conduire l'ambassadeur à l'audience publique'; Richelieu's sketch provides many details on the ceremonies; compare the generalised 1708–1709: 'Instruktion für eine Kaiserliche Audienz-Kommission' in HHStA ÄZA K 22, fols. 432–435; and the variety of court dignitaries taking part in the niceties of receiving and escorting in ÄZA K 3 'Varia, Empfangen, Audienzen', concentrated on the imperial electors in Prague 1651–1654.

and magnitude of ceremony at court. For the seventeenth century we find no parallel for the voluminous but less well-ordered notes so typical for the hierarchically better-placed French ceremonial officers.

The institutional settings were quite different; can we say the same for the preoccupations of the ceremonial agents, or for the forms of ceremony encountered in these sources? The similarity of themes addressed in these differently organised ceremonial establishments is remarkable: the *Zeremonialprotokol*, Sainctot's registers and their parallels in both realms list basically the same ceremonies.[47] We encounter all forms of dynastic state ceremonial: the dynasties' personal and political life cycles form a major part of the materials both in France and in Vienna. The familiar ecclesiastical ceremonies and the orders of chivalry occupy a steady, yet smaller place. In France, ecclesiastical routines seem to have become less dominant in the eighteenth century, a development occurring only after 1765 in the Habsburg domains.[48] The reception of sovereigns and their representatives looms larger and larger. In the printed as in the unpublished works in France, and in the Viennese manuscript sources, we get the impression that diplomatic ceremony was rapidly expanding in the decades following the peace of Westphalia.[49] Theodore Godefroy's 1619 volume only incidentally refers to encounters between sovereigns, and more often discusses the *rangs et séances* of princes – the conspicuous 'internal' sovereigns. The 1649 volumes published by Denys Godefroy more frequently allude to diplomatic ceremony. Most later compilations of ceremony, from the German *Zeremonialwissenschaft* to Rousset and Du Mont's comprehensive 1739 volumes, devote much space to diplomatic encounters of every conceivable sort – Rousset and Du Mont, typically, chose 'cérémonial diplomatique' as their title. Simpler ceremonial works, especially those printed for German princes fighting for a place among the recognised European sovereigns, simply offer a catalogue of ranks, matching the indigenous hierarchies with those of other courts.[50] The German princes were unable to be admitted on the basis of equality among the sovereign rulers, yet operated in practice as territorial rulers, only marginally limited in their sovereign rights by the constraints of the empire. The electors, in particular, did the utmost to be recognised as equals of royal sovereigns, and be granted the *honores regii*. In Vienna, therefore, 'dynastic' and 'diplomatic' ceremony merged in the imperial

47 BN MS naf 818: 'Collection générale des cérémonies qui ont été observées et des Fêtes qui ont été données sous le règne de Louis XIV. Avec la description des monumens élevés à sa gloire', *c.* 1730, gives a table of ceremonies and festivals, the first nine points well reflect the bias of the ceremonial archives, the last five points indicate the overlapping of ceremony with festive forms and general representation: 1. *sacre, inauguration*; 2. *mariages*; 3. *baptêmes*; 4. *cérémonies à l'église*; 5. *Te Deum*; 6. *entrées*; 7. *entrevûes*; 8. *réceptions*; 9. *Ambassadeurs, leurs entrées et leurs audiences*; 10. *fêtes et festins*; 11. *carrousels*; 12. *feux d'artifice*; 13. *funerailles et services*; 14. *monumens élevés à la gloire de Louis XIV*.

48 Compare Antoine, *Louis XV*, pp. 486–487, and Kovacs, 'Kirchliches Zeremoniell'.

49 See Klaus Müller, *Das kaiserliche Gesandtschaftswesen im Jahrhundert nach dem Westfälischen Frieden (1648–1740)*, Bonner Historische Forschungen 42 (Bonn 1976); Vec, *Zeremonialwissenschaft*; Bély, *Société des princes*.

50 See, for example, *Ceremoniale Palatinum wie bey der Regierung von Caroli Ludovici sich solches befunden* (Freiburg 1700).

ceremonies, and the near-sovereign princes of the empire were key actors both in the imperial ceremonies and in the diplomatic ceremonies at court. Yet in Vienna too, diplomats were becoming a more marked presence at court. The 1651 reform was partly prompted by ambassadors' complaints about disorders, and other efforts to render the court more orderly invariably addressed the problem of receiving and escorting diplomats, defining their place in the courtly system of ranks.[51]

Was ceremony increasingly dominated by the transactions among European princes? Had the near-sovereigns within the realm, so markedly present in earlier ceremonial conflicts, indeed successfully been integrated into the state?[52] A subtle yet perceptible shift is suggested by the sources, but we should note that at both courts the ruler's relatives, and the grandees, were major actors in ceremony.[53] Princes and members of the royal family observed the routines of *lever*, *coucher*, and public dining just as would the ruler. In Vienna as in France, diplomats and incidental visitors progressed with their audiences and visits through the whole 'dynastic complex' after visiting the sovereign. Nor was the French king always averse to supporting the sovereign pretensions of his relatives, as long as they loyally supported the grandeur of French monarchy in its international entanglements. The highest echelons of French nobles, the princes and the *ducs-pairs*, were developing into elite groups within a more or less unified state, yet the princes in particular still cherished the appurtenances of sovereignty. Ceremonial conflicts with diplomats, with fellow-princes, and with the groups contiguous in rank, moreover, remain in evidence. In France, the royal family, quite numerous in the later eighteenth century, asserted its place in ceremony as well as in other spheres – not always in support of their ruling relative.

Diplomacy, with its ever-changing balances and levels of power, was hardly a new factor in court life. Yet it gained force from the later seventeenth century onwards, and was one of the factors motivating the courts to adhere to stricter norms: representatives of other sovereigns put a premium on the court's dignity and display, and they had to be integrated into its system of ranks. Diplomacy connected the ranking at all major European courts, hierarchical conflicts at one court could disrupt the hierarchies elsewhere. A need for conformity in

[51] See AVA, Harrach Historica 797, 'Guettachten', p. 5 (point 14), and on pp. 7–8, *Obersthofmeister* Dietrichstein's commentary, where the difficulties are presented as one of the reasons for the institution of the secretary for ceremonial matters; p. 11 for the further elaboration of a *Zeremonialprotokoll*; pp. 14–15, point 11, of the comments on the marshal's instruction describes the disorders, the lack of clarity in the arrangements for receiving ambassadors, and their complaints.

[52] See David Parrott 'A 'prince souverain' and the French Crown: Charles de Nevers, 1580–1637', in *Royal and Republican Sovereignty in Early Modern Europe: Essays in Memory of Ragnhild Hatton*, ed. R. Oresko, G. C. Gibbs, and H. M. Scott (Cambridge 1997), pp. 149–187, for an illuminating perspective on 'sovereign subjects'.

[53] See AN K 1712 no. 14 (1741): 'Mémoire sur des difficultés entre les princes du sang et les electeurs'; no. 15, discussing the same in 1775, concentrating on the duc de Chartres and the prince de Conti vis-à-vis the elector of Bavaria. Nos. 16, 18, 19, 20, 23, 27, and 28 again prominently include the royal family and *princes du sang*. Princes and Electors, we may conclude, were still not neatly to be fitted into the categories either of full sovereigns, or of subjects.

treatment of the higher ranks at all courts emerged; the drawn-out discussions on the question whether the *enfants de France* held the same position versus visiting diplomats as the archdukes and archduchesses in Vienna exemplify the importance of such issues for these courts.[54] To be sure, the highest echelons within the realm always still added their share of ceremonial strife, yet the battle for rank and precedence at court was now frequently caused by diplomatic niceties, or by the interconnected interactions of diplomats and domestic grandees at all courts. The essential forms of diplomatic ceremony – private and public audiences, the entry – show as great a continuity as do the dynastic state ceremonies, and were basically European in outlook. Private audiences reflected the papal audience, with three reverences on bended knee in coming and going – the latter always facing the ruler. Rulers received diplomats leaning against a table on a dais and under a canopy. The public audience, with its *harangue*, presents, and compliments, usually in a presence- or throne room, was likewise roughly similar. Details of receiving and escorting could vary according to the occasion, as would the rules for carriages – alternatively drawn by two, four, or six horses. When diplomats ate at the court's tables, attended performances, or took part in hunts and festivities, however, their presence could lead to complications, as they would confront their colleagues as well as courtiers in less codified situations where rank was nevertheless at stake.

In addition to the prevalent dynastic and diplomatic ceremonies, and the instances of ceremonies related to the church and orders of chivalry, we incidentally find the court's routines in the registers. Yet when we find details about the table or the chamber, they are mostly put forward in connection with great dynastic or diplomatic occasions, or because of serious conflict over precedence. When more private 'domestic' rules are discussed, such as the empress' return into the court after giving birth, or the consummation of a dynastic marriage, the dynastic life cycle was at stake. The routines of table and chamber are conspicuously missing in the records. Indeed, a committee instituted in 1715 by Charles VI to re-establish order in the apartment vainly scanned the *Zeremonialprotokolle* for preceding discussions, without finding any materials outlining this crucial domestic routine.[55] Nor would a similar attempt to find the order for daily meals have been more successful. The various registers compiled by French masters of ceremony show the same tendency: they include many detailed descriptions

[54] For example, HHStA, Staatenabteilung, Frankreich, K 26: Berichte 1688, 1698–1700; Weisungen 1680–1688, 1698–1699, 1698. Second point of Waldstein's questions about Leopold's instruction, fols. 2–4, 2v: as Villars refused to visit the archdukes uncovered, Waldstein wondered how he should visit the *dauphin*'s children; this was to be a lasting problem, compare AN K 1712 28 (1773) last three pages: 'La difference est donc palpable. A Vienne, nos envoyez extraordinaires ne voient point en ceremonie les Archiducs. A Versailles les envoyez extraordinaires de l'Empereur ont en ceremonie audience des Enfans de France . . .'.

[55] ZA Prot 8, fol. 266r, somewhat ambivalent, the text refers to the 'Obristhoffmeister Ambtsprotocollo' but this seems to indicate the *Zeremonialprotocoll*, not the other protocol, variously labelled *Hoff- Amts*, or *Partheyen-protokoll*, that would not logically include such matters. Moreover, the registers of the ZA Prot volumes clearly convey the same focus.

of solemn occasions, but rarely even hint at domestic conventions.[56] A short description of the tasks performed by the masters of ceremonies included in the 1712 *état* confirms this focus:

Ils se trouvent au Baptême du Roy . . . , ils se trouvent aussi à sa Majorité, à son Sacre, à son Mariage; aux Baptêmes des Dauphins et des Enfants de France, aux ouvertures des Etats, le Jeudy Saint à la cérémonie de la Cêne, aux prémières et dernières Audiances des Ambassadeurs Extraordinaires, à la conduite des Reines ou des Princesses, aux Obsèques et aux Pompes Funèbres des Rois et Reines, des Princes & Princesses, où ils ordonnent de tout ce qui appartient aux cérémonies, & ont le soin du rang & de la préséance que chacun doit avoir.[57]

The bias of the ceremonial archives clearly indicates that the competence and special responsibility of ceremonial agents was limited to preparing and overseeing the greater public events. Table and chamber were controlled by the traditional court officers in charge of these spheres, in Vienna as in France. Sainctot and his colleagues were not supposed to meddle with the daily details of *lever* and *coucher*, or the king's meals: the great nobles holding the relevant charges would not tolerate such interference. The chapel and the stables occupy a slightly different position, as the ruler's activities in these spheres were more structurally public, and frequently demanded ceremonial expertise. The pages and musicians of the stables had as marked positions in ceremonies as the guards at court. The ruler's devotions represented a significant share of his public appearances, and the *grand maître des cérémonies* and his staff did have a role to play in addition to the *grand aumônier*. Yet these officers could force themselves upon the great courtiers only in the context of the major ceremonies, and we should not overstate their daily impact at court, or forget the more elevated status of the officers truly overseeing the ruler's daily activities. In Vienna this situation emerges more forcefully because the small ceremonial office within the steward's staff was not even headed by a noble court officer, and the *ceremoniarius*' responsibilities were limited to the ecclesiastical sphere.

Thus, the rise of the ceremonial officers in France and the *Zeremonienamt* in Vienna was connected mainly to the great dynastic ceremonies, most of them redefined, codified, and embellished in the course of later Middle Ages and becoming ever more prominent in the sixteenth century. Up to the 1740s the rhythm of such ceremonies remained relatively unchanged in the empire and in the assortment of territories under the rule of the Austrian Habsburgs. The *Reichstag* convened permanently in Regensburg from 1663 to 1806; the habitual

56 *Lever*, *coucher*, with the *entrées* and specific graces, or the ceremonies for daily meals, are conspicuously missing in AN KK 1440, an exhaustive 'table alphabetique des matières contenües dans les 50 cartons cottés & qui sont du depot des archives de la pairie au Louvre' – now to be found in AN KK 1423–1439.

57 I, pp. 644–646; the financial extras granted to the masters of ceremony confirm the occasions listed here, see Dangeau, *Journal*, VIII, p. 61 (20 March 1701): 'Ces casuels sont les mariages, les baptêmes, les pompes funèbres et les *Te Deum*'.

ceremonies tied to the dynasty and its rule over the constituent parts of the *monarchia austriaca* continued unchanged. The mid-eighteenth-century crisis, however, changed the ties both between the empire and Vienna, and between Vienna and the components of the monarchy. Even before the Prussian and Bavarian challenges to Habsburg power, the Electors were hesitant to come to Vienna for their *Belehnung*; none did so in the years following the mid-century war. The whole 'Belehnungsgeschäfft', high steward Ulfeld noted in 1766, was in serious crisis.[58] Attempts to reanimate it by enticing the elector of Braunschweig-Lüneburg (the king of England) with a new *Erzamt* did not prove successful.[59] Kings were not keen to swear loyalty on bended knee to the emperor, yet lesser princes, or their representatives, continued to flock to Vienna to do homage. Likewise, *Erbhuldigungen* changed in character after the mid-century crisis, a development reflecting the diminished power of the regional estates, and the stronger central institutions in Vienna.[60]

In France, however, the development and intensification of similar dynastic state ceremonies in the sixteenth century contrasts markedly with their apparent decline in the seventeenth century. No meeting of the estates general was summoned after 1610–1614. Louis XIII and his son, evidently, were baptised, crowned, married, and buried; yet Louis XIV himself did not engage in urban entries after the great Parisian spectacle of 1660, and after the 1673 *lit de justice* forty years would pass without this ceremony. Had the Sun King's personal rule obviated the need for such incidental but potentially recurring points of contact between the political elites and the dynasty? Could household and government in their newly consolidated form fully absorb the necessity for such interaction? Major specialists in this field have indeed interpreted the Sun King's court as a new phase in the development of ceremony. A 'script' coordinating daily routines at court, so the argument runs, partly replaced the solemn re-enactments of the ties between ruler and realm that had been so prominent in the preceding centuries.[61]

Several questions arise. A marked difference in the political relevance and the frequency of important ceremonies appears well-attested; yet did such discontinuity characterise all great public ceremonies? Only in the case of the estates general, is this unambiguously clear. In the last years of the Sun King's reign, the *lit de justice* re-emerged, and it would remain characteristic for eighteenth-century legal-political culture. The *entrée*, mostly confined to the first years of any ruler, was not fully absent for Louis himself after 1660 as he 'entered' the cities

58 Khevenhüller, *Tagebuch*, VI, p. 519, in n. 190, a 4 November 1766 *Vortrag* on the *Mantelkleid*, to Joseph II.

59 Khevenhüller, *Tagebuch*, VII, pp. 243–313, n. 39, with explicit comment on the crisis of the *Belehnungen* on pp. 252–253.

60 A research project in Vienna, under the auspices of Grete Walter-Klingenstein, will help to identify changes in the rhythm and character of *Erbhuldigungen*.

61 See Boureau, 'Ritualité politique', in *L'Etat ou le roi*, ed. Bulst *et al.*, pp. 9–25, discussing the 'historiographie cérémonialiste'.

Besançon (1674) and Strasbourg (1681). Foreign princes or princesses marrying into the dynasty, moreover, would habitually enter one of the cities after crossing the borders of the realm. Upon his accession to the Spanish throne, Louis' grandson Philippe, duc d'Anjou, was escorted to Spain by his brothers, the duc de Bourgogne and the duc de Berry: together, they entered several cities. The last Bourbon kings would respect this custom.[62] Through the ages forms changed fundamentally, from the entry of a roaming band exacting contributions, via the typical *joyeuse entrée* outlining the ruler's rights as well as his duties, to the stylised glorification of rulership: yet the entry itself did not disappear. Finally, in the Sun King's reign the public ceremonies connected to the ecclesiastical year continued without serious interruptions, as did the ceremonies of the orders of chivalry, or those occasioned by the incidents of dynastic demography – nor did his successors abolish them, notwithstanding the gradual emergence of more critical attitudes. The celebration of victories, in the form of *Te Deum* settings, some of them in the king's company, became increasingly prominent in the seventeenth century.[63] Thus, not all was discontinuous, and much of the apparent discontinuity finds a natural explanation in the length of Louis XIV's reign.

Undoubtedly, both in Versailles and in Vienna, there was a 'script' for court life, a series of conventions structuring the daily routine of the ruler. Was it an echo of preceding generations, or an innovation conceived by the ruler and his advisers? For Vienna the question seems fully redundant, as tradition went uncontested until the advent of Maria Theresa, and was treated with great circumspection until the days of Joseph II. The Sun King's domestic ceremonies, however, have often been presented either as an innovation, or as a highly conscious adaptation of tradition. Yet the *lever* and *coucher*, as well as the ritualised meal, have a long pedigree. When Henry III codified the ceremonies of table and chamber, he did not invent them, but added system and distance to proceedings that were long since accepted. He restructured the habits of an open style of kingship to conform to his desires of order, piety, and most of all liberation from the permanent bustle of uninvited grandees, petitioners, and advisers. Henry III's ordinances, moreover, include many minutiae more often associated with the Sun King's court, such as the *triage* affected by the subsequent *entrées*, and

62 BN MS naf 818, pp. 17–44, discusses the entries, mentioning among others Louis XIV's entries in Besançon (1674) and Strasbourg (1681), and the series of entries in the context of Philip V's voyage to Spain. See, for example, the entry of the princesse de Savoie, the new *dauphine*, in Lyon, Dangeau, *Journal*, VI, p. 12 (19 October 1696), reported with much detail in the *Mercure* for October 1696, pp. 317–324; November, pp. 225–254. For the entries of Louis XVI and Marie-Antoinette, first as *dauphin* and *dauphine* in June 1773 and later as ruling couple in February 1779, see *Correspondence secrète entre Marie-Thérèse et le Cte de Mercy-Argenteau*, I, pp. 458–459 (14 June 1773); *Journal de l'abbé de Véri*, II, pp. 177–178; *Journal inédit du duc de Croÿ*, IV, p. 156. Compare Anne Spagnolo-Stiff, *Die 'Entrée Solennelle'. Festarchitektur im Französischen Königtum* (1700–1750) (Weimar 1996); and Alain-Charles Gruber, *Les grandes fêtes et leurs décors à l'époque de Louis XVI* (Geneva 1972).

63 See Fogel, *Les cérémonies d'information*, and her *L'Etat dans la France moderne de la fin du XVe siècle au milieu du XVIIIe siècle* (Paris 1992), for example, pp. 39–61.

the presentation of *serviette* or *chemise*. Even the less familiar *débotté* (or taking off of the king's boots) after the hunt, organised along the same norms of hierarchically regulated access, was instituted by the last Valois.[64]

The presentation of *serviette* and *chemise* was routinely observed in Héroard's *Journal*, suggesting that the less ceremonially inclined first two Bourbons did respect the logic of a tradition antedating their immediate Valois predecessor.[65] The late medieval practice of noble officers serving the rulers' table, reaching a momentary highpoint at the Burgundian court, indicates that the stately forms of dining hardly were a seventeenth-century specialty. Louis XIV's court followed customs that were representative of early modern court life as a whole, including service by high noblemen, assaying, and the presentation of water-bowl and napkin – only the combined form of the preceding, the moist serviette, was reportedly added by Louis XIV, an innovation more practical than dignified.[66] In Vienna, we find comparable forms for the public meals, and entrance into the appartement ideally was even more stringently connected to rank. Only in the rituals of the bedchamber had the French court developed a style that differed markedly from most other courts, both in accessibility and complexity – although it would be imitated elsewhere from the later seventeenth century onwards. The ingenious seating arrangements, most notably the *tabourets* so coveted by the duchesses, can be seen as yet another variant of the tensions implicit in court life, and whereas the specific form may have been a novelty,

[64] The ordinances of 1578 and 1585, the last in *AC*, pp. 321 and 324 for the *serviette*, p. 331 for the *robbe* parallel to the *chemise* at the *coucher*; p. 311 for the *débotté*; compare Besongne, *Etat* 1687, pp. 228–229: 'Un valet de chambre tire la bote du pie droit, & un valet de garderobe celle du pie gauche. Au *dêboté* du roy peuvent entrer les personnes qui ont les entrees au lever de S.M.' See BN MS naf 2004 fols. 258–264, for Charles IX's 24 October 1572 initiative approaching the *entrées*, and the previous Aragonese (*leges palatinae*) and Burgundian examples discussed in Kruse and Paravicini, eds., *Höfe und Hofordnungen*.

[65] Héroard, *Journal*, I, chemise: for example on pp. 117, 142 (for the young *dauphin*), 145, 411; *serviette*: for example on II, pp. 239–240. For the continuity of ceremonial customs, see Knecht's description of *lever*, *chemise*, and *coucher* in *Renaissance Warrior and Patron*, p. 128; and Knecht, 'The Court of Francis I', p. 9; Gaston Zeller, *Les institutions de la France au xvie siècle* (Paris 1948), p. 99, contains descriptions of the 'Chemise' for Charles IX in 1564.

[66] *Couvert du Roi*, p. 33; compare the *Mémoires de Mademoiselle de Montpensier* in *Nouvelle collection des mémoires pour servir a l'histoire de France*, ed. Michaud and Poujoulat (Paris 1850), IV, pp. 1–523 (1627–1686), at p. 281: Anne of Austria saying that her son 'n'aimoit pas les cérémonies, et qu'il voulut qu'on mangeât à son plat', a quote proffered by *Mademoiselle* in the context of an extraordinarily unceremonious *collation* (to her tastes) following a masked ball in 1658. Her remarks may be explained both by the youth of the king, and by the joyous occasion. Similar occasions were disorderly even in Louis' later years, compare the descriptions in AN O 1 822, pp. 60–63, a masked ball in 1700. On the relaxation of ceremonial or *bienséance*, see Jaeglé, *Correspondance de Madame*, I, p. 247 (11 February 1700):

> Il y a deux raisons pour lesquelles le respect disparaît de partout: la première, c'est que Monseigneur [the Dauphin] ne se soucie de rien, et quelque grandes que soient les familiarités qu'on se permet à son endroit, il n'y trouve jamais à redire. Secondement le lansquenet y est pour beaucoup aussi. On veut avoir du monde pouvant jouer gros jeu, or les gens de haute lignée ne sont pas les plus riches. On joue donc avec toute sorte de racaille, pourvue qu'ils aient de l'argent. On permet à toutes les femmes, jusqu'au femmes de chambre inclusivement, de mettre à la réjouissance, et pour qu'elles puissent rester au jeu on leur fait prendre place, des lors les femmes de qualité ne peuvent rester debout; tout le monde est donc assis, sans distinction de rang, ni de qualité! Tout est sens dessus dessous. Le roi seul a conservé la politesse. A cette unique exception près, elle est totalement banni de la cour.

the principle surely was not. The same can be said for the detailed demarcation of responsibilities between the valets of the chamber and the wardrobe, the chamber taking care of the right side, leaving the slightly less honourable left side to the wardrobe. In such cases, moreover, it is not clear what exactly was new: the detailed written accounts, or the practices themselves. Nor is it obvious that the dignified routines existing on paper were always adhered to in practice.

If the form of most domestic ceremonies was not new, were such ceremonies implemented with more strictness? The sheer quantity and the detail of the ceremonial registers convey the image of a world ruled by punctilio; of the ceremonial officers as the high priests of a rigidly ritualised order.[67] Which conclusions can we draw from the materials assembled and created by the ceremonial agents, and how can we assess the consequences of the *Verschriftlichung* of ceremony? Ceremonial expertise was most stringently invited when conflict threatened: the registers give countless details of ceremonies, but the selection of instances may have been determined by the desire to prevent and solve ceremonial disputes, leaving aside the occasions and rules that went unchallenged. This may explain long blanks and an uneven distribution of notes in the registers: when ceremony continued without excessive complication, and no great dynastic events occurred, there was no reason to take notes. The same holds true for ordinances and incidental rulings: they were not intended to describe daily habits, but to counter disorder at court. By doing so repeatedly, and in weary terms, they give us a chaotic and querulous idea of the court. On the other hand, there is no reason whatsoever to mistake prescriptive descriptions of ceremony for scenes from court life. These manuscripts, limited as they are, stay closer to the realities of the court than do the idealised descriptions to be found in print, which were close to the machinery of representation, and had no interest in disturbing details.

It does not come as a surprise that an early seventeenth-century French manuscript discussing ceremonies stressed the remaining uncertainties:

> nul ne sçait comment il doit aller, ni où il doit se mettre, aux autres royaumes, ou états les rangs sont differement exprimez et réglez, l'angleterre est la maîtresse en cette science, chacun y sçait son rang, et en France chacun porte le sien en incertitude et en la volonté du prince souvent persuadé et tourné par le conseil et ceux qui n'y entendent rien, et qui le font juger par la faveur et non par la raison. De tout temps la France a été sujette à ses disputes . . .[68]

[67] A comparison frequently found in the literature, see, for example, Evelyne Lever in the introduction to Breteuil's *Mémoires*, p. 31.

[68] AN K 1712 21, 'Mémoire pour les rangs des princes et grands', quotation on p. 5; a copy of the same text can be found in BN MS naf 7236, p. 221ff. A positive evaluation later added in the margin of the manuscript attributes the text to Villeroy (Nicolas de Neufville, seigneur de Villeroy, 1542–1617) Henry IV's *sécrétaire d'état aux affaires étrangères*, but this seems dubious.

A generation later, Denys Godefroy, continuing his father's ceremonial works, seemed well aware of the marginal success of earlier attempts to create an unambiguous rule for precedence in ceremonies and elsewhere. The goal of his 1649 work, he noted in the *avertissement au lecteur*: 'n'est pas autre que pour servir à appaiser & terminer tant de debats qui surviennent chaque jour en matières de preseances'.[69] While we have reason to doubt the conspicuous success of the English or other nations in solving the problem of precedence, we can readily accept that conflicts for precedence were endemic at the French court. Denys Godefroy had assembled abundant materials for a third volume, but the outcry of those aggrieved by his delineation of *rangs et préséances* in the first two volumes of the 1649 *cérémonial* kept him from pursuing his ambition.[70]

Ceremonial strife hardly disappeared with the advent of Louis XIV. The Sun King's courtiers, we read in almost all contemporary descriptions, tended to be obedient and deferential towards their master, in sharp contrast with the insolence and open rebellion prevailing in critical phases of the regency or Louis XIII's reign. Well-placed courtiers could find their positions threatened when they misbehaved, and exile was more than once forced upon them. The reduction of the numbers of court officers, finally successful in Louis XIV's personal reign, well fits such observations: we have every reason to expect more deferential and orderly procedures in other domains of court life. Yet the battles for precedence continued unabated, at all levels of the courtly hierarchy. Frequently, they were caused by an opaque division of labour among the king's servants. Thus, in 1667 the *officiers du gobelet* complained that the *courreur de vin* had served the king a *collation* in the gardens, whereas he could only do so outside the palace grounds. The *courreur*, moreover, had to give precedence to the *conducteur de la haquenée* when the king desired a more substantial outdoor meal. In the chamber, the rights of the *bouche* and the chamber staffs in serving the dinner *à petit couvert* could lead to conflicts.[71]

Among the masters of ceremonies, Nicolas de Sainctot stands out. The notes of Louis XIV's master of ceremonies, moreover, recur in printed works that determined much of our image of the court. Did his unflagging dedication improve the situation? Saint-Simon saw in Sainctot an obsequious upstart hardly qualified to mix with the ranks of the great French nobles, and derided his activities, pointing to the 'friponnerie avérée de ses registres, qu'il fut forcé d'avouer et de réparer'.[72] The little duke, whose far more palatable literary

[69] *Cérémonial François*, 1649, *avertissement*, iii. [70] Godefroy-Ménilglaise, *Les savants Godefroy*, p. 167.

[71] BN Clair 814, p. 843: Règlement entre les officiers du Gobelet et le courreur de vin. Le 17 Mars 1667: the *courreur* had the right only to serve 'les colations que sa Majesté faisoit aux chasses, et autres lieux ou il ny avois que des viandes froides'; AN O 1 751, no. 81, adds that while the *courreur* served a small collation, the *conducteur de la haquenée* would have the right to transport a more substantial meal. See BN Clair 814, p. 819, for an earlier 'Règlement entre les valets de Chambre et les officiers du Gobelet le 4eme jour d'octobre 1643'.

[72] Saint-Simon, *Mémoires*, I, p. 93 (1692); V, pp. 5–20 (1698); XXIV, pp. 10–12 (1713) quote on p. 11. Luynes, who (states Boislisle in Saint-Simon, *Mémoires*, V, 19–20, n. 3) possessed a copy of texts by Sainctot, was also critical: see *Mémoires*, II, p. 119, and VIII, p. 345: the registers were contradictory, and the relevant details were not well described.

reminiscences reveal a spirit as punctilious and as litigious as that of Nicolas de Sainctot himself, founded his ambitions upon his rank, whereas Sainctot used his function to further his career. Sainctot's registers show an impressive range of quarrels he himself had with other officers at court, including an 'exempt' of the *gardes du corps*, the *grand maître des cérémonies*, his co-*introducteurs*, and later even ambassadors.[73] Such disputes were no exception: the demarcation of competences and rights between grand master and master of ceremonies; between these and the *introducteurs*, and between the *introducteurs*, frequently caused troubles, and led to new rulings.[74] Yet Sainctot's belligerent attitude was remarkable even within this general context. He made it a point of honour to better his superior, and Saint-Simon was probably right when he claimed that Sainctot sold his office partly because of a notorious 1690 quarrel with his superior Blainville.[75]

Blainville had ventured to assert more strongly the hierarchical difference between the charges of grand master and master. Thus, he suggested that only the grand master took orders from the king himself, and that the master and aide for ceremonies waited for his orders; that the master served as his lieutenant only; that the difference in rank had to be visible in dress, position in ceremony, and tasks; and finally that the remuneration should be commensurate with this clear hierarchy. Sainctot's lengthy reply, heavily larded with quotes and descriptions from previous ceremonial authors, trumped Blainville.[76] The king's decision implied a middle way, granting some territory to the grand master while still basically maintaining the relative independence of the master. Thus, Trabouillet's 1712 *Etat* stated that:

> Le Grand Maître & le Maître assistant à toutes les Cérémonies, & exercent concurrement toutes les fonctions: ils sont assis et marchent sur même ligne, le Maître étant à la gauche du Grand Maître des Cérémonies.[77]

The documentary legacy of Sainctot's litigations does not tell us much about the level of ceremony at court, yet it shows that the agents of ceremony had their own agenda, not invariably supportive of their master's representation.

[73] See AN KK 1431 pp. 63/335–101/373; AN O 1 753, pp. 197–256, on the major quarrel between Sainctot and Blainville; AN O 1 753, pp. 347–348, on Bonneuil's widow; BN MS f 16633, fols. 207–208 with St Mory, exempt 'des gardes du corps'; AN K 1712, fols. 4–5, gives a list of quarrels between masters of ceremony and introducteurs; Dangeau, *Journal*, VII, p. 60, reports a dispute between Sainctot and Breteuil; see Saint-Simon, *Mémoires*, XXIV, p. 11, n. 3, for the discussion of Sainctot's 1695 attempt to outdo the ambassadors, and his memoir in AN K 1326, 9, and BN MS f 6679, pp. 402–411. Quarrels between grand master and master, and between them and the *introducteur* were a structural phenomenon, recurring as frequently in the sources as the *règlements* to prevent them.

[74] For example, KK 1431, fol. 48: 'De charge, fonction et rang des introducteur des ambassadeurs, et fonction du grand maitre des ceremonies ou de celuy qui sert en son absence aux receptions et audiences des ambassadeurs chez le roy et la reine'; fol. 60: 'Reglement du Roy pour les differents qui peuvent survenir entre les grands maitres et maitre des ceremonies et les conducteurs des ambassadeurs'.

[75] Saint-Simon, *Mémoires*, XXIV, p. 12 (1713): 'il eut tant de discussions avec Blainville du temps qu'il étoit grand maître des cérémonies, auquel il tachoit toujours de s'égaler, qu'il fut contraint de vendre sa charge de maître des cérémonies'.

[76] Sainctot versus Blainville: see AN KK 1431, fols. 63/335–101/373, and O 1 753, pp. 197–256.

[77] I, pp. 644–646.

The ambivalence of the sources give special relevance to the incidental confessions of the ceremonial agents themselves. Louis-Nicolas Le Tonnelier, baron de Breteuil, sharing the charge of *introducteur* with Sainctot, complained that the French court: 'est celle de toute l'Europe où on a le moins d'attention aux cérémonies, et ou les officiers de la maison du Roi s'appliquent le moins à les savoir'. His task as *introducteur*, moreover, apparently was far from easy: 'dans la plupart de nos fonctions, je chemine en aveugle, et je ne sais pas trop quelle route je dois tenir pour la plus sre'.[78] Sainctot, as could be expected, was unwilling to share his experiences with his new colleague, and may have been waiting to profit from Breteuil's mistakes. Breteuil decided to support his perplexing tasks by keeping an accurate record of his activities. His statements are echoed by other ceremonial officers. Halfway through the eighteenth century, *introducteur* Verneuil resorted to the same strategy. In the dedication of his *Journal*, he explained why he thought it wise to keep track of his activities:

> Je dois l'idée du travail dont ces mémoires sont le fruit à l'expérience que j'ai faite de l'embarras où mon père s'est trouvé plusieurs fois dans l'exercice de la charge d'introducteur des ambassadeurs par le peu d'éclaircissements qu'il a tirés des mémoires de ses prédécesseurs... Quoique j'aie étudié avec exactitude tout ce qui avait rapport au cérémonial concernant les ambassadeurs, je ne me sens point la capacité nécessaire pour vouloir prescrire sur cela des règles.[79]

The abundance of memoirs could not lead even specialists through the dense forest of ceremonial conventions, and their repeated attempts to fill the gap by adding personal notes may only have augmented the bewilderment of successors. The proliferation of ceremonial texts, conventionally seen as evidence for the consummate state of the ceremonialised court, can better be understood as an indication of lingering confusion. Or can we read the perplexity of the ceremonialists as the consequence of ever-increasing levels of ceremoniousness, forcing them to include the most minute details of court life? Reading Luynes' memoirs, written a generation after those of Dangeau or Sourches, one does get the impression that day-to-day detail had become more important. Yet this change did not entail greater consensus or clarity. In a discussion of the presentation of the Evangel to the king, a highly traditional and conspicuously ritualised act, Luynes could still argue that: 'On a aucune attention à écrire les faits qui se passent journellement, et l'on oublie souvent les faits qui se sont passées l'année d'auparavant; à plus forte raison ignore-t-on les faits anciens'.[80] Similar instances in his memoirs mention conflicts about the arrangements of major officers behind the sovereign's chair, or the parallel details in the chapel.[81]

[78] Breteuil cited in Dangeau, *Journal*, XVIII, appendices, p. 344; Breteuil, *Mémoires*, pp. 30–31.
[79] Quoted in Boppe, *Les introducteurs*, p. 9.
[80] Luynes, *Mémoires*, IX, pp. 73–75, in the context of a discussion of the presentation of the Evangel to the king (quote on p. 74).
[81] See the instances cited in Luynes, *Mémoires*, I, pp. 215, 261; II, pp. 56–57, 70.

Had even such familiar matters to be contested over and over again? In August 1754, Luynes wearily reported new quarrels over the arrangement of the officers behind the chair of king and queen – the protagonists, moreover, did not consult ceremonial registers, but asked Luynes' permission to use his journal in support of their contentions.[82] Halfway through the eighteenth century, the comte de Charolais, younger brother of M. le Duc and for more than a decade replacing the latter's minor son as acting *grand maître de France*, wrote a sharply critical letter to the master of ceremonies, Desgranges, chastising him for misconstruing the position of the *princes du sang* in ceremony – a topic heatedly debated at least since the sixteenth century. The ensuing little correspondence well conveys the continuity of the problems.[83] As to the levels of *Verschriftlichung*: an 'ancien cérémonial des princes du sang' in the archives of the grand master of ceremonies includes the intriguing marginal note that it was provided by the same comte de Charolais, stating without further confirmation that that it had been dictated by Louis XIV.[84]

Lesser staff was apparently not always able or eager to strictly adhere to the rules their superiors found so hard to implement. The *premiers gentilshommes*' registers repeatedly stress that *huissiers* had to be told before each new quarter that they should not to admit unknown persons to the king's chamber. Besongne's 1687 *état* adds a justifying note to the rules for the *entrées* that:

Il est du devoir de l'Huissier de demander le nom & la qualité à ceux qu'il ne connoit pas: & lorsqu'il le demande, qui que ce soit ne le doit trouver mauvais: parce qu'il est de sa charge de connoître tous ceux qu'il laisse entrer.

We find ushers being pushed aside by haughty courtiers.[85] Nor were the ushers the only servants faced with the pressure of persons striving to be admitted; the arrangements for a Versailles *bal masqué* in January 1700 show that great pains were taken to shield the festivities from unwanted participants, because the *garçons* of the *chateau* were apt to admit people through secondary entrances. A more remarkable entry in the register of the *premiers gentilshommes* recommends that the *huissier* take care that no stranger stand behind the king's *chaise* during supper, another points out that no *placets* should be offered to the king by his chamber staff. All such pious wishes are familiar from a range of earlier ordinances; they testify to the persistence of the problems.[86]

82 Luynes, *Mémoires*, XIII, pp. 323–325, 440.

83 AN K 1712, nos. 16 and 18, the first containing a letter from Charolais to Maurepas denying the *dauphin*'s right to be escorted by *princes du sang* dated 26 October 1746; the second containing the correspondence (copies) between Charolais and Desgranges discussing the right of the princes to stand near the king on his estrade (12 December 1757 and 24 December 1757). See also 19, 20, 23, and 28, likewise concerning princes and *sang royal*, now clashing among others with electors and archdukes – two other ranks not wholly comfortable within the emerging two-layered system of sovereigns and subjects.

84 AN O 1 1042 'papiers du grand maître des cérémonies', no. 63 pp. [1–7]: 'La copie de ce cérémonial a été donné par M. le Comte de Charolois, qui a dit qu'il avoit été dicté par le Roy Louis 14'.

85 Luynes, *Mémoires*, XIII, pp. 440–441.

86 AN O 1 822, pp. 12–13, 60–63; Besongne's 1687 *état*, pp. 202–203.

Was ceremony a less troubling pursuit in Vienna? The Austrian Habsburgs had a reputation for austere ceremony. Palaces, rooms, decorations, and dress may have been less brilliant than those of the Bourbon court, yet visitors were impressed by the dignified and aloof ceremonies. The initiative of 1651–1652, most notably the institution of the office for ceremony and its protocol, gave the court a more reliable framework for ceremony. The functional ranks of *Räte* and *Kämmerer*, and their internal hierarchies following dates of nomination, provided a relatively stable basis for ceremony at court. The *neue Fürsten* could disturb ceremonial order when they demanded recognition of their superiority within this system of ranks, overruling the seniority of their fellow chamberlains or councillors. Scions of several princely families had declined to ask for confirmation of their rank as chamberlain after Charles VI's death; their temporary disaffection was appeased in 1745 by granting princely chamberlains precedence over their senior colleagues.[87] On the whole, such disputes were less persistent than in France, and the share of diplomats and foreign princes – notably those from the imperial territories – was proportionately larger.[88] Nevertheless, the impressive number of *Referate* and *Extracte* in the *Zeremonialakten*, discussing the same themes over and over again, conveys a sense of uncertainty not far removed from that expressed by the French ceremonial agents.

When we find explicit statements about the level of implementation of ceremonial measures, they are pervaded by the same weariness recurring in the instructions. After the accession of Charles VI, the rules for entering the series of rooms in the state apartment were revised in a lengthy and complicated process. Two major problems were noted: the system of ranks never was either clear cut or universally acceptable, and any solution would be challenged. On the other hand, whatever the order finally proposed, the implementation of the rules threatened to be submerged in the day-to-day routines. How could the ushers recognise any person? As in the French system of *entrées*, they were undoubtedly supposed to bar the way to those unknown, asking their name and waiting for the chamberlain's decision. Yet would they dare to confront haughty noblemen in this way? How could they check those intent upon crossing the hierarchical borders, using their conversation or relationship to higher-ranking persons, or proceeding quietly from one entrance to the screen shielding the next entrance, and slipping through unnoticed? The topography of the apartment, such as the existence of a corridor and entry for staff, brought more problems. Most troubling, however, was the discouraging experience that any order, whether

[87] Khevenhüller, *Tagebuch*, II, pp. 43–45 (April 1745), pp. 116–117 (6 October 1746), p. 154 (May 1747). When Khevenhüller mentions trouble or Disgusto, we usually find either *Fürsten*, or foreign princes and diplomats.

[88] Compare Winkelbauer, *Fürst und Fürstendiener*, pp. 288–320, for hierarchical conflicts with the *Fürsten* in the first half of the seventeenth century; and for the following period Susanne Claudine Pils, 'Hof/Tratsch. Alltag bei Hof im ausgehenden 17. Jahrhundert', *WRGB* 53 (1998), pp. 77–99, with a discussion of *Rangstreitigkeiten* at pp. 96–97; Goloubeva, *Glorification of Emperor Leopold I*, chapter 3 on pp. 71–73, confirms the preponderance of the German and Italian princes, and diplomats in ceremonial strife.

rigid or flexible, would slowly crumble in everyday practice. The committee pointedly asked the emperor whether he wanted the 'neue Ordnung mit allem rigor, oder aber mit mehrerer indulgence und nachsehung eingerichtet'. It seems likely that in most cases, rigour was the intention, indulgence the inevitable practice, and disorder the consequence – offering a starting point for yet another revision.[89]

Thirty years later, Khevenhüller more than once deplored the complete decline of ceremony and courtly forms. Grave initial troubles kept Maria Theresa from paying attention to ceremony, a neglect which inevitably led to 'Unordnungen und Mißbräuch', not to be mended easily. The temporary loss of the imperial title further complicated the changeover from Charles VI's court to that of Maria Theresa; nor was the young court much tempted by the sombre forms of its predecessor.[90] In 1745, Khevenhüller fretfully announced measures to limit entry into the *Retirada*, as the habitual restrictions were wholly neglected by the court. In July 1746, he stated that even the recovery of imperial dignity – Francis Stephen had been elected emperor in September 1745 – had hardly improved the deplorable state of *decorum* at court, notwithstanding the continual effort of court dignitaries. War and reform further changed the aspect of the court. The military presence at court, recognised but marginal in earlier *Kammerordnungen*, became much more notable. In 1751 military dress was accepted at court, and in the years following military ranks were fitted into the chamberlain–councillor hierarchy.[91]

Obviously, when Joseph II from 1765 onwards received more responsibilities, Khevenhüller complained perennially about his new sovereign, 'welcher alle alte Gebrauch für eitel Préjugés haltet'. In 1766, Joseph took communion on Maundy Thursday without the habitual *Mantelkleid*, and in the next year he declined to wash the feet of the 12 poor men, who had to be sent away with two ducats.[92] Maria Theresa convinced him to change his ways, and we find the *pedilavium* explicitly noted for most years of his reign – with only 1787, 1788, and 1789 as notable exceptions. In 1774 Khevenhüller reported the absence of the *Hofstaat* in the Corpus Christi procession, a fact much commented upon, and a bad omen for ceremony at court.[93] It seems to have been quite as difficult to uproot the basic forms of ceremony, as it had earlier been to uphold the

89 HHStA ZA Prot 8, fol. 266v; see fol. 273r 'daß Eür KM die . . . Cammerordnung, mit Abstellung der zeither darunter eingeschlichenen confusionen von nun an von neuen eingeführt, und auffs genaueste beobachtet haben wollen', versus the preceding remarks on fol. 270v: the earlier *Ordnung* was 'zerfallen' because it had not been implemented, and 'es mit diesen Unordnung und confusionen so wheit kommen daß ein jeder, wo es ihme nur eingefallen, oder gefällig gewesen, indistincte hingelaufen ist'. Compare the Saxon envoy's remarks in 1651 cited above: 'in demevorhero fast menniglich indifferenter in die antecamera hinein geloffen, aniezo aber alle in ein buch verzeichnet werden'; Hauptstaatsarchiv Dresden, Loc. 8241/1 (Des kursächs. Residentensam kaiserl. Hofe Schreiben 1648–52), Bl. 181 (29 March 1651).

90 Khevenhüller, *Tagebuch*, II, pp. 187–188 (November 1743); p. 16 (16 March 1745); pp. 102–103 (July 1746).

91 Hochedlinger, 'Mars Ennobled', pp. 151–152; HHStA ÄZA K 45, *Kammerordnung* (20 November 1745).

92 Khevenhüller, *Tagebuch*, VI, pp. 231–232 (April 1766). 93 *Ibid.*, p. 29 (9 June 1774).

demands of ceremony.[94] In Joseph's years, court costume changed, the sequence of religious observances became less dense, galas were abolished except for the gala on the first day of the year. Yet other members of the dynasty partly took over Joseph's role, and the demands of diplomacy secured the maintenance of basic ceremonies. Indeed the *Zeremonialprotokolle* suggest relative continuity.[95] Courtiers were apt to find new forms of distinction in dress and deportment. The *Kämmerer* were granted the right to wear the symbol of their charge, the golden key, on their coats, an innovation later copied for the *Truchseße*, who obtained the right to do so with a newly invented symbol of their charge: two staffs.[96] Only towards the end of 1787 did Joseph more clearly seek to break the bonds of ceremony by abolishing a range of forms he regarded as 'Spanish' influences: the *baise-main* or *Handkuß*, the compliment on bended knee, and official *Hofkleidung* or court dress for the *Appartements*.[97] Most of his measures would not survive him.

Domestic routines did not belong to the field of the ceremonial agents; they remained largely within the purview of the relevant court dignitaries. Can they still be pictured as the ingenious tool for manipulation, following the classic image? In innumerable settings, the king could multiply small graces, distributing them at will – a policy explicitly embraced by Louis XIV in a well-known digression on the distinctions attached to rank:

> c'est d'ailleurs un des plus visible effets de notre puissance, que de donner quand il nous plaît un prix infini à ce qui de soi-même n'est rien . . . d'excellens hommes ont blamé les derniers temps de n'en avoir pas assez; il est à propos, non seulement d'user de ceux que nos pères ont introduites, quand nous le pouvons, mais même d'en inventer de nouvelles, pourvu que ce soit avec jugement, avec dignité, comme vous verrez ailleurs que j'ai taché de vous en montrer l'exemple.[98]

Domestic ceremonies could serve as the backdrop for such policies. Did the king methodically use the *entrées*, the presentation of *serviette, bougeoir*, and

94 *Ibid.*, p. 207, *Mantelkleid* abolished, Ulfeld's fruitless attempt to save it, pp. 518–522, n. 190. Compare Joseph's later decision p. 538, n. 229: 'Ich werde bey dieser Audientz in Campagne Kleid sambt denen Hof Chargen erscheinen, bei weiteren sich zu ereignenden fällen werde ich schon das erforderliche befehlen'.

95 ZA Prot 32–37 include most of the familiar categories in the register, nor do the basic descriptions differ as much as Khevenhüller's complaints suggest. Compare ÖNB cod. 12955–12958 'Cérémoniale' for the last decades of the eighteenth century, with the habitual Holy Week ceremonies, 40-hour devotions, etc.

96 Khevenhüller, *Tagebuch*, VII, pp. 7, 14, and p. 233, n. 27. Compare ÄZA K 70, 28 and 30 June 1765: an earlier decision to allow the chamberlains to carry the key in their *boutonnière* when not wearing the *Mantelkleid*; and Khevenhüller, *Tagebuch*, VI, p. 156, where Khevenhüller disapprovingly notes that *Toisonisten*, knights of the Golden Fleece, carried their chain during their ride to the church, to compensate for the absence of the dignified *Mantelkleid*.

97 ÄZA K 91: Letter from Joseph to high steward Starhemberg, 30 December 1786, fol. 1–4: 'Expedirt an sämtliche hofstellen, dann obersten Hofämter', 2 January 1787, and duly reported in ZA Prot, 37, fol. 50. On fol. 207, and in ZA Prot 38, fols. 14, 97, we again find the *pedilavium*.

98 Grouvelle, *Œuvres de Louis XIV* (Paris 1806), I, p. 143, compare the often cited passage in Dreyss, *Mémoires de Louis XIV*, II, p. 15, a well-formulated summary of the impact of conspicuous demonstration of *rangs et séances* on a populace willing to be convinced by the senses only. Reputation, rank, and decorum are the keywords of the memoirs, recurring in many key passages.

chemise? In addition to the king's immediate relatives, only those responsible for the *chambre*, the *chambellan*, the *premiers gentilshommes*, and the *maîtres de la garderobe* had functional access to the most intimate settings in the *chambre*; the *princes du sang* were granted the right of access by the *entrées familières*, introduced after Louis XIV's death. *Monseigneur* had to plead with his father to invite Condé father and son, and Conti, to the Trianon or Marly.[99] Thus, outside the ceremonies connected to the table, even the Condé *grand maître* was dependent upon the king's graces allowing him more private access; *a fortiori*, the same held true for the Conti, who did not hold high office at court during the larger part of Louis XIV's reign.[100] Nor was rank always decisive for special vestiary distinctions such as the *justaucorps à brevet*, for invitations to Marly, or in Louis XV's days to *petits soupers*. Before being eligible for the *petits soupers*, however, one had to be presented to the king, an honour usually reserved to those who could prove their nobility to the king's genealogist.

For most ceremonies, as well as for the less public scenes of court life, rank remained the most fundamental criterion. The *tabourets* were the consequence of princely or ducal rank: they could not be withheld, but the king rarely could grant a *tabouret de grâce*. If a lady received this right by the king's personal favour, however, she would henceforth hold ducal rank, as did Mme de Pompadour after 1752, although she still styled herself *marquise*. The right to present the *chemise* during the *lever* or *coucher*, or the *serviette* during meals was granted to the highest-ranking person present. Only the presentation of the *bougeoir*, relevant when *lever* and *coucher* took place in dark hours, was explicitly left to the king's discretion.

It is not untrue, but certainly limited, to picture the endemic quarrels among courtiers as an ideal opportunity for the king to meddle with their ranks. When in March 1688 the *premier gentilhomme* and the *grand maître de la garderobe* disputed the right to hand the king his coat, Dangeau tells us, 'Le roi ne voulut point décider, et ne prit le surtout des mains d'aucun des deux'.[101] Such conflicts, recurring frequently, were uncomfortable and hardly brought superb chances for manipulation. Nor did the king's judgement always prevail. Luynes reports that Livry, *premier maître d'hôtel*, entered the cabinet against the express orders of Richelieu, the serving *premier gentilhomme* and the king – to Luynes' regret, Louis XV left Livry's transgression unpunished, annulling his previous decision

99 Dangeau, *Journal*, II, p. 107 (11 February 1688), and Saint-Simon's more sweeping addition. Dangeau more often mentions *Monseigneur* asking graces for the princes, compare, for example, I, p. 142 (27 March 1685).

100 See, for example, Dangeau, *Journal*, I, p. 350 (15 June 1686): 'Le roi donna les grandes entrées à M. le Duc, qui les souhaitoit depuis longtemps, et qui a été fort sensible à cette grace là', and the lengthy addition of Saint-Simon on the same page. The marriages between the princes and the *legitimées* were the most common ground for the granting of the *grandes entrées*.

101 Dangeau, *Journal*, II, p. 123 (25 March 1688): 'Il y eut une contestation à Saint-Cyr (Salut) entre M. de la Rochefoucault, grand maître de la garderobe, et le marquis de Gesvres, premier gentilhomme de la chambre, à qui donneroit le surtout au roi. Quand le roi est hors de sa chambre, c'est au premier gentilhomme de la chambre à lui donner son manteau ou sa casaque; M. de la Rochefoucault prétend qu'un surtout c'est un justaucorps.'

and eroding his authority.[102] When Louis XVI and Marie-Antoinette wanted to simplify the rituals surrounding their young child, their plans were thwarted by the opposition of Mme de Guéménée, *gouvernante des enfants de France*, and in the end nothing changed.[103] Courtiers, clearly, had their own agendas in ceremonial matters.

Saint-Simon's presentation of the Sun King's astute manipulations cannot universally be discarded. It was highly relevant in all situations where the king – or any of his fellow monarchs – had the right to grant or withhold special favours. Leopold, not a manipulative character, would recognise the impact of invitations to *Wirtschaften*, sleigh rides, private hunts, or *Kammerfesten*, as well as he could see the attraction of the Golden Fleece. Yet even here, respect for established rank was among the rulers' necessary considerations, although their efforts in this direction were not invariably appreciated. Khevenhüller relates in January 1748, after hasty invitations for earlier sleigh rides had given rise to protests among princes, councillors, and their widows, all such dignitaries and their widows were meticulously invited. This led to even greater problems, as many widows perceived the invitation to such an occasion for couples as a crude mockery of their deprivation.[104] While the exclusivity of *Kammerfesten* and *Toisonfesten* guaranteed the prestigious nature of these occasions, the same may not invariably have applied to the sleigh rides or *Wirtschaften*. We have examples where Charles VI ordered several of his chamberlains to take part in a *Bauernhochzeit*, simply to fill the ranks; high court officers and knights of the Golden Fleece were interested only in the more exclusive occasions, chamberlains had to establish their place, and could not be unduly selective.[105]

Access to the ruler inevitably figured among the graces a ruler could distribute, as it indicated favour, rank, and proximity to benefits. Yet rulers were interested above all in maintaining a dignified and undisturbed ceremonial order at court, nor would they easily engage in tactics potentially harmful to their stature as hub of the ceremonial universe. Could they systematically be so shrewd and detached that they could play the roles of masterminds distant contemporaries and later observers so often attribute to them? It will not do to construe Saint-Simon's examples of the ruler's manipulations as the major motivation for a set of habits that in practice remained firmly based on rank. Nor is it helpful to depict the incidental use of ruses in the domestic *mise-en-scène* as the everyday rule, forgetting the fact that the ruler, too, needed a level of companionship and comfort in the more sheltered moments of court life. Indeed, the access granted

[102] Luynes, *Mémoires*, XIII, pp. 440–441.
[103] *Journal de l'abbé de Véri*, II, pp. 162, 171. Compare Louis XIV's *de facto* abolition of the charge of master of ecclesiastical ceremonies after the opposition of the other ceremonial officers.
[104] Khevenhüller, *Tagebuch*, II, p. 204 (January 1748): 'ja, eine erst unlängst gewordene Wittib brache sogar in Thränen aus, gleich ob mann mit ihr und ihrem neuerlichen Verlust nur ein Gespött treiben wolte, also zwar, daß mann alle Mühe gehabt, ihr Raison capiren zu machen'.
[105] Pecar, 'Ökonomie der Ehre', pp. 207–214.

to the highest servants was the supreme benefit, the advantage of belonging to an inner circle that was closest to the fountain of honour, an ideal path to intimacy and friendship – yet never a guarantee. Contemporaries gave as the first rationale for ceremony the collective demonstration of the hierarchy vis-à-vis a populace that was less susceptible to other forms of discourse. They tended to present court nobles as the participants, not as the audience, and surely not as the victims, of ceremony. This picture may be too simple, as the audiences for ceremony differed according to the occasion, but it is more plausible than the habitual overstatement of manipulation. Ceremonial graces, however, could and would be used to consolidate or redefine the system of ranks. If a court was indeed a meeting place of high-ranking visitors from the realm, it tended to develop into a major battlefield of rank, allowing the ruler to serve as arbiter and judge. Whatever the powers of king or emperor, such policies could never be executed in disregard of commonly accepted hierarchies: Louis and Leopold were keen on granting their loyal servants their due, but carefully distinguished between appropriate rights and additional graces. If they used their position as the arbiter of ceremonial conflict, they would mostly do so by asking their ceremonial officers to scan their records for earlier examples, and follow the logic indicated there.[106]

The fact that the bedchamber in France was more public than it was in Vienna made its rituals more susceptible to machinations on the king's part: without an audience such actions made less sense. Yet there were other, more important grounds for the *entrées* than these exceptional tricks. Louis XIV, residing in relatively open and crowded palaces, wanted the rank of the major participants in ceremonies to stand out for less elevated spectators, and the *entrées* well suited this purpose. Visiting grandees, particularly crowned heads or their accredited personal representatives, moreover, would demand a place in domestic ritual that befitted their standing, roughly conforming to the practices of their own, usually more secluded courts. They would be loath to accept an undifferentiated *pêle-mêle* arrangement when they came to pay their respects – only when this allowed them to interact freely with those higher placed, would it have been an enviable opportunity. The increasing presence of diplomats, who habitually formed part of the everyday court life instead of sticking to the bare minimum of their designated tasks, undoubtedly strengthened the sense of permanent representation in court life. The intensified presentation in print of the court's routines, and its reputation among travellers, moreover, had created a pattern

[106] The Viennese sources clearly indicate this, but we find the same mentality in France, see, for example, AN KK 1448, fol. 231: Colbert asks the master of ceremonies to write a memoir on the ceremonies following the death of Madame in 1626, allowing the king to judge the current 'differend survenu entre madame la duchesse de Noailles et monsieur de Brancaz'. In 1690, the *Europische Mercurius*, I, pp. 213–215; II, pp. 24–25, reported at length the confusions caused in France by the untimely death of the *dauphine*, and noted that the desperate search for a previous similar instance went back up to 1446.

that had to be obeyed to a certain extent. Louis, highly sensitive to anything that could either enhance or menace his reputation, would respect that logic.

The domestic ceremonies regulating access were further differentiated and refined in the reign of Louis XV. Luynes' digressions on the *entrées*, *petits soupers*, and other niceties to be found in the sources, such as the right to attend the *poudré du roi*, seem closer to the image habitually given of Versailles in its heyday than are the simpler descriptions to be found in the sources of Louis XIV's age, and the same holds true for the *honneurs de la cour* connected to presentation, including the right to enter the king's *carrosse*.[107] Moreover, we also find frequent discussions of dinner parties, balls, or other pleasures and *raffinements* of court life. The sociable, half-public setting of court life looms larger in eighteenth-century descriptions than in those of the preceding century; conversely, the traditional heritage of dynastic state ceremonies and religious feasts had become somewhat less dominant. These traditional forms of ceremony, moreover, were increasingly subject to criticism and mockery. The strengthening of the intermediate forms in the continuum between intimacy and display changed the focus and definition of ceremony, bringing it closer to polished social mores, or brilliant style. In Louis XV's years, the domestic setting became more refined, and was more closely observed. Yet by that time, the relationship between king and court nobles had again markedly changed. Louis XV may have used such artifices as a defence against court nobles ruling him as much as he ruled them. Yet Luynes and most other witnesses frequently deplored the king's indecisiveness, or his lack of *fermeté* in implementing his decisions, ceremonial as well as 'political'. Our conventional image of the Sun King's court took form in the reign of Louis XV; in retrospect it can be likened to a pastiche, including elements from various periods, joined together to present a scenery that never actually existed.

Having established the outlines of ceremony, I will not indulge in further haphazard archaeology of the field so dominant in contemporary sources. At a certain point, any student of ceremony at the early modern court will be confronted with a challenge not unlike that which faced the *ancien régime* guardians of ceremony. Can we conceivably establish a set of general rules for ceremony that contains solutions for most if not all potential problems? Time and again

[107] For example, Luynes, *Mémoires*, I, pp. 138–139 (*coucher*); I, pp. 262–264; II, pp. 34–35; XIII, pp. 218–219 (*entrées*); I, pp. 399–400 (*carrosses*), II, p. 70 (audiences); II, p. 194 (*petits soupers*); X, pp. 231–232 (presentations). Examples can be multiplied *ad libitum*. Disputes about the right to attend the *poudré du roi* can be found in the *premiers gentilshommes*' register of ceremonies, AN O 1 822, p. 184 (December 1740): the comte de Noailles cannot attend the 'poudré du roi'. This source, a true 'register' only from the 1750s onwards, lists the presentations, and gives descriptions of all major ceremonies in the *chambres*, an overview presented as the practices around 1688 on pp. 4–10; further description, rarely wholly consistent with these, follow, for example *entrées* on pp. 87–90 (1723), pp. 127–128 (1727); compare O 1 820 (*Grand Chambellan*) likewise with information about *chemise* no. 1, pp. 37–38; *entrées*, *débotté* etc. no. 8, pp. 1–3, listing 5 *entrées* for *lever*, adding that there were no formal *entrées* during the *coucher*; people were admitted at the *premier gentilhomme*'s discretion, both procedures inconsistent with the descriptions in O 1 822.

such efforts foundered on the rocks of unanticipated contextual detail or of a slowly changing table of ranks. Shying away from the uncertain general approach, most agents of ceremony cited ever more instances, seeking to rigidly establish conventions by multiplying examples. Yet the abundance of examples did not lighten the burden of their successors.

Comparing the courts in France and the Austrian Habsburg lands over time, it is likely that court life became more orderly at both, and evident that great ceremonies had reached a high level of codification by the seventeenth century. In Vienna, the relatively closed palace harboured a *Hofstaat* that in its frequent outings necessarily interacted with its urban environment. Versailles, a more open palace, accommodating a larger group of residents as well as visitors, had escaped from its urban confines – yet Parisians and tourists found it within their reach. The most conspicuously public moments at these courts were also the most ceremonialised instances of court life. The French court had long since offered divertissements and companionship to the elites; the Habsburg court would slowly open up after 1740, providing a setting for festivities, soirées, and dinners. Courts never became wholly ceremonial, but it is more than probable that the impact of permanent diplomacy, the availability of printed digests of domestic rules, and the increasing prevalence of a style of court life *in mezzo publico*, helped to strengthen the ceremonial side in the continuum ranging from display to intimacy.[108] Yet ceremony always fell short of the reiterated written expectations and demands of the ceremonial agents, and was always susceptible both to regressions and to the changing individual inclinations of rulers, high officers, and lower staff. The temple of ritual kingship was staffed not by automatons, but by persons of flesh and blood: the splendid image of the untouchable ceremonial ruler could in practice easily succumb to a jumble of human idiosyncrasies and ambitions.

CONCLUDING REMARKS

Studying daily life at court and the solemn ceremonies closely attached to the dynastic household, we may be surprised at the suave quality habitually attached to court life. While this fits the images emanating from the opposing but connected spheres of courtier and anti-courtier literature, the realities of life in the household of a sovereign as reflected in ordinances and decrees let us glimpse another world – possibly as querulous as the negative image, surely not as sophisticated as the idealised image suggests, and, most of all, far more human, variable, and lively. Rulers were interested in their reputation, and sought to enhance it by demanding the unswerving loyalty and dignity of their retinues. Our

[108] In *Theater, Feste und Feiern*, p. 226, Khevenhüller notes that in January 1765, the court went to theatre 'in mezzo publico'.

materials suggest that they were never quite successful. Yet the literary images clung to the court, and undoubtedly were a force in the education of courtiers and more generally nobles. In the intriguing interaction of discourse and practice, propaganda and day-to-day life, we need to take the concrete starting point more seriously than its literary emanations.

Ceremonial practices were only the relatively modest and constant nucleus of a 'fabrication' of rulership, to be discussed briefly in the last chapter of this book. A purified and embellished version of the court and its ceremonies was broadcast to an audience unaware of its less than perfect original. The most relevant innovation was the changing form of publicity, now reaching those who did not participate in, nor even witness, the events from a certain distance. Whoever had been the intended audiences of court ceremonies and festivities – court nobles as the direct participants; diplomats as the more aloof, but socially close observers; the multitudes, attracted by the spectacle and rewarded with largesse, food, and drink – now a broader and geographically dispersed group could be informed and impressed. The court may have travelled less; its representation in words and images more than compensated for this. In the long run, the Viennese court followed the same pattern, yet as in so many other respects, the main innovative impulses came only in Maria Theresa's reign. Ceremony was not necessarily as expensive a pursuit as the building of palaces. Indeed, when exceptionally high outlays characterised a ceremony – usually one of the great dynastic state ceremonies with its attendant festivals – we can invariably point to a specific rival or ambition, and a specific audience. Motives for such especially lavish ceremonies and festivals can usually be found in the competitive European sphere, or alternatively for the German princes in the geographically more limited but equally agonistic context of the *Reich*.

Clearly, ceremony did not end – not with the onset of more critical notions about religious rites or splendour at court, nor with the Revolution or the Restoration. The continuity of forms at both courts is more surprising than the adaptation to new standards, a process compressed in Vienna in the reigns of Maria Theresa and Joseph II, longer and thus less concentrated in the later eighteenth century in the French case. Yet conspicuous splendour was increasingly criticised as uneconomic, while court ceremony and the interminable troubles over precedence were regarded with reservation.[109] Malesherbes advised Louis XVI to reduce the splendour of his household, stating that 'ce n'est point par la pompe, par la magnificence, qu'un roi de France est respecté . . .'. A reduction of the court and its ceremonies, he continued, 'ne fera qu'augmenter la vénération qu'il [the king] inspira à ses sujets et aux étrangers . . .'.[110] Similar feelings

[109] Volker Bauer, *Hofökonomie. Der Diskurs über den Fürstenhof in Zeremonialwissenschaft, Hausvä terliteratur und Kameralismus* (Vienna, Cologne, and Weimar 1997); Vec, *Zeremonialwissenschaft*.

[110] AN O 1 749, no. 51, 1775 memoir.

surfaced in Maria Theresa's reign, though only after the death of Francis Stephen did they become more dominant.

Changing religious feelings made the ceremonies connected to the liturgical year, so fundamental for the household in earlier ages, seem outdated and even awkward. Much to the regret of Maria Theresa, the Jesuit order was abolished in the Austrian lands as it had been elsewhere, surely a sign of changing attitudes, highly relevant for rulers traditionally invoking divine protection and legitimation.[111] Ceremonies enacting the bond between rulers and the regions under their authority – *Erbhuldigungen* and *entrées* – likewise changed, stressing the authority of the centre rather than the rights of the periphery. Nor did the ruler do all the travelling: frequently, representatives of the regions were asked to come to the centre to pay their respects, or the ruler let himself be represented by his agents. Rulership adapted to the changes, as did the make-up of the elites in both realms. Ceremony itself, we may expect, would slowly have adapted to the emerging vocabulary of state and utility, freely mixing them with bits and pieces from the traditional religious and dynastic idiom – as it did when the dust of Revolution and empire had settled.

[111] Khevenhüller, *Tagebuch*, VIII, p. 12: Maria Theresa and Khevenhüller discussing the abolition effected in 1773, compare *Tagebuch*, VII (Vienna 1925), p. 181, 31 August 1773 (the papal bull had arrived 21 July) and pp. 256–262, n. 218.

Figure 1 A view of the stables at Versailles from the *cour des ministres*, late seventeenth century

Figure 2 Scenes from Ferdinand III's coronation as king of Hungary, 1625. Note at the top the '*ausgeworffne Müntz*' – coins distributed for the occasion

Figure 3 The Lower Austrian estates in the *Ritterstube* for Ferdinand IV's *Erbhuldigung*. Note the two canopies, one for Emperor Ferdinand III, the other for King Ferdinand IV

Figure 4 Joseph I's *Huldigungsact* in the *Ritterstube*, 1705, J. C. Hackhofer

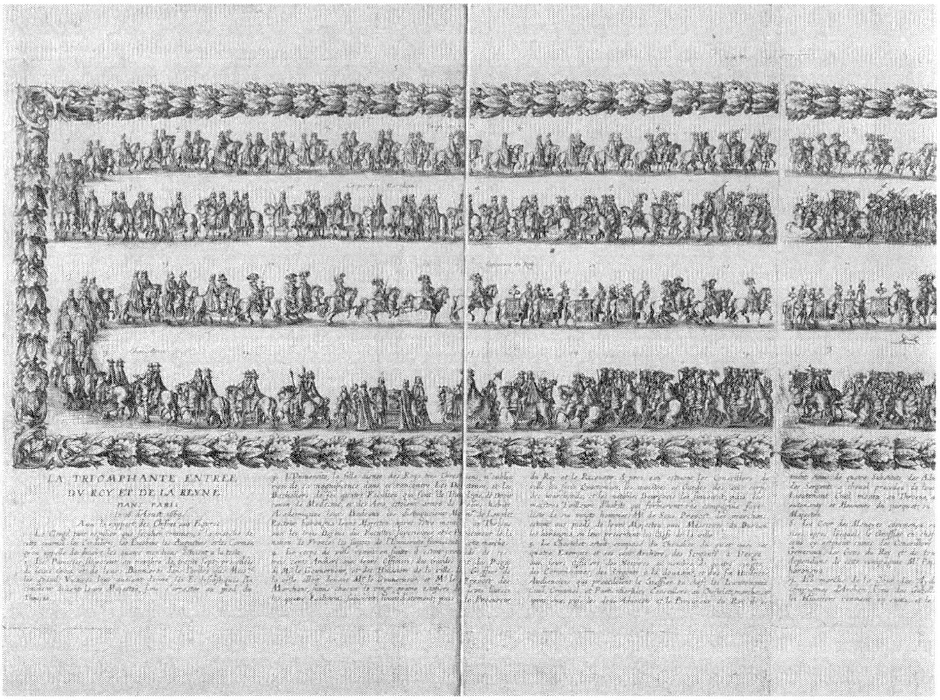

Figure 5 A typical S-form depiction of a hierarchically ordered procession, for the entry of Louis XIV and Maria Teresa into Paris, 26 August 1660, Jean le Pautre

Figure 6 *Erbhuldigung* of the Lower Austrian estates for Charles VI, a procession from the Graben to the Stephansdom. Compare Louis XIV's 1660 *entrée*

Figure 7 The great *Rossballett* in the Hofburg's inner court, January 1667, part of the series of ceremonies and entertainments to celebrate Leopold's marriage to his Spanish bride

Figure 8 Theatre in the Favorita, with designs by Burnacini

Figure 9 Fireworks, with Louis XIII and Anne of Austria in attendance, 1642, Gabriel Lebrun

Figure 10 Fireworks in Vienna, 1709

Figure 11 The great hall at the court in Vienna laid for a banquet on the occasion of the *Erbhuldigung* for Ferdinand IV in 1651, a peak year of court activities after years of war

Figure 12 Banquet given for the convalescence of Louis XIV in the *hôtel de Ville*, Paris 1687, Pierre Le Pautre

Figure 13 The emperor's table in the *Ritterstube*, *Erbhuldigung* 1705, J. C. Hackhofer

Figure 14 The entry of the Ottoman delegation into the Hofburg, February 1689

Figure 15 Public audience of the Dutch ambassador, Jacob Hop, with the young Louis XV, 1719, Wagenaar, *Vaderlandsche Historie, vervattende de geschiedenisse der vereenigde Nederlanden* (Amsterdam 1729)

Figure 16 *Das Ritterschlagen*: promotion into the order of the Golden Fleece under Rudolf II

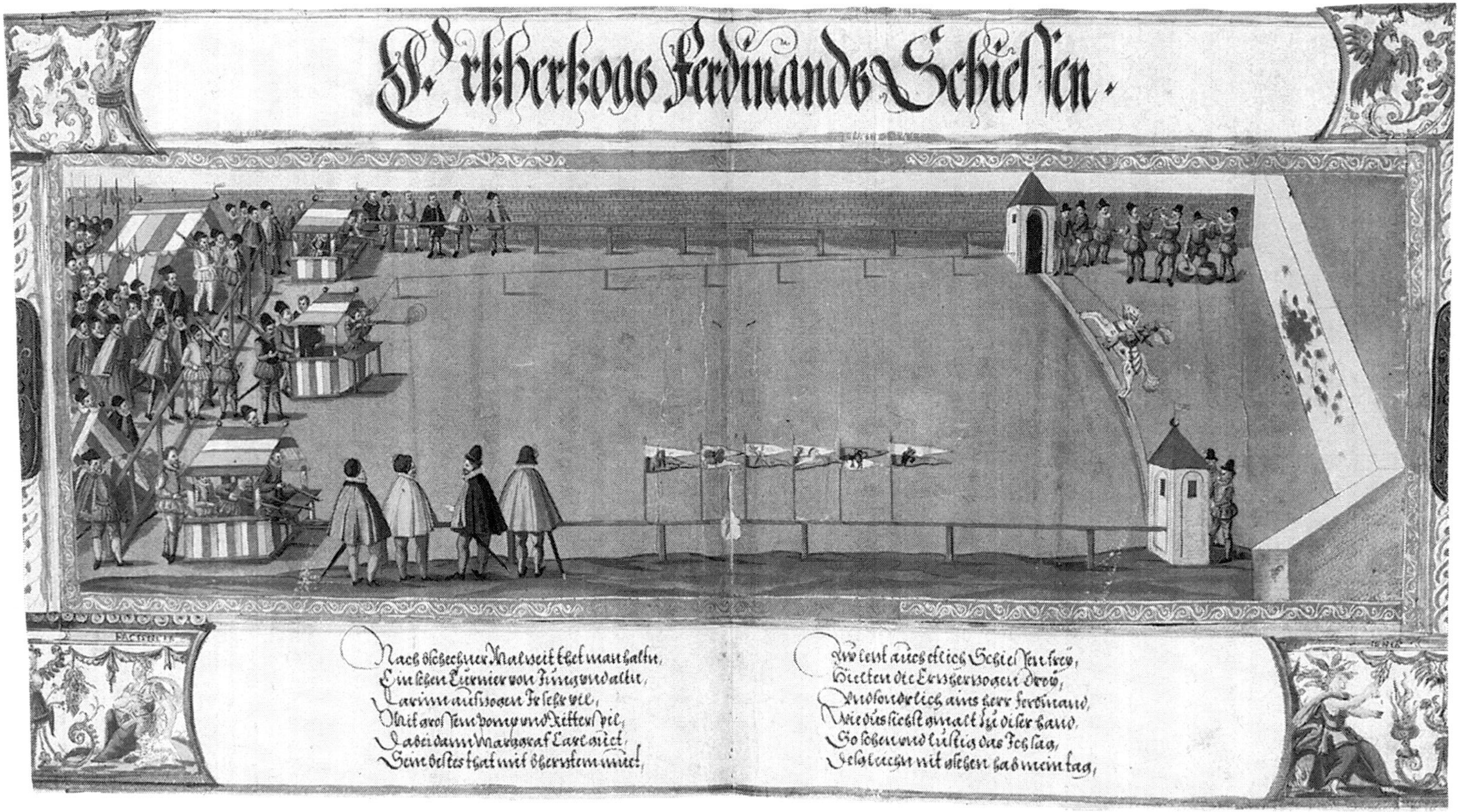

Figure 17 Shooting at targets during the festivities of the Golden Fleece, Prague 1590

Figure 18 Reception of the *chevaliers* of the *Saint-Esprit* in the chapel of Versailles, 1689, Sebastien Leclerc

Figure 19 The chapel of Versailles, with courtiers watching Louis XIV accepting the oath of Dangeau as grand master of the orders of Mont Carmel and Saint Lazare, 18 December 1695, Antoine Pezay

Figure 20 Laxenburg *c.* 1720, the spring hunting lodge of the emperors, famous for its *Reiherbeize* or heron hunt, Salomon Kleiner

Figure 21 Boar hunting in the Prater, December 1666, on the occasion of Leopold's marriage

Figure 22 Louis XIV and his entourage, hunting near Meudon, Adam Frans van der Meulen

Figure 23 The *botter* during Louis XV's hunt, 1735, with (centre group, l. to r.) the *grand écuyer*, the king, and the *premier écuyer*, J. B. Oudry

Figure 24 Louis XV's *lever*, anonymous, eighteenth century

Figure 25 A ball at the court of Henry III, 1581, to celebrate the marriage of Anne de Joyeuse and Marguerite de Lorraine

Figure 26 Louis XIV and the ladies of the court, seventeenth century, anonymous

Figure 27 Table with a collation for the court's *appartement*, late seventeenth-century Versailles, Antoine Trouvain

Figure 28 Louis XIV playing billiards during the *appartement*, late seventeenth-century Versailles, Antoine Trouvain

Figure 29 The game of Portique, late seventeenth-century Versailles, Antoine Trouvain

Figure 30 The Infanta Maria Anna and the young Leopold receiving the *schwarzen Skapulier* for his convalescence

Figure 31 Louis XIV presenting the *dauphin* to the court at Fontainebleau, 1661, Jean Le Pautre

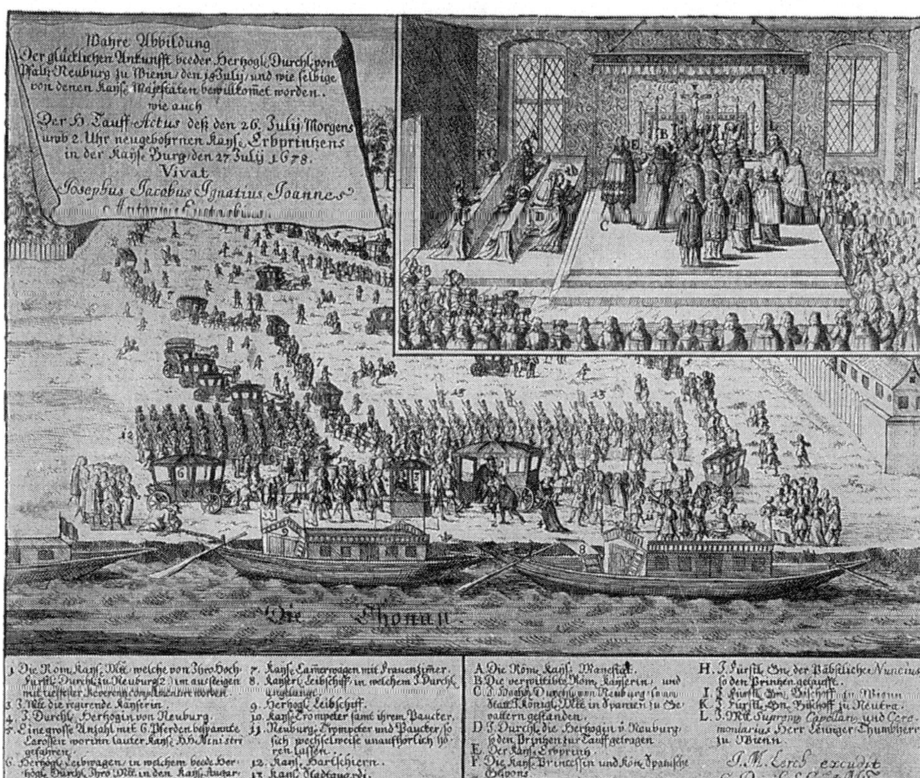

Figure 32 Joseph I's baptism in 1678, and the arrival of the duke of Pfalz-Neuburg

Figure 33 Louis XIV's death: the *chambre du trépas*, 1 September 1715

Figure 34 A procession around the Stephansdom, Vienna, 1614

Figure 35 *Te Deum* in Notre Dame, on the occasion of the entry of Louis XIV and his Spanish bride into Paris, 26 August 1660, Jean Marot

Figure 36 *Te Deum* in the Hofburg chapel, on the occasion of Joseph I's *Erbhuldigung* 1705, J. C. Hackhofer

Figure 37 A familiar scene for many rulers: Joseph I kneels before the cortège with the sacrament for the dying, 1703, Caspar Luyken

Figure 38 A late eighteenth-century *Fronleichnamsprozession* on the Graben

Figure 39 Cup with Leopold's arms, for the 1699 *Pedilavium* or *Fusswaschung*

Figure 40 The survival of tradition: Francis Joseph washing the feet of twelve elderly poor men, 1902

PART IV

Power

CHAPTER 7

Levels and forms of power at court

INTRODUCTION

Household staff attended to the rulers' personal needs; councillors and ministers, usually convening in or near the rulers' apartment, helped them to govern their territories and finance their ambitions. Agents of government visited the court to pledge loyalty and receive orders; regions and corporations of the realm renewed their ties with the ruling house, whether by visiting the court, or by inviting it to their territories. Diplomats represented other sovereigns at court, advancing their interests by formal speeches and requests as well as by mixing in court faction. The rulers' patronage attracted multitudes seeking employment or advancement in the hierarchies of court, administration, church, and army. Others flocked to the court to plead a cause, to find support for their litigations, to request financial assistance, or simply to behold its majesty. This confluence almost always served to turn the court into a central theatre of power. Both in France and in the Habsburg lands, it was the main focus for those intent upon carrying high responsibilities. At court, they would find themselves competing with others pursuing similar ambitions. This chapter will shed light on the levels and forms of power and competition at court; a subsequent chapter will situate the court as a locus of power in the realm, and discuss the components of its centripetal potential.

In reconstructing the court as the central arena for decision-making, we need to distance ourselves from several common assumptions. In the later Middle Ages and the early modern age the strengthening of written procedures and the advent of specialised administrative personnel unmistakably changed the routines of the court. Around the key monarchical responsibilities of justice and warfare, moreover, a web of new challenges and tasks emerged. Many of these were connected to the increasing levels of contact as well as rivalry among the dynasties of Europe: warfare, diplomacy, competition through courtly splendour. The sources of income of patrimonial monarchy were woefully inadequate for the rising costs of warfare; an unending sequence of new taxes and *ad hoc* measures proved necessary. Wars remained endemic throughout the early modern age, and their pressures on state finances did not abate: reform usually was the consequence of financial crisis generated by military expenditure. The triad of war, foreign affairs, and finances was the predominant concern of ministers and their staffs, in addition to the domains of justice and religion.

The 'great' age of the European court occurred in a period rightly known for the development of government by paper, and for the ascent of ministers and secretaries. Yet the spheres of household and government were never wholly separated in personnel, social status, or mentality. The household staff was subject to the same 'administrative spirit' and paperwork characteristic of the emerging bureaucracies: the preceding chapters have hinted at the ongoing efforts of court servants to lay down rules for household expenses, and establish codices for disciplined behaviour. Instructions for court staffs stress thrift, loyalty, diligence; the 1665, 1681, and 1726 instructions for the Sun King's table dwell longer on provisioning, parsimony, and ways to prevent embezzlement or loss of tableware than on the rules for dignified service.

Councillors and secretaries were not necessarily unassuming, industrious, and incorruptible, nor were court dignitaries always haughty and incompetent spendthrifts. Ministerial office, held as a family speciality and possession throughout the seventeenth century, allowed younger scions of these dynasties to secure high court office, membership in royal orders, and marriages among the *fine fleur* of French nobility. The dynastic affectations of the Colbert, Le Tellier, Phélypeaux closely followed the *épée* example. Ministerial officeholding tended to become less dynastic in the eighteenth century, and to this exclusive echelon, few new names were added. The emperors' senior state servants were likewise ennobled but did not match the conspicuous success of their French counterparts. In the Austrian domains, however, many noble dynasties were noted for service in government and finance. In their careers, they would combine honorary court office with a progression of tasks and offices in a variety of other fields: high court office came as a reward for loyal service in non-courtly spheres as much as a recognition of high noble rank. In France, noble families would be less tempted to follow a slow *cursus honorum*; the *survivance* usually guaranteed office, and lessened the need to earn the king's approval. Thus, while court office in France was habitually combined with army command, regional government, and diplomacy, it was never close to the typically *robin* domain of lesser administrative service: only the supreme responsibility of a minister would appeal to the vested *épée* families at court.

Honorary office and 'ceremonial' strife, on the other hand, pervaded the administrative institutions as well as the household. Venality of office in France, and the proliferation of honorary office in the Austrian Habsburg lands were pervasive in each of these domains, and the same holds true for conflicts over rank, rights, and competences, or their minute external signs. 'Administrative monarchy' and Montesquieu's monarchy based on honour are two sides of the same phenomenon: we cannot simply draw the line between a fading 'feudal' household based on honour, and an expanding 'modern' bureaucracy animated by the ideals of efficiency and hard work; nor is it easy to pinpoint a period marking the changeover from the first to the second style. In France, surely the restoration after the *Fronde* brought changes, limiting both the open and recognized political role of the household and the right of princes to enter the council. In the Habsburg domains the Haugwitz reforms of 1749, and their multiple successors throughout the century, fundamentally changed the balance between household and government – yet the admixture of the spirits of honour and administration, differently proportioned in various ages and among various groups and persons, remains the defining characteristic for early modern monarchy in its entirety.

The *Refeudalisierungsthese* for the German territories in the early seventeenth century and the notion of an 'aristocratic reaction' in eighteenth-century France can be seen as answers to questions generated by the overstatement of sudden and decisive change.[1] In textbooks as well as in learned studies, the catchword absolutism serves as the endpoint of one phase of state building, the completion of an imposing edifice that later was to crumble under revolutionary pressures. Resurgence of noble power and princely opposition in the eighteenth century are frequently connected to the collapse of the edifice, but rarely to Louis XIV's careful redefinition and consolidation of noble status and power. For the history of the court, the divide of 1660–1715 has been particularly insurmountable. The invaluable *Residenzenforschung* volumes do not go beyond the early seventeenth century; two other major recent conference volumes devoted to the history of the court concentrate on the period antedating Louis XIV's personal reign.[2] Did the problems confronting rulers in the eighteenth century differ fundamentally from those their predecessors faced? Had they mastered the challenges of court faction, could they do without favourites and brokers, did they rule in splendid isolation from their wives, mistresses, household dignitaries, and lesser servants? Was the end of the *ancien régime* in France announced and prefigured by the end of the traditional courtly politics of a dynasty surrounded by myriads of families pursuing their own ambitions and interests, whether at court, in the administrative institutions, or elsewhere? If we find no affirmative answers to such questions, we should leave open the notion of a basic continuity

[1] See the perceptive studies of William Beik, 'A Social Interpretation of the Reign of Louis XIV', in *L'Etat ou le roi*, pp. 145–160, and Stefan Ehrenpreis, 'Österreichischer Adel, habsburgische Höfe, und kaiserliche Zentralverwaltung', in *Europäische Adel im Ancien Régime*, pp. 235–261.

[2] Asch and Birke, eds., *Princes, Patronage, and the Nobility*; J. H. Elliott and L. W. B. Brockliss, eds., *The World of the Favourite* (New Haven and London 1999) – the latter overstepping the age of 'absolutism' but typically including contributions on eighteenth-century history, almost as an afterword. Solnon, *Cour de France*, Dickens, *Courts of Europe*, and Adamson, *Princely Courts*, overstep the limits, but do not focus on the problems mentioned here. In Dickens' *Courts of Europe*, contributions by different authors discuss the two phases. Campbell, *Power and Politics*, explicitly addresses the problem, stressing continuity more than change; Béguin, 'Louis XIV et l'aristocratie', offers a plausible revision of Louis XIV's decision to rule without first minister.

of court life, without denying the slow but critical changes in the routines of government.

It is easier to point to omissions in historiography than to rectify them with well-researched alternatives. The 'political history of the court' has yet to be written: most central administrative institutions have been dealt with effectively in monographs, but the more elusive and largely unrecorded processes of decision-making at court can be reconstructed only where we have an abundance of correspondence and memoirs, supplementing and correcting the usually bland official records. Such an effort demands an erudition and concentration that do not fit within the compass of this study. Nor can I follow the *histoire événementielle* of the countries under discussion at close range: I seek patterns and changes, recurring tensions and positions; the careers of individual rulers, ministers, and courtiers have to remain subservient to this goal.

THE SILENT CENTRE

Rulers were frequently attributed a sphinx-like character. Reticence and elusive words recur in contemporary portrayals. These have been interpreted either critically as indecisiveness, or respectfully, as a masterful ruse, the choice between the alternatives depending mostly on the general perception of a reign, whether or not with the doubtful benefit of hindsight: the silence of the successful was masterful, those who failed were simply indecisive. Such judgements, by historians and contemporaries, obscure the basic similarity in the outlook of most kings and emperors.

Silence was among the most conspicuous characteristics of rulers. Luynes was frequently irritated by Louis XV's 'manque de fermeté', leading the king to remain silent and passive when prompt action was necessary.[3] Argenson perceived the king's diffidence as the inclination to pose as enigmatic. Many observers stress the contrast between the kings' intelligence, and their less impressive record of putting this quality to good use.[4] Véri dubbed Louis XVI 'le maladroit' and thought he matched Louis XV in taciturnity:

> Il [Louis XVI] garde le silence lorsqu'on le presse. Et le silence sec qui était la qualité dominante de Louis XV dans tous les embarras, jette les ministres et les affaires dans l'incertitude.[5]

Strained silence frequently was the king's only refuge – when difficult decisions had to be taken, but also in other uncomfortable situations. Maurepas

[3] Luynes, *Mémoires*, for example, XIII, pp. 430, 441–441, 446–447; compare Antoine, *Louis XV*, for example, p. 108 for Louis' young years.

[4] Hardman, *Louis XVI*, p. 61, on Louis XV citing Argenson, *Mémoires*, ed. Rathéry, IV, p. 42; Besenval, *Mémoires*, III, pp. 328–329, on Louis XVI (see quote below).

[5] *Journal de l'abbé de Véri*, I, pp. 244–245, 221 (quote), 378; II, pp. 43–44; II, pp. 101–102 ('le maladroit'); compare his negative assessment of Louis XIV's rule in II, pp. 224–226.

admonished his timid royal patron to take greater care of his dignity during public appearances. Croÿ, on the other hand, interpreted Louis XVI's silence during a *débotté* as undue formality, out of tune in an age where the 'ton de réprésentation était trop passé'.[6]

Louis XIV knew better how to adapt his attitudes to circumstances: he could be imposing as well as easygoing – yet he was hardly known for his verbosity. Saint-Simon reports that 'je verrai' was the king's habitual answer to requests. The Sun King explicitly advised his son to always listen carefully, but say little, while preferably sticking to obliging and noncommittal words.[7] He cautioned him that 'Ceux qui l'approchent [the king] de plus près, voyant les premiers sa faiblesse, sont aussi les premiers qui en veulent profiter'. Louis XIII, finally, was likewise known for his silence, and was reticent and cryptic in writing as well as in his stammered speech.[8] We recognise the same elements in Vienna. Leopold invariably answered petitioners 'in terminis generalissimis'; reportedly emperors favoured the phrase 'euch wird Recht werden'.[9] Leopold and Charles were frequently described as constrained; unfavourable witnesses represent Charles VI as dumbfounded, uttering inarticulate sounds instead of coherent replies, notwithstanding his proficiency in languages.[10] Maria Theresa, not by inclination well disposed towards games of cards and dice, advised her children to engage in these activities during the court's *appartements*, as 'toujours parler au milieu de 100. personnes qui cherchent à vous éplucher, est trop difficile, pour s'y soutenir à la longue'.[11]

Such advice indicates that the ruler's pivotal position at court was a strength as well as a liability. Many rulers, imbued with the pious and glorious examples of their forebears, dreaded less the negative consequences of silence or passivity than the hazard of rash judgements or impulsive deeds. There was more to the ruler's central position than his hierarchical pre-eminence, demonstrated in the household's public activities. The pull towards the centre of decision-making and distribution of honours was the essential feature of a politically successful court; yet frequently it proved a heavy burden. Distribution of honours was a vital ligament of the state: the traffic between the centre and the provinces, with the loyalties and expectations it engendered, ideally enabled the ruler to befriend, oblige, and snub as he saw fit, within the limits of his resources, and the dictates

6 *Journal de l'abbé de Véri*, I, pp. 242–243; *Journal inédit du duc de Croÿ*, IV, p. 137.

7 Dreyss, *Mémoires de Louis XIV*, I, pp. 196–197; II, pp. 64–65.

8 A. Lloyd Moote, *Louis XIII. The Just* (Berkeley and Los Angeles 1989), pp. 3, 139.

9 Pufendorf, *Bericht über Kaiser Leopold*, p. 59; Volker Press, 'Österreichische Großmachtbildung und Reichsverfassung. Zur kaiserlichen Stellung nach 1648', *MIÖG* 98 (1990), pp. 131–154, at p. 146.

10 Lhotsky, 'Karl VI und sein Hof', pp. 63–64.

11 Maria Theresa in ÖNB cod. ser. n. 1713, fol. 77r; compare Dreyss, *Mémoires de Louis XIV*, II, p. 404, and p. 288. Luuc Kooijmans, *Liefde in opdracht. Het hofleven van Willem Frederik van Nassau* (Amsterdam 2000) a political biography of Willem-Frederik, Stadhouder of Friesland and Groningen in the Dutch Republic. The *stadhouder*, hardly a *grand monarque*, succinctly captured the connection between rulership and silence, when he noted 'mij wat dom houden' in his diary as guideline for future behaviour at his miniature court.

of hierarchical thinking. The management of this process demanded a constant effort, exceeding the character and talent of many a ruler. Unbalanced liberality provoked resentment; sharing the burden with confidants could make things worse by inviting jealousy and distrust among rivals. Foreclosing this possibility by evading responsibilities, however, would render useless the court's centripetal potential.

Reiterated instructions forbidding personal servants to pass on requests are indicative of the desire of kings and emperors to be left alone. When Joseph II in 1781 radically transformed the status of his serving *Kämmerer*, he nevertheless basically echoed the stipulations of a 1651 instruction for *Kammerdiener*: both stress the need for secrecy, and forbid eavesdropping, inquisitiveness; most relevantly, they stress that the chamber staff should not intrude upon the emperor, neither with personal requests nor as go-betweens carrying requests for others.[12] Roughly 300 years before Joseph's admonition, an Innsbruck instruction already stated that the *Kämmerer*, *Truchseßen*, *Kammerdiener*, usher, and all others: 'so zu unnser person geordnet sein, sol keiner einich suplication einnehmen...'[13] For the Capetian court, the 1318 *ordonnance de Bourges* likewise sought to limit solicitations, an attempt repeated with far greater precision in Henry III's 1578 and 1585 ordinances; later we find the procedures outlined in the printed *Etats*. Choisy suggests that Alexandre Bontemps, Louis XIV's favourite *premier valet de chambre*, gained the king's confidence because he took care never to ask favours.[14] An eighteenth-century register of the *premiers gentilshommes* stresses that no *placets* should be handed to the king without their permission.[15] The instruction for a banquet following a *bal masqué* in 1700 in the same register includes an intriguing gloss stressing the desirability to limit the king's exposition to unfamiliar persons: 'Nota: Eviter autant qu'il se peut de mettre des visages inconnus au roi sur l'échaffaud qui est vis à vis de lui'.[16]

Government by paper aggravated the plight of kings and emperors. How could the monarch effectively control his ministers without submerging himself in paperwork, neglecting ceremonial and social components of his craft? How could he determine the general direction of policies, decide among the alternatives

[12] OMeA Sr 74 Instruktionen Varia, 11 instruction 2 March 1651, pp. 1–3, p. 1: 'ferners sollen weder sie, noch der leibbarbier, cammerheitzer, und andere dergleiche cammerpersohnen von denen Partheyen Memorial annehmen, noch dieselbe übergeben, oder bey Uns sollicitirn, noch etwas in ihrem nahmen an- oder vorbringen, auch anderer gestalt nicht, als befragter, mit uns reden und antworthen'; ÖNB cod. 12957 opens the 1781 ceremonial with an 'instruction für die von S. K. M. ausgewählten 36 dienstkammerherren' (fols. 1–4); under the ninth point, we find the echo of the 1651 instruction, the chamberlains cannot request favours or plead a cause without the intermission of the *Oberstkämmerer*, who alone could grant them a formal audience.

[13] Bojcov, 'Sitten und Verhaltensformen', in *Höfe und Hofordnungen*, ed. Kruse and Paravicini, p. 267.

[14] Choisy, *Mémoires*, pp. 183–184.

[15] Lalou, 'Ordonnances de l'hôtel des derniers Capétiens', in *Höfe und Hofordnungen*, ed. Kruse and Paravicini, p. 101; BN Brienne 256 (MS naf 7225) *règlement* 1578, fol. 56; *règlement* 1585, *AC*, pp. 309, 312, 325–326; see the reiteration of the familiar formula in the last printed *Etat de la France*, 4 vols. (Paris 1749), I, p. 373; the *premiers gentilshommes*' remarks in AN O 1 822, p. 4 (1688), repeated on p. 14.

[16] AN O 1 822, the *premiers gentilshommes*' register: 'cérémonies de toute espèce'; pp. 60–63 'Bal masqué du 27 janvier 1700', note in the margin of p. 63.

presented to him in the council? How could he prevent his more knowledgeable servants from preparing their positions before the council session, overruling him by the well-orchestrated presentation of their proposals and interventions? Finally, how to trust advisers who might choose to defend the specific interests of their affiliations at court against their better knowledge of the interest of state and dynasty? Discussing the distribution of honours, to him the essence of kingship, Louis XIV argued that even his wisest councillors: 'peuvent raisonnablement être suspects en celle-ci, parce que plus les places qu'il faut remplir sont importantes, plus l'envie qu'ils ont d'y porter dépendants d'eux . . .'.[17] Rulers could err either by trusting their ministers without reservation, or by not sufficiently trusting them. The *juste mesure*, or alternatively, the ideal set of advisers, was a rare asset, never to be taken for granted.

The king or emperor governed advised by his council; administrative institutions executed the decisions taken in council. Councils tended to expand, and to diversify. When the number of councillors had expanded, a nucleus of advisers within the council tended to serve as an 'inner', or 'privy', council. Expansion and redefinition of the council occurred frequently at the Austrian Habsburg court, where the 'privy council' and later the *Konferenz* served as the true medium for advice, and the larger council finally attained a ceremonial status. Other, more specialised councils had long since emerged to deal with finance, war, and matters pertaining to the empire – but the emperor would not as a rule attend these councils, and when necessary their presidents could be invited to the *Konferenz*. Nor were all affairs decided in council meetings with the councillors offering advice to the emperor: he could choose to have them write down their individual or collective opinions, consider them in seclusion, and present his decision as a comment in the margin of their proposals.[18] Between the council meeting and solitary study, stood the option to deliberate matters with an individual councillor or informal adviser.

In France, where *sécrétaires d'états* and their departments had developed earlier, the basic principle of the council was not so different. Again, we see the expanding unwieldy council that inevitably led to the formal or informal establishment of a smaller inner group; and the proliferation of specialised councils, not necessarily attended by the king.[19] After the proliferation of councillors in Anne of Austria's regency, Louis XIV restructured and limited the council, stipulating that only those invited by the king could attend the *conseil d'en haut*, thus abrogating the right of the princes to sit in his innermost advisory bodies – creating a situation that was common practice at the Habsburg court. French kings, too, would prepare council meetings in solitary study, and could invite ministers for deliberations in the sessions indicated first as the *liasse*, later as the *travail*

[17] Dreyss, *Mémoires de Louis XIV*, II, pp. 341–342. [18] See Sienell, *Die Geheime Konferenz*.

[19] See Antoine's lucid summary of government institutions and procedures in *Louis XV*, pp. 180–211.

du roi. If a senior minister attended the *travail du roi* of his fellow ministers, he could develop a special responsibility as intermediary between king and ministers, or first minister. Extending his position to the spheres of household and distribution of graces, he became a minister and a favourite, and frequently a source of annoyance to those against whom he shielded the king.

In his memoirs, Louis XIV pointed out that even an unfounded perception of a favourite ruling his sovereign seriously undermined the latter's prestige.[20] His determination to rule without first minister, however, forced him to spend much time studying and discussing affairs of state, a situation exacerbated by his decision to abolish the office of *surintendant des finances* after Fouquet's disgrace. Louis proposed to his son various solutions to deal with this problem. Unwavering hard work helped him to follow the outlines of his ministers' policies; incidental probes into the details of their *liasses* allowed him to test their assiduousness and loyalty. The king stressed that he never relied on one minister, but always sought the advice of others: competition among the ministers would check their ambitions.[21] Yet, he admitted, the key problem of finding the right advisers probably was a matter of fortune more than insight.[22] In the decades following the death of Louvois in 1691, Louis XIV experienced the stress of protracted crisis with less lucky ministries, and increasingly relied on the active support of Madame de Maintenon. She turned into an informal variant of the *premier ministre*, the inevitable go-between and 'fidèle interprète des pensées du roi'; a situation exacerbated by the deaths in the royal family.[23]

Leopold, relying on his *Aio* and *Obersthofmeister* Portia in his early years, asserted parallel ambitions after the latter's death:

> Io bin ich entschlossen kein primo ministro oder valido zu haben, sondern mein eigner primado selbsts zu sein, doch etlich Räthe zu den meisten oder allen Negotien zu ziehen, et hoc ex multus causis: 1o bin ich noch jung und kann wohl arbeiten, 2o bleibe ich Herr und kann einander nit vantiren, dass alles von Ihm dependire, 3o kann ich es besser verantworten, dann alles ich mir selbst attribuiren muess.[24]

Like Louis XIV, Leopold I stressed that it was not sufficient not to have a favourite; nobody should be allowed to plausibly pose as a favourite, suggesting that he was the sole intermediary with the ruler, and everything thus depended

20 Dreyss, *Mémoires de Louis XIV*, II, pp. 270–271.

21 The gist of a much-abused quote from Dreyss, *Mémoires de Louis XIV*, II, p. 267: 'La jalousie de l'un sert souvent de frein à l'ambition de l'autre'.

22 Dreyss, *Mémoires de Louis XIV*, II, pp. 266–268.

23 Mark Bryant, 'Françoise d'Aubigne', quote from Villars' memoirs, cited on p. 274.

24 *Privatbriefe*, I, pp. 104–107 (18 February 1665) after Portia's death; see Arthur Levinson, *Nuntiaturberichte vom Kaiserhofe Leopolds I*, 2 vols. (Vienna 1913–1918), for frequent reports on Leopold's reliance on Portia, and the incompetence of the favourite, for example, in I, no. 398 (15 April 1664), p. 222: 'Wenn der Kaiser nicht einen Regierungswechsel eintreten lassen wird, läuft er Gefahr, Krone und Reich zu verlieren, da es unglaublich ist, wie unfähig und fahrlässig sein erster Minister ist. Er lebt dahin, erfüllt von Argwohn und Eifersüchteleien, traut niemandem, will alles allein machen und bringt niemals etwas gutes zustande. – Der Kaiser weiß es zwar, doch tut er nichts, aus Liebe und Hinneigung zur Portia und weil er an dessen guten Willen glaubt.'

on him. The emperor remained loyal to his decision, yet he was dismayed to notice that he had nobody in whom to confide, or with whom to share his grief over Portia's death:

ich ... bin recht imbroglirt, noch mehr aber, weilen ich fast mit niemand hievon reden kann, weil alle hiebei interessirt sein, chi per un verso, chi per un altro, ma spes mea deus, in hoc ego confido ...[25]

Leopold defended his ministers against charges of bribery and treason, usually with the Spanish as accuser, the French as the alleged tempter. Yet his defence was uneasy, and he admitted to his friend, the ambassador to Spain Count Pötting: 'Ich fürchte wohl es gehe nit allzeit Recht zue'.[26] Not only had Leopold to defend his ministers: the accusations implied that he himself was governed by his corrupt ministers, and thus indirectly by the French envoy Grémonville. The emperor responded that he listened to all his ministers, but did not depend on any of them.[27] Annoyed to hear the same suggestion over and over again, he later stated sharply: 'Ich thue, was recht ist und frag um niemand. Sollete aber ich ein Prob haben, dass ein Minister ein Schelm seie, so wuerde sein Kopf bald zue Boden liegen.'[28] Johann Weikhard Auersperg's downfall and exile followed within months. Ruling 'alone', without the comfort of a coordinator and intermediary, the emperor found himself quite busy. Once, Leopold wrote to Pötting that he could only write a few lines, as he had already been working at his writing desk for five hours.[29] Elsewhere, he noted his hope to soon visit Laxenburg for outdoor recreations, adding: 'habe es wohl vonnöthen, dann die occupationes häufen sich merklich, ma das ist mein obligatio et mea professio, zu welcher mich Gott deputirt hat'.[30] Indeed, the hunting fervour of monarchs may have been heightened by the strenuous and often frustrating burden of government. Typically, after the misfiring of the *assemblée des notables* in the spring of 1787, Louis XVI hunted more than ever, engaged in immoderate meals, and daily wept in the queen's apartment.[31]

Trusting ministers was necessary, but also necessarily limited; could the ruler more easily confide in others? His spouse, of foreign extraction, with her own establishment and loyalties, represented a dynastic alliance in the first place, and was not necessarily a close companion. Instead of speaking directly to Margarita Teresa, Leopold I, a devoted husband, suggested that his ambassador in Spain communicate to the Spanish court his misgivings about the attitudes of her Spanish following.[32] Respect and reserve were more typical than either

[25] *Privatbriefe*, I, p. 107. [26] *Ibid.*, I, p. 143 (21 July 1665); compare I, p. 420 (7 November 1668).
[27] *Ibid.*, I, p. 390 (20 June 1668). [28] *Ibid.*, II, p. 28 (Laxenburg 22 May 1669).
[29] *Ibid.*, I, p. 375 (11 March 1668), compare Dickson, *Finance and Government*, I, p. 322, for the 'tendency for the ruler to be swamped by the growing volume of state business', and the reservations Maria Theresa and Joseph had about delegating responsibilities.
[30] *Privatbriefe*, I, p. 118 (15 March 1665). [31] Hardman, *Louis XVI*, p. 126.
[32] *Privatbriefe*, I, pp. 264–265 (9 December 1666).

the recurring conflict of Louis XIII and Anne of Austria, or the companionship of Maria Theresa and Francis Stephen. Relying on the support of the queen or empress, moreover, tended to be perceived as a sign of weakness, as spouses were not expected to mingle openly in government, or have more than the habitual share in religious patronage. Nor were mothers always trusted. The three queen-mothers temporarily ruling France only hesitantly passed on the reins of power to their sons, and represented a force to be reckoned with in the early years of their sons' reigns. In Vienna, dowager-empresses tended to be formidable presences, with more impressive establishments than ruling spouses; their relations with their daughters-in-law were rarely free from rivalry. Passer noted that Ferdinand III's widow, Eleonora II Gonzaga, was loath to see her step-son Leopold's third wife Eleonora Magdalena take over her title as queen of Hungary in 1681.[33] Such situations could confront young rulers with conflicts of loyalty, forcing them to take sides with their mother or spouse, or keep their distance from both.

Brothers and uncles in the male line, archetypical rivals in patrilineal societies, surface as leaders in rebellions throughout the early modern age. In France, the erosion of their traditional role in decision-making after the *Fronde* did not prove lasting, nor did their relations with the king lose their potential for conflict. Dynastic proximity, and rights of succession, pernicious in the case of the agnates, also strained the ties between ruler and his male offspring, particularly in long reigns. How could an elderly king or emperor gradually introduce his successor into government without creating impatience if his life lasted longer than expected? – barring the prince from councils and commands did not alleviate the problem. In the Habsburg lands, the election of the eldest son as King of the Romans, consolidating the Habsburg monopoly of the elective imperial worthy, introduced the king as a serious factor in court life – short-lived in the case of Ferdinand IV, lasting fifteen years for Joseph I. Joseph's *Hofstaat* and advisers represented an alternative course in Leopold I's last years, more or less like the group surrounding the duc de Bourgogne, son of the *grand dauphin*, in the same years. Joseph II voiced misgivings about his lengthy sharing of Maria Theresa's sovereignty after his father's death. Other children had to be suitably provided for. Monarchs experienced a typical variant of a noble dilemma: safeguarding succession by frequent childbirth, or limiting the number of children to prevent destabilisation of family wealth and harmony. French kings' illegitimate children further complicated the patterns, as their fathers usually created vested positions for them that inevitably aroused the anger of legitimate offspring and courtiers alike. Families, not without conflict in any society or social group, were a hotbed of tensions at court, and dynastic scions were frequently connected to major forces of opposition, or represented passive

[33] Passer, 'Berichte', p. 313.

foci for those advocating a change of course, or simply waiting to profit from the new ruler's favours. Nevertheless, blood ties were strong, and the dynastic network remained the core of court life. Whether or not the ruler chose to confide in his relatives, he had to reckon with their rank and proximity. Confiding in them, and listening to their advice, was as hazardous as it was natural.

A monarch was particularly vulnerable in the opening and closing years of his lifecycle. First confrontations with the burdens of rulership were rarely easy. In 1648, nine-year old Louis XIV wept in the Parlement de Paris when the speech he had learnt by heart went astray. Leopold grew up in a more sheltered environment – he seems to have held his first public speech in 1663, almost 23 years old and after ruling for over five years.[34] Typically, both rulers decided to rule without first minister only after the deaths of their first mentors; and both reportedly were becoming more dependent upon their consorts in the decade preceding their deaths, while their courtiers were realigning in anticipation of the new reign.[35] The sequence was repeated for both eighteenth-century French kings, respectively relying first on Fleury and Maurepas, later on Pompadour and Marie-Antoinette. Joseph's rule was too short, and Charles' or Maria Theresa's dependencies do not closely fit this image. After having survived the critical first phase of her reign, however, Maria Theresa looked back on her early years, stating that she had been inexperienced, timid, and insecure. She stressed her indebtedness to a handful of devoted servants:

> Bartenstein und Haugwitz gaben mir vor den Staat und Erhaltung der Monarchie das Benöthigte an die Hand, Tarucca und Koch dieneten mir zu meinem Trost, Rath und particular-Auskundschaften, zu meiner erkanntnüss und Correction: Und werde so lange ich lebe, an dieser Ihren Personen, Kindern, und Kindes-Kindern erkennen, was sie mir und dem Staat vor Dienste geleistet.[36]

In 1767, two years after the death of her beloved husband, Maria Theresa wrote to one of these confidants, Sylva Tarouca 'qu'il lui était aussi nécessaire dans sa vieillesse et décrépitude que dans sa jeunesse et etourderie'.[37] Five years later, Khevenhüller reported with relish Maria Theresa's 'epanchement de cœur'. The partition of Poland and worries about Joseph's and Kaunitz's policies had severely strained the empress, who was, Khevenhüller feared, 'auf Extrema' and

[34] *Privatbriefe*, I, p. 11 (2 May 1663); for Louis' crying during the 1648 *Lit de Justice* see Orest Ranum, *The Fronde: A French Revolution 1648–1652* (New York and London 1993), p. 91.

[35] See Coenraad van Heemskerck's reports in *Weensche Gezantschapsberichten van 1670 tot 1720*, ed. G. von Antal and J. C. H. de Pater, 2 vols. Rijks Geschiedkundige Publicatiën 67, 79 (The Hague 1929–1934), I, pp. 494–499 (letter 226, 13 November 1691) mentioning the increasing influence of the empress, on the emperor as well as on Joseph; see Mark Bryant, 'Françoise d'Aubigné', for the preponderant position of Mme de Maintenon in Louis XIV's later years, particularly after 1712.

[36] Alfred Arneth, 'Zwei Denkschriften der Kaiserin Maria Theresia', *AÖG* 47, 2 (Vienna 1871), pp. 267–354, at pp. 285, 307 (quote).

[37] *Correspondence secrète entre Marie-Thérèse et le Cte de Mercy-Argenteau*, I, pp. 146–147 (the empress reporting the death of Sylva-Tarouca to Mercy, 1 April 1771), quote in n. 1.

might even think of 'die Crone vollends par dégoût et désespoir niederzulegen'.[38] In 1773, the tired sovereign herself wrote to Hatzfeld:

J'avoue, ma situation devient presque intolérable; ce n'est que quelques personnes et ministres attachés a moi, qui me retiennent encore; vous y êtes aussi, dont j'espère encore le plus de secours.[39]

Greater dependence, more opportunities for confidants to gain exceptional power, and a marked tendency for power struggles at court usually characterised childhood as well as old age – even for astute rulers.

PROXIMITY AND FAVOUR

The image of a centre surrounded by concentric circles, divided into compartments like those between the spokes of a wheel, has frequently been evoked to describe the conjunction of spheres around the ruler.[40] The household staffs as well as the institutions of government included persons in steady contact with the ruler, both at the highest level of their hierarchies of rank and function, and at the lower but not necessarily less intimate level of daily service. To this image of the institutionally segmented wheel, we can add the continuum between display and intimacy described in chapter 5. Access to the ruler in intimate settings could bring familiarity and favour: it was surely one of the most direct channels to power. Yet access, favour, and power were not necessarily parallel. Neither did all persons favoured by the ruler become powerful; nor did all powerful ministers or courtiers have the rights of easy access, and the benefit of intimacy.

For most rulers, it must have been imperative to find a level of support and friendship in their daily environment. Confidence and intimacy could entail dependence, and the mere semblance of the ruler's dependence was sufficient to unsettle a court. In whom could the ruler confide without risking manipulation and defamation? Unobtrusive characters were ideal confidants, as they offered easy companionship at low risk. Court jesters and dwarves form a remarkable example of this category. Dwarves, ubiquitous at the Spanish Habsburg court, were also present at the early seventeenth-century French court, the *états* listing several *nains* and *naines* in the chamber staff. In Vienna their presence was more notable and lasted longer: the seventeenth-century payrolls include governors and servants for the *Kammerzwergen*, though not usually the dwarves themselves. Pufendorf reports Leopold fervently clubbing foxes in the company of his dwarves; Charles VI still reckoned among his intimates a 'Baron Klein' or 'Hansl', who had accompanied him to Spain, and later shared his hunting

[38] Khevenhüller, *Tagebuch*, VII, pp. 128–130 (20–25 May 1772); with an exchange of letters in nn. 153 and 154, pp. 422–423. Compare Beales, *Joseph II*, pp. 288–289, 350–351.

[39] *Briefe Maria Theresia an Ihre Kinder und Freunde*, ed. Alfred von Arneth, 4 vols. (Vienna 1881), IV, pp. 298–299.

[40] For example, in Sergio Bertelli, *The Courts of the Italian Renaissance* (Milan 1985), pp. 26–27; Salvadori, *Chasse*, p. 220.

trips.[41] Lesser servants, valets, and ushers, familiar but socially distant and politically harmless, could offer easy companionship at low risk. Philip Lang, Rudolf II's *oberste Kammerdiener*, however, so blatantly abused his position that he became a serious liability: he sold positions in the household, asked for money to arrange audiences, and offered his personal influence with the emperor to the highest bidder. In 1608, he fell from power, and two years later died in jail.[42] For the Austrian Habsburgs, these lower-level intimates mostly remain anonymous, and their influence must usually have remained limited. For France several names are reported, most obviously the successful dynasties of valets in the chamber, but also a range of others such as D'Aigremont, the *porteur de devant* of the sedan chair Louis XIV had to use in his later years, or sieur Antoine, the *porte-arquebuse* in whose company he fed and petted his dogs before sleeping.[43] A counterpart for the valets in the chamber existed in the cabinet. The number of personal secretaries in the ruler's cabinet or 'study', after the extreme inflation in France during the early decades of the seventeenth century, remained small throughout the *ancien régime*. Toussaint Rose, one of Louis XIV's four secretaries of chamber and cabinet, was thought to have some influence: Saint-Simon notes that 'il était compté et ménagé même par tous les ministres. Sa plume l'avoit entretenu dans une sorte de commerce avec le roi, et quelquefois d'affaires qui demeuroient ignorées des ministres.' Secretaries were important at the Habsburg court, but only halfway through the eighteenth century did a *geheime Kabinetssekretär* emerge. Ignaz Koch, mentor and confidant of prince Eugene after 1723, and Maria Theresa's cabinet secretary from 1742 to 1763, was a notable and respected adviser.[44] In 1754, she implored Kaunitz to keep Koch well-informed, as 'ich ihm von Allem rede und er der einzige ist, mit welchem ich mein Herz ausschütten kann'.[45]

[41] See 'Hansl' in Khevenhüller, *Tagebuch*, V, p. 100 (2 May 1759); *Briefe Maria Theresia an Ihre Kinder und Freunde*, II (22 May 1777), when a relative sought her protection: 'Il était neveu du fameux baron Klein, nain que j'ai tant estimé'; Mitis, *Jagd und Schützen*, p. 35; *Wienerisches Diarium* (September 1703), an annex reporting Charles' voyage to Spain; other frequent references to *Kammerzwergen und Narrendiener* in the Hofzahlamtsbücher, for example, HKA, HZAB 1662/107, fols. 251v–252r; 1675/119, fol. 155v–r; Leopold hunting with dwarves in Redlich, 'Tagebuch Esaias Pufendorfs', p. 568; BN Clair 837, p. 3309: three *nains* after 1590; on pp. 3355–3426 in Marie de Medici's *état*, and on p. 3409 in Anne of Austria's *état*; see the parallel in Griselle, *Etat de la maison du roi Louis XIII*, p. 142, nos. 5288 and 5289 (Louis XIII's 1638 *état*), p. 127, no. 4712 (Anne of Austria); p. 75, nos. 2976–77 (Marie de Medici) and anonymous *naines* in the same *état* on p. 60, no. 2409. Father Marin and son Claude Noué; *portemanteau* and *nain* for Marie de Medici and Anne of Austria respectively, later *nain du roi*.

[42] Friedrich Hurter, *Philip Lang, Kammerdiener Kaiser Rudolfs II. Eine Criminalgeschichte aus dem Anfang des siebenzehnten Jahrhunderts* (Schaffhausen 1851), pp. 52–87, with the indictment printed in the annex.

[43] *Couvert du roi*, p. 113; Besongne, *Etat* 1687, I, p. 243. See the moderate but repeated pensions granted to Antoine and his relatives AN O 1 630 pensions 1683–1718, fols. 2–3.

[44] For Rose or Roze, Louis XIV's *sécrétaire du cabinet* (*d*. 1701) see, for example, Choisy, *Mémoires*, p. 150; Saint-Simon, *Mémoires*, VIII, a lengthy portrayal on pp. 22–34 and further details in Boislisle's nn. 1 and 2 on p. 22, quote on p. 24. Compare Antoine, *Louis XV*, pp. 201–202, in the concise and lucid discussion of government institutions, and Bély in *DAR*, p. 1144; in the *états*, however, the four *sécrétaires d'état* were frequently listed as the four *sécrétaires de la chambre et du cabinet*. For Vienna see Sienell, *Geheime Konferenz*, for biographical data on secretaries in Leopold's time, and Dickson, *Finance and Government*, I, p. 338 and n. 25 on Koch.

[45] *Briefe Maria Theresia an Ihre Kinder und Freunde*, IV, p. 249 (13 November 1754), similar remarks in III, p. 111.

Confessors and other clerics, doctors and surgeons, or scholars and artists of all kinds, usually of indifferent rank, could rise to favour because of their special status and skills. The confessor's function made him familiar with the rulers' most intimate deeds and feelings, and he thus represented a potential force – ideally remaining potential, because of the constraints inherent in his office. Yet the mere assumption that he held the keys to the ruler's mind, if not always to his deeds, inevitably made him the object of the ambitious as well as the curious. When the confessor in France held the *feuille des bénéfices*, or the responsibility for ecclesiastical patronage, he was one of the steady points of orientation within the courtly constellation of power.[46] In the seventeenth century, the *feuille* habitually was in the confessor's hands; eighteenth-century confessors were less influential. Choisy recounts how *Père* La Chaise entertained Louis XIV with his *médailles* during the *après-dinées* of his protracted 1686 illness; having come closer to the king, he strengthened his grip on the *feuille des bénéfices*, shared earlier with the archbishop of Paris in the *conseil de conscience*.[47] Saint-Simon perceived Father Tellier, succeeding La Chaise in 1709, as an awesome presence.[48] Wilhelm Lamormaini, Ferdinand II's confessor for 13 years after 1624, was a notable presence and influence at the Viennese court; Leopold's Jesuit confessor Müller, and the Capuchin friars Emmerich Sinelli and later Marco d'Aviano were likewise recognised as important.[49]

Infirmity and dangerous ailments could be alleviated by doctors and surgeons taking care of the ruler and his kin. Héroard's *journal* conveys the daily closeness of doctor and king. The *journal de la santé de Louis XIV* misses the sense of personal proximity, but shows the king's frequent illnesses and medication.

[46] Barbiche, *Institutions*, p. 245, gives as the king's patronage for 1789 129 bishoprics and archbishoprics, more than 750 abbeys for monks, almost 1,000 abbeys for nuns. On the confessor in general, see Minois, *Confesseur du Roi*.

[47] Minois, *Confesseur du roi*; Choisy, *Mémoires*, pp. 187–188; compare Oroux, *Histoire ecclésiastique de la cour de France*, II, p. 507: 'François de la Chaize (Forez, 25 août 1624) famille noble, petit neveu du père Coton, confesseur de Henri IV et Louis XIII'; II, pp. 527–529, the same story about the medals and the *feuille*. In II, pp. 483–486, Oroux prints an excerpt from Louis XIV's memoirs dealing with the distribution of ecclesiastical benefices. On the *feuille des bénéfices* see Raymond Darricau, 'Bénéfices', in *DGS*, p. 185, and Michel Pernot, 'Confesseur du roi', in the same volume on pp. 383–385, on p. 384 mentioning private sessions of Louis XIV with confessor Annat, discussing the distribution of benefices.

[48] Saint-Simon, *Mémoires*, general XVII, pp. 55–64; role in distribution of graces and quarrels with Mme de Maintenon XVII, p. 226; XX, pp. 75–78. Compare the negative assessment in Oroux, *Histoire ecclésiastique*, II, p. 556, stressing Tellier's ambitions.

[49] Robert Bireley, *Religion and Politics in the Age of the Counterreformation: Emperor Ferdinand II, William Lamormaini S. J., and the Formation of Imperial Policy* (Chapel Hill 1981); Elisabeth Kovács, 'Einflüsse geistlicher Ratgeber und höfischer Beichtväter auf das fürstliche Selbstverständnis, auf Machtbegriffe und politische Entscheidungen österreichischer Habsburger während des 17. und 18. Jahrhunderts', *Cristianesimo nella storia* 4 (1983), pp. 79–102; B. Dudik, ed., 'Correspondenz Kaisers Ferdinand II. Und seiner erlauchten Familie mit P. Martinus Becanus und Wilhelm Lamormaini, kaiserl. Beichtvätern S. J.', *AÖG* 54 (1876), pp. 79–102; Arthur Levinson, *Nuntiaturberichte vom Kaiserhofe Leopolds I.* (Vienna 1913–1918), I: 1657 Februar bis 1669 Dezember; II: 1670 Mai–August 1679 printed from *AÖG* 103 and 106. II, pp. 141 and 232 (letters 101 and 286), mention Sinelli's influence, p. 225 (letter 273) mentions confessor Müller. The manuscript diary by the Swedish resident Esaias Pufendorf, HHStA Handschriften Weiß 324, discusses the influence of Sinelli and others at length, see the selection published by Redlich, 'Tagebuch Esaias Pufendorfs', p. 570, and the somewhat more formal report by Pufendorf, *Bericht über Kaiser Leopold, seinen Hof, und die Österreichische Politik 1671–1674*, ed. Karl Helbig (Leipzig 1862), pp. 17, 52, 70–76, discussing the influence of several groups and individuals at court.

Louis XIV's famous operation in 1686 brought nobility and favour for Félix, *premier chirurgien*, and laid the foundation for the rise to favour of Fagon, who would replace Daquin as *premier médecin* in 1693.[50] Sourches and Saint-Simon suggested that Daquin lost office because he was too pushy in asking favours for himself and his family. He wanted an archbishopric for his son, and after a clear rebuttal by the king, unwisely tried to convince Father la Chaise to intercede for him.[51] Favour, apparently, should never be pushed too far, and confessors were more important than doctors. *Leibärzte* at the Viennese court, we may assume, could likewise hold a special position. The king's or emperor's interests and likings, for music, reading, painting, building, gardens, jewellery, and a variety of other pursuits, would bring him into contact with the pertinent specialists, and could lead to friendship. Leopold's letters to his librarian Lambeck show the vivid interests of the emperor, and his friendly disposition towards the guardian of his books.[52] The *Kapellmeister* and his counterpart the superintendent of the king's musical chapel, or talented *virtuosi* could charm their sovereign patrons, particularly when they themselves were devoted performers. The 1687 *état de la France* listed Jean Baptiste Lully in the *première entrée*, 'par une grace particulière attachée à sa personne'.[53] The role of musicians was more marked at the Habsburg court than it was in France. In general, however, while doctors and highly skilled artisans could expect special benefits, they would rarely come close to power.

Formative experiences undoubtedly helped to create and fortify close relationships. Youth friends and playmates, usually of high rank, were frequently perceived as more trustworthy and less dangerous than others, and could become much more influential than most low-profile confidants discussed above. Saint-Simon's finest hour came when Philippe d'Orléans, the companion of his early years, rose to power and finally granted the responsibilities that had previously eluded him. The high-ranking *gouvernantes* caring for children in their first years, and the governors taking over the reins for the education of princes upon their seventh year, likewise left a strong imprint. The son of Louis XIV's governor Villeroy grew up with the king, remained close to him, and was duly appointed governor to Louis XV. Johann Ferdinand Portia, Karl Theodor Otto von Salm, first archdukes' *Aios* or governors, became exceptionally influential high stewards upon their masters' accession to the imperial throne – a record matched in form though not in influence by Anton Florian von Liechtenstein.

50 Choisy, *Mémoires*, pp. 251–252.

51 Dangeau, *Journal*, IV, pp. 388–390, with Saint-Simon's addition, and Sourches, *Mémoires*, IV, pp. 281–282. Saint-Simon states that Daquin had been Mme de Montespan's protégé, and that Fagon was supported by Mme de Maintenon; he also adds that the king had been particularly friendly to Daquin the evening before his disgrace – probably a typical Saint-Simonian embellishment.

52 See Th. G. von Karajan, 'Kaiser Leopold und Peter Lambeck', *Almanach der Kaiserlichen Akademie der Wissenschaften* 18 (Vienna 1868), pp. 101–156, on pp. 132–133, 135, suggesting a close bond between Leopold and Lambeck, and the latter's influence on political affairs.

53 Besongne, *Etat* (1687), I, p. 201.

Dubois and Fleury, preceptors of Philippe D'Orléans and Louis XV respectively, later served as their first ministers.[54]

Menins or chamberlains, serving as noble companions in the establishment of princes, could likewise hope to follow the rise of their masters to supreme power – a tendency obscured by the frequency of premature deaths of *dauphins* in France. Henry IV had placed Charles d'Albert among the *dauphin*'s companions – he would rise to power and acquire the dukedom of Luynes as Louis XIII's first favourite, helping the diffident young king to assert himself, displacing his mother and her Italian favourites.[55] In 1694, when Joseph's establishment as King of the Romans was substantially expanded, several chamberlains in his staff rose to the court offices they would still hold after 1705.[56] From 1633, Maximilian von Trautmannsdorf was Hungarian and Bohemian king Ferdinand's high steward, an office he would consequently hold until 1650 under Ferdinand III's imperial rule. Auersperg, like Trautmannsdorf among Ferdinand III's most respected advisers, was well positioned for the next reign, serving as high steward for the emperor's son and namesake from 1645 onwards; his hopes and ambitions were thwarted only by Ferdinand IV's untimely death in 1654, leaving the field unexpectedly to archduke Leopold's *Aio* Portia.

The ruler's first military campaigns could be equally formative, creating strong ties of loyalty and friendship. The constellation of Henry III's favourites was moulded during the bloody siege of La Rochelle and the eventful Polish sojourn.[57] Charles VI's Spanish adventure formed the basis of his lasting proximity with Michael Johann Althann and Rocco Stella.[58] On a more limited scale, hunting, the almost daily exercise and joy of most Habsburg and Bourbon rulers, represented a similar experience. It brought danger as well as intimacy: Charles in 1732 shot his own master of the stables Adam Schwarzenberg in a much deplored hunting accident, and in his diaries he referred to his hunting companions with affectionate nicknames: 'Hartl', 'Gund', and 'Jost' among others.[59] Louis XIII's hunting fervour may have encouraged his fancy for Saint-Simon, the memorialist's father, who allegedly obtained his grace by sounding the hunting horn and teaching him how to change horses without dismounting.

Joseph I's *Oberststallmeister* Leopold Matthias von Lamberg assisted his master in his amorous exploits, surely a basis for confidence in the devout Habsburg environment, less used to such behaviour than the French court. Joseph appreciated Lamberg highly, and considered nominating him first minister in 1709, after

[54] Antonio Feros, *Kingship and Favoritism in the Spain of Philip III 1598–1621* (Cambridge 2000), a detailed analysis of Lerma's power under Philip III, mentions that both Lerma and Olivares based their rise on their favour with the successor, and positions in the successor's household.

[55] Lloyd Moote, *Louis XIII*, p. 80. [56] Sienell, 'Wiener Hofstaate zur Zeit Leopolds I', pp. 106–108.

[57] Le Roux, *Faveur du roi*, pp. 125–161.

[58] See the notes in Charles' diary, cited in Lhotsky, 'Karl VI und sein Hof', pp. 67–68, on Althan: 'mein Trost, mein treyster Diener, mein Herzensfreundt, der mich wie ich ihn 19 Jahr geliebt in wahrer Freundschaft'; on Rocco Stella: 'Stella gestorben, Minister, trey, auf den mich meist verlassen, vertraut'.

[59] Mitis, *Jagd und Schützen*, pp. 30, 34–35.

Salm's withdrawal.[60] Mistresses are not in evidence for most other Habsburgs in these centuries, though Vehse cites Charles VI's affection for Althann's wife Marianna Pignatelli as a matter of fact, a suggestion conceivably supported by Pöllnitz who dwelt at length on the emperor's fondness for Pignatelli's children.[61] Joseph I's licentiousness was as exceptional among the Habsburgs as Louis XVI's fidelity was for Bourbon kings. Even before Henry IV's open concubinage with Gabrielle d'Estrées, the illicit liaisons of kings had become part and parcel of French court life, as had the children arising from these frequent encounters. Indeed, not the existence of mistresses, but the extent of their influence on their royal lover, or the status of the royal bastards would lead to debates or defamation. The complication of illegitimate offspring was absent from Louis XIII's male friendships, yet whether or not his turbulent liaisons with François de Barradat, Henri d'Effiat marquis de Cinq-Mars, and others, were sexual, they provoked an uneasiness if anything stronger than did the flirtations of kings with mistresses. These sentiments were exacerbated by Cinq-Mars' ambitions and intrigues.[62]

The amorous domain, uncomfortably situated between serious historiography and gossip-mongering, cannot be neglected when discussing favouritism. The tendency to dismiss female actors from the central stage of decision-making by suggesting that they did not mingle in such typically male occupations was surely as present in seventeenth-century discourse as it was in older historiography, but for all practical purposes, we should discard it. Female protagonists themselves frequently hid behind the mantle of the 'natural' limitations of their femininity, but this did not keep them from intervening when they saw fit. Legitimate spouses, mothers, and sisters, were as keen on protecting their dynastic interests and affiliations as were their ruling relations. They would affect their spouses by ties of loyalty, compassion, and physical attraction, or could choose to use their position at court more autonomously. The last option was not available for mistresses: their power was usually contingent upon their sexual dominion over the ruler.[63] Surely, physical attraction and sexual contact can create ties and dependencies more exclusive and pervasive than those arising from shared administrative work with a minister, or more to the point, the shared excitement of hunting. As long as these ties lasted, and particularly when they were reinforced

60 Georg Heilingsetzer, 'Prinz Eugen und die Führungsschicht der österreichischen Großmacht', *Österreich und die Osmanen. Prinz Eugen und seinen Zeit*, ed. Erich Zöllner and Karl Gutkas, Schriften des Instituts für Österreichkunde (Vienna 1988), pp. 120–137, at p. 133; Pecar, 'Ökonomie der Ehre', p. 87; see the description of the court in 1709 by the Saxon envoy, Christoph Graf Wackerbarth, Sächsisches hauptstaatsarchiv Dresden, Geheimes Archiv Loc. 9936/37, to be published by Katrin Keller in *Frühneuzeit Info* 2001.

61 Vehse, *Geschichte der deutschen Höfe*, II, 6, pp. 206–209; Pöllnitz, *Mémoires*, pp. 237–240.

62 Lloyd Moote, *Louis XIII*, pp. 283–290.

63 See the discussion of women at court in Barbara Harris, 'Women and Politics in Early Tudor England', *Historical Journal* 33, 2 (1990), pp. 259–281; more recently Magdalena S. Sánchez, *The Empress, the Queen and the Nun: Women and Power at the Court of Philip III of Spain* (Baltimore 1998), and various contributions to Hirschbiegel and Paravicini, eds., *Frauenzimmer*; Antoine, *Louis XV*, pp. 484–510, 886–888, gives a concise discussion of Louis XV's mistresses, their connections at court, and their impact on court faction.

by friendship and respect, the mistress was a force to be reckoned with, on a par with ministers or influential courtiers.

Louis XIV warned his son that the mistress was the most dangerous of all favourites, yet at the same time he confidently stated that he would never mix *esprit* and *cœur*, or love and statecraft. We may doubt his success in achieving this ambition. Mme de Montespan offers a typical example of at least one of the dangers inherent in the mistress, in Louis' own words: 'il faut, pour la contenter elle seule, mécontenter tout le reste du monde'.[64] Mme de Maintenon, as Louis XIV's morganatic wife, is less typical a case. Towards the end of Louis XIV's reign, her veiled empire over ecclesiastical nominations as well as other decisions had reached impressive dimensions.[65] While previous mistresses had usually come from the group of noble ladies already present at court, attending princesses or taking care of children, Mme de Pompadour – the other inescapable model – was an outsider in all respects. Louis XV had to introduce her into the court first, giving her the rank appropriate for a *maîtresse déclarée*, who could join him on public occasions as a matter of fact. The *marquise*, receiving the *tabouret* in 1752, was initially welcomed with some indulgence, and found grace in the eyes of Luynes, who noted her humane attitude towards the queen.[66] She clearly exerted control over the king's patronage, however, and scandalised opinion with her relatively low birth as well as her insouciance. By serving as the king's *entremetteuse* with lesser mistresses of bourgeois background and without formal presence at court, the *marquise* maintained her position more than ten years after her sexual contact with the king had ended.[67] Most other mistresses were less successful: when their physical charm faded, their fall from favour could be rapid and cruel.

In this wide spectrum of favour and proximity, articulate advisers and high-ranking court dignitaries occupied positions differing markedly, but sharing one characteristic. Both the high rank of court dignitaries, and the propinquity to state secrets of the ministers, made the rulers' favour risky: it could lead to a critical accumulation of power in the hands of such favourites. The dangers were partly on the side of the ruler, who risked being perceived as a *roi fainéant*

[64] See Dreyss, *Mémoires de Louis XIV*, II, pp. 313–316. The Soissons in Louis XIV's reign lost offices to Mme de Montespan's children and relatives – the exile of the comtesse de Soissons finally led to the conspicuous role of her younger son Eugène de Savoye in imperial service. The duc de La Rochefoucauld had to sell his office of *grand veneur* to the comte de Toulouse in 1714 – admittedly a belated consequence of Louis' predilection for Mme de Montespan. My thanks go to Leonhard Horowski for bringing these instances to my attention.

[65] Mark Bryant, 'Françoise d'Aubigné'; compare the diverging judgement of Bluche, 'Maîtresses', in *DGS*, pp. 945–946. See *Correspondance de Madame duchesse d'Orléans*, ed. Ernest Jaéglé, 2 vols. (Paris 1880), letter of 10 November 1700, I, p. 260: 'On m'a assuré que le roi a amené hier publiquement la pantocrate [i.e. Mme de Maintenon] au conseil; cela a paru un peu étrange aux courtisans'.

[66] See, for example, the intercession of Argenson as well as Pompadour in Croÿ's successful attempts to obtain a *gouvernment*, *Journal inédit du duc de Croÿ*, I, pp. 240–244; Thomas E. Kaiser, 'Madame de Pompadour and the Theatres of Power', *FHS* 19, 4 (1996), pp. 1025–1044, particularly the introduction, pp. 1025–1027.

[67] Antoine, *Louis XV*, pp. 493–502; Antoine's careful discussion repeats the notion that Pompadour left aside politics, and 'only' mingled in the distribution of honours.

when he left the business of government to grandees or senior state servants. It did not need the acuity of the Sun King to discover the fact that, particularly after a period of marked unrest and subsequent rule by a cardinal-minister, the patent combination of supreme rank and political control would undermine the reputation of independence and personal power he wanted to establish. His delimitations of the princes' power in council and government, following his decision to rule by himself, first and foremost were attempts to eliminate remaining doubts as to his personal government. Participation in the highest level of decision-making, whether or not combined with high rank, was as prestigious as it was hazardous: the frequently insecure and isolated ruler was a dangerous neighbour. For the highest state servants it was difficult to end serenely a phase of proximity to the ruler and knowledge of the *arcana imperii*. In France particularly, exile, confiscations, punishments awaited those whose loss of confidence was rightly or wrongly interpreted as treason; and even if dismissed ministers escaped from chastisement and were benevolently allowed to retire peacefully to their estates, the court rejoiced in their downfall and eagerly prepared to reap the benefits of change. In the Habsburg lands, service as a trusted councillor or as a court dignitary could end without much ado, yet exceptional confidence, or the exceptional abuses of power this could entail, incidentally led to disgrace and exile. After 1618, Matthias' confidant Melchior Khlesl spent years in prison and exile before he was again allowed to return to Vienna; councillor Auersperg in 1669 and high steward Lobkowitz in 1674 had to retire to their estates upon their fall from power; and in 1680 *Hofkammerpräsident* Georg-Ludwig von Sinzendorf was condemned for mismanagement and embezzlement and had to pay a huge fine.[68]

High court dignitaries without open political responsibilities, but daily serving the ruler during their term, were less exposed to such mishaps. Lengthy loyal service, untarnished by immoderate ambitions or manipulations, could engender confidence and friendship – alternatively, the ruler's friendship could lead to promotion into these ranks. Saint-Simon frequently mentions Louis XIV's great fondness for François VII de La Rochefoucauld. The king made him *grand maître de la garderobe* in 1672, added the charge of *grand veneur* in 1679, and showered him with gifts. Typically, Saint-Simon once used the word *privance* to describe La Rochefoucauld's position – from the Spanish *privanza* usually connected to more conspicuous favourites such as Lerma or Olivares.[69] In France, high charges were turning into semi-hereditary dynastic possessions, and life-long service would be the usual situation. In Vienna promotion from one court office to another and shifts to other responsibilities were more frequent; the spheres of domestic and ministerial offices intertwined, and we cannot truly

[68] On Sinzendorf, see Bérenger, *Finances et absolutisme*, pp. 365–373.

[69] Saint-Simon, *Mémoires*, XVII, pp. 329–331, stressing the solidity of the king's friendship for La Rochefoucauld, and the multiple advantages the latter gained in the process.

separate the two groups of state servants. At both courts, the highest court dignitaries, not necessarily close to the formation and execution of royal policy, usually were closer to the distribution of honours, and their dynasties were conspicuously prominent among the receivers of ecclesiastical benefices, high offices in the army, diplomacy, and regional government.[70] Their dynastic status was safeguarded and demonstrated by the theatre of ceremony and rank around the ruler; their long-term dynastic interests benefited from their proximity to the distribution of charges. Special favour, or an important share in decision-making, could be a boon to personal prestige and family fortune, but brought risks, and was hardly indispensable from a long-term perspective.[71]

FAVOURITES AND FIRST MINISTERS

Low-profile intimates profited from the ruler's grace without tarnishing his reputation; mistresses, ministers, and high court dignitaries were far more powerful, but less safe candidates for conspicuous confidence. Yet the confidant, unobtrusive or conspicuous, was inevitably present at court: a volatile and ill-assorted variety of persons would share in the ruler's favour, in all spheres and at all levels. Only if one among them successfully barred others from direct access to the ruler, did he or she turn into a true favourite. Such favourites quickly became notorious, even more so should they be of low birth or foreign extraction, and charges against them often carried sexual connotations. The fanciful accusations against Mazarin typically embroidered his Italian background and his proximity to the queen-mother with stories of his sexual empire over Anne of Austria, and even his rape of the young king.[72] Meteoric rise and fall dominate the literary convention surrounding the favourite.[73] At this supreme level of favour, the profits and the risks were indeed extremely high: violent death awaited many favourites, and threatened nearly all of them. As soon as their ruling patron was disenchanted, or temporarily rendered powerless, exile or death were imminent. Marie de Medici's Italian favourite Concino Concini, marquis d'Ancre, was murdered with Louis XIII's connivance in 1617, and his powerful wife Leonora

[70] Horowski, 'Obersten Chargen', pp. 36–38, nn. 16 and 20, presents percentages based on the 34 highest charges of the king's *maison*, and another 20 of the queen's establishment. His initiative deserves a wider-ranging prolongation for both courts under discussion here. On p. 43 Horowski notes that the friends and followers of ministers, upon their death or dismissal were frequently taken over by the grandees close to them. In the Habsburg domains, connections between the army and court office were less strong than in France, a situation changing in the course of the eighteenth century, see Hochedlinger, 'Mars Ennobled'.

[71] Compare the priorities of Richelieu quoted in Campbell, *Power and Politics*, pp. 108–109.

[72] For the alleged sexual assault on the young Louis XIV in 1652, see the *Mémoires de P. de la Porte, premier valet de chambre de Louis XIV contenant plusieurs particularités des règnes de Louis XIII et de Louis XIV* (Paris 1850), in *Nouvelle Collection des mémoires pour servir à l'histoire de France*, third series, vol. VIII, pp. 1–57, most notably at p. 51.

[73] Elliott and Brockliss, eds., *The World of the Favourite* is strong on the imagery surrounding the favourite, see part III, pp. 159–235, and James Boyden's contribution on pp. 26–37.

Galigai executed shortly afterwards. On a European scale, we find many parallels for the fate of the Concinis, and other favourites well knew the stakes were high.

In the Habsburg lands, this ultimate form of favour was rare, if not absent. Melchior Khlesl, the bishop and later cardinal dominating Matthias' reign, may be the only more or less plausible candidate. Wallenstein's death, planned by the emperor and his councillors, did end a striking accumulation of power in his hands, yet the victim had never been the emperor's confidant or favourite in the ordinary sense. Most Habsburg favourites did not come near any monopolisation of access and power, neither did they achieve the notoriety of their French, English, or Spanish counterparts. Both Eggenberg and Lamormaini were important for Ferdinand II – Eggenberg overnight becoming Bohemia's greatest landowner thanks to the emperor's favour. Trautmannsdorf and Auersperg were Ferdinand III's major advisers, the former remarkable not only for his devoted service, but also for his disinterestedness, and aloofness from hierarchical infighting. Portia's favour was limited in time, and based on his imperial pupil's youth and inexperience. The decade after Portia's death witnessed sharp fluctuations in the power of court dignitaries, yet not even during the half decade separating Auersperg's disgrace in 1669 from Lobkowitz's fall in 1674 can we picture the flamboyant Bohemian high steward as an all-powerful mediator and manager. Court Chancellor Hocher was able and influential, and the Capuchin friar Emmerich Sinelli was close to the emperor.[74] During Leopold's later reign, we find many influential courtiers and state-servants, a variety of friends and confidants, but no towering figures. High steward Salm's empire over Joseph was never unchallenged, and his advanced age diminished his power before his death in 1710. Charles VI's favourites Althann and Rocco Stella had to reckon with the considerable sway of Prince Eugene in the army as well as in the conference. Later instances suggest similar, more moderate forms of favour, usually shared among a heterogeneous group of persons.

In France, the multifaceted phenomenon of favouritism has usually been perceived through the narrow prisms of either the mistresses, or the cardinal-ministers, twin icons in the hagiography of the state. Typically, the first category was presented as a moral weakness forgivable for much-burdened rulers, and usually of little import to matters of state; the second as a necessary intervention, bridging a critical phase in the development of 'administrative monarchy'.[75] Richelieu and to a lesser extent Mazarin were seen as great builders, not to be compared either with Renaissance cronies and *mignons*, or later *grands-commis*. The contrast, reflecting different stages in the development of the French state, is not unfounded, but tends to be overstated. Anne de Montmorencey had served

[74] Helbig, *Bericht über Kaiser Leopold*, pp. 17, 70–76.

[75] This position seems to return in Elliott and Brockliss, eds., *World of the Favourite:* fundamental comparative and long-term questions are discussed in Brockliss' conclusion, but his caveats against the older position do not lead to a serious revision. The volume, moreover, does not address the sexual dimension of favour.

as *1er conseiller* to both Francis I and Henry II; the Guise brothers held much the same position under Francis II, though without the title. Henry IV's dominant minister Sully took care of most government affairs, but Henry left foreign affairs to Villeroy, and let them compete in the council. The title of *premier* or *principal ministre* emerged only in the 1620s, first as a general term for senior ministers, equivalent to the later *ministre d'état*. In spring 1624 Richelieu obtained the title *principal ministre*, restyled *premier ministre de l'état* in a 1630 council decree. After 1642, Mazarin would be the last seventeenth-century titular.[76] In August 1722, the title was reinstated for Dubois, who died within a year, leaving his supreme responsibility to the former regent. In another six months, Philip too was dead, and the Condé high steward, M. le Duc took over.[77] Upon the duke's disgrace in June 1726 Louis XV conspicuously abolished the title – yet in practice allowed Fleury to do exactly what a *premier ministre* was expected to do. Maurepas, serving Louis XVI between 1774 and 1781, somewhat resembled a first minister. Finally, in 1787–1788 Loménie de Brienne again formally held the title.

A tract redefining the key domains of the *principal ou premier ministre* written for Dubois explicitly looked to the example of his two more famous predecessors. The argument can be summarised in one general statement:

> Le premier ou principal ministre est le dépositaire de l'autorité du prince; il est le canal immédiat par où le prince fait passer aux sujets toutes ses volontés, et par où les sujets doivent parvenir jusqu'au prince.

Most of all, the four secretaries, chancellor, keeper of the seals, and *contrôleur-général* had to abide by this rule:

> les ministres ou ceux qui ont part à la direction des affaires ne raportent point au prince qu'en la presence du Premier Ministre, & lorsqu'ils l'en ont prevenu.

Foreign affairs, the 'soul of the state', were to be the cardinal's special responsibility, yet no major decisions in other fields were to be taken without his prior 'aveu ou approbation'. Nor was this the only field where Dubois' monopoly should be guarded:

> Si le Premier Ministre est le seul organe pour toutes sortes d'affaires, il est aussi le seul canal à qui l'on s'adresse pour toutes les graces tant militaires que civiles. Tous les Placets présentés à l'ordinaire au Roy doivent estre portés à M. le Cardinal pour en faire le renvoy à ceux à qui la connoissance en appartient. S.E. a chez Elle plusieurs sécrétaires ou premiers commis pour ces differentes natures d'affaires.

In subsequent passages, the same points return, with a particular emphasis on the distribution of graces:

[76] See Barbiche, 'Principal Ministre', in *DAR*, pp. 1020–1022.

[77] When M. le Duc was *premier ministre*, the duc d'Antin replaced him as *grand maître*; after the death of M. le Duc in 1740, his younger brother the comte de Charolais acted as *grand maître* for M. le Duc's son, the Prince de Condé (1736–1818). The duc de Saint-Aignan temporarily took over his governorship of Burgundy.

La distribution des graces ou des charges fait le point le plus essentiel et le plus jaloux d'un premier ministre. Il n'est véritablement grand ni véritablement maistre, qu'autant qu'il sçait établir non seulement l'opinion de son crédit, mais celle d'une dispensation juste, ferme et exacte des bien faits ou des recompenses comme des disgraces.[78]

Wielding power as a *premier ministre*, then, was defined by controlling direct access to the king, managing the distribution of honours, and supervising key sectors of policy. It was contingent upon the unreserved confidence of the king: as soon as the king's confidence was undermined, others could break through the monopoly.

Was a monopoly of favour ever within reach? In practice most French favourites and 'first ministers' had permanently to deal with courtiers' cabals, and the changing infatuations of their royal patrons. Nicolas Le Roux's *Faveur du Roi*, meticulously charting the forms of friendship and favour at Henry III's court, shows that there never was a single favourite, and underlines the mutual ties among the favourites as well as their closeness to the king. The favourites operated as a collectivity of the king's friends, a trusted group of loyals. Among them, Joyeuse and Epernon gradually emerged as *archimignons*, more seriously monopolising royal favour. Their meteoric elevation, flowing from Henry's friendship and trust, was also part of the king's attempt to redefine noble rank and service: it was meant to inculcate the image that loyal service could offer a more secure and rapid avenue to power than did rank.

Richelieu's rise to power, carefully unravelled by Joseph Bergin, suffered many setbacks; the cardinal knew how to flatter, withdraw, and adapt. Even in his years of relatively unchallenged power after the test of 1630, he had to reckon with passing favourites, court factions, and grandees. His success in dealing with these persistent concerns arose not from his superior vision, but from his ability as a political operator, tending his power base and surviving setbacks.[79] From 1627 onwards, Henri II de Condé thought it wise to join forces with Richelieu, and both parties profited from their new alliance.[80] The tempestuous waters accompanying royal minorities go a long way to explain both the Concini's and Mazarin's rise to power. While Concini's power did not long survive the majority of Louis XIII, Mazarin emerged victoriously from the contest of the Fronde, consolidated his power and gained the loyalty, or at least respect, of the new king. The incumbencies of Dubois, Philip of Orléans, and M. le Duc were too short or atypical to fit within this little catalogue.

[78] BN MS f 25135, pp. 1, 3, 7, 17, and Campbell, *Power and Politics*, p. 182.

[79] See the detailed analysis in Bergin, *Cardinal Richelieu, Power and the Pursuit of Wealth* (New Haven and London 1985). Richelieu, Bergin concludes in *Rise of Richelieu*, p. 266, was closer to his Renaissance predecessors than to later *grands-commis*.

[80] Béguin, *Princes de Condé*, pp. 38–47, and her conclusion, stressing that the Fronde obscures the continuity between the pragmatic attitudes of the Condé after 1627 and 1659, combining their forces with Richelieu as well as the later ministers. Treasure, *Mazarin*, p. 332, n. 2, pictures Condé's choice, and the marriage of his son to Richelieu's niece Mlle de Brézé as a sign of the grandees' increasing dependence.

One detail, illustrating the potential impact of court office as well as the stature of M. le Duc, may be worth mentioning. When after a conflict with M. le Duc in December 1725, Fleury withdrew to Issy, Louis XV immediately asked his preceptor to return to court. The king allegedly was convinced to do so by his serving *premier gentilhomme* the duke of Mortemart, whose intervention thus helped to tilt the balance between the rising and declining favourites.[81] Fleury's rise to power in 1725–1730 was possible thanks only to his ability to appease or isolate the dominant factions at court, and after 1737 his exclusive role was slowly undermined, again leaving more room for court factions.[82] The last great cardinal-minister, however, followed the priorities sketched by Dubois: foreign affairs and the distribution of graces – with a special eye to church affairs. Maurepas later attempted to achieve the same position with the same methods, though without the formal title, and far less successfully.[83]

In 1974 Jean Bérenger noted the pervasiveness of the *valido* or favourite in the early seventeenth century, and the decline of the phenomenon in later reigns.[84] His wide-ranging analysis recently served as the starting point for a conference, and a volume published by J. H. Elliott and L. W. B. Brockliss. Its focus is on the late sixteenth and early seventeenth centuries: the later seventeenth century is christened the 'twilight' of the favourite. This reinforces the notion that powerful favourites rose at a critical point in the development of administrative monarchy, marking the changeover to more solidly established forms. The critical accumulation of pressures arising from religious turmoil, civil strife, warfare, and the growing burden of government by paper may have overwhelmed rulers not noted for their intellect or dexterity, leading them to undue reliance on trusted advisers and companions. When after the 1650s a measure of stability returned to most states, the favourite did not disappear, but became less conspicuous. Favour was inevitable at a court revolving around a single dynastic ruler, inflated to superhuman proportions in a show of rank and power, but often daunted by his task and longing for support. Favour was based not on special circumstances, but on the recurring structures

81 Campbell, *Power and Politics*, p. 98.

82 Campbell, *Power and Politics*; compare Luynes' surprised remark that during Fleury's illness in 1738 even the *capitaine des gardes* left the king alone with his favourite, *Mémoires*, II, p. 51.

83 John Hardman, *Louis XVI and his French Politics 1774–1789 from the Accession of Louis XVI to the Fall of the Bastille* (London 1995).

84 Jean Bérenger, 'Pour une enquête européenne: le problème du ministériat au XVIIe siècle', *Annales ESC*, 29, 1 (1974), pp. 166–192; Elliott and Brockliss, eds., *The World of the Favourite*; compare Hamish Scott, 'The Rise of the First Minister in Eighteenth-century Europe', in *History and Biography: Essays in Honour of Derek Beales*, ed. T. C. W. Blanning and David Cannadine (Cambridge 1996). The conclusions of the Elliott and Brockliss volume return in a monograph by one of their contributors, Antonio Feros, *Kingship and Favoritism in the Spain of Philip III 1598–1621* (Cambridge 2000), which stresses the continuity between the methods of Philip II's favourites, and more particularly between Lerma and Olivares. While Feros redresses the exaggerated contrast between Lerma and Olivares – the first usually depicted as a nonentity, the second as a powerful minister – he repeats the habitual contrast between these favourites and those succeeding them. 'Personal' methods of government were supplanted by 'institutional' methods, and Spanish kings followed the familiar advice of Louis XIV's memoirs.

of court life. Besenval couched his discussion of Louis XVI's insecurity in general terms:

obligé de donner continuellement des décisions, il se trouve sans cesse dans un embarras assez commun au rois, qui, succédant de droit au trône, s'y asseyent sans les notions qu'on n'acquiert que dans l'usage de la société, sans connoître même les lois fondamentales de l'Empire. Incertains comment prononcer, ils se laissent guider par le ministre auquel ils croient devoir donner leur confiance, ou par la maîtresse, le confesseur, le favori, qui les a subjugués.[85]

Notwithstanding the fact that the combined patronage of state and household by far surpassed the patronage of internal rivals, and could be administered with somewhat greater precision, this first cause of favouritism remained unaltered. In protracted critical phases, or with more vulnerable rulers, the favourite would return in many guises; more orderly procedures for council and administration did little to change this. Dubois' tract revolves around the double meaning of 'grace' resounding in the history of the court: the ruler's personal favour, and the benefits he could distribute. By taking hold of these, a favourite ruled, whether he styled himself first minister and accepted the coordination of royal policies, or simply amassed offices and wealth, gratifying his dependents; whether he helped ruling a realm torn by strife, or a relatively pacified kingdom. The favourite is not the equivalent of the first minister, but neither of the two functions disappeared with the consolidation of monarchies in the second half of the seventeenth century, nor did mistresses or lower-level multiple favourites disappear.

The reputation of favouritism among contemporaries and later observers was dubious at best, and often downright bad. Yet favourites could serve as a prop, when they astutely managed the patronage of an insecure ruler, wisely advised him, or simply helped him to seek respite at limited costs. Such positive favourites were as vulnerable as their more greedy and ambitious compeers. Like ministers, all favourites risked disgrace, and could serve as scapegoats, their disgrace or exile deflecting the negative consequences of unpopular decisions, or simply pleasing an unfriendly populace. They did not seek favour with the ruler, however, to allow the latter to play this trick upon them. Consequently, we cannot turn the logical sequence upside down by presenting this stratagem as a *raison d'être* for favouritism: it was one outcome only of the vulnerable bond between a conspicuous favourite and his patron. Possibly, the fact that Habsburg rulers were by tradition granted more shielded lives, made them less susceptible to seeking escape in the arms of confidants, or alternatively allowed such moves to pass unnoticed. In Vienna, gossip was undoubtedly as present as in Versailles, but the close observation and relentless speculation suggested by numerous memoirs and letters on the French court remained unknown or at least went unrecorded

85 Besenval, *Mémoires*, III, pp. 328–329.

among the Viennese. On the whole, a different mentality and make-up of the rulers, and different styles of service and decision-making, helped to make the favourite less provoking a presence in Vienna than in Versailles.

FACTION AT COURT

Access and favour rarely were a wholly individual affair. Ministers and mistresses could be pawns of courtiers seeking to gain a foothold in the ruler's proximity, or champions of a court faction. Persons reckoned among the ruler's intimates could expect to find themselves enlisted by others at court: they were perceived as vital channels of information and influence. Competition at court was thus to a large extent structured by the dynamics and perceptions of favour: intrigues were more likely to succeed when they were supported by those close to the ruler in his various pursuits. The monarchical ideal, however, did not leave much room for debates at court. The monarch's decisions were not expected to be moulded by others than his councillors and confidants. Nor were they allowed to raise doubts about their sovereign's policy, at court or elsewhere. When groups of courtiers systematically sought to influence the ruler's decisions, their effort would soon reach the limits of accepted behaviour – frequently 'faction' was used not as an indication of inoffensive horse-trading at court, but as the degeneration of the court, and an offence against the ruler's prerogatives. Therefore, cabals of courtiers usually operated in the margin – known to insiders, but rarely publicly acknowledged and listed. Open manifestations of partisanship occurred mostly in periods of crisis. More often, we find the contours of friendships and enmities at court tentatively reported by memorialists and diplomats. Diplomats, by their profession committed to penetrate the alliances and rivalries at court, habitually tried to identify those closest to the ruler, most influential in the councils, or particularly well connected among court grandees. Frequently, they presented their lists of names as groups, pitting one set of advisers and courtiers, with their lesser supporters at court, against an alliance of their rivals. Such lists reflect a variety of incongruous oppositions: lasting and fleeting rivalries, vehement as well as mild conflicts.

Detailed descriptions of faction, such as Saint-Simon's famous discussion of the court in 1709, have been used to draw diagrams of rivalries and loyalties.[86] The detail in the descriptions as well as in the drawings based on them may confer a false sense of precision. Was the constellation momentary, dictated by a specific bone of contention? Or did it reflect lasting oppositions between families or groups at court? Today's friends could be tomorrow's rivals: as the focus of

[86] Factions in Saint-Simon, *Mémoires*, for example IX, pp. 39–43; XV, pp. 1–23; XVI, pp. 11–14; XVIII, pp. 5–8; XXXVIII, pp. 278–279, 282–284 graphically presented in Le Roy Ladurie, 'Auprès du roi, la Cour', *AESC* 38, 1 (1983), pp. 21–41; compare the diagram in Linda and Marsha Frey, *A Question of Empire: Leopold I and the War of Spanish Succession 1701–1705* (New York 1983), p. 90.

conflict shifted from matters of rank, to policy choices, or nominations. Nor did the conflicts within each of these fields necessarily lead to stable oppositions. On the contrary, in each conflict, the patterns of allegiance and enmity could change. This would happen not only because of individual caprice: different settings engendered different loyalties. One layer of the hierarchy at court could be pitted against another, each defending the rights connected to its stratum; yet at other moments social equals within such a horizontal alliance would find themselves competing for the same rewards. Ministers could defend their specific interests against court dignitaries, yet at other times their 'functional' loyalty succumbed to rivalry within the ministry.[87] Conflict at court cannot be subsumed under one heading. The changeable panorama of loyalties and conflicts defies any rigid taxonomy: we need to assess different sources of loyalty and conflict.

RANK OR CLAN: HORIZONTAL VERSUS VERTICAL LOYALTIES

Noble dynasties with their friends, servants, and followers, often with a regional basis, formed relatively durable groupings. Their most distinguished members could be present at court, where they sought to strengthen family fortunes by office, favour, and marriage. While we can readily understand that relatives close or distant with their clients looked to each other for support, it is far from clear whether such loyalties dominated faction at court. They offered a focus for vertical solidarity, cutting through the horizontal layers of the social hierarchy, but were a loose grouping of which only the summit was present at court, where they met their compeers. Horizontal solidarity, based on the ranking of the court, offered another, contrasting focus for loyalties. Persons within a layer of the hierarchy – i.e. *princes du sang*, *ducs et pairs*, or *Fürsten*, *Räte*, *Kämmerer* – could collectively defend their rights against infringements, usually by contiguous ranks. Saint-Simon frequently protested the incursions of royal bastards and *princes étrangers*, two layers uncomfortably situated between the dukes and the princes. His complaints about the ascendancy of the ministers he perceived to be of execrably low birth were even more vehement. In the Habsburg lands, the *neue Fürsten* repeatedly proved reluctant to accept the place granted to them on the basis of the court's general yardstick of rank: seniority as chamberlain or councillor. Their demand for special distinctions clashed with the obvious desirability of leaving the twofold system of ranking unchanged; usually discreet compromises helped to reduce pressure. While ceremonial registers in both realms, discussed at some length in previous chapters, abound with examples of

[87] In France 'functional' loyalty can, at least for the larger part of Louis XIV's reign, be seen as horizontal loyalty, the *robe de conseil* occupying most ministerial places; in the eighteenth century the balance changed. In the Habsburg monarchy, the groups overlapped, and while the functional separation became more marked in the course of the eighteenth century, ministers and courtiers were largely recruited from the same groups.

such conflict, they also show that disputes for precedence within one layer of the hierarchy were widespread, as seniority was apt to be complicated by charges and responsibilities. Hierarchies of rank and function, moreover, never fitted easily, and conflict could occur between court officers sharing similar responsibilities (e.g. table servants), or when the chain of command was confusing (e.g. conflicts between *grand* and *premier* offices in France, or between captains of the guards and the high steward in Vienna).

Vertical and horizontal loyalties, clan and rank, were routinely tested in two spheres: competition for the ruler's patronage, and conflicts over precedence. The loyalties of rank, bringing together great nobles of one clan with their peers from another, would usually crumble under these everyday pressures. Indeed, conflict over precedence gained force from the vertical dividing lines of the noble networks. The great patrons were social near-equals, competing for the same distinctions of rank. Such distinctions, moreover, could confer closer access, and thus a better hold on the distribution of honours, vital sustenance for the *nébuleuses*. The *sang royal* itself was a competitive arena *par excellence*. Tension frequently surfaced in the upper stratum of the *famille royale*, notably between the ruling king and his brothers, but it was endemic among the *princes du sang* – Orléans, Condé, Conti – and between each of these dynasties and the king's bastards. Louis XIV's full assimilation of his bastards into the *princes du sang* in 1714 disturbed the regency and the early years of Louis XV. The regent orchestrated the abrogation of the rights of succession of the bastards, and nearly obliterated the special position granted by Louis XIV to the duc du Maine. In 1726, supporters both of Orléans, the regent's son, and du Maine rejoiced when M. le Duc, head of the house of Bourbon-Condé, fell from power.[88] The fiercely competitive princely dynasties were closely related by male as well as female connections. The dowager-duchesses of Orléans and Bourbon-Condé were illegitimate daughters of Louis XIV and Mme de Montespan, and sisters of his *bâtards* Maine and Toulouse; the dowager-princess of Conti was daughter of Louis XIV and Louise de la Valliere; Maine himself was married to a Bourbon-Condé princess. These women, long outliving their men, turned into powerful matrons defending the honour of their houses.[89]

The greatest court grandees, Lorraine, Rohan, and Bouillon, matched the querulous record of the princes: they were perennially testing each other, newly

[88] See the analysis in Campbell, *Power and Politics*; the troubled relations among the Orléans, Bourbon-Condé, and bâtards loom large in Dutch envoy Cornelis Hop's long and perceptive April 1724 letter describing the French court, see Algemeen Rijksarchief Den Haag (ARA) Collectie van der Hoop (1.10.42), inv. no. 191. I owe this reference to Olaf van Nimwegen. Luynes frequently reports uneasiness of princes vis-à-vis the ruler, in 1749 he noted they rarely visited Versailles, where the expanding royal family occupied the most attractive *logements*, *Mémoires*, X, p. 115 (April 1749).

[89] The same holds true for the Maréchale de Noailles, M.-F. de Bournonville (1656–1748) coaching the fortunes of her family. The Noailles were related by marriage to the comte de Toulouse, Louis XIV's well-liked and influential bastard, whose household in Rambouillet frequently offered hospitality to Louis XV, see Campbell, *Power and Politics*, pp. 41–42, 72, 102, 130, 168–169.

establishing their status and sway in ceremonial conflict.[90] Only slightly below their level, a sequence of noble dynasties, among which the Noailles were conspicuously successful in the eighteenth century, repeated the same pattern. The existence of noble networks could both reinforce and mitigate conflicts over precedence at court: friends in one affiliation could choose not to quarrel over the keenly cherished outward attributes of rank, or would more easily forget their passing antagonism; rivals would be apt to engage in protracted struggles.

In Vienna, we miss the characteristically unmanageable echelon comprised in France of the lower fringes of the royal family and the highest levels of court officers. The incidents of Habsburg dynastic demography led to the near-disappearance of this group in the course of the seventeenth century. After 1619, strife within the dynasty occurred only in notably exceptional situations, such as Leopold-William's possible candidacy for the imperial dignity, Joseph I's restiveness towards the end of his father's long reign, or Charles' and Joseph's contrasting interests and policies in Joseph's reign. By strengthening Bavarian and Saxon ambitions for the Habsburg succession, however, the marriages of Joseph's daughters, posed a serious but distant threat to dynastic peace. In Vienna, a wider echelon of noble families was eligible for supreme office at court, and they competed for the emperor's graces, but the game seems to have been muted in comparison with France, as was the battle for rank. The emperor, moreover, had more leeway in his choice of court officers, and his nomination of the younger members of all families as chamberlain, or councillor, determined seniority within the simple twofold hierarchical system. The regional connections of court grandees were relevant for France, as the Noailles' ties to Languedoc show; yet in Vienna they may still have had a stronger impact. The composite nature of Habsburg dominion and the distances between the various parts engendered more marked differences in style as well as policy priorities for the 'nations' represented at court. In a 1751 *Denkschrift*, Maria Theresa censured the strength of regional loyalties of her ministers, that had prevented her from acting rapidly in the 1740s, and made clear her intention to put an end to collusion between the central state servants in Vienna and the regional estates.[91]

MINISTERS AND COURTIERS

When Luynes in July 1754 outlined the 'parties' within the ministry formed by Machault and D'Argenson respectively, he noted pointedly that the latter, secretary for war, had: 'beaucoup d'amis, mais non pas dans le ministère et fort peu

[90] See, for example, Véri's observation on the Lorraine, Bouillon, and Rohan, *Journal de l'abbé de Véri*, I, pp. 131–132.

[91] 'Zwei Denkschriften', mostly pp. 300–302.

dans les courtisans qui approchent du roi'.[92] Slightly earlier, he had commented upon the close connections of Machault's party with the king's mistress-turned-into-friend Mme de Pompadour. Besenval and Croÿ later discussed the parties of Choiseul and d'Aiguillon in the same vein; the former was ousted from the ministry of war in December 1770 partly by the intrigues of d'Aiguillon, supported by Mme du Barry.[93] The chances of parties at court, we may infer, depended on their connections in the ministry, as well as among the courtiers in the king's proximity – with the mistress in Louis XV's later days as the most significant factor.

Does this reflect earlier practice? For Louis XIV's days, the ministers have usually been depicted as a group of powerful mandarins, antagonising the collectivity of great nobles by their haughty demeanour – Louvois most of all, as his responsibility for the army combined with his crudeness made clashes with noble commanders inevitable. Court grandees frequently and loudly proclaimed their indignation about these social climbers. In his memoirs Louis made clear his intention to separate supreme rank from ministerial office, a goal maintained with diminishing rigour throughout his reign. In practice loyalty among the ministers succumbed to pressures quite like those dividing the great officers at court. Noble courtiers were willing to cooperate backstage with the mandarin *usurpateurs*, enlisting their support against fellow-grandees. Saint-Simon, mouthpiece of collective indignation, befriended ministers whenever he could. The most consistently reported rivalry of Louis XIV's court, in addition to the tensions within the *sang royal*, moreover, was that between Colbert and Louvois and their descendants, heading their carefully maintained networks.[94] The ministers as well as the courtiers followed the logic of dynastic competition, seeking support against those vying for the same rewards. The patronage connected to their ministries, and the family alliances they cultivated, resembled the parallel methods of the court grandees. A lasting commitment of Louvois or Colbert to their collective status as minister is hard to find; indeed, some of their conflicts may be explained by the tension inherent in the competition between the priorities of war and finance, which functional competition strengthened the rivalry engendered by their social proximity. In the eighteenth century, the social distance between the descendants of these ministers and courtiers lessened,

92 Luynes, *Mémoires*, XIII, pp. 430–431, 436–437 (July 1754), quote on p. 437 about Pierre-Marc de Voyer de Paulmy, comte d'Argenson, secretary for war, and Jean Baptiste Machault d'Arnouville, *contrôleur-général* and *garde des sceaux*.

93 Besenval, *Mémoires*, II, pp. 20–55; *Journal inédit du duc de Croÿ*, II, pp. 454–459, Aiguillon and Du Barry, pp. 462, 474; Aiguillon's nomination as secretary for foreign affairs, pp. 505–506, 513–514; the *anéantissement* of Choiseul's party on p. 515. Etienne-François comte de Stainville, duc de Choiseul, occupying a range of ministerial positions in the preceding decades, achieved a position not far removed from the *premier ministre*, before he was ousted by combined efforts of Mme du Barry and Emmanuel Armand de Vignerot du Plessis duc d'Aiguillon, foreign secretary 1771–1774, minister for war 1774.

94 The rivalry between the clans of Louvois and Colbert is well-attested, see Mettam, *Power and Faction*, pp. 93–98, 156–157, 241–243. On p. 97 Mettam suggests the professional rivalry of the two departments as a possible explanation; Spanheim, *Relation*, pp. 312, 314, 315, 316, 336, 362, 366, 367, 369, 552–554; Saint-Simon: *Mémoires*, III, p. 28; IV, pp. 40, 264; VI, p. 364; VIII, p. 16; X, p. 46; XI, p. 50; XIV, p. 314; XV, p. 85; XVII, p. 416; XXVIII, pp. 11, 54–56.

and we again find high nobles in ministerial office. Thus, it becomes increasingly unlikely to construe a lasting functional opposition between ministers and courtiers. Indeed, we should be careful not to accept without scrutiny the existence of other functional foci of loyalty at court: 'church' or 'army' reflected fields of competition more than a unified interest or 'lobby'. Confessor Tellier's dislike of Mme de Maintenon, reported by Saint-Simon, may have been caused by her strong hold on the distribution of ecclesiastical benefices. The nominations of army commanders, reported at length in Sourches or Luynes, indicates the most recurring concern of army officers, and were a source of rivalry.

For Vienna the contrast between 'bourgeois' ministers and noble courtiers makes even less sense than it did for France. The spheres of household and administration remained intimately connected deep into the eighteenth century; when halfway through the century a functional separation was emerging, we consistently find noble as well as non-noble state-servants. The principle of *Stiftsfähigkeit*, granting ecclesiastical places only to those able to prove sixteen quarters of spotless descent, prevented German high nobles from allowing social climbers to marry into their dynasty. This seriously limited the potential for assimilation, and it may not have been a coincidence that Chancellor's Strattmann's daughter married Count Batthyány, a Hungarian noblemen untroubled by such strictures. There was no outcry against the social ascent of chancellors though irritation surfaced about their pedantry or *parvenu* manners.[95] The predominantly noble elites at court and in the administrative gremia were clearly less concerned about the incursions of non-nobles than were their French counterparts. Incidentally we find labels for faction indicating an opposition between courtiers and ministers. Senior minister as well as general, Prince Eugene was never close to Charles VI. This predicament invited frequent attempts to oust him from office. His faction of 'ministers' – a label explained by Eugene's authority among conference ministers – was opposed by a faction of 'courtiers', notably including Charles' favourite Althann and supported by a 'Spanish' faction.[96] In Maria Theresa's later days, a sense of opposition may have existed between old style servants like Khevenhüller and new style administrators closer to Joseph – yet this matches more closely the recurring conflict between the 'old' court of an ageing ruler and the 'young' court of the successor.[97] Ministers rarely formed a single front at the Viennese court; nor can we picture the influence of clerics as the collective defence of a sectional interest. The prominence of a variety of shades of Catholic beliefs, each with its own differently oriented clerics, made alliances the exception instead of the rule. Pufendorf's observation that Leopold's

[95] *Weensche Gezantschapsberichten*, II, p. 318, on Hofkanzler Seilern: 'cependant il n'est pas du goût de tout le monde et il n'y en a qui trouvent à redire à ses manières'; Heilingsetzer, 'Führungsschicht', pp. 128–130, mentions the nobles' dislike of the pedantry of ennobled state servants.

[96] See Gehling, *Europäischer Diplomat*, pp. 44–116.

[97] Bourgogne and Joseph I are the evident examples; see Campbell, *Power and Politics*, for example, pp. 52, 66–67, discussing the cabale of the duc de Chartres/Orléans, and the 'vieille cour' consisting of the remainders of the ministry and favourites of Louis XIV's reign.

Jesuit confessor Müller and his Capucin confidant Sinelli belonged to different factions again supports the general conclusion that those closest in rank or function tended to choose opposite sides.[98]

THE INTERNATIONAL DIMENSION

Religious schism and internal strife made the splendid isolation of the ruler's collegial decision-making improbable. The Protestant challenge and the quest for counter-reform connected to the Spanish Habsburgs dominated the vocabulary of faction into the seventeenth century. The legacy of the French *ligue* did not end with the accession of Henry IV, and a moderate prolongation of its tenets may be found among the *dévôts* – mostly the combination of anti-Huguenot and pro-Habsburg policies. The *dévôts*, however, represented a broad religious phenomenon much more than a court faction or a vehicle of noble clans. Richelieu, usually depicted as their determined adversary, can equally well be seen as a *dévôt*, notwithstanding his policies in the European arena.[99] The religious factor remained important in French court quarrels: yet the 'dévot' label changed into a wider variety of competing religious groups and leanings, inextricably mixed with political attitudes. In the eighteenth century the conflicts engendered by the papal bull *Unigenitus* Rome as well as the internal political ramifications of ultramontanism, gallicanism, and jansenism were among the most heatedly debated topics – yet Spain was now wholly irrelevant to these issues. In reaction to Louis XV's early promiscuity, something like a 'dévôt' faction surfaced, briefly holding sway during Louis XV's embarrassing 1744 confessions and apologies in Metz. By that time, however, open conflict over policies had become common at court, and the *sécrétaires d'état* threatened to turn into 'candidates of aristocratic factions'.[100] The expulsion of the Jesuits by the Choiseul ministry had antagonised the *Mesdames de France*, Louis XV's daughters. Brought in by the same minister, the new *dauphine* Marie-Antoinette by her rank and position challenged the king's daughters' supremacy among women at court, and they proved distinctly unreceptive: she soon became a major target of their *dévot* grouping, attached to Choiseul's rival Aiguillon, and not averse to using the king's new mistress Mme du Barry.[101]

Arguably, warfare, as the quintessential noble trade, aroused the active concern of courtiers more than most other policy decisions. The vagaries of the War of Spanish Succession led to opposition between hawks and doves; the peace of

[98] Redlich, 'Tagebuch Esaias Pufendorfs', p. 570.

[99] Compare the reassessment in Bergin, *Rise of Richelieu*, pp. 113–115, with the more conventional presentation in *DGS*, pp. 472–473.

[100] Campbell, *Power and Politics*, p. 175; see Hardman, *Louis XVI*, for a more sceptical view about courtiers' power.

[101] *Correspondence secrète entre Marie-Thérèse et le Cte de Mercy-Argenteau*, see pp. xvi–xvii; II, p. 22 (Mercy to Maria Theresa, 14 August 1773); II, p. 178 (Maria Theresa to Mercy 16 June 1774); II, p. 344 (Marie-Antoinette to Maria Theresa 22 June 1775); compare Besenval, *Mémoires*, II, pp. 20–55, on Choiseul's disgrace, and the rivalry between Choiseul and Aiguillon, the latter supported by Mme Du Barry.

Utrecht inaugured friendly relations with England, and left the remnants of the 'old system' based on warfare against the sea powers and the emperor in disarray; the Spanish marriage gave rise to another sequence of troubles, as did the mid-century wars and the *renversement des alliances*.

The standing rivalry with Spain and the ongoing wars made open Spanish influence more suspect in France than it was at the Habsburg court in most periods. Pejorative references to a 'Spanish party' in the Habsburg lands were particularly strong in the long prelude to the Bohemian rebellion. The label, however, was used as a rallying cry, coined to unite those forces averse to Spanish or counter-reformatory influences. We have to ascertain whether their unfriendly allegations were well founded. Did Lobkowitz, Martinitz, Slawata, and their friends truly form a 'Spanish party' or did they simply share Catholic beliefs and *Kaisertreue*? – the latter seems far more likely.[102] The cluster of dynastic, religious, and political associations clinging to Spain remained in evidence at both courts throughout the early seventeenth century, but we should take care not to overstate the levels either of Spanish influence, or cooperation among such affiliations.

In general, it is difficult to disentangle the positions chosen by a ruler and his advisers from the real or alleged influence of diplomats or court factions. Spanish ambassadors were not necessarily the most active or dominant diplomats at court. French diplomats, after 1648 and 1659 representing a triumphant and expansive state, ostentatiously flaunted their power in Europe's capitals. The French court itself represented not only the centre of power of the French realm, but an increasingly dominant point of orientation for European – and more incidentally, African or Asian – diplomats. In Vienna electors and their agents were notably present, and could hope to generate support among court nobles. Papal nuncios and Venetian ambassadors were particularly respected, and we habitually find them with their Spanish colleagues as the participants or spectators of ceremonies and festivities. French envoys were notoriously active. Spanish sources readily perceived Leopold's ministers as the cronies of Grémonville, French envoy after 1664, and we have seen that the emperor, while countering such accusations, was never wholly at ease with his ministers.[103] Grémonville was active both in befriending the emperor's councillors, and in inciting the Hungarian malcontents. His record was far from unique: ambassadors, lesser diplomats, and spies certainly tried hard to find support for their causes; they systematically used bribes and were not invariably averse to employing force to get their way.[104]

102 Compare other labels for factions, for example the *importants* of 1643, see Jean-Marie Constant in *DGS*, p. 746. Discussions with Ivo Cerman (Prague) helped me to put into perspective the notion of a 'Spanish' party.

103 Only after 1715 would the French send ambassadors to the Austrian Habsburgs; before that date the supremacy granted by the emperors to the ambassadors of their fellow Spanish Habsburgs prevented this.

104 See, for example Lucien Bély, *Espions et Ambassadeurs au temps de Louis XIV* (Paris 1990). See See Pecar, 'Ökonomie der Ehre', pp. 140–141, for the 1,320,255 fl Luis Duque de Ripperda distributed in 1725 to find support for Spanish interests.

Vienna was more than once confronted by the Ottoman as well as the French military challenge. A war on two fronts would stretch the monarchy's limited means to the utmost, and thus choices had to be made: whom to pacify, whom to fight? As long as this situation persisted, it could give rise to faction at court. Conceivably, the location of the heartlands of the protagonists at court influenced their preferences: were they more likely to profit from war against the French, or from war against the Ottomans? The juxtaposition of 'Easterners' and 'Westerners', however, conveys a rigid and simplistic image of the shades of opinion at court.

The first task of diplomats was to discover whose proximity to decision-making justified further friendly inducements. Diplomats reportedly tried to manipulate Prince Eugene, an obvious target for such manoeuvres, through his friend, the widow Countess Eleonore Batthyány (Strattmann's daughter), and through his personal secretaries. Such practices, soliciting the support of women as well as of staff, mirrored the styles used to approach the ruler at a lower level.[105] When diplomats were not successful in finding or buying support in the highest echelons, they could hope to influence decisions by strengthening those courtiers more favourably disposed towards their goals, either as groups or as individuals – usually a slow and uncertain process at best. Only incidentally would the enticements of diplomats tilt the scales between competing groups at court. The prying and meddling of diplomats, however, was a lasting ingredient of factional strife at court.

Talk of Spanish or other foreign 'parties' at court frequently hid a reality relatively distant from policy choices or diplomacy. Foreign advisers in the ruler's proximity, or the presence of foreign households, would convince others of unsavoury intrigues, which were misleading the ruler, and most particularly, conquering his grace(s). Those who felt excluded sought to counter such perceived intrigues by loudly denouncing them. Ferdinand I's formative court ordinances were decreed partly as an answer to complaints by the estates, who suspected him of breaking with indigenous tradition as well as with local dignitaries, preferring his Spanish and Flemish advisers. In the late 1660s Margarita Teresa's following, disrupting the Viennese quartering system, annoyed courtiers and gave rise to grumblings about a 'Spanish camarilla'. After Charles VI's return to Vienna, the Dutch resident noted sharp discontent among the local nobles, who observed with anger the favours given to the emperor's Spanish following.[106] A

105 Gehling, *Europäischer Diplomat*, pp. 32–33, 67–68.

106 See Paula Sutter Fichtner, *Ferdinand I of Austria: The Politics of Dynasticism in the Age of Reformation*, East European Monographs, no. C (New York 1982), pp. 28–30; Christiane Thomas, 'Von Burgund zu Habsburg. Personalpolitische und administrative Verflechtungen in den Herrschaftskomplexen des Hauses Österreich', in *Archiv und Forschung. Das Haus-, Hof- und Staatsarchiv in seiner Bedeutung für die Geschichte Österreichs und Europas*, ed. Elisabeth Springer and Leopold Kammerhofer (Vienna and Munich 1993), pp. 35–48; Spielman, *City & the Crown*, pp. 96, 99, 118; *Weensche Gezantschapsberichten*, II, pp. 541–542; Lhotsky, 'Kaiser Karl VI. und sein Hof', p. 65; Hadamowsky, *Barocktheater am Wiener Kaiserhof*, p. 46.

'Spanish' party, based on Charles' Iberian experiences and advisers, did arise in the following years; in the other cases mentioned, the presence of foreigners, and their competition for favours usually reserved for locals, was in itself sufficient to generate opposition. The notion of foreigners as improper competitors was present in the outcry against Concini, and later in the furious attacks against Mazarin. Was this an exception in the French context? Suriano, a Venetian ambassador, describing the French kings' sources of power shortly after Francis II's death, commented positively on the Salic law, preventing foreign princes from ascending the French throne, and argued that the French loved their king most of all because he 'has the patronage of an enormous number of titles, offices, judgeships, Church benefices, grants, pensions, gifts, and other good jobs and honors, . . . and he assigns all of them to his own subjects . . .'. This contrasted markedly with the practice at other courts, the ambassador concluded.[107] Towards the end of the seventeenth century, moreover, the French court was notably less cosmopolitan in its composition than the Habsburg court.

Open conflict over policy decisions was an affront to the monarchical state and its councillors. It occurred in unsettled times, when the ruler's legitimacy was eroded by religious schism or protracted malpractice, or during minorities and succession crises – periods when the notorious favourite, too, was apt to surface, usually connected to one or more factions, provoking the fierce opposition of others. Yet while crisis at court might be recurring, or persisting, at a lower level debates over policy must have continued in more stable periods. It is far from clear whether the decisions reached in the council were prefigured by discussions among courtiers, or by rivalry between existing alignments. We can assume the interest as well as the influence of a select group of courtiers, but under a strong ruler, their position was contingent upon discretion. The connection with previously discussed forms of competition cannot be forced into any fixed mould. Only when specific policies were expected to affect the status and power of an existing alignment at court, can we expect its involvement as a group. On the whole, no single model of court faction can be accepted, only an enumeration of recurring themes, and several lasting contradictions.

CONCLUSION

There is no reason to picture the court as a Hobbesian fight of all against all, but competition definitely was a common occurrence, both among individuals and among their changing alignments. In this ambitious environment, the vulnerability and loneliness of rulers strike the eye. Their predicament made it difficult to find a balance between emotional isolation and trust; between overworking

[107] See Suriano's relazione in J. C. Davis, *Pursuit of Power: Venetian Ambassadors' Reports on Spain, Turkey, and France in the Age of Philip II* (New York 1970), pp. 185–187.

themselves and leaving their responsibilities to others. A variety of persons in their proximity, from relatives and sexual intimates, to servants in all ranks and segments of the court, was most likely to find favour with them. When trusted confidants among these intimates dominated the ruler, and sought to withhold favours and access from others, this temporary solution to isolation usually only served to exacerbate the problems of rulership. Most rulers discussed here were dependent on senior advisers – often previous mentors – in the early stages of their reign, and tended to seek the support of their legitimate, morganatic, or illegitimate spouses in their later years.

Intermediaries were inevitable for more distant petitioners. They could use their attachment to noble houses, or connections to staffs and departments, to ask for intercession. The 'vertical' ties of family networks, confronting noble clans, and the 'horizontal' orientation flowing from the hierarchical stratification, defending the rights of their position in the ranking, exerted contradictory pressures, and could lead to conflicting loyalties. Nevertheless, those closest to each other in rank and function most frequently found themselves competing for graces, as well as for the visible attributes of rank. No clear-cut conclusion can be drawn about the more incidental alignments involving policy decisions. Dividing lines, moreover, were never rigid, and could change according to the occasion. Only in unsettled times, when low-profile everyday competition had escalated, and inhibitions were weakened, would faction approach insubordination, by openly and blatantly seeking to change the ruler's course. In the Habsburg monarchy such moments were rare; more examples can be found in France during the regencies, and in the second half of the eighteenth century. Most court factions combined elements of many forces cited in this chapter. They were more conspicuous when a ruler was insecure – coalesced around his close relatives, around other persons in the proximity of the ruler, or as a defensive move against the perceived ascendancy of another group. For faction as well as for the favourite, it helps to differentiate between the unavoidable and pervasive forms, and their more exceptional exacerbations. Most contemporary observers suggest that cabals and intrigues pervaded court life, and were the rule instead of the exception. Competition for places and nominations was endemic, and did not necessarily lead to the 'menées secrettes & illicites' and 'conduite détournée' given in the *Encyclopédie* under 'cabale' and 'intrigue' respectively.

Who held power at court? Who influenced decisions? These two superficially parallel questions hint at different problems. The court ostentatiously demonstrated noble power, as well as noble subservience to the sovereign summit of nobility. Court offices conveyed immense prestige, conferred access to the distribution of graces, and brought propinquity to decision-making. When we take all three to represent power, court nobles were a power elite *par excellence* in France as in the Habsburg monarchy; when we more narrowly define power as the demonstrable influence on major policy decisions, the balance changes considerably. In Vienna, where court and ministerial offices could be shared among the members of one extended noble family, only a limited number of conference ministers and secretaries would mould the emperor's policies at any particular time. In France, the same held true for a handful of supreme state servants – *sécrétaires d'état*, *chancelier*, *garde des sceaux and contrôleur-général*. French court nobles, moreover, did not as a rule serve as *ministre d'état*, or secretary of state. Such service became more usual in the course of the eighteenth century, but it still cut a meagre figure in comparison with the record of Habsburg nobles. At the time the political role of traditional court officers slowly diminished in Vienna, however, their counterparts in Versailles were again present in ministerial positions, and court faction a manifest influence on policy-making.

Discussing the nomination of a captain of the guards at court, Véri voiced an opinion that was clearly gaining strength in the last decades of the eighteenth century:

Peu importe au public que ce soit tel ou tel qui occupe ces sortes de charges, si propres à contenter la vanité servile des gens de cour et si insignifiantes dans l'administration générale.[108]

Court office, indeed, did not in itself lead to predominance in the *administration générale*, though major courtiers could strive to exert influence through a variety of channels. Probably, most French courtiers were happy to hold prestigious office, strengthen the position of their families, and acquire regional governments, army commands, or diplomatic charges. This fitted their noble way of life, reflecting a more inclusive, or 'social' definition of power.[109] Nevertheless, some of them held office as minister or secretary, while others must have exerted power informally and indirectly. The informal and unrecorded stages of decision-making need more study, but their very secrecy makes conclusive results unlikely: influence can only be established on an individual basis, after intensive research. Court nobles formed a vested elite, including conspicuously powerful as well as wholly insignificant persons; no student of power structures and processes in early modern monarchy can safely disregard them.

108 *Journal de l'abbé de Véri*, II, p. 216.

109 See Campbell, *Power and Politics*, p. 108, quoting the correspondence of the duc de Richelieu – who is presented as quite influential on p. 22, alas without further detail. The Noailles would be an evident example of a family permanently close to power and very well connected.

CHAPTER 8

The court as focus of the realm

INTRODUCTION

Faction did not stop at the palace gates. The contests at court can only be understood in the context of the court's position in a larger whole. The same holds true for the dynamics of court office and royal orders, or for ceremony. The preceding chapters have hinted at these connections, but concentrated mainly on the stubborn human details of the household, stressing continuity in forms as well as in mentality. Nevertheless, the position of the court in the larger whole underwent important changes, in France as well as in the Habsburg lands. It does not suffice to ascertain continuities in the make-up of the household: we have to integrate them into the developmental picture of state building, and the diverging trajectories of the two realms under discussion. Did the court strengthen its position as a social, political, and cultural point of reference for groups and regions connected to the dynasty? Did the position of nobles in the regional power structures change, and can such changes be connected to the household?

Courts have frequently been presented as 'instruments of power' alongside the army and the bureaucracy; as minor or major assets in the hands of rulers determined to establish a strong state.[1] Such statements are tautologies as well as half-truths. We cannot easily separate the early modern court from the state; for most purposes this conglomerate of persons, institutions, and interests was the major theatre where the 'state' took form. It is seriously misleading to picture the court either as an army led into battle by a ruler striving to overcome the opponents of 'absolutism', or as a luxurious prison for disarmed opponents. The court was a steady point of contact for the major players of a realm, and although no single person determined the connections amongst them, the ruler was by definition a principal actor. This pivotal position, as we have seen, froze many rulers into inaction. The structural assets connected to their central position were a heavy burden for flesh and blood incumbents, awed by their sacral

[1] See, for example, Jürgen von Kruedener, *Die Rolle des Hofes im Absolutismus*, Forschungen zur Sozial- und Wirtschaftsgeschichte 19 (Stuttgart 1973).

stature as well as constrained by the unrelenting practical demands. Power, at court and elsewhere, was a process reflecting changing balances among groups and persons, never a fixed outcome, or an artefact – Norbert Elias took that perceptive notion as point of departure for his analysis, only to stifle it under his replication of absolutist mythology.

At court a variety of overlapping relationships were made visible: ruler and nobles, ruler and ministers, ruler and church, ruler and subjects, centre and provinces, Europe's sovereign rulers among each other. Clearly, we cannot always read such representations as reflecting, let alone transforming, reality, but the images themselves could have considerable influence. Likewise, hierarchies established at court filtered into noble hierarchies by various means. Finally, by providing a point of contact as well as a symbolic centre, the court could be of utmost importance. Nothing in this enumeration was wholly new in the early modern age, and in the course of the centuries the traditional forms may simply have adapted to changes engendered by forces outside of the limited compass of the court itself – but we should address the possible connections between the household and change. A brief overview of the changing balances between centre and periphery, ruler and regional elites, may prove of use. On a different level, we have to ask ourselves whether the busy machinery of court life was central for observers in the country at large, and could indeed structure their cultural preferences and ideals.

CENTRE AND REGIONS

Entrées and *Erbhuldigungen* invested a new prince with the titles and powers he held over the components of his dominion. Coins must have made him vaguely familiar for many of his subjects. Yet how often did agents of royal government encroach upon these subjects' daily lives? Did regional governors or governing bodies, pledging loyalty to the sovereign,[2] see themselves as ruling their territories in their own right, or as his representatives? Were their actions reported to the sovereign, and corrected or annulled when the ruler deemed necessary?

FRANCE

For France, we can establish a steady strengthening of a chain of command connecting the regions to the centre.[3] Royal governors, the king's personal representatives in the provinces connected to military command as well as government,

[2] See AN O 1 713 'Répertoire Alphabetique des charges qui pretent serment entre les mains du Roy, avec le montant desdits sermens', including the governors, who paid between *c.* 6,000 and 14,000 (only Guyenne) upon pledging their oath. With at least 10,000 lt governors of the traditional provinces and the *pays d'états* paid most, significantly more than the chancelier (8,000) or the highest court officers.

[3] See the third part of Barbiche, *Institutions de la monarchie française*, pp. 313–406, on pp. 313–319 outlining the various superimposed but frequently incongruent administrative entities: *gouvernement*, *généralité*, *intendance*.

emerged in the fourteenth century. They provided provinces with a prestigious central figure, supplanting the largely judicial powers of the older *baillis* and *sénéchaux*, or usurping the powers of previous sovereigns in newly annexed provinces. These governors tended to be recruited from among the king's relatives, frequently from among royal bastards, and from families with strong ties to the regions they governed. The connections of such families were fitted into the edifice of royal government, with evident benefits for both sides. The king used the regional support of these families to strengthen the connections between regions and royal power; the families wielded regional power and consolidated their prestige. In sixteenth-century France, governors imitated the increasing elaboration of royal ceremonies, and entered cities with the habitual appurtenances of sovereignty, notably the canopy.[4]

The rank of governor was never either a venal proprietary 'office' or a charge held by commission. The governor was the king's personal representative, the most prestigious agent of royal government in the provinces, yet in theory he could instantly be dismissed. Women as well as men held the honour: we find queens and duchesses governing provinces, a practice abandoned after Anne of Austria.[5] Ideally the domain of princely dynasties, it was regularly invaded by the king's lesser-ranking special favourites – Henry III's *archimignons* and their kin held major *gouvernements*. In the early modern age, the number of such regional governorships increased from 12 to almost 40 – an expansion concentrated in the century after 1550. Within these entities ruled by governors, smaller *places* and forts also called *gouvernements*, were held by other nobles. The extent of each government in territories and responsibilities was never wholly clear, and the king could subdivide governments – as Louis XIII did for the successors of Epernon in 1622.[6] Governors frequently served simultaneously as army commander, councillor, or court dignitary, and were often absent: in these instances; they were replaced by a second echelon of royal representatives, the *lieutenants-généraux*. In the course of the seventeenth century, *lieutenants-généraux* came to serve permanently as deputy-governors. In the most important governments, a *commandant en chef*, serving on the basis of revocable commission, maintained order and commanded troops. Lieutenants and commanders usually were high nobles, closely following the governor in duties as well as in status. A figure of entirely different make-up was to become the main pillar of everyday regional administration: the intendant. In the later sixteenth century governors were supported by robe specialists in various administrative matters, notably law

[4] Robert R. Harding, *Anatomy of a Power Elite: The Provincial Governors of Early Modern France* (New Haven and London 1978), pp. 8ff.; Michel Antoine, 'Gouverneurs de Province', in *DGS*, pp. 667–671, with list of incumbents 1589–1715, and Antoine's 'Les gouverneurs de province en France (XVIe–XVIIIe siècle)', in *Prosopographie et génèse de l'état moderne. Actes de la Table ronde de Paris, 22–23 oct. 1984*, ed. F. Autrand (Paris 1986), pp. 185–194.

[5] Compare the *landvoogd(es)* in the Dutch provinces under Spanish rule: frequently women related to the dynasty, or the *stadhouders* ruling the various provinces for the Habsburg prince, usually with strong ties to these provinces.

[6] Antoine, 'Gouverneurs de province', in *DGS*, p. 667.

and taxes. These specialists were chosen mostly among the *maîtres des requêtes*, and would later be called intendants. The intendants inserted a measure of bureaucratic paperwork and continuity into an intensely personalised system of government.

In the early seventeenth century, there was a marked change in the position of the governors: their regional followings became less secure, as their patronage of lesser governments in their provinces diminished, partly because of the razing of forts, decreed in 1626. Finally, the governors tended to reside more frequently in Paris, at court, leaving their provinces to the lieutenants.[7] Absenteeism entailed a reorientation more than a loss of power: the closer connection to the court helped the governors to restore their position as patrons for the provinces, acting as the broker of provincial interest at court. This change coincided with the weakening of the governors' noble military clientage, and a steady increase in the intendants' share in provincial administration.[8] During the civil wars a disobedient governor could carry with him an entire province. With the exception of the great southern provinces, rebellions of governors, concentrated in the years 1614–1620, 1630–1632, and the *Fronde*, were less effective because of the diminished military potential of the governors.[9] Nevertheless, relations between governors and royal power were turbulent deep into the seventeenth century. Of the 19 governors in office when Richelieu rose to power, four remained in 1642, the others having been replaced, disgraced, or executed.[10]

Writers such as du Tillet or Loyseau had complained about abuses of power by governors, and called for remedies. The 1629 *Code Michaux* had stated that no intendant should be appointed to a province ruled by a governor to whom he had previously been connected.[11] After the 1630s the sequence of intendants serving in regional government was rarely broken. The intendants, however, cannot simply be seen as the king's men, outmanoeuvering presumptuous governors at the ruler's behest. They sought to bring order into regional government, partly by repairing and propping up an institution that was still of great importance for the monarchy as well as for the families holding it. In practice, the status of the principal governors was such that the intendants were still frequently enrolled in their service; critical voices censured the intendant of Provence in the 1640s for acting more as if he were intendant of the governor's household than truly an 'homme du roi'.[12] Mostly, governors and intendants cooperated: the

7 Harding, *Anatomy*, pp. 199–202; the estates general of Blois in 1614 suggested the razing of forts in the interior provinces, a 1626 edict prescribed it, underlining the savings made in garrison duties.

8 See Harding, *Anatomy*, pp. 203–204, for noble clientage general on p. 199 with the apt description: 'Yet, although it cannot be shown that anyone in the central government consciously projected such a change, the more bureaucratic system superseded the patrimonial one'. On pp. 123–124, 206, there are other general revisionist assessments.

9 See Harding, *Anatomy*, pp. 204–205, for the governors' military clientage.

10 See Barbiche, *Institutions*, p. 328.

11 Harding, *Anatomy*, p. 191, citing article 81 of the 1629 *Code Michaux*.

12 Harding, *Anatomy*, p. 207.

intendant serving as the principal actor in the king's regional administration, the governor as his higher-placed personal representative.[13] Curiously, the intendant indirectly strengthened the governor: he was held responsible for unpopular royal measures, or misbehaving royal agents. This allowed the governor to act effectively as the king's go-between with regional dignitaries, representing the interests of the communities and groups in his region at court, and seeking compromises acceptable to all parties.

In the aftermath of the *Fronde*, the power of governors was further delimited: Louis XIV decreed in 1661 that governors did not have life tenure: their charge was 'à trois ans renouvelable'; moreover, they had to ask permission to reside in their province.[14] In practice, the measures strengthened the tendency of governors to reside at court, without necessarily undermining their power. Even notorious *frondeurs* continued their service as governors, but safeguards were found to secure their loyalty as well as to set limits to their regional power bases.[15] Condé, condemned for *lèse majesté* in 1654, was reinstated to the government of Burgundy and Bresse, but he lost Berry, and his son Henry-Jules took over his charge of high steward in a somewhat diminished form.[16] The Longueville, anything but loyal during the *Fronde*, had strong support in Normandy, and the king could not give the province another governor without risking disturbances. Therefore, Louis and Mazarin formally left the duke his governorship, but had his functions exercised by a royal deputy. They placated the duke by adding a peerage to his duchy, and by promising to acknowledge the Longueville, who were Valois bastards, as *princes du sang*.[17] High nobles remained the typical candidates for governorships – though Louis was more careful with princes, displacing them in regional government with his illegitimate children or loyal favourites. The marquis de Dangeau, of solid but simple nobility,

[13] George Cuer, 'Gouverneurs, gouvernements', in *DAR*, pp. 604–608; p. 605 suggesting the intendant as representative of the council, the governor as the king's personal representative, respectively covering the 'administrative' and the 'social' sphere – a repartition nicely matching the developments at court, where the 'administrative' component waxed alongside the long more prestigious personal sphere of the ruler. Compare Barbiche, *Institutions*, p. 391.

[14] See Béguin, 'Louis XIV et l'aristocratie', pp. 500–501, citing a new edition of the *Mémoires pour l'instruction du dauphin* (Paris 1992), pp. 137–138. Marion, *dictionnaire*, p. 260, cites a 23 June 1750 ordinance stipulating that governors had to ask permission to reside in their governments; the same is said about Louis XIV in all relevant texts, yet without further reference to dates or decisions. It is not clear to me whether this attitude is inferred from the memoirs, or was truly dictated by the king in a concrete measure. In any case, Béguin makes amply clear that in Louis XIV's reign the tenure of governors became, if anything, far more stable, showing the same tendency as high court offices, i.e. clinging to specific dynasties.

[15] See Dreyss, *Mémoires de Louis XIV*, pp. 401–402, against the excessive authority of governors, suggesting the use of garrisons to check their power.

[16] Béguin, *Princes de Condé*, pp. 153–155.

[17] Bluche, 'Longueville', in *DGS*, p. 890; Mettam, *Power and Faction*, pp. 85–86; compare Mettam's discussion of La Rochefoucauld, pp. 92–93, mistaken in one respect: the office of *premier maître de la garderobe* was new only in the sense that one single high officer held the charge since 1669, now assisted by two other *maîtres* – it was created not for La Rochefoucauld, but for Chaumont de Guitry, see BN MS f 7859, fol. 220v: 'reglement des fonctions de Grand Mtre et Mtre de la Garderobe du 26 novembre 1669'. The charge was held by Chaumont de Guitry until his death in the *passage du rhin*; from October 1672 François VII de la Rochefoucauld was grand master of the wardrobe, and the office would remain vested in this house.

obtained the government of Touraine in 1667, and this nomination was not an isolated phenomenon.

While Louis XIV's nominations to governorships can be seen as a conscious but circumspect adaptation of tradition, his successors reinstated the *princes du sang* alongside the *maréchaux de France* as the typical governors for major provinces. Upon Dangeau's death in 1720, the comte de Charolais, M. le Duc's cadet brother, was given Touraine. Louis Armand de Bourbon, prince of Conti, had been granted the government of Poitou in 1717 – his ancestors had not enjoyed such honours in Louis XIV's personal rule.[18] The regent bestowed the government of Dauphiné on his son Chartres in 1719; the Orléans would retain it until the Revolution. In 1776, finally, an ordinance reduced the staff of the governors, and redefined the dignity as a 'grâce militaire', without great responsibilities. Eighteen major governments were strictly reserved for princes and marshals, who received a *traitement* of 60,000 lt; 21 others were to be given to generals of the royal army.[19] Intendants and the noble substitutes of the governor, the *commandants en chef*, were now clearly the main characters responsible for the king's government in the provinces. As soon as the intendants had secured this position, however, they too were likely to act as the provincial spokesmen with the council as well as the royal administration's man in the province.

In most parts of the realm, governors and intendants, whether competing or cooperating, had to cope with a range of vested corporations cherishing their responsibilities in taxation, law, and finance. The disappearance of the estates general after 1615 foreshadowed the fate of regional assemblies of the three estates. Provincial assemblies, numerous in the sixteenth century, were reduced in the seventeenth century. Royal agents, the *élus*, had been made responsible for the levying of taxes from the fourteenth century onwards, without taking away the fiscal rights of the *états*. In the seventeenth century, the territorial expansion of the *élus*, or *élections*, first eroded the fiscal competence of the estates, and then slowly displaced them – though the two regimes could coexist, as they did in Normandy into the seventeenth century.[20] By the end of the century, a range of minor assemblies in the north-east and south-west of France, and four major estates in Bretagne, Bourgogne, Languedoc, and Provence remained. In these *pays d'états*, the governor, commander, and intendant had to work through the estates; in Languedoc, the archbishop of Narbonne presided over the assembly, and his colleague from Toulouse had an equally important role. While these characteristic *corps intermédiaires* could no longer refuse to assent to the contributions asked by the king, they remained responsible for the repartition

18 See Antoine, *Louis XIV*, p. 240; Luynes, *Mémoires*, V, p. 58, discusses pecuniary graces attached to the government of Poitou granted to Conti's son in 1743.
19 Marion, *Dictionnaire*, pp. 259–261; Cuer, 'Gouverneurs, gouvernments', *DAR*, p. 607.
20 Barbiche, *Institutions*, pp. 98–105; compare Jean Bérenger, 'Etats provinciaux', in *DGS*, pp. 559–561.

and collection of the taxes. Their share in government secured the right to present *cahiers de doléances* providing an outlet for provincial complaints and demands.

Governments did not neatly fit the boundaries of either the traditional provinces and the ecclesiastical provinces, or the *généralités* forming the basis of financial administration. The intendancies, finally, overlapped with the *généralités* in the *pays d'élection*, with the provinces in the *pays d'états*.[21] More complications and competing claims arose from the regional powers of the *cours souveraines*. While estates were reduced in number, the *cours souveraines*, with competences pertaining to law and finance, expanded. The most notable of these bodies, the Parisian *parlement* and *chambre des comptes* had emerged from the *Curia Regis* in the fourteenth century. The *parlements*, five towards 1500, numbered thirteen on the eve of the revolution; the other *cours souveraines* likewise expanded: we find six *chambres des comptes*, four *cours des aides* in 1789 – while more such bodies were attached to *parlements*.[22] The *parlements* registered and published the king's laws, yet they could temporarily halt this process when they deemed a law to be in violation of the *lois fondamentales*. Their remonstrances, issued upon such occasions, could be broken by the king in a *lit de justice*. While the sovereign held the final decision in his hands, the complications, publicity, and delay entailed by a *lit de justice* could be painful. Louis XIV limited and controlled the rights of remonstrance by a 1667 ordinance, followed by a further declaration in 1673.[23] Remonstrances could now be submitted only after the registration of his measures, and within a limited time-span. Throughout his reign the Parisian *parlement* refrained from the practice, yet the provincial *cours souveraines* did present their remonstrances according to the king's rules. In 1715, the regent boosted the *parlementaires* by restoring their right of remonstrance before registration: his measures inaugurated a lengthy phase of political activity in the *cours souveraines*, mounting tension in the 1730s, and grave clashes with royal power in the last decades of Louis XV's reign.

Several other corporations or groups, without a strictly regional character, were of great relevance for regional as well as central government. The first order, present in the remaining provincial estates, obtained a status that had eluded the estates-general: regular conventions, and a series of permanent institutions. After 1560, when the first *décimes* contract was signed, the first order convened

[21] Barbiche, *Institutions*, pp. 315–316.

[22] See the excellent overviews by Olivier Chaline, 'Parlements', in *DAR*, pp. 960–965; and Barbiche, 'Cours souveraines ou supérieures', *DAR*, pp. 362–364, and *Institutions*, pp. 335–358, for the *parlements*, pp. 359–383 for the financial *cours souveraines*; well-balanced accounts on critical phases of *parlementaire* history by Albert N. Hamscher, *The Conseil Privé and the Parlements in the Age of Louis XIV: A Study in French Absolutism*, Transactions of the American Philosophical Society 77-II (Philadelphia 1987); Julian Swann, *Politics and the Parlement of Paris under Louis XV 1754–1774* (Cambridge 1995); more generally also David Parker, 'Sovereignty, Absolutism and the Function of the Law in Seventeenth-Century France', *Past & Present* 122 (1989), pp. 36–74; Bailey Stone, *The French Parlements and the Crisis of the Old Regime* (Chapel Hill and London 1986) underlines the cooperation between *parlements* and government.

[23] Barbiche, *Institutions*, p. 110: *ordonnance civile* 1667 (art. 2 and 5 of first 'titre'); declaration of 24 February 1673. John J. Hurt, *Louis XIV and the Parlements: The Assertion of Royal Authority* (Manchester 2002).

to discuss matters theological as well as practical – heresy, the balances between pope and king; *décimes*, the *don gratuit*.[24] In 1625, the meetings became more regular, with representatives of France's fifteen ecclesiastical provinces convening every five years. The clergy successfully defended its fiscal autonomy, and secured a level of influence in royal policies pertaining to religion. Likewise connected to the royal fisc, were the operatives alleviating the regime's permanent cash shortage. The collection of indirect taxes was traditionally subject to *affermage* by tax farmers. Financiers obtained the treaty or contract to collect a variety of rights and indirect taxes after paying a lump sum into the king's coffers; the same group provided loans to the crown. The financiers, or *traitants*, were subject to vehement criticism, and inspired public fury and rioting – yet they persisted throughout the *ancien régime*. In 1726, as a consequence of the attempt to restore financial stability following the turmoil of the Law system, a *ferme générale* or semi-public company of *fermiers généraux* was instituted. Thereafter the *ferme* with its huge staff, operating nominally under the direction of the *contrôleur-général*, acted as chartered intermediary between the state and its taxpayers, following the interests of its members more often than those of the state.

Towards the end of the seventeenth century, the French state, strengthened internally as well as expanded externally, and enjoying relative peace within its borders, was ruled by a king who did not have to fear serious rivals in his realm. Estates sent deputations to Versailles to pay their respects to the king, as did the representatives of the clergy, and other major corporations. Princely and ducal houses were thoroughly embedded in the structures of the state. The contrast with the century of troubles preceding 1650 could hardly have been more marked. The reconstruction of royal authority had been reached partly by coercion and the royal army – yet it was to be safeguarded and stabilised by compromises and rewards. Louis XIV's power was built on the notions of hierarchy and privilege as well as on obedience and administrative efficiency. If the *grands* were willing to forswear the principle and practice of revolt, exacerbated in generations of religious and civil strife, the king expected them to resume their dominant position in the upper echelons of the state.[25]

The ravages of the religious wars and more particularly the *Fronde* obscured the continuity of a noble elite becoming increasingly focused on the royal court: they gave a long-term development the appearance of an abrupt change. The recent experience of open revolt helps to explain the ubiquitous comments about the submissiveness of nobles at the Sun King's court – yet many of such proud-warriors-turned-courtiers had long since opted for a pragmatic course,

[24] Barbiche, *Institutions*, pp. 96–98, 48, 50, 244–246; Pierre Blet, 'Assemblées du clergé', in *DAR*, pp. 93–96; Blet, 'clergé', and 'Assemblées du clergé', in *DGS*, pp. 337–338, 123–125.

[25] See, for example, Arlette Jouanna, *Le devoir de révolte: La noblesse française et la gestion de l'état moderne 1559–1661* (Paris 1989).

A classic image of the Sun King's reign: the carriage of king and queen crushing rebellion

allying with ministers and consolidating their dynastic power by seeking court office – Henri II de Condé offers a prominent example.[26] Loyalty and deference to those higher in the hierarchy, moreover, were as typical for the noble ethos as martial valour and fiercely guarded independence; although religious strife temporarily upset the balance between these forces. The increased power of the centre limited the leeway of the regions and corporations. New extraordinary direct taxes, the *capitation* and the *dixième* were levied without waiting for their consent – a significant yardstick for the erosion of the particularist position.[27] On the whole, however, the machinery was effective thanks to continuing processes of give-and-take between regions, corporations, elites, and the centre – the dialogue never turned into a monologue. In the centre, in the king's household, moreover, regional grandees had been conspicuously successful in securing their power.

The turmoil following Louis XIV's death without adult successor led to a subdued variant of the problems which had marked most previous regencies. The king's traditional partners-in-government, the *cours souveraines* as well as the princes were appeased, as the regent needed their support to underpin his legitimacy. This set the tone for a century of further administrative growth in a context still largely dominated by traditional practices and precepts. Montesquieu's ideal of a monarchy retaining its vitality thanks to the spirit of honour and the intervention of *corps intermédiaires* was far from wholly alien to the practices of Louis XIV's reign. In the eighteenth century, it would rule with increasing strength – until it finally succumbed to its enlightened mirror image, the state ideally ruling with efficiency and equity over its citizens.

From the princes in supreme office to the dukes and peers following them, dynasties of court nobles maintained their hold on court office and strengthened their position in regional government – almost all major dynasties at court – among them Condé, Bouillon, Rohan, Guise, Noailles, Richelieu, Luxembourg, Villeroy – held or gained important governorships throughout the eighteenth century, as did *princes du sang* and *bâtards*. Courtiers' dynasties were heavily overrepresented among generals and marshals. The predominance of nobles in the upper echelons of the army entailed costs both in blood and money for many a family; moreover, it indicated that their martial values had effectively been integrated into the machinery of *gloire* and warfare coordinated by the king's ministers. The military stance of France's nobles, at court and elsewhere, was an

26 Béguin, *Princes de Condé*, stresses Henry's pragmatic and profitable choice, and allows us to see the *Fronde* as a passing stage, temporarily offsetting a process well under way.

27 Taxation without consent: see, for example, Richard Bonney, 'France, 1494–1815', in *The Rise of the Fiscal State in Europe, c. 1200–1815*, ed. R. Bonney (Oxford 1999), pp. 131, 146; Julian Swann, 'War and Finance in Burgundy in the Reign of Louis XIV, 1661–1715', in *Crises, Revolutions and Self-Sustained Growth: Essays in European Fiscal History, 1130–1830*, ed. W. M. Ormrod, M. Bonney, and R. Bonney (Stamford 1999), pp. 294–322, indicates on p. 321 that in Burgundy, the limited scale of opposition against Louis XIV's fiscal policies may be explained by the fact that 'they had worked largely to the advantage of the Burgundian propertied and office-owning elites'.

important asset for the French army – there is no reason, however, to picture the integration of *épée* valour into an army ruled by discipline, firepower, siege warfare, and manoeuvring as a bad omen for noble power in general.[28] French nobles, moreover, profitably meddled in finance, frequently seen as the domain solely of *robins* or *roturiers*. Directly or indirectly several of the major dynasties of courtiers – Bouillon, Rohan, Guise, La Trémoille, Richelieu – were lastingly involved in supporting monarchy's frail pecuniary foundation.[29] Finally, senior diplomatic missions were frequently granted to high nobles, as their rank made them particularly fit to represent the king in person. The *maréchal-duc* de Richelieu, combining diplomatic missions, court office, army command, and a major regional government in his long career, in addition to the multiple intrigues attributed to him, represented a type that can hardly be depicted as powerless.

The status of court nobles in these fields, as well as their proximity to the king, made them ideal go-betweens for regions, corporations, and individuals seeking the king's ear. Petitioners outside the charmed circle of the ruler, not entitled by rank or office to seek his presence, were dependent on their intercession. Audiences might sometimes have been granted to such persons or corporations, and as a rule they could submit written requests – yet their pleas were more likely to meet with favour when they were accompanied by approving words of well-connected courtiers or administrators.[30] The dynamics of intercession connected the courtiers and their combinations to the realm at large. Many persons at court were routinely asked to support causes for a variety of groups and individuals, as their correspondence shows. Courtiers as well as ministers may have been weary of this incessant demand for support, but knew that it arose from the perception of their power and credit with the ruler, and thought it wise to cultivate it. The starting point of such patterns, typical of power centres in any age, was likely to be either a pre-existing loyalty to a noble house and its affiliations, or previous service in a staff connected to a higher officer present at court. Both domains could serve as stepping-stones for clients, and 'constituencies' for patrons. In provincial governments, army units, and staffs of high court officers, the domains came together.

It is difficult to reconstruct more than the bare outline of dynastic networks and their dependents. Katia Béguin's recent study of the seventeenth-century Condé from Henry II to Henry Jules provides an analysis as well as a prosopographical annex of the Condé household and clientage. For most other major

[28] This tends to be the case in the superb study by John Lynn, *Giant of the Grand Siècle: The French Army 1610–1715* (Cambridge 1997), for example p. 606; see Parrott, *Richelieu's Army*, for a plausible and well-founded revisionist view, limited to the first half of the century.

[29] Dessert, *Argent, Pouvoir et Société*, pp. 341–368 and conclusion; compare in general Hillay Zmora, *Monarchy, Aristocracy, and the State in Europe, 1300–1800* (London 2001).

[30] Audiences or less formal conversations themselves were, of course, more easily obtained by the intercession of the servants in the chamber, most notably the *premiers gentilshommes* and the *Oberst-kämmerer*, conceivably their assistants.

families at court, princes of the blood or great ducal houses, such works are not available, and we have to glean details from a variety of sources.[31] Dynastic networks represented a potential for mutual support, rarely the daily practice of such support. Around the fixed points of orientation of such connections, senior members of the most important families, moved a volatile cloud of lesser entities – the French expression *nébuleuse* well conveys this. Ties long somnolent could unexpectedly revive when crisis threatened, or high rewards were promised. Lesser clients saw no harm in changing sides when their masters' services proved disappointing; closer friends might hesitate longer before seeking attachment with other patrons. At court, only a small upper segment of the *nébuleuses* would be present, others might be active in *parlements* and estates, in church, army, or finance; their followers in a mixture of other pursuits. Kinship, friendship, honour, and loyalty formed the backbone of these ties; they were frequently based on the court grandees' provincial connections. The basic contours of dynastic networks tended to change slowly, mostly through the dynamics of marriage and office. The benefits of protection, patronage, and intercession nourished them in the long run.

Did noble brokerage end with the strengthening of state structures and procedures? Surely, the habit persisted, but it may have become less important a force in the functioning of the state. Towards the end of the seventeenth century, the most important noble affiliations in France were strongly oriented towards the court, and thrived because of their proximity to the ruler's patronage. While this could lead to a decrease in the numbers attached to great nobles' own households, it did not necessarily diminish their importance. The connections among noble dynasties, and the practices of patronage are well attested throughout the *ancien régime*, yet we will have to await further study before we can effectively gauge the longevity, scope, and bearing of such connections. We cannot ignore the ascendancy of princely and ducal clans in the eighteenth century, and their recurring impact on court faction and royal policies; the same holds true for the *cours souveraines*. Were these a sign only of the temporary breakdown of royal authority in a monarchy ruled by the precepts of Weberian bureaucracy, or do they indicate the continuity of habits and structures long thought to have been obliterated by Louis XIV's strong hand? The question begs the answer.

[31] Béguin, *Princes de Condé*, did not include the court offices in the high steward's power added by Blanquie, 'Dans la main'; see recently Béguin's 'Louis XIV et l'aristocratie'; compare Duma, *Les Bourbon-Penthièvre*, and several older studies: R. Forster, *The House of Saulx-Tavannes: Versailles and Burgundy 1700–1830* (Baltimore 1971); W. Weary, 'The House of La Trémoille, Fifteenth Through Eighteenth Centuries: Change and Adaptation in a French Noble Family', *JMH* 49 (1977), D1001; Nancy Barker, 'Philippe d'Orléans, Frère Unique du Roi: Founder of the Family Fortune', *FHS* 13 (1983–1984), pp. 145–171. See Dessert, *Argent, Pouvoir, et Société*; Mettam, *Power and Faction*; Bergin, *The Making of the French Episcopate 1589–1661* (New Haven and London 1996); Michel Antoine, *Le gouvernement et administration sous Louis XV. Dictionnaire biographique* (Paris 1978), including a table of 'familles alliées' on pp. 283–319; Christophe Levantal, *Ducs et Pairs et duchés-pairies à l'Epoque moderne (1519–1790)* (Paris 1996); Horowski's analytically strong 'obersten Chargen', and Newton, *Espace du roi*, like Levantal's book, offering many data.

THE EMPIRE AND THE HABSBURG DOMINIONS

The ties of the components of Habsburg monarchy to its centre in Vienna present a far more complicated picture.[32] First of all, the principalities of the empire, slowly nearing levels and practices of sovereignty eluding princely dynasties existing within the framework of other European composite states, would never have accepted the idea that they formed part of a Habsburg 'monarchy'. They ruled their territories increasingly independently from the suzerainty of the elected emperor, and under the loose control only of imperial institutions in Vienna and elsewhere. The power of the electors and major princes resembled that of sovereign territorial rulers: the familiar processes of state building occurred in their domains, not on the imperial level. 'Imperial' armies and contributions were to remain subject to bargaining between the constituent parts of the empire, whereas within the territories a greater level of central control over such important assets could be achieved. The contributions and armies of the greater principalities were becoming more important in proportion to those generated by the empire as a collectivity. A welter of smaller principalities, worldly and spiritual, likewise followed the course of 'territorialisation', even though their existence made sense only within the larger compass of the Holy Roman Empire.

Notwithstanding the approximation of sovereignty reached by the components of the empire, imperial institutions remained of great importance. One lasting focus emerged in Regensburg, around the general diet or *Reichstag* permanently convening since 1663; ten regionally organised *Kreise*, or circles of the empire, were important for the organisation of collective defence, and a variety of other pursuits. The strong legal basis of the empire was exemplified by two thriving rival courts of appeal, the *Reichskammergericht* (1495: imperial cameral court) largely nominated by the *Reichsstände* and the Vienna *Reichshofrat* (1498: imperial aulic council), dominated by the emperor's nominees.[33] The interminable litigations in these courts seemed to become the most favoured means of

[32] Evans, *Making*, pp. 157–308; Dickson, *Finance and Government*, I, pp. 257–329, and Dickson, 'Monarchy and Bureaucracy', are the most authoritative general accounts of Habsburg government, both assimilating knowledge from an immense range of specialised studies. James van Horn Melton, 'The Nobility in the Bohemian and Austrain Lands, 1620–1780', offers a useful overview of nobles, lordships, and estates in the period. For the empire, the concise overviews by Peter Wilson, *The Holy Roman Empire*, and Helmut Neuhaus, *Das Reich in der Frühen Neuzeit*, offer a helpful and up-to-date guides to the intricacies of the empire as well as to the literature on the subject. Evans' *Making* and Dickson's *Finance and Government* offer the major basis for these paragraphs, yet conversations with Géza Pálffy (Budapest) and Petr Mat'a (Prague) were a welcome and helpful addition.

[33] See Neuhaus, *Das Reich in der Frühen Neuzeit*, pp. 48–53, and the extensive older study of O. von Gschliesser, *Der Reichshofrat. Bedeutung und Verfassung, Schicksal und Besetzung einer obersten Reichsbehörde von 1559–1806* (Vienna 1942) and von Gschliesser, 'Das Beamtentum der hohen Reichsbehörden (Reichshofkanzlei, Reichskammergericht, Reichshofrat, Hofkriegsrat)', in *Beamtentum und Pfarrerstand 1400–1800. Budinger Vorträge 1967*, ed. Günther Franz (Limburg and Lahn 1972), pp. 11–26; see also *Reichshofrat und Reichskammergericht: ein Konkurrenzverhältnis*, ed. Wolfgang Sellert, Quellen und Forschungen zur Höchsten Gerichtsbarkeit im Alten Reich 34 (Cologne 1999), for example the contribution by Eva Ortlieb, 'Reichshofrat und kaiserliche Kommissionen in der Regierungszeit Kaiser Ferdinands III. (1637–1657)', pp. 47–81.

solving a variety of conflicts within the empire. Apparently, the emperor as well as the ill-assorted mélange of electors, princes, prince-bishops, abbots, counts, and cities of the empire appreciated the collective institutions. For the emperor, they were the most evident channel for exerting his feudal overlordship. Imperial commissioners represented the emperor's interests in the diet and the circles. The *Reichshofrat* was a crucial if slow-moving asset for the emperor, attracting litigants both Protestant and Catholic, though mostly from the southern parts of the empire, whereas the *Reichskammergericht* remained more influential in the north. The electors cultivated their special status by meeting separately, a right confirmed in the Golden Bull. The smallest entities, particularly those who held *Reichsunmittelbarkeit* based on the vestiges of an independent existence, clung to the imperial institutions as the only way to safeguard themselves against the greed of their greater territorial neighbours. All components of the empire used the institutions – whether to assert their position, to combine against the emperor, or to protect themselves against foreign invasion.

The combined forces of 'territorialisation', religious schism and international rivalry effectively foreclosed greater unity under Habsburg sway – though the geographical scope and diversity of the empire probably never made this a likely development. France championed 'Germanic liberties' to prevent broad support for the emperor in the sixteenth and seventeenth centuries; it continued this practice into the eighteenth century, frequently finding support in the Wittelsbach domains of Bavaria and Cologne and elsewhere. During the long phase of warfare between France and the emperor, and particularly after the ravaging of the Palatinate in 1688–1689, anti-French sentiments made Leopold more popular in the empire – but this was always contingent upon the emperor's respect for the niceties of the 'imperial constitution', and the rights of his ruling quasi-subordinates.[34] Powerful princes in the empire supported Habsburg causes with their armies to obtain higher status – a course that secured a royal crown for the rulers of Prussia as well as Savoy.

Leopold's relatively successful legalist phase of imperial recovery was followed by a reorientation towards other territories: Italy, with its rich legacy of papal-imperial struggles and intact framework of feudal obligations; and in the south-east the lands conquered from the Ottomans after their retreat from Hungary. Arguably, the extension of Habsburg rule into the Balkans made the empire less relevant in the long run; yet rule in the Italian possessions relied strongly on imperial rights. Neither the rising status of the electors and major princes, who were now increasingly unwilling to come to Vienna to do homage on bended knee to the emperor, nor the shifting of the geographical balance of Habsburg possessions, should lead us to underestimate the value of the imperial dignity. At the height of the War of Austrian Succession, French secretary for

[34] Goloubeva, *Glorification*, pp. 143–154, and pp. 123–141 for Leopold's wars against the Turks.

foreign affairs d'Argenson could still claim that: 'Il est aise de sentir que l'objet p[rinci]pal de cette guerre a este et est encore de faire perdre a la cour de Vienne la dignite Imp[eria]le'.[35] The three-tiered structure of imperial government – emperor, territorial ruler, subject – was highly relevant for the Habsburgs: it influenced their international alignments as much as their policies regarding the household and noble hierarchies. The right to confer imperial nobility, and an important say in nominations to the benefices of the *Reichskirche*, were important assets for the emperor. A busy traffic remained between Habsburg institutions and the empire – evident in the personnel of court, administration, and army. Chancellors in the Austrian *Hofkanzlei* as well as staff in the *Reichshofkanzlei* were often recruited from the empire, most notably but never exclusively from its south-western and western fringes. According to one estimate up to 50 per cent of the officers serving in the Habsburg army originated in the empire.[36] Yet the connections between Vienna and the empire present a picture wholly different from the closer and more hierarchical ties that had emerged in France between centre and regions.

The Habsburgs enjoyed direct sovereignty in the duchies of Lower and Upper Austria, Inner Austria comprised of Styria, Carinthia and Carniola, Tyrol and Further Austria, together the *Erblande* or hereditary lands.[37] Lower Austria fulfilled a role more or less comparable to the *Ile de France*: the province most closely associated with the centre of government and the court. The government of this province was more frequently listed in the manuscript *Hofstaatsverzeichnisse* of the later seventeenth century than any other provincial government – only the regional chambers for finance connected to the central *Hofkammer* usually received the same treatment. Vienna, however, was hardly as thriving an urban centre as Paris; while in the ecclesiastical hierarchy this bishopric did not match the archbishoprics of Salzburg, Prague, or Esztergom. Nevertheless, Vienna was pivotal in Lower Austria, and that province overshadowed Upper Austria, centred on the city of Linz. Graz and Innsbruck retained importance as the main centres of the other provinces. The crown of Wenceslas included notably Bohemia, with Prague as its proud urban centre, Moravia with Brünn (Brno) and Olmütz (Olomouc), Silesia geographically and ethnically closer to the German principalities, and the Lusatias, ceded to Saxony in 1635. St Wenceslas' crown had been a hereditary Habsburg possession since the *verneuerte Landesordnung*

[35] Marquis d'Argenson, to Delaville, minister in The Hague, Versailles 4 April 1745. Archives des Affaires Etrangeres (AAE), Correspondence Politique (CP), Hollande 455. I kindly thank Dr Olaf van Nimwegen for this reference.

[36] Evans, *Making*, p. 279, for the emperor's patronage over the *Reichskirche*; pp. 292–299 for other flows between empire and Viennese institutions; Hochedlinger, 'Mars Ennobled', for the army; generally the articles by Volker Press listed in the bibliography.

[37] *Niederösterreich*, *Oberösterreich*, *Innerösterreich*, Tyrol and *Vorlande*; see Dickson, *Finance and Government*, I, p. 259; Erich Zöllner, *Der Österreichbegriff* (Vienna 1988), pp. 48–53, on the complications concerning 'Oberösterreich' a label that could also be used for the combined territories of Further Austria and Tyrol. Another customary translation for the *Vorlande* or *Vorderösterreich* is Outer Austria.

of 1627, and thus Bohemia may be assimilated into the hereditary lands from that date onwards.[38] Hungary, in contrast to the preceding territories, was never a part of the Holy Roman Empire; its St Stephen's crown, initially elective as that of Bohemia, became hereditary in the Habsburg male and female lines after 1687.[39] Although it was the richest province under Habsburg rule in the sixteenth century, the Ottoman occupation left only a substantial slice of its territory connecting Croatian Zagreb and its temporary capital Pozsony (Pressburg) near Vienna to a large chunk of territory situated between Transylvania and Poland. Only after 1683 did the Habsburgs recover the Hungarian kingdom, from its historic capital Buda to the outlying province of Transylvania and a part of Wallachia.[40]

After the War of Spanish Succession, the Habsburgs acquired the southern Netherlands, Milan, Naples, and Sicily. Sicily and Naples were lost in 1735, but Tuscany was secured for a junior branch of the dynasty after the extinction of its Medici dukes in 1737 – leading to a concentration of Habsburg possessions in northern Italy. Finally, Maria Theresa lost most of Silesia to Frederick II, but gained Galicia following the first partition of Poland (1772–1773), and the adjacent Bukovina in the Russian-Turkish peace of 1774. Vienna never was the sole centre of this assemblage, but it eclipsed Prague after Rudolf's reign, Graz after Ferdinand II's accession to the imperial throne, and Innsbruck after the extinction of the Tyrolean line in 1665. Not even excluding the dispersed *Vorlande*, did the Habsburg territories present a contiguous area: clerical immunities small and huge broke up the territorial unity. The archbishopric of Salzburg, wedged in between Lower and Upper Austria on one side and the Tyrol on the other side, retained its conspicuous independence until the end of the Holy Roman Empire.

It is quite possible to construct a rise of Habsburg power centred in Vienna, around several well-known points of orientation. A phase of militant Protestantism and unruly estates, complicated by recurring war with the Ottomans, and exacerbated by the Habsburg *Bruderzwist* after 1608, ended after the battle of the White Mountain (1620), subduing the Bohemian revolt and its Austrian parallels. The early successes in the Thirty Years' War underpinned Habsburg authority in the *Erblande* and Bohemia, while the confiscations of territories belonging to Protestant nobles allowed the emperor to reconstruct an elite including loyalist scions of old families, *émigré* generals, and a minority of

[38] Petr Mat'a's (Prague) forthcoming book comparing the structures and practices of the regional governments belonging to the Bohemian crown, as well as his other project concentrating on the prosopography of major noble dynasties, will shed new light on various themes discussed in this chapter.

[39] Dickson, *Finance and Government*, I, p. 288.

[40] See in general Evans, *Making*, pp. 235–274; Pálffy, 'Der Wiener Hof und die ungarischen Stände'; although Hungary was quite rich, it could not pay for the costly defences against the Ottomans, and needed Habsburg support, see Géza Pálffy, 'Der Preis der Verteidigung der Habsburgermonarchie in Mitteleuropa: Die Kosten der Türkenabwehr in der zweiten Hälfte des 16. Jahrhunderts', a forthcoming article the author provided in unpublished form.

ennobled administrators. The example of their success attracted many remaining Protestant nobles into the Catholic camp, others saw themselves forced to choose between conversion and emigration. Loyal Catholic magnates from Bohemia and the *Erblande* became the mainstay of Leopold's reign. The very predicament that led to the Habsburg crackdown in Bohemia, created room for the Hungarian magnates, who were left in charge of defence against the Turks and remained free in their religious adherence for the decades following. In the seventeenth century, a handful of Hungarian magnates served as chamberlain at court, or held the office of Hungarian chancellor or vice-chancellor; this strengthened the status of these dynasties in their homeland, but did not markedly bolster Viennese presence in Hungary. Only after the inauspicious end of the *Magnatenverschwörung* in 1670–1671 did Leopold seek a more marked Habsburg presence in Hungary, including counter-reformatory policies. Ferenc II Rákóczi's rebellion in 1703–1711 ended in a compromise that re-established Habsburg rule, but confirmed freedom of religion, and prevented further centralisation for some time.

Haugwitz's reforms following the War of Austrian Succession remodelled and strengthened central government in Vienna. As in the decades around the battle of the White Mountain, the Bohemian and Hungarian experiences were quite different: Bohemia lost its separate chancellery, and was integrated into the Austrian administrative structures, whereas Hungary retained its separate institutions as well as a level of autonomy under the overarching structure of Habsburg monarchy. The rejuvenation of Habsburg power in the Austrian core lands and their dependencies coincided with a weakening of the Habsburg hold on the empire, surfacing blatantly in the acts both of King Frederick II and Charles-Albert of Bavaria. Within the monarchy the balance between Hungary and Bohemia shifted perceptibly; more generally, the imperial dimension of Habsburg rule never wholly recovered from its mid-century breakdown. Joseph II's frenzied law-making and reform were connected overwhelmingly with the consolidated hereditary domains, not with the empire. His rule provides a suitably administrative and national apogee, yet many of his reforms proved abortive, and restoration followed under Leopold II. Finally, the Holy Roman Empire would dissolve in the crucible of revolutionary and Napoleonic warfare, giving rise to an Austrian empire based on the territories more closely tied to Habsburg rule.

As a broad indication of the Habsburg's rights over the components of their realm, this may suffice – yet it tells us nothing about either the resilience of regional institutions, or about noble power in localities subject to Habsburg rule. In the Austrian and Bohemian lands, we find lieutenants of the emperor with their staffs and advisory bodies at the level of the regions; the lieutenants held an ambivalent position as they served both the Habsburg ruler and the estates. In all provinces, we find estates assemblies, usually bringing together four groups: prelates, *Herren* (lords), *Ritter* (knights), and towns.[41] The powers of the estates were much greater than those of the remaining French *états*. Their fiscal right was not limited to a decorous consenting to the ruler's requests: consent came only as a consequence of due recognition of the estates' corporate power. The Habsburgs, perennially short of money, were not in a position to change this, nor did they seem intent upon doing so in the period between the 1620s and the crisis of the mid-eighteenth century. The implementation of the decrees of central government was left to the agents of the estates. Permanent committees carried out important day-to-day administrative tasks for the estates. When the estates consented to the contribution financing the emperor's army, these committees and their employees would assess and collect it; army recruitment, quartering, and provisioning were likewise among their responsibilities. At the village level, the lord's authority was the dominant force in the Bohemian and Moravian lands, where lordships were all-important. In the Austrian duchies, *Gutsherrschaft* was less prevalent, and noble landownership more fragmented; yet seigneurial rights represented a rising force here as well. In fact, not only was lordship the level where the policies of central government had to be implemented: *Polizeiordnungen* occasionally originated there, and were passed on through the estates to the court.[42] Thus, we find the starting point of a *Quellengattung* habitually connected to the disciplining force and motivation of absolutism at a level more frequently associated with either opposition or with sullen compliance.

[41] I leave aside here the diverging courses of Protestant and Catholic nobles, as well as the decline of the *Ritter*, or lower nobility, and the parallel rise of the *Herren*, charted in a range of works, see, for example, Karin J. MacHardy, 'Der Einfluss von Status, Konfession und Besitz auf das politische Verhalten des niederösterreichischen Ritterstandes 1580–1620', in *Spezialforschung und 'Gesamtgeschichte' Beispiele und Methodenfrage zur Geschichte der frühen Neuzeit*, ed. Grete Klingenstein and Heinrich Lutz, Wiener Beiträge zur Geschichte der Neuzeit 8 (Munich 1982), pp. 56–83; MacHardy, 'Cultural Capital, Family Strategies and Noble Identity in Early Modern Habsburg Austria 1579–1620', *Past & Present* 163 (1999) and her forthcoming book: *Statebuilding, Religion and Court Patronage: Social and Cultural Dimensions of Political Interaction in Habsburg Austria, 1521–1622* (Palgrave/Macmillan Press, 2002). The author kindly allowed me to read the introduction of her book. Herbert Knittler, 'Adelige Grundherrschaft im Übergang. Überlegungen zum Verhältnis von Adel und Wirtschaft in Niederösterreich um 1600', in *Spezialforschung und 'Gesamtgeschichte'*, pp. 84–111; Thomas Winkelbauer, 'Krise der Aristokratie? Zum Strukturwandel des Adels in den böhmischen und niederösterreichischen Ländern im 16. und 17. Jahrhundert', *MIÖG* 100 (1992), pp. 328–353.

[42] Van Horn Melton, 'Nobility', in *The European Nobilities*, ed. Scott, II, pp. 110–143, at pp. 124–126, 133; Winkelbauer, 'Sozialdisziplinierung und Konfessionaliserung durch Grundherren in den österreichischen und böhmischen Ländern im 16. und 17. Jahrhundert', *Zeitschrift für Historische Forschung* 19 (1992), pp. 318–319, 338, and Winkelbauer, 'Grundherrschaft, Sozialdisziplinierung und Konfessionalisierung in Böhmen, Mähren und Österreich unter der Enns im 16. und 17. Jahrhundert', in *Konfessionalisierung in Ostmitteleuropa. Wirkungen des religiösen Wandels im 16. und 17. Jahrhundert in Staat, Gesellschaft und Kultur*, ed. Joachim Bahlcke and Arno Strohmeyer, Forschungen zur Geschichte und Kultur des östlichen Mitteleuropa 7 (Stuttgart 1999), pp. 307–338; Winkelbauer prepares an extensive source collection on Lordship and the rules decreed by *Grundherren*. Thus, the mentioning of *Polizeiordnungen* in court ordinances, mostly in the points pertaining to the *Hofmarschall*, may have been a concession to estates frowning upon the disorders of the court more than the court's own initiative – my thanks go to Josef Pauser (Vienna) for enlightening me on the nature of *Polizeiordnungen*. Likewise, Winkelbauer's study of noble conversion in *Fürst und Fürstendiener*, pp. 66–158, tends to stress a late sixteenth-century Catholic revival as an important force, in addition to the concrete influence of Habsburg patronage and coercion on noble conversions.

The estates remained the heart of Habsburg regional government until Haugwitz's reforms. Thereafter, they continued to perform important tasks, but no longer provided the sole agents of Habsburg power in the regions, nor could they effectively oppose the reforms delimiting their power. Intransigent estates, common in the sixteenth and early seventeenth centuries, were rare from the later seventeenth century onwards – the alliance between the Habsburgs and loyal magnates made conspicuously strong central government unnecessary, opposition irrelevant or fleeting.[43] This compact between nobles and dynasty did not fall prey to the crisis of the 1740s, but strong measures were now indispensable to solve the monarchy's problems, and the arm of government was extended into the localities. Revenues doubled, and the number of state employees rose steeply between 1740 and 1765.[44] As in the 1620s, crisis and reform opened opportunities for relative outsiders, and the small group of vested elites serving the emperor was once more revitalized by the influx of colleagues of less distinguished stock. The Habsburg army emerged as a new focus for loyalties and social mobility, and it cast its net wider than did the court. Army officers and civil servants found their place next to their senior colleagues holding court office. A bureaucracy was born that would continue to display some of the features earlier reserved to the court: honorary offices, inflation of places, niceties of protocol, slow processes of decision-making.[45] Finally, while the Bohemian chancellery was absorbed into the new central structures, the estates of the lands of the Bohemian crown had to accept a marked reduction of their role in regional government – arguably, they paid dearly for their homage to Charles Albert in 1741. Hungary maintained a distinct place in the commonwealth of Habsburg hereditary lands, as the only dominion somewhat aloof from the increasingly active policies of the centre. Hungary's special status, and the integrative force of the army, would figure among the main characteristics of Habsburg monarchy in the nineteenth century.

For all practical purposes, the noble families serving the Habsburgs since the seventeenth century in the highest offices of administration and household, well represented in the church as well as in regional offices of crown and estates, formed the backbone of Habsburg government in the regions. They embodied the connections between centre and region; their prestige, strengthened by high court office in the proximity of the ruler, helped to orient the regions towards the centre. Yet as a rule they saw themselves and behaved as loyal and devoted servants of a regime that knew how to reward them – if usually belatedly, and sometimes not at all. Undoubtedly, families had their methods

[43] Paraphrasing Evans' illuminating comment in *Making*, p. 169: 'It might appear odd that seventeenth-century Austria lacked both strong government and strong opposition . . .'.

[44] Dickson, *Finance and Government*, I, p. 309.

[45] *Ibid*., I, p. 314, the *Registratur* (evolving in court offices at the same time), pp. 320–321, the complaints about *Vielschreiberei*; Dickson, 'Monarchy and Bureaucracy', p. 324.

and strategies to strengthen dynastic fortunes, and protect their interest at all levels of the realm; there is little we can say about *nébuleuses* because as yet no studies have systematically addressed the ties of loyalty among families and their dependents – prosopographical details, moreover, are more dispersed than in France.[46] Even without the benefit of such data, it is clear that members of key families remained close to power, and had a lasting impact on Viennese decision-making.

The different structures and practices of office-holding and landownership in France and in the Habsburg lands affected the nature of noble power and noble connections. Venality was an important asset of court officers, provincial governors, and army commanders in France; whereas the extent and nature of landownership as well as the more impressive power of regional estates may have directed the patronage of Habsburg grandees. In Vienna, we find no parallel to the power bases created by the major French ministerial dynasties, who successfully constructed their own networks of fidelity, based on their departments, and strengthened by their increasingly close ties with vested noble dynasties. Only further prosopographical study of the *nébuleuses* as well as the processes of formal and informal decision-making at court can add substance to the brief outlines offered here; the same holds true *a fortiori* for a more penetrating comparison of these phenomena in the two realms discussed here.

ENTICEMENTS AND MANIPULATIONS

Regional administration sheds light on the balance between noble families and central government. Yet rulers had at their disposition a wider range of means to influence nobles, reflecting the ideally close connections between a ruling house and its loyal noble servants, and securing nobles' loyalty by circumspectly tying them to dynastic interests. Distribution of material graces and offices was undoubtedly the most conspicuous of these assets. Several specific forms of the rulers' grace deserve special attention here, because they were closely tied to the household, strengthening its influence on noble hierarchies and attitudes: the right to confer noble rank, orders of chivalry, and the rulers' patronising of noble marriages and their offspring.

[46] See at http://www.univie.ac.at/Geschichte/wienerhof/wienerhof2/index.htm information about a research project studying clientage around the mid-seventeenth-century court, concentrating on noble connections based on several *Hofstaatsverzeichnisse* in the reigns of Ferdinand II and III, notably including the share of noble women in these networks; another important project has now been initiated to study the *Hofstaatsverzeichnisse* in Leopold's reign, including all members and social groups at court, but probably without studying the ties connecting this group to the outside world. See Winkelbauer's comprehensive 'collective biography' of the *neue Fursten*, in the form of a biography of Gundaker von Liechtenstein, *Fürst und Fürstendiener*; more generally about noble attitudes and mentalities, bringing into the picture a variety of themes and artefacts usually neglected in historiography, see Beatrix Bastl, *Tugend, Liebe, Ehre. Die adelige Frau in der Frühen Neuzeit* (Vienna, Cologne and Weimar 2000); Mark Hengerer's (Konstanz) forthcoming dissertation, focusing on nobles at court from Ferdinand II to Leopold's first decade, will shed light on financial transactions and noble networks as well as ceremony.

Ennobling loyal servants, typically after bravery on the battlefield, was an important prerogative. In the early modern age, it offered a source of additional income as well as a means to upset or reconstruct noble hierarchies. Venality of offices conferring nobility in France exemplifies both: it brought important revenues, yet threatened to antagonise sword nobles who looked with contempt on their pseudo-peers. The office of *sécrétaire du roi*, or *savonnette à vilains* cleansing *roturiers* of their lowly origins was only the most conspicuous of a welter of venal offices in all sectors of society, conferring nobility in return for cash payment. Receiving a title from the Habsburg ruler, in his capacity of *Landesfürst* or emperor, entailed payment of substantial taxes carefully stipulated in *Taxordnungen*.[47] Noble society, carefully watching its rank and privileges, was likely to be annoyed by inflation of honours in the lower fringes of nobility; the ruler's meddling with supreme ranks, however, was far more distressing, as it threatened to overturn internal noble hierarchies. If a ruler was able to place his favourites and robe servants in the upper echelon of nobility, or could indeed create a new supreme level of nobility, he held a powerful card.

In France, the *ducs et pairs* came to occupy a special station between nobles and royal family, that could indicate lineage as well as favour or service. The traditional six *pairs ecclésiastiques* and six *pairs laïques*, comparable in status to the electors of the empire, enjoyed special rights in *sacre* and coronation. In the course of the sixteenth century, the *ducs-pairs* broadened into a group of royal favourites.[48] They were now effectively becoming a royal creation, exemplifying the king's power to promote *gentilshommes* loyally serving him to a rank ideally reserved for the greatest feudatories, or at least for the eldest lineages. Henry III conspicuously demonstrated this power in 1581 when he made Anne de Joyeuse *duc-pair* and bestowed upon him the first rank after the *princes du sang* and *princes étrangers*. Favourites such as Epernon, Luynes, or Saint-Simon *père*, and a range of loyal administrators of relatively obscure origins would likewise be rewarded with a *duché-pairie*. In addition to the *ducs-pairs*, we find the *ducs vérifiés* or *ducs héréditaires* without peerage, and the lesser-ranking *ducs à brevet*, holding the ducal rank only for their lifetime.

The dukes-peers reflect a change of focus within noble hierarchies from pedigree to royal favour.[49] The preceptor of a mid-eighteenth century scion of the

[47] See, for example *ÖZV*, I, 3, no. 36, a June 1683 *Taxordnung* for the *Hofkanzlei*, pp. 1–17, notably the amounts on pp. 10–14; and the 1720 *Universaltaxordnung* on pp. 388–397.

[48] Jean-Pierre Labatut, *Les ducs et pairs de France au XVIIe siècle: étude sociale* (Paris 1972); Levantal, *Ducs et pairs*; Labourdette, 'Ducs et pairs', in *DAR*, pp. 448–450: the *pairs ecclésiastiques*: Reims, Langres, Laon, Beauvais, Noyon, Chalons-sur-Marne; the *pairs laïques*: Bourgogne, Normandie, Guyenne, Flandres, Toulouse, Champagne – in both categories, the first three had the rank of dukes, the second three of counts.

[49] A development not contradicting the changes described by Ellery Schalk, *From Valor to Pedigree: Ideas of Nobility in France in the Sixteenth and Seventeenth Centuries* (Princeton 1986); the monarchical attempt to redefine and verify the criteria of nobility connects the two. The unpublished *Magisterarbeit* of Shannon Hunt, 'Zur Definition ständischer Grenzen unter den frühen Stuarts – John Seldens "Titles of Honor" im historischen Kontext' (Münster 1999) well explains the relationship between the creation of noble titles and *Vorzugsrecht*.

La Trémoille, among the early ducal creations of French monarchy as well as among the eldest families of France, advised his pupil to stress his lineage instead of his dukedom vis-à-vis non-ducal *noblesse d'ancienne race*. Such nobility would respect the La Trémoille more for their pedigree, than for the rank of duke-peer:

Elle voit avec indignation des familles d'une origine obscure élevées au premier rang par la dignité de duc et pair. De la leur mépris et leur mauvaise humeur contre les ducs. Ils feront plus de cas de votre naissance que de votre duché.[50]

Saint-Simon, son of a favourite-created-duke and himself a courtier *manqué*, stood uncomfortably between non-ducal nobles with impressive lineages, and social climbers reaching ducal station in his time. His staunch defence of the *duché-pairie* represented a vulnerable compromise between the principle of pedigree and monarchical meddling with ranks. The monarchs' initiatives had turned a group composed both of high nobles and loyal lesser families into a caste acting as a buffer between the royal family and the nobility at large. Membership conferred visible honours and privileges at court; major courtiers were recruited mostly among the *ducs-pairs*.

In the Habsburg lands, similar processes can be observed. Emperors could create counts and princes of the empire, the latter functioning as the upper layer of nobility in the Habsburg domains as well as in the empire. Between 1582 and 1806, 160 *neue Fürsten* were nominated. Whereas the French reinvention of the feudal *ducs-pairs* occurred in the context of an increasingly unified monarchy, the emperor's creatures had to find a place in a group of independently-minded *Reichsfürsten*. These territorial rulers sought to limit the ascent of the emperor's protégés, by barring them from the final accolade of princely power, *Sitz und Stimme* in the *Reichsfürstenrat* of the imperial diet. Aspirant-princes needed to acquire territories in the empire to justify their ambitions, and the vested princes had secured a voice in judging whether these possessions warranted promotion into this bastion of their rank. Only 19 new princes were duly admitted with full rights of vote and session between 1653 and 1754; thus the immediate political influence of this group remained limited.[51] Nevertheless, promotion into this rank, sometimes accompanied with the *Palatinat*, conferring a variety of sovereign rights including the *Münzrecht* (right of mintage) represented a formidable prize for service at the imperial court. Many dynasties of supreme high officers and ministers serving the Habsburgs were rewarded with princely rank in the course of the seventeenth and eighteenth

50 Cited in Labourdette, 'Ducs et pairs', in *DAR*, p. 450. Compare Harold A. Ellis, 'Genealogy, History and Aristocratic Reaction in Early Eighteenth-Century France: The Case of Henri de Boulainvilliers', *JMH* 58, 2 (1986), pp. 414–451, and Ellis, *Boulainvilliers and the French Monarchy: Aristocratic Politics in Early Eighteenth-Century France* (Ithaca and London 1988). Compare Chaussin and Nogaret, eds., *Noblesse au XVIIIe siècle*.

51 Neuhaus, *Reich in der Frühen Neuzeit*, pp. 17–18, literature cited on pp. 82–83; Pecar, 'Ökonomie der Ehre', pp. 361–362, lists relevant promotions between 1608 and 1711.

centuries; the most successful among them created their own principalities in the empire – the Liechtenstein's sovereign possessions outlived the Habsburgs as a ruling dynasty.[52] Whereas the French kings were wary of their great courtiers' princely ambitions, the emperor served his own interests by promoting his loyal dignitaries to princely rank in the empire, as this underlined his supremacy over the ruling territorial princes.

Both Leopold I and Charles VI, however, forbade the new princes to use or demand formulae conspicuously reserved for sovereign rulers in their correspondence.[53] Whereas the *neue Fürsten* enjoyed precedence over senior chamberlains or councillors without princely rank during imperial ceremonies in the empire, at court in Vienna, their status was a moot point. They normally had to assume positions deriving from their seniority in the ranks of councillors and chamberlains. Only the functional rights of the major court dignitaries usually overrode the hierarchy based on seniority in the two ranks; though the princes strove to assert their supremacy in practice, and their efforts were at times endorsed by the rulers.[54] The emperor controlled the ranking of chamberlains and councillors: the moment of nomination lay in his hands. This allowed him to influence the ranking at court more easily than would a system based more generally on noble rank, always a compromise between noble hierarchies and the rulers' meddling. Moreover, the function of the two honorary offices at court offset the negative consequences of their rapid inflation. Multiplication had rendered the title of chamberlain or councillor less prestigious – yet the fact that seniority among them served as basis for the ranking at court still made it vital to secure an early nomination. Finally, even for those not interested in pursuing an active career at court, the rank of chamberlain was attractive because it could help one outdo local rivals. Pöllnitz stated that Bohemian nobles coveted the chamberlain's honorary key mostly because it assured precedence for their spouses.[55]

Closely connected to ennoblement as well as to honorary court office, and related to activities annually recurring at court, were the orders of chivalry patronised by the ruler.[56] After the Burgundian dukes, Spanish kings became grand-masters of the order of the Golden Fleece. The order in its early stages expanded from 24 to 30 and finally to 50 knights, but it retained its restrictedness

52 See Winkelbauer, *Fürst und Fürstendiener*, chapter 8 for Gundaker's attempts to obtain *Sitz und Stimme*; and Evans, *Making*, pp. 171–178, in general on the Liechtenstein and other loyalist princely dynasties.

53 Winkelbauer, *Fürst und Fürstendiener*, p. 319. (pluralis maiestatis; 'von Gottes Gnaden', etc.); see also chapter 7 for the princes at court.

54 Khevenhüller, *Tagebuch*, II, discussing Maria Theresa's attempts to convince the princes to serve as chamberlains by granting them precedence over senior non-princely chamberlains, pp. 43–45 (April 1745); pp. 116–117 (6 October 1746); p. 154 (May 1747); see *Tagebuch* 1764–1767 (Vienna 1917), p. 141 (September 1765), for a short digression on supreme court office and seniority.

55 Pöllnitz, *Mémoires*, I, p. 279.

56 See in general D. A. J. D. Boulton, *The Monarchical Orders of Knighthood in Later Medieval Europe 1325–1520* (Woodbridge 1987).

and renown.[57] All scions of the Habsburg dynasty were knights of the order, and emperors could ask this grace for their noble servants. A substantial proportion of the dynasties loyally serving the Austrian Habsburgs can be found in the lists of the order. Membership never became a right, and could be expected only in an advanced stage of a courtier's career. The repetition of the same families over the generations in the lists suggests, however, that it must have been far easier for sons of *Toisonisten* to enter the order.[58] In the sixteenth and early seventeenth centuries, the order was dominated by names from Spain, Italy, and the southern Netherlands, sprinkled more thinly with nominations representing the hereditary lands and the empire. During the seventeenth century the balance changed perceptibly, and names familiar from high court office recur. After the War of Spanish Succession, Charles VI and Philip V both acted as grand-master of the order. Two competing orders now evolved, and while both maintained a cosmopolitan outlook, the membership of the two orders tended to conform more closely to the nations and dynasties connected to the Spanish-Bourbon and Habsburg crowns respectively. The *Toisonisten* formed the supreme rank in the multi-layered structure of honorary office at the Habsburg court. They were listed in the printed *Schematismen*; as were their female counterparts, the members of the order of the *Stern Kreuz* or Starry Cross, patronised by the dowager-empress. Halfway through the century, the great military effort gave rise to new orders, rewarding outstanding service on the battlefield: the order of Elisabeth Theresa, founded in 1750 by Charles VI's widow; and more notably the order of Maria Theresa founded in 1757. In 1764, the royal Hungarian order of St Stephen was instituted – an honour notably absent for Bohemia's Wenceslas crown.[59]

In France membership in the order of Saint-Michel, 36 upon its creation by Louis XI in 1469, and expanded to 50 by Charles IX in 1565, rapidly inflated in the course of the religious and civil wars: it became known as the *collier à toutes bêtes*. Henry III, so crucial for the structures of the court, also renovated the principle and practice of the orders of chivalry, by founding the order of the *Saint-Esprit* in December 1578. The knights of the Holy Ghost included the royal family, in addition to four officers, nine prelates, and 87 loyal Catholic nobles. The order's officers received *gages*; all members received an annual *commande* of 3,000 lt. Aspirants obtained the *collier* of Saint-Michel before their installation

57 *Toison d'Or ou recueil des statuts et ordonnances*, pp. 275–276; see the recent discussion and bibliography in Gert Melville, 'Rituelle Ostentation und Pragmatische Inquisition. Zur Institutionalität des Ordens vom Goldenen Vließ', in *Im Spannungsfeld von Recht und Ritual. Soziale Kommunikation in Mittelalter und Früher Neuzeit*, pp. 215–271.

58 See on orders of chivalry Lünig, *Theatrum Ceremoniale*, II, 9, XXXVI, vol. II, p. 1071, to vol. III, p. 1163. For the general structure, rulings, and changes of the order of the Golden Fleece, *Toison d'Or ou recueil des statuts et ordonnances*; see a list of the order's knights in *La Toison d'or. Cinq siècles d'art et d'histoire* (Bruges 1962). See Pecar, 'Ökonomie der Ehre', pp. 353 and 363–364, for an analysis of provenance and rank of the knights, as well as their attendance of the order's festivities in Vienna for the years 1712–1739.

59 Dickson, *Finance and Government*, I, p. 326, provides a wider context of decisions in favour of Hungary.

as knight of the *Saint-Esprit*, and thus were usually called *chevaliers des ordres du roi*. Their *cordon bleu* was to become a coveted grace, yet outside of the order's processions at court, it did little to influence hierarchies at court. Only royal blood guaranteed membership, though more distant *princes du sang* and *princes étrangers* could expect nomination. Among the knights, French court nobles, great noble soldiers, and governors predominate; but foreign sovereigns and ambassadors also occasionally received the honour. The order of Saint-Michel was examined in 1661–1664, and thereafter purged of its less eminent members: numbers sharply declined from *c.* 1,500 to 100.[60] A tendency to adopt stricter genealogical norms, suggested by the institution of the *généalogiste du roi* working for the king's orders as well as for the pages in the *écuries* and the *chambre*, and by the methodical exposition of *faux nobles* in the provinces, coincided with a marked broadening of royal orders. The order of Saint-Michel would progressively lose its noble character as it was granted mostly to writers, artists, and magistrates.[61] In 1693, Louis founded the order of Saint-Louis, rewarding the devoted service of Catholic army officers. The order introduced the hierarchy of *chevalier-commandeur-grand croix* and was open to roturiers. Among the 17 grand crosses, 52 commanders, and 1,800 knights created by Louis XIV, an estimated 50 per cent died in battle. Finally, Louis XV founded the order of *Mérite Militaire* in 1759 to reward Protestant foreigners serving in the French army.

The Golden Fleece truly matched the *Saint-Esprit* as the prime noble order of the realm after 1712, when the emperor himself could act as patron of his branch of the order. This most prestigious category reflected the need to generate loyalty and support among the major nobles. The Golden Fleece and the *Saint-Esprit* retained their exclusive character. Conferring a knighthood in these orders would be used to reward unswerving loyalty; withholding or delaying it to show discontent. The lists suggest, however, that even these nominations, quintessentially within the ruler's discretion, increasingly remained limited to a stable set of families, with minor additions reflecting extraordinary service. In Louis XIV's as well as in Maria Theresa's years, we find a new stress on military merit, evident not only in the institution of military orders, but also in the increasing prestige of elite guards at court. The guards in Vienna never reached numbers comparable to those around Versailles, but the old *Hartschieren* and *Trabanten* were pushed aside by several more prestigious guards, and elite units connected to the several components of the monarchy. These helped to make the military profession

[60] Isambert, *Recueil général*, XVIII, no. 446, pp. 44–48: 'Statut et ordonnance pour le rétablissement de l'Ordre de Saint-Michel', and various edicts pertaining to the examination of noble lineage, mostly with fiscal motives, in the same volume; compare on the *faux nobles* in the provinces, likewise purged for fiscal motives, for example Caumartin, *Recherches de la noblesse de Champagne* (Chalons 1673). No reliable lists of seventeenth-century knights survive, an indication of the uncontrolled inflation of the order.

[61] See the relevant articles in *DAR*, pp. 1125–1126, 1384–1388 (with list of the *Saint-Esprit*), 1392, 1395, and *DGS*, pp. 939–940.

more attractive for a nobility that had previously been of a disposition less martial than its French counterpart. The bonds between the court and the military were strengthened in other ways; a concordance was established among ranks of courtiers, administrators, and soldiers. The introduction of military court attire by Joseph II neatly fitted into this broader perspective. Nor did the initiatives remain limited to nobles: by rewarding service on the battlefield with nobility, the military orders restored the ties between the *impôt de sang* and promotion into noble rank – a connection strengthened in the Habsburg domains by the decision to grant hereditary nobility to lifelong officers.[62]

Marriage alliances and godparenthood were central issues in the networks of noble families: they indicated lasting loyalties and entailed major transactions in income and landed wealth. The court was the central meeting place for dynasties from the various regions. In the centre, at the apex of the hierarchy of descent, the ruling dynasty acted as the major patron. Noble dynasties present at court sought the approval of the king and emperor or their spouses for their marriage alliances. The ruler's *Bewilligung* or *agrément* came to be regarded almost as requisite for marriages among courtiers and their families; in principle this allowed the ruler to meddle with noble alliances. It is difficult to find out whether this opportunity was systematically pursued. Henry III used marriages to support his *mignons*, by connecting them to his own lineage, and by concluding most prestigious and lucrative alliances for them – and among them.[63] Louis XIV systematically connected royal bastards with legitimate princes of the blood; he also intervened in marriages among ministers and high court nobles, though his policy was more ambiguous there.[64] In 1699 Louis XIV declined his minister Pontchartrain the honour of connecting his family to Bourbon blood, by refusing to grant permission for the marriage of Mlle de Malauze, of distant and illegitimate Bourbon stock, to the young Phélypeaux – a slight in which Saint-Simon took great delight.[65] The notorious marriage of Louis XIV's friend and

[62] See Hochedlinger, 'Mars Ennobled', for Habsburg reforms halfway through the eighteenth century; Rowlands, 'Louis XIV, Aristocratic Power and the Elite Units', for France in Louis XIV's rule.

[63] Le Roux, *Faveur du roi*, pp. 479–485.

[64] See Béguin, 'Louis XIV et l'aristocratie'; Mettam, *Power and Faction*, pp. 88–93; examples on another level in Robert Oresko, 'The Marriages of the Nieces of Cardinal Mazarin: Public Policy and Private Strategy in Seventeenth-Century Europe', in *Frankreich im europäischen Staatensystem der Frühen Neuzeit*, ed. Rainer Babel (Sigmaringen 1995), pp. 109–151; see Chaussinand-Nogaret, *La noblesse au XVIIIe siècle* pp. 163–179, at p. 167, and more generally Anne Lefebvre-Teillard, 'Mariage', in *DGS*, p. 971. Bastl and Heiss, eds., 'Hofdamen und Höflinge', particularly p. 206; Beatrix Bastl, *Tugend, Liebe, Ehre. Die adelige Frau in der Frühen Neuzeit* (Vienna, Cologne, and Weimar 2000), pp. 34–83, particularly pp. 36–37 and for Patenschaft, pp. 500–503; p. 153 cites Anton Florian von Liechtenstein stating: 'der König seye König, und er seye vatter yber seyn Kindt', while rejecting his daughter's marriage to a Lamberg scion, notwithstanding the emperor's *Bewilligung* and advocacy of the union. I warmly thank Beatrix Bastl for her patient and invariably well-informed answers to my recurring questions on these and other matters. Compare, however, Ferdinand I's 1563–1564 post-tridentine disavowal of the marriage arranged between Nikolaus von Lobkowitz and Katharina von Gutnstein: Ferdinand brought them to court, but the proceedings were dropped after the emperor's death, see Petr Vorel, 'Aristokratické svatby v čechách a no moravě v 16. století jako prostředek společenské komunikace a stavovské diplomacie', *Opera Historica* 8 (2000), pp. 191–206, with a summary in German. I thank Pavel Kral for this reference.

[65] Béguin, 'Louis XIV et l'aristocratie', pp. 510–511, citing Saint-Simon.

courtier François VII de La Rochefoucauld's son, the duc de La Rocheguyon, to Mlle de Louvois in 1679, on the other hand, has been construed as royal policy, yet there is no evidence that the king initiated this union: he may only have endorsed it. Two decades later, moreover, the same duke of La Rochefoucauld 'fit opiniatrément la sourde oreille' when the king, eager to join the families of his friend and wife, proposed the union of the duke's grandson Marcillac to Mlle d'Aubigné, a relative of Mme de Maintenon.[66]

The ruler's role in the marriage market at court could incidentally be outspoken and active, more often unobtrusive and limited. Consent was routinely asked, and routinely given. Dangeau frequently reports marriages, often citing dowries, and sometimes including the king's signature of the contract, or his gifts for the new couple, without further comment.[67] Nobles themselves, however, may have wondered whether their alliances were likely to appeal to the ruler, while the latter could express surprise at the prospect of certain unions. Marriages were a major factor in the power balances among families at court as well as in the country at large; thus, even such minor and indirect influences should not be dismissed lightly. Baptism offered another occasion for the ruling dynasty to extend to the newly-born children of their noble servants protection as godfather or godmother – *Paten*, *Patin*, *parrain* or *marraine*. When members of the imperial family were willing to act as godparents, this was a special favour, never extended to the court nobles as a group, and indicative of the special standing of a family. At the French court, however, godparenthood was extended to a more mixed group of families, with the *premier gentilhomme de la chambre* usually serving as the king's representative.[68] Allowing children to serve at court as *enfants d'honneur*, as the companions of royals, would certainly show great favour – and boded well for future favour.

[66] Saint-Simon, *Mémoires*, XVII, p. 329, noting that the king 'mourut d'envie' to effect the union, but met with cold responses from both sides. Saint-Simon is not wholly consistent: in *Mémoires*, V, pp. 123–124, he again stresses the king's eagerness, adding that La Rochefoucauld 'n'y consentit que par respect et par complaisance' and that the cold attitudes from both parties stopped the king. Françoise Charlotte Amable d'Aubigné (1684–1739) married into the Noailles family in 1698; Leonhard Horowski brought these examples to my attention, and his detailed prosopographical data helped me to reconsider several statements in the paragraphs on marriage and godparenthood.

[67] References to marriages abound in Dangeau and Luynes; see for example in Dangeau, *Journal*, IV (1692), pp. 7, 28–29, 31–32 (Chartres-Mlle de Blois) and 22, 45 (Maine-Mlle de Charolais), both marriages with the active involvement of the royal family; lesser instances on pp. 54, 58, 65, 67, 71, with explicit references to the king's role on pp. 58 and 71; likewise in 1699, pp. 26, 27 and 43, 52, in the first instance with active involvement (in annulling the marriage) of Mme de Maintenon, in the last two instances with the king's involvement – on p. 52 it is explained that the prince de Chimay and Mlle de Nevers married in secret because the king of Spain had not assented to their union; Luynes, *Mémoires*, for example II (1738), pp. 21–22, 25–26, with explicit references to the king's refusal to endorse the marriage of the elderly duke of Brancas, and the compromise on p. 50, or XIII (1755), pp. 9, 82–83, 239, 241, in the last instance explicitly mentioning the king's signature. Typically, the king's half-refusal to sign Brancas' marriage contract was connected to the hierarchy of dukes.

[68] My basis for these statements is small; godparenthood is less frequently referred to than marriages, see, for example, in Luynes, *Mémoires*, I (1737), p. 351; XIII (1755), p. 9, with the *dauphin* as *parrain* in both cases, madame as *marraine* in the first, the queen in the second instance. Among noble families, godparenthood was a means to cement connections and loyalties.

Ennoblement, the granting of exclusive ranks and titles to nobles, the institution of orders of chivalry, and princely patronage over marriages offer only a small selection of the more subtle forms and means available to rulers to connect their household to the wider environment of nobles and noble hierarchies. In many respects, they have the same dual character as groups and distinctions attached more directly to the household: honorary officers, pages, ladies-in-waiting; presentations or invitations for special occasions. Rewards and honorary memberships create obligations: all such inducements may be interpreted either as the consequence of a close relationship, or as a calculated attempt to bind elites – most likely a rather traditional and unpremeditated mixture prevailed. Recognizing rank as well as rewarding distinguished service helped to orient the beneficiaries towards the court. In various guises, such habits would survive monarchy itself – they underline the need of any political system to generate loyalty by appeasing vested interests and rewarding merit.

THE COURT AS A CULTURAL CENTRE

The gradual strengthening of the machinery of power at court slowly tilted the balance between regions and centre in favour of the latter; rewards and enticements moulded noble hierarchies and could attract nobles to the court. The accumulation of noble splendour at court, it has often been argued, helped to charm populations into obedience; its conspicuous presence offered an example for the entire culture, setting standards for arts, language, dress, and deportment. The essentials of the courtly environment, however, seem to reside in a sharp sense of rank and honour, a strong presence of religious traditions, keen hunting ardour, and recurring eruptions of merry spectacle more than in any of the achievements we commonly connect to the notion of 'high' culture. Admittedly, music was among the preferred activities of many a ruler, most of them were involved in restructuring their palaces, and took an interest in the decoration of their interiors – some of them saw no harm in reading a variety of works in addition to the obligatory state papers, or might even pursue specific intellectual interests. There is no point, however, in presenting the arts, learning, or even good manners, as the essence of a 'court culture' aloof from daily practice in the dynastic households of early modern Europe. The magnificent representations of rulership to wider audiences, however, could strengthen the position of the court as the visible centre of power and rank in the realm. I cannot systematically chart the reception of the various media propounding dynastic majesty here, yet their impact needs to be included in a discussion of the court as a focus for wider territories. Finally, some thought has to be given to the exemplary role often ascribed to the court in restructuring manners among the elites.

The public manifestations of the household, in their magnificent indoor or outdoor settings, had impressed spectators in earlier ages. The great ceremonies and festivities, reported in the Godefroy volumes for France, in more incidental publications and manuscript sources for the Habsburgs, attracted participants as well as spectators. Around the inner circle of ruler and high court nobles, central in the proceedings, we find a second echelon of honorary officers and nobles attached more loosely to the court, yet still clearly participants more than spectators. Beyond their ranks, an ill-defined audience could watch, usually kept at bay by rows of guards, or held at a distance by gates and walls. These spectators were gratified not only by the splendour of the show: largesse was distributed among them, fountains spouted wine, and oxen were roasted.[69] For specific occasions, such as the king's touch in France, they could expect other rewards; in the Maundy Thursday *pedilavium* and meal, a minute part of the populace was singled out to take a notable if passive part in ceremony. To a certain extent, onlookers were always vital participants at the same time, as public festive or ceremonial acts were painfully inadequate without them. Indeed, a splendid occasion unattended by crowds conveyed a dismal message.[70]

Large-scale festivities were typically organised around great dynastic ceremonies, notably marriages or coronations. They could include *carrousels* or *Ringlrennen*, mock naval or land battles, large-scale equestrian ballets, open-air concerts, operas and plays, fireworks, illuminations, banquets, and smaller-scale entertainments for the intimates. Depending on the nature of the occasion, and the particulars of the location, audiences could be smaller or larger. Such occasions frequently were accompanied by printed booklets, explaining the emblems of the show for the onlookers, or providing texts and cast. These prints, or their counterparts published afterwards, could reach more distant audiences, as did descriptions of the dynastic feats that gave rise to the festive exuberance. Certainly, rulers wanted their outlay and programme to be admired by subjects as well as by their rivals beyond the borders. The printed dissemination of courtly splendour had a long pedigree: dynastic ceremonies and joyous festivals had been described in printed pamphlets since the late fifteenth century.[71] Maximilian I and Rudolf II, and all late Valois kings, had created typical forms of representation, including both the visual arts and the medium of print.

In the course of the centuries, forms and styles changed. Castles became palaces; the tournaments became more stylised, via *Ringlrennen* or carrousels turning into elegant, near balletic forms of equestrian bravery, finally dissolving

[69] See Passer and Godefroy quotes above on p. 184.

[70] See the perceptive comments on 'failed' ceremonies in Duchhardt, 'Krönungszüge', in *Im Spannungsfeld von Recht und Ritual*, ed. Duchhardt and Melville, pp. 291–301; Pecar, 'Ökonomie der Ehre', pp. 283–285, points out that the audiences in Vienna seem closer to participants than to spectators.

[71] See recently the overview edited by Pierre Béhar and Helen Watanabe-O'Kelly, *Spectaculum Europaeum: Theatre and Spectacle in Europe*, Wolfenbütteler Arbeiten zur Barockforschung 31 (Wiesbaden 1999); and the bibliography *Festivals and Ceremonies: A Bibliography of Works Relating to Court, Civic, and Religious Festivals in Europe 1500–1800*, ed. Helen Watanabe-O'Kelly and Anne Simon (London and New York, 2000).

into court opera, court theatre, and masked balls.[72] Most important of all, the essentially ephemeral forms of the great festival, with its processions, temporary structures, solemn ritual, dashing performances, illuminations and fireworks, were now given a more durable form in stone, image, and writing. In the course of the seventeenth century, such efforts were to become both more comprehensive, and more methodical. Noteworthy activities of the French Bourbon kings and their environment were reported in print, either in laudatory descriptions written at their behest, in sponsored journals such as the successive *mercures* published after 1611, *gazettes*, and other periodicals.[73] The great outdoor festivals organised in the early years of the Sun King were represented in Felibien's lavishly illustrated tomes and by the *Mercure*. By imitating and elaborating the Italian example of academies, state-sponsored groups of writers and artists came into being.[74] Academies instituted by the ruler set new standards for language, arts, and sciences alike, with their efforts contributing to the sovereign's radiance. Medals celebrated highpoints of the dynasty and its glorious pursuits, and later became the subject of learned study.[75] In the Habsburg lands, the quantity of publications was less impressive, and the emperors seem to have been reticent in initiating major efforts themselves.[76] Periodicals arose slightly later, and more hesitantly in Vienna. After 1622 the *Ordentliche Postzeitungen* reported news from the court, but its publication would be halted halfway through the century. From 1671 onwards the German *Currier* and the Italian *Corriere* were published, while from 1703 onwards the *Wienerisches Diarium* provided a lasting outlet for the news of the court.[77] Jesuits were an active force in disseminating the emperors' reputation in print – possibly more active than the dynasty itself. From the introduction of the order in the second half of the sixteenth century to its

[72] Khevenhüller, *Geheimes Tagebuch 1548–1605*, gives an idea of the frequence and importance of *Ritterspiele*, and suggest the differences with the later type of festivities; see Helen Watanabe-O'Kelly, *Triumphall Shews: Tournaments at German-Speaking Courts in their European Context 1560–1730* (Berlin 1992).

[73] See Eugène Hatin, *Bibliographie historique et critique de la presse périodique française* (Paris 1866), including French gazettes published in the Dutch Republic, and Monique Vincent, *Mercure Galant. Extraordinaire Affaires du temps. Table analytique de tous les articles publiés 1672–1710* (Paris 1998).

[74] Burke, *Fabrication*, gives a succinct overview of the process, outlined earlier in Jürgen Voss, 'Mäzenatentum und Ansätze systematischer Kulturpolitik im Frankreich Ludwigs XIV.', in *Europäische Hofkultur*, ed. Buck *et al.*, II, pp. 123–132. Compare more general works on royal propaganda, Jeffrey K. Sawyer, *Printed Poison, Pamphlet Propaganda, Faction Politics, and the Public Sphere in Early Seventeenth-Century France* (Berkeley and Los Angeles 1990); Joseph C. Klaits, *Printed Propaganda under Louis XIV: Absolute Monarchy and Public Opinion* (Princeton 1976).

[75] C.-F. Menestrier, *Histoire du Roy Louis le Grand. Par les Médailles, Emblèmes, Devises, Jettons, Inscriptions armoires et autres* (Paris 1691).

[76] Though Leopold did commission a history, by Galeazzo Gualdo Priorato, *Historia di Leopoldo Cesare*, 3 vols. (Vienna 1670), see the circumstances of Gualdo Priorato's 'sabbatical' in HKA HZAB, fol. 257r, where we find in the extraordinaria 12,200 fl for 'Herr Conte Gualdo Kaijl. Historico wegen seines zuverfertigung habenden Buchs'; compare Goloubeva, *Glorification*, pp. 60, 102.

[77] Goloubeva, *Glorification*, p. 59; see *Wienerisches Diarium* in ÖNB, 393–052 B-D-E Kat or microfilm 226. Compare at the level of the empire and Europe Merian's *Theatrum Europaeum* (electronically available in the Augsburg university library http://digbib.bibliothek.uni-augsburg.de/2/) and another Frankfurt periodical, the *Diarium Europaeum*, or, for example, Dutch periodicals such as the *Europische Mercurius*, a well-informed six-monthly volume published from 1690 onwards.

demise in 1773, it was one of the pillars of Habsburg power. The role of Jesuits was conspicuous at least until the end of Charles' reign, but in 1774 Maria Theresa and Khevenhüller deplored the end of the order, remembering its invaluable services to the dynasty.[78]

Major occasions, such as the celebrations following Leopold's marriage to Margarita Teresa of Spain in December 1666, with festivities lasting into 1668, certainly reached wider audiences. *Libretti* were printed by court printer Mattheus Cosmoverius, and the highpoints were reported in the European periodical press.[79] Less spectacular dramatic performances were frequent, and found their way into the world. Leopold sent *libretti* to Pötting in Madrid, and to relatives and ambassadors elsewhere, urging them to further distribute the booklets.[80] The festive cycles of the 1664 Versailles *plaisirs de l'isle enchantée* and the celebrations in Vienna 1666–1668 indicated the rivalry of the Bourbon and Habsburg dynasties over the Spanish heritage. In this battle of images, Leopold's chances were decidedly more favourable than they would have been in the case of open military competition. Likewise, when Charles VI chose to turn the 1723 Bohemian coronation into a major occasion, he must have had in mind the festive challenges previously articulated by the electoral courts of Dresden and Munich during the celebrations of marriages with the daughters of Joseph I. In many of these instances courtly festivals were expected to brace dynastic power; they were most brilliant when succession was at stake, or in sequences of challenge and response. The European society of princes was the motor of court spectacle in its grander forms.

In print and image, the courts' magnificence could be enjoyed even by those in the provinces, or beyond the borders. Yet around the palaces a tourist industry emerged, offering accommodation or guided tours; travellers busily copied their predecessors' notes, inserting them into their own frequently published impressions. In the eighteenth century, a true travel literature appeared, that was centred on the great dynastic centres of Europe – Pöllnitz's stylised letters, or Monicart's description of Versailles may serve as examples.[81] Visitors to Vienna were apt to contrast the superb collections and excellent musical performances with the outmoded and austere Hofburg. Matthaeus Merian's *Topographia Germania* marvelled at the imperial *Schatzkammer*, and thought highly of the

[78] Evans, *Making*, frequently discusses individual Jesuits, and the order's contribution to the dynastic 'universal enterprise', pp. 41–2, for the introduction; Goloubeva, *Glorification*, pp. 52–56; Khevenhüller, *Tagebuch*, VII, pp. 181 and n. 218; VIII, p. 12, conversation of Khevenhüller and Maria Theresa during an audience, 2 March 1774.

[79] Goloubeva, *Glorification*, pp. 103–120, on Cosmoverius pp. 51–52; see Francesco Sbarra's texts in Cosmoverius' editions for these years in the ÖNB; contemporary descriptions of the range of festivities accompanying the marriage of Leopold and Margarita Teresa in Vehse, *Geschichte der deutschen Höfe*, II, 5, pp. 117–155; compare Richard Alewyn and Karl Sälzle, *Das Grosse Welttheater. Die Epoche der höfischen Feste in Dokument und Deutung* (Hamburg 1959), pp. 103–119.

[80] *Privatbriefe*, I, p. 382, further instances in Goloubeva, *Glorification*, p. 48.

[81] Pöllnitz, *Mémoires*; Jean-Baptiste de Monicart, *Versailles immortalisé par les merveilles parlantes de bâtimens, jardins, bosquets, parcs, statues, termes & vases* (Paris 1720).

Stattliche musica in the chapel, yet noted that the Hofburg was 'nicht sonders prächtig erbaut/und für einen solchen mächtigen und höchsten Potentaten/und eine so grosse Hoffhaltung zimblich eng . . .'. These judgements would be echoed by many authors. The Hofburg, not far below the standards of European palaces after Leopold's early improvements, tended to lag more seriously behind its major rivals in the decades around 1700 – the very years characterised by opulent building projects of Vienna's court aristocracy. In the half-century following 1683, major court aristocrats built splendid palaces both in the centre and on the outskirts of Vienna. The Hofburg looked unassuming and uncomfortable when compared with the major examples of aristocratic building, most strikingly Eugene's Belvedere. Montesquieu quipped that he was disposed to admire a realm in which the nobles' houses outshone that of the sovereign.[82] In Charles' reign, the Hofburg was expanded and embellished, yet his religious building projects were at least as ambitious, as the examples of the Karlskirche and Klosterneuburg show. Continuity and tradition were particularly important for a dynasty cherishing an elective title over a feudal commonwealth as its supreme honour, and this may have helped the Hofburg, with its appropriately traditional structures, to remain the major residence of the Habsburgs. Only under Maria Theresa, when the balances between the empire and the hereditary lands had undergone rapid changes, would Schönbrunn take on the allure of a second major residence, on a par with the fashionable palaces of major princes in the empire, and other European sovereigns, and even then, it never eclipsed the venerable Hofburg.

The Habsburgs cherished a pious, austere, and hard-working image – lavish expenditure on court opera and hunt, much favoured pursuits of both Leopold and Charles, tended to be dealt with apologetically more than proudly. Reticence was made easier by the active support of the Jesuits, and more generally by the close link between dynasty, religion, and tradition. Austerity, frequently dictated by the perennial shortage of funds, seems to have obtained a rhetoric of its own. Rinck's biography of Leopold, and Küchelbecker's description of Charles' court dwelt on the modesty of the court more than on its splendour. Monarchy, long

[82] Matthaeus Merian, *Topographia Germania – Österreich* (Frankfurt 1649–1656; repr. Kassel 1963), pp. 44–45; similar comments are to be found in Casimir Freschot, *Mémoires de la Cour de Vienne, contenant les remarques d'un voyage curieux sur l'état de cette Cour, & sur ses interêts* (Cologne 1706), pp. 4–5; Küchelbecker, *Allerneueste Nachricht*, pp. 213–219; Pöllnitz, *Mémoires*, I, pp. 287, 304; Pribram, 'Berichte eines Franzosen', pp. 273, 295; and Lhotsky, 'Kaiser Karl VI. und sein Hof', p. 57; Montesquieu, *Pensées*, no. 6, *Œuvres Complètes* (Paris 1964), p. 855: compare Montesquieu's praise of aristocratic palaces in *Voyages en Europe*, in the same volume on p. 212. Brown, *A Brief Account*, p. 153, and Charles Patin, *Relations historiques et curieuses de voyages, en Allemagne, Angleterre, Hollande, Bohème, Suisse, & c.* (Amsterdam 1695), p. 3, however, are more commendatory. The mediocrity of the Hofburg was most marked in the very decades of opulent aristocratic building, between 1680 and 1720: before that time the Leopoldine Tract was acceptably grand, later Charles' additions improved the Hofburg's stature. See a fine analysis of noble palaces and representation in Pecar, 'Ökonomie der Ehre', pp. 311–336 and pp. 365–369; on the imperial residences see Friedrich Polleroß, 'Tradition und Recreation. Die Residenzen der österreichischen Habsburger in der Frühen Neuzeit', *Maiestas* 6 (1998), pp. 91–148, and several contributions in volume 51 (1997) of the *Österreichische Zeitschrift für Kunst und Denkmalpflege*.

the object of scorn and fears in the empire, must have been more palatable to them in this modest appearance, relatively close to the feudal imperial traditions. Pöllnitz wondered why the emperor left his state apartment almost unadorned, even though he probably was able to furnish it in grand style using his rich collections. The apparent modesty imparted an appropriately dignified aura to the nominally highest worldly ruler of Christendom, who saw no need to flaunt his riches.[83] Yet it also served as a powerful counterimage to the fashionable 'vanities' of the French court, spreading across Europe. In the empire, Protestants might feel closer to the style of their traditional opponent than to the more dazzling style of the self-appointed Gallic defender of Germanic liberties.

For French visitors, used to the massive scale and rich furnishings of Versailles, the contrast must have been striking. Palace architecture, interior decoration, and gardens attained new heights in Versailles: it provided a splendid setting for the court; its statues, picture galleries, and lavish decorations glorified the dynasty and its martial exploits in a language more grandiose than words could offer. De la Court appreciated the paintings, but was amazed by the abundance of gold, silver, and marble – it was all truly royal, he noted, and much better than the fusty Louvre.[84] Yet the Leiden manufacturer was equally impressed by other palaces in the vicinity of Paris: Meudon and Saint-Cloud among them. Indeed, Fouquet's palace at Vaux-le-Vicomte had pioneered some of the artistic innovations of Louis XIV's Versailles. Alternatives to the king's artistic programme would recur later; the Grand Condé's improvements of Chantilly offer a major example, not on the same scale as Versailles, but certainly on the same artistic level. The same would hold true for other palaces owned by royal family. Neither of these, however, could approach the royal domicile in grandeur, nor could any of the other palaces in the vicinity of Paris. Versailles conveyed a message differing markedly from that of the Hofburg, with its stress on tradition and modesty: it exuded personal grandeur and martial imagery. Equestrian statues, typical in Louis XIV's effort to spread the image of his strong rulership, or explicit references to crushed rebellions – snakes trampled underfoot by the king – were exceedingly rare for Habsburg rulers. Leopold's proskynesis, or reverent submission to heavenly powers, beseeching their support against the plague or the Turks, has no parallel in Ludovician imagery. *Pestsäulen*, or 'plague pillars', were as typical for Leopold's attitude as equestrian statues were for Louis' posture.

The imagery of these rivalling dynasties, their building projects, printed propaganda, and institutional forms of patronage, have been reconstructed in some detail. The sources provide a comfortable basis for discussing the creation of images around court, and their echoes at other European courts. The impact of the Habsburg and Bourbon models in the peripheries of France, or in the

[83] Küchelbecker, *Allerneueste Nachricht*, pp. 213–219; Pöllnitz, *Mémoires*, I, pp. 287, 304, with echoes in most other descriptions; see the illuminating discussion in Pecar, 'Ökonomie der Ehre', pp. 291–341.

[84] *Reizen der de la Courts*, pp. 49–55.

hereditary lands respectively, however, remains to be charted. Sources allowing us to address this vital question are unevenly distributed, and necessarily spread over the whole territory under discussion. We are faced with a situation analogous to the study of absolutism in its early orthodox phase, when the decrees emanating from the ruler were studied, and their implementation was taken for granted. Regional studies have now corrected this image, but their efforts have rarely included the cultural field. The rare instances studying regional reception, or the attitudes of other social groups, vis-à-vis the cultural images of the centre, indicate that responses were not always favourable, and policies not necessarily successful.[85] The social and geographical 'penetration' of the court's images needs more study; we cannot infer it from the central example itself. Nor should we take for granted the compliant acceptance of the court's images among the audiences reached.

Even the well-attested influence of Bourbon and Habsburg examples among the princes of the empire is not as straightforward as it may seem. All courts in the empire were bound by political and ceremonial traditions pertaining to the empire; they formed a closely interacting commonwealth of states within the whole of Europe. Princely residences included *Kaisersäle*, waiting to receive the emperor on his travels through their territories. Princely state-apartments followed the same ceremonial principles as did the emperor's apartment in the Hofburg, tying entry into the enfilade of rooms to rank, and reserving a relatively private space for the ruler. Court staffs were organised basically along the same lines as were those at the Habsburg court, though the marshal was frequently more important than the steward. Were these the remnants of a collective past, consequences of the standing interactions among the princes of the empire, or effects of a Habsburg model? In this mixture direct Habsburg influence may have been a minor ingredient. The question becomes more troubled when styles and fashions are introduced. Can Baroque be equated with Habsburg influence, Classicism with a French model? The platitude does not seem helpful. Newly built palaces might combine dominant French influences with the splendid Baroque styles of Fischer von Erlach or Hildebrandt. At the same time, their princes might sport French clothes, invite French theatre companies, prefer French-style cooking and wines, host a French-inspired salon life at court, or introduce a *lever* and *coucher* along French lines. These French examples, however, were readily imitated by Amsterdam patricians as well. Evidently,

85 See Goloubeva, *Glorification of Emperor Leopold I*; Franz Matsche, *Die Kunst im Dienst der Staatsidee Kaiser Karls VI. Ikonographie, Ikonologie und Programmatik des 'Kaiserstils'*, 2 vols. (Berlin and New York 1981); a range of works by Friedrich Polleross, and a comparative long-term perspective in Thomas H. von der Dunk, *Das deutsche Denkmal: eine Geschichte in Bronze und Stein vom Hochmittelalter bis zum Barock* (Cologne 1999); Burke, *Fabrication* and Sabatier, *Versailles ou la figure du roi*. The limits of the central example and the resilience of local traditions were pointed out by Roger Mettam, whose work ranges from the social-political to the cultural domains, see his 'Power, Status and Precedence'. Compare the rather sceptical and well-founded assessment of royal propaganda in Engels, *Königsbilder*.

France had displaced Italy as the major influence in a variety of fashions and items of elite life all over Europe. Vienna never came close to playing such a role, and after 1740 gave up resistance to the French example: it adopted many of the fashionable items of court life that had earlier been embraced by other German princes – French language notable among them. Yet for ceremony, the principalities of the empire were necessarily oriented more strongly towards Vienna than towards Versailles – even if they came to adopt some of the domestic peculiarities of French court life into their markedly different ceremonial setting.

What exactly did the court export to the provinces, or to the courts of rivals? Voltaire, praising the high culture of the courts in the Italian Renaissance and in Louis XIV's France, seems to have been interested mostly in the spread of art and learning. Yet he also connected the example of the courts to the rise of good manners. Court life did play a marked role in several literary traditions connected to *politesse* and civility. At one end, the anti-courtier literature criticised the noble community around the ruler, censuring its vanity, ambition, and pretence: implicitly, it sketched an ideal of 'inner' nobility, unaffected by these base concerns. At the other end, we find manner books using the icons of courtly rank and deportment to instruct social climbers. The extremes use the same categories for opposed purposes: the first dismantling a world of deceit and intrigue, the second simply paving the way to success in that same environment. Most works stand in the middle, offering both aspects in varying proportions. Castiglione, outlining an ideal community of male and female courtiers testing their strengths in smart discourse, allows one of his characters to suggest one should dash forward on the battlefield only when the ruler could be expected to behold and reward this heroic act.

The ideals and anti-ideals connected to the courtier, with elevated moral as well as thoroughly pragmatic perspectives, call to mind a string of notions, such as *curialitas*, *urbanitas*, *cortegiania*, *honnêteté*, *civilité*, *politesse*. Each of these represents a different phase in an ongoing literary discourse, seeking its models and arguments more in the preceding tradition than in the examples of court life. The court and the nobility inevitably figured among the prime categories, but so did the church, the urban milieu, or the satisfyingly contrasting bucolic scenery. The *topos* of the court in literary traditions throughout the ages must have had some connections with the practices of court life, yet these should not be pictured in too straightforward a way. In current variants of this discourse, we could substitute for 'court' the conspicuous centre either of the political structures, or the cosmopolitan-metropolitan *beau monde*, with similarly opposed ideals of fashionable yet superficial vanities and 'inner' values, and similar dynamics of repulsion and attraction. How to lead a *vita activa* without succumbing to earthly vanities, that seems to be the recurring underlying question.

Did this hybrid literary tradition, itself a distant and distorted reflection of court life, influence the manners and examples of the population at large? Those eager to make their way into the world of rank and privilege may have used manner books, more or less like diplomats might use ceremonial compilations, or voyagers could consult travel books: to grasp the details of a world unknown to them. A variety of other works dealing with architecture, household management, cooking, table service, and the like, undoubtedly helped to disseminate fashions and items in vogue at the Italian or French courts to a wider readership. In the course of the eighteenth century, when the solemn ceremonial forms of the court were perceived as obsolete by increasing numbers in the upper echelons, the example of the *raffinements* of court dining, pertaining more to social niceties than to the food itself, could still be imitated, and the same holds true for the splendours of its furnishings and decorations. The extremes from down-to-earth camaraderie to solemn ceremonial, so typical for earlier court life, were now pushed aside by an image of affected everyday luxury that would remain dominant in subsequent interpretations of court life.

In the context of late nineteenth- and early twentieth-century Germany, the discourse of the courtier obtained a curious national finale, with 'superficial' French *civilisation* being opposed to 'deep' German *Kultur*. Norbert Elias' works on the court and on civilisation were an attempt to transcend this opposition, by integrating Rankean, Weberian, and Freudian models in a visionary image of humanity's progress towards a world less hampered by eruptions of irrational drives and impulses. He understood civilisation as *Affektbeherrschung*, reached in a process starting with *Fremdzwang* or external force reining in behaviour, leading to *Selbstzwang* and positive identification with the new style of behaviour. The cliché of tamed nobles at court formed the ideal illustration of this process. The preceding chapters have outlined that nobles at court were far from caged and impotent; the preceding paragraphs have cautioned against reading courtiers' manuals as descriptions of court life. Courts could be conspicuous centres of high culture, yet we should not confound this general notion with Elias' specific interpretation of civilisation as *Affektbeherrschung*. We should not take for granted that the court or its reputation in print and image led the way in processes of change that may equally well have arisen in response to more general developments, or the examples of other sectors of society – notably the church, and urban culture.

Were forms we tend to see as 'courtly' in fact pioneered at court and diffused by its example? The religious domain, so dominant in household routines, became particularly crucial in the century of strife and reform after 1550. The church, more than any other institution, seems traditionally to have harboured suspicions against the economy of human drives, and the experiences of heresy and conversion will have increased this both on the individual and the institutional level. Thriving urban communities and an expanding world of lay intellectuals, likewise well-represented in rulers' households, exerted their own influences. Paris was a centre and example in its own right, never wholly congruent with the court. In Vienna, noble society was indubitably organised around the court, yet until deep into the eighteenth century, noble social life was concentrated in the aristocratic palaces more than at the Hofburg.

This maze of interconnections and influences cannot be cast into the simple form of example and imitation. The urban oligarchies in the Dutch Republic followed patterns of cultural change reflecting the general European development, though the stadholder's court was neither permanently present nor always culturally or politically significant. Courts could for a short time outshine all rival centres, yet such phases of near-monopolistic brilliance were rare and usually short-lived. Moreover, they were the consequence of the confluence of major groups and institutions at court. If the court could effectively attract major nobles, clergymen, administrators, soldiers, artisans, and scholars into its orbit, it profited from the accretion of prestige and talent without necessarily diminishing the status of the visitors and their affiliations. As soon as the court's power to attract declined, its prestige would inevitably be undermined, and the autonomy of other corporations in the state would become manifest. Concentrating more on the realities of court life than on its reputation, we cannot but conclude that the importance of the court was inflated in the artistic representations of rulership, taken at face value by some contemporaries as well as by later historians. The Bourbon and Habsburg courts were successful centres for much of the seventeenth and eighteenth centuries, yet neither of them was ever as omnipotent or unchallenged as the triumphant images of the 1670s and 1680s suggest.[86] The court's propaganda and cultural patronage may have been successful in radiating an image of omnipotence, but this image always had to contend with images originating in other spheres, propounded by other media. In this plurality of public spheres, no lasting dominance could be achieved.

Two developments spanning the entire early modern age did much to shape the position of the court. The first development emerged from the court itself: the increasing use of media allowing audiences distant in time and space to marvel at the splendour or dignity of the dynasty. The interaction of rulers, courtiers, servants; visitors, diplomats, and spectators was enlarged and embellished in a printed representation of court life that communicated its messages to an infinite world of secondary observers, most of whom were never present or even personally represented at court. The second more profound development did not necessarily have much to do with the court, but had weighty consequences. We may choose to label it civilisation, *Entzauberung*, rationalisation; we can limit it in time by calling it Enlightenment, or in theme by pointing to the strengthened ideas and institutions of 'rational' government. The changing environment inevitably had an impact both on the court itself, and on the perception of the

[86] In Blanning, *Culture of Power and the Power of Culture*, Louis XIV's 'culture of power' comes out rather grand, which allows the author to stress the contrast with the emerging 'power of culture', unchecked by the king, in the eighteenth century.

courtly traditions in the world at large. The court was a bulwark of tradition and conservatism, as well as a motor of innovation and change – tradition had often been the preferred framework of decision-making, innovation the indispensable *ad hoc* answer to crisis. In the course of the eighteenth century the dialogue of courts and cultural change became increasingly relevant: how could this institution adapt its forms and media to the exigencies of a changing outlook, among its habitués as well as among others in the upper layers of society? The changes in the make-up and presentation of the Habsburg court and the various elites connected to it contrast markedly with the less easily transformed world of the Bourbon court and its elites. When after the watershed of 1789–1815, European courts re-emerged triumphantly, both the representation of the court and the public voice of its opponents reached a higher pitch.

PART V

Epilogue

CHAPTER 9

Conclusions and conjectures

INTRODUCTION

Towards the end of the Middle Ages, the households of the French kings and the Habsburg king-emperors were quite similar as well as radically different, and this ambivalent situation would hold sway until the French Revolution. Both dominions showed a largely comparable heritage of court staffs and offices, routines and ceremonies. Not only did the structures and practices of these courts present many resemblances; the phases of construction, redefinition, crisis, and reform frequently followed a parallel rhythm, dictated by the Protestant challenge and the restoration of Catholicism as the dominant creed, as well as by the pace of European warfare. Yet at the highest levels of the state complexes, a different measure of integration was long since becoming evident. French *pairs* were no equals to German electors, and French princes were losing the territorial powers their counterparts in the empire were consolidating. It may not be possible to point out where the fate of these two commonwealths came to diverge irreversibly, but after the Peace of Westphalia the territorial power of the major princes of the empire was a foregone conclusion, whereas the French grandees by that time had opted for a strategy more clearly subservient to the royal court. The emperor's status was based on his power over the hereditary lands, his support in the empire, and his *renommée* eamong the princely courts of Europe; for the French king, the intermediate level was absent. The imperial dimension, and the elective nature of Habsburg rule in the empire were formative for many habits at court in Vienna.

The incongruity introduced by the imperial structures allows us to see a basically similar institution developing in two different environments. It shows the household with its feudal appurtenances slowly adapting to the distinct exigencies entailed by change in both realms. This process gave rise to a multicoloured mosaic of recurring tensions and alternatives, of which the familiar imagery of Versailles retained only the shrillest tints. My endeavour was first and foremost to restore the historical palette in its full range, but it will not do to stop there. Below, I will provide a *précis*, seguing into a more thoughtful expansion of analytical remarks previously scattered throughout the text. My conclusions do not fit easily with Versailles' reputation for unqualified royal power, and they indicate that the emperor's court was in some ways more conspicuously successful. Finally, they underline the need for more comparative, intercultural studies of phenomena long confined within narrow boundaries by a nationally oriented and frequently teleological historiography. Courts are the most general arrangement of power in pre-modern society, and deserve to be analysed in this wider perspective.

CONTOURS

The French inner *maison du roi* including chapel, chamber, table, and smaller elements of other services, doubled from 300 to 600 in the early sixteenth century, and rose to 1,100 in the last two-thirds of that century. In the seventeenth century, the curve was more irregular, with peaks after Henry IV's death, reductions after 1625, inflation in the 1630s, and a sharp climax at 2,000 in 1650. In the decade after 1654 reductions were decreed, as they had been throughout the first half of the seventeenth century, yet they were to be vigorously implemented in the course of the 1660s and 1670s. The inner *maison* was severely curtailed, finally reaching levels around 900. Hunt and stables, recorded in different series, followed the same curve of expansion and reduction, though royal hunting fervour apparently made it particularly difficult to implement reduction in the staffs for the hunt. In 1699, hunts, *prévôté*, stables and the king's inner *maison* numbered 2,120 *officiers*. Secondary establishments within the dynasty, from the queen's household to the substantial *maisons* of male and female relatives and more distant *princes du sang*, usually added another 1,000–2,000 persons to the court. In the course of the seventeenth century, however, with two *dauphins* surprised by their fathers' deaths at an early age, the independent *maison* of the successor came to be replaced by a smaller establishment, staffed mostly by the king's own servants. Finally, we have to take into account the *maison militaire*. In addition to the traditional court guards, several companies and regiments had emerged mostly as elite units of an expanding army, but their officers were close to the court. If we follow the most detailed contemporary assessments available by adding a number of somewhat fewer than 3,000 persons for the other *maisons* and guards, Louis XIV's wider court may be estimated at *c.* 5,100 persons in 1699. In the stables, the hunt, the musical chapel, and the services for building, others served the court on the basis not of office, but of commissioned labour. It is more difficult to assess their numbers, but particularly in the stables, such lower staff was numerous. The eighteenth-century court stayed close to these numbers and proportions, though dynastic demography could lead to rapid changes in the constellations of secondary *maisons*.

The court of the Austrian Habsburgs took form only in the course of the sixteenth century, as the successor to various territorial Habsburg courts as well as the imperial court. In the later fifteenth and early sixteenth centuries, the household of the king-emperor approached 600 persons, a level it would reach again only in the last, imperial phase of Ferdinand I's rule. In Rudolf's reign, the court expanded from 700 to almost 1,200. In 1615, Matthias tried to reduce numbers, and his court, including councils, but without hunt or other households, seems to have been close to 800 persons. In Leopold's early years, the aggregate of court staffs, now without councils, was still around 800. It would soon expand, first largely through the proliferation of honorary chamberlains, later by a more steady growth of all staffs, most notably the stables. The junior status of the Austrian Habsburgs within the Habsburg family compact, a situation without parallel for either Valois or Bourbon kings, may have set limits to their courtly outlay, as the Viennese court started its most protracted phase of expansion in the last decades of the seventeenth century, when the Spanish branch had lost its ascendancy. In the last years of Leopold's reign, the household, including the honorary chamberlains, had risen to almost 1,500, and it approached the 2,000 level in last years of Charles VI. The critical mid-century decades witnessed a temporary reduction of the court, but towards 1760, Maria Theresa's court again matched that of her father, and in 1780 it exceeded 2,000. This number, excluding the numerous honorary chamberlains, notably included 737 new guards, introduced by Maria Theresa and Joseph. This expanded military establishment was still no match for the French *maison militaire*. While the expansion of the core staffs at the Habsburg court had significantly reduced the gap between the two courts, no parallel existed in Vienna for the secondary *maisons* within the Bourbon dynasty. The empresses had a 60–80-person household; dowager-empresses, prominent between 1651 and 1750, had more sizeable establishments, expanding from *c.* 250 in the later seventeenth century to 350 in the first half of the eighteenth century. In addition, only the King of the Romans was expected to build a serious household after his election – Joseph I's reached *c.* 400 in the year of Leopold's death. In post-1740 Vienna, the tendency was to fuse the major secondary establishments with the central household, as had been the case for Francis Stephen after 1740, and for Joseph II after 1765. Otherwise, young archdukes and archduchesses had modest staffs largely for personal care and education. They were expected to marry and depart, or rule outlying territories in the name of their sovereign relative. Thus, in Vienna guards and secondary household never loomed as large as in France, and the numbers of the wider court remained closer to the numbers cited above for the household.

In comparison to the household, the core services of the central 'bureaucracies' in France and the Habsburg lands long remained small. In Leopold's reign, the councils and their staffs expanded from 225 to 400, mostly by the increasing numbers of honorary councillors. All administrative institutions, especially those dealing with finance, expanded slowly in Charles' reign, but only after 1749 did the balance truly change. In Maria Theresa's reign, the size of central government quickly approached that of the household, and in Joseph's personal reign it would go beyond it by a small margin. This rapidly changing constellation cannot be observed in France, where the 'six departments' of the *sécrétaires d'état*, the *contrôleur-général,* and the chancellor were close to 700 for most of the late seventeenth and eighteenth centuries. The *ferme générale* in France and the staffs of all regional institutions in the Habsburg lands were far more impressive, but they cannot be seen as central government agencies, nor could they unequivocally be directed by these central agencies. The same holds true for the countless holders of venal offices so dominant in France. If numbers are to be accepted as an indicator of the relative weight of institutions, we should hesitate to place central administration before the household.

The expenses of the household were a major item in the budgets of Bourbon and Habsburg rulers. Court-related outlay was almost invariably the third-largest category, following war and debt service – the latter predominantly caused by war. General budgets are an unmanageable affair, for early modern administrators as well as for historians; within the controversial development of aggregate government expenditure, it is quite arbitrary to draw a line around 'court expenses'. In addition to the wages of court staffs and the cost of feeding, lodging, and entertaining the court, and the maintenance of palaces, came the wildly variable extraordinary expenses for marriages or deaths, and the equally unsteady outlay for building. Most difficult to disentangle are the ruler's secret expenses, and the payments of pensions and gratifications. In Vienna, it is frequently unclear whether pecuniary graces were repayments of loans, or truly gifts; in neither of these realms can we – without massive research – clearly distinguish pensions given to courtiers from pensions given to those in other sectors of government. Major courtiers often doubled as army commanders, provincial governors, diplomats, or senior ministers; thus it may not be very helpful to ask in which quality they received their recompenses. Whereas such payments tended to be moderate in Vienna, the aggregate of special pecuniary rights and graces formed a more significant share of the French court budget.

War determined short-term change in court expenditure: it shrunk significantly in wartime, and could peak after the peace, when finances were reshaping, outstanding payments had to be made, and rewards were expected. The combined benefits of peace and victory were most conducive to conspicuous outlay. Short-term fluctuations caused mostly by warfare obscure long-term trends: court outlays varied between 3 per cent and 40 per cent of the total budget. There is insufficient material to present a long-term chart of court expenses, and the available absolute numbers need to be corrected with information on monetary policies or inflation. Thus, the following figures should be treated with circumspection: they should be seen as rough and tentative approximations. In France, overall average court expenditure was around 18 per cent in the seventeenth century, and probably did not stray far from this level in the eighteenth century – we have less sound a basis here. In Vienna, averages suggest a slow decline in court expenditure as a share of the total budget, from *c.* 18 per cent in the first half of the seventeenth century, to *c.* 13 per cent in the second half of the seventeenth century, and close to 10 per cent for the years 1729–1784. This tendency, however, was caused not by a decline in court expenditure, but by a rise in the total expenditure of the Habsburgs. In the second half of the eighteenth century the salaries of the expanding bureaucracy in Vienna would surpass court expenses; in the drastic reforms of both courts in the 1780s the proportion of the court in the budget would shrink more significantly. The costs for the military *maison*, sizeable secondary establishments within the royal family, and high pensions help to explain the higher French percentages. We have to keep in mind, moreover, that the total revenues and expenditures of the Habsburgs represented a sum much smaller than did those of the French crown: Habsburg court expenditure demanded a smaller share of a budget that itself represented only between 15 per cent and 30 per cent of the French budget.

The household serving the ruler was comprised of a majority of non-noble servants, a small upper echelon of noble dignitaries, and a more varied intermediate layer of mostly noble honorary servants. The heads of the court staffs, and their high-ranking substitutes, more numerous at the Bourbon court than in Vienna, stood at the pinnacle of this three-tiered pyramid. The divides were never impenetrable; service specialists and personal servants from the broad non-noble basis of the pyramid were apt to rise by the ruler's favour, and might successfully seek to have their favour transformed into hereditary rank. At its lower edges, the pyramid dissolved into a world of purveyors and artisans loosely attached to the court. The middle layer of honorary servants was the most volatile layer of the household: its changing structures and numbers can help to trace the ties of the household with the nobility, as will be discussed in some detail below. The highest court dignitaries took their oath to the ruler in person, and received the oath of many among their staff. This accurately reflects their stature at court, based both on the lineage of their families, and on the proximity of their offices to the ruler. They headed relatively autonomous staffs; in France, the power of these officers over their staffs was, if anything, more impressive than in Vienna. At the Habsburg court, however, the challenge of robe ministers was hardly an issue: from the later seventeenth century onwards, the relatively few newcomers found themselves in a massively noble environment both at court and in the administrative gremia. Even in the 1770s, after a phase of decline of the household officials vis-à-vis their brethren in the administration, the high steward in Vienna was still reckoned to be the first servant of his imperial masters. Rapid social ascent of ministerial dynasties caused annoyance in seventeenth-century France, exacerbated by the temporary removal of court grandees from the king's inner council. In the eighteenth century traces of these tensions remained, but the grandees had effectively secured their supremacy at court.

In Vienna, all members of the *Hofstaat* lost their office upon the death of the emperor – they had to be confirmed by the new emperor, who was free to choose others in all cases except that of the imperial vice-chancellor. In practice, a new ruler indeed brought a wholesale change in the highest court charges, though administrators and lower staff at court might retain their positions, while others found themselves taken up in the reconstituted and expanded dowager-empress' court. In France, such practices, deriving from the personal bond of homage, were slowly disappearing after the late fifteenth century. Henry II was expected to retain at least an important proportion of his servants, and in the course of the seventeenth century charges at court, never fully integrated into the system of venality as they formally depended on the king, nevertheless became hereditary in practice through the *survivance*. In Vienna, where venality was never widely implemented outside of the offices pertaining to finance, no family held rights to high court office; although at lower levels, dynasties of court servants did serve for long periods. Interestingly, while in France courtiers retained their offices under a new ruler, ministers were usually replaced; whereas in Vienna senior courtiers normally lost their position, but leading advisers were not necessarily dismissed.

For all courtiers and servants, ordinary wages were depressingly low, increasingly so as they were only rarely adjusted for inflation. To make things worse, wages were frequently in arrears, particularly during wars. At the same time, however, all *commensaux* or members of the *Hofgesinde* profited from a range of immunities and privileges, received allowances for food or clothing, could expect special gratifications from the ruler, and were likely to extract substantial additional revenue from visitors to the court, or from petitioners seeking their help. Gratuities were an inevitable and fiercely defended component of court staffs' income, seen as a vested right more than as a transgression. For the lower levels of the household, support in old age or illness was ideally made available; widows and children of servants likewise can be found on the court's payroll. Remuneration for the highest court officers was differently organised in Vienna and Versailles. The French grandees holding high court office enjoyed rights over the transactions with offices in their staffs, and pocketed a handsome profit from these *casuels*. Moreover, the pensions and extras they received in addition to their low *gages ordinaires* were steadily paid. While the ordinary wages of court dignitaries in Vienna were at a marginally more acceptable level, the extras were less secure, and remained more clearly dependent on the ruler's grace. In Vienna, wealth was a precondition more than an outcome of high noble court office, notwithstanding the fact that it could bring huge profits. The best-paid servants in the vicinity of both courts undoubtedly were those responsible for finance – yet they were also expected to use their personal capital to prop dynastic interests, especially in Vienna. Pay was least impressive for the middle group of honorary noble servants: their wages were not invariably superior to those of non-noble servants, and did not come close to compensating them for the outlay necessary for staying at court.

Honorary office, indeed, needs further thought. It was responsible for most rapid fluctuations of the court. Throughout the sixteenth century, the French chamber staff expanded, its *chambellans* and *gentilshommes* serving as the ruler's confidants and representatives. While the staffs of chamber and wardrobe became smaller and more stable after Henry III's reign, the honorary servants for the table, *maîtres d'hôtel* and *gentilshommes servants*, multiplied in the first half of the seventeenth century. After a protracted phase of inflation, peaking in the 1650s, they were sharply reduced. Hundreds of noble servants for the table disappeared, and a maximum of 12 *maîtres* and 36 *gentilshommes*, 3 and 9 respectively serving per quarter, was carefully maintained. Nor did the numbers of ladies-in-waiting, the female equivalent of male honorary office in the households of queens or princesses, grow. In the same decades, many servants of lesser station lost their status of *commensaux du roi*: their *charges* were reformed into commissions, and they disappeared from the *états*. Both measures helped to reduce tax privilege, and this was among the explicit motivations cited by Louis XIV. Among the lower servants retaining their charges, service was frequently rewarded with the status of *écuyer*, conferring nobility. As a consequence, the household, purged of its loose noble extensions as well as of its lowest fringes, and more solidly ennobled in its middle ranks, became ever more prestigious and exclusive. The luxurious household in Versailles became the hub of a courtly universe inviting the admiring glances of many visitors – nobles as well as *roturiers*; French as well as foreigners. In an age characterised by widespread sales of offices, it is difficult to picture Louis XIV's reticence as an oversight or missed opportunity: he apparently wanted his household to be small, predominantly noble, and striking in allure. Only in the ranks of the pages in the stables and the chamber, controlled by a genealogist since 1643, and in the guards at court, did the king tolerate expansion. These exceptions were closely connected to the king's martial exploits, and indicate his preference for a nobility of military stance and career.

After the sharp sequence of expansion and reduction in the early seventeenth century, a steadier expansion from the second half of the seventeenth century onwards occurred in the two distinctive honorary offices of the Viennese court: chamberlains and councillors. The proliferation of chamberlains had started in the reign of Ferdinand II, but continued at a more rapid pace in Leopold's reign. In the 1670s their numbers were close to 500; after which inflation spread into the previously more exclusive group of the councillors. Their numbers expanded from 30 to 164 in the last three decades of Leopold's reign. Later rulers in Vienna copied the practice, nominating chamberlains upon major occasions in their reign, councillors at a more variable pace. The establishment daily serving the Habsburgs, however, retained its traditional composition, employing huge numbers of non-nobles and only a small upper echelon of nobles. To this horizontal segment in the upper tier of the household's social pyramid, the myriads of honorary officers were attached. Chamberlains ideally served a full year; for most chamberlains, a few weeks' service was more likely, while others held the rank without serving at all. Their numbers alone made it improbable that a clear-cut system such as service per quarter could succeed. Essentially, the rank of chamberlain indicated access at court, and entry into the imperial *cursus honorum*, more than actual service at court. Councillors were usually nominated only after loyally serving the dynasty at court or elsewhere. The two honorary offices determined rank at court: councillors held precedence over the chamberlains; and seniority settled the ranking within each group.

While honorary office was expanded to include almost all major families from the hereditary lands as well as a significant group of families from the empire at the Viennese court, it was reduced in Versailles. The more secluded court, ruling over more widely dispersed territories, became more inclusive in its definition of honorary membership; at the open court ruling over a more contiguous and unified territory, honorary office was sharply reduced, and the household as a whole became more exclusive as well as more predominantly noble.

COURT LIFE

The structure of the household with its noble connections needs to be placed in the context of the daily life and ceremonies at court: for each setting, the court showed a different composition, and expected different audiences. Not only have historians tended to equate the court with the noble sphere of honorary office, thus leaving aside the ordinary household staffs; they have likewise presented court life as an ongoing feast, an everlasting ceremony – forgetting the daily routines of the ruler, servants, and administrators. Life at these courts followed a pattern roughly similar: it was dominated by the routines of rising, eating, sleeping, as well as by the alternation of devotions, deliberation with ministers, audiences, and hunting. Yet one major difference stands out: access was far more limited in the Hofburg than it was in Versailles.

The outlines of Habsburg reticence were already present in the ordinances promulgated by Ferdinand I, stipulating that the king's bedroom was not as a rule open to anyone except his most trusted intimates. His imperial successors refined the rules. Rights of entry into the state apartment – from the *Ritterstube*, through two antechambers, into the council chamber – were carefully defined, with each threshold demanding higher rank. The emperor's private apartment, beyond the council chamber, was not included in the classification. The Habsburg ruler dined publicly in the *Ritterstube* on major festivities, and on a variety of incidental occasions; yet his daily meals in the chamber were never watched by spectators. Public ceremonies were clearly demarcated highpoints in a usually more secluded setting. Interestingly, court ordinances often show clusters of words such as 'decorum', 'reputation', 'ceremonial', and 'public'. The Latin script of these words stands out in German manuscripts, as did the public ceremonies in the ongoing rhythm of household routines. Nobles at court, whether or not holding office, were expected to join the emperor in his public excursions, and attend the temporary visits of outsiders into the palace. They were hardly courtiers, however, in the sense that they lived in the palace, or daily shared entertainments with members of the dynasty. The Hofburg's capacity to lodge courtiers was extremely limited. Until the reign of Maria Theresa, moreover, there was no recurring programme of dinners, *soirées*, balls, and comedies. Except for the *Fasching*-festivities in the first months of the year, divertissements were incidental. Processions and public devotions were the most frequent points of contact of the *Hofstaat* with the Viennese: they took place almost every week, reaching an impressive density in Holy Week and at Pentecost.

The French court was traditionally more open, allowing courtiers as well as visitors to approach the king upon rising, while he ate, and before he went to sleep. Christine de Pisan reported a disorderly *lever* in the early fifteenth century; in an oft-cited 1530 edict against theft, Francis I noted the daily bustle of visitors in his apartment. Henry III sought to restrict access, in an effort to underline his supreme status; a palpable dislike of the impertinences of courtiers and spectators pervades his ordinances. Most characteristics attributed to the innovations and ruses of Louis XIV were present in Henry's texts, yet the Sun King seemed far less distressed by the multitudes at court. He prided himself on the *honnête familiarité* of French kings with their nobles, contrasting it with the more aloof style of the Spanish Habsburgs. Nor does the court seem to have become a more closed environment at Versailles, where the king repeated Francis I's decree, once more citing the 'affluence des gens de toutes sortes, faineans & sans aveu qui abordent de toutes parts à notre Cour'.[1] Visitors could habitually be found wandering through the gardens and the palace. An ongoing sequence of entertainments formed part of the French court from the sixteenth into the eighteenth century, and Versailles, with its dependencies, was able to lodge an estimated 3,000 persons.

It is far from easy to connect the open style of the French court, or the closed style of the Habsburgs with ceremony. The Habsburg style, common at German courts, as Hugh Murray Baillie pointed out long ago, created distance between ruler and subjects; the French style stressed accessibility. Distance can help to convey an impression of sanctity, and thus the closed style may seem to be more 'ceremonial' than the open style. Yet distance made room for intimacy and family life as well, by reserving a secluded sphere for the ruler and his kin with their companions. Such levels of privacy were more elusive for French kings, and this exerted considerable pressures. In an environment stressing openness, barring

[1] BN Clair 828 (Prévôté), pp. 1253–1259.

access could be perceived as a slight, particularly by high-ranking courtiers. When French kings sought refuge against the bustle, sharing intimacy with relatives or confidants, those excluded from this smaller circle tried to gain admission for two reasons: it conspicuously showed their rank and favour, and it allowed them to find the king's ear under ideal circumstances. This process formed the basis of the domestic rituals of the French court, and, while it allowed the king to toy with his courtiers by inventing an infinity of special occasions and rights, this was neither his first intention, nor the usual practice of court life.

How likely, or easy, was it for the ruler to resort to manipulation? Did conflicts of rank and competence indeed strengthen his authority? The abundance of regulations striving to solve and prevent such conflicts, suggest that they were first and foremost a nuisance. Quarrelling servants, one strongly suspects, made kings feel more uncomfortable than shrewd. We tend to repeat a handful of dubious instances suggesting the Sun King's active manipulation, whereas we forget the examples showing embarrassment and passivity. Manipulation of domestic rituals, it seems to me, was an unpredictable instrument at best, most often used ineffectively and defensively by individuals who felt harassed and anxious. The familiar scenes from Saint-Simon, usually presented as the 'ceremonies' of the French court, were the domestic routines of a relatively open court, characterised by a highly competitive upper echelon. The ceremonies of the French court form a nearly exact parallel to the Habsburg ceremonies: the traditional public highpoints re-creating the ties between commonwealth and dynasty. The ceremonial compilations by Godefroy father and son, published in 1619 and 1649 respectively, rarely refer to the domestic setting, nor does it form more than a minute part of the immense manuscript heritage of Nicolas de Sainctot, Louis XIV's master of ceremonies. Routines in the chamber and at the king's table, moreover, were controlled not by the special agents of ceremony, but by the relevant court dignitaries – that is, by the very persons conventionally depicted as the victims of ceremony.

In the course of the seventeenth century, contacts between the courts of Europe became far more frequent, and a measure of compatibility was necessary among the ceremonial settings of these courts. Diplomats, especially ambassadors, would demand a treatment visibly underlining their sovereign status, in all spheres of court life where they were admitted. Thus, a major effort in the 1650s to improve the ceremonial stature of the Habsburg court was explicitly connected to complaints of ambassadors. It was relatively easy to secure these changes at the Habsburg court, where social occasions were limited, and the dynasty lived in relative privacy. In France, the very openness of the court, and its more frequent occasions standing halfway between solemn ceremony and dynastic privacy, escalated the potential for conflict of rank. The high proportion of above-stairs noble servants, as well as the prestige of the families holding the highest court offices, further exacerbated the situation. Thus, while in Vienna conflict over precedence usually involved either diplomats or princes from the empire, in France the locals had a lasting, large, and vehement share.

Rank was a dominant concern in humdrum court life as well as in ceremonies. Situational details indicated rank in both contexts: sitting– standing, covered–uncovered, left–right, and the unending array of similar distinctions. Nevertheless, we need to separate the solemn or festive ceremonial occasions from daily interaction at court. The border line was relatively precise in Vienna; whereas in France the more frequent intermediate stages between intimacy and display tended to blur it. The extremities of public presentation and privacy, however, were commonplace for rulers at both courts. In fact, the strongest case for 'ceremonialisation' of the court can be made if we connect it to two factors: the impact of permanent diplomacy, itself driven by the competition among European courts, and the increasing density of intermediate-level social events at court in the eighteenth century. We should note, however, that these developments coincided with the erosion of traditional ceremonies – a process slow in France, later and more abrupt in the Habsburg lands. The re-enactments of the ties between centre and regions, and the rituals connected to the annual liturgical calendar, in particular, became less frequent.

Finally, ceremony and court life never were as well-ordered as prescriptive sources suggest. In the ordinances and rulings of both courts, one is surprised by the verbatim repetition of complaints about conflicts, disorders, and bad behaviour. Ceremonial registers tend to focus on problems; ordinances likewise tried to correct abuses: thus, these sources may convey an excessively rowdy impression – but they present a more plausible and lively image than the superficial equations of ceremony and court life found in contemporary descriptions, and uncritically copied in much recent court history. All ceremonial arrangements tended to be forgotten or violated in the long run; rules for entry into the chamber, or arrangements for courtiers in the chapel and at the public table, were reiterated periodically, usually in weary tones. In the eighteenth century, Luynes and Khevenhüller, acknowledged guardians of ceremony, were stupefied by the inability of their contemporaries to understand and adhere to the basic rules of ceremony.

POWER

One crucial domain remains to be discussed: the ties between household and council, and the practices of decision making. A variety of administrative institutions had long since been important in the vicinity of the court, either emerging out of its compass as autonomous corporate bodies responsible for justice and finance, or serving at court to record and structure collegial decision-making. The various councils with their chancelleries in Vienna, or the secretaries and their departments in France, enjoyed a status separate from the household staffs, even if in Vienna this was not always clearly recognised in the manuscript overviews. My endeavour was not to deny the vital process of state building with its accompanying mentalities, but to restore the household as the main theatre of this process: from the institutional point of view, separation of services is evident and needs no further debate.

The personnel in the administrative services, and the changing hierarchical relationships between household and administration, complicate the picture. In Vienna, the heads of most of the administrative staffs remained socially close to the household officers, and were hierarchically situated below the high steward – the latter, moreover, chaired sessions of the inner council into the eighteenth century. The *geheime Räte*, the core group of the decision-making process, formed the first rank for ceremonial occasions at court. Even after Haugwitz's reforms, we cannot picture the household as an a-political environment, though its role in formal decision-making was clearly becoming less impressive. No marked social differences, however, characterised the upper layers of household and 'bureaucracy', and dynasties of courtiers took an active part in the reorientation of Habsburg monarchy. *Vielschreiberei* and proliferation of offices, characteristic vices of the old court, would soon be as typical for the Habsburg bureaucracy. In France, where fewer high nobles were attracted to service in the administrative gremia, a marked antagonism arose between *robe* and *épée*. The inner council, collegially discussing policies, formed a link between the two domains, as it was usually composed both of robe councillors and noble courtiers. This vital link was temporarily brought to an end in Louis XIV's reign, but major courtiers recaptured it in the regency, would retain a voice in the council throughout the eighteenth century, and held ministerial office in the second half of that century.

The practices at court, finally, were likely to turn the neat institutional separation into a hopeless jumble. The ideal of the hardworking servant, impervious to bribes and flattery, and austerely serving his ruler, was to be found among courtiers as well as among ministers: notions of efficiency and financial prudence are evident in many court ordinances. Courtiers may have sidestepped such rules to extract maximum profit from their charges, but so could ministers – whether highly competent or ineffectual, they usually had their own schemes for enrichment of their family and its supporters. Rank and hierarchy, as well as conspicuous consumption, were relevant for both spheres. Most important of all, the ruler remained the centre of the service establishment catering for his person, as well as that of the government agencies. Inevitably, the preferences and weaknesses of kings, queens, emperors, and empresses could overturn any institutional arrangement. Ministers needed the ruler's confidence, and were ineffective or even helpless without it. Personal servants or trusted intimates, close to the ears of their sovereign, could destroy ministries, or isolate talented advisers. Therefore, the domestic environment needs to be taken into account even if it can institutionally and socially be isolated from the formal trajectory of decision-making.

The informal web of friendships and influences can never fully be grasped, if only because most relevant communications will not have been put into writing. With a massive array of sources, we can try to reconstruct factions and intrigues at court for a short time span. For longer periods, we can hope to uncover recurring sources of influence, and establish patterns of conflict. David Starkey's equation of access and power helped to highlight the 'political' relevance of domestic service and intimacy. Access to the ruler, however came in many forms and at many levels of hierarchy: youth friends, mentors, confessors, chamber servants, companions of military adventures or otherwise formative experiences, councillors, and mistresses were among those most likely to achieve lasting influence. Lower-ranking servants and companions offered relatively untroubled solace to rulers: chamber valets were prominent at both courts, dwarves conspicuously present at the Habsburg court. Senior domestic officers and important ministers certainly had the opportunity to find the ruler's ear, but their high status or knowledge of state secrets made confidence probable as well as dangerous – no ruler wanted to be perceived as a *roi fainéant*. In France, exceptional favour and sharp disgrace were never far apart, as the tragic ending of many favourites and the habitual exiles of French ministers indicate.

Favour and faction are two sides of the same phenomenon. While factions are reported at both courts throughout the early modern age, we have reason to doubt the solidity and longevity of alignments. Diplomats, professionally committed to uncovering intrigues at the courts they visited, may have perceived combinations that would have surprised the alleged allies, and the same may hold true for the reports of courtiers fretting over the successes of their rivals. Party labels were often invented as a slur: factions did not publicize their secretive activities and were rendered manifest mostly by the outcry of their opponents. Faction in Vienna has often been connected to provenance, with Germans, Spaniards, Italians, and Bohemians recurring from Ferdinand I to Maria Theresa. These regional labels were thought to partly overlap with policy orientations, the hereditary lands versus the empire; war against France or war against the Ottomans. In her 1751 political testament Maria Theresa condemned the overly close ties of ministers and courtiers with their native provinces. Closer scrutiny suggests that connections among the main actors in household and government were frequently more personal and more volatile, changing according to the occasion. We tend to define 'politics' as top-level decision-making; ambitious persons at court, whether in Vienna or in Versailles, were often looking for something else. They were interested more in finding a suitably prestigious office, and supporting their dynastic interests, than in meddling in the details of policy.

Only in particularly challenging choices, or when decisions had a direct impact on their interests, would larger groups be drawn into policy matters. In other situations, they were happy to leave the details to specialists and devoted advisers. The day-to-day distribution of graces, material as well as honorific, occupied the minds of most court-related elites more often than did the formulation of policies. Conflicts over precedence, or over coveted nominations, moreover, might give rise to other combinations than decisions pertaining to religion, warfare, or taxation.

Serious instances of factional strife in France, especially during regencies, inevitably included *princes du sang*, royal bastards, and the highest dynasties of courtiers. Nor did this tendency disappear after the *Fronde*. Proximity to succession structured alignments in the last decade of Louis XIV's reign, and determined the conflicts of the Orléans, Condé, and royal bastards in the early eighteenth century. Louis XV's last decades were troubled by a renewed *fronde des princes*, albeit without military clashes. Louis XVI's reign likewise would be soured by royal siblings. The royal family, evidently, was rife with potential for conflict. In Vienna the role of dynastic siblings was less marked, and courtiers never came near that elevated rank. After Rudolf's tragic ending, archdukes were usually loyal, yet distant, ruling their own provinces in the name of their crowned relative. There are several exceptions: the death of emperor-elect Ferdinand IV suddenly turned Leopold William into a serious rival for young Leopold's imperial election. Towards the end of Leopold's reign Joseph was anxious to assert himself, and his group of reformers served as a shadow cabinet, more or less like the circle around the duc de Bourgogne. Joseph's unexpected death in 1711, may have prevented a conflict with his brother Charles, who would have needed a rich appanage or an otherwise suitably prestigious accommodation upon returning to Vienna after his Spanish misadventure. In the eighteenth century, archdukes and archduchesses resident in Vienna were never as constant and vocal a force of opposition as the French princes – though the co-regency of Maria Theresa and Joseph was far from easy.

Were the dynamics of access and favour less important after 1700? Did the strengthening of administrative institutions somehow render less relevant the personal element in decision-making? In France, we find more notorious instances of favourites to a certain extent able to monopolise access than in the Habsburg lands, yet favour in its various forms was near the heart of these courts from the sixteenth into the eighteenth century. The ruler's isolated central position secured a persistent need for trust and intimacy. Typically, favourites held sway either in the early years of an inexperienced young ruler, or in the last years of an elderly ruler confronted with declining health and an eager successor. I see no difference here between the familiar eighteenth-century instances, and earlier examples. Monarchy became more stable after the protracted phase of religious upheaval, and administrative institutions carried a larger share of the machinery of governance. The operation of these institutions, however, was still based on the personal setting of power around the dynastic ruler.

VIENNA AND VERSAILLES

In many respects, the Habsburg court was a more serene environment than the French court. Most of all, the relation between the emperor and his senior noble servants was more stable than that of the French king with his grandees. 'It might appear odd that seventeenth-century Austria lacked both strong government and strong opposition', Robert Evans noted in the *Making of Habsburg Monarchy*.[2] The statement aptly captures the atmosphere at court. After the clash of the 1620s, the emperor, weak if his rule is seen in terms of bureaucratic power or bold action, was rarely challenged by his elites. Indeed, his courtiers were far more deferential towards their overlord than were their French counterparts. While courtiers habitually advised the emperor, they had no vested right to a place in the council. Court servants and honorary officers lost their office upon the death of the emperor. The new emperor could influence hierarchies at his court by the timing of his nomination of new councillors and chamberlains. High court office, shared among a group of high noble families, stood at the end of a long career. The emperor was free to nominate whomever had served him well, and no single family could demand court office. His court staffs were at least in theory subject to one general budget, overseen by his financial chamber. Senior courtiers do not seem to have enjoyed well-defined rights of nomination, though the emperor would probably have tended to confirm their nominees. The income of the highest court charges in Vienna remained limited, and only special rewards, given at the emperor's discretion, would make court service truly attractive from a financial point of view.

The French dynasties dominating court office clashed more frequently with royal power than did nobles in the Habsburg lands. Indeed, the century after 1560 was characterised by recurring conflict, rendering more demonstrative both noble opposition and royal authority. The 1650s were not as disruptive for French nobles as the 1620s had been for nobilities in the Habsburg lands, yet the more recent heritage of revolt and restoration left its mark on the ties between sovereign and courtiers from the 1660s onwards. This made contemporaries as well as historians highly sensitive to the fate of princes and dukes at court. From a longer-term perspective, the shift of high nobles to the court seems neither new nor harmful. Robert Harding long ago suggested the increasing orientation of provincial governors on the court around 1600, underlining that they profitably used their frequent stays at court to cement local networks. Katia Béguin has more recently showed that by the late 1620s the Condé were

[2] Evans, *Making*, p. 169.

already cultivating their ties with ministers. The comparison with Vienna further reduces the impression of sudden capitulation or decline surrounding French noble courtiers. Louis XIV's reform of the council, allowing only his personal nominees into his inner council, introduced a practice long since common in Vienna. The French king could promote and demote, but the seniority among dukes and peers was less easily manipulated than that of Habsburg honorary officers. From the Viennese perspective, it is not the impotence, but the vested position of the French supreme officers that strikes the eye. They controlled their own budgets, and held unambiguous rights over charges in their staffs – indeed, the value of their offices was partly determined by the extent of such rights or *casuels*. The Condé high stewards saw their rights limited only marginally after 1659; they enjoyed rights over hundreds of persons in their staff, and accepted the oath of loyalty from others. The financial autonomy of all major staffs, and the income flowing from transactions with venal offices, offered lucrative opportunities for the leading courtiers. Leading noble dynasties obtained a *de facto* monopoly for their charges in the later seventeenth century: their sons would obtain the *survivance* during their father's lifetime, and hold office upon his death. The offices were clearly seen in terms of family property. A variety of special rights and rewards were listed in the *états* as a matter of fact, tied to the dynasties. In the eighteenth century, the vested position of these dynasties was seen in terms of rights more than in terms of royal grace.

The Condé, Bouillon, Lorraine, and Rohan scions holding high court office in France were hierarchically closer to the king than the princes and counts holding court office in Vienna were to the emperor. These dynasties, and the major ducal families closely following them at court, usually held senior governorships as well as high military command, and were also often active in finance. Around 1700 Viennese court dignitaries were invariably of high noble stock, but they had received princely status in the course of recent service to the Habsburgs. As upstart princes of the empire, they were at pains to secure their position in a group of near-sovereign territorial rulers that looked at them coldly. Most of them never received full rights of session and vote in the imperial diet, the final confirmation of princely status. The elder princes of the empire, ranking below the emperor, but above his supreme domestic officers, jealously protected their rights against both. Inevitably, the rivalry of this distant intermediate layer strengthened the bond between the emperor and the new princes serving at his court. In mentality as well as in activities, Habsburg courtiers were closer to a service elite than were French courtiers, and they rarely were as troublesome and haughty.

In addition to the pressures of territorial princes of the empire, there was another reason for the easy compliance of Habsburg courtiers: until the reforms of Haugwitz, regional and local government was almost wholly in the hands of the regional estates and the noble lordships. In the lands of the Bohemian crown, and in Hungary, the immense landholdings of a handful of dynasties connected to the Viennese court underline that, for them, serving the emperor was hardly an economic necessity. In general, extensive landed income was a precondition for obtaining high court office. The impressive number of palaces in the city and outskirts of Vienna after the 1680s shows that these dynasties saw no apparent contradiction between demonstrating their dynastic ambitions, and loyally serving the emperor. Interestingly, neither do the emperors seem to have been bothered by the splendid palaces of their noble servants, as they sought legitimation more in tradition and religion, than in personal grandeur. Thus, while at court the French grandees held a more exalted position, in the country at large the dynasties of Habsburg courtiers remained more powerful. Most French dynasties of court dignitaries, moreover, were probably more dependent on the income generated by serving at court. On the whole, not the impotence, but the conspicuous power of French dynasties of courtiers became a problem. In the eighteenth century they were effectively taking hold of the sources of income and prestige engendered by the court. In Vienna, at the same time, senior dynasties remained more subservient, were traditionally more committed to the machinery of administration, and proved to be less averse to reform.

The reduced, exclusive establishment at Versailles, and the expanding, inclusive household in Vienna, were successful as points of orientation for nobilities only marginally present at these courts. Court office, held by the upper noble layers, was the *non plus ultra* of rank and power in both realms – even if it did not necessarily bring direct political influence. In addition to the honorary officers, not permanently or even frequently residing at court, we can draw further concentric circles around the nucleus of the ruler and his permanent household: visitors who were admitted into the court, to its hospitality, celebrations, or to audiences; spectators, allowed to look but clearly not part of the *höfische Gesellschaft*; and those distant audiences beholding the court only through its printed dissemination. For each of these levels, the courts in Vienna and Versailles struck a different balance, and the balances changed over time. Surely, nobles seeking to be admitted at court and taking part in its activities were more plentiful in Versailles than in Vienna, most markedly so before Maria Theresa's reforms slowly opened the court. The numerous Habsburg chamberlains, in status as well as the duration of their stay at court, stood between the select group of honorary table servants serving *par terme* and the numbers of nobles 'presented' to the king in France – yet the presentation was structured more or less methodically only in the course of the eighteenth century. Spectators were ubiquitous in Versailles, but surely less permanent and dominating a presence in the secluded Hofburg. Yet the emperor with his *Hofstaat* frequently visited churches in his urban environment, and the Viennese could expect to encounter their ruler's processions. The printed glorification of the French court, finally, was earlier, more systematically organised, and more abundant than that of the imperial court. Closed and open, protective and projective, exclusive and inclusive, passive and active: these labels differ for each of the concentric circles of the courtly structure. Only by combining the various levels can we understand the court, as a pivot in a culture animated by hierarchy and rank, and as a centre of redistribution for those intent upon improving their status.

Open rebellion became a rare aberration in the later seventeenth century, yet in the centre of ceremonial splendour as well as of the increasingly strengthened bureaucratic structures and procedures, the ruler remained vulnerable. The long-term processes we can now carefully chart, were not usually present in the minds of rulers, who muddled through an unending sequence of routine decisions and greater challenges, hoping to make ends meet. I see no masterminds hiding behind a screen of silence, no weaklings incapacitated by their character flaws, but individuals confronted with a burden that was frequently too much for them. Surrounded by advisers and servants who well knew that their power depended partly on princely favour, rulers were at a loss to find persons in whom they could confide. Those who approach the king, Louis XIV noted in his memoirs, are the first to see his weaknesses, and are likely to take advantage of them.[3] The dynamics of favour would gradually subside only when the rulers themselves were sidestepped by the new combination of representative assemblies and bureaucracies, and the relevance of personal attendance lessened with the weakening of its dynastic centre.

AFTERWORD: A 'MODEL' FOR COURTS?

Around conspicuous leaders in any age, phenomena may develop that show striking similarity to those outlined here in the specific settings of two early modern courts. Power, representation, distribution of honours, flattery, favour, and faction can be seen to operate in any conceivable setting; yet it makes no sense to use 'court' as a bland equivalent for group dynamics around leaders. Even the main parts together forming the rigid clockwork of the model of Versailles, shown to be false in many respects here, can be applied to almost all political systems. A symbolic political centre helps to integrate elites, whether in cultures based on the notion of lineage and social representation, or on the ideals of democracy and elected representatives. Have we been 'domesticated' by a state hiding behind the fig leaf of the popular vote? Are representatives debating in a 'gilded cage', ensnared by mutual rivalries, and increasingly disconnected from their constituencies? The discomfort caused by these *questions mal posées* may help to put into perspective the curious terminology surrounding Versailles. Yet it also points out that most categories used to explain the court have a far wider relevance, particularly for the worlds of power and fashion. What, then, are the

[3] Dreyss, *Mémoires de Louis XIV*, II, p. 404.

defining characteristics of the early modern court in particular, or the court in general?

The minimum defining elements seem to be the permanent admixture of domestic service to a single person, and the government of territories pledging loyalty to him – or more rarely, her. The significance of domestic service is connected to a dynastic mentality, where house, *Haus*, *maison*, *domus*, *oikos*, and their equivalents indicate the family as well as the domestic establishment, and its place of abode – by extension the realm under its control. A close link of the ruling dynasty with sanctity and religion; a widely shared mentality acknowledging inequality as the basis of society, and the marked presence of other noble dynasties, may also be accepted as typical, though not universal, characteristics. This enumeration does not go very far as a definition, yet it already excludes many courts, such as the contemporary establishments of constitutional monarchs, or the Egyptian court, where no fully hereditary nobility developed and status remained linked to offices held in lifetime.

The early modern court was a traditional dynastic household slowly adapting to govern larger territories. Both the administrative and the representative domains expanded in the process; they remained in steady contact and were subject to the same pressures. Status and influence at court evolved from the interplay of proximity to the throne, functional hierarchies in household or administration, and hierarchies defined wholly or partly outside of the court. Intimacy acted as a dynamic factor in hierarchies at court, allowing those closest to the ruler to trump higher officers operating at greater distance. This was relevant for the household as well as for the administration, although favour may have supplanted high rank somewhat more easily than it did special skills. The courts in Versailles and Vienna were both successful in moulding noble hierarchies throughout the realms they governed, fitting them increasingly into a court-based – or court-demonstrated – system of rank. This coincided at both courts, however, with a massive accumulation of power and status by those nobles holding court office. Thus, integration seems to be a more suitable term than domestication, with its connotations of taming and subduing.

To these first characteristics – the intensely personal character of power, the variable ties between household and government, and the volatile interplay of proximity, functional hierarchies, and non-courtly hierarchies at court – we may add other recurring features. Yet most of these need to be seen as questions, as variables that can only be determined precisely by referring to concrete examples. The nature of 'belonging' to the court, with a hierarchy of permanent servants, and more distant members appearing for great occasions, offers one example. These loose ties, not necessarily limited to the nobility, underline the cohesive, centripetal potential of the court; yet we will find examples where this potential was never relevant. The contrast between actual court life and its embellishment in words and images is another example of a spectrum in which each court will strike a different balance – the literary and artistic discourses around the court, however, seem to be as ubiquitous in history as the court itself.

Adding more substance to these very general statements, we threaten either to get lost in the unending variety of courts, finding different outcomes of comparable processes, or fall into the trap of reducing the court to a set of related characteristics too rigid to accommodate its varieties – the very same dilemma that so frustrated the ceremonialists trying to lay down rules for rank and ceremony. The more systematic approaches to the court have the disadvantage that their functional categories leave little room for the sense of taking part in a world that surely was more than a mechanism for domination, even for those kept at bay by rows of guards. With all its attendant vanities and hard-nosed power struggles, the court was still the centre of a society animated by hierarchies that were demonstrated, re-enacted and renegotiated in its recurring calendar of ceremonies. When this basis for early modern court life was questioned, and rulers could choose to promote themselves as first ministers, this marked a profound change.

In the aftermath of revolution and empire, European monarchs adapted to the new situation, initially continuing (or reinventing) at a somewhat lower profile most habitual items of the courtly heritage. Their position was soon to be questioned by the rise of liberal and democratic sentiments. Post-revolutionary liberals regarded as stifling and sterile the protocol and pomposity of nineteenth-century courts, and their understandable judgement would reverberate in the first academic studies of the early modern state. When this prolific and influential generation of historians looked at the origins of their states, they carried with them an image of the household as a feeble coterie around the monarch, distant from the central arenas of political debate and decision. Nationalist sentiment proved more conducive to monarchical pageantry, and in the last decades of the nineteenth century, European court life experienced a revival. The new glamour of royalty, however, did not alter the marginal position of the household in the state, and was unlikely to change the perspective of later historians.[4] After the end of the Habsburg empire, the thorny heritage of the Baroque court was cast aside for two generations; in France Versailles was incorporated in a nationalist mystique that was long left unquestioned.

[4] The history of the (British) court in the nineteenth century is discussed by David Cannadine, 'The Context, Performance, and Meaning of Ritual: The British Monarchy and the Invention of Tradition c. 1820–1977', in *The Invention of Tradition*, ed. E. Hobsbawm and T. Ranger (Cambridge 1983), pp. 101–165; see *Hof und Hofgesellschaft in den deutschen Staaten im 19. und beginnenden 20. Jahrhundert*, ed. Karl Möckl, Deutsche Führungsschichten in der Neuzeit 18 (Boppard am Rhein 1990), and more recently Johannes Paulmann, *Pomp und Politik. Monarchenbegegnungen in Europa zwischen Ancien Régime und Erstem Weltkrieg* (Paderborn and Munich 2000).

Manuscript sources

ARCHIVES NATIONALES, PARIS

K 885; K 1326; K 1712; KK 209; KK 544; KK 547; KK 548; KK 1394; KK 1423–1439; KK 1448; M 608; MM 817; O 1 15; O 1 120; O 1 630; O 1 653; O 1 656; O 1 711; O 1 712; O 1 713; O 1 715; O 1 730; O 1 731; O 1 747; O 1 748; O 1 749; O 1 751; O 1 753; O 1 755; O 1 756; O 1 762; O 1 793; O 1 820; O 1 822; O 1 858; O 1 872; O 1 889; O 1 970; O 1 976; O 1 1042; O 1 1076; O 1 3715; O 1 3794; O 1 3794; Z 1 A 472–523.

BIBLIOTHÈQUE NATIONALE, PARIS

Baluze 182; Brienne 256; Clairambault 814; 827; 828; 830; 836; 837; 1216; 1220; Dupuy 218; 489; Mélanges Colbert 318; MS f 3515; 4581–4582; 6679; 7859; 14117–14120; 14128; 16633; 22713; 25135; 26289; MS naf 818; 819; 2004; 7225; 7236; 7857; 9703.

BIBLIOTHÈQUE MAZARINE, PARIS

MS 2658; 2737–2751.

BIBLIOTHÈQUE DE L'INSTITUT, PARIS

Godefroy 379–483 (394; 400; 446; 453; 461; 479; 481 in the notes)

HAUS- HOF- UND STAATSARCHIV, VIENNA

Staatenabteilung Frankreich, K 8, K 26; OMa A I K I (1564–1712); K 519 (1656–1689); Hofakten des Ministeriums des Inneren, K 14–16; OMeA Sr. 73–74; 181–189; 367; OMeA Prot 1–9; ZA Prot 1–10, 33, 34, 35, 36, 37, 38; ÄZA 1–10, 12, 17, 22, 24, 25, 26, 45, 70, 89; Familienakten III K 100; Handschriften Weiß 324, 1032, 1095; Blau 386; Bibliothek 38 K 2; ÄZA K 26 (fols. 2–14); OMeA Sr K 74, no. 16, Familienakten K. 102, repaginated together 26 March 1997.

ÖSTERREICHISCHE NATIONALBIBLIOTHEK, VIENNA

Codices 8025; 14233; 12388; 12955–12958; 14027; 14071; 14209; 14443; 14676; 14725; 14848; cod ser. n. 1713; 1849; 4411.

ALLGEMEINES VERWALTUNGSARCHIV, VIENNA

Harrach 323, Harrach Historica 796–797; Harrach Handschriften 145.

HOFKAMMERARCHIV, VIENNA

Hofzahlamtsbücher: 1570/24; 1610/61; 1615/64; 1616/65; 1619/68; 1620/69; 1622/71; 1623/72; 1624/73; 1631/78; 1633//80; 1640/86; 1646/92; 1647/93 I-II; 1648/94 I-II; 1649/95 I-II; 1650/96 I-II; 1651/97 I-II-III; 1652/98 I-II; 1653/99; 1655/101; 1660–61/106; 1662/107; 1669/112; 1670/113; 1670/114; 1675/119; 1685/130; 1686/131; 1690/135; 1693/138; 1694/139; 1697/140; 1699/142; 1702/ 144; 1703/145; 1704/146; 1706/148; 1710/152; 1713/155; 1714/156; 1714/267; 158; 165/1763.

ALGEMEEN RIJKSARCHIEF, THE HAGUE

Collectie van der Hoop (1.10.42), inv. no. 191.

Printed sources

Almanac ou calendrier pour l'année... Où sont marquez les Eclypses, le lever & le coucher du soleil le mouvement de la lune, les jours des foires, le journal du palais, la demeure des messagers, le depart des couriers, le tariff des monnoies & la liste des bureaux de messieurs des finances, & leurs departments (1699–).

Anselme [Pierre de Guibours, dit le père d'Anselme], *Histoire généalogique et chronologique de la maison royale de France*, 9 vols. (Paris 1726–1733; repr. New York 1967).

Benoit, Marcelle, *Musiques de cour: chapelle, chambre, écurie, 1661–1733* La vie musicale en France sous les rois Bourbons 20 (Paris 1971).

Besenval [Pierre Victor, baron de], *Mémoires de M. Le baron de Besenval, Lieutenant-Général des armées di roi, sous Louis XV et Louis XVI... écrits par lui-même*, 4 vols. (Paris 1805–1806).

Boislisle, A. M. de, *Correspondence des contrôleurs généraux des finances avec les intendants des provinces*, vol. III (Paris 1897).

Brown, Edward, *A brief account of some travels in divers parts of Europe...* (London 1687).

Breteuil [Louis Nicolas, Baron de], *Mémoires*, ed. Evelyne Lever (Paris 1992).

Calendrier de la cour tiré des éphémérides pour l'annee... Imprimé pour la famille royale et maison de sa majesté (1701–1791).

Castiglione, Baldesar, *The Book of the Courtier* (New York 1959).

Catherine de Médicis, *Lettres de Catherine de Médicis*, ed. Hector de la Ferrière, vol. II (Paris 1885).

Caumartin, *Recherches de la noblesse de Champagne* (Chalons 1673).

Ceremoniale Palatinum wie bey der Regierung von Caroli Ludovici sich solches befunden (Freiburg 1700).

Choisy, *Mémoires de l'Abbé de Choisy*, ed. Georges Mongrédien (Paris 1966).

Cimber, Danjou, ed., *Archives curieuses de l'histoire de France*, serie I, vol. X (Paris 1836).

Clément, Pierre, *Lettres... de Colbert*, vol. II (Paris 1863).

Code des commensaux ou recueil general des edits, declarations, ordonnances, lettres patentes, arrests, & reglemens: portant etablissement & confirmation des privileges, franchises, libertez, immunitez, exemptions, rangs, préséances, & droits honorifiques des officiers-domestiques & commensaux de la maison du roy, des maisons royales, & de leurs veuves (Paris 1720).

Croÿ [Emmanuel, duc de], *Journal inédit du duc de* Croÿ, *1718–1784*, ed. Paul Cottin Grouchy, 4 vols. (Paris 1906–1907).

Dangeau [Philippe de Courcillon, marquis de], *Journal du marquis de Dangeau . . . avec les additions inédites du duc de Saint-Simon*, ed. E. Soulié and L. Dussieux, 19 vols. (Paris 1854–1860).

Davis, J. C., *Pursuit of Power: Venetian Ambassadors' Reports on Spain, Turkey, and France in the Age of Philip II* (New York 1970).

Dictionnaire de l'Académie (Paris 1694).

Diderot and D'Alembert, eds., *Encyclopédie ou dictionnaire raisonné des sciences, des arts et des métiers* (Paris 1756).

Driessen, Felix, ed., *De reizen der de la courts 1641–1700–1710* (Leiden 1928).

Du Bois, *Moi, Marie Du Bois. Gentilhomme Vendômois valet de chambre de Louis XIV*, ed. François Lebrun (Rennes 1994).

Carafa, see Hurter, *Friedensbestrebungen* in secondary literature.

Etat de la France, contenant tous les princes, Ducs & Pairs, Maréchaux de France . . . (Paris 1649–1749) with varying titles and compilers.

Europische Mercurius behelzende al het voornaamste 't geen zo omtrent de zaaken van staat als oorlog, in alle de koningrijken en landen van Europa, en ook zelfs in verscheidene gewesten van d'andere deelen der wereld, is voorgevallen (Amsterdam 1690–1739).

Fellner, Thomas, and Kretschmayr, Heinrich, eds., *Die österreichische Zentralverwaltung.* I. *Abteilung Von Maximilian I. bis zur Vereinigung der Österreichischen und Böhmischen Hofkanzlei (1749)*, 3 vols., Veröffentichungen der Komission für neuere Geschichte österreichs 5–7 (Vienna 1907).

Forbonnais, F. Véron de, *Recherches et considérations sur les finances de France depuis l'année 1595 jusqu'à l'année 1721*, 2 vols. (Basel 1758).

Freschot, Casimir, *Mémoires de la Cour de Vienne, contenant les remarques d'un voyage curieux sur l'état de cette Cour, & sur ses interêts* (Cologne 1706).

Furetière, Antoine, *Dictionnaire Universel contenant generalement tous les mots françois . . .* (Paris 1690).

Godefroy, Denys, *Le Cérémonial François*, 2 vols. (Paris 1649).

Godefroy, Theodore, *Cérémonial de France* (Paris 1619).

Greppi, comte de, *Notes de voyage du comte Giandemaria envoyé du duc de Parme la cour de Louis XIV (1680)* (Paris, s.d.).

Griselle, Eugène, *Etat de la Maison du Roi Louis XIII . . . comprenant les années 1601 à 1665* (Paris 1912).

Héroard, *Journal de Jean Héroard sur l'enfance et la jeunesse de Louis XIII 1601–1628*, ed. E. Soulié and E. de Barthélemy, 2 vols. (Paris 1868).

Hézecques, Félix de, *Souvenirs d'un page de la cour de Louis XVI* (Paris 1998).

Isambert, F., *Recueil général des anciennes lois françaises depuis l'an 420, jusqu'à la révolution de 1789*, vol. XIV (Paris 1829).

Kayserlicher Hof- und Ehren-Kalender . . . Zum Gebrauche des Kaiserl. auch Kaiserl. Königl. Hofes (Vienna 1715–), 'Hofkalender'.

Kayserlicher und Königlicher, wie auch Erz-herzoglicher und dero Residenzstadt Wienn Staats- und Standskalender / auff das Jahr MDCCII. Mit einem noch nie dergleichen gesehenen Schematismo geziert (1704–), 'Schematismus'.

Keyszler, Johann Georg, *Nieuwe Reizen door Duitschland, Bohemen, Hongarije . . . Uit het Hoogduitsch vertaalt*, 4 vols. (Amsterdam 1753–1755).

Khevenhüller, *Hans Khevenhüller kaiserlicher Botschafter bei Philipp II Geheimes Tagebuch 1548–1605*, ed. Georg Khevenhüller-Metsch and Günther Probszt-Ohstorff (Graz 1971).

Khevenhüller-Metsch, Johann Josef, *Aus der Zeit Maria Theresias. Tagebuch des Fürsten Johann Josef Khevenhüller-Metsch, kaiserlichen Obersthofmeisters 1742–1776*, ed. R. Khevenhüller-Metsch and H. Schlitter, 7 vols. (Vienna 1907–1925).

Aus der Zeit Maria Theresias. Tagebuch des Fürsten Johann Josef Khevenhüller-Metsch, kaiserlichen Obersthofmeisters 1742–1776, 1774–1776 und Nachträge, ed. M. Breunlich-Pawlik and H. Wagner (Vienna 1972).

Theater, Feste und Feiern zur Zeit Maria Theresas 1742–1776, Grossegger, Elisabeth, ed., Österreichische Akademie der Wissenschaften Philosophisch-Historische Klasse Sitzungsberichte 476, Veröffentlichungen des Instituts für Publikumsforschung no. 12 (Vienna 1987).

Küchelbecker, Johann Basilius, *Allerneueste Nachricht vom Römisch-Kayserl. Hofe* (Hanover 1732).

La Porte, *Mémoires de P. de la Porte, premier valet de chambre de Louis XIV, contenant plusieurs particularités des règnes de Louis XIII et de Louis XIV*, in *Nouvelle collection des mémoires pour servir à l'histoire de France*, ed. Michaud, Poujoulat, 3rd series, vol. VIII (Paris 1850), pp. 1–57.

Leopold I, *Privatbriefe Kaiser Leopold I an den Grafen F. E. Pötting 1662–1673*, ed. A. F. Pribram and M. Landwehr von Pragenau, 2 vols., Fontes Rerum Austriacarum 56–57 (Vienna 1903–1904).

Levinson, Arthur, *Nuntiaturberichte vom Kaiserhofe Leopolds I*, 2 vols. (Vienna 1913–1918).

Lhotsky, Alphons, 'Kaiser Karl VI. und sein Hof im Jahre 1712–13', *MIÖG* 66 (1958), pp. 52–80.

Loménie de Brienne, Etienne-Charles, *Compte rendu au roi Au moi de Mars 1788, et publié par ses ordres* (Paris 1788).

Louis XIV, *Mémoires de Louis XIV pour l'instruction du Dauphin*, ed. Charles Dreyss, 2 vols. (Paris 1860).

Œuvres de Louis XIV, ed. M. Grouvelle, 6 vols. (Paris 1806).

Louis XV, *Lettres de Louis XV à son petit-fils l'infant Ferdinand de Parme*, ed. Philippe Amiguet (Paris 1938).

Loyseau, Charles, *Les Œuvres du Maistre Charles Loyseau, Avocat en Parlement. Contenant les cinq livres du droit, des offices, les traitez des Seigneuries, des ordres & simples dignitez, du déguerpissement & delaissement par Hypotheque, de la garantie des rentes, & des abus des justices de village* (Paris 1678).

Lünig, Johann Christian, *Theatrum Ceremoniale historico-politicum oder historisch und politischer Schau-Platz aller Ceremonien . . .*, 3 vols. (Leipzig 1719–1720).

Luynes [Charles Philippe d'Albert, duc de], *Mémoires du duc de Luynes sur la cour de Louis XV*, ed. L. Dussieux and E. Soulié, 17 vols. (Paris 1860–1865).

Maria Theresa, *Briefe Maria Theresia an Ihre Kinder und Freunde*, ed. Alfred von Arneth, 4 vols. (Vienna 1881).

Correspondence secrète entre Marie-Thérèse et le Cte de Mercy-Argenteau, avec les lettres de Marie-Thérèse et de Marie-Antoinette, ed. Alfred von Arneth and M. A. Geffroy, 3 vols. (Paris 1874–75).

'Zwei Denkschriften der Kaiserin Maria Theresia', ed. Alfred von Arneth, *AÖG* 47, 2 (1871), pp. 267–354.

Mathon de la Cour, Charles-Joseph, *Collection de comptes rendus, pièces authentiques, états et tableaux concernant les finances de la France depuis 1758 à nos jours* (Lausanne 1788).

Mavidal, M. J., and Laurent, M. E., eds., *Archives Parlementaires de 1787 à 1860*, prémière série, vol. XXVII (Paris 1887).
Menčík, see secondary literature.
Menestrier, C.-F., *Histoire du Roy Louis le Grand. Par les Médailles, Emblèmes, Devises, Jettons, Inscriptions armoires et autres* (Paris 1691).
Merian, Matthaeus, *Topographia Germania – Österreich* (Frankfurt 1649–1656; repr. Kassel 1963).
Molesworth, Robert, *Etat du Royaume de Danemark, tel qu'il etoit en 1692* (Amsterdam 1695).
Monicart, Jean-Baptiste de, *Versailles immortalisé par les merveilles parlantes de bâtimens, jardins, bosquets, parcs, statues, termes & vases* (Paris 1720).
Montesquieu [Charles-Louis de Secondat, Baron de la Brède et de Montesquieu], *Œuvres Complètes* (Paris 1964).
Montpensier, *Mémoires de Mademoiselle de Montpensier*, in *Nouvelle collection des mémoires pour servir a l'histoire de France*, ed. Michaud, Poujoulat (Paris 1850), IV, pp. 1–523.
Necker, Jacques, *Compte rendu* (Paris 1781).
De l'administration des finances de la France, 3 vols. (Lausanne 1784).
Orléans [Elisabeth-Charlotte de, Madame], *Briefe*, ed. Wilhelm Ludwig Holland, Bibliothek des Literarischen Vereins 88, 107, 122, 132, 144, 157 (Stuttgart 1867–1881).
Correspondance de Madame duchesse d'Orléans, ed. Ernest Jaéglé, 2 vols. (Paris 1880).
Oroux, *Histoire ecclésiastique de la cour de France. Où l'on trouve tout ce qui concerne l'histoire de la chapelle & des principaux officiers ecclésiastiques de nos rois*, 2 vols. (Paris 1776–1777).
Pacichelli, G.-B., *Memorie de' Viaggi per l'Europa Christiana, scritte à diversi In occasion de' suoi Ministeri dall'abate* (Naples 1685).
Passer, 'Berichte des Hessen-Darmstädtischen Gesandten Justus Eberhard Passer', ed. L. Baur, *AÖG* 37 (1867), pp. 273–409.
Patin, Charles, *Relations historiques et curieuses de voyages, en Allemagne, Angleterre, Hollande, Bohème, Suisse, &c.* (Amsterdam 1695).
Pisan, Christine de, *Le livre des fais et des bonnes mœurs de sage roy Charles V*, ed. S. Solente (Paris 1936; repr. Paris 1977).
Pöllnitz, *Mémoires de Charles-Louis Baron de Pöllnitz*, 2 vols. (Amsterdam 1734).
Potter, David, and Roberts, P. R., 'An Englishman's View of the Court of Henri III, 1584–1585: Richard Cook's Description of the Court of France', *FH* 2 (1988), pp. 312–344.
Pribram, A. F., ed., 'Aus dem Berichte eines Franzosen über den Wiener Hof in den Jahren 1671 und 1672', *MIÖG* 12 (1891), pp. 270–296.
Pufendorf, Esaias, *Bericht über Kaiser Leopold, seinen hof, und die Österreichische Politik 1671–1674*, ed. Karl Helbig (Leipzig 1862).
'Das Tagebuch Esaias Pufendorfs, schwedischen Residenten am Kaiserhofe von 1671 bis 1674', ed. Oswald Redlich, *MIÖG* 37 (1917), pp. 541–597.
Rinck, G. E., *Leopold des Grossen Röm. Kaysers wunderwürdiges Leben und Thaten aus geheimen Nachrichte eröffnet* (Cologne 1713).
Rousset de Missy, Jean, and Du Mont, Jean, *Le Cérémonial Diplomatique des Cours de l'Europe ou collection des actes, mémoires et relations qui concernent les Dignitez, Titulatures, Honneurs et Prééminences; les fonctions publiques des souverains, leurs*

sacres, couronnemens, mariages, batêmes, & Enterremens; les Investitures des grands Fiefs; les Entrées publiques, Audiences, Fonctions, Immunitez & Franchises des Ambassadeurs et autres Ministres publics; leurs Disputes & Démelez de Préséance; Et en général tout ce qui a rapport au Cérémonial & à l'Etiquette, 2 vols., Supplément au Corps Universel Diplomatique du Droit des Gens 4–5 (Amsterdam and The Hague 1739).

Saint Maurice, Marquis de, *Lettres sur la cour de Louis XIV*, ed. Jean Lemoine (Paris 1910).

Saint-Simon [Louis de Rouvroy, duc de] *Mémoires*, ed. A. de Boislisle and Léon Lecestre, 42 vols. (Paris 1879–1930).

Siéyès, Emmanuel, *Qu'est ce que le Tiers Etat*, ed. R. Zappéri (Geneva 1970).

Sourches [Louis François du Bouchet, marquis de], *Mémoires du marquis de Sourches sur le règne de Louis XIV*, ed. Gabriel-Jules de Cosnac, 13 vols. (Paris 1882–1893).

Stollberg-Rilinger, Barbara, and Krischer, André, eds., *Das Hofreisejournal des Kurfürsten Clemens August von Köln 1719–1745* (Siegburg 2000).

Theatrum Europaeum oder ausführliche und wahrhaftige Beschreibung aller und jeder denckwürdigen Geschichten, so sich hin und wider in der Welt zugetragen haben (Frankfurt am Main 1635–).

Tillet, Jean du, *Recueil des Roys de France leurs couronne et maison, ensemble le rang des grands de France* (Paris 1611).

Toison d'Or ou recueil des statuts et ordonnances du noble ordre de la Toison d'Or, leurs confirmations, changemens, additions, ceremonies, immunitez, exemptions, prééminences, . . . depuis l'institution jusques à présent (Cologne 1689).

Véri, *Journal de l'abbé de Véri publié avec une préface et des notes par le baron Jehan de Witte*, 2 vols. (Paris s.d.).

Visconti, Giovanni Battista Primi, *Mémoires de Primi Visconti sur la cour de Louis XIV, 1673–1681*, ed. J.-F. Solnon (Paris 1988).

Weensche Gezantschapsberichten van 1670 tot 1720, ed. G. von Antal and J. C. H. de Pater, 2 vols. (The Hague 1929–1934).

Wicquefort, *L'Ambasadeur et ses Fonctions* (Cologne 1690).

Wienerisches Diarium (Vienna 1703–).

Zedler, Johann Heinrich, *Grosses vollständiges Universal-Lexikon aller Wissenschaften und Kunsten . . .* (Leipzig and Halle 1732; repr. Graz 1961).

Bibliography

Abraham, Claude Kurt, *Gaston d'Orléans et sa cour: étude litteraire*, Studies in the Romance Languages and Literatures 41 (Chapel Hill n.d.).

Adamson, John, ed., *The Princely Courts of Europe: Ritual, Politics, and Culture under the Ancien Régime 1500–1750* (London 1999).

Adelige Sachkultur des Spätmittelalters. Internationaler Kongress Krems an der Donau 22. bis 25. September 1980, Veröffentlichungen des Instituts für mittelalterliche Realienkunde Österreichs 5 (Vienna 1982).

Alewyn, Richard, and Sälzle, Karl, *Das Grosse Welttheater. Die Epoche der höfischen Feste in Dokument und Deutung* (Hamburg 1959).

Alföldi, Andreas, *Die monarchische Repräsentation im römischen Kaiserreich* (Darmstadt 1980).

Antoine, Michel, 'Les gouverneurs de province en France (XVIe–XVIIIe siècle)', in *Prosopographie et génèse de l'état moderne. Actes de la Table ronde de Paris, 22–23 oct. 1984*, ed. F. Autrand (Paris 1986), pp. 185–194.

Le gouvernement et administration sous Louis XV. Dictionnaire biographique (Paris 1978).

Louis XV (Paris 1989).

Aretin, Karl Otmar von, *Das Alte Reich 1648–1806. II Kaisertradition und Österreichische Großmachtpolitik (1684–1745)* (Stuttgart 1997).

Arnade, Peter, *Burgundian Ceremony and Civic Life in Late Medieval Ghent* (Ithaca 1996).

Asch, R. G., *Der Hof Karls I. Vom England. Politik, Provinz und Patronage* (Cologne, Weimar, and Vienna 1993).

Asch, R. G., ed., *Der Europäische Adel im Ancien Régime. Von der Krise der ständischen Monarchien bis zur Revolution* (Cologne, Weimar, and Vienna 2001).

Asch, R. G., and Birke, A., eds., *Princes, Patronage and the Nobility: The Court at the Beginning of the Modern Age c. 1450–1650* (Oxford and London 1991).

Aymard, Maurice, and Romani, Marzio A., eds., *La cour comme institution économique* (Paris 1998).

Baillie, Hugh Murray, 'Etiquette and the Planning of State Apartments in Baroque Palaces', *Archaeologia or Miscellaneous Tracts Relating to Antiquity* 101 (1967), pp. 169–199.

Barbiche, Bernard, *Les institutions de la monarchie française à l'époque moderne* (Paris 1999).

Barker, Nancy, 'Philippe d'Orléans, Frère Unique du Roi: Founder of the Family Fortune', *FHS* 13 (1983–1984), pp. 145–171.

Barthélemy, Edouard de, *Les Grands Ecuyers et la Grande Ecurie de France avant et depuis 1789* (Paris 1868).

Bastl, Beatrix, 'Das Österreichische Frauenzimmer. Zur Rolle der Frau im höfischen Fest- und Hofleben 15. bis 17. Jahrhundert', *Opera Historica* 8 (2000), pp. 79–105.

'Feuerwerk und Schlittenfahrt. Ordnungen zwischen Ritual und Zeremoniell', *WRGB* 51 (1996), pp. 197–229.

Tugend, Liebe, Ehre. Die adelige Frau in der Frühen Neuzeit (Vienna, Cologne, and Weimar 2000).

Bastl, Beatrix, and Heiss, Gernot, 'Hofdamen und Höflinge zur Zeit Leopolds I. Zur Geschichte eines vergessenenen Berufsstandes', *Opera Historica* 5 (1996), pp. 187–234.

'Tafeln bei Hof: die Hochzeitsbankette Kaiser Leopolds I', *WRGB* 50 (1995), pp. 181–206.

Bauer, Volker, *Die höfische Gesellschaft in Deutschland von der mitte des 17. bis zum Ausgang des 18. Jahrhunderts. Versuch einer Typologie* (Tübingen 1993).

Hofökonomie. Der Diskurs über den Fürstenhof in Zeremonialwissenschaft, Hausväterliteratur und Kameralismus (Vienna, Cologne, and Weimar 1997).

Repertorium territorialer Amtskalender und Amtshandbücher im Alten Reich. Adreß-, Hof-, Staatskalender und Staatshandbücher des 18. Jahrhunderts, vol. II, Heutiges Bayern, Osterreich, Liechtenstein. Ius Commune, Sonderheft 123 (Frankfurt 1999).

Baulant, M., 'Le salaire des ouvriers du bâtiment à Paris de 1400 à 1726', *AESC* 26 (1971), pp. 461–483.

Beales, Derek, *Joseph II: In the Shadow of Maria Theresa 1741–1780* (Cambridge 1987).

Beattie, John, *Bunyoro: An African Kingdom* (New York 1969).

Béguin, Katia, 'Louis XIV et l'aristocratie: coup de majesté ou retour à la tradition', *Histoire, économie et société* 19, 4 (2000), pp. 497–512.

Les princes de Condé. Rebelles, courtisans et mécènes dans la France du grand siècle (Paris 1999).

Béhar, Pierre, and Watanabe-O'Kelly, Helen, eds., *Spectaculum Europaeum: Theatre and Spectacle in Europe*, Wolfenbütteler Arbeiten zur Barockforschung 31 (Wiesbaden 1999).

Beik, William, *Absolutism and Society in Seventeenth-Century France: State Power and Provincial Aristocracy in Languedoc* (Cambridge 1985).

Louis XIV and Absolutism: A Brief Study with Documents (Boston and New York 2000).

Bély, Lucien, *Espions et Ambassadeurs au temps de Louis XIV* (Paris 1990).

La Société des Princes xvie–xviiie siècle (Paris 1999).

Benedik, Christian, 'Die Herrschaftlichen Appartements. Funktion und Lage Während der Regierungen von Kaiser Leopold I. bis Franz Joseph I', *Österreichische Zeitschrift für Kunst und Denkmalpflege* 51 (1997), pp. 552–570.

Benoit, Marcelle, *Versailles et les musiciens du roi, 1661–1733: étude institutionnelle et sociale* (Paris 1971).

Bérenger, Jean, 'A propos d'un ouvrage récent: les finances de l'autriche à l'époque baroque (1650–1740)', *Histoire, economie et société* 3, 2 (1984), pp. 221–245.

Finances et Absolutisme Autrichien dans la seconde moitié du XVIIe siècle (Paris 1975).

'Pour une enquête européenne: le problème du ministériat au XVIIe siècle', *AESC* 29, 1 (1974), pp. 166–192.
Bergin, Joseph, *Cardinal Richelieu, Power and the Pursuit of Wealth* (New Haven and London 1985).
The Making of the French Episcopate (1589–1661) (New Haven and London 1996).
The Rise of Richelieu (New Haven and London 1991).
Berns, J. J., and Rahn, Th., ed., *Zeremoniell als höfische Ästhetik in Spätmittelalter und Früher Neuzeit* (Tübingen 1995).
Bertelli, Sergio, *The Courts of the Italian Renaissance* (Milan 1985).
Beutler, Corinne, 'Bâtiments et salaires: un Chantier à Saint-Germain-des-Prés de 1644 à 1646', *AESC* 26 (1971), pp. 484–517.
Bireley, Robert, *Religion and Politics in the Age of the Counterreformation: Emperor Ferdinand II, William Lamormaini S.J., and the Formation of Imperial Policy* (Chapel Hill 1981).
Blanning, T. C. W., *The Culture of Power and the Power of Culture* (Oxford 2002).
Blanquie, Christophe, 'Dans la main du Grand maître. Les offices de la maison du roi, 1643–1720', *Histoire & Mesure* 13, 3–4 (1998), pp. 243–288.
Bloch, Marc, *Les Rois thaumaturges. Etude sur le caractère surnaturel attribué à la puissance royale particulièrement en France et en Angleterre* (Paris 1983).
Bonney, Margaret, and Bonney, Richard, *Jean-Roland Malet premier historien des finances de la monarchie française* (Paris 1993).
Bonney, Richard, ed., *The Rise of the Fiscal State in Europe, c. 1200–1815* (Oxford 1999).
Bonney, Richard, Bonney, Margaret, and Ormrod, W. M., eds., *Crises, Revolutions and Self-Sustained Growth: Essays in European Fiscal History, 1130–1830* (Stamford 1999).
Boppe, A., *Les introducteurs des Ambassadeurs 1585–1900* (Paris 1901).
Bosher, J. F., *French Finances, 1770–1795: From Business to Bureaucracy* (Cambridge 1970).
Bouchenot-Déchin, Patricia, *Henry Dupuis, jardinier de Louis XIV*, Les Métiers de Versailles (Versailles 2001).
Boucher, Jacqueline, *Deux épouses et reines à la fin du XVIe siècle. Louise de Lorraine et Marguerite de France* (Saint-Etienne 1995).
La cour de Henri III (Rennes 1986).
'L'évolution de la maison du Roi: des derniers Valois aux premiers Bourbons', *XVIIe Siècle* 137 (1982), pp. 359–379.
Boulton, D. A. J. D., *The Monarchical Orders of Knighthood in Later Medieval Europe 1325–1520* (Woodbridge 1987).
Boutier, Jean, Dewerpe, Alain, and Nordman, Daniel, *Un tour de France royal: le voyage de Charles IX (1565–1566)* (Paris 1984).
Bryant, Lawrence M., *The King and the City in the Parisian Royal Entry Ceremony. Politics, Ritual, and Art in the Renaissance* (Geneva 1986).
Bryant, Mark, 'Françoise d'Aubigné, Marquise de Maintenon: Religion, Power and Politics: A Study in Circles of Influence during the Later Reign of Louis XIV, 1684–1715', unpublished Ph.D. thesis, London (2001).
Bucholz, R., *The Augustan Court: Queen Anne and the Decline of Court Culture* (Stanford 1993).
Bucholz, R., and Sainty, J. C., eds., *Officials of the Royal Household, 1660–1837. Part I: Department of the Lord Chamberlain and Associated Offices* (London 1997).

Buck, A., Kaufmann, G., Spahr, B. L., and Wiedemann, C., eds., *Europäische Hofkultur im 16. und 17. Jahrhundert. Vorträge und Referate gehalten anlässlich des Kongresses des Wolfenbütteler Arbeitskreises für Renaissanceforschung und des Internationalen Arbeitskreises für Barockliteratur in der Herzog August Bibliothek Wolfenbüttel vom 4. bis 8. September 1979*, Wolfenbütteler Arbeiten zur Barockforschung 8 (Hamburg 1981).

Buisseret, David, *Henry IV* (London 1984).

Bulst, N., Descimon, R., and Guerreau, A., eds., *L'Etat ou le roi. Les fondations de la modernité monarchique en France (xive–xviie siècles)* (Paris 1996).

Burke, Peter, *The Fabrication of Louis XIV* (New Haven and London 1992).

Campbell Orr, Clarissa, ed., *Queenship in Europe 1660–1815: The Role of the Consort* (Cambridge 2004).

Campbell, Peter R., *Power and Politics in Old Regime France, 1720–1745* (London 1996).

Chaussinand-Nogaret, Guy, *La noblesse au XVIIIe siècle. De la Féodalité aux Lumières* (Paris 1976).

La vie quotidienne des femmes du roi (Paris 1990).

Christiane, Thomas, 'Von Burgund zu Habsburg. Personalpolitische und administrative Verflechtungen in den Herrschaftskomplexen des Hauses Österreich', in *Archiv und Forschung. Das Haus-, Hof- und Staatsarchiv in seiner Bedeutung für die Geschichte Österreichs und Europas*, ed. Elisabeth Springer and Leopold Kammerhofer (Vienna and Munich 1993), pp. 35–48.

Claessen, H. J. M., and Skalnik, P., eds., *The Early State* (The Hague 1978).

Coreth, Anna, *Pietas Austriaca. Ursprung und Entwicklung barocker Frömmigkeit in Österreich* (Vienna 1959).

Cosandey, Fanny, *La reine de France. Symbole et pouvoir xve–xviiie siècle* (Paris 2000).

Dessert, Daniel, *Argent, pouvoir et société au grand siècle* (Paris 1984).

Dessert, Daniel, and Journet, J.-L., 'Le lobby Colbert: un royaume ou une affaire de famille', *AESC* 30 (1975), pp. 1303–1336.

Dickens, A. G., ed., *The Courts of Europe: Politics, Patronage and Royalty 1400–1800* (London 1977).

Dickson, P. G. M., *Finance and Government under Maria Theresia 1740–1780*, 2 vols. (Oxford 1987).

'Monarchy and Bureaucracy in Late Eighteenth-Century Austria', *English Historical Review* 110 (1995), pp. 323–367.

Dictionnaire de l'Ancien Régime, ed. Lucien Bély (Paris 1996).

Dictionnaire du Grand Siècle, ed. François Bluche (Paris 1990).

Die Lust am Jagen. Jagdsitten und Jagdfeste am Kurpfälzischen Hof im 18. Jahrhundert (Ubstadt-Weiher 1999).

Doyle, William, *Venality: The Sale of Offices in Eighteenth-century France* (Oxford 1996).

Dreger, Moriz, *Baugeschichte der K.K. Hofburg in Wien bis zum XIX. Jahrhunderte*, Österreichische Kunsttopographie 14 (Vienna 1914).

Dubost, Jean-François, *La France Italienne XVIe–XVIIe siècle* (Paris 1997).

Duchhardt, Heinz, 'Krönungszüge. Ein Versuch zur "negativen Kommunikation"', in *Im Spannungsfeld von Recht und Ritual. Soziale Kommunikation in Mittelalter und früher Neuzeit*, ed. H. Duchhardt and G. Melville (Cologne 1997), pp. 291–301.

Duchhardt, Heinz, Jackson, Richard, and Sturdy, David, eds., *European Monarchy: Its Evolution and Practice from Roman Antiquity to Modern Times* (Stuttgart 1992).

Duindam, Jeroen, 'Ceremony at Court: Reflections on an Elusive Subject', *Francia. Forschungen zur westeuropäischen Geschichte* 26, 2 (1999), pp. 131–140.

Myths of Power: Norbert Elias and the Early Modern European Court (Amsterdam 1995).

'Norbert Elias und der frühneuzeitliche Hof. Versuch einer Kritik und Weiterführung', *Historische Anthropologie* 6, 4 (1998), pp. 370–387.

'The Court of the Austrian Habsburgs: Locus of a Composite Heritage', *MRK* 8, 2 (1998), pp. 24–58.

Duma, Jean, *Les Bourbons-Penthièvre (1678–1793): Une nébuleuse aristocratique au xviiie siècle* (Paris 1995).

Dunk, Thomas H. von der, *Das deutsche Denkmal: eine Geschichte in Bronze und Stein vom Hochmittelalter bis zum Barock* (Cologne 1999).

Durand, Y., 'Recherches sur les salaires des maçons à Paris au XVIIIe siècle', *Revue d'Histoire Economique et Sociale*, 44 (1966), pp. 468–480.

Elias, Norbert, *Die höfische Gesellschaft. Untersuchungen zur Soziologie des Königtums und der höfischen Aristokratie. Mit einer Einleitung: Soziologie und Geschichtswissenschaft* (Darmstadt and Neuwied 1969).

Elias, Norbert, *Über den Prozeß der Zivilisation. Soziogenetische und Psychogenetische Untersuchungen*, 2 vols. (Bern 1969).

Ellenius, Allan, ed., *Iconography, Propaganda, and Legitimation* (Oxford 1998).

Elliott, J. H., *Spain and Its World 1500–1700: Selected Essays* (New Haven and London 1989).

'Tediums and Te Deums', *Times Literary Supplement*, 28 April 2000, p. 27.

Elliott, J. H., and Brockliss, L. W. B., eds., *The World of the Favourite* (New Haven and London 1999).

Elliott, J. H., and Brown, Jonathan, *A Palace for a King: The Buen Retiro and the Court of Philip IV* (New Haven and London 1980).

Ellis, Harold A., *Boulainvilliers and the French Monarchy: Aristocratic Politics in Early Eighteenth-Century France* (Ithaca and London 1988).

'Genealogy, History and Aristocratic Reaction in Early Eighteenth-Century France: The Case of Henri de Boulainvilliers', *JMH* 58, 2 (1986), pp. 414–451.

Engels, Jens Ivo, *Königsbilder. Sprechen, Singen und Schreiben über den französischen König in der ersten Hälfte des achtzehnten Jahrhunderts*, Pariser Historische Studien 52 (Bonn 2000).

Evans, Robert J. W., *The Making of the Habsburg Monarchy 1550–1700: An Interpretation* (Oxford 1979).

Feros, Antonio, *Kingship and Favoritism in the Spain of Philip III 1598–1621* (Cambridge 2000).

Festivals and Ceremonies: A Bibliography of Works Relating to Court, Civic, and Religious Festivals in Europe 1500–1800, ed. Helen Watanabe-O'Kelly and Anne Simon (London and New York 2000).

Fidler, Katharina, 'Mäzenatentum und Politik am Wiener Hof: das Beispiel der kaiserin Eleonora Gonzaga-Nevers', *Innsbrucker Historische Studien* 12, 13 (1990), pp. 41–68.

Fogel, Michèle, *Les cérémonies d'information dans la France du XVIe au XVIIIe siècle* (Paris 1989).

L'Etat dans la France moderne de la fin du XVe siècle au milieu du XVIIIe siècle (Paris 1992).

Forster, R., *The House of Saulx-Tavannes: Versailles and Burgundy 1700–1830* (Baltimore 1971).

Frêche, Genevièvel, and Frêche, George, *Les prix des grains des vins et des légumes à Toulouse (1486–1868). Extraits des Mercuriales suivis d'une bibliographie d'histoire des prix* (Paris 1967).

Frey, Linda, and Frey, Marsha, *A Question of Empire: Leopold I and the War of Spanish Succession 1701–1705* (New York 1983).

Geertz, Clifford, *Negara: The Theatre-state in Nineteenth-Century Bali* (Princeton 1980).

Gehling, Theo, *Ein Europäischer Diplomat am Kaiserhof zu Wien. François Louis de Pesme, seigneur de Saint-Saphorin, als englischer Resident am Wiener Hof 1718–1727*, Bonner Historische Forschungen 25 (Bonn 1964).

Giesey, Ralph E., 'The King Imagined', in *The French Revolution and the Creation of Modern Political Culture*. I *The Political Culture of the Old Regime*, ed. K. M. Baker (Oxford and New York 1987), pp. 41–59.

Giesey, Ralph E., *The Royal Funeral Ceremony in Renaissance France* (Geneva 1960).

Godefroy-Ménilglaise, *Les savants Godefroy. Mémoires d'une famille pendant les xvie, xviie & xviiie siècles* (Paris 1873).

Goloubeva, Maria, *The Glorification of Emperor Leopold I in Image, Spectacle and Text*, Veröffentlichungen des Instituts für Europäische Geschichte 184 (Mainz 2000).

Goubert, Pierre, *Mazarin* (Paris 1990).

Graf, Henriette, 'Das kaiserliche Zeremoniell und das Repräsentationsappartement im Leopoldinischen Trakt der Wiener Hofburg um 1740', *Österreichische Zeitschrift für Kunst und Denkmalpflege* 51 (1997), pp. 571–587.

Graham, Victor E., and McAllister Johnson, W., eds., *The Royal Tour of France by Charles IX and Catherine de Medici: Festivals and Entries 1564–1566* (Toronto, Buffalo, and London 1979).

Griselle, Eugène, *Ecurie, Vénerie, Fauconnerie et louveterie du roi Louis XIII* (Paris 1912).

Gruber, Alain-Charles, *Les grandes fêtes et leurs décors à l'époque de Louis XVI* (Geneva 1972).

Gschliesser, O. von, 'Das Beamtentum der hohen Reichsbehörden (Reichshofkanzlei, Reichskammergericht, Reichshofrat, Hofkriegsrat)', in *Beamtentum und Pfarrerstand 1400–1800. Budinger Vorträge 1967*, ed. Günther Franz (Limburg Lahn 1972), pp. 11–26.

Der Reichshofrat. Bedeutung und Verfassung, Schicksal und Besetzung einer obersten Reichsbehörde von 1559–1806 (Vienna 1942).

Guillaume, Jean, ed., *Architecture et vie sociale. L'Organisation intérieure des grandes demeures à la fin du moyen age et à la renaissance. Actes du colloque tenu à Tours du 6 au 10 juin 1988* (Paris 1994).

Hadamowsky, Franz, *Barocktheater am Wiener Kaiserhof. Mit einem Spielplan (1625–1740)* (Vienna 1955).

Ham, Claudia, 'Die Verkauften Bräute. Studien zu den Hochzeiten zwischen Österreichischen und Spanischen Habsburgern im 17. Jahrhundert', unpublished dissertation, Vienna (1995).

Hamann, Brigitte, ed., *Die Habsburger. Ein biographisches Lexikon* (Vienna 1988).

Hamscher, Albert N., *The Conseil Privé and the Parlements in the Age of Louis XIV: A Study in French Absolutism*, Transactions of the American Philosophical Society 77-II (Philadelphia 1987).

Hanley, Sarah, *The* Lit de Justice *of the Kings of France: Constitutional Ideology in Legend, Ritual and Discourse* (Princeton 1983).
Harding, Robert R., *Anatomy of a Power Elite: The Provincial Governors of Early Modern France* (New Haven and London 1978).
Hardman, John, *Louis XVI* (New Haven and London 1993).
Louis XVI: The Silent King (London and New York 2000).
Harris, Barbara, 'Women and Politics in Early Tudor England', in *Historical Journal* 33, 2 (1990), pp. 259–281.
Harris, Robert D., *Necker: Reform Statesman of the Ancien Régime* (Berkeley, Los Angeles, and London 1979).
Hartmann, Peter C., *Kulturgeschichte des Heiligen Römischen Reiches 1648 bis 1806. Verfassung, Religion, Kultur* (Vienna, Cologne, and Graz 2001).
Haslinger, Ingrid, *Küche und Tafelkultur am Kaiserlichen Hofe zu Wien. Zur Geschichte von Hofküche, Hofzuckerbäckerei und Hofsilber- und Tafelkammer* (Bern and Vevey 1993).
Hatin, Eugène, *Bibliographie historique et critique de la presse périodique française* (Paris 1866).
Hatton, Ragnhild, ed., *Louis XIV and Europe* (London 1976).
Haupt, Herbert, 'Kunst und Kultur in den Kameralzahlamtsbüchern Kaiser Karls VI: die Jahre 1715 bis 1727', *MÖStA* 12 (1993), pp. 7–186.
Hausenblasová, Jaroslava, 'Die "Höflinge" des Kaisers Rudolf II. – Beitrag zur Begriffsbestimmung', in *Rudolf II, Prague, and the World: Papers from the International Conference, Prague, 2–4 September, 1997*, ed. Lubomir Konecny, Beket Bukovinska, and Ivan Muchka (Prague 1998), pp. 239–243.
'Nationalitäts- und Sozialstruktur des Hofes Rudolfs II. im Prager Milieu an der Wende vom 16. zum 17. Jahrhundert', in *Berichte und Beiträge des Geisteswissenschaftliches Zentrums Geschichte und Kultur Ostmitteleuropas e. V. 1999. Öffentliche Vorträge 1998–1999* (Leipzig 1999), pp. 20–37.
'Seznamy dvoranu císare rudolfka II. Z let 1580, 1584 a 1589', in *Paginae Historiae. Sborník Státino Ustredniho archivu v Praze* 4 (Prague 1996), pp. 39–151.
Heilingsetzer, Georg, 'Prinz Eugen und die Führungsschicht der österreichischen Großmacht', *Österreich und die Osmanen. Prinz Eugen und seinen Zeit*, ed. Erich Zöllner and Karl Gutkas, Schriften des Instituts für Österreichkunde (Vienna 1988), pp. 120–137.
Heinig, Paul Joachim, *Kaiser Friedrich III (1440–1493). Hof, Regierung und Politik* (Cologne 1997).
Hengerer, Mark, 'Adelsintegration am Kaiserhof 1620 bis 1665', *MRK* 10, 1 (2000), pp. 21–32.
Himelfarb, Hélène, 'Versailles: fonctions et légendes', in: *Les lieux de mémoire*, ed. Pierre Nora, II *La Nation* (Paris 1986), pp. 235–292.
Hirschbiegel, Jan, and Paravicini, Werner, *Das Frauenzimmer. Die Frau bei Hofe in Spätmittelalter und früher Neuzeit 6. Symposium der Residenzen-Kommission der Akademie der Wissenschaften in Göttingen* (Stuttgart 2000).
Hobsbawm, Eric, and Ranger, Terence, eds., *The Invention of Tradition* (Cambridge 1983).
Hochedlinger, Michael, 'Mars Ennobled: The Ascent of the Military and the Creation of a Military Nobility in Mid-Eighteenth-Century Austria', *German History* 17 (1999), pp. 141–176.

Hofmann, Christina, *Das Spanische Hofzeremoniell von 1500–1700*, Erlanger Historische Studien 8 (Frankfurt, Bern, and New York 1985).

Holl, Brigitte, *Hofkammerpräsident Gundaker Thomas Graf Starhemberg und die österreichische Finanzpolitik der Barockzeit (1703–1715)*, AÖG 132 (Vienna 1976).

Horowski, Leonhard, 'Pouvez-vous trop donner pour une chose si essentielle? Eine prosopographische Studie der Obersten Chargen am Hof von Versailles', *MRK* 11, 1 (2001), pp. 32–53.

Huizinga, Johan, *Herfsttij der Middeleeuwen. Studie over levens- en gedachtenvormen der veertiende en vijftiende eeuw in Frankrijk en de Nederlanden* (Haarlem 1963).

Hunt, Shannon, 'Zur Definition ständischer Grenzen unter den frühen Stuarts – John Seldens, Titles of Honor' im historischen Kontext', unpublished Magisterarbeit Münster (1999).

Hurt, John J., *Louis XIV and the Parlements: The Assertion of Royal Authority* (Manchester 2002).

Hurter, Friedrich, *Friedensbestrebungen Kaiser Ferdinand's II. Nebst des Apostolischen Nuntius Carl Carafa Bericht über Ferdinand's Lebensweise, Familie, Hof, Räthe und Politik* (Vienna 1860).

Philip Lang, Kammerdiener Kaiser Rudolfs II. Eine Criminalgeschichte aus dem Anfang des siebenzehnten Jahrhunderts (Schaffhausen 1851).

Jackson, Richard A., *Vive le Roi! A History of the French Coronation from Charles V to Charles X* (Chapel Hill and London 1984).

Jäger, Wolfgang, '"Menschwissenschaft" und historische Sozialwissenschaft. Zur Rezeption von Norbert Elias', *Archiv für Kulturgeschichte* 77 (1995), pp. 85–116.

Jouanna, Arlette, *Le devoir de révolte: La noblesse française et la gestion de l'état moderne 1559–1661* (Paris 1989).

Jousselin, Roland, *Au couvert de roi XVIIe–XVIIIe siècles* (Paris n.d.).

Kagan, Richard L., and Parker, Geoffrey, eds., *Spain, Europe and the Atlantic World* (Cambridge 1995).

Kaiser, Michael, *Politik und Kriegsführung. Maximilian von Bayern, Tilly und die Katholische Liga im Dreißigjährigen Krieg* (Münster 1999).

Kaiser, Thomas E., 'Madame de Pompadour and the Theatres of Power', *FHS* 19 (1996), pp. 1025–1044.

Keller, Katrin, 'Der Wiener Hof von außen. Beobachtungen zur Reflexion des Kaiserhofes im Reich im 17. und 18. Jh.', *Frühneuzeit Info* 12 (2001), pp. 21–31.

Kettering, Sharon, *Patrons, Brokers and Clients in Seventeenth-century France* (Oxford 1986).

Klaits, Joseph C., *Printed Propaganda under Louis XIV: Absolute Monarchy and Public Opinion* (Princeton 1976).

Kléber Monod, Paul, *The Power of Kings: Monarchy and Religion in Europe 1589–1715* (New Haven and London 1999).

Kleinman, Ruth, 'Social Dynamics at the French Court: The Household of Anne of Austria', *FHS* 16 (1990), pp. 517–535.

Knecht, R. J., *Renaissance Warrior and Patron: The Reign of Francis I* (Cambridge 1994).

'The Court of Francis I', *European Studies Review* 8, 1 (1978), pp. 1–22.

Kooijmans, Luuc, *Liefde in opdracht. Het hofleven van Willem Frederik van Nassau* (Amsterdam 2000).

Kovács, Elisabeth, 'Einflüsse geistlicher Ratgeber und höfischer Beichtväter auf das fürstliche Selbstverständnis, auf Machtbegriffe und politische Entscheidungen österreichischer Habsburger während des 17.und 18. Jahrhunderts', *Cristianesimo nella storia* 4 (1983), pp. 79–102.

'Kirchliches Zeremoniell am wiener Hof des 18. Jahrhundert im Wandel von Mentalität und Gesellschaft', *MÖStA* 32 (1979), pp. 109–142.

Kruedener, Jürgen Freiherr von, *Die Rolle des Hofes im Absolutismus*, Forschungen zur Sozial- und Wirtschaftsgeschichte 19 (Stuttgart 1973).

Kruse, Holger, *Hof, Amt und Gagen: die täglichen Gagenlisten des burgundischen Hofes (1430–1467) und der erste Hofstaat Karls des Kühnen (1456)*, Pariser historische Studien 44 (Bonn 1996).

Kruse, Holger, and Paravicini, Werner, eds., *Höfe und Hofordnungen 1200–1600. 5. Symposium der Residenzen-Kommission der Akademie der Wissenschaften in Göttingen* (Sigmaringen 1999).

Kühnel, Harry, *Die Hofburg zu Wien* (Graz and Cologne 1964).

La Hetraie, *La Chasse. Vénerie – Fauconnerie. Suivi de notices et d'un vocabulaire général des termes de la chasse du cerf* (Paris 1945).

La Toison d'or. Cinq siècles d'art et d'histoire (Bruges 1962).

Labatut, Guy de, *La Cour de Monsieur Frère de Louis XIV. Portraits et documents inédits* (Paris 1927).

Labatut, Jean-Pierre, *Les ducs et pairs de France au XVIIe siècle: étude sociale* (Paris 1972).

Laferl, Christopher F., '"En tierra ajena" Spanier in Wien zur Zeit Ferdinands I. (1522–1564)', *WRGB* 52 (1997), pp. 1–14.

Le Roux, Nicolas, *La faveur du roi. Mignons et courtisans au temps des derniers Valois (vers 1547–vers 1589)* (Paris 2000).

Le Roy Ladurie, Emmanuel, 'Auprès du roi, la Cour', *AESC* 38, 1 (1983), pp. 21–41.

Saint-Simon ou le système de la cour (Paris 1997).

Levantal, Christophe, *Ducs et Pairs et duchés-pairies à l'Epoque moderne (1519–1790)* (Paris 1996).

Lexikon des Mittelalters ed. Liselotte Lutz et al., 12 vols. (Munich 1977–1999).

Lindert, Peter H., Hoffman, Philip T., Jacks, David, Levin, Patricia A., 'Prices and Real Inequality in Europe since 1500', University of California – Davis, Agricultural History Center, Working Paper No. 102 (October 2000).

Lloyd Moote, A., *Louis XIII. The Just* (Berkeley and Los Angeles 1989).

Loeb, Edwin M., 'Die Institution des Sakralen Königtums', *Paideuma* 10 (Wiesbaden 1964), pp. 102–114.

Lynch, John A., and Reitan, E. A., 'From Revenue to Civil List, 1689–1702: The Revolution Settlement and the "Mixed and Balanced" Constitution', *Historical Journal* 13 (1970), pp. 571–588.

Lynn, John, *Giant of the Grand Siècle: The French Army 1610–1715* (Cambridge 1997).

MacHardy, Karin J., 'Cultural Capital, Family Strategies and Noble Identity in Early Modern Habsburg Austria 1579–1620', *Past & Present* 163 (1999), pp. 36–75.

MacHardy, Karin J., *Statebuilding, Religion and Court Patronage: Social and Cultural Dimensions of Political Interaction in Habsburg Austria, 1521–1622* (Palgrave/Macmillan Press, forthcoming).

Malettke, Klaus, and Grell, Chantal, eds., *Hofgesellschaft und Höflinge an europäischen Fürstenhöfe in der Frühen Neuzeit(15.–18. Jh.)* (Münster 2001).

Mansel, Philip, 'Monarchy, Uniform, and the Rise of the Frac', *Past & Present* 96 (1982), pp. 103–132.

Marion, Marcel, *Dictionnaire des institutions de la France aux XVIIe et XVIIIe siècles* (Paris 1923; repr. 1979).

Matsche, Franz, *Die Kunst im Dienst der Staatsidee Kaiser Karls VI. Ikonographie, Ikonologie und Programmatik des 'Kaiserstils'*, 2 vols. (Berlin and New York 1981).

May, Wolfgang, 'Reisen "al incognito". Zur Reisetätigkeit Kaiser Josephs II', *MIÖG* 93 (1985), pp. 59–91.

Mecenseffy, Grete, *Im Dienste dreier Habsburger. Leben und Wirken des Fürsten Johann Weikhard Auersperg (1615–1677)* (Vienna and Leipzig 1938).

Menčík, Ferdinand, 'Beiträge zur Geschichte der Kaiserlichen Hofämter', *AÖG* 87 (Vienna 1899), pp. 447–563.

Mensi, Franz von, *Die Finanzen Österreichs von 1701 bis 1740 nach archivalischen Quellen dargestellt* (Vienna 1890).

Mettam, Roger, *Power and Faction in Louis XIV's France* (Oxford and New York 1988).

'Power, Status and Precedence: Rivalries Among the Provincial Elites of Louis XIV's France', *Transactions of the Royal Historical Society* 38 (1988), pp. 43–62.

Mikoletzky, Hanns Leo, 'Hofreisen unter Kaiser Karl VI', *MIÖG* 60 (1952), pp. 265–285.

Miller, Rotraut, 'Die Hofreisen Kaiser Leopold I', *MIÖG* 75 (1967), pp. 66–103.

Minois, Georges, *Le confesseur du roi. Les directeurs de conscience sous la monarchie française* (Paris 1988).

Mitis, Oskar von, *Jagd und Schützen am Hofe Karls VI* (Vienna 1912).

Morineau, Michel, 'Budgets de l'Etat et gestion des finances royales au XVIIIe siècle', *Revue Historique* 104 (1980), pp. 288–336.

Mörke, Olaf, *'Stadtholder' oder 'Staetholder'?: die Funktion des Hauses Oranien und seines Hofes in der politischen Kultur der Republik der Vereinigten Niederlande im 17. Jahrhundert* (Münster 1997).

Müller, Klaus, *Das kaiserliche Gesandtschaftswesen im Jahrhundert nach dem Westfälischen Frieden (1648–1740)*, Bonner Historische Forschungen 42 (Bonn 1976).

'Habsburgischer Adel um 1700: Die Familie Lamberg', *MÖStA* 32 (1979), pp. 78–108.

Müller, Rainer, *Der Fürstenhof in der frühen Neuzeit* (Munich 1995).

Necipoglu, Gülru, *Architecture, Ceremonial, and Power: The Topkapi Palace in the Fifteenth and Sixteenth Centuries* (Cambridge, MA, and London 1991).

Neuhaus, Helmut, *Das Reich in der frühen Neuzeit* (Munich 1997).

Newton, William Ritchey, *L'Espace du roi. La cour de France au château de Versailles 1682–1789* (Paris 2000).

Noflatscher, Heinz, *Räte und Herrscher. Politische Eliten an den Habsburgerhöfen der österreichischen Länder 1480–1530*, Veröffentlichungen des Instituts für europäische Geschichte 161 (Mainz 1999).

Oresko, Robert, 'The Marriages of the Nieces of Cardinal Mazarin: Public Policy and Private Strategy in Seventeenth-Century Europe', in *Frankreich im europäischen Staatensystem der Frühen Neuzeit* ed. Rainer Babel (Sigmaringen 1995).

Oresko, R., Gibbs, G. C., and Scott, H. M., eds., *Royal and Republican Sovereignty in Early Modern Europe: Essays in Memory of Ragnhild Hatton* (Cambridge 1997).

Oßwald-Bargende, Sybille, *Die Mätresse, der Fürst und die Macht. Christina Wilhemina von Grävenitz und die höfische Gesellschaft*, Geschichte und Geschlechter 32 (Frankfurt and New York 2000).

Pállfy, Géza, 'Der Wiener Hof und die ungarischen Stände im 16. Jahrhundert', *MIÖG* 109 (2001), pp. 346–381.

Paravicini, Werner, ed., *Zeremoniell und Raum. 4. Symposium der Residenzen-Kommission der Akademie der Wissenschaften in Göttingen* (Sigmaringen 1997).

Paravicini, Werner, and Werner, Karl Ferdinand, *Histoire comparée de l'administration (ive–xviiie siècles). Actes du XIVe colloque historique franco-allemand Tours, 27 mars-1er avril 1977*, Beihefte der Francia 9 (Zurich and Munich 1980).

Parker, David, 'Sovereignty, Absolutism and the Function of the Law in Seventeenth-Century France', *Past & Present* 122 (1989), pp. 36–74.

Parrott, David, *Richelieu's Army: War, Government and Society in France, 1624–1642* (Cambridge 2001).

Paulmann, Johannes, *Pomp und Politik. Monarchenbegegnungen in Europa zwischen Ancien Régime und Erstem Weltkrieg* (Paderborn and Munich 2000).

Pecar, Andreas, 'Die Ökonomie der Ehre. Resources, Zeremoniell und Selbstdarstellungspraxis des höfischen Adels am Kaiserhof Karls VI. (1711–1740)', unpublished dissertation Cologne (2001), forthcoming as *Die Ökonomie der Ehre. Der höfische Adel am Kaiserhof Karls VI. (1711–1740)*, Symbolische Kommunikation in der Vormoderne 5 (Darmstadt 2003).

Persson, Fabian, *Servants of Fortune: The Swedish Court Between 1598 and 1721* (Lund 1999).

Pikl von Witkenberg, Wilhelm, *Kämmerer-Almanach. Historischer Rückblick auf die Entwicklung der Kämmerer-Würde. Zusammenstellung der Kaiserlichen Kammerherren seit Karl V. bis zur Gegenwart* (Vienna 1903).

Pils, Susanne Claudine, 'Hof/Tratsch. Alltag bei Hof im ausgehenden 17. Jahrhundert', *WRGB* 53 (1998), pp. 77–99.

Polleroß, Friedrich, 'Tradition und Recreation. Die Residenzen der österreichischen Habsburger in der Frühen Neuzeit', *Maiestas* 6 (1998), pp. 91–148.

'Zur Repräsentation der Habsburger in der bildenden Kunst', in *Welt des Barock*, ed. Elisabeth Kovacs and Rupert Feuchtmüller (Vienna 1986).

Pommier, Edouard, 'Versailles, l'image du souverain', in *Les lieux de mémoire*, ed. Pierre Nora, II *La Nation* (Paris 1986), pp. 193–234.

Potter, David, *A History of France 1460–1560: The Emergence of a Nation State* (Houndmills and Basingstoke 1995).

Press, Volker, 'Josef I. (1705–1711) – Kaiserpolitik zwischen Erblanden, Reich und Dynastie', in *Deutschland und Europa in der Neuzeit. Festschrift für Karl Otmar Freiherr von Aretin zum 65. Geburtstag*, ed. R. Melville and C. Scharf (Stuttgart 1988), I, pp. 277–297.

'Kaiser und Reichsritterschaft', in *Adel in der Frühneuzeit. Ein regionaler Vergleich*, ed. Rudolf, Endres, Bayreuther Historische Kolloquien 5 (Cologne and Vienna 1991), pp. 163–194.

'Österreichische Großmachtbildung und Reichsverfassung. Zur kaiserlichen Stellung nach 1648', *MIÖG* 98 (1990), pp. 131–154.

'The Habsburg Court as a Center of the Imperial Government', *JMH*, 58 supplement (1986), pp. 23–45.

'The System of Estates in the Austrian Hereditary Lands and in the Holy Roman Empire: A Comparison', in *Crown, Church and Estates: Central European Politics in the Sixteenth and Seventeenth Centuries*, ed. R. J. W. Evans and T. V. Thomas (London 1991), pp. 1–22.

Pribram, Alfred Francis, Geyer, Rudolf, and Koran, Franz, *Materialien zur Geschichte der Preise und Löhne in Österreich* (Vienna 1938).

Price, David, 'The Palace and its Institutions in the Chiefdom of Ngambe', *Paideuma* 31 (1985), pp. 85–103.
Ranum, Orest, *The Fronde: A French Revolution 1648–1652* (New York and London 1993).
Reinhard, Wolfgang, *Power Elites and State Building* (Oxford 1996).
Riley, James C., *The Seven Years War and the Old Regime in France: The Economic and Financial Toll* (Princeton 1986).
Roche, Daniel, and Reytier, Daniel, eds., *Les écuries royales du xvie au xviiie siècle* (Paris 1998).
Rogister, John, 'From Louis XV to Louis XVI: Some Thoughts on the Petits Appartements', in *The Art and Architecture of Versailles*, ed. Robert P. Maccubin and David F. Morill, *Eighteenth Century Life* n.s., 17 (1993), pp. 147–166.
Rösener, Werner, 'Hofämter an mittelalterlichen Fürstenhöfen', *Deutsches Archiv für Erforschung des Mittelalters* 45 (1989), pp. 485–550.
Rowlands, Guy, 'Louis XIV, Aristocratic Power and the Elite Units of the French Army', *FH* 13 (1999), pp. 303–331.
Rule, John C., 'A Career in the Making: The Education of Jean-Baptiste Colbert, Marquis de Torcy', *FHS* 19 (1996), pp. 967–996.
Sabatier, Gérard, *Versailles ou la Figure du Roi* (Paris 1999).
Salvadori, Philippe, *La Chasse sous l'Ancien Régime* (Paris 1996).
Sánchez, Magdalena S., *The Empress, the Queen, and the Nun: Women and Power at the Court of Philip III of Spain* (Baltimore 1998).
Saunders, Steven, *Cross, Sword, and Lyre: Sacred Music at the Imperial Court of Ferdinand II of Habsburg (1619–1637)* (Oxford 1995).
Sauzet, Robert, ed., *Henri III et son temps. Actes du colloque international du Centre de la renaissance de Tours, octobre 1989* (Paris 1992).
Sawyer, Jeffrey K., *Printed Poison, Pamphlet Propaganda, Faction Politics, and the Public Sphere in Early Seventeenth-Century France* (Berkeley and Los Angeles 1990).
Schalk, Ellery, *From Valor to Pedigree: Ideas of Nobility in France in the Sixteenth and Seventeenth Centuries* (Princeton 1986).
Schilling, Heinz, 'Reichs-Staat im frühneuzeitliche Nation der deutschen oder teilmodernisiertes Reichssystem. Überlegungen zu Charakter und Aktualität des Alten Reiches', *Historische Zeitschrift* 272 (2001), pp. 377–395.
Schindling, A., and Ziegler, W., eds., *Die Kaiser der Neuzeit 1519–1918. Heiliges Römisches Reich, Österreich, Deutschland* (Munich 1990).
Schmidt, Georg, *Geschichte des alten Reiches. Staat und Nation in der Frühen Neuzeit 1495–1806* (Munich 1999).
Scholten, Helga, *Der Eunuch in Kaisernähe. Zur politischen und sozialen Bedeutung des praepositus sacri cubiculi im 4. und 5. Jahrhundert n. Chr*, Prismata 5 (Frankfurt 1995).
Schreiber, Renate, 'Erzherzog Leopold Wilhelm', unpublished dissertation, Vienna (2001).
Schwerhoff, Gerd, 'Zivilisationsprozeß und Geschichtswissenschaft. Norbert Elias' Forschungsparadigma in historischer Sicht', *Historische Zeitschrift* 266 (1998), pp. 61–105.
Scott, Hamish, 'The Rise of the First Minister in Eighteenth-century Europe', in *History and Biography: Essays in Honour of Derek Beales*, ed. T. C. W. Blanning and David Cannadine (Cambridge 1996).

Scott, Hamish, ed., *The European Nobilities in the Seventeenth and Eighteenth Centuries*, 2 vols. (London 1995).

Seeliger, Gerhard, *Das deutsche Hofmeisteramt im spaeteren Mittelalter* (Innsbruck 1865).

Sellert, Wolfgang, ed., *Reichshofrat und Reichskammergericht: ein Konkurrenzverhältnis*, Quellen und Forschungen zur Höchsten Gerichtsbarkeit im Alten Reich 34 (Cologne 1999).

Sienell, Stefan, *Die geheime Konferenz unter Kaiser Leopold I: personelle Strukturen und Methoden zur politischen Entscheidungsfindung am Wiener Hof*, Beiträge zur Neueren Geschichte Österreichs 17 (Frankfurt 2001).

'Die kaiserlichen Beratungsgremien und die spanische Erbfolgefrage 1699/1700)', *MÖStA* 47 (1999), pp. 117–145.

Solnon, Jean François, *La Cour de France* (Paris 1987).

Spagnolo-Stiff, Anne, *Die 'Entrée Solennelle'. Festarchitektur im Französischen Königtum (1700–1750)* (Weimar 1996).

Spielman, John P., 'Status as Commodity: The Habsburg Economy of Privilege', in *State and Society in Early Modern Austria*, ed. Charles Ingrao (West Lafayette Indiana 1994), pp. 110–118.

The City & the Crown: Vienna and the Imperial Court 1600–1740 (West Lafayette Indiana 1993).

Starkey, David, ed., *The English Court from the Wars of the Roses to the Civil War* (London 1987).

Stollberg-Rilinger, Barbara, 'Zeremoniell, Ritual, Symbol. Neue Forschungen zur symbolischen Kommunikation in Spätmittelalter und früher Neuzeit', *Zeitschrift für historische Forschung* 27, 3 (2000), pp. 389–405.

Stone, Bailey, *The French Parlements and the Crisis of the Old Regime* (Chapel Hill and London 1986).

Straub, Eberhard, *Repraesentatio Maiestatis oder Churbayerische Freudensfeste. Die höfischen Feste in der Münchner Residenz vom 16. bis zum Ende des 18. Jahrhunderts*, Miscellanea Bavarica Monacensia 14 (Munich 1969).

Sutter Fichtner, Paula, *Emperor Maximilian II* (New Haven and London 2001).

Ferdinand I of Austria: The Politics of Dynasticism in the Age of Reformation, East European Monographs C (New York 1982).

'Habsburg Household or Habsburg government? A Sixteenth-Century Administrative Dilemma', *Austrian History Yearbook* 26 (1995), pp. 45–60.

'To Rule Is Not To Govern: The Diary of Maximilian II', in *The Mirror of History. Essays in Honor of Fritz Fellner*, ed. Solomon Wank and Heidrun Maschl (Santa Barbara and Oxford 1988).

Swann, Julian, *Politics and the Parlement of Paris under Louis XV 1754–1774* (Cambridge 1995).

Tambiah, S. J., *Culture, Thought and Social Action: An Anthropological Perspective* (Cambridge MA 1985).

Tardits, Claude, 'L'Espace, indicateur historique, révélateur structural: l'exemple Bamoum (Cameroun)', *AESC* 40, 6 (1985), pp. 1261–1287.

'L'Etiquette à la cour royale Bamoum (Cameroun)', in *Culture et idéologie dans la genèse de l'état moderne. Actes de la table ronde organisée par le centre national de la recherche scientifique et l'école française de Rome* (Rome and Paris 1984), pp. 179–198.

Thomas, Christiane, 'Von Burgund zu Habsburg. Personalpolitische und administrative Verflechtungen in den Herrschaftskomplexen des Hauses Österreich', in *Archiv und Forschung. Das Haus-, Hof- und Staatsarchiv in seiner Bedeutung für die Geschichte Österreichs und Europas*, ed. Elisabeth Springer and Leopold Kammerhofer (Vienna and Munich 1993).

Thurley, Simon, *The Royal Palaces of Tudor England* (New Haven and London 1993).

Treasure, Geoffrey, *Mazarin: The Crisis of Absolutism in France* (London and New York 1995).

Vale, Malcolm, *The Princely Court: Medieval Courts and Culture in North-West Europe, 1270–1380* (Oxford 2001).

Vec, Milos, *Zeremonialwissenschaft im Fürstenstaat. Studien zur juristischen und politischen Theorie absolutistischer Herrschaftsrepräsentation* (Frankfurt am Main 1998).

Vehse, Eduard, *Geschichte der deutschen Höfe seit der Reformation* (Hamburg 1851–1860). *Zweite Abtheilung: Oestreich. Geschichte des Österreichischen Hofs und Adels und der Österreichischen Diplomatie*, 8 vols. (Hamburg 1851–1852).

Vincent, Monique, *Mercure Galant. Extraordinaire Affaires du temps. Table analytique de tous les articles publiés 1672–1710* (Paris 1998).

Vorel, Petr, 'Aristokratické svatby v čechách a no moravě v 16. století jako prostředek společenské komunikace a stavovské diplomacie', *Opera Historica* 8 (2000), pp. 191–206.

Wade, Mara R., *Triumphus Nuptialis Danicus: German Court Culture and Denmark. The Great Wedding of 1634*, Wolfenbütteler Arbeiten zur Barockforschung 27 (Wiesbaden 1996).

Wagner, Hans, 'Royal Graces and Legal Claims: The Pension Payments of Maria Theresa and their Withdrawal by Joseph II', in *Intellectual and Social Developments in the Habsburg Empire from Maria Theresa to World War I. Essays Dedicated to Robert A. Kann*, ed. Stanley Winters and Joseph Held, East European Monographs, 11 (New York and London 1973), pp. 5–29.

Wailly, Nathalis de, *Mémoire sur les variations de la livre Tournois depuis le règne de Saint-Louis jusqu'à l'établissement de la monnaie décimale*, Extrait des Mémoires de l'Académie des Inscriptions et des Belles Lettres 21, 2éme partie (Paris 1857).

Watanabe-O'Kelly, Helen, *Triumphall Shews: Tournaments at German-Speaking Courts in their European Context 1560–1730* (Berlin 1992).

Weary, W., 'The House of La Trémoille, Fifteenth through Eighteenth Centuries: Change and Adaptation in a French Noble Family', *JMH* 49 (1977), *D1001.

Wilson, Peter H., *The Holy Roman Empire, 1495–1806* (Basingstoke 1999).

Winkelbauer, Thomas, *Fürst und Fürstendiener. Gundaker von Liechtenstein, ein österreichischer Aristokrat des konfessionellen Zeitalters* (Vienna and Munich 1999).

'Grundherrschaft, Sozialdisziplinierung und Konfessionalisierung in Böhmen, Mähren und Österreich unter der Enns im 16. und 17. Jahrhundert', in *Konfessionalisierung in Ostmitteleuropa. Wirkungen des religiösen Wandels im 16. und 17. Jahrhundert in Staat, Gesellschaft und Kultur*, ed. Joachim Bahlcke and Arno Strohmeyer, Forschungen zur Geschichte und Kultur des östlichen Mitteleuropa 7 (Stuttgart 1999), pp. 307–338.

'Krise der Aristokratie? Zum Strukturwandel des Adels in den böhmischen und niederösterreichischen Ländern im 16. und 17. Jahrhundert', *MIÖG* 100 (1992), pp. 328–353.

'Sozialdisziplinierung und Konfessionaliserung durch Grundherren in den österreichischen und böhmischen Ländern im 16. und 17. Jahrhundert', *Zeitschrift für Historische Forschung* 19 (1992), pp. 318–319.
Winterling, Aloys, *Der Hof der Kurfürsten von Köln 1688–1794. Eine Fallstudie zur Bedeutung 'absolutistischer' Hofhaltung* (Bonn 1986).
Winterling, Aloys, ed., *Comitatus: Beiträge zur Erforschung des spätantiken Kaiserhofes* (Berlin 1998).
Zwischen 'Haus' und 'Staat'. Antike Höfe im Vergleich, Historische Zeitschrift, Beiheft 23 (Munich 1997).
Wolf, Adam, *Die Hofkammer unter Leopold I* (Oktoberhefte des Jahrganges 1853 der Sitzungsberichte der Philos.-histor. Classe der kais. Akademie der Wissenschaften, 11, pp. 440 ff., separately published).
Woolgar, C. M., *The Great Household in Late Medieval England* (New Haven 1999).
Zeller, Gaston, *Les institutions de la France au xvie siècle* (Paris 1948).
Zmora, Hillay, *Monarchy, Aristocracy, and the State in Europe, 1300–1800* (London 2001).
Zolger, Ivan, *Der Hofstaat des Hauses Österreich*, Wiener staatswissenschaftliche Studien 14 (Vienna and Leipzig 1917).
Zöllner, Erich, *Der Österreichbegriff* (Vienna 1988).

Index

1359902R0

Printed in Great Britain by
Amazon.co.uk, Ltd.,
Marston Gate.